ACCESS
BOSTON

P9-BZZ-332

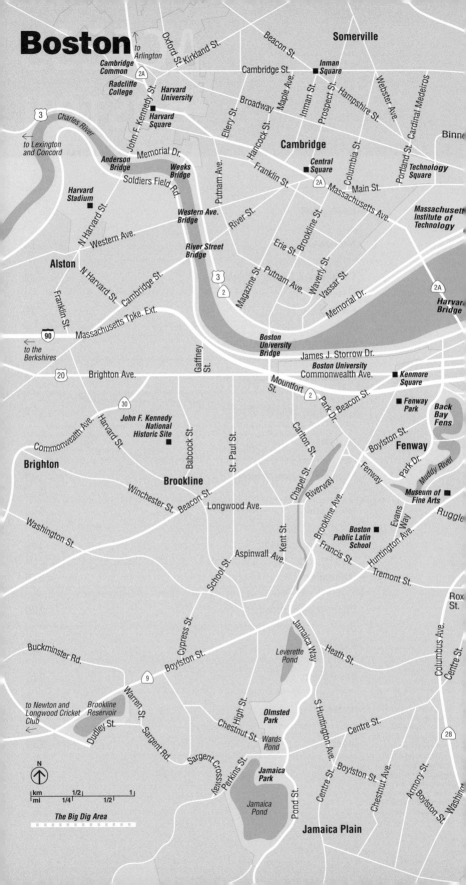

ORIENTATION

B oston is the 24th-largest city in the country, but its grandeur—based on more than 375 years of history—is genuinely impressive. The **Freedom Trail** alone connects 16 historical sites from colonial and Revolutionary days, including the **Old State House, Paul Revere House,** and the **Old North Church.** Such events as the Boston Massacre, the Boston Tea Party, Paul Revere's midnight ride, and Samuel Adams's impassioned protests against taxation without representation have all left their mark on the city and its residents.

Despite its historical ambience, Boston's student population—more than 300,000 a year flock to the city and nearby Cambridge—keeps the city's spirit young and in flux. Many are tempted to stay on, and do. "It's so livable," they marvel, meaning walkable and packed with odd pleasures—not that the shortest distance between two points is ever a straight line here. The older parts of Boston, particularly **Beacon Hill** and the **North End,** as well as **Cambridge** (across the Charles River), were laid out helter-skelter along cow paths, Native American trails, and the ghosts of long-gone shorelines (from the very start, the city has stretched its limits with landfill). Logic is useless in assailing the maze, but getting "lost" is half the fun.

You could spend a day wandering the narrow and sometimes cobblestoned streets of Beacon Hill and never run out of charming 18th- and 19th-century town houses. Furnish your own dream abode out of the grab bag of **Charles Street** antiques stores in Beacon Hill, or while away a lazy afternoon sampling the market wares in the North End—here a nibble of fresh mozzarella, there a briny olive, and virtually everywhere a cappuccino and biscotti with lively conversation. Eventually you'll gravitate, as the natives do, to the banks of the **Charles River,** where runners, walkers, bicyclists, and skaters whip by.

Though the climate is trying at times (the seaborne weather can be capricious), it's never boring. Summer's lush abandon cedes gradually to bracing autumns and bitter-cold Februaries. But greenery and sanity reemerge in April with the magnolias abloom along magnificent **Commonwealth Avenue** and the willows weeping around the **Public Garden** lagoon.

After a day on your feet, you'll be anxious to dive into a seafood feast (one of Boston's trademarks) or perhaps a gourmet meal. As recently as 20 years ago, you might have had trouble coming up with more than a handful of interesting restaurants in Boston; now the problem is choosing among them. Literature likewise provides rich repasts. **Harvard Square** is said to boast the largest concentration of quality bookstores in the country, and readings often draw crowds in the hundreds.

And finally there are the Boston sports teams: the **Celtics,** the **Bruins,** and the 2004 World Series champions, the Boston **Red Sox.** The Sox win over the St. Louis Cardinals was Boston's first Series victory since 1918. As frustrated as they may have been with the players, Red Sox fans were inevitably caught up in the romance of **Fenway Park,** a classic stadium dating from the golden age of ballpark design. But this should come as no surprise to anyone who knows a born-and-bred Bostonian. They savor the intimacy, the authenticity, and the history of their lovely city—and rightly so.

How to Read This Guide

ACCESS® BOSTON is arranged by neighborhood so you can see at a glance where you are and what is around you. The numbers next to the entries in the following chapters correspond to the numbers on the maps. The type is color-coded according to the kind of place described:

Restaurants/Clubs: Red

Hotels: Purple | Shops: Orange

◐ Outdoors: Green | Sights/Culture: Blue

Ġ Wheelchair accessible

WHEELCHAIR ACCESSIBILITY

An establishment (except a restaurant) is considered wheelchair accessible when a person in a wheelchair can easily enter a building (i.e., no steps, a ramp, a wide-enough door) without assistance. Restaurants are deemed wheelchair accessible *only* if the above applies and if the rest rooms are on the same floor as the dining area and can accommodate a wheelchair.

RATING THE RESTAURANTS AND HOTELS

The restaurant star ratings take into account the quality, service, atmosphere, and uniqueness of the restaurant. An expensive restaurant doesn't necessarily ensure an enjoyable evening; a small, relatively unknown spot could have good food, professional service, and a lovely atmosphere. Therefore, on a purely subjective basis, stars are used to judge the overall dining value (see the star ratings at right). Keep in mind that chefs and owners often change, which sometimes drastically affects the quality of a restaurant. The ratings in this guidebook are based on information available at press time.

The price ratings, as categorized at right, apply to restaurants and hotels. These figures describe general price-range relationships among other restaurants and hotels in the area. The restaurant price ratings are based on the average cost of an entrée for one person, excluding tax and tip. Hotel price ratings reflect the base price of a standard room for two people for one night during the peak season.

RESTAURANTS

★	Good
★★	Very Good
★★★	Excellent
★★★★	An Extraordinary Experience
$	The Price Is Right (less than $15)
$$	Reasonable ($15–$20)
$$$	Expensive ($20–$25)
$$$$	Big Bucks ($25 and up)

HOTELS

$	The Price Is Right (less than $120)
$$	Reasonable ($120–$180)
$$$	Expensive ($180–$250)
$$$$	Big Bucks ($250 and up)

MAP KEY

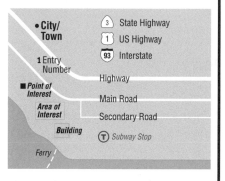

A Note About Telephone Calls

The entire 10-digit phone number—including the area code—must be used to make a call, local or long distance. Boston, Cambridge, Somerville, and Brookline are in area code 617. Close-in suburbs are mostly 781.

For all sections, the area code is 617 unless otherwise noted. Remember, area code *must* be dialed with the local number.

Getting to Boston
Airport

Located in East Boston, two miles east of downtown Boston on a peninsula across the harbor from the city, **Logan International Airport (BOS)** services more than 40 domestic and international airlines. The airport is fully accessible to people with disabilities, but is often a logistic and traffic nightmare owing to work on new roads, parking areas, and terminals. Construction is winding down on the $4 billion project that gave us some 3,000 new parking spaces and a $500 million terminal. You can learn about construction updates, rerouted airport roads, parking lot status, and things like ground transportation rates and availability by calling 800/23.LOGAN. The website www.massport.com has much information on traffic, parking, weather, and flight tracking.

You might consider flights into and out of airports in Providence, RI (888/268.7222, www.pvd-ri.com), Manchester-Boston Regional Airport in Manchester, NH (603/624.6556, www.flymanchester.com), Worcester, MA (888/359.9672, www.massport.com/ airports), or Hanscom Field in nearby Bedford (888/999.3273, www.massport.com/airports). Remember too that Amtrak (800/872.7245) offers comfortable, high-speed Acela Express trains on the Boston–New York–Philadelphia–Washington, DC, corridor. Downtown-to-downtown is awfully nice.

The **Logan Airport Hilton and Towers,** a 600-room property at the center of the airport, opened in 1999. The 10-story hotel offers views of the Boston skyline, a health club with an indoor pool, a business center, and shops and restaurants. For information call 800/HILTONS.

LOGAN AIRPORT SERVICES

Airport Emergencies 567.2233

Currency Exchange 569.4635

Customs 568.1810

Ground Transportation Hotline 800/235.6426

Information 561.1800

Lost and Found...561.1714

Health Center 568.6500

PAGING

Terminal A 568.8403

Terminal C 561.1806

Terminal D 561.8403

Terminal E 561.1804

Parking..561.1670

Police 561.1700

Traveler's Aid 567.5385

AIRLINES

Aer Lingus 800/474.7424

Air Canada 888/247.2262

Air France...800/237.2747

Air Jamaica...800/523.3515

Air Nova 888/422.7533

Air Tran...800/247.8726

Alitalia 800/223.5730

America West 800/235.9292

American/American Eagle 800/433.7300

British Airways 800/247.9297

Cape Air...800/352.0714

Cayman 800/422.9626

Comair...800/354.9822

Continental..800/525.0280

Delta 800/221.1212

Delta Express 800/325.5205

Frontier..800/432.1359

Icelandair...800/223.5500

Jet Blue 800/538.2583

KLM 800/374.7747

Lufthansa 800/645.3880

Midwest Express 800/452.2022

Metrojet 888/638.7653

Northwest...800/225.2525

Olympic 800/223.1226

TACA 800/535.8780

Swiss Intl 877/359.7947

United 800/241.6522

US Airways 800/428.4322

Virgin Atlantic 800/862.8621

Getting to and from Logan International Airport

By Boat

The **Airport Water Shuttle** (439.3131, 800/23.LOGAN) travels across Boston Harbor between the **Logan Boat Dock** and **Rowes Wharf** and **Long Wharf** at Atlantic Avenue on the edge of downtown Boston. A separate MBTA water shuttle goes from Logan to Quincy (222.6999). A free shuttle bus runs between the airline terminals. The water shuttle, 7AM–7PM, is a favorite way to and from the airport for several reasons: It's fast (a 10-minute trip, including the bus); the one-way adult fare is only $10, round-trip $17; it's scenic; and it avoids traffic.

By Car

On top of airport construction, road work and cleanup left over from the massive, officially finished, **Big Dig** project can sometimes make driving to and from Logan a challenge. It's best to avoid Logan between 4PM and 6PM on a weekday—especially on Fridays—and on Sundays. Legendary traffic snarls can make the trip via the Callahan Tunnel (to Logan) or the Sumner Tunnel (out of the airport) seem to take forever. Always give yourself extra time. The 1.6-mile Ted Williams Tunnel under Boston Harbor, which connects South Boston to East Boston and the airport, is usually a better traffic bet and costs the same small toll on the way into the city. From the tunnel, you can connect with I-90 (the Massachusetts Turnpike) west, or I-93 north and south. Much of this traffic advice, unfortunately, went out the window in 2006, when defects in Big Dig construction were discovered. A woman died when part of a new-tunnel roof fell on the car in which she was riding. Investigators found hundreds of potentially dangerous defects in new tunnels beneath the South Boston water-front. The old reliable Callahan and Sumner tunnels to Logan Airport were unaffected, but the new tunnels linking the Ted Williams Tunnel (and Logan) with I-90 (the Massachusetts Turnpike) and I-93 were shut for safety reasons until defects could be corrected. Traffic was routed through city streets and the old tunnels.

To get to Boston from Logan via the Sumner, bear left on the first ramp coming out of the airport and follow the signs to Sumner Tunnel (there's a toll). At the end of the tunnel is the North End. Look for signs for I-93. Take the I-93 North exit for Back Bay and points west; for downtown, head in the direction of I-93 South.

To get to the airport from downtown, follow the I-93 ramp sign posted "Airport" to the Callahan Tunnel (there's no toll in this direction). A large horseshoe-shaped road takes you past all terminals. There's long-term parking in the middle of the horseshoe and short-term parking at terminals A, B, and Central. You can get up-to-date parking information by tuning to Logan Radio, 1650AM, as you approach the airport.

RENTAL CARS

Free shuttle buses will transport you from outside the terminals' baggage-claim areas to car-rental counters (all open 24 hours).

Avis 800/331.1212

Budget 800/527.0700

Hertz 800/654.3131

National 800/227.7368

Thrifty..800/367.2277

BY LIMOUSINE

A luxurious transportation alternative, limousine service between Logan International Airport and downtown Boston can cost about $115 (includes tip and toll). Contact one of the following companies for further information:

A&A Limousine/Carey of Boston 623.8700

Boston Coach 387.7676

Custom Transportation 848.6803

BY SUBWAY

The **Massachusetts Bay Transportation Authority** (MBTA; 222.3200, 800/392.6100), the T, is the least expensive way to travel to and from the airport, and one of the quickest. Take the Blue Line subway to the Airport station (a 10-minute ride from the Aquarium or Government Center stops in downtown) and connect with free Massport shuttle buses that make stops throughout the airport (look for a sign on each bus indicating which terminal). Travel time to the terminals from the MBTA Airport station is about 10 minutes. There's also the T's (usually) rapid Silver Line waterfront bus service, to and from Logan, with stops at the World Trade Center, the Moakley federal courthouse, and South Station. You can board the Red Line subway at South Station.

BY TAXI

Cab stands are at all airport terminals; the common practice is to share a ride with others headed your way, as traffic congestion can easily run up the cost of the trip. Fares—about $15 to $25 to downtown—can skyrocket during peak travel times. An economical alternative, if you're headed to/from the suburbs, is Massport's Logan Express (800/235.6426)—a clean, direct bus between the airport and suburbs. The big coaches go directly to/from Logan and stop at all terminals. A one-way adult ticket is $11; round trip is $20. Riders 65 and over get $1 off each way and kids under

12 ride free. Communities served are Braintree (south), Framingham (west), and Peabody and Woburn (north).

Getting Around Boston

The major ways of getting around Boston are bus, foot, subway (the "T"), and taxi. Walking is highly recommended because of Boston's compact size. The T works well if the stations are convenient to your destination.

BICYCLES

Bikers have several scenic options in Boston. Two particularly appealing paths are the **Greenbelt Bikeway** and the **Dr. Paul Dudley White Bikeway.** The Greenbelt outlines the entire perimeter of Boston's famous **Emerald Necklace,** an eight-mile chain of parkland extending from Boston Common to Franklin Park. The Dudley starts along the Charles River, then traverses several sections of town. You can rent mountain bikes and hybrids (a cross between a touring bike and a mountain bike) at **Community Bike Shop** (496 Tremont St, at E Berkeley St, 542.8623), **Back Bay Bicycles & Boards** (333 Newbury St, between Hereford St and Massachusetts Ave, 247.2336). Maps of local trails are available at the bike shops or from **Hosteling International** (12 Hemenway St, between Haviland and Boylston Sts, 536.9455). Also see "Boston by Bike: Plum Paths for Pedal Pushers" on page 78.

BUSES

The **MBTA** (722.3200, 800/392.6100) operates the city's buses, subways, streetcar lines, commuter trains and boats, and vans for riders with special needs. Crosstown and local buses travel throughout greater Boston and Cambridge. Subway tokens are being replaced by an automated fare collection system called the Charley Ticket or Charley Card. You can buy cards from vending machines in most T stations.

The **South Station Bus Terminal** (700 Atlantic Ave, between Kneeland and Summer Sts) is part of the South Station Transportation Center. Bus lines that service Boston include:

Bonanza ....800/556.3815, www.bonanzabus.com, (northeast US)

Concord Trailways ....800/636.3317, www.concordtrailways.com, (New Hampshire)

Greyhound ....800/231.2222, www.greyhound.com, (nationwide)

Peter Pan Bus Lines ......800/237.8747, www.peterpanbus.com, (central Massachusetts, New York City)

Plymouth and Brockton ..508/746.0378 (Cape Cod)

Vermont Transit..............800/552 8737, www.vermonttransit.com, (Montreal, New England)

DRIVING

If you have a choice, don't drive. Boston is a pedestrian city, with confusing street patterns in many neighborhoods.

Even if you have the derring-do to compete with Boston's notoriously brazen drivers, be forewarned that signage here is poor and that there are lots of one-way streets. Right turns on a red light are permitted in Massachusetts except where prohibited by posted signs. Tolls are charged for the **Massachusetts Turnpike (Interstate 90),** various bridges, and tunnels to/from **Logan International Airport.**

For information on weather and traffic conditions on the Massachusetts Turnpike, check www.massturnpike.com; for information on traffic conditions on the Pike and in greater Boston, call 374.1234, *1 on many cell phones, or see www.smarttraveler.com.

PARKING

Street parking is limited and highly regulated, so read signs carefully. Many neighborhoods—particularly Beacon Hill and the North End—have almost no parking for nonresidents. It's common to be ticketed and/or towed to Boston's hinterlands. If your car is towed, retrieving it will be costly and time-consuming. Driving in Boston is difficult.

There are numerous **parking garages** in town, and various open lots, some of which are listed below. Prices vary widely for hourly and day rates, with the most expensive in the Financial District/Downtown and Back Bay areas. Parking at Red Sox home games is difficult, and the price at one lot near Fenway Park hit an astounding $90 in 2006.

IN BOSTON

Auditorium Garage 50 Dalton St (at Scotia St). 247.8006

Back Bay Garage Clarendon St (between St. James Ave and Boylston St) and St. James Ave (between Berkeley and Clarendon Sts). 266.7006

Boston Common Garage Charles St (between Boylston and Beacon Sts). 954.2098

Boston Harbor Garage 70 East India Row (at Milk St). 367.3847

Copley Place Parking 100 Huntington Ave (between Garrison and Stuart Sts). 369.5025

Government Center Garage 50 Sudbury St (between Congress and Cambridge Sts). 227.0385

Post Office Square Parking Garage Post Office Sq (entrances on Pearl and Congress Sts). 423.1430

Prudential Center Garage 800 Boylston St (between Exeter and Dalton Sts). 236.3060

IN CAMBRIDGE

Charles Square Garage 5 Bennett St (between Eliot St and University Rd). 491.0298

Harvard Square Parking Garage Eliot St (between John F. Kennedy and Winthrop Sts). 354.4168

SUBWAYS

Boston's subway system—known locally as the "T"—is the nation's oldest. Four major lines—Red, Blue, Orange, and Green—radiate from downtown. The symbol **T** outside the entrance indicates stops. Inbound trains go to central downtown stations: **Park Street, Downtown Crossing, State,** and **Government Center;** outbound trains head away from these stops. Tokens (available for purchase at stations), exact fare, or passes (see below) must be used. Tokens should be replaced in 2007 with an automated fare-collection Charley Ticket or Charley Card. You'll be able to buy the card at most T stations. The MBTA asked in 2006 to raise fares from $1.25 to $1.70 for subways and trolleys and from 90 cents to $1.25 for buses. The new rates were to take effect in January 2007, and may be in effect by now.

The **T** has minor eccentricities. For example, on the Green Line, many of the street-level stations do not have ticket booths, so you must have exact change ready (tokens—or the card—are also accepted, supplemented by change). Drivers do not make change, although passengers might. Note: Certain inbound lines charge higher fares from outlying stations; always ask. And going outbound on the Green Line, no fare is charged if you board at an aboveground station. Smoking is not allowed in stations or on trains.

MBTA subway trains operate Monday through Saturday from 5AM to 12:45AM, and Sunday and holidays from 6AM to 12:45AM. (Expanded late hours were tried, then abandoned. Officials blamed budgets, but the general thinking—perhaps a remnant of the Yankee-Puritan past— is that decent folk wouldn't be out and about at such hours.) Discount passes for senior citizens are available at the Downtown Crossing Concourse; student passes are sold at schools (children 5 to 11 pay half fare, children under 5 ride free). The **Boston Visitor Pass** is valid for unlimited travel on the subway, local bus, and inner harbor ferry and can be purchased for one, three, or seven days ($7.50, $18, $35). The visitor pass is sold at the Boston Common Visitor Information Center, 147 Tremont St (daily from 9AM to 5PM), Logan airport station, at a variety of locations, or by mail with an order form available at the MBTA website, www.mbta.com.

TAXIS

There are usually plenty around town, except between 3 and 7PM (especially on Friday) and in the worst weather. They're easiest to find near major hotels, on Newbury Street, and at Downtown Crossing and Faneuil Hall Marketplace. Available cruising taxis have a lighted sign on the roof. Some local companies are:

IN BOSTON

Boston Cab	262.2227
Checker Taxi	536.7000
Red and White Cab	242.8000
Red Cab	734.5000
Town Taxi	536.5000

IN CAMBRIDGE

Ambassador Brattle	492.1100
Cambridge Yellow Cab	625.5000
Checker Cab of Cambridge	497.9000

TOURS

Tours in Boston focus on the city's charm and rich historic legacy. There are, naturally, walking tours, as well as harbor and Charles River excursions. Trolley tours make a circuit past some of the city's—and the country's—historic landmarks, and have reboarding stops convenient to most Freedom Trail sites and in Back Bay. Here's a sampling of some leading tours:

Boston's Beginning: The **Freedom Trail** is Boston's most famous and popular walking tour. Although it is designed as a self-guided tour (pick up a map and brochure at the Boston Common Visitor Information Centr) and several guided walks are available for a fee. There are also free 1.5-hour walking tours of Revolutionary sites led by National Park Service rangers. With a ranger, you'll visit the Old South Meeting House, Old State House, Faneuil Hall, Paul Revere House, and Old North Church. Daily, mid-April to mid-November. Tours from the NPS Information Center, 15 State Street, next to the Old State House (242.5642, www.nps.gov/bost). **Boston by Little Feet** (367.3766) offers a child's-eye view of the Freedom Trail, including an introduction to architecture and history. Colonial-costumed members of The Histrionic Academy offer tours on the **Freedom Trail** four times daily. Meet at the Boston Common Visitor Center and end at Faneuil Hall. Tours are $12 for adults, $6 children, with senior and student discounts (938.7289, www.thehistrionicacademy.com).

Other walking tours cover specific neighborhoods. The excellent **Boston by Foot** tours (367.3766, www.boston-byfoot.com), which run from May through October, explore the narrow streets and markets of the North End and expose visitors to the sights and sounds of this predominantly Italian community. Fee. The Foot people cover the Freedom Trail, Beacon Hill, Victorian Back Bay, the Waterfront, Boston Underground, Literary Landmarks, and Boston by Little Feet. Also in the North End, Michele Topor reveals neighborhood secrets on her **North End Market Tours** (523.0932, www.cucinare.com). A chef and long-time resident, Topor takes small groups on an afternoon tour of the neighborhood's Italian markets, shops, and hideaways. Along the way, she offers food tastings, shopping tips, restaurant finds, and historical insights. She details the big difference between "Italian" restaurants and "Italian-American" restaurants. Fee. Reservations required (Wednesday, Friday, and Saturday).

The Histrionic Academy has a $30 walking tour Wednesdays along the **Irish Heritage Trail**, including lunch at an Irish pub. From the Boston Irish Visitors Center, 25 Union Street, at 11AM. 938.7289, www.thehistrionicacademy.com.

Bus and trolley tours are another popular way of seeing the city. **Old Town Trolley** (269.7010) offers many tours through the Boston area. Its Cambridge tour covers Harvard Square, MIT, Tory Row, and Longfellow House. Old Town's John Kennedy–themed JFK Boston trolley tour stops at places where the nation's thirty-fifth president spent his formative years, including his Brookline birthplace and Harvard University. The three-hour, reservation-only tour also includes a visit to the John F. Kennedy Library and Museum. Sunday from Memorial Day to Columbus Day.

You can enjoy the Boston skyline from the deck of one of the city's many harbor cruises. **Bay State Cruises** (748.1428) specializes in great views and fascinating history; excursions include a stop at Georges Island, site of a restored Civil War-era fort. Free water taxis that make a circuit to several other harbor islands leave from Georges Island. **The New England Aquarium** (973.5281, www.neaq.org) offers thrilling whale-watching adventure narrated by naturalists aboard private charters (April through November). In addition to sunset and moonlight tours, **Massachusetts Bay Lines** has four-hour-long whale-watch trips from Rowes Wharf (behind the Boston Harbor Hotel) to Stellwagen Bank National Marine Sanctuary (542.8000, www.massbaylines.com). For a fun, amusing excursion on land and sea, take a **Duck Tour** (723.3825, www.bostonducktours.com), an 80-minute trip that includes a drive around the city—and into Boston Harbor—in a quacking amphibious vehicle. Ducks leave from the Museum of Science and the Prudential Center.

Gray Line (236.2148) is one of the largest sightseeing operators covering areas beyond the city limits, offering coach excursions to Cape Cod, Concord, Gloucester, Lexington, Plymouth, and Salem.

TRAINS

MBTA (722.3200, 800/392.6100) commuter trains leave from **North Station** (Causeway St, between Beverly St and Lomasney Way) for destinations north and west of the city. This is where droves of Bostonians catch the Rockport Line to the North Shore and its beaches. Nicknamed "The Beach Train," it fills up fast on hot summer days. The MBTA **Green** and **Orange Line** subways also stop here.

Amtrak (800/872.7245) trains depart from **South Station** (Atlantic Ave and Summer St) and stop at Back Bay Station (145 Dartmouth St, between Columbus Ave and Stuart St) and at Route 128 Station in Westwood, 15 minutes west of Boston.

You can avoid the hassles of Logan Airport and eliminate the congestion of La Guardia (and the taxi ride to the city) by taking Amtrak to New York—or to Philadelphia, Washington, DC, and stops in between. There's the comfortable Metroliner and the high-speed Acela Express. Acela offers conference tables and other business amenities. Schedules, fares, and reservations are at 800/872.7245; www.acela.com. You can even take the comfortable Downeaster train from North Station to Portland, Maine, and, on the same ticket, be whisked by The Cat, a high-speed ferry to scenic Nova Scotia, Canada (www.amtrakdowneaster.com).

Commuter trains also leave from South Station for points south of the city. The **Red Line subway** stops at South Station and the **Orange Line** stops at Back Bay/South End Station (which also serves as Amtrak's Back Bay Station). You can take the Red Line to Cambridge (MIT and Harvard Square) and to Davis Square in Somerville and Alewife station in Arlington.

WALKING

Much of the city could be walked briskly in a day, so a lot of your sightseeing is best done on foot. Half the fun is wandering along the twisting, nonsensical streets. If you would prefer a more premeditated route, you can follow the Freedom Trail (see "Tours" above). In Boston, you are never much more than a few blocks from parkland, thanks to Frederick Law Olmsted's **Emerald Necklace,** or from water, thanks to Boston's harborfront and the **Charles River Esplanade.**

FYI

ACCOMMODATIONS

In addition to the hotels listed in each chapter, there are a variety of guest houses and bed-and-breakfasts in Boston and Cambridge. There are also many **bed-and-breakfast referral organizations** serving a number of neighborhoods and towns. Some of these include:

A Cambridge House
Bed-and-Breakfast Inn 491.6300, 800/232.9989

Bed & Breakfast Agency of Boston...............720.3450,
800/248.9262

Bed & Breakfast
Associates 720.0522, 800/347.5088

Bed and Breakfast Cambridge 720.1492

New England Bed & Breakfast Inc. 244.2112

CLIMATE

Boston's weather can be capricious: Summer can be very hot and humid, although sea breezes provide some relief; winter is usually cold and either damp with snow and ice or brisk and sunny. The most comfortable times are spring and fall, but each season has its charms.

Months	Average Temperature (°F)
December-February	30
March-May	46
June-August	71
September-November	53

DRINKING

You must be 21 years old to legally buy liquor. Laws vary in Cambridge and Boston, and also depending on the establishment's license, but in general, no liquor is sold in bars after 2AM or before noon on Sunday. In stores, no liquor is sold after 11PM Monday through Saturday, and none is sold on Sunday except near the New Hampshire border.

HOURS

Opening and closing times for shops, attractions, coffee-houses, and so on are listed by day(s) only if normal hours apply (opening between 8 and 11AM and closing between 4 and 7PM). In unusual cases, specific hours are given.

MONEY

Boston banks do not commonly exchange foreign currency, so handle such transactions at foreign-money exchanges at **Logan International Airport** (Terminals B, C, and E). Banks, many stores, and restaurants accept **traveler's checks,** generally requiring a photo ID. You can purchase checks at American Express (1 State St, at Washington St, 723.8400) and at most major banks. Banks are generally open Monday through Friday from 9AM to 4PM.

PERSONAL SAFETY

Always keep an eye on the traffic, as Boston drivers—and cyclists—are aggressive and often run red lights. Use common sense, and be careful if you venture off well-worn paths in the city. The subways are generally safe within Boston, Cambridge, and Brookline, but be smart. After dark, avoid parks, alleys, and dimly lit side streets.

PUBLICATIONS

Local newspapers and periodicals include *The Boston Globe* (daily), the tabloid *Boston Herald* (daily), the *Christian Science Monitor* (Monday through Friday), the unstuffy *Weekly Dig* (weekly), the *Boston Phoenix* (weekly, published on Friday), *Improper Bostonian* (weekly), the gay *Bay Windows* (weekly), *Boston Magazine* (monthly), and the *Tab* (weekly, with editions for specific neighborhoods). Especially helpful for events information are listings in the *Weekly Dig* and the *Boston Phoenix*, the *Herald*'s Friday "Scene" section, and the *Globe*'s Thursday "Calendar" section.

RADIO STATIONS

AM:

590	WEZE	Religious talk
680	WRKO	Talk
850	WEEI	Sports, Red Sox
890	WAMG	ESPN and local sports
1030	WBZ	News radio, traffic
1090	WILD	Adult urban contemporary
1120	WBNW	Financial news, talk
1260	WEZE	Religious talk
1300	WBZ	News, traffic

FM:

89.7	WGBH	National Public Radio, classical, jazz
90.9	WBUR	National Public Radio, talk, BBC, local news
91.9	WUMB	U Mass., Boston: folk and roots music
92.5	WXRV	Alternative rock
94.5	WJMN	Hip-hop
95.3	WHRB	Harvard University, classical
98.5	WBMX	Adult contemporary
99.5	WKLB	Country

101.7	WFNX	Alternative rock
102.5	WCRB	Light classical
104.1	WBCN	Rock/Alternative
107.9	WXKS	Teen pop

RESTAURANTS

Reservations are essential at most trendy or expensive restaurants, and it's best to book far in advance at such dining spots as L'Espalier and Rialto. If you want to avoid crowds, ask about late seatings. In general, jackets and ties are not required except at posh places, and most establishments accept credit cards.

SHOPPING

Boutiques and galleries bedeck Back Bay's upscale **Newbury Street.** A longer—and not quite so elite—shopping thoroughfare is **lower Boylston Street,** also in Back Bay. For clothing fashions for college students, you can't beat **Cambridge,** which is also the place to track down hard-to-find books. Nirvana for bargain hunters is the original **Filene's Basement** (426 Washington St, at Summer St, 542.2011) at Downtown Crossing in the **Financial District.** There are shopping complexes throughout Boston, including **Faneuil Hall Marketplace** (bounded by Commercial St and Faneuil Hall Sq, and Chatham and Clinton Sts), **Copley Place** (100 Huntington Ave, between Garrison and Dartmouth Sts), and the **Prudential Center** (800 Boylston St, between Exeter and Dalton Sts); in Cambridge, visit shops in and around **Harvard Square** and, for chain operations the **Cambridgeside Galleria** (First St and Cambridgeside Pl).

SMOKING

As a public-health measure, Massachusetts bans smoking in restaurants, cafés, coffee shops, food courts, bars, taverns, or any other place where food or drink is sold.

IRISH PUBS

Even as Boston has become a majority-minority city, fascination with the image of an Irish Boston remains. The old days of Irish domination of state and city politics are past, but census results show that Irish-Americans are still the largest single ethnic group (23% state and 17% city). Nationwide, about 11% of people claim Irish ancestry.

Links between Boston and Ireland are deep. Boston's police chief, Kathleen O'Toole, agreed in 2006 to become the chief inspector of Ireland's national police. Aer Lingus has 11 summer flights each week between Boston and Ireland. It sometimes seems there's an Irish pub on every other corner. But the political power of Italian-Americans, the second-largest, and other groups is on the rise. Mayor Thomas Menino was elected to his fourth term in 2005.

There's a lot more to Irish Boston than the pubs, but there's no denying that many of those pubs have extraordinary charm. And unlike bars of the past, Boston's Irish pubs today are often beautiful inside.

There's a concentration of lively Irish pubs around the **BankNorth Center** (jammed on game nights) and less hectic watering spots on and around **Broad Street** in the Financial District. Of course there are still old-style corner bars with an Irish accent, places like the **Eire Pub** in Dorchester (795 Adams St at Gallivan Blvd; no phone), a neighborhood hangout with photos of visits by Presidents Clinton and Reagan, or the enticing **Doyle's** in Jamaica Plain (3484 Washington St, between Williams and Gartland Sts, 524.2345). On the other hand, places like **Kitty O'Shea's,** across from the Custom House Tower (131 State St, at India St, 725.0100), **Daedalus** in Cambridge on the edge of Harvard Square (45 1/2 Mt Auburn St, between Plympton and DeWolf Sts, 349.0071; www.daedalusrestaurant.net), and **Kennedy's Midtown** near Downtown Crossing (42 Province St, between Bosworth and School Sts, 426. 3333; www.kennedysmidtown.com) are more 21st-century sophisticated Dublin restaurant than 1950s Boston bar.

Best Irish Pub

Boston attorney Richard J. Sinnott (whose father, Richard, as licensing chief during the 1960s was Boston's last city censor) favors **Mr. Dooley's Boston Tavern** (★★$ 77 Broad St, Financial District, 338.5656) for the good food, talk, drink, and, on Thursdays, a no-music mix heavy with well-dressed downtown lawyers, local and federal law-enforcement people, journalists, prosecutors, and occasional politicians. There's live music and young professionals t he other six nights, and Irish breakfast Sundays 11AM to 4PM.

Best Live Irish Music

Michael Quinlin of the Boston Irish Tourism Association (696.9880) recommends **The Burren Music Pub and Restaurant** (★$, lunch and dinner daily, 247 Elm St, Davis Square, Somerville, 776.6896; www.burren.com) for the live Irish music. There's usually a crowd of college students about the bar Friday and Saturday nights, but on unhurried evenings and afternoon and evening Sundays you can relax with a pint, talk, and listen to authentic live Irish music without charge. The back room (admission) is open seven nights, often with bands direct from Ireland.

STREET PLAN

Logic won't help you figure out the maze of Boston's thoroughfares. It's best to get a good detailed map of the city; even longtime residents have to haul one out when planning to stray from familiar paths.

TAXES

In Massachusetts, a 5% **sales tax** is charged on all purchases except services, food bought in stores (not restaurants), and clothing under $175 per item. A 5% **meal tax** is added to all restaurant bills. There's a 12% **hotel tax.**

TELEPHONE

The **area code** for Boston, Cambridge, Brookline, and other Greater Boston communities is **617.** You must use the area code with *all* calls, local and long distance. Massachusetts has other area codes and the list is growing. They are **508** (for Cape Cod and other parts of eastern Massachusetts), **781** (for some close-to-Boston suburbs, North Shore and South Shore, that previously had the 617 area code), **978** (for some northeastern and central Massachusetts communities that previously had the 508 area code), and **413** (for the western part of the state).

TICKETS

Ticketmaster (931.2000) is a computerized ticket service for Boston-area sports, theater, concerts, and other events. The **Hub Ticket Agency** (240 Tremont St, at Stuart St, 426.8340) also handles sports and theater happenings. **Concertix** (876.7777) sells tickets for the Regattabar jazz performances.

If you prefer paper to plastic, and want a same-day bargain, stop at a BosTix outlet at Faneuil Hall or Copley Square (Dartmouth and Boylston Sts) for cash-only half-price tickets (482.BTIX, www.artsboston.org).

TIME ZONE

Boston is in the **eastern time zone,** the same as New York. **Daylight saving time** is observed from the first Sunday in April to the last Saturday in October.

TIPPING

Leave a 15 to 20% gratuity in restaurants and for personal services. Taxi drivers expect at least a 15% tip.

VISITORS' INFORMATION OFFICES

The main visitors' information center is the **Greater Boston Convention and Visitors Bureau** at Copley Place (2 Copley Place, Suite 105, 536.4100, 888/SEE.BOSTON, www.bostonusa.com). It is open Monday through Friday from 9AM to 5PM. There's also a branch on Boston Common (at Tremont St, no phone) that's open every day except Christmas. Other sources include the **Cambridge Visitor Information Booth** (daily, 9-5, next to the T station in Harvard Sq, Cambridge, 497.1630, www.cambridge-usa.org), the **Charlestown Navy Yard Visitor's Center** (Charlestown Navy Yard, Bldg 5, Charlestown, 242.5601), and the **National Park Service Visitor Center** (15 State St, at Devonshire St, 242.5642). All are open daily from 9AM to 5PM.

Phone Book

EMERGENCIES

Ambulance/Fire/Police	911
AAA Emergency Service	800/222.4357
Dental	636.6828

HOSPITALS

Beth Israel/Deaconess Medical Center	632.7000
Brigham and Women's Hospital	732.5500
Massachusetts General Hospital	726.2000

PHARMACIES

CVS (Beacon Hill)	523.1028 (daily until midnight)
CVS (Cambridge)	876.4032 (open 24 hours)
Walgreen's (Back Bay)	236.1692
Walgreen's (Dorchester)	282.5246 (open 24 hours)
Poison Control	232.2120
Rape Crisis Hotline	492.7273
(Spanish	800/223.5001)

VISITORS' INFORMATION

American Youth Hostels (AYH)	731.5430
Amtrak	800/872.7245
Bay State Cruise Company (ferry service)	723.7800
Better Business Bureau	426.9000
Disabled Visitors' Information	800/462.5015
Greyhound Bus	526.1810
Mass Bay Lines (ferry service)	542.8000
Massachusetts Bay Transportation Authority (MBTA)	722.3200
Daily conditions	222.5050; 800/392.6100
National Park Service	242.5642
Road Conditions	374.1234
State Forests and Parks	727.3180
Time	637.1111
US Customs	565.6133
US Postal Service	451.9922
Weather	936.1111

MAIN EVENTS

January

Chinese New Year (sometimes celebrated in February), Chinatown; **Old Sturbridge Village Yankee Winter Weekends,** Sturbridge; **Boston Cooks,** a week-long chefs' festival. January also kicks off a three-month series of food and wine festivals called **Boston Overnight.**

February

Harvard's Hasty Pudding Club Awards, Cambridge; **Inventor's Weekend,** Museum of Science; **New England Boat Show,** Bayside Expo Center; **Valentine's Festival,** various hotels.

March

Evacuation Day (17 March), commemorating the British army's retreat from Boston in 1776; **St. Patrick's Day Parade** (17 March), South Boston; **New England Spring Flower Show,** Bayside Expo Center.

April

Annual Lantern Hanging (third Monday), Old North Church; **Boston Marathon** (third Monday in April); **Patriot's Day** (third Monday in April), commemorating battles of the American Revolution with a reenactment of the Battle of Lexington, Paul Revere's/William Dawes's rides, a parade, and other events; **Swan Boats** return to the Public Garden Lagoon (mid-April, Patriot's Day weekend); **Earth Day,** Charles River Esplanade, Hatch Shell; **baseball season** begins, Fenway Park; **whale-watching cruises** begin; **Arts Festival,** Harvard University, Cambridge; **American Indian Day,** The Children's Museum; **Artists' Ball,** the Cyclorama in the South End; **The Big Apple Circus,** Fan Pier.

May

All Walks of Life (AIDS walk); **Art Newbury Street** (open galleries); **Beacon Hill Hidden Garden Tour; tulips bloom** in the Public Garden; **Boston Pops** season begins, Symphony Hall (through June); **Brimfield Outdoor Antiques Show,** Hamilton; **Lilac Sunday,** Arnold Arboretum; **Boston Kite Festival,** Franklin Park; **polo matches** at Myopia Hunt Club, Hamilton (on Sunday through October); **Walk for Hunger.**

June

Blessing of the Fleet, Provincetown and Gloucester; *Boston Globe* **Jazz Festival,** Hatch Shell and other locations; **Bunker Hill Day,** Charlestown (17 June); **Dairy Festival,** Boston Common; **Gay Pride March; Irish Connections Festival,** Irish Cultural Center in Canton.

July

USS *Constitution* Turnaround (4 July); **Boston Harborfest; Chowderfest,** City Hall Plaza (4 July weekend); **Boston Pops Esplanade Orchestra Concerts,** Charles River Esplanade (3-5 July); **Tanglewood Music Festival,** Boston Symphony Orchestra in the Berkshires (through August); **Bastille Day,** Marlborough Street in Back Bay (14 July); **Brimfield Outdoor Antiques Show,** Hamilton; **Lowell Folk Festival,** Lowell; **North End Italian Feasts** (most weekends through August); **US Pro Tennis Championships,** Longwood Cricket Club, Brookline.

August

Salem Heritage Days, Salem.

September

Boston Film Festival/Cambridge River Festival, Charles River bank, Cambridge; **The Big "E" Eastern States Exposition,** Springfield; **King Richard's Renaissance Fair,** South Carver.

October

Topsfield Fair, Topsfield; **Haunted Happenings,** Salem; **Head-of-the-Charles Regatta** (next-to-last Sunday of month); **Cranberry Festival,** Cranberry World, South Carver; **ice-skating** at the Frog Pond on Boston Common and at the Public Garden Lagoon (end of month).

November

Thanksgiving Day parade and celebration, Plymouth; **Boston Ballet's** *Nutcracker,* The Wang Center; *Boston Globe* **Book Festival,** Hynes Center; **Boston Ski and Travel Show; Plymouth Plantation Thanksgiving dinner** reenactment in authentic costumes, Plymouth.

December

Christmas Tree Lighting, Prudential Center; **Boston Common Tree Lighting; Christmas Revels** at Harvard University's Sanders Theater; **Boston Tea Party Reenactment; First Night** (31 December until midnight).

BEACON HILL

In one of North America's most European cities, Beacon Hill is the most continental of neighborhoods. This redbrick quarter of handsome houses crowded along crazy-quilt streets is a walker's dream (and a driver's nightmare). It offers intriguing architecture, interesting historical sites, and exquisite squares in abundance as well as unusual shops and a handful of fine eateries.

A stroll across **Boston Common,** a grassy blanket that Bostonians have used since the city's birth, is the perfect prelude to a morning or afternoon spent poking about the nooks and crannies of historic Beacon Hill. The neighborhood's slopes are easiest to navigate in good weather, but it's well worth a bit of slipping and sliding to enjoy winter stillness here. (Along **Mount Vernon Street,** iron handrails fastened to buildings assist those making the steep climb.)

In colonial times, what is now a fashionable enclave was infant Boston's undesirable outskirts, crisscrossed with cow paths and covered with brambles, berry bushes, and scrub. The Puritans called it Trimountain because of its three-peaked silhouette. But the

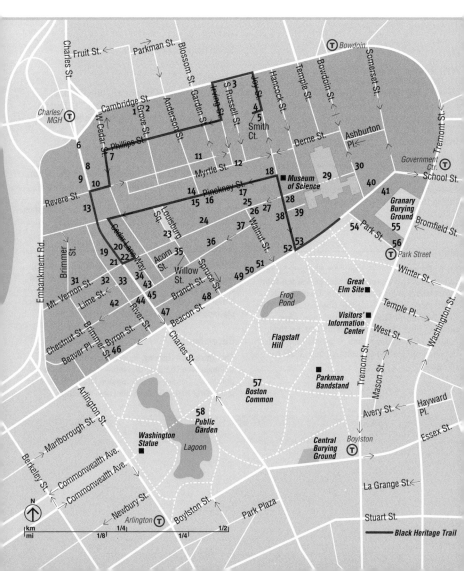

land was whittled away by early developers to create new lots and landfill, and only one hill remains today. The completion in 1798 of the majestic **State House,** designed by **Charles Bulfinch,** drew attention to the area's potential. Affluent Brahmins and a number of cultural luminaries were drawn here as Beacon Hill blossomed in the first half of the 19th century and the city's intellectual and artistic renaissance unfolded.

Beacon Hill is composed of approximately three districts. **The flats,** the newer, more orderly section, runs down to the Charles River from Charles Street. Up from Charles Street is the sunny **south slope,** extending from Beacon Street to Pinckney Street, and the shady **north slope,** descending from Pinckney to Cambridge Street. While the south slope's mansions and row houses exude Brahmin privilege, the north slope's smaller houses and former tenement walk-ups reflect a history of ethnic diversity and the struggle of many groups—especially African-Americans—to make their way here. Coursing through Beacon Hill, infusing it with vitality, is **Charles Street,** an eclectic, surprisingly friendly thoroughfare where most of the area's shops, services, and businesses are located.

In older cities, the chicken-or-the-egg question is: Which came first, the streets or the dwellings? It's clear that the houses came first on the hodgepodge "Hill," and that the streets have simply made do. As you wend your way over bumpy brick sidewalks, you'll probably agree that Beacon Hill wouldn't be so appealing without the jigs and jogs of the streets, the surprise of **Louisburg Square,** and the glistening river glimpsed below. In this intimate, people-scaled place, small details reveal the layers of lives that have enriched the brick and granite. Gardens enliven rooflines; ornate door knockers, boot scrapers, and wrought-iron embellishments dress up some of the most modest façades; and tunnels lead to concealed courtyards and hidden houses.

Most of the homes are Greek Revival or Federal in style, but refreshing upstarts sneaked in here and there. Master carpenters, called "housewrights," built most of the structures when the trained American architect was a brand-new breed. Notice the many graceful bowfronts—a local innovation. Officially declared a historic district in 1955, the neighborhood and its precious repository of buildings is today zealously watched over by the Beacon Hill Civic Association, which even dictates exterior color choices. Come back in 30 years, and the structures will look the same. But as buildings change hands, there's less single ownership, and more condos and luxury apartments belong to young professionals instead of "Proper Bostonians." Today this area is home to Jewish and Italian immigrants and their descendants, bohemian artists, and college students as well as Boston's famous "First Families"—the Cabots, Lodges, Codmans, and Lowells, to name a few—which held sway over Beacon Hill for generations.

After thoroughly immersing yourself in Beacon Hill's tranquil charm, watch the world go by over an espresso at **Caffè Bella Vita,** find that slip of a street called **Acorn,** then come down from the heights and take an afternoon promenade in the **Public Garden.**

1 HARVARD GARDENS

★ $$ Near Mass General, Harvard Gardens (no link to Harvard University) can be crowded after work, especially Thursdays, with single 20- and 30-somethings unwinding and checking out possible new close friends. There's also an undistinguished passable dining room with candles on the tables. ♦ American. ♦ Daily, dinner; M-F, lunch 11:30 AM-5PM. 316 Cambridge St (between Grove St and Lindall Pl). 523.2727; www.harvardgardens.com

2 ANTONIO'S CUCINA ITALIANA

★★$ Here is a friendly, unpretentious place—a nice, family-owned Italian restaurant right across from the North Grove Street entrance to Mass General. It's as if the 50-seat place were picked up from the North End and deposited here—without the North End prices and parking problems. Think veal Marsala, steak pizzaola, and fettuccine Alfredo. ♦ Italian ♦ M-Sa, lunch and dinner. Reservations recommended. 286 Cambridge St. 367.3310

3 VENICE RISTORANTE

★$ This is the kind of place you can walk past a hundred times without noticing, but stop in once and try the food and you're a regular. Crisp-crusted pizzas topped with ultrafresh ingredients even come in a "personal" size for one. Or choose from a selection of salads, pastas, subs, and daily specials. There's free delivery. ♦ Pizza/Takeout ♦ Daily, lunch and dinner. 204 Cambridge St (at S Russell St). 227.2094 ċ

4 WILLIAM C. NELL HOUSE

America's first published African-American historian and a member of **William Lloyd Garrison**'s circle, Nell boarded in this farmhouse from 1851 to 1856. He led the crusade for integrated public schools in the city, and his Equal School Association organized the boycott of the neighboring **Abiel Smith School** (now the **Museum of Afro American History,** see below) until the state legislature abolished restrictions on black children's access to public schools. African-American clothing dealer James Scott, who purchased Nell's house and ran it as a rooming house starting in 1865, sheltered fugitive slaves here. It is now a National Historic Landmark, but it is closed to the public. ♦ 3 Smith Ct (just west of Joy St)

5 MUSEUM OF AFRO AMERICAN HISTORY

The **Abiel Smith School,** the first grammar and primary school for black children in Boston, opened here in 1834, replacing the school that had met in the **African Meeting House** basement (see below). It was named for a white businessman who bequeathed the funds for its construction. The school closed 20 years later when the state upheld the demand for integrated schools, ending the practice of taxing blacks to support schools that excluded their children. Visitors may tour the building, although there aren't many artifacts on display. Exhibits of photographs by African-American photographers or with African-American themes are mounted here as well. ♦ Free. M-F; daily in summer. 46 Joy St

(at Smith Ct). 725.0022. www.afroammuseum.org

5 AFRICAN MEETING HOUSE

Free African-American artisans built this meeting house in 1806, and **Asher Benjamin**'s architecture influenced its town-house style. A National Historic Landmark, it's the oldest black church still standing in the US. Nicknamed "Black Faneuil Hall" during the abolitionist era, this is where William Lloyd Garrison founded the **New England Anti-Slavery Society** on 6 January 1832. Late in the 19th century, the African-American residents of the neighborhood began migrating to the South End and Roxbury; by the 1920s, Irish and Jewish immigrants had moved in. The meeting house was sold to a Jewish congregation and remained a synagogue until it became part of the **Museum of Afro American History** (see above) in the 1970s. ♦ Free. Daily. 8 Smith Ct (just west of Joy St). 739.1200

6 THE JOHN JEFFRIES HOUSE

$ A former residence for nurses, this gracious hotel at the foot of Beacon Hill (named for a founder of the nearby Massachusetts Eye and Ear Infirmary) is a charming, European-inspired bed-and-breakfast inn, decorated in late-19th-century Federal style. It accommodates patients and families attending to the infirmary and other hospitals, along with ordinary visitors. Most of the 46 units include a kitchenette complete with refrigerator, stove, and microwave. They range from cozy single rooms to deluxe suites boasting country French fabrics and kitchenettes, private baths, TVs, and telephones. Nonsmoking. There's free wireless Internet access and complimentary continental breakfast. The inn is convenient to public transportation and within walking distance of many of Boston's major attractions. ♦ 14 Mugar Way (at Cambridge and Charles Sts). 367.1866; fax 742.0313; www.johnjeffrieshouse.com ċ

7 LEWIS HAYDEN HOUSE

Fugitive slaves themselves, Lewis and Harriet Hayden became noted abolitionists, and their 1833 home was a station on the **underground railroad.** William and Ellen Craft, a famous couple who escaped by masquerading as master and slave, stayed here. And in 1853 **Harriet Beecher Stowe,** who had already published Uncle Tom's Cabin, visited the Haydens and was introduced to 13 newly escaped slaves—the first she'd ever met. The house is still a private home and is closed to the public. ♦ 66 Phillips St (between Grove and W Cedar Sts)

8 THE KING & I

★$$ What started as a fling in the 1980s between Boston and Thai restaurants has turned into a passionate affair. The offspring of this affair are scattered throughout the city, but this bright restaurant with courteous staff has always stood out for dishes like its delicate versions of Paradise beef. For an after-dinner treat of a different sort, cross Charles Street and enter the passage to the left of the Charles Street Animal Clinic. You'll see an arch framing trees, the river, and passing cars. Enter here and admire the curved charm of **West Hill Place,** another of the neighborhood's quaint and narrow streets. ♦ Thai ♦ M-Sa, lunch and dinner; Su, dinner. Reservations recommended for dinner. 145 Charles St (between Revere St and George Washington Cir). 227.3320

9 DANISH COUNTRY ANTIQUE FURNITURE

Here brightly colored rugs, tableware, crafts, and folk art can be found in, on, and among handsome blond furniture dating from the mid–18th century onward. So often antique furniture cringes from returning to active service, but owner James Kilroy's Danish desks, armoires, tables, chests, and chairs sturdily welcome the prospect. His shop is cheery when compared with many other dark and dour Hill establishments. ♦ Daily. 138 Charles St (between Revere St and Embankment Rd). 227.1804

9 MARIKA'S

You'll need to navigate very carefully through this crowded collection of glassware, furniture, paintings, tapestries, and treasures from all around the world. Owner Matthew Raisz's grandmother, Marika, emigrated from Budapest and founded this shop in 1944. It's prized particularly for its extraordinary jewelry. ♦ Tu-Sa. 130 Charles St (between Revere St and Embankment Rd). 523.4520

10 PERIOD FURNITURE HARDWARE COMPANY

This almost-80-year-old shop is aglow with gleaming surfaces to stroke. Many antiquers have abandoned their wearisome Holy Grail quest for such-and-such genuine wall sconce from such-and-such period for the almost-as-satisfying pleasures of these reproductions of hardware from the 18th century onward. If only the price tags weren't the real thing. ♦ M-F; Sa until 2PM. 123 Charles St (between Revere St and George Washington Cir). 227.0758

10 BOSTON ANTIQUE COOP I & II

These two cooperatives in one building set out a tempting smorgasbord of American, Asian, and European antiques. The place has all the ambience of a garage sale, but it's great fun—and local antiques dealers snoop about here, too. Downstairs at Coop I, four dealers display sterling, porcelain, paintings, jewelry, bottles, vintage photography, bric-a-brac, and more. Upstairs at Coop II, eight dealers specialize in decorative items, vintage clothing, and textiles. ♦ Daily. 119 Charles St (between Revere St and George Washington Cir). Coop I: 227.9810, Coop II: 227.9811. www.bostonantiqueco-op.com

11 ROLLINS PLACE

Countless passersby have glanced down this cul-de-sac off Revere Street and been charmed by the little white house tucked snugly at its end. But the inviting Southern-style façade is really a false front. The architectural trompe l'oeil masks a cliff that runs between Revere Street and the lower Phillips Street. Continue down the same side of Revere Street and slip into **Goodwin, Sentry Hill,** and **Bellingham Places,** all charming dead-end streets that also disguise the cliff, but without such fanciful deceit. ♦ 27 Revere St (between Garden and Anderson Sts)

12 MYRTLE STREET

When Brahmin elegance begins to stultify, seek this narrow, down-to-earth street. Tenements and Greek Revival row houses commune along this stretch with laundries, markets, shoe repair shops, a playground, a pizza parlor, and other unfashionable establishments that make it the neighborhood's most for-real street. Look at the rooflines and spot the funky gardens that aren't found on any "Hidden Gardens of Beacon Hill" tour. Perched here in the heights, you can see the lazy **Charles River** and **Massachusetts Institute of Technology** over in Cambridge. ♦ Between Hancock and Revere Sts

13 HELEN'S LEATHER

Care to prance about in python or buckle on some buffalo? You can even opt for ostrich at this leather emporium, which boasts an exotic collection of handmade boots. In case you didn't know, the mammoth wooden boot out front tells you you've arrived at New England's biggest Western boot dealer. Also for sale are popular brands of shoes, clothing, briefcases, backpacks, and other leather whatnots. ♦ Closed Tu. 110 Charles St (between Pinckney and Revere Sts). 742.2077

14 BOSTON ENGLISH HIGH SCHOOL

The first interracial public school in Boston (boys only) opened in this austere cruciform edifice—now divided into condominium units—in 1844. ♦ 65 Anderson St (at Pinckney St)

15 PINCKNEY STREET

Begin at its base, and with luck you'll arrive at the summit just as the late-afternoon sunlight turns golden, and the trees become sparkling lanterns stretching down toward the Charles River. Called the "Cinderella Street" of Beacon Hill by one author, it was once the dividing line between those who were and those who were not. There are both handsome and humble buildings here, and all are utterly delightful. ♦ Between Joy St and Embankment Rd

16 62 PINCKNEY STREET

Built in 1846 and owned by George S. Hilliard, this residence was a stop on the **underground railroad** that ran through Boston in the 1850s. Whether Hilliard knew fugitive slaves were harbored in his home is debatable, but his staunchly abolitionist wife, **Susan Tracy Hilliard,** certainly did. Workmen discovered the secret attic chamber in the 1920s. The house is still a private residence and is closed to the public. ♦ Between Joy St and Louisburg Sq

16 PIE-SHAPED HOUSE

The interior reveals what the exterior conceals: Squeezed between its neighbors, this house comes to a point like a piece of pie. Look at the roofline for a clue. ♦ 56 Pinckney St (between Joy St and Louisburg Sq)

17 HOUSE OF ODD WINDOWS

When **Ralph Waldo Emerson**'s nephew renovated this former carriage house in 1884, he succumbed to an inexplicable burst of artistry and turned the façade into a montage of windows, each singular and superbly positioned. Notice the quirky eyebrow dormer at the top. ♦ 24 Pinckney St (between Joy St and Louisburg Sq)

17 20 PINCKNEY STREET

Bronson Alcott—mystic, educator, "otherworldly philosopher," and notoriously bad provider—brought his wife and four daughters to live here from 1852 to 1855. The close-knit family and their struggle with poverty inspired daughter Louisa May's *Little Women.* ♦ Between Joy St and Louisburg Sq

18 9½ PINCKNEY STREET

The Hill's hodgepodge evolution created labyrinthine patterns of streets and housing that led to hidden gardens and even hidden houses (No. 74½ Pinckney Street is the famous "Hidden House," left to your imagination). The iron gate here opens onto a tunnel that passes through the house and into a courtyard skirted by three hidden houses. Crouch down for a glimpse. ♦ Between Joy and Anderson Sts

18 MIDDLETON-GLAPION HOUSE

George Middleton, an African-American jockey, horse-breaker, and Revolutionary War veteran, and hairdresser Louis Glapion collaborated in the late 1700s on this minute clapboard house, so untouched by time that you'll think the pair might have strolled out the front door this morning. ♦ 5 Pinckney St (between Joy and Anderson Sts)

19 JAMES BILLINGS ANTIQUES & INTERIORS

James Billings concentrates on 18th-century English furniture and decorative arts. Lise Davis, his wife and partner, is an interior decorator who specializes in the ever-more-popular English country house look. The couple—who belong to the British Antique Dealers Association and have been in business in Essex, England, since 1961, and in Boston since 1982—blend their talents in this opulently appointed shop. ♦ M-Sa. 88 Charles St (between Mount Vernon and Pinckney Sts). 367.9533

19 EUGENE GALLERIES

It's easy to lose all track of time in this enthralling emporium, which specializes in Boston views and maps: old prints, sketches, postcards, and photographs. Stop here after touring the city—it's the ideal place to see how your favorite sights have been captured through the centuries. You'll also find oddments of every sort—a Victorian dustpan, sheet music, paperweights, fire-and-brimstone sermons, and a *History of the Great Fire of Boston*, to name a few. ♦ Daily. 76 Charles St (between Mount Vernon and Pinckney Sts). 227.3062

20 THE SEVENS

★★$ No wonder this is the neighborhood's favorite pub. Often crowded, with free-for-all conversations bouncing between the bar and the booths, it's a gregarious place meant for sitting back and sipping a draft when the rest of the world seems a little lonely. Try the pub lunch—a generous, satisfying sandwich and bargain-priced mug of draft beer. ♦ American ♦ Daily until 1AM. Cash only. 77 Charles St (between Mount Vernon and Pinckney Sts). 523.9074

21 CHARLES STREET MEETING HOUSE

An octagonal belfry crowns the rectangular central tower, a handsome ensemble by **Asher Benjamin,** the architect who designed Faneuil Hall and inherited Bulfinch's unofficial role of architect laureate of Boston. The meeting house's first congregation was the **Baptist Society,** which found the nearby

Charles River convenient for baptisms. Later, although abolitionists—including William Lloyd Garrison, Frederick Douglass, Harriet Tubman, and Sojourner Truth—often orated from the pulpit, church seating was segregated. **Timothy Gilbert,** a member of the congregation, challenged the tradition and was expelled for inviting several African-American friends to sit in a white pew. (Gilbert then founded the **Tremont Temple** in 1842, Boston's first integrated place of worship.)

The **African Methodist Episcopal Church** met here from 1867 until the 1930s, and the **Unitarian Universalists** moved in after the Depression. Later, when the **Afro-American Culture Center** was located here, poet Langston Hughes gave readings. The Meeting House was renovated in 1982 by John Sharratt Associates and put on the National Register of Historic Places. Shops and private offices have replaced the church and community activities that took place here. ♦ 121 Mount Vernon St (at Charles St)

22 LaLa Rokh

★★★$$ The Persian/Eastern Mediterranean cuisine here is aromatic, flavorful, and subtly spiced. Parts of the owner family's collection of Persian miniatures from the 14th to the 16th century, calligraphy from the 8th to the 16th century, and European maps of the region from the 16th century are on display. ♦ Persian ♦ M-F, lunch; daily, dinner. Valet parking. 97 Mount Vernon St, a few doors up the hill from Charles St (at Charles and Mount Vernon Sts). 720.5511; www.lalarokh.com

23 Louisburg Square

Suddenly, the houses open wide and strollers find themselves at the edge of one of Boston's most serenely patrician spots. The redbrick row houses (built between 1835 and 1847) and the oval park they overlook aren't extraordinary in themselves; it's the square's timeless aura that has always appealed to Bostonians. Deteriorating statues of Aristides the Just and Columbus coolly survey all comers. Many famous people have crossed the thresholds of houses on this street. After becoming a literary success, **Louisa May Alcott** brought her perennially penniless family to **No. 10,** where mercury poisoning (she got it while a Civil War nurse) slowly crippled her. **No. 20** is a happier address: Here soprano **Jenny Lind** ("The Swedish Nightingale"), who skyrocketed to fame with the help of P.T. Barnum, was married in 1852 to her accompanist. **Samuel Gray Ward,** a representative of Lind's London bankers, also lived at **No. 20;** among his banking coups was arranging America's purchase of Alaska

from Russia for $7.2 million. ♦ Between Mount Vernon and Pinckney Sts

24 Harrison Gray Otis House, 1802

Ever an onward-and-upward kind of fellow, Otis abandoned a spanking-new manse on Cambridge Street, also designed by **Charles Bulfinch,** to take up residence in this fashionable neighborhood of his own making. One of the only houses in the area with ample elbow room, this towering structure was intended to set a Jones's standard of freestanding mansions on generous landscaped grounds, but Boston's population boom soon made this impossible. It is now on the National Register of Historic Places, but is not open to the public. ♦ 85 Mount Vernon St (between Joy St and Louisburg Sq)

25 Nichols House Museum

Remarkable **Miss Rose Standish Nichols,** niece of sculptor Augustus Saint-Gaudens, spent most of her genteel life in this house, built in 1804 by **Charles Bulfinch.** A gardening author, world traveler, peace advocate, and pioneer woman landscape architect who earned her own living, Nichols also founded the **International Society of Pen Pals** in her front parlor. Stop in to see the furnishings, memorabilia, and ancestors' portraits—collected by her family over centuries—which Nichols bequeathed to the public along with her home. The witty curator, William Pear, takes visitors on an entertaining tour of the only Beacon Hill home open to the public. ♦ Admission. Feb-Dec (call for days and hours). 55 Mount Vernon St (between Joy St and Louisburg Sq). 227.6993 ♿

Within the Nichols House Museum:

The Beacon Hill Garden Club

The club's annual spring **Hidden Gardens Tour** is the public's chance to roam through greenery that otherwise can only be glimpsed beyond brick walls. ♦ 227.4392. www.beaconhillgardenclub.org

26 John Callender House

One of the first houses on the street, Callender's small abode cost $2,155 for the lot and $5,000 to $7,000 for construction when it was built in 1802. A new roof was affixed to the Federal-style brick house and the entrance moved slightly, but it's still standing. A lavish garden blooms in the back. A private residence, it's closed to the public. ♦ 14 Walnut St (at Mount Vernon St)

Restaurants/Clubs: Red | Hotels: Purple | Shops: Orange | Outdoors/Parks: Green | Sights/Culture: Blue

27 32 MOUNT VERNON STREET

Julia Ward Howe and Dr. Samuel Gridley Howe took up housekeeping here in the 1870s. Dr. Samuel is best known for founding the Perkins Institute for the Blind, but he also organized the Committee of Vigilance to protect runaway slaves, helping hundreds of fugitives and pulling off an occasional daring rescue when word arrived that slaves were aboard the ships pulling into Boston Harbor. Julia composed "The Battle Hymn of the Republic" as well as many volumes of poetry. A suffragist and social reformer, she wrote and lectured on the rights of women and African-Americans. General Ulysses S. Grant and writer Bret Harte were among the couple's notable houseguests. It's still a private residence and is closed to the public. ◆ Between Joy and Walnut Sts

28 LYMAN PAINE HOUSE

This understated house's distinctive character comes from its intriguing asymmetrical windows and refined Greek Revival ornamentation. ◆ 6 Joy St (at Mount Vernon St)

29 THE STATE HOUSE

The 23-karat gilded dome of the Massachusetts State House (pictured below) glitters above the soft, dull hues of Beacon Hill, luring the eye. In fact, it was the capitol building (always called "the State House," never "the Capitol") that first drew wealthy Bostonians away from the crowded waterfront to settle in this more salubrious neighborhood, which was still considered "country" at the start of the 18th century.

Architect **Charles Bulfinch** spun out his remarkable designs at a breathtaking rate,

leaps and bounds ahead of city officials in his brilliant urban-planning maneuvers. Completed in 1798, the State House is his finest surviving gift to Boston. When construction began, Governor **Samuel Adams,** the popular Revolutionary War patriot, laid the cornerstone with the help of **Paul Revere.**

Facing the Common, the imposing south façade is dominated by a commanding portico with 12 Corinthian columns, surmounting an arcade of brick arches. Topping the lantern—which is illuminated on evenings when the state legislature is in session—above the dome is a gilded pinecone, a symbol of the vast timberlands of northern Massachusetts, which became the state of Maine in 1820.

This striking neoclassical edifice cut a much less flashy figure in Bulfinch's time. The two marble wings were added more than a century later by **Chapman, Sturgis, and Andrews.** The dome was originally made of whitewashed wood shingles, replaced in 1802 with gray-painted copper sheeting installed by Paul Revere and Sons; gilding wasn't applied until 1874. The dome was briefly blackened during World War II to hide it from moonlight during blackouts, so it wouldn't offer a target to Axis bombers.

If you look to your left across the street from the State House steps, by the way, you'll see the building used as Ally McBeal's supposed law office in the set-in-Boston TV series.

In 1825 the redbrick State House walls were painted white (a common practice when granite or marble was too costly); in 1845 they were repainted yellow; and in 1917 they were painted white again to match the new marble wings. Not until 1928 was the

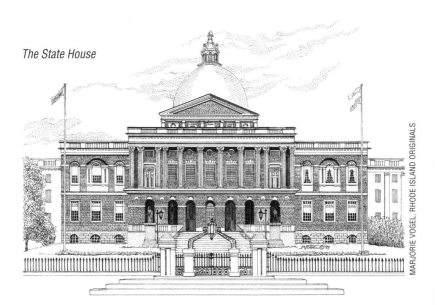

The State House

red brick exposed once more. Around the back, safely out of sight from Beacon Street, is the monstrous yellow-brick heap of an extension, six times the size of the original building.

Statues of the spellbinding orator and US senator **Daniel Webster,** educator **Horace Mann,** and Civil War general **Thomas Hooker** on his charger stand beneath the central colonnade. On the lawns below are more pensive images. There's **Anne Hutchinson** (below the left wing), who was banished from Boston in 1645 by the Puritan community for her freethinking religious views. (Not until 1945 did the Great and General Court of Massachusetts revoke the edict of banishment.) And there's Quaker **Mary Dyer** (below the right wing), who was hanged on the Common for protesting Anne's banishment. Note also the statue of a serious, striding **John F. Kennedy.**

Climb the steps and enter by a door to the far right. This leads to Bulfinch's **Doric Hall** (named for its 10 colossal columns) on the second floor under the dome. The hall's main doors open only when a US president visits or a Massachusetts governor leaves the building for the very last time.

Visitors may see the rest of the building on guided tours. On the third floor is the resplendent **House of Representatives gallery.** Here hangs the **Sacred Cod** carved in pine, presented to the legislature in 1784 by Boston merchant Jonathan Rowe as a reminder of the fishing industry's importance to the state economy. This wooden fish effigy garnered such ridiculous reverence that in 1895, when the House of Representatives was relocated within the State House, the fish was wrapped in an American flag and carried to the new seat of government by four messengers, escorted by a committee of 15 House members. And on 26 April 1933, when the fish was "codnapped" by the *Harvard Lampoon* as a prank, all business in the House was suspended for several days, the members fuming over their missing fish. The thieves relented and phoned to tell the House that their mascot was concealed in a closet beneath their chamber.

In the barrel-vaulted **Senate Reception Room** (the original Senate Chamber) each of four original Ionic columns by Bulfinch was carved from a single pine tree. Directly beneath the gold dome is the sunburst-ceilinged **Senate Chamber,** where Angelina Grimké became the first woman to address a US legislative body when she gave an antislavery speech in 1838. ♦ Free. M-F; tours by reservation. Beacon St (between Bowdoin and Joy Sts). 727.3676 &

30 THE FILL-A-BUSTER

$ Gracious Vaios Grigas's friendly crew serves hearty fare with Greek highlights—egg-lemon soup, spinach-cheese pie, and kabobs—for a clientele of pols and media types. The breakfast specials are bountiful, and you can smell Grigas's famous homemade muffins a block away. Once you're a regular here, they'll have your coffee poured before you've crossed the threshold. ♦ Greek/American/Takeout ♦ M-F, breakfast and lunch. 142 Bowdoin St (between Beacon St and Ashburton Pl). 523.8164

31 THE CHURCH OF THE ADVENT

The story goes that flamboyant parishioner **Isabella Stewart Gardner,** founder of the museum in the Fenway, scrubbed this Episcopal church's steps during Lent as penance. The tale also goes that proper Bostonians sniffed and wondered why Isabella wasn't required to scour the entire edifice. The Gothic Revival structure (completed in 1888 by **Sturgis and Brigham**) distributes its great girth on an awkward site through a chain of conical-roofed chapels, accommodating nearby domestic architecture as a good Beacon Hill neighbor should. The interiors are also ingeniously arranged and splendidly embellished. The church boasts one of the finest carillons in the country. There's also a lovely garden in the rear. ♦ M-F (enter through church office); Su, 7:30AM-1PM. 30 Brimmer St (at Mount Vernon St). 523.2377. www.theadvent.org

32 SUNFLOWER CASTLE

Remodeled in 1878 by **Clarence Luce,** this amusing Queen Anne cottage began life in 1840 as an anonymous little plain Jane of a building; now it takes its name from the enormous, gaudy sunflower ornament pressed on its brow. Maybe boredom with Beacon Hill's de rigueur palette and mincing details inspired Luce to paint the stuccoed first floor brilliant yellow and sheath the second story in China-red tile. His whimsy unleashed, he added exuberantly carved brackets and posts, and a griffin. It's still a private home and is closed to the public. ♦ 130 Mount Vernon St (at River St)

33 CHARLES STREET SUPPLY

A really good hardware store is an alluring place. Even if you've never gone to war with weeds or handled a two-by-four, you'll itch to tackle some project, any project, at the sight of all those home-improvement aids spilling onto this overstuffed store's sidewalks. Sure, the prices are high, but owner Richard Gurnon and his staff offer plenty of how-to's along with the tools. ◆ Daily. 54-56 Charles St (between Chestnut and Mount Vernon Sts). 367.9046

33 BLACKSTONE'S OF BEACON HILL

Owner Richard Dowd provides reproductions to historical societies all across the US, so this is the place to come for brass and mahogany trivets, candlesnuffers, and door knockers. Also available are porcelain and enamel renditions of the Public Garden's famous **Swan Boats,** designed for the shop by Limoges and Crummles, clothing, and stained-glass picture frames. ◆ Daily. 46 Charles St (between Chestnut and Mount Vernon Sts). 227.4646. www.blackstonesbeaconhill.com

33 PARAMOUNT STEAK HOUSE

★$ This is a Greek diner squeezed into a Charles Street shoe box. A gathering spot for locals, it offers typical greasy-spoon breakfasts (self-serve and cheap) that one is expected to consume with dispatch during busy hours. Its appeal is elusive, but so many are dedicated to the place that there's surely something here. Nothing on the menu is small—try the Greek salad, moussaka, or souvlaki. ◆ Greek/American/Takeout ◆ Daily, breakfast, lunch, and dinner. 44 Charles St (between Chestnut and Mount Vernon Sts). 720.1152 ⑁

33 FIGS

★★$$ There are just a dozen tables at this cozy cousin to the popular Olives in Charlestown, but it's certainly worth the wait. Fig and prosciutto pizza with rosemary crust; semolina dumplings baked in spaghetti squash, ham, sage, and Parmesan; and fresh Maine lobster with leek risotto and cream sauce are some of the favorites at this popular brick-walled eatery. ◆ Italian ◆ M-F, dinner; Sa, Su, lunch and dinner. 42 Charles St (between Chestnut and Mount Vernon Sts). 742.3447. Also at 10 City Sq (at Park and Main Sts), Charlestown. 242.2229 ⑁

34 RISTORANTE TOSCANO

★★★$$ Conscientiously patrolled by its ultracivilized owners, this brisk, friendly Florentine trattoria offers a diverting lineup of daily specials, headlining such luscious stars

as carpaccio, smoked-salmon pasta, and rack of lamb. And this is one of the only places in town you're likely to encounter *bollito misto* (boiled meats). Sophisticated and self-assured, this restaurant is one of Boston's favorites. There's valet parking evenings. ◆ Italian ◆ M-Sa, lunch and dinner; Su, dinner. Reservations recommended. 41-47 Charles St (between Chestnut and Mount Vernon Sts). 723.4090

35 ACORN STREET

Stand at the crown of this street, one of Boston's skinniest, and watch cars shimmy and shake as they climb its cobbled length. On one side, look up at the trees waving from hidden gardens backing **Mount Vernon Street;** opposite are diminutive houses that belonged to coachmen serving families in mansions on Chestnut and Mount Vernon Streets. Study the entrances to **Nos. 1, 3,** and **5** and notice the ornamental acorns that correspond in number with each address. The original homeowners would be pleased to know that their humble houses now hobnob with the best on the real-estate market. ◆ Between Willow and W Cedar Sts

36 29A CHESTNUT STREET

In 1865 tragedian **Edwin Booth** was enjoying a successful run in *The Iron Chest,* a drama about a murderer haunted by his crime, and was staying here at the home of the theater

Acorn Street

MARJORIE VOGEL, RHODE ISLAND ORIGINALS

manager. But on the eve of Edwin's last performance, brother **John Wilkes Booth** murdered President Abraham Lincoln. Edwin's last performance was canceled, and he left secretly for New York, not appearing before an audience for nearly a year. The house is still a private residence and is closed to the public. ♦ Between Walnut and Willow Sts

37 13, 15, AND 17 CHESTNUT STREET

Architect **Charles Bulfinch** was kept busy building for patrons' daughters, and, in fact, this most famous trio of row houses was dubbed the "Daughter Houses." In 1805, while her husband, Colonel James Swan, cooled his heels in a French debtors' prison, Boston heiress **Hepsibah Swan** had these houses built as wedding gifts for her daughters. No. 13 is a National Historic Landmark. All are private homes and are closed to the public. ♦ Between Walnut and Willow Sts

38 APPALACHIAN MOUNTAIN CLUB

Founded in Boston in 1876, the AMC provides information on outdoor recreation in Boston and New England and organizes hikes, river trips, family outings, and conservation activities. ♦ M-F. 5 Joy St (between Beacon and Mount Vernon Sts). 523.0636. www.amcboston.org

The Eliot & Pickett Houses

Bed & Breakfast

39 THE ELIOT & PICKETT HOUSES

$ Conveniently located at the top of Beacon Hill, these two adjoining 1830s brick town houses feature 20 comfortably appointed guest rooms, most with private baths. There's a fully stocked kitchen for guests who prefer to eat in. In season, guests have access to the roof deck with its grand views of the city and the nearby gold-domed **State House.** ♦ 6 Mount Vernon Pl (just east of Joy St). 248.8707; fax 742.1364 &

40 15 BEACON

$$$$ This 61-room luxury boutique hotel opened in 2000, and something about the XV Roman numerals on the marquee tells you it will be expensive. It can be ($395 basic to $1,005 for a two-bedroom suite), but, after all, you get what you pay for. From 1923 to 1999, the 10-story property housed the Boston School Committee, and today it advertises peerless

personal service with the intimacy of a private residence. Two studios are outfitted for guests with disabilities. ♦ 15 Beacon St (between Bowdoin and Somerset Sts). 670.1500; fax 670.2525; www.xvbeacon.com &

Within the 15 Beacon hotel:

THE FEDERALIST

★★★★$$$$ This plush 125-seat restaurant serves dishes like a Colorado rack of lamb with Portobello mushrooms and goat cheese tart ($45). A delectable mix of Continental dishes and New England classics makes this a dining experience to be savored. ♦ M-F, lunch; daily, dinner. Jackets recommended, of course. 15 Beacon St. 670.2515; fax 670.2525 &

40 BLACK GOOSE

★★$$ Crowds gather regularly for the Coliseum-size Caesar salads and abundant plates of pasta with pesto served in the midst of Corinthian columns. In good weather, find a sun-warmed table out front for lunch and watch scholars and book browsers coming and going beneath the dignified sandstone façade of the **Boston Athenaeum** across the way. ♦ Italian ♦ M-F, lunch and dinner; Sa, dinner. Reservations recommended. 21 Beacon St (between Somerset and Bowdoin Sts). 720.4500 &

41 THE BOSTON ATHENAEUM

Although **Edward Clark Cabot** modeled the 1849 building after Palladio's Palazzo da Porta Festa in Vicenza, Italy, the Athenaeum is a Boston institution to its bones. Enlarged and rebuilt in the early 1900s by Henry Forbes Bigelow, the structure is now a National Historic Landmark. Only 1,049 ownership shares exist to this independent research library, founded in 1807, and all can be traced to their original owners. Nonmembers are invited to tour the building and look at—but not touch—books on the first and second floors, and to visit the **Athenaeum Gallery,** which offers ongoing exhibitions. Take a tour and visit Boston's most pleasant place for musing, the high-ceilinged, airy **Reading Room** on the fifth floor, with its sunny alcoves. As poet David McCord wrote, the room "combines the best elements of the Bodleian, Monticello, the frigate *Constitution,* a greenhouse, and an old New England sitting room." Also be sure to step out onto the **fifth-floor terrace,** with its gorgeous plantings and fine view of the Granary Burying Ground. The superb collections here include George Washington's private library and Confederate imprints, as well as history, biography, and English, American, and Gypsy literature. There's a notable mystery collection too.

Members and visitors who've gained special dispensation can handle many of the books, but may receive a lesson in the proper way to remove a volume from its shelf (work your fingers around its sides, don't pull it out from the top!). Take a ride in the charmingly **hand-painted elevator,** a former employee's handiwork, with its framed bookplate display. Part of the library's appeal is the way Oriental carpets and art treasures are strewn about. Keep an eye out for the wonderful **statue of Little Nell** on the first floor next to the stairs. ♦ Admission free. M-Sa. Tours by reservation. Open only to members and qualified researchers, but special exhibits and receptions—many open to the public—are mounted Sept-June. 10½ Beacon St (between Park and School Sts). 227.0270 ₺

42 75 CHESTNUT

★★★$$$$ This romantic, hidden gem serves elegant contemporary American cuisine in an intimate, 55-seat setting with etchings and oils of old Beacon Hill on its hunter-green walls and candlelight warming its mahogany woodwork. ♦ Contemporary American ♦ Daily, dinner; Su, jazz brunch, Sept-June. Reservations recommended. Complimentary validated parking in Boston Common Garage. 75 Chestnut St (off Charles St between River and Brimmer Sts). 227.2175; fax 227.3675; www.75chestnut.com ₺

43 CEDAR LANE WAY

When evening has nearly crept over the Hill, enter this skinny lane from Chestnut Street. Say hello to the cats in the windows of the tiny dwellings and try to sidestep the residents' trash cans and potted plants while you look up and admire their gardens spilling over brick retaining walls. The lane turns to cobblestones after crossing Pinckney Street and ends beneath a lantern's intimate glow. ♦ North of Chestnut St

44 BEACON HILL HOTEL

$$$ This full-service boutique hotel in two connected 19th-century town houses is just 50 paces from Boston Common. Built in 2000, the hotel offers 13 guest rooms from $245 for a small room with charming views to $365 for an in-room suite, with same price for single or double occupancy. Includes full breakfast in the **Bistro** (below). Room service is available 7AM to midnight. ♦ Smoking only on mahogany roof terrace. 25 Charles St (at Chestnut St). 617/723.7575; fax 617/723.7525; www.beaconhillhotel.com ₺ (One room and all public areas wheelchair accessible)

Within the Beacon Hill Hotel:

BEACON HILL BISTRO

★$$ In the style of a French bistro, the Beacon Hill is decorated with mahogany paneling and mosaic tile floors, and serves bistro classics like steak *frites* and roast duck with an extensive, reasonably priced wine list. ♦ Daily, breakfast, lunch, and dinner (until 11PM); Su, brunch ₺

45 CAFFÈ BELLA VITA

★$ We'll tell you up front that the service is inexplicably harried in this redbrick storefront café, and the pastries and cappuccino are only so-so. But look around, and you'll know right away why you came. Long after the last drop of espresso is memory, people linger here gazing out at the Charles Street parade. Every table is near a plate-glass window, making this a good place to write a long letter on a winter afternoon. Plus, the biscotti di Prato (say "almond cookies," or you'll get a blank look) are great dunkers. ♦ Café ♦ Daily, 9AM-11PM. 30 Charles St (at Chestnut St). 720.4505 ₺

45 TORCH

★★$$$ One of the good ones. Floor-to-ceiling windows in this intimate, 46-seat restaurant overlook Charles Street (a block in from Beacon Street) and décor hews to the torch theme, with copper wainscoting and burgundy walls. Deep-blue ceilings put a relaxing temper to the flame. There's also a private dining area for 12. ♦ Modern French with Asian and Italian influences. ♦ Tu-Su, 5PM-10PM. Reservations recommended. On-street parking (if you're lucky) and valet parking. 26 Charles St. 723.5939 ₺

46 THE HAMPSHIRE HOUSE

Built by **Ogden Codman** in 1909, this town house borrows from Greek and Georgian Revival and Federal styles, and is best known for housing two of Boston's most popular restaurants. ♦ 84 Beacon St (at Brimmer St). www.hampshirehouse.com

Within The Hampshire House:

LIBRARY GRILL

★★★$$$ The silver-spoon spirit still thrives in this bar/restaurant above Cheers/Bull & Finch, with the polished paneling, leather chairs, and moose heads creating a men's-club ambience. Sunday live jazz brunch is the only meal served, aside from holiday openings and private functions. The décor becomes more and more pleasant when the splendid eggs Benedict and crisp corned-beef hash arrive. Have a second impeccable Bloody Mary, listen to the piano music, and let the morning slip away. ♦ American ♦ Su, brunch, 11:30AM-2:30PM, Sept.-June. Reservations recommended. 227.9600

BULL & FINCH

★$ This is the basement bar that inspired the long-running TV sitcom *Cheers.* All the brouhaha eclipsed a lot of the pub's authentic charm, but if you time it right, you can sidestep the boisterous throngs of tourists and college students. Slip in at a quiet hour for a beer and some pub-style fare (the burgers are great). One of Boston's nicest bartenders, Eddie Doyle, works here days. A DJ plays pop hits for dancing on Friday and Saturday nights. ♦ American ♦ Daily, lunch and dinner. Bar: daily, 11AM-1AM. 227.9605. www.cheersboston.com &

47 DE LUCA'S MARKET

This grocery store carries all sorts of gourmet fixings for a sumptuous picnic on the esplanade or supper by a fire. There's a little bit of every-thing here, and if you can't find your favorite treat, they'll order it. Of course, quality commands a high price. In business since 1905, the market wangled a wine and liquor license (a major feat on the Hill) some years back and purveys an extensive selection. ♦ Daily, 7AM-10PM. 11 Charles St (between Beacon and Branch Sts). 523.4343. Also at 239 Newbury St (at Fairfield St). 262.5990

48 WILLIAM HICKLING PRESCOTT HOUSE

Built in 1808, this graceful pair of brick bowfronts, now joined, is adorned with many of the delicate Greek architectural details favored by architect **Asher Benjamin.** The left-hand house, now a National Historic Landmark and headquarters for the National Society of the Colonial Dames of America,

inspired the setting for *The Virginians* by British author **William Makepeace Thackeray** (houseguest of a former owner). During Wednesday guided tours, visitors can peruse the colonial and Victorian artifacts collected and preserved by the Dames. ♦ Admission. W and Th only; tours by reservation. 54-55 Beacon St (between Spruce and Charles Sts). 742.3190

49 HARRISON GRAY OTIS HOUSE, 1805

This is the last and largest of the three imposing residences designed by **Charles Bulfinch** for the larger-than-life grandee **Harrison Gray Otis,** a Boston mayor, US senator, and one of the city's first big-time developers. Otis, who believed in the good life, added a fourth repast to his regular meals, breakfasted daily on pâté de foie gras, and—surprise—suffered with gout for 40 years. Otis feted all of fashionable Boston in his magnificent rooms. Each afternoon the politicians and society guests who gathered in the drawing room consumed 10 gallons of spiked punch. The house didn't have plumbing. (Bathwater was considered a health menace because it supposedly attracted cockroaches, so tubs weren't allowed until the 1840s.) The American Meteorological Society is the current resident; visitors may walk through the interior, but there are no exhibits. ♦ Free. ♦ M-F. 45 Beacon St (between Walnut and Spruce Sts)

50 SOMERSET CLUB

Painter **John Singleton Copley** lived in a house that stood on this site, until he went to England in 1744 and never returned. Today, the Greek Revival granite bowfront that replaced Copley's house aggressively protrudes beyond its neighbors' façades, and houses an exclusive private club. **David Sears** erected the right-hand half in 1819, adding the left half in 1831, doubling **Alexander Parris**'s original design and spoiling it in the process. Look for the baronial iron-studded portal with its lion's-head knockers—a very showy touch for Beacon Hill. Closed to the public. ♦ 42 Beacon St (between Walnut and Spruce Sts)

51 APPLETON-PARKER HOUSES

Built in the early 1800s by **Alexander Parris,** these two Greek Revival bowfronts were the abodes of Boston's merchant prince Nathan Appleton, of the textile-manufacturing family, and his former partner, Daniel Parker. **Henry Wadsworth Longfellow** courted and married Fanny Appleton in her family's front parlor in 1843. And at one Appleton soiree, sardonic **Edgar Allan Poe,** characteristically misbehaving before the ladies, was given the heave-ho. Both

BEST SUSHI—IN BOSTON?

Members of the Internet-based Boston Sushi Society (BSS) say the "best" sushi restaurants range from a busy, no-frills sushi bar in Cambridge's Porter Square to an upscale sushi bar in Boston's Eliot Hotel.

Charles Richmond, who maintains the BSS members list and web page, www.iisc.com/bss, nominated **Kotobukiya** sushi bar (492.4655) and **Blue Fin** restaurant (497.8022) (in the Porter Exchange building, 1815 Massachusetts Ave, Cambridge). Porter Exchange, a converted 1920s Sears, Roebuck building, with Leslie University and Harvard-Smithsonian offices on upper floors, draws Japanese residents and students seeking the authentic shops and restaurants on the first floor.

Near the Tampopo noodle shop open to passersby, Kotobukiya is fast and cheap with fresh, fresh, fresh sushi and sashimi. "And the full-service Japanese restaurant, Blue Fin, has cooked food, sushi, sake, and Japanese beer. The staff is Japanese, and the place makes me feel like I am sitting in a family restaurant and *sushiya* in Chiba [Tokyo]," Richmond said. "The food is great and the sushi is excellent, with very fresh *uni* [sea urchin]. Both are accessible for people with disabilities." Richmond also praised the esteemed **Sakura Bana** in Boston's Financial District (57 Bond St at Milk St, 542.4311).

Member and sushi fan William Bardwell chose **Uni** sashimi bar in Clio restaurant (in the Eliot Hotel, 370 Commonwealth Ave at Massachusetts Ave, 536.7200). Top-rated Clio serves French-American cuisine. Uni has eight tables and a seven-seat sushi bar. "Uni," Bardwell said, "has seriously upscale sashimi and creative raw-fish creations. Very tasty, real wasabi, top-quality fish—and you *will* impress your guest."

Bardwell also loves **Sushi Island** in suburban Wakefield (397 Main St, 781/224.3479). "This is the best sushi in town, consistently excellent rice and fish, and lots of special fish." Stalwart Dan Lochter also voted for Sushi Island, and added little **Toraya** in Arlington (up Mass Ave from North Cambridge at 890 Massachusetts Ave, just past Arlington High School, 781/641.7477). The small **Shino Express Sushi** (144 Newbury St, Boston, 626.4530) got a nod from Richmond and member Vince Del Vecchio. Sushi praise also went to **Ginza** (Chinatown at 16 Hudson St, 338.2261, or Brookline at 1002 Beacon St, 566.9688).

houses are National Historic Landmarks, but are closed to the public. ♦ 39-40 Beacon St (between Walnut and Spruce Sts)

On the Appleton-Parker Houses:

PURPLE WINDOWPANES

A number of homes along this stretch of Beacon Street boast unusual lavender-hued windowpanes. The famed "purple panes" of Beacon Hill are prized historical artifacts and the proud possession of only a handful of houses on the Hill. Actually, the treasured tint was a fluke—in shipments of glass sent from Hamburg to Boston between 1818 and 1824, manganese oxide reacted with the sun to create the color. Although numerous copies exist, very few authentic panes have survived. (They can also be seen at **29A Chestnut Street** and **63 Beacon Street**.)

52 LITTLE, BROWN AND COMPANY

Established in 1837, this venerable Boston publishing house has on its backlist Louisa May Alcott, John Bartlett (of that household tome *Bartlett's Familiar Quotations*), J.D. Salinger, Evelyn Waugh, Fanny Farmer (of cookbook fame), Margaret Atwood, and Berke Breathed, creator of the retired Bloom County cartoon strip. The firm moved its headquarters here in 1909, and although the Adult Trade division decamped to New York several years ago, certain imprints remain. ♦ 34 Beacon St (at Joy St)

53 GEORGE PARKMAN HOUSE

In one of the most sensational murders of the century, Dr. George Parkman was killed in 1849, allegedly by Harvard professor John Webster, a fellow Boston socialite who had borrowed money from him. Lemuel Shaw, the judge, was related to the victim, and sent Webster to his hanging. After the furor, Parkman's son, George Francis Parkman, retreated from public scrutiny with his mother and sister, remaining a recluse in this house until his death in 1908. Built in 1825 by **Cornelius Coolidge,** the house overlooks Boston Common. Parkman must have found solace in this unchanging landscape because he left $5.5 million in his will for the Common's maintenance. For generations, Boston mayors lived in this house, which belongs to the city; it is now used for civic functions. ♦ 33 Beacon St (between Bowdoin and Joy Sts)

54 PARK STREET

Called Sentry Lane in the 17th century, this was the pathway the sentry took to the top of Beacon Hill, where a bucket of tar mounted on a post in 1634 was ever ready for emergency lighting (until it blew down in 1789). An almshouse, a house of correction, an insane asylum, and a "bridewell" (a lovely name for a jail) stood along this street when it was part of Boston's outskirts; now Park Street is home to a number of decidedly reputable institutions.

In 1804 architect **Charles Bulfinch** straightened out the lane and designed nine residences facing the Common that became known as Bulfinch Row. Only the **Amory-Ticknor House** at the corner of Beacon Street survives, although it's disastrously altered. ◆ Between Tremont and Beacon Sts

On Park Street:

THE UNION CLUB

Formerly separate 19th-century mansions owned by two of Boston's most illustrious families, the Lowells and Lawrences, this is now a private club where members meet to converse over lunch. The right wing was demolished in 1896 and later replaced. ◆ No. 8 (at Park St Pl)

54 NO. 9 PARK

★★★★$$$$ Much-praised chef Barbara Lynch offers cuisine from France and Italy, billed as European classic country. The casually elegant European bistro atmosphere is in a 1940s setting of rich greens, blues, and chocolate brown. There's a popular 30-seat bar in a separate area with fun offerings like oysters and fondue (not in same dish). ◆ M-Sa, lunch and dinner. 9 Park St, across from the State House (between Tremont and Beacon Sts, just a short walk from Red Line Park St T stop). 742.9991. www.no9park.com ♿

55 GRANARY BURYING GROUND

Nestled next to the **Park Street Church** (see right), this graveyard was named for the 1738 granary that the church replaced. Created in 1660, it is the third-oldest graveyard in the city. In this shady haven lie the remains of many Revolutionary heroes—among them **Samuel Adams, John Hancock, James Otis, Robert Treat Paine,** and **Paul Revere**—although the headstones have been moved so often you can't really be sure who's where. The five victims of the Boston Massacre (including black patriot **Crispus Attucks**), philanthropist Peter Faneuil (for whom Faneuil Hall is named), Benjamin Franklin's parents (he's in Philadelphia), and Elizabeth "Mother Goose" Foster are also here. Judge Samuel Sewell likewise rests easy here, having cleared his conscience as the only judge to ever admit publicly that he was wrong to condemn the Salem witches.

The best reason to visit this two-acre necropolis is to examine (and just examine: rubbings are forbidden here) the tombstones' extraordinary carvings of skeletons, urns, winged skulls, and contemplative angels. In this haunting place, you will be transported back to the 17th century, from which the earliest tombstones date. The winged hourglasses

carved into the Egyptian-style granite gateway (designed in 1830 by Solomon Willard) were added later in the 19th century. ◆ Free. Daily. Tremont St (between School and Park Sts)

56 BRIMSTONE CORNER

The intersection of Park and Tremont Streets was supposedly given this name because of the fire-and-brimstone oratory of the Park Street Church's Congregational preachers—including abolitionist **William Lloyd Garrison,** who gave his first antislavery address here in 1829. But a more banal explanation is that brimstone, used to make gunpowder, was stored in the church's crypt during the War of 1812. ◆ Park and Tremont Sts

At Brimstone Corner:

PARK STREET CHURCH

People heading northeast along the Common can't help but look at this majestic 1809 Congregational church, looming opposite the subway station. Henry James heaped praise on the elegant late-Georgian edifice, pronouncing it "perfectly felicitous" and "the most interesting mass of brick and mortar in America." Influenced by his illustrious English compatriot Christopher Wren, architect **Peter Banner** capped the crowning glory of his career with a stalwart 217-foot-tall telescoping white steeple that points to the sky. Locals have always relied on its easy-to-read clock for time and a rendezvous point. The illustrious Handel & Haydn Society, formed here in 1815, drew many of its voices from the church choir over the years. And here the anthem "America" was first sung on 4 July 1831; 24-year-old Samuel Francis Smith reputedly dashed off its lyrics a half hour before schoolchildren sang it on the church steps. The church once stood next to a workhouse, the Puritan answer to homelessness and poverty. ◆ Tu-Sa July-Aug; by appointment only Sept-June. Services Su, 9AM, 10:45AM. 1 Park St. 523.3383 ♿

57 BOSTON COMMON

The oldest public park in the country encompasses 50 sprawling acres. Now the city's heart, it was once Boston's hinterland. In the early 1600s the grounds were part of a farm belonging to **The Reverend William Blaxton,** the first English squatter on the Shawmut Peninsula. A reclusive bachelor in the style of Thoreau, Blaxton shattered his own blissful solitude by generously inviting the city's Puritan founders to settle on his peninsula and share its fresh water. Then, finding his neighbors too close for comfort, Blaxton sold them the land in 1634 and retreated to Beacon Hill. There the city's first—but not

---

Restaurants/Clubs: Red | Hotels: Purple | Shops: Orange | Outdoors/Parks: Green | Sights/Culture: Blue

last—eccentric tended to his beloved orchard, reputedly riding about on his Brahma bull for recreation. But when the busybody Puritans tried to convince Blaxton to join their church, he fled south to Rhode Island.

The park has belonged to Bostonians ever since. Cattle grazed its grass until the practice was outlawed in 1830. Justice (of a sort) was meted out here with whipping posts, stocks, and pillories. Indians, pirates, and persecuted Quakers were hanged here, as was Rachell Whall in the late 1700s, for the crime of highway robbery (she stole a 75¢ bonnet). This is where Redcoats camped during the Revolution and where Civil War troops once mustered. Until 6 July 1836, African-Americans couldn't pass freely through the land. General Lafayette returned to the US in 1824 and shot off a ceremonial cannon here, and the Prince of Wales, future King Edward VII, reviewed the troops on these very same grassy lawns in 1860.

Long the site of great public outdoor theater—which has seen sermons, duels, puppet shows, balloon ascensions, promenades, hopscotch championships, fire-engine and flying-machine demonstrations, horse races, antislavery meetings, fireworks, hoop rolling, and ox roasting—the Common still offers some of Boston's best people-watching.

Arrive before nine on a sunny morning and relish your leisure while working folk push on to their jobs, leaving you to saunter among the magicians, musicians, mounted police, artists, babies in strollers, religious proselytizers, in-line skaters, soapbox orators, pigeons, and pushcart vendors along the park's walkways. Return some summer evening to watch a softball game in one corner, while in another corner an unofficial dog-walking group meets after work to chat as their pets romp. One cautionary note: As is true in most urban areas, the park is not a safe place to be after dark. ♦ Bounded by Tremont, Park, Charles, Boylston, and Beacon Sts

Within Boston Common:

PARK STREET STATION

Designed by **Wheelwright and Haven,** the first subway system in the US opened here to incredible fanfare on 1 September 1897. "First Car Off the Earth!" trumpeted *The Boston Globe.* (The subway line originally ran only as far as today's Boylston Station, just one stop across Boston Common.) Before you hurry aboveground to escape the popcorn and doughnut smells and the throngs on the platforms, look for the mosaic mural by the turnstiles. It depicts the first subway car—actually a streetcar that became an underground railway here—entering the tunnel, with a woman rider holding aloft that day's

Globe. Aboveground, the two copper-roofed, granite-faced kiosks are National Historic Landmarks. ♦ Park and Tremont Sts

VISITOR INFORMATION CENTER

Head a short distance down Tremont Street to this freestanding center, where information is available on museum exhibitions, helicopter rides, and whale-watches. This is also the place to pick up a map of Boston's renowned **Freedom Trail.** ♦ Daily. 536.4100

THE FREEDOM TRAIL

Begin the famous self-guided tourist pilgrimage at the **Visitor Information Center** and track an elusive red line connecting 16 historical sites from colonial and Revolutionary times, including **Paul Revere's House** and the **Old North Church** (see the map on page 30).

BOSTON COMMON RANGER STATION

Situated behind the **Visitor Information Center** (see above), this is the place to obtain details about the many walks and tours led by park rangers. Offerings include **historic tours** of the Common and the Granary Burying Ground; a **What's in Bloom? walk** and a **Family Stroll** in the Public Garden; the **Make Way for Ducklings tour,** which includes a reading of the famous children's storybook (the walk starts at the Garden's bronze ducklings); and the **Horse of Course program,** which traces a day in the life of a park ranger's trusty steed. ♦ Free. Daily. 635.7383, 635.7412

PARKMAN PLAZA

This plaza's bronze figures enshrine Puritan values. The path to the left of *Industry* is called **Railroad Mall,** because in 1835 it led to the terminal of one of Boston's first railroads. A brief, lovely stroll down Railroad Mall leads to the recently renovated neoclassical **Parkman Bandstand,** the site of Shakespeare in the Park performances during the summer (call 888/SEE.BOSTON for information).

CENTRAL BURYING GROUND

Follow **Railroad Mall** to find history etched on 18th-century tombstones. Legend has it that American soldiers who died at the Battle of Bunker Hill and British soldiers who succumbed to illness during the Siege of Boston lie here. At least a dozen Boston Tea Party guests are also buried in this graveyard, as is portrait artist **Gilbert Stuart,** who painted Martha and George Washington. Stuart died in poverty, having been eclipsed by less talented but more socially skilled painters. The inscriptions that mention "strangers" refer to Irish Catholic immigrants buried here. In early colonial graveyards like this one, headstones often face east—whence would come the Day of Judgment trumpet call—and are paired with footstones, creating a cozy bed for the occupant's eternal rest.

FLAGSTAFF HILL

Climb the Common's highest point, atop which the **Soldiers and Sailors Monument** commemorates Civil War combatants. Gunpowder was stored here long ago.

FROG POND

True, it's a frogless, sometimes empty concrete hollow instead of the marshy amphibian abode it once was (Edgar Allan Poe derisively called Bostonians "Frogpondians"), but it has become a popular winter ice-skating spot and in steamy weather the pond is filled with children cavorting under its fountain. (Even the cynical Poe called the Common "no common thing.")

BEACON STREET MALL

In the shadow of the **State House,** this wide, dappled promenade along the Common's north side is where Ralph Waldo Emerson and Walt Whitman once paced back and forth, arguing about whether or not to take the sex out of Whitman's *Leaves of Grass*. Though Emerson was utterly convincing, Whitman concluded, "I could never hear the points better put—and then I felt down in my soul the clear and unmistakable conviction to disobey all, and pursue my own way." Despite their disagreement, the friends went off together to partake of "a bully dinner."

ROBERT GOULD SHAW MEMORIAL

Across from the main entrance to the State House, sculptor Augustus Saint-Gaudens's monument honors the 54th Massachusetts Regiment, the nation's first black regiment, which enlisted in Boston. The troops fought in the Civil War under the command of 26-year-old Shaw, son of a venerable Boston family. For two years, until a shamefaced Congress relented, members of the 54th refused their pay because they received only $10 a month instead of the $13 paid to white soldiers. Shaw and half his men died in an assault on Fort Wagner, South Carolina, in 1863. Saint-Gaudens took 13 years to complete this beautifully wrought bas-relief, which Shaw's abolitionist family insisted must honor the black infantrymen as well as their son. Erected in 1897, the monument today seems somewhat patronizing for its portrayal of the white Shaw as a heroic figure on horseback, towering above the black troops, but it was, in fact, remarkably liberal in its day. Draw near to study the portraitlike treatment of the men's expressive faces. The Angel of Death hovers above. The story of Shaw and his brave regiment

is recounted in the 1989 film *Glory*. Charles McKim, of the architectural firm **McKim, Mead & White,** designed the memorial's classical frame. It sits on a small plaza whose granite balustrade overlooks the park.

BLACK HERITAGE TRAIL

A guided 1.6-mile walking tour that traces the history of Boston's 19th-century black community begins at the **Robert Gould Shaw Memorial**. The first Africans arrived as slaves in Puritan Boston in 1638, eight years after the city was founded. By 1705, when a free black community was beginning in the North End, the city had more than 400 slaves. But after the American Revolution, the first federal census in 1790 showed Massachusetts as the only state to record no slaves. ◆ Call the Boston African American National Historic Site for more information. 742.5415. www.afroammuseum.org

58 PUBLIC GARDEN

You can't lounge as freely on the grass here as on the Common, but this park is an idyllic, lush retreat that always seems larger than it truly is. Artists love the garden's manicured look, and the advertising and film communities stage photo shoots all over it. Several out-of-the-way bowers offer havens from urban tumult, and there's no better place for a springtime romance to bloom.

One of the oldest botanical gardens in America, the property began as desolate, soggy salt-marsh flats located along a great bay of the Charles River estuary. Ropewalks spanned the area, and Bostonians clammed and fished when the tides allowed. In April 1775 British soldiers embarked by boat for Lexington and Concord from a spot near the garden's Charles Street Gate.

There's also a remarkable history of outspoken citizen involvement enshrined in this spot. Throughout the early 1800s, real-estate developers hankered after its 24 acres, only to be thwarted again and again by vigilant citizens dreaming of a magnificent botanical garden. Bostonians finally ratified a bill in 1859 that deemed the garden forever public. That same year, **George Meacham,** a local novice architect, won $100 for his English-inspired vision of a public garden dominated by a sinuous pond and ribboned with paths. His grandiloquent scheme was modestly altered in the final form. Today the garden is watched over and beautified by garden angels: The Friends of the Public Garden, formed in the 1970s. Plantings change seasonally, beginning with hearty pansies and tulips that triumph over Boston's uncertain spring weather. ◆ Bounded by Charles, Boylston, Arlington, and Beacon Sts

---

Restaurants/Clubs: Red | Hotels: Purple | Shops: Orange | Outdoors/Parks: Green | Sights/Culture: Blue

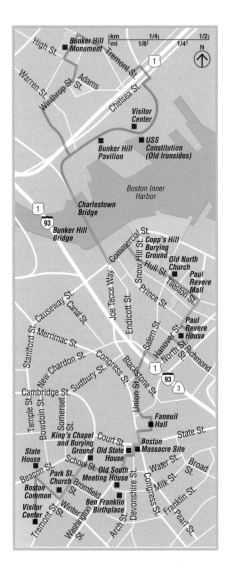

downtown stretch in the distance along Tremont Street. From bridgeside, watch Boston's entire socioeconomic and cultural spectrum pass by on the surrounding walkways.

SWAN BOATS AND LAGOON

One of Boston's most famous sights, the Swan Boats cruise serenely by while dozens of chatty ducks wait for handouts on the four-foot-deep, four-acre lagoon. A pair of real swans, ceremoniously escorted to the lagoon every spring, also sail snootily about. Rowboats, canoes, and a little side-wheeler named the *Dolly Varden* once plied these waters, but the Swan Boats have reigned alone now for more than a century. Their creator, **Robert Paget,** an English immigrant and shipbuilder, was inspired by Wagner's opera *Lohengrin,* in which the hero crosses a river in a boat drawn by a swan.

Paget's descendants still own the quaint fleet he launched in 1877. The six existing boats now carry up to 20 passengers per boat instead of the original four, and weigh two tons. The oldest, *Big Bertha,* dates from 1918. Children are thrilled by the 15-minute figure-eight voyage, pedal-powered at 2 miles per hour, and it's a fine way to rest your feet. In the winter, the lagoon becomes a picturesque ice-skating pond. ♦ Nominal fee. Daily from mid-Apr to late Sept. Swan Boats 522.1966; skate rentals 482.7400

PLANTS AND TREES

Amble amid the colorful legacy of **William Doogue,** the garden's controversial superintendent from 1878 to 1906, who instituted its famous Victorian floral displays, which are rotated seasonally. Some Bostonians griped about Doogue's extravagant use of showy hothouse plants, including palms, cacti, and yucca—in 1888, some 90,000 plants were laid out in 150 beds—but most people were thrilled, and Doogue's style has endured, though on a more modest scale. Nearly 600 trees of more than 100 varieties grow in the garden, most labeled with their Latin and common names. The garden's weeping willows offer splendid shade for reading.

DUCKLINGS

The best-loved garden sculptures (unveiled in 1987) are Boston artist Nancy Schön's larger-than-life bronzes of Mrs. Mallard and her eight ducklings, the heroes of Robert McCloskey's illustrated children's tale *Make Way for Ducklings* (published in 1941). As the story goes, after stopping all traffic on Beacon Street, the canard clan marches off to rendezvous at the

Within the Public Garden:

FOOTBRIDGE

Enter the garden by taking the ceremonial **Haffenreffer Walk** off Charles Street and step onto the spunky, whimsical footbridge, designed in 1867 by **William G. Preston.** It's an appealing exaggeration of the engineering marvel of its day, the suspension bridge. Repaired and reinforced, the bridge's spiderweb cables are only decorative now. Lean back against the baby bridge and gaze across the garden toward Beacon Street, ignoring the ugly

---

Restaurants/Clubs: Red | Hotels: Purple | Shops: Orange | Outdoors/Parks: Green | Sights/Culture: Blue

lagoon with Mr. Mallard. It's easy to spot the ducks along the path between the lagoon and the gateway at Charles and Beacon Streets—look for children sitting on them, embracing and patting them, or waddling nearby quacking. When one of the ducklings was stolen in 1989, a pair of bartenders, Eddie Doyle of the nearby Bull & Finch (aka "Cheers") pub and Tommy Leonard of Kenmore Square's Eliot Lounge, started the "Bring Back Mack" fund-raising campaign. Now Mack is back with his pack.

Since the 17th century, the Boston Harbor islands have served as sites for public facilities (quarantine hospitals, pauper colonies, immigration stations, almshouses, reform schools, and prisons)—and, occasionally, for illegal businesses. In the 19th century one island was the site of a factory where local girls produced cigars that Bostonians were led to believe were made in Spain and for which they were charged premium prices.

THE BIG DIG

The most expensive, over-budget local transportation project in US history is over, sort of. The official end of the **Central Artery/Tunnel Project** came in 2005. But 2006 saw clean-up work, repairs, and the indictments of several contractors for shoddy work and allegedly fraudulent billing. More serious was the closure of connector tunnels beneath the South Boston waterfront in 2006 after a falling concrete slab crushed a car and killed a passenger. But the long-awaited **Rose Kennedy Greenway**—a downtown ribbon of parkland over the now-underground I-93—should be in place in 2007. The 30-acre string of parks in place of the ugly elevated roadway goes 1.5 miles from Causeway Street near North Station and the North End to Kneeland Street in Chinatown. The North End and the waterfront, isolated for years by the expressway, are easily accessible to the rest of the city again.

The $15 billion Big Dig began in 1986 to fix Boston's traffic-choked highways and end daily traffic jams. Building 10 lanes of highway under the heart of the city and extending Interstates 90 and 93 made chaos of many downtown streets, especially in the North End and the Financial District.

Traffic is, indeed, better. The trip from Logan Airport to downtown or the suburbs, for example, is noticeably shorter and easier (when all the tunnels are open). But in rush hour, you can still expect traffic delays. The Rose Kennedy Greenway is one of the best things to come out of the project; the North End, Waterfront, and South

Boston will no longer be cut off from the rest of the city by an ugly elevated expressway.

The project was called the Big Dig because some 15 million cubic yards of dirt and rocks was excavated to make room for the new highway. The Dig built tunnels under the city and Boston Harbor and worked around subways—while they were running. It built the Ted Williams tunnel linking Logan Airport with I-90, the Fort Point Channel tunnel, the new Broadway bridge into South Boston, and the Summer Street bridge. It changed neighborhoods and changed lives. In addition to smoother traffic and the Rose Kennedy Greenway, it gave us the graceful **Leonard P. Zakim Bunker Hill Bridge** from I-93 over the Charles River. With supporting cables like white webbing, the short-but-beautiful 10-lane bridge is the world's widest cable-stayed span.

It's still true—despite the changes—that cars and Boston usually mean trouble. If you must drive, check the traffic web sites for help. Try www.masspike.com and www.boston.com/traffic.

Boston has always been a beautiful walking city, and it's more so now with the Greenway. Don't bring a car if you can avoid doing so. Parking is scarce and expensive. Driving can make you frantic—and late—even without the detours, road closings, and barriers of the Big Dig. Besides, you can more easily get around town by taxi or on the clean and reasonably efficient subway system called the T.

Restaurants/Clubs: Red | Hotels: Purple | Shops: Orange | Outdoors/Parks: Green | Sights/Culture: Blue

GOVERNMENT CENTER/FANEUIL HALL

This part of town is not so much a neighborhood as it is a collection of interesting sights sprinkled among impersonal office towers and heavily trafficked, characterless streets. More or less bound by State, Court, and Cambridge Streets to the south, the tangle of highways at the edge of the Charles River to the west and north, and the now-underground I-93/Central Artery to the east, the main attractions here are **Faneuil Hall Marketplace,** with its blend of history and contemporary consumer delights; **Blackstone Block,** a tiny remnant of "Old Boston"; and the **TD Banknorth Garden,** home of the Celtics basketball team, the Bruins hockey team, the circus, boxing matches, and high-profile music acts.

Established communities were swept away during the 1950s and '60s, when the city tried to rejuvenate itself through drastic, painful, and, many say, wrong-headed urban renewal, forcing thousands of residents to move. Architect **I.M. Pei**'s master urban design plan imposed monumental order on 56 acres: 22 streets were replaced with six; slots for big, bold new buildings were carefully plotted; and a vast plaza was created and crowned with an iconoclastic city hall symbolizing "New Boston."

The name **West End,** nearly forgotten now, at one time referred to the 48 vibrant acres stretching from the base of Beacon Hill to North Station. The West End's fashionable days ended in the 19th century, and by the 20th century city officials considered the area a slum. Yet more than 10,000 people—mostly Italians and Jews, with Russian, Greek, Albanian, Irish, Polish, and Lithuanian immigrants—inhabited brick row houses on the lively, intimate streets. Older Bostonians recall when Government Center was the raucous **Scollay Square,** where Boston's racier nightlife crowd caroused in saloons, burlesque shows, shooting galleries, adult theaters, pawnshops, tattoo parlors, and cheap hotels. Physically, much of the West End looked like today's treasured Beacon Hill, albeit with less money. Many still regret that this historic, freewheeling square was obliterated to make way for businesses and federal, state, and city offices.

Incredibly altered and dislocated from its past, this area now seems oddly situated. Abutting the history-drenched Waterfront, North End, and Beacon Hill, Government

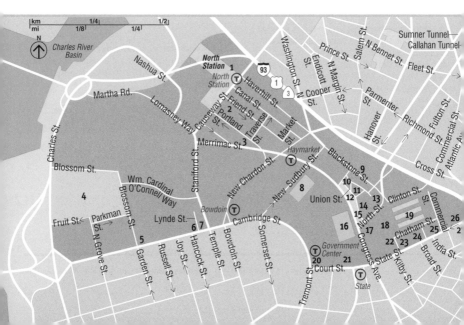

Center is more a passageway to other destinations than a place to linger. Only vestiges of the past remain, like **Old West Church,** the **Harrison Gray Otis House,** the **Bulfinch Pavilion** and **Ether Dome** at Massachusetts General Hospital, and the famous **Steaming Kettle** landmark. Most of the contemporary architecture has a 1960s look, often alienating and aloof. The newest buildings still can't decide what they're doing here. The old, authentic languages, layers, color, and complexity are gone.

1 NORTH STATION

Trains operating from here transport sports fans and daily commuters to and from the North Shore and western suburbs. In summer, the station (under the TD Banknorth Garden) has crowds waiting for the beach train (the route stopping at Beverly, Manchester, Gloucester, Rockport, and other towns with spacious public beaches). Five commuter lines and Amtrak's Downeaster service to New Hampshire and Maine pull in here. Construction to double the size of the often-crowded station should be finished in 2007. Across from the station's main entrance is the MBTA's Green Line and Orange Line, subway lines that carry riders in and out of central Boston. City planning being what it is, the subways don't go into North Station; you have to walk across the street, climb the stairs (there's an elevator for wheelchair access), and board the clunky subway cars. Station expansion plans aren't scheduled to change this. ♦ Causeway St (at Canal St). 723.3200

At North Station:

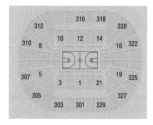

TD BANKNORTH GARDEN

This squat-looking, $160 million home to the Boston Celtics and NHL Boston Bruins opened in the 1995-1996 season as the Fleet Center. It became the Banknorth Garden in 2005. The 755,000-square-foot arena and entertainment complex rests above North Station. Like its predecessor, the old Boston Garden, the arena hosts family events like the circus, the Ice Capades, and concerts year-round. Unlike the Garden, however, the arena offers air conditioning and access by elevator and escalator. The Garden's parquet floor—built during World War II when only short wood was available—was moved to the arena, along with a rafterful of championship banners and the retired numbers of legendary Celtics players Bill Russell, Bob Cousy, John Havlicek, and Larry Bird, and Bruins players Bobby Orr, Johnny Bucyk, and Phil Esposito. The garden, highly visible from north and south, features grand-scaled windows looking out over the city's inner harbor. After a game, many fans choose from the slew of nearby bars. Others, looking for more than bistro food, make their way to restaurants in the nearby North End (see page 46). ♦ Recorded information: 624.1000 &

THE SPORTS MUSEUM OF NEW ENGLAND

On the fifth and sixth floors of the Banknorth Garden, the Sports Museum encapsulates top moments in New England sports history. Holdings include more than a thousand hours of film and video highlights, action-packed displays, interactive exhibits, and life-size statues of sports legends. ♦ Closed M. Museum tickets sold at the Garden box office. 624.1235; www.sportsmuseum.org

2 HILTON'S TENT CITY

What began as a modest army surplus store in 1947 has ballooned into the USA's biggest source of tents, with five floors of tents and accessories for camping and backpacking. It also sells men's and women's clothing and footwear for skiing, mountaineering, and backpacking. ♦ Daily. 272 Friend St (between Valenti Way and Causeway St). 227.9242; www.hiltonstentcity.com

3 101 MERRIMAC STREET

Boston's first faux-historic building, this 10-story office complex—which looks like a conglomeration of rehabbed warehouses—was, in fact, designed from scratch by The Architects Collaborative in 1991. Duck inside to catch New York muralist Richard Haas's trompe l'oeil palm court, a domed winter garden eked out in two dimensions. The ubiquitous **au bon pain** (248.9441) has a small café here, should you wish to rest and nosh awhile. ♦ At Lancaster St

3 ANTHEM

★★$$$ Upscale Anthem replaced the old, noisy Commonwealth Brewing Company a few years ago with floor-to-ceiling windows, comfortable décor, fancier food and, yes, higher prices. A lot of people still come here before and after games and events at the Garden. There's awfully good comfort food and a more discriminating crowd has found the restaurant. ◆ American ◆ Daily, lunch and dinner. 138 Portland St (between Valenti Way and Causeway St). 523.8383; www.anthemboston.com &

4 MASSACHUSETTS GENERAL HOSPITAL

Although a hospital is rarely a voluntary destination, this medical center—considered to be one of the nation's best general hospitals—is worth a look. The main hospital building, the **George R. White Memorial Building** on Fruit Street, was built in 1939 by **Coolidge, Shepley, Bulfinch, and Abbott.** The late–Art Deco structure is now a city landmark. The most noteworthy edifice in the medical complex, however, is the **Bulfinch Pavilion.** To find this National Historic Landmark amid the "Mass General" maze, enter from North Grove Street off Cambridge Street, or ask directions in the main hospital building.

In 1817 Boston's trailblazing architect **Charles Bulfinch** won the commission to create this edifice of Chelmsford granite, quarried by inmates of the state prison. Questions persist about Bulfinch's actual role in the pavilion commission, since it was his last project before he was called to Washington, DC, by the president to design the Capitol rotunda. His assistant, **Alexander Parris**—who later gained fame in his own right, particularly for designing Quincy Market—prepared the working drawings and supervised construction, probably influencing the pavilion's final form much more than its name suggests. Delayed by the War of 1812, the building's cornerstone was laid in 1818 and the first patient admitted in 1821. The building is still used for patient care, offices, and research.

Progressive for its day and gracefully proportioned, the Greek Revival building's enduring fame derives from the medical achievements that took place in the amphitheater beneath the sky-lit dome. It was in this theater, the hospital's operating room from 1821 to 1867 (now called the **Ether Dome**), that the first public demonstration of the use of ether in a surgical procedure took place. On 16 October 1846, Dr. John C. Warren, cofounder of the hospital and its first surgeon, operated on a patient suffering from a tumor in his jaw. A dentist named Thomas Green Morton administered the ether with his own apparatus, after supposedly almost missing the operation because he was having last-minute adjustments made to the inhaler device. When the procedure was finally finished, the patient awoke and said he had felt no pain. Within a year, ether was in use worldwide to prevent surgical pain.

The amphitheater is also home to **Padihershef,** a mummy brought here from Thebes, Egypt, in 1823. It was the first Egyptian mummy in the US. The hospital's original fund-raiser, Padihershef is also the only remaining witness to the Ether Dome's finest moments. To visit the Ether Dome, call ahead to be sure it's not in use. ◆ 55 Fruit St (between N Grove and Charles Sts). 726.2000

5 HOLIDAY INN SELECT– GOVERNMENT CENTER

$$ Adjacent to **Massachusetts General Hospital,** this 14-story hotel on the edge of Beacon Hill has 303 rooms, with the nicest on the executive level. There's an outdoor pool; rooms for nonsmokers and people with disabilities are available. **Foster's Bar and Grill,** across from the hotel lobby, offers breakfast, lunch, and dinner. The location is convenient for sightseers, who can walk to Faneuil Hall Marketplace or cross Cambridge Street and meander over to Beacon Hill. Discounted parking is also available. ◆ 5 Blossom St (at Cambridge St). 742.7630, 800/465.4329; fax 742.7804 &

6 HARRISON GRAY OTIS HOUSE, 1796

This house—a trial run for Otis and his architect of choice—was the first in a series of three increasingly lavish residences that **Charles Bulfinch** designed for his friend, who had a taste for flamboyant living and fine architecture. Otis lived here for four years before moving his family to grander quarters on **Mount Vernon Street** (see page 20), followed by another move to **Beacon Hill** (see page 14). When he lived in house number one, Harry Otis was a prestigious lawyer and freshman member of Congress. He became Boston's third mayor and a major land speculator who transformed rustic Beacon Hill into a wealthy enclave, again with Bulfinch's help. Set in what was briefly fashionable Bowdoin Square, this Federalist mansion is austerely handsome, much more opulent inside than out. By the end of the 19th century, Bowdoin Square's elegance had frayed, and Otis's former home endured a spotty career as a Turkish bath, then a patent medicine shop, and finally a boardinghouse defaced with storefronts.

In 1916 the **Society for the Preservation of New England Antiquities** (SPNEA) acquired the house—now one of 34 New England properties the group runs—and restored it to its former splendor. The society is headquartered here, and the building houses the SPNEA's architectural and photographic archives. The house's décor dates from 1790 to 1820 and includes some Otis family belongings. With its next-door neighbor, the **Old West Church** (see below), the Otis House is a reminder of the early years of the Republic; the two are lonely survivors that refuse to be overwhelmed by their high-rise surroundings. ♦ Admission. W-Su. Guided tours every 30 minutes, 11AM-4:30PM. 141 Cambridge St (at Lynde St). 227.3956; www.historicnewengland.org

7 OLD WEST CHURCH

A 1737 wood-framed church stood on this site until the British razed it in 1775, suspicious that Revolutionary sympathizers were using the steeple to signal the Continental troops in Cambridge. The decorous redbrick Federal replacement, a National Historic Landmark designed by **Asher Benjamin** in 1806, is kin to Charles Bulfinch's Massachusetts State House and St. Stephen's Church, and to Benjamin's Charles Street Meeting House—all flat surfaced and delicately ornamented with classical motifs. Formerly Unitarian and now Methodist, the church exudes quiet composure in the midst of Cambridge Street's physical and architectural chaos. Inquire about concerts featuring the fine Charles Fisk pipe organ. ♦ Daily; Su service 11AM. 131 Cambridge St (at Lynde St). 227.5088

8 JOHN F. KENNEDY FEDERAL OFFICE BUILDING

Indifferent and impersonal in appearance, this one-million-square-foot building, designed in 1967 by The Architects Collaborative (Walter Gropius's firm) and Samuel Glaser Associates, is a perfectly appropriate home for the Internal Revenue Service, the Federal Bureau of Investigation, and many of the other federal agencies one doesn't want to tangle with. A Robert Motherwell mural marks the spot where the 26-story tower is connected to its long, low-rise mate. ♦ New Sudbury St (between Congress Ave and Cambridge St)

9 EBENEZER HANCOCK HOUSE

This three-story redbrick house (one of Boston's rare surviving late-18th-century

downtown residences) was probably completed in 1767 by John Hancock's uncle, Thomas, from whom John later inherited it. Here John's younger brother, Ebenezer, lived and maintained his office as deputy paymaster of the Continental Army. His biggest duty came in 1778, when Admiral D'Estaing's fleet conducted two million silver coins from King Louis XVI of France to pay local troops, salvaging their morale. Restored, the house is now lawyers' offices and not open to the public. ♦ 10 Marshall St (at Creek Sq)

9 THE HAYMARKET

They were hard-pressed during Big Dig construction, but on Friday and Saturday a fleet of pushcart vendors selling fruit, vegetables, and fish sets up for open-air business along Blackstone Street by the Rose Kennedy Greenway. The narrow sidewalk is often clogged with shoppers. Saturday is busiest. Come for bargains, especially at the end of the day, but be forewarned that vendors will treat you brusquely if you pick over their merchandise. They fill the bags; you just pay, European style. So what if a tomato is the worse for wear? You get what you pay for, but it's satisfying to avoid supermarket sterility. Along this stretch are old establishments purveying meats and cheeses that complement the Haymarket's offerings. ♦ F, Sa, dawn–mid-afternoon. Blackstone St (between Creek Sq and Hanover St)

10 BELL IN HAND TAVERN

$ Operating since 1795, though not always at this site on the Freedom Trail, this is the oldest tavern in the US. Its moniker is illustrated by the curious old sign on its plain façade, much like pubs in Great Britain. It was named by original proprietor Jim Wilson, Boston's town crier until 1794, who rang a bell as he went through town announcing the news. Benjamin Franklin's childhood home once stood on this site. Expect a line at the door, a DJ, and contemporary bands at night. On a cold afternoon, duck in for a draft and a burger or sandwich. (Kitchen hours vary, so food isn't always available.) ♦ American ♦ Daily. 45 Union St (between Marshall and Hanover Sts). 227.2098

10 GREEN DRAGON TAVERN

★$ First opened in 1657, this place was once deemed "the headquarters of the Revolution" by Sam Adams, Daniel Webster, and Paul Revere. Occupying British soldiers kept a close watch on the tavern, but the Sons of Liberty were nevertheless able to plan the Boston Tea Party here. Today the old place is Irish in ambience, with wood-plank floors and lace-curtained windows. Popular menu specials

---

Restaurants/Clubs: Red | Hotels: Purple | Shops: Orange | Outdoors/Parks: Green | Sights/Culture: Blue

include beef stew, beer-batter fish-and-chips, bangers and mash, and an Irish grill. There are 13 varieties of beer on draft. ♦ Irish/American ♦ Daily, lunch and dinner until 2AM. 11 Marshall St (between Union and Hanover Sts). 367.0055

11 UNION OYSTER HOUSE

★★$$$ Dine in one of the few spots in Boston where time refuses to move forward. The city's oldest restaurant (founded circa 1715) and the oldest in continuous operation in the US, this eatery has served seafood at this spot since 1826. When the restaurant's original owners opened their oyster-and-clam bar, they installed the current half-circle mahogany bar that supposedly became Daniel Webster's favorite haunt. Webster reputedly downed each half-dozen oysters with a tumbler of brandy and water, and usually consumed six platefuls at a sitting.

Today this is a one-of-a-kind place, best on a cold winter's day when you can follow chilled oysters with steaming chowder or oyster stew and your choice of fresh seafood entrées. The first-floor booths are original, with a plaque adorning the booth where JFK liked to dine. Even if you don't stop to eat, look in and watch the oyster shucking at the bar. ♦ Seafood/American ♦ Daily, lunch and dinner. Reservations recommended. 41 Union St (at Marshall St). 227.2750. www.unionoysterhouse.com & (first floor only)

11 HENNESSY'S IRISH PUB

★$ Between Faneuil Hall and the Union Oyster House, Hennessy's is a popular, Irish-run pub with good food, a wide selection of beers, and entertainment most nights. Dishes go beyond the usual pub grub, with selections like scallop and mushroom pie. The popular dance club "Q" is on the second floor. ♦ Irish/American ♦ 11AM-2AM. 25 Union St (next to the Holocaust Memorial). 742.2121

12 NEW ENGLAND HOLOCAUST MEMORIAL

Dedicated in 1995, the 50th-anniversary year of the end of World War II, the quiet, haunting memorial is the result of a group effort by Nazi concentration camp survivors living in the Boston area. The stark memorial is the work of San Francisco architect **Stanley Saitowitz**, and comprises six five-story glass towers, each representing the gas chambers of the major Nazi death camps. Etched on tinted-glass panels are the numbers one to six million to represent the number of Jews killed in the Holocaust. Also on the panels are quotations and stories from survivors. Saitowitz sought to create a memorial that was ambiguous, open-ended, and hopeful. ♦ Union Park, Congress St (between North and Hanover Sts) &

13 BLACKSTONE BLOCK

A charming snippet of Old Boston, this tiny neighborhood is laced with winding lanes and alleys whose names—Salt Lane, Marsh Lane, and Creek Square—recall an era when water still flowed here. The area was once on the narrow neck of land—frequently under water—that led from Shawmut Peninsula to the North End. The block's history dates to colonial times; its architecture spans the 18th, 19th, and 20th centuries. People, chickens, geese, hogs, garbage, and carts laden with goods from nearby ships once commingled on the block's dirt streets. Meat markets flourished here throughout the city's history, and still do along Blackstone Street, named for Boston's first settler, William Blaxton (his name was spelled both ways). ♦ Bounded by Blackstone and Union Sts, and North and Hanover Sts

13 MILLENNIUM BOSTONIAN HOTEL

$$$$ Intimate, gracious, and across the courtyard from **Faneuil Hall,** this is one of the most pleasant places to stay in Boston. A $14-million renovation in 2007 should keep it that way. Much of the charm comes from its residential scale and the way it blends with the historic Blackstone block. Incorporated into the hotel complex is a structure dating from 1824 and an 1890 warehouse built by **Peabody and Stearns** (architects for the **Custom House Tower**). Many of the 201 rooms (11 with canopy beds) have French doors opening onto private balconies that overlook the marketplace. The lobby is appealingly low-key, with historic displays on loan from the Bostonian Society. There's a first-rate restaurant on the premises (see below),and the airy **Atrium** cocktail lounge is a comfortable place to snack on appetizers and listen to live jazz. (No jeans or sneakers.) Amenities include baby-sitting and complimentary overnight shoe shines and morning airport limos. Nonsmoking floors are available, as are rooms equipped for people with hearing impairments. Overnight valet parking is $40. ♦ North and Blackstone Sts. 523.3600, 800/343.0922; fax 523.2454; e-mail bostonian@mhrmail.com; www.millennium-hotels.com/boston &

Within the Millennium Bostonian Hotel:

SEASONS

★★★★$$$$ The swank, glass-enclosed dining room atop the hotel offers generous cityscapes and views of Quincy Market's gold dome, the famous Faneuil Hall weather vane, and the Custom House Tower's glowing clock; newcomers to Boston will be dazzled. This dining spot is famous as a training ground for Boston's top chefs (Lydia Shire, Jasper White, Gordon Hamersley, et al.). As befits its name, Seasons' menu changes quarterly and has

THE WOMEN'S HERITAGE TRAIL

The achievements and contributions of women have enriched the city of Boston for almost four centuries, yet the significance of women and their stories has often been overlooked. The Boston Women's Heritage Trail, established in 1990, is an attempt to remedy that situation. In a city known for its walking tours, the development of a women's trail seemed a natural way to trace women's rightful place in the history of Boston. Seven walks have been established, each one focusing on a particular neighborhood: Downtown, the North End, South Cove/Chinatown, Beacon Hill, the South End, Jamaica Plain, and Roxbury. The trails are described in a self-guided tour booklet, which includes maps of the sites and details about the women associated with each; the booklet is available at some bookstores and at the shop of the National Park Service Center (15 State St, at Devonshire St; 242.5642). Descriptions of the four trails located in central areas of Boston follow.

North End: A Diversity of Cultures

This walk spans Boston history from Revolutionary times to the influx of immigrants during the 19th and early 20th centuries. It focuses on the lives of women from the variety of ethnic groups that populated the North End during that period. Beginning with Yankee women active in support of the Revolutionary War (such as **Rachel Walker Revere,** the resourceful spouse of patriot Paul Revere), it continues with the activities of the Irish (including **Rose Fitzgerald Kennedy,** who was born here), Jewish, and Italian women who made the North End their first home in Boston.

Downtown: The Search for Equal Rights

Boston's early-17th century struggles over religious freedom are examined in this walk through the stories of **Anne Hutchinson** and **Mary Dyer.** Statues of the two women—to date, the only public statues of women anywhere in Boston—stand in front of the Massachusetts State House on Beacon Hill. Plaques affixed to the statues briefly outline the women's lives. Anne Hutchinson (1591-1643) and her husband, William, arrived in Boston on 18 September 1634. They built a home on the site of the original Old Corner Bookstore. Anne Hutchinson became popular, prominent, and powerful, and respected as a midwife—she herself had 15 children. She was a brilliant thinker and a leader of the controversial Antinomian sect, which took issue with prevailing Puritan thought. Hutchinson believed that men and women could receive grace only from God, and accused the ministers of preaching that "good works" signified holiness. She was taken to court for her beliefs and in 1637 was banished for heresy. Like most religious refugees of the era, she and her family fled to Rhode Island.

Like her friend Anne Hutchinson, Mary Dyer, a mother of five, disagreed with the all-male Puritan ministry. She was twice banished to Rhode Island. The third time she returned to Boston (in 1660), she was hanged.

Also covered in the Downtown walk is **Phillis Wheatley** (1753-1784), the first published African-American woman poet. Soon after arriving in Boston in 1761 on the slave ship *Philli,* the young girl was purchased at auction by the Wheatley family. Her mistress, Suzannah Wheatley, became her mentor, and by 1771 the former slave had become a member of the Old South Meeting House. In 1773 Phillis gained international fame when her book of poems was published. In 1784, at about the age of 30, she died destitute. The museum at the **Old South Meeting House** has an exhibit about her life and a copy of her book of poems.

South Cove/Chinatown: Action for Economic and Social Justice

The lives of the three **Peabody sisters** are the focus of this tour. Elizabeth, who introduced kindergartens to Boston, ran a bookshop at 15 West Street (today the West Street Grill). Her younger sisters were each married in the family parlor behind the store: Sophia, an artist, became the wife of author Nathaniel Hawthorne, and Mary, an educator, became the wife and associate of educator Horace Mann.

Beacon Hill: Writers, Artists, and Activists

This journey traces the ways in which women writers and artists living on Beacon Hill used their talents to further social causes—from the abolition of slavery to peace. Also covered here are the stories of African-American women who were abolitionists, among them **Edmonia Lewis,** a well-known sculptor, and **Harriet Hayden,** a survivor and then activist in the underground railroad. Hayden and her husband, also an escaped slave, owned a house on Beacon Hill at 66 Phillips Street. When she died in 1893, Harriet bequeathed a scholarship for "needy and worthy colored students" to Harvard Medical School.

Although not based on the Women's Heritage Trail specifically, two **free guided walking tours** that also focus on women are available. Park rangers (242.5642) give tours of sites on Boston Common and adjacent streets that have connections with Louisa May Alcott, Julia Ward Howe, Lucy Stone, Elizabeth Peabody, Margaret Fuller, Mary Dyer, Anne Hutchinson, "Mother" Elizabeth Goose, and Phillis Wheatley. In addition, Boston National Historical Park rangers (242.5688) offer a tour called **Remembering the Women,** which features women during the American Revolution period, in particular Abigail Adams and Rachel Revere.

Restaurants/Clubs: Red | Hotels: Purple | Shops: Orange | Outdoors/Parks: Green | Sights/Culture: Blue

THE BEST

Ed Gordon

Former executive director, Gibson House Museum/president, Victorian Society in America, New England Chapter

Chatting with friends in the courtyard at a **Gibson House Museum** "Twilight Talks" reception.

Admiring **"painted ladies"** in Boston neighborhoods during Victorian Society walking tours.

Visiting art galleries on **Newbury Street**.

Antiquing on **Charles Street**.

Browsing and buying collectibles at the **Cyclorama Flea Market** in the South End.

Lining up at the **Commonwealth Pier** on a hot summer morning for the ferry to Provincetown.

Watching the sun stream through the aquamarine opalescent stained glass of **Trinity Church's** Ascension window.

Watching the world go by while enjoying a Sam Adams beer at **Milano's Italian Kitchen** on Newbury Street.

Buying fresh flowers and homemade desserts at the fall **Copley Square Farmers Market**.

Drinking Irish beer and dining at the authentic 1880s **Doyle's Cafe** in Jamaica Plain.

Visiting artist lofts during the annual Fort Point Channel, South End, and Cambridgeport **open studios tours**.

Strolling through the grounds of **Mount Auburn Cemetery** in the spring and fall.

Visiting the **Vietnamese restaurants** and stores of the Harvard Avenue area in Allston.

---

featured such New England and international treats as duckling with ginger and scallions, roasted rack of lamb and pumpkin couscous, baked swordfish with olive compote, and wild mushroom tartlet. Service is gracious. But Seasons' glory days are past. It was once one of the city's few top-tier restaurants to offer the very best. Today, fortunately, there are many first-class restaurants in Boston. With this in mind, the hotel plans to replace Seasons in 2007 with a more modern, 70-seat, fine-dining restaurant on the first floor. We expect the quality to continue. ♦ Daily, breakfast, lunch, and dinner. No jeans or sneakers at dinner. Reservations recommended. 523.4119

CHURCHILL'S CIGAR BAR

★$$ Off the lobby and separate from other hotel facilities, Churchill's attracts a well-dressed, mostly male crowd with its dark-wood interior, high-backed leather chairs, and cigars of all types. You can buy them at the bar with a drink, and smoke them without feeling guilty. With windows overlooking **Faneuil Hall,** the bar is popular with businesspeople and sports figures. ♦ Daily.

13 THE RACK

★★$$ With 22 pool tables, two bars, beer, loud live music every night, inexpensive bar food served to 1AM, demistars like local radio DJs, no admission charge, and a location next to **Faneuil Hall Marketplace,** this post-teen, young-professional meeting place is wildly popular. Daily, lunch and dinner. ♦ No shorts, sneakers, T-shirts, baseball caps, or jeans on Saturday nights. Management also likes collars on shirts. 24 Clinton St (at North St, across from Millennium Bostonian Hotel). 725.1051

14 BLACKSTONE GRILL

★★$$ When the **Union Oyster House** (see page 36) is too crowded or too much for your wallet, come to this popular spot (which used to be called Marshall House). You may still have a wait, but it won't be as long. This place actually opened in 1982, yet looks as if it has been here a century, with plenty of brass and wood. Eat informally at the bar or bar tables, or in the snug rear dining room. Start with selections from the raw bar—oysters, steamers, cherrystones, littlenecks—and proceed with fresh seafood entrées prepared in the open kitchen. There are two lobster specials daily, a wide choice of beers, and big burgers and sandwiches. The food stops around 11:30PM, but the pleasant bar—without loud music or loud, young patrons, is open until 2AM. ♦ Seafood/American ♦ Daily, lunch and dinner. 15 Union St (between North St and Salt La). 523.9396

15 JAMES MICHAEL CURLEY PARK

Follow North Street to an amiable little park tucked between Union and Congress Streets, which features two statues of Boston's controversial but beloved mayor James Michael Curley (1874-1958) by Lloyd Lillie. In one, Curley is seated on a bench in a very approachable pose; many a photo has been taken of the mayor "chatting" with whoever plops down next to him. The other portrays an upright Curley as the man of action and orator. Four-time mayor, four-time congressman, and one-time Massachusetts governor, the man fondly called "The Rascal King" was born in Boston's South End. Curley gave Bostonians plenty to admire, gossip about, and remember him by. He was the first Irish-American—a Catholic—to become mayor, in 1914, beating an oppressive Yankee-Protestant apparatus that had long ruled. Signs declaring "No Irish need apply" were not uncommon before him. Curley ran Boston's infamous and powerful Irish political machine. Edwin O'Connor had Curley in mind when he wrote *The Last Hurrah*. But Curley was also known as the "Mayor of the Poor," and his civic contributions included establishing Boston City Hospital. ◆ Union Park, North St (between Union and Congress Sts)

16 BOSTON CITY HALL

Towering over a windswept brick plain, **Kallmann McKinnell & Wood Architects'** massive, cold structure looks like what it is: a factory where Boston governmental operations crank along. Gerhard Kallmann and Michael McKinnell, also architects for the Hynes Auditorium in Back Bay and the Boston Five Cents Savings Bank on School Street, won a national competition for this project, the eye-catching centerpiece of New Boston. The plaza, however, was named as the worst public space in the world by the nonprofit Project for Public Space. A gray concrete slab now covers the plaza's tiered fountain, which never worked properly.

The 1968 building's exterior communicates the functions and hierarchies of what's happening inside. Its sprawling, open lower levels house departments that directly serve the public, while more aloof bureaucracy is on the upper floors, and the publicly accountable mayor and city council offices are suspended between. Summertime concerts, public celebrations, and political events spill onto **City Hall Plaza.** Although its interior is somewhat dim and neglected-looking, and there are frequent calls for the building of a new city hall, this municipal building remains an edifice of heroic intentions. ◆ City Hall Plaza, Court and Cambridge Sts. 635.4000

17 DOCK SQUARE

The open area between Congress Street and Faneuil Hall earned its name in colonial times when it was young Boston's landing place and an important threshold to the New World. People and goods constantly passed across the square as they traveled to and from the boats docked near its edge. The town dock was eventually extended into Town Cove and later the cove was filled in to create more land. On the way to Faneuil Hall, look for Anne Whitney's 1880 bronze of Samuel Adams. ◆ Congress Ave and North St

18 FANEUIL HALL

From the heights of the steps behind City Hall, look for the most familiar of Boston's many curious objects of affection: Spinning in harbor-sent breezes and glinting in the sun atop Faneuil Hall is master tinsmith **Deacon Shem Drowne's** gold-plated grasshopper, a weather vane modeled in 1742 after a similar one topping London's Royal Exchange. Grasshoppers symbolize good luck, and in a city where many a fine old building has been lost to fire or progress, this critter has done right by Faneuil Hall. In 1740, when American **Peter Faneuil,** who sympathized with the French Huguenots and made his fortune trading with the English, offered to erect a market building for the town at his own expense, citizens voted on his proposal. It passed 367 to 360—a lukewarm welcome for a landmark that has been a historic center of Boston life ever since.

Painter **John Smibert** designed the original structure. Built in 1742, it housed open-market stalls, a meeting hall, and offices. All were gutted by fire in 1761, but an identical building was soon rebuilt. Peddlers and politicians have peacefully coexisted here, inspiring local poet Francis W. Hatch to write: "Here orators in ages past have mounted their attack / Undaunted by proximity of sausage on the rack." As the Revolution approached, the impassioned oratory of patriots such as Samuel Adams and James Otis fired up the populace, drawing huge crowds and earning Faneuil Hall the nickname "Cradle of Liberty." At a 1772 town meeting here, Adams proposed that Boston establish the Committee of Correspondence and invite the other colonies to join, thus establishing the clandestine information network that promoted united action against British repression. The hall's nickname was further cemented when Boston's famous antislavery orator Wendell Phillips presented his first address here in 1837. William Lloyd Garrison and Massachusetts senator Charles Sumner joined the abolitionist cause from the same rostrum.

In 1806, when the crowds just couldn't squeeze in anymore, **Charles Bulfinch** handsomely remodeled and enlarged the cramped hall. He preserved its stalwart simplicity but doubled its width, added a floor, and created a marvelous second-floor galleried assembly room that citizen's groups use to this day. Among dozens of portraits of famous Americans hung around the room, look for George P. A. Healy's *Liberty and Union, Now and Forever*, depicting Massachusetts senator Daniel Webster on the floor of the US Senate defending the Union in 1830 against a Southern senator's contention that states could veto federal laws. Gilbert Stuart's portrait of George Washington

Faneuil Hall Marketplace

COURTESY OF CARLOS DINZ ASSOCIATES

taking Dorchester Heights from the Redcoats is also here. On the third floor is the headquarters and museum of the **Ancient and Honorable Artillery Company of Massachusetts** (227.1638, www.ahacsite.org), a ceremonial organization with a proud past as the oldest chartered military organization in the Western Hemisphere; it was chartered in 1638 by Massachusetts's first governor, John Winthrop. On display is the company's vast collection of arms, uniforms, documents, and memorabilia. The museum is open weekdays; there's no admission charge.

Back at ground level, make a quick tour of the souvenir shops and food counters that have replaced more down-to-earth produce and feed stalls. The adaptable hall continues to thrive. Its political pulse also beats strong; during election years, contenders debate here. ♦ Daily. Faneuil Hall Sq, North St (between Clinton St and Congress Ave)

Next to Faneuil Hall:

1 FANEUIL HALL SQUARE

Representative of New Boston's sometimes cavalier attitude toward the city's history,

this building by **Graham Gund Associates,** built in 1988, strives to relate to the other marketplace structures. But as hard as it tries, it comes off as a new kid on the block, with too much style and not enough substance. Inside are branches of national chain stores: places like **Abercrombie & Fitch,** featuring casual clothing for outdoorsy types; **Express,** a sportswear shop for women and men; and **Bath & Bodyworks,** an emporium selling soaps, lotions, and bath accessories. ♦ Daily. 742.6838

BOSTIX

Stop by this outdoor kiosk to purchase tickets to many of Boston's arts and entertainment events. The tickets are half-price on the day of performance. The in-person, cash-only service sells tickets for visiting Broadway shows and dozens of local theater, dance, and music performances, plus comedy clubs, sports events, jazz concerts, nightclubs, dinner theaters, tourist attractions, and festivals. ♦ Tu-Su. Also at Copley Sq, Dartmouth St (between St. James Ave and Boylston St). 482.BTIX; www.artsboston.org

19 FANEUIL HALL MARKETPLACE/ QUINCY MARKET

Beyond **Faneuil Hall** stands a long, low trio of buildings bursting with international and specialty food stalls, restaurants, cafés, boutiques, bars, and an army of pushcarts with wares to tempt impulsive buyers. Officially named Faneuil Hall Marketplace but often called Quincy Market (the name of its main building), the complex offers everything from junk food to gourmet meals, kitsch to haute couture. The extravaganza attracts more than 20 million visitors a year, inviting comparisons to Disney World. But touristy and slick as it is, the marketplace possesses the authentic patina of history. It has lived a long, useful life, having served as a meat and produce market for more than 150 years before its current incarnation.

The marketplace's 535-foot-long granite centerpiece, a National Historic Landmark, is **Quincy Market.** It is named for Josiah Quincy, the Boston mayor who revitalized the decrepit waterfront by ordering major landfills, six new streets, and construction of a market house to supplement overcrowded Faneuil Hall. Architect **Alexander Parris** crowned the 1826 Greek Revival central building with a copper dome and planted majestic Doric colonnades at either end. The building projected a noble face seaward, for it was right at the harbor's edge in those days. Two granite-faced brick warehouses, today called the **North and South Markets,** later rose on either side, according to Parris's plans. For 150 years the ensemble was the dignified venue for meat and produce wholesale distribution and storage.

By the 1970s, however, the marketplace was decaying and in danger of demolition. Benjamin and Jane Thompson of **Benjamin Thompson & Associates** convinced the city and developers that the complex could become Boston's gathering place again if it were recycled to suit contemporary urban life. The firm restored most of the marketplace in 1978, adding festive signage and glass canopies, and transforming vegetable and meat stalls into fast-food outlets and cafés, bars and boutiques. Boston lost its meat-and-potatoes-style market to colorful abundance of another sort.

The main Quincy Market building is now a runway of fast foods from around the world. As you stroll down the **Colonnade** (center aisle) of the alleylike building, you'll pass concessions selling baklava, barbecue, chowder, fudge, gourmet brownies, pizzas, salads, sausage on a stick, oysters, Indian pudding, french fries, ice cream—the whole gastronomic gamut. Visitors make their purchases at the counters and then search for a table in the large central rotunda. On the sides of Quincy Market are two glassed-in walkways filled with cafés, take-out eateries, and pushcart vendors.

The two rows of buildings flanking Quincy Market, the North and South Markets, also were upgraded considerably from their original state as warehouses. The shops they now house are a mix of highbrow and informal, traditional and bizarre.

When winter finally gives up, **sidewalk cafés** dot the cobbled pedestrian streets between the three buildings. An outdoor **flower market** near the north side of Faneuil Hall blankets the cobblestones with greenery, bringing colors and smells of each season: autumn pumpkins, Christmas trees and poinsettias, spring bunches of welcome daffodils, and summer bouquets. And crowds often gather around the cobblestoned square between Faneuil Hall and Quincy Market's **West Portico,** the prime spot for musicians, jugglers, and other entertainers.

In short, the scheme to gently breathe life back into the old buildings has been a model for renewal projects around the world. While some people are turned off by the throngs and the "buy, buy, buy" mood of this shop-and-snack mecca, it deserves a visit—if only to see the worthy old buildings and enjoy the outdoor spectacle of pedestrians and street performers. An **information desk** is under the South Canopy. It isn't easy to spot among the pushcarts, and the staff can be indifferent, but pick up the helpful printed directory. ♦ Daily. Bounded by Commercial St and Faneuil Hall Sq, and Chatham and Clinton Sts. 338.2323; www.faneuilhallmarketplace.com

Within Quincy Market:

THE COMEDY CONNECTION

This club attracts the under-30 crowd, especially college students, with established stand-up comedians and new talent. Drinks and snacks served during shows. ♦ Admission. Nightly. Th-Sa; cash only at the door. Second floor. 248.9700. www.symfonee.com/comedyconnection/boston &

NED DEVINE'S

★★$ A huge, lively Irish-themed, industrial-look tavern owned by the same people who

---

Pronunciations of "Faneuil" abound, with little agreement about which is correct. Is it *Fan-yool, Fannel, Fan-you-ill, Fan-yul,* or *Fan-ee-yul?* Who knows? But the first two are by far the most common.

---

run **Solas,** the upscale Irish bar in the **Lenox Hotel.** ◆ Pub food ◆ Daily, 11AM-2AM; Sa, Su, Irish breakfast. Bar: Daily until 2AM. Within Ned Devine's is a dance club with DJs and bands. ◆ Cover charge. Upper Rotunda. 248.8800

DICK'S LAST RESORT

★$$ Dallas-based Dick's became a popular restaurant chain by running barely controlled frat parties. The beers are large, the patrons encouraged to be loud, and the food comes piled up. But people seem to love it, and the theatrical abuse from wait staff. The restaurant took three floors in 2006, moving from the Prudential Center after 12 years. They advertise "Live music. No cover. No dress code. No class." ◆ 267.8080; www.dickslastresort.com &

THE SALTY DOG SEAFOOD BAR AND GRILLE

★★$$ Get some of the best oysters in town, good chowder and fried clams, and other fresh and undisguised seafood in this noisy little hut of a place. There's no pastry cart here, and they don't take reservations, but you can dine alfresco from April through November. A lot of regulars stay away during the summer to avoid the inevitable throngs. ◆ Seafood/American ◆ M-Sa, lunch and dinner; Su, brunch and dinner. Lower level. 742.2094

CHEERS CAFÉ

★$ Remember *Cheers,* the popular TV show set in a Boston bar? Only exterior shots were done in Boston. Interior scenes were filmed in Los Angeles. Here's a duplicate of the *Cheers* Hollywood set with real bartenders offering pub food and helpful clerks hawking *Cheers* merchandise. ◆ American. ◆ Daily. South canopy. 227.0150; www.cheersboston.com

---

There's only one Faneuil Hall—the brick building with the grasshopper on top—but the entire marketplace is collectively called Faneuil Hall, too. To add to the confusion, it's also known as Quincy Market (the name of the main historic market building).

The Boston Stone, set in the foundation of a shop on Marshall Street, is a millstone brought from England during the 1600s. Originally used to grind colored powders into paint, it became to Boston what its counterpart, the London Stone, was to that city—the official point from which all distances from Boston were measured.

BOSTON CHIPYARD

The award-winning chocolate chip cookies are fresh and delicious. Choose the traditional favorite or variations with peanut butter, extra chocolate, nuts, oatmeal, or raisins. A California mom opened the shop here some 30 years ago, using her own recipe, a favorite of her son and his friends. Come for a late-night fix of milk and cookies. ◆ Daily. North Canopy. 742.9537; www.chipyard.com

Within Faneuil Hall Marketplace:

DURGIN-PARK

★★$$ Come to this restaurant for true Yankee cooking and a taste of Boston's bygone days. Don't listen to detractors who say this place is overrated; give it a try and enjoy a fast-paced, filling meal. Founded in 1827, this cranky, creaky, but well-loved institution dates from the marketplace's old days, when produce held the spotlight. Notice the ancient plank floors and tin ceilings. Waitresses legendary for their brisk manner serve raw clams and oysters, phonebook-size prime rib, starchless fish chowder, Boston scrod (with baked beans, of course), chops, steaks, fresh seafood, chicken potpie, and more solid old favorites. Save room for the scrumptious fresh strawberry shortcake, made on premises, or the rich Indian pudding. Everybody dines family style at tables set for 16 and decked out in red-checkered cloths. ◆ American ◆ Daily, lunch and dinner. Validated parking. Second floor. 227.2038; www.durgin-park.com

Downstairs at Durgin-Park:

THE OYSTER BAR AT DURGIN-PARK

★★$ Serving appetizers and sandwiches only, this is a great alternative to the noisy place upstairs if you want a light repast and a little calm. Try the soothing clam chowder and briny steamers. There are no tables; just the bar and counters. Dessert is not on the menu, but just ask and someone will bring it down from the restaurant. ◆ American ◆ Daily, lunch and dinner. 227.2038

GEOCLASSICS

Featuring an unusually broad array of fossils, minerals, and gemstones, this shop offers simple and tasteful necklaces and rings as well as semiprecious stones set in silver or gold. Though owner Claudio Kraus prices some children's offerings at $1 or $2, other pieces can run $1,000 and up. There are also some unusual paperweights and more run-of-the-mill sundries. ◆ Daily. Street level. 523.6112

McCORMICK & SCHMICK'S SEAFOOD RESTAURANT

★★$$ The menu at this outpost of the national chain is updated twice daily to feature the freshest seafood. There are also steak, chicken, and pasta dishes. ♦ Seafood ♦ Daily, lunch and dinner. Bar open to 2AM. 720.5522; www.mccormickandschmicks.com ঙ. Also at the **Park Plaza Hotel,** 34 Columbus Ave, 482.3999

ZUMA'S TEX-MEX CAFE

★$$ Subdued it's not: The very first sight that greets visitors as they enter this basement café is a sandpit artfully sporting an O'Keeffe-style cattle skull. The small, packed space is abuzz with neon accents and scattered video monitors broadcasting surfer tapes. The mission—to serve "foods of the sun"—is carried out in a menu that offers everything from sizzling fajitas and quesadillas zapped with hot, hot sauce to Italian pasta and Japanese teriyaki. Try one of the fresh-fruit "neon" margaritas. ♦ Tex-Mex/International ♦ Daily, lunch and dinner. Basement. 367.9114

Within South Market:

KINGFISH HALL

★★$$$ The noise level can be high, but there's some very nice seafood here, some of it exciting and Asian influenced. ♦ Seafood ♦ Daily, lunch and dinner. Reservations recommended. Validated parking. 523.8862; www.toddenglish.com ঙ

PLAZA III STEAKHOUSE

★★$$$ This quality-beef restaurant is flooded with light from the large windows on three sides. A giant fiberglass steer hangs from the ceiling, but ignore the kitsch—the prime steaks are very good. Seafood too. Meats are flown to Boston directly from Kansas City. Some outdoor tables. ♦ American ♦ Daily, lunch and dinner. 101 South Market building. 720.5570; www.plazaiii.com ঙ

20 SEARS CRESCENT BUILDING

A holdover from old Scollay Square, this gracefully curving 1816 building, renovated in 1969 by **Don Stull Associates,** moderates **City Hall**'s aggressive stance and softens nine-acre City Hall Plaza's impersonality. The building recalls the days when Boston streets sprouted every which way and the city didn't

care that the shortest distance between two points is a straight line. Built by **David Sears,** whose Beacon Hill mansion is now the Somerset Club, this block was once Boston's publishing center, where Emerson, Hawthorne, and other literary types gathered. Cozying up to this structure is the little **Sears Block** building (completed in 1848), where Boston's homey landmark the gilded **Steaming Kettle** puffs around-the-clock. The city's oldest animated trade sign, the kettle was cast in 1873 by coppersmiths Hicks and Badger, and commissioned by the Oriental Tea Company. Fed steam by a pipe from the company's boiler room, the kettle was an instant curiosity when it was hung in Scollay Square. Its big day came when Oriental Tea held a contest to guess its mascot's capacity. Weeks of fervent speculation ended on 1 January 1875, when more than 10,000 people gathered to watch William F. Reed, city sealer of weights and measures, decree the official measure of 227 gallons, two quarts, one pint, and three gills—now engraved on the kettle's side. Eight winners shared the prize: a chest of premium tea. Reporting on the event, the *Boston Sunday Times* referred to the famous Boston Tea Party and bragged, "The tea-kettle excitement has run nearly as high as the tea excitement of old, and is almost a historical incident in the career of our noble city." Once Scollay Square was razed, the kettle was relocated in 1967 to the Sears Block. Now a landmark, it graces a Starbucks coffee shop (formerly the Steaming Kettle Coffee Shop). ♦ 63-65 Court St (at Cambridge St)

21 AMES BUILDING

Fourteen stories high, this proud and distinctive structure—now on the National Register of Historic Places—was once the tallest office building on the Eastern seaboard. Abounding with arches, modulating from the weighty ones at the base to the delicate chain under the cornice, the vigorous building was designed in 1889 by Henry Hobson Richardson's successor firm, **Shepley, Rutan, and Coolidge.** Although the great architect had died a few years earlier, his influence clearly was not forgotten, especially in the Romanesque architectural details and lacy carvings.

One of Boston's first skyscrapers, the sturdy building is supported by nine-foot-thick masonry walls, not the light-steel frame that became popular soon afterward. It's the second-tallest structure built this way in the world. The building only briefly dominated the city's skyline and is now dwarfed by 20th-century behemoths, but it exerts an enduring presence. ♦ 1 Court St (at State St)

BOSTON'S TEA PARTIES

Few would disagree that as tea parties go, Boston's is the best known. The only contender might be the Mad Hatter's in Lewis Carroll's *Alice in Wonderland.* But that was fantasy—unlike the Boston Tea Party, during which 340 chests of fine tea shipped from England were dumped into Boston Harbor, forever linking the city with tea.

Once the war was over, Bostonians once again sought the pleasurable ritual of afternoon tea practiced for centuries by their British ancestors. Today there are still a number of spots in Boston where visitors can indulge in their own tea parties.

The Boston Harbor Hotel

Not far from the site of the original Boston Tea Party, this hotel serves tea in the Café Intrigue overlooking the waterfront. You'll have a view of the harborfront, the cruise ships, and the water shuttles tied up outside. The room is large and furniture is on a grand scale; classical music plays in the background. The complete tea includes warm scones, clotted Devonshire cream, and fruit preserves. ◆ M-F 2:30-4PM. 70 Rowes Wharf, Atlantic Ave (between Northern Ave and East India Row). 439.7000; www.bhh.com

The Boston Park Plaza Hotel

Afternoon tea is offered in Swan's Court, located at the far end of the handsome lobby. Finger sandwiches, tea cake, scones, and fresh sliced strawberries with whipped cream accompany your choice of tea. ◆ Daily 3-5PM. 64 Arlington St (between Columbus Ave and Park Plaza). 426.2000; www.bostonparkplaza.com

The Four Seasons Hotel

Traditional afternoon tea is served in the spacious Bristol Lounge. The setting is refined yet relaxed, the service gracious. Finger sandwiches, Viennese pastries, scones, and English tea breads are served separately, after a choice has been made from the broad spectrum of regular, herbal, and decaffeinated teas. Tea here (rather than drinks after work) has become a favorite meeting option among the local business community. For leisurely lingerers, live piano music begins at 5PM. ◆ Daily 3-4:30PM. 200 Boylston St (between Charles St S and Hadassah Way). 338.4400; www.fourseasons.com/boston

The Ritz-Carlton Hotel

This hotel has been offering formal afternoon tea since it opened in 1927. Tea is taken on the second floor in the Tea Lounge, an interior room with the intimate atmosphere of a comfortable drawing room. The lime, pink, and cream décor has appealing sconce and lamp lighting, and the walls are hung with 19th-century oil paintings. During the week, a harpist provides a backdrop to the hushed conversations. Ingredients for a full tea come to the table attractively arranged on a multistoried compote. Service begins with a selection of open-face sandwiches—miniature works of art that are tasty as well as pretty—followed by tea breads, pastries, and scones with clotted cream and strawberry preserves. ◆ M-F, seating at 2:30 and 4PM; Sa-Su 1, 2:30, and 4PM. 15 Arlington St (between Newbury St and Commonwealth Ave). 536.5700; www.ritzcarlton.com

22 BERTUCCI'S

★★$ Another spacious outpost of the very popular local pizza and pasta chain, this branch hops in tune with nearby Faneuil Hall Marketplace. Count on tasty fresh pizzas, calzones, and salads. Look for the fun mural, depicting pizza-making, above the bar. ◆ Pizza/Italian/Takeout ◆ Daily, lunch and dinner. 22 Merchants Row (north of State St). 227.7889. Also at 21 Brattle St (between Palmer and Church Sts), Cambridge. 864.4748

Clarke's

23 CLARKE'S

★$$ On one side, there's a big neighborly saloon where crowds flock to watch sports events on TV, eye prospective dates, or wind down after work; on the other, there's a comfortable, no-frills restaurant and bar where you can order straightforward New England dishes like broiled scrod or big sandwiches and burgers with a side of great fries. A shuttle bus takes patrons to FleetCenter events. Co-owner Dave DeBusschere, formerly of the New York Knicks, sometimes drops by to watch the Celtics play. ◆ American ◆ Daily, lunch and dinner. Reservations recommended for large parties. 21 Merchants Row (at Chatham St). 227.7800

24 CUNARD BUILDING

The boldly inscribed name on this Classical Revival building built in 1901 by **Peabody and Stearns** recalls another bright moment in Boston's past. The building was once the headquarters for the famous Cunard Line, which pioneered transatlantic steamship routes. Boston was proud to beat out New York City as the first American city to enjoy the innovative service. Nautical motifs aplenty—crowned Poseidon heads, anchor-and-dolphin lighting stanchions, a wavelike ornamental band—add an adventurous air to an otherwise sober structure. ♦ 126 State St (between Chatham and Merchants Rows)

25 THE BLACK ROSE

★$ Its name is the English translation of Roisin Dubh, a Gaelic allegorical name for Ireland that symbolizes the repression of Irish Catholics by the British. Famous Irish faces and mementos line the walls, and Irish music accompanies bargain-priced homestyle meals such as meat loaf, lamb stew, fish-and-chips, Yankee pot roast, and boiled lobster (don't look for gourmet here). The big, hospitable bar offers numerous beers and stout on tap and there's live Irish music nightly. It's a place to meet friends after work, sing along with some folk musicians, watch a game on the big-screen TV, or linger over a pint of Guinness or an Irish coffee. ♦ Irish-American ♦ Daily, lunch and dinner. 160 State St (at Commercial St). 742.2286

26 MARKETPLACE CENTER

This gauche, gate-crashing building, erected in 1985 by the **WZMH Group,** tries to look as if it belongs on this important historic site, even mimicking its venerable neighbors somewhat in materials and style. Though it could have been worse, the building is awkward, especially its graceless atrium gateway with makeup-mirror-style fixtures. Although the opening preserves the pedestrian walk-to-the-sea leading to Boston Harbor at Waterfront Park, the too-tall, too-wide building creates a barrier where none existed before. The marketplace's stockpile of shops includes many chain stores. ♦ 200 State St (between Atlantic Ave and Commercial St). 478.2030

Within Marketplace Center:

CHOCOLATE DIPPER

Watch thick streams of fragrant, gooey chocolate blending away here while the staff readies luscious fresh fruit and truffles for dipping. Try strawberries, raspberries, cherries, grapes, banana, pineapple, or orange slices dipped in dark, milk, or white chocolate. The extra-rich truffles come in more than a half-dozen flavors, and a wide variety of other chocolates are also made on the premises. ♦ Daily. Street level. 439.0190. Also at Washington and School Sts. 227.0309

27 SANCTUARY

★$ This trendy lounge and restaurant on three floors has a mostly 20-something clientele. Menu choices range from tacos and burgers to cashew chicken and steaks. Popular martinis have names like Lusty Latte, Satan's Vice, and Purgatory's Pleasure. Free tacos weekdays from 5 to 7PM, and a DJ Thursday through Saturday. Reservations let you ignore the line at the door. No sneakers, hats, or torn jeans. ♦ American ♦ M-Sa, 4:30PM-2AM. 189 State St. 573 9333; www.sanctuaryboston.com

NORTH END

You'll know you've wandered into the North End when you hear the strains of a tenor wafting over the streets. The sidewalks—in what might still be America's most Italian neighborhood, even with gentrification—are abuzz with food shoppers and elders who haul their lawn chairs down to summer sidewalks to create an alfresco living room. Gala window displays brighten the rows of redbrick façades and alluring aromas from *pasticcerie, trattorie, ristoranti, mercati,* and *caffè* escape into the tangled streets. The banter of children can be heard, switching between English and Italian depending on whether they're talking to school friends or family. And within this insular, proud Italian enclave winds the red ribbon of the **Freedom Trail,** directing tourists to the **Paul Revere House,** the **Old North Church,** and other vestiges of colonial Boston.

This is the spirited, colorful, bursting-at-the-seams North End. Don't even attempt to come here by car. Take a taxi. Getting here by foot used to be tricky with Big Dig construction, but now the old elevated Central Artery/Fitzgerald Expressway (I-93) is in a tunnel underneath the Rose Fitzgerald Kennedy Greenway and most construction is finished. From Government Center, the Haymarket subway stop, or the Financial District, you can skip across the parkland into the Waterfront or the North End.

The heart of this vivacious, voluble district is Mediterranean, but Italians have held sway here only since 1920 or so. This is Boston's original neighborhood, where the city's early Puritan residents settled during the 17th century, their eyes on the sea. As piers, wharves, and markets sprang up along the Waterfront, the North End became the

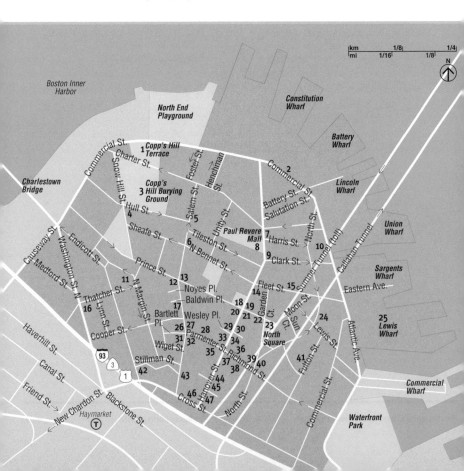

wealthiest, most populous, and in every way the most important part of town. It has undergone many changes. The glory days ended with the Revolution, when the area's aristocratic Tory population fled to England and elite Bostonians moved to Beacon Hill and Bay Village. The black community gradually migrated to the Hill as well. In the 19th century, waves of immigrants—first Irish, then Eastern European Jews, then Portuguese, then Italians—poured into the North End, which had deteriorated into a slum. Over some 70 years, Italian-Americans have restored the neighborhood. Their traditions, rituals, and festivals—focused around the family, the church, and the cafés—have become the North End's bulwark. Gentrification and moves to the suburbs are changing the neighborhood again.

Most of the neighborhood's streets follow a jumbled 17th-century pattern. When infant Boston still fit onto the Shawmut Peninsula, the North End was a second peninsula, almost an island, divided from the first by Mill Creek. Today the 1.5-mile Greenway, like the expressway it replaced, follows the old creek's track.

Changes are already afoot, so spend some time here while the fascinating cultural layers remain in place. Many of the people you pass on the streets are still the children and grandchildren of *paesani* from villages in Sicily, Abruzzi, and Calabria. On **Hanover Street,** the main commercial thoroughfare, café jukeboxes play Italian pop music. Parallel and to the left is **Salem Street,** where meat and provisions shops (and authentic Italian restaurants) do a brisk business. A block to the right brings you to quaint **North Square** and **North Street,** which originally followed the shoreline (they're now blocks away from the water, thanks to subsequent landfill projects).

Notice the loaded laundry lines (you won't see those on Beacon Hill), minimal building ornamentation (except for a bit of wrought iron here and there), and dearth of green space (aside from some well-used parks and rooftop gardens). Glance up: More than one elderly North Ender will be leaning out a window to check on who's coming, who's going, and who's doing what they shouldn't be doing. This is a close-knit place where people watch out for one another and strangers get the once-over more than once. But don't let that intimidate you.

Be sure to visit the North End in July and August when each weekend there's a festival dedicated to a different patron saint. Join the throngs for one of these *feste,* when North Enders commandeer the streets for morning-till-night processions, dancing, and eating.

1 COPP'S HILL TERRACE

This graceful plaza, set into the sloping hill near Copp's Hill Burying Ground, has been beleaguered by neglect and vandals. It's still a wonderful architectural progression, most frequented by the youngest and oldest neighborhood residents. There are a few outdoor stone tables with chessboards laid in them. In the field below, by the harbor, male residents of the North End gather day and night to play their game of passion: boccie. ♦ Charter St (between Foster and Commercial Sts)

2 BAY STATE LOBSTER COMPANY

In business for more than 70 years, this is the East Coast's largest retail and wholesale seafood operation. The biggest draw here is lobster—you can buy the tasty crustaceans live on the spot to cook for tonight's dinner, or have a few shipped via UPS to anywhere in the continental US. Seafood of every kind—including shellfish prepared with all the trimmings, the company's own clam and fish chowders, and lobster pies—is also sold here and can be packed for traveling. As you might guess, it's often a madhouse. ♦ Daily. 379 Commercial St (between Battery and Hanover Sts). 523.7960

3 COPP'S HILL BURYING GROUND

One of Boston's many wonderful outdoor pantheons, this cemetery not only offers the finest gravestones in Boston, but also some of the best views of the city's most elusive feature—the Waterfront. From this promontory you can see down to the boat-clogged Boston Harbor and over to Charlestown and its **Navy Yard,** where the venerable warship "Old Ironsides"—the USS *Constitution*—is berthed. This cemetery was established in 1659 when **King's Chapel Burying Ground** got too crowded. Once an Indian burial ground and lookout point, "Corpse Hill" (as it is also known) has accommodated more than 10,000 burials. In colonial days black Bostonians settled at the base of the hill in what was called "New Guinea." A granite pillar marks the grave of Prince Hall, black antislavery activist, Revolutionary War soldier, and founder of the Negro Freemasonry Order.

Sexton Robert Newman, who flashed the signals from Old North Church—and was imprisoned by the British for doing so—is also buried here. And the Mathers—Increase, his son Cotton, and Cotton's son Samuel—that formidable dynasty of Puritan churchmen and educators, rest in a brick vault near the Charter Street gate. (Increase was awarded the first doctor of divinity degree conferred in America.) During the Revolution, British generals directed the shelling of Bunker Hill from here and their soldiers used the gravestones for target practice, as visitors can still discern. Look for Captain Malcolm's bullet-riddled marker. His patriotic epitaph particularly incensed the British soldiers: "a true son of Liberty / a friend to the Publick / an enemy to oppression / and one of the foremost / in opposing the Revenue Acts on America." Legend tells of two tombs that were stolen here: Interlopers ejected the remains of the graves' rightful owners, whose names were carved over with those of the thieves for future burial. ◆ Snowhill St (between Hull and Charter Sts)

4 HULL STREET

Leading up the hill from the Old North Church and abutting the **Copp's Hill Burying Ground** is this tree-lined, winding street, one of the North End's most pleasant roads. It was named after Boston's first mint master, John Hull, who coined the city's famous "pine-tree shillings" and had an estate that encompassed this neighborhood. ◆ Between Salem and Snowhill Sts

The Great Molasses Flood occurred on 15 January 1919 on Commercial Street below Copp's Hill Burying Ground. A four-story tank containing 2.5 million gallons of molasses burst, releasing a lavalike torrent that destroyed several buildings, killed 24 people, and injured 60. It took a week to clear the streets after the explosion, and a sticky-sweet aroma clung to the neighborhood for decades. Some North Enders say they can smell molasses from time to time.

On Hull Street:

No. 44

Located across from the Hull Street entrance to Copp's Hill Burying Ground is a circa-1800 house that is indisputably the narrowest in Boston, one window per floor at the street end, squeezing up for air between its stout companions. An amusing tale claims that this house was an act of revenge, built solely out of spite to block the light and view of another house behind. In truth, this is a lonely survivor of a breed of modest dwellings called "10 footers," sometimes depicted in old prints of colonial Boston Town. The picturesque dwelling is nine feet, six inches wide, to be precise. A floral wrought-iron fence leads to its charming entry.

5 OLD NORTH CHURCH (CHRIST CHURCH)

Called the Old North Church by nearly everyone, this is the oldest church building in Boston (pictured at right) and the second Anglican parish founded in the city. Architect **William Price,** a local draftsman and print dealer, emulated Christopher Wren quite nicely in this 1723 brick edifice, now a National Historic Landmark. Coping with a tiny site in cramped quarters, Price gave the church needed stature and eminence by boldly attaching a 197-foot-high, three-tiered steeple—one of New England's earliest.

What points to the sky today, however, is the 1955 replica of the original steeple, which was toppled by a gust of wind in 1804 and once again in 1954. The weather vane on top was made by colonial craftsman Deacon Shem Drowne. The eight bells that ring from the belfry were cast in 1744 by Abel Rudhall of Gloucester, England, and range in weight from 620 to 1,545 pounds. Their inscription recalls long-extinguished aspirations: "We are the first ring of bells cast for the British Empire in North America, Anno 1744." The oldest and sweetest-sounding church bells in America, they have tolled the death of every US president since George Washington died in 1799. When **Paul Revere** was 15, he and six friends formed a guild to change-ring the bells (a specific form of bell ringing). The tradition stuck, and the Old North Guild of Change Ringers still exists. Practice takes place on Saturday beginning at 11:30PM, with formal ringing after the 11AM Sunday service.

Years later, Revere starred in the celebrated drama that has enveloped this landmark building with enduring legend, though a lot of the facts are cloudy. On the night of 18 April 1775, Revere rode on horseback to warn the Minutemen at Lexington and Concord of the approaching British troops. And as Revere arranged before departing (or so the story goes), the church's sexton, Robert Newman, hung two signal lanterns in the belfry to alert the populace that the British were on the move. Although a number of other messengers, including William Dawes, rode out into the towns, Paul Revere has eclipsed them all in fame. **Henry Wadsworth Longfellow** can take the real credit for Revere's glory. Spellbound by the nearly forgotten tale, he wrote the inaccurate but entertaining poem "Paul Revere's Ride," published in *The Atlantic Monthly* in 1861. Every April, on the eve of Patriots' Day, descendants of Revere or Newman hang lanterns in the church belfry to commemorate that spring night. An unresolved controversy, however, concerns whether this is the real Old North Church, or whether the Second Church of Boston on North Square—nicknamed "Old North" and later burned down by the British—truly held the leading role in the events on the eve of the American Revolution. If the other church were ever proven to be the real thing, it would require a major rerouting of the Freedom Trail, so no one is rushing to verify this theory.

No matter what the truth is, a sad and genuine chapter in this church's past was the divided loyalties of its Episcopalian congregation. Once the Revolution ignited, the church was closed until 1778 because of the tensions unleashed between Patriot and Tory parishioners.

The structure's white interior shimmers with light entering through pristine glass windowpanes. It's too bad there's rarely a chance to enjoy the unusual serenity and architectural clarity in solitude. The tall box pews—originally owned by parishioners, with brass plaques indicating which was whose—were designed to hold the warmth of hot bricks and coals during the winter. Look for the Revere family pew—No. 54. Inscriptions abound in the church and on the walls of the Washington Memorial Garden in back. Many offer interesting slants on colonial Boston. The clock ticking reassuringly at the rear of the gallery was made by a parishioner in 1726, and it's the oldest still running in an American public building. The brass chandeliers, also gifts, were first lighted on Christmas day, 1724. To the right of the apse, a 1790 bust of **George Washington** rests in a niche. When General Lafayette returned to Boston in 1824, he noticed this bust and said, "Yes, that is the man I knew, and more like him than any other portrait." Before leaving the church, look for the tablet on the left side of the vestibule, which identifies 12 bricks set into the wall. These were taken from a cell in Guildhall in Boston, England, where William Brewster and

other Pilgrims were held after attempting to flee that country in 1607. In 1923, on the church's 200th anniversary, the mayor of Boston, England, sent the bricks as a gesture of friendship.

To the left as you exit is a curious **museum and gift shop** amalgam (open daily) housed in a former chapel built in 1917 to serve the North End's tiny community of Italian-speaking Protestants, now vanished. In front of the chapel's street entrance, notice the amusing, stout little columns resting on the pair of lions' backs. Inside the museum, look for the **Vinegar Bible,** a gift of King George II in 1733 and so nicknamed for its famous typo: On one page heading, the "Parable of the Vinegar" appears instead of the "Parable of the Vineyard." Tea retrieved from the boots of a Boston Tea Party participant is also on display. There are lots of fun things to buy here, from spice gumdrops and maple sugar candy to copies of Longfellow's poem and Wedgwood china decorated with the church's image. (Giftshop: 523.4848)

Behind the church on both sides are charming small gardens nestled among clusters of nearby residences. In early summer the courtyard of the **Washington**

Old North Church

Restaurants/Clubs: Red | Hotels: Purple | Shops: Orange | Outdoors/Parks: Green | Sights/Culture: Blue

Memorial Garden is awash in the fragrance of roses. Among its many commemorative tablets, one intriguingly states, "Here on 13 Sept. 1757, John Childs, who had given public notice of his intention to fly from the steeple of Dr. Cutler's church, performed it to the satisfaction of a great number of spectators." Said Childs did indeed leap from on high, strapped to an umbrella-like contraption that carried him safely for several hundred feet.

Cross Salem Street and look back at the church. Ever since its completion, the steeple has towered over the swath of redbrick that makes up the North End's fabric. The church's colonial neighbors are gone now, but unlike the State House, it has not been overwhelmed by 20th-century urbanism. None of the newer buildings in the area exceeds five stories, so you still get a vivid picture of the early 18th-century landscape. Historical talks are offered by staff every 15 minutes. ♦ Daily; Su services 9AM, 11AM (with choir). 193 Salem St (between Tileston and Charter Sts). 523.6676; www.oldnorth.com

6 NORTH BENNET STREET SCHOOL

Founded in 1881 by Pauline Agassiz Shaw, this school was originally designed to help North End immigrants develop job skills. No longer a social service agency, it now offers classes in furniture making, carpentry, piano tuning, violin making and restoration, bookbinding, jewelry making, watch repair, and other fields. Students are trained in traditional methods and graduates are respected throughout New England. ♦ 39 N Bennet St (at Salem St). 227.0155

7 LUCIA RISTORANTE

★$$ Popular here since 1977, Lucia has a faithful following. The reasonably priced fare—mostly dishes from Abruzzi—is good, but not exceptional. One pasta dish reproduces the Italian flag with a white cream, red tomato, and green pesto sauce. On the walls are reproductions of Italian masterpieces. Upstairs is the opulent pink marble barroom, whose ceiling is painted with scenes from the Sistine Chapel. ♦ Italian ♦ M-Th, dinner; F-Su, lunch and dinner. Reservations recommended. Valet parking available. 415 Hanover St (next to St. Stephen's Church at Harris St). 367.2353; www.luciaristorante.com

8 PAUL REVERE MALL (THE PRADO)

Laid out in 1933 by Arthur Shurcliff, this tree-shaded park could have been plucked from Italy. It offers residents a comfortable cushion of space in their jam-packed quarter, and sight-seeing pilgrims a pleasant passage from

St. Stephen's Church to the Old North Church looming up ahead on Salem Street. The modest, slightly scruffy park has more personality than many of Boston's grander spaces. Though it isn't very old, it has a very lived-in look. The mall's brick walls and paving carve out a restful realm in which all generations of North Enders cheerfully converge. A serious game of checkers or cards often goes on among the elders while baby strollers are wheeled past, kids play, and dogs race about. The bronze equestrian statue of Paul Revere (designed by Cyrus E. Dallin in 1885 and erected in 1940) towers near the Hanover Street edge, giving the young park a historical stamp. Hardworking, pragmatic artisan that he was (not to mention unremarkable in physique), Paul Revere wouldn't recognize himself in this dashing figure. On some of the side walls, plaques commemorate North Enders' contributions to their city.

The mall ends at Unity Street; cross and enter the gate leading into the courtyard behind the Old North Church. On the way, look for the Clough House at 21 Unity Street. Built in 1715, it was the home of Ebenezer Clough, one of the Sons of Liberty, a Boston Tea Party "Indian," and a master mason who laid the bricks for the church. The courtyard itself occupies the former site of 19 Unity Street, which Benjamin Franklin bought for his two widowed sisters. ♦ Between Hanover and Unity Sts

At Paul Revere Mall:

MAURIZIO'S

★★★$$ Bright, quiet, and understated, this restaurant serves some of the best Mediterranean cuisine in Boston. In addition to traditional pasta dishes like penne al salmone e vodka (with fresh and smoked salmon, sautéed shallots, and sun-dried tomatoes in a light vodka cream sauce) and linguine al frutti di mare (with shrimp, scallops, clams, mussels, and calamari in a spicy tomato sauce), the menu offers meat selections like filetto di vitello al forno (pan-roasted veal tenderloin in a sun-dried tomato, brandy, and orange sauce) and daily fresh fish specials such as bistecca di tonno al limone e rosmarino (grilled tuna steak with lemon, rosemary, capers, and extra-virgin olive oil). Artwork on display is by local artists and is available for purchase. Owners Linda and Maurizio Loddo provide a satisfying and tasteful dining experience. ♦ Italian ♦ Daily, dinner; Sa, lunch and dinner. 364 Hanover St. 367.1123

9 ST. STEPHEN'S CHURCH

Located on the sunny side of Hanover Street's bend is Charles Bulfinch's sole surviving church in Boston. In 1804 Bulfinch transformed a commonplace meeting house

ART ALFRESCO

Boston and Cambridge boast a wealth of outdoor sculptures that adds to the charm and character of this history-rich area.

Each of the nine blocks of the Commonwealth Mall features a memorial sculpture. Among them are historian **Samuel Eliot Morison** by Penelope Jencks (between Exeter and Fairfield Streets) and explorer **Leif Erickson** by Anne Whitney (between Massachusetts Avenue and Charlesgate East). The Viking sculpture was donated in 1887 by philanthropist Even N. Horsefod, who believed that Erickson had landed in Cambridge in the year 1000, making him the true European discoverer of America.

Although female sculptures are few in number, animal subjects abound. The most famous is the **Make Way for Ducklings** family in the Public Garden. The figures, sculpted by Nancy Schön, are representations of the drawings from the children's book by Robert McCloskey. Schön also created **Tortoise and Hare** in Copley Square. Other animal sculptures in town include the **112-pound bronze bear** that was moved from the sidewalk outside FAO Schwarz, now gone to Children's Floating Hospital, and **Paint & Henry,** a pair of abstract horses sculpted from welded sheet copper at Copley Place.

The huge bronze equestrian sculpture of **George Washington** in the Public Garden facing Commonwealth Mall was dedicated in the 1860s. Sculptor Thomas Ball, who had studied sculpture in Florence, prided himself on the detail of the steed upon which the general sits. Two other beloved equestrian sculptures in Boston, both by sculptor Cyrus Edwin Dallin, are **Paul Revere** (Paul Revere Mall, between Hanover and Unity Streets) in the North End, and **Appeal to the Great White Spirit,** a moving sculpture of a Native American on horseback, in front of the Museum of Fine Arts (Huntington Avenue, between Forsyth Way and Museum Road).

Widely acknowledged as Boston's most outstanding piece of public art is the **Robert Gould Shaw/54th Regiment Memorial,** sculpted by Augustus Saint-Gaudens. The work, which stands in Boston Common across from the State House, honors Shaw, a Boston native and colonel of the first free black regiment in the Union Army (whose story is told in the 1989 film *Glory*). The compelling bas-relief piece, which took 14 years to complete and was dedicated in 1897, depicts Shaw and 23 members of his volunteer company, many of whom were killed in their 1863 attack on Fort Wagner, South Carolina.

Quest Eternal is the name of the sculpture of the heroic-size mythological Everyman by Donald DeLue that stands in front of the Prudential Tower (Boylston Street, between Exeter and Dalton Streets). Reaching heavenward with his left hand, the muscular, five-ton bronze male is an impressive sight, especially when the sun makes him shimmer.

Boston Celtics legend **Red Auerbach** and the powerful and charismatic **Mayor James Michael Curley** may also fall under the heroic (or at least the legendary) heading. Auerbach's intimate portrait in bronze is at Faneuil Hall Marketplace. Curley, the controversial mayor who ruled the city three times between 1914 and 1949, has two bronze memorials, one sitting on a park bench and one standing, in Union Park (just north of Faneuil Hall). A bust of another local hero, **Arthur Fiedler,** the legendary conductor of the Boston Pops, can be found on the Charles River Esplanade. Located across from the Arthur Fiedler Footbridge (Beacon Street and Embankment Road), this depiction is six cubic feet in size, mounted on a pedestal. The sculptor, Ralph Helmick, used 80-inch-thick metal sheets that were designed by computer. When seen from too close a range, the image is fuzzy; viewers need to step back before the remarkable likeness resolves itself. Helmick's intent was to show Fiedler as he was: a person who didn't choose to get close to people.

The **Free at Last** sculpture, dedicated to the memory of Martin Luther King Jr. (1929-1968), stands in front of Boston University's Marsh Chapel on Commonwealth Avenue. Dedicated to the "Distinguished Alumnus and Nobel Laureate for Peace" and sculpted by Sergio Castillo, the work features 50 abstract doves—one for each state—rising in formation.

An easy walk or ride across the Charles River from Boston is the Massachusetts Institute of Technology campus, which offers many outdoor artistic expressions. Situated among the buildings that abut Memorial Drive fronting the river is Alexander Calder's **The Great Sail.** The campus boasts two Henry Moore pieces: **Three-Piece Reclining Figure—Draped** and **Working Model for Lincoln Center.** Louise Nevelson's **Transparent Horizon** and Picasso's **Figure Decoupée** can also be found, as can several works by Jacques Lipchitz and one by Beverly Pepper.

Restaurants/Clubs: Red | Hotels: Purple | Shops: Orange | Outdoors/Parks: Green | Sights/Culture: Blue

called the New North into an elaborate, harmonious architectural composition, for which the Congregational society in residence paid $26,570. **Paul Revere** cast the bell that was hung in the church's belfry in 1805.

Although Bulfinch was usually drawn to English architecture, Italian Renaissance campaniles also inspired him in this work—an architectural foreshadowing of the North End's future ethnic profile. The dramatic tower crowds to the front of the wide-hipped façade, a bold counterpoint to the subtle Federal architectural gestures inside. Notice how the windows and column styles metamorphose as they move toward the gracefully curving ceiling. Most of the woodwork is original, including the pine columns. The 1830 organ was restored by Charles Fisk of Gloucester, Massachusetts, a famous American organ conservator.

In 1862 the Roman Catholic Diocese of Boston bought the church to serve the North End's enormous influx of Irish immigrants and gave it its present name. In 1869 the entire building was moved back approximately 12 feet to accommodate the widening of Hanover Street, and in 1870 the structure was raised six feet so that a basement church could be installed. Rose Kennedy, the Kennedy family matriarch, was christened here. In 1964 Cardinal Richard Cushing launched a successful campaign to renovate and restore the church to Bulfinch's design (**Chester F. Wright** carried out the restoration), respectfully returning the edifice—now on the National Register of Historic Places—to its original prominence. ♦ Daily. 401 Hanover St (at Clark St). 523.1230

10 DAVIDE

★$$$$ Davide has been serving the North End since 1982, with a fine wine list. The interior features accents of exposed brick and oak. The menu changes seasonally (uncommon in the North End). Try the duck in a port sauce flavored with figs, risotto with seafood, or panfried bass with lemon-caper butter. ♦ Italian ♦ M-F, lunch and dinner; Sa, dinner. Jackets required. Reservations required. Valet parking available. 326 Commercial St (between Clark and North Sts). 227.5745; www.daviderestaurant.com

11 PIZZERIA REGINA

★$$ Everybody but everybody knows Boston's most famous (though not necessarily best) pizza joint, in business since 1926. This is brick-oven pizza of the thin-crust, oily variety. Customers from New York and Florida fly home with as many as eight pies. Even with the red and white sign over the sidewalk, it can be tricky finding the curved corner building. But any North Ender can point you in the right direction.♦ Pizza/Takeout ♦ Daily, lunch and dinner. No credit cards accepted. 11½ Thacher St (at N Margin St). 227.0765. Also at Faneuil Hall Marketplace (upstairs), Quincy Market (742.1713), Prudential Center food court (424.1115), South Station (261.6600), and suburban locations

12 SALEM STREET

This intimate, bustling street was dominated in the 19th century by the millinery and garment businesses owned by Jewish immigrants who settled in this area. Now butcher shops, restaurants, and great produce markets, many with no signs and run by proprietors who serve all customers—North Enders or not—with the same brusqueness, are tucked into tiny shopfronts. Most of the people you see lugging parcels are returning from this street; here one gets a glimpse of daily North End goings-on. Some of the most authentic Italian (as opposed to Italian-American) restaurants are on this street. The south end of Salem Street offers a great view of the Greenway. Enjoy your pedestrian freedom. Between Cross and Charter Sts.

12 A. PARZIALE & SONS BAKERY

This is a businesslike shop, and its business is to make lots of great bread. The place is bursting with it. The Parziale family sells a thousand loaves a day of French bread alone. But why not stick to the Italian varieties and try a handsome loaf of scali, bostone, or fragrant, rich raisin bread? The pizzelle and anisette toasts are great too. ♦ Daily. 80 Prince St (at Salem St). 523.6368

Enrico Caruso loved the North End. When the Italian tenor came to Boston, he often ate at a restaurant on Hanover Street called the Grotta Azzura (now closed). A famous anecdote tells how Caruso wasn't able to cash a check at a neighborhood bank because he had no acceptable identification. The tenor launched into "Celeste Aida," immediately delighting and convincing the skeptical bank manager.

The most popular of the North End's summer weekend *feste* are the "Big St. Anthony" in late August and the colorful Feast of the Madonna del Soccorso (nicknamed the "Fisherman's Feast") in mid-August. The *feste* have become increasingly commercial over time, and many North Enders avoid them because they draw hordes of outsiders and turn the neighborhood into a circus. But try to attend one anyway: They're the fullest expression of North End culture you'll ever encounter.

THE BEST

David R. Godine

Publisher

First, everyone should read Walter Muir Whitehill's *Boston: A Topographical History.*

For entertainment, check out **Jordan Hall** at the New England Conservatory of Music; free faculty and student concerts are scheduled here.

Spend at least a day walking around **Cambridge** and visiting its many museums.

Eat at least one dinner or lunch at **Locke-Ober.**

Also consider tea at the **Ritz-Carlton Hotel**—very relaxing.

In winter, spend time at the **Isabella Stewart Gardner Museum.** It's much less expensive than going to Florida.

Finally, attend a Sunday morning service at **King's Chapel** or **Trinity Church** in Copley Square.

12 BOVA ITALIAN BAKERY

Suffer from insomnia? Why not discover what the North End is like at four in the morning with a trip to the Bova family's corner shop, which is open around the clock? For more than 70 years this clan has been baking all its bread and pastries right on the premises. There's nothing fresher. There are many famous bread and pastry shops in the North End, but the locals go to Bova. ♦ Daily, 24 hours. 134 Salem St (between Noyes Pl and Prince St). 523.5601

13 SAGE

★★★$$$ Rich regional Italian and New American cuisine in a warm and elegant little restaurant, seating 25, with attentive service. Try the homemade-pasta sampler appetizer.♦ Italian/New American ♦ M-Sa, dinner. Reservations are a must. 69 Prince St (at Salem St). 248.8814: www.northendboston.com/sage ♿

14 GIACOMO'S

★★$$$ The open kitchen is close, but not too close, which means you're enveloped in tantalizing, spicy-sauce aromas, but you won't leave this cozy bistro drenched in the smell of garlic and smoke. The grill's the thing here— meaty swordfish and tuna steaks arrive succulent and smoky from the charcoal flame, and grilled chicken and sausage are a fine duo; or try linguine with *frutti di mare* (seafood), a house specialty, with "Giacomo" sauce, a feisty combination of white and red sauces. The unfinished brick walls and refinished wood floors—signs of gentrification throughout the North End—suit owner Jack Taglieri's unpretentious place. A handsome tin-stamped ceiling, oil-on-wood paintings of Rome and Venice, and black-and-white café curtains add warmth and character. No credit cards and no reservations. ♦ Italian ♦ Daily, dinner. 355 Hanover St (between Prince and Fleet Sts). 523.9026. Also at 431 Columbus Ave (between Braddock Park and Holyoke St). 536.5723

15 PREZZA

★★★$$$$ Prezza, a town in Italy's Abruzzi region, is the hometown of chef/owner Anthony Caturano's grandmother. His sophisticated Abruzzi-inspired menu tempts with dishes like lamb rack, broccoli rabe, roasted potato and red wine sauce, or an appetizer of roasted oysters with mascarpone, radicchio, and scallions. There's an extensive, quality wine list too. ♦ Italian ♦ Tu-Su, dinner. 24 Fleet St (between Hanover and North Sts). 227.1577; www.prezza.com

16 JOE TECCE'S

★★$$ This is North End traditional, a Neapolitan red-sauce favorite for more than 50 years and so much a part of the city that street signs say "Joe Tecce Way." Politics has been a part of the restaurant's life; specials are named for people like John A. Nucci, clerk magistrate (baked calamari with spicy shrimp and clam stuffing, with a light tomato sauce over linguine). Valet parking or validated parking at nearby Parcel 7 garage. ♦ Daily, lunch and dinner. 61 N Washington St (between Cooper and Thatcher Sts). 742.6210; www.joetecces.com ♿

17 LO CONTI'S

★★$ If you like your Italian fare fresh and light, and are not keen on the heavy trappings of typical bordello-style décor, try this small, bright restaurant with teal-laminate wooden tables and modernist leanings. Specialties include *gnocchi mascarponi* (potato dumplings tossed in a rich cheese sauce) and *calamari bianco* (fresh squid simmered with white wine). The service is brisk and no-nonsense, the pricing and portioning quite generous. ♦ Italian ♦ Tu-Su, lunch and dinner. 116 Salem St (at Baldwin Pl). 720.3550 ♿

Restaurants/Clubs: Red | Hotels: Purple | Shops: Orange | Outdoors/Parks: Green | Sights/Culture: Blue

18 St. Leonard's Church Peace Garden

With flowers and statuary that are lighted at night, this looks more like a garden center than a garden. It's a cheery spot, especially when decked out with lights at Christmastime. Planted at the close of the Vietnam War and maintained by Franciscan friars, the garden contains two shrubs that stood on the altar on Boston Common when Pope John Paul II celebrated mass in 1979. The adjacent church, designed in 1891 by **William Holmes,** was the first Italian church erected in New England. ♦ Daily until 1PM in winter; until evening in summer. Hanover and Prince Sts. 523.2110

FLORENTINE CAFE
BAR - BISTRO

19 Florentine Cafe

★$$$ The modern glassed-in room across from **St. Leonard's Church Peace Garden** (above) is great for watching the scene along the North End's main thoroughfare. It's also a dependable spot for good pasta: Top choices include crabmeat cannelloni, lobster ravioli, and Maine crab lasagna roll. Meat lovers might try the grilled prosciutto-wrapped black Angus filet mignon or the veal marinated in Marsala wine. The place takes on a particularly lively atmosphere in warm weather, when the floor-to-ceiling windows are opened to the sidewalk. ♦ Italian ♦ Daily, lunch and dinner. 333 Hanover St (at Prince St). 227.1777; www.florentinecafeboston.com

20 Caffè dello Sport

★$ No question about which sport this sunny café's name refers to: Fluttering everywhere are pennants for Italian soccer teams. Take a windowside seat and sip an intense espresso or foamy cappuccino while you join in the North End's favorite pastime: people watching. It gets ever more lively as the day progresses. ♦ Café ♦ Daily, 7AM-midnight. 308 Hanover St (between Wesley Pl and Prince St). 523.5063 ♿

21 Daily Catch

★★$$ That's the tiny restaurant's official moniker, but the name Calamari Cafe and the portrait of a squid lovingly hand-painted on the front window tell the real story. Owners Paul and Maria Freddura have dedicated their culinary careers to promoting this cephalopod, which can be devoured here in many delicious ways. The menu's supporting cast includes Sicilian-style seafood options. The linguine with white or red clam sauce is another hit. Half a dozen or so tables flank the open kitchen, so enjoy the show as young chefs deftly, flamboyantly toss your meal together (there's a lot of garlic in practically every dish). The drawback: There's no bathroom (but it doesn't take much resourcefulness to find neighboring facilities). There's usually a line at this popular eatery, so come in good weather when you feel gregarious or dine early. ♦ Italian ♦ Daily, lunch and dinner. No reservations and no credit cards. 323 Hanover St (between Lothrop Pl and Prince St). 523.8567. Also at 2 Northern Ave in the Harborwalk patio of the Moakley federal courthouse. 338.3093; 441 Harvard St (between Coolidge and Thorndike Sts), Brookline. 734.2700; www.dailycatch.com

22 Artú

★★★$$ Don't let the unobtrusive door of this tiny, casual place fool you. Owner/chef Donato Frattarolli serves dishes that rival the best food anywhere, whether it's *quazzetto alla Donato* (shrimp, squid, mussels, clams, and sole in a stew) or *agnello arrosto* (roast leg of lamb with marinated eggplant and roasted peppers). Take-out orders are available. ♦ Italian ♦ Daily, lunch and dinner. 6 Prince St (between North Sq and Hanover St). 742.4336, fax 248.0808. Also at 89 Charles St (between Pinckney and Mt. Vernon Sts), 227.9023; www.artuboston.com

23 North Square

Idiosyncratic interpretations of the civic "square" abound in Boston. This plaza is, in fact, a cobbled triangle. Nearly overwhelmed by the massive chain along its perimeter—a heavy-handed nod to a nautical past—the square is still winsome, made more so by its circular garden. A stone's throw from the waterfront and part of the first section of the North End to be settled, the square was frequented by a diverse community of artisans, merchants, seafarers, and traders. By late colonial times this had become a prestigious neighborhood. Boston's two most lavish mansions overlooked the square, then called Clark Square. The Second Church of Boston, seat of the powerful, preaching **Mather** family, once stood where Moon Street enters the square. Nicknamed "Old North," the church was torn down by the British in 1776. Today 17th- to 20th-century structures commune here. Around the corner is **4 Garden Court,** home for eight years to **John F. "Honey Fitz" Fitzgerald,** ward boss, congressman, Boston mayor, and one of the city's most famous citizens. His daughter Rose, President John F. Kennedy's mother, was born here in 1890, in what she described as "a modest flat in an eight-family dwelling." While in residence at No. 4, Honey Fitz began his political ascent; he was elected to Congress in 1894 and soon acquired the nickname "Napoleon of the North End." After leaving Garden Court, Honey Fitz took his family to **No. 8 Unity Street,** also in this neighborhood. Honey Fitz spoke so often of the "dear old North End" that North Enders were dubbed the "Dearos"; the name was also adopted by the Irish political and social organization Fitzgerald led.

Honey Fitz was born nearby on Ferry Street in 1863. (Both the Fitzgeralds and the Kennedys emigrated from Ireland in the mid-1800s to escape the island's potato famine. Honey Fitz's father became a grocer on North Street and on Hanover Street.) US senator **Ted Kennedy** has reminisced about how he and brothers John and Robert used to play a game to see who could cross Hanover Street first "in a hop, a skip, and a jump." ♦ At North St, Moon St, and Garden Ct

On North Square:

MAMMA MARIA

★★★$$$$ The dining rooms of this 19th-century brick row house are models of intimate, understated elegance. Diners make the pilgrimage here for the food, which is complex without being fussy. Recommended pasta dishes include *ravioli con tartufi* (handmade truffle-scented ravioli with grilled asparagus and Portobello mushrooms) and *pappardelle con coniglio* (homemade pasta tossed with a traditional Tuscan sauce). For an entrée, consider roasted game hens with risotto and wild mushrooms, the oven-baked pork chop with chestnut polenta, or the *carpaccio bistecca alla Fiorentina* (paper-thin slices of beef tenderloin with Reggiano cheese and extra-virgin olive oil). There are also daily specials and a good selection of Italian and American wines. For a truly romantic evening, complete with captivating views of the Boston skyline, ask to be seated at table 99. ♦ Italian ♦ Daily, dinner. Reservations recommended. No. 3 (at Prince St). 523.0077; www.mammamaria.com

MARINERS' HOUSE

Dedicated to the service of seamen, this respectable Federalist edifice was erected in 1838 and converted into a seamen's boarding-house in the 1870s. It's a remnant of Boston's great and now long gone seafaring days, which fueled the city's rapid growth and many Bostonians' fabulous fortunes. From the cupola atop its roof, mariner residents reputedly kept watch on the sea, much nearer then than it is today (due to landfill). Bona fide seamen still board here. The building is closed to the public. ♦ No. 11 (at Garden Ct)

SACRED HEART CHURCH

Walt Whitman described this former bethel (a place of worship for seamen) as "a quaint ship-cabin-looking church." It opened in 1833, and for 38 years seamen flocked to hear the legendary Methodist preacher **Father Edward Taylor,** once a sailor himself. "I set my bethel in North Square," said Taylor, "because I learned to set my net where the fish ran." Whitman came to the services, calling Father Taylor the only "essentially perfect orator." Ralph Waldo Emerson anointed Taylor "the Shakespeare of the sailor and the poor" and often spoke from his close friend's pulpit. On one of his Boston visits, Charles Dickens made a special trip to hear the preacher, accompanied by Longfellow and Charles Sumner, abolitionist and US senator. In 1871 the bethel was sold, enlarged, and converted into a Catholic church, which it remains today. ♦ Daily. No. 12 (at Moon St). 523.1225

CARMEN

★★★$$$ This small (32-seat), casual redbrick gem of a restaurant also has a small wine and tapas bar. It's kitch free, with attentive service and outstanding rustic Italian cuisine. ♦ Tu-Sa, dinner; F,Sa, lunch. 33 (North Square), 742.6421

PAUL REVERE HOUSE

America's most famous messenger hung his hat here. A descendant of Huguenots named Revoire, Paul Revere was a versatile gold- and silversmith, as well as a copper engraver and a maker of cannons, church bells, and false teeth—reputedly including a set for George Washington.

Busloads of tourists stream in nonstop, but it doesn't take long to see the humble rooms in Revere's tiny, two-story wooden clapboard abode (pictured on page 56). It's worth inching along with the crowd, because this house and the **Pierce-Hichborn House** next door (see page 56) are remarkable rare survivors of colonial Boston.

Built in 1680, rebuilt in the mid-18th century, and renovated by Joseph Chandler in 1908, this National Historic Landmark has been restored to what it looked like originally, before Paul added an extra story to accommodate his big family. Revere and his second wife, Rachel (who gave birth to 8 of his 16 children), owned the house from 1770 to 1800 and lived here for a decade until the war-ruined economy forced them to move in with relatives. From here Revere hurried off to his patriotic exploits, including participating in the Boston Tea Party. By the mid-19th century, the house had slipped into decrepitude and become a sordid tenement with shabby storefronts. The wrecking ball loomed at the start of this century, but a great-grandson of Revere's formed a preservation group that rescued the house.

From across North Square, look toward the medieval overhanging upper floor and leaded casements. These throwbacks to late-16th-century Elizabethan urban architecture are reminders that architectural styles were exported to the colonies from England and adapted with Yankee ingenuity long after they were out of fashion in Europe. Built after the devastating Boston fire of 1676, the fashionable town house violated the building code because it was made of wood, not brick. Today 90 percent of its frame and one door are genuine; its clapboard shell and interior are reproductions. See how artfully the house tucks into its tiny site in the colonial North End, where rabbit-warren clusters of small houses are linked by a maze of alleyways. The dark, low-ceilinged, heavy-beamed rooms with their oversize fireplaces bear few traces of the Revere family, but recall colonial domestic arrangements. The pretty period gardens in back are equally interesting; study them with the help of the posted key and a pamphlet sold at the ticket kiosk. The multipurpose plants—with old-time names

Paul Revere House

COURTESY OF PAUL REVERE MEMORIAL ASSOCIATION

like Johnny-jump-up, bee balm, Dutchman's-pipe, and lady's mantle—remind visitors that gardens were once common-place sources of pharmaceuticals, food, and domestic aids. ◆ Admission. Daily; closed M Jan-Mar, and major holidays. No. 19 (between Bakers Alley and Prince St). 523.1676; www.paulreverehouse.org

PIERCE/HICHBORN HOUSE

This stalwart structure to the left of Paul Revere's house was home to Paul's cousin, a boatbuilder by the name of Nathaniel Hichborn. A prized colonial urban relic, the house was built around 1710 by a glazier named Moses Pierce. Although built just 30 years later than Revere's Tudor, this English Renaissance brick structure represents a huge stylistic leap. Even the central stair is innovative—simple and straight instead of windy and cramped like that of the Revere House. The pleasing three-story residence reflects a pioneering effort to apply formal English architectural principles to early Boston's unruly fabric. When the house left Hichborn's family in 1864, it, too, fell on hard times, becoming a tenement until it was restored in 1950. Four rooms are open to the public for guided tours given twice daily, the only times to see the interior. Enter at the Revere House gate. ◆ Admission. Tours daily at 12:30 and 2:30 PM, but call beforehand to confirm; closed M Jan-Mar and major holidays. No. 19 (at Bakers Alley). 523.1676

Around the corner from the Pierce/Hichborn House:

BAKERS ALLEY

Walk down this alley to a pretty residential plaza ingeniously tucked in among the back sides of apartment buildings. The lucky residents have a number of handsome specimens of that scarce North End commodity: trees.

RACHEL REVERE PARK

This tiny park is used as a playground for schoolchildren. It was dedicated to the patriot's wife by the Massachusetts Charitable Mechanics Association, a philanthropic group that was founded in 1795 with Revere as its first president. ◆ At North St

24 PICCOLO NIDO

★★★$$ Owner Pino Irano has developed an imaginative and tempting table of Northern and Southern Italian entrées at this trattoria. Try the *brodetto di pesce* (fish stew), semiboneless roast duck served in port wine with cherries, or the *crespelle al funghi di bosco* (wild mushroom–filled crepes with Madeira and thyme sauce). The in-depth wine list is not only laudable, it's applaudable. ◆ Italian ◆ M-Sa, dinner. Reservations required. 257 North St (at Lewis St). 742.4272 ⟁

25 LEWIS WHARF

In the mid–19th century, Boston's legendary clipper-ship trade centered on this wharf, named for Thomas Lewis, a canny merchant who acquired much of the city's waterfront property after the American Revolution. Ships carried tea to Europe and foodstuffs to California, where they were sold at exorbitant rates to Gold Rush prospectors. The warehouse, attributed to architect **Richard Bond,** was built of Quincy granite between 1836 and 1840 and renovated in the late 1960s by **Carl Koch and Associates,** at which time the graceful gabled roof was replaced with an unwieldy mansard one. The building now houses residential and commercial units.

To the right stretches an attractive **harborside park** where members of the Boston Croquet Club set up their wickets—a genteel sight that reminds us how long gone the city's seafaring era is. Local lore has it that Edgar Allan Poe's tale "The Fall of the House of Usher" was inspired by events that took place on the wharf's site in the 18th century. Two lovers, a sailor and another man's wife, were trapped by the angry husband in their rendezvous, a tunnel underneath the Usher house. When the structure was torn down in 1800, two skeletons locked in embrace were discovered behind a gate at the foot of the tunnel steps.

Set back at the Boston Harbor end of the wharf is the **Boston Sailing Center** (227.4198; www.bostonsailingcenter.com), which offers a variety of sailing and racing lesson packages as well as captained harbor cruises aboard 23- to 30-foot sailboats. Boats also embark on day sails among the Boston Harbor Islands and on overnight trips to Provincetown, Martha's Vineyard, Newport, and Block Island. The sailing center also will arrange more extensive charters. ◆ Atlantic Ave (between Commercial Wharf E and Eastern Ave)

26 L'OSTERIA RISTORANTE

★★$$ This family-owned Northern Italian place serves delectable entrées made from the freshest ingredients. House specialties include chicken *finiziare* (served with veal, shrimp, and assorted vegetables) and veal *bocconcini* (rolled and stuffed with tomato cream sauce). There is a large dining area downstairs that is ideal for business meetings or festive gatherings. ◆ Italian ◆ Daily, lunch and dinner. Reservations recommended. 104 Salem St (at Cooper St). 723.7847; www.losteria.com ੬

27 AL DENTE

★★$$ Be as casual as you please. This restaurant is run by sausage-cart king Joe Bono, who, needless to say, knows real Italian-American home cooking (and lots of it) influenced by Sicily, Calabria, and the northern regions, with dishes like chicken, veal, and shrimp with red and yellow peppers in a white-wine sauce. Bono's mother, Lauraine, makes the wonderful tiramisù for dessert. ◆ Regional Italian ◆ Daily, 11AM-11PM. Nearby validated parking. 109 Salem St (at Parmenter St), near the Freedom Trail. 523.0990; www.aldenteboston.com ੬

28 BOSTON PUBLIC LIBRARY, NORTH END BRANCH

Come by when the library is open to inspect the remarkable 14-foot-long plaster model diorama of the Doge's Palace in Venice. This creation was the consuming passion of Henrietta Macy, who taught kindergarten in this neighborhood before moving to Europe. After she died in Venice, her handiwork was presented to the library. Painted settings and dolls enacting 16th-century scenes were added by Louise Stimson of Concord, Massachusetts. Architect **Carl Koch**'s attention to Italian-American cultural heritage in this 1965 building has tempered and transformed the coldness of 1960s modernism into an extraordinary neighborhood addition. The library's atrium is cobbled like an Italian piazza, with plants and a small pool, and a bust of Dante on the wall. Umbrella-like concrete vaults supported by nine columns form a roof, raised to create a clerestory that illuminates the library interior. The brick exterior is punctuated by colored glass ceramics, adding festive notes to what is an otherwise drab streetscape. ◆ M-F. 25 Parmenter St (between Hanover and Salem Sts). 227.8135

29 RISTORANTE SARACENO

★$$ Neapolitan recipes are featured at this family-owned and -operated multifloor restaurant. In addition to the antipasti and entrée lineup, specialties include good veal saltimbocca, shrimp and lobster *fra diavolo,* and linguine with seafood. The scrolled menus add pretension to an otherwise straightforward and pleasant place, which is recommended by many North Enders. Ask for a table in the small upstairs room; downstairs, with its gaudy murals of Capri, the Bay of Naples, and Amalfi, is rather confining. ◆ Italian ◆ Daily, lunch and dinner. Reservations recommended. 286 Hanover St (at Wesley Pl). 227.5888 ੬

Restaurants/Clubs: Red | Hotels: Purple | Shops: Orange | Outdoors/Parks: Green | Sights/Culture: Blue

29 Caffè Vittoria

★$ This place is almost too much, with *un cortile* that isn't really a courtyard, *un grotto* that isn't really a grotto, and more-lurid-than-life murals of Venice and the Bay of Sorrento in the back. But a little braggadocio isn't all bad, and this café—Boston's first, they claim—exerts a full-bodied charm. The antique coffee grinders are absolutely authentic, as are the black-and-white photos of North Enders on the walls, and the opera-singing espresso makers (people, not machines) by the windows. Venture beyond cappuccino; try an anisette, grappa, Italian soda, or maybe a gelato. Come during the day when your companions will be older men lingering over newspapers and chatting in Italian; you'll quickly get a sense of how deeply rooted Italian culture is in this neighborhood. At night it's a different place, festive and boisterous. ♦ Café ♦ Daily, 8AM-midnight. No credit cards. 294 Hanover St (between Wesley Pl and Prince St). 227.7606 &

29 Mike's Pastry

★$ Every type of caloric Italian treat—cream cakes, candy, cookies, breads, cannoli—along with that most un-Italian of baked goods, the oat-bran muffin, is sold at this perpetually busy bakery. Tourists love it and since this place is trying to cover all the bases, quality varies. You should scout out the smaller *pasticceria* in the shop for your favorite sweets. That said, the biscotti di Prato are very good and cinnamony here. Or try a "lobster tail," a particularly diet-devastating concoction of pastry with cheese, custard, and whipped cream. There are some tables, and Freedom Trail pilgrims find this to be a convenient spot to rest their weary feet and fuel up with a cup of coffee before continuing their trek through local history. ♦ Café ♦ M-Sa, 9AM-9PM; Su, 8AM-9PM. 300 Hanover St (between Wesley Pl and Prince St). 742.3050; www.mikespastry.com

30 Pomodoro

★★★$$ Seating up to 24 diners, this cozy restaurant is a joy. Chef Seth Trafforo prepares such classic dishes as chicken carbonara with wild mushrooms and prosciutto, and seafood *fra diavolo* (clams, mussels, and other shellfish in a spicy red sauce over linguine). Whimsical modern art and a full list of Italian wines complete the sensory experience. No credit cards. ♦ Italian ♦ Daily, lunch and dinner. 319 Hanover St (between Lothrop Pl and Prince St). 367.4348

Terramia

31 Terramia

★★★★$$$ Nestled along narrow Salem Street is one of Boston's smallest (39 seats) but very best restaurants. Owner and chef Mario Nocera has won the hearts and palates of sophisticated critics and diners alike. Don't look for veal parmigiana here; Nocera prepares *authentic* Italian cuisine. (Italians visiting the US have been known to fly in to Boston just to eat here.) Featured are dried salted cod, reconstituted with potato and onions in white truffle oil; roast quail risotto with porcini and shiitake mushrooms; and swordfish stuffed with pine nuts and raisins. It's all served in an elegant but spare setting, with views of the copper-laced Old World kitchen. ♦ Italian ♦ M-W, Su, dinner; Th-Sa, lunch and dinner. 98 Salem St (at Bartlett Pl). 523.3112

32 Polcari's Coffee

A fragrant North End fixture since 1932, congenial Ralph Polcari's shop sells more than a hundred spices from all over the world as well as a fine selection of coffees. Innumerable specialty items fill every inch of shelf and floor space: chamomile flowers, *ceci* (dried chickpeas), Arborio rice, flaxseed, carob and vanilla beans, pine nuts, braided garlic, and bunches of fresh oregano. Polcari's wares are the stuff of alchemy in everyday cooking. ♦ M-Sa. 105 Salem St (at Parmenter St). 227.0786

33 Gelateria

Some 50 flavors of the Italian ice-cream favorite are available from the sidewalk or inside the yellow-walled café. The gelato is made there daily by a *Maestro dio Gelati* from Naples. (Gelato has less butterfat, no eggs, and is lighter than American ice cream.) There's also a choice of coffee drinks, juices, pastries, and sorbets. ♦ Daily, 11AM-10PM. 272 Hanover St (between Parmenter St and Wesley Pl). 720.4243 & (Staff will assist with step.)

The Associated Daughters of Early American Witches, founded in 1987, is a society of women who are descended from someone accused, tried, or executed for witchcraft prior to 31 December 1699 (the Salem Witch Trials took place in 1692).

Just off North Square is Boston's most charmingly named intersection: the celestial meeting of Sun Court and Moon Street.

34 CAFFÉ GRAFFITI

★$ Depending on the time of day, stop in for a glass of wine, a generous calzone, or one of Boston's best cappuccinos, along with a tasty, award-winning homemade pastry. ♦ Café ♦ Daily, 7:30AM-midnight. 307 Hanover St (at Lothrop Pl). 367.3016

35 FRATELLI PAGLIUCA'S

★$$ There's nothing fancy about the brothers Joe, Freddy, and Felix Pagliuca's popular place. A goodly number of locals eat here, as do businesspeople who know their way around. This is satisfying, stick-to-the-ribs Italian red-sauce cuisine served in a family atmosphere. Favorites include the chicken-escarole soup, chicken Marsala, and sweet roast peppers with provolone and sausage, which come in large portions for reasonable prices. Don't look for the four basic food groups here: pasta and meat, not veggies, get priority. ♦ Italian ♦ Daily, lunch and dinner. Reservations recommended for parties of four or more on weekends. 14 Parmenter St (between Hanover and Salem Sts). 367.1504

36 SALUMERIA ITALIANA

It's crowded with imported-from-Italy olive oils, cheeses, coffees, pastas, sauces, rice, cured meats, and kitchen tools. But many residents of the one-third-square-mile North End would shop nowhere else. Many who moved to the suburbs (and their grown children) drive in every weekend. They'll ship web orders. ♦ M-Sa. 151 Richmond St (between North and Hanover Sts) on the Freedom Trail about a minute from **Paul Revere House.** 800/400.5916; www.salumeriaitaliana.com

36 MONICA'S

★★$$ This family-run authentic Italian restaurant in a storefront offers freshly made pastas, heavenly breads, and sophisticated dishes on a seasonal menu. Pizza too. ♦ Italian ♦ Daily, dinner from 5:30PM. Valet parking ($20) and validated parking. 143 Richmond St (between Hanover and North Sts). 227.0311 &

37 LA PICCOLA VENEZIA

★★$ Forget décor, forget romance, forget trendy angel-hair pasta concoctions—there are other reasons to frequent this no-frills spot. First, there's the hearty Italian home cooking, which runs the gamut from familiar favorites—lasagna, spaghetti with meat sauce, sausage cacciatore—to such hard-to-find, traditional Italian fare as gnocchi, polenta, tripe, *baccala* (salt cod), and scungilli. Second, everything's inexpensive, and third, portions are enormous. When your wallet is light but your appetite is immense, this place is perfect. ♦ Italian ♦ Daily, lunch and dinner. No credit cards. 263 Hanover St (between Mechanic and Richmond Sts). 523.3888

38 VILLA-FRANCESCA

★$$ This restaurant on the Freedom Trail claims its share of star diners, including a slew of Red Sox players, and a seat by one of the large open windows is a summer pleasure. The food is nothing special—large portions spruced up with lots of lemon and white wine—but if you want a little schmaltz with your romance, try this place. ♦ Italian ♦ M-Sa, dinner; Su, lunch and dinner. 150 Richmond St (between North and Hanover Sts). 367.2948; www.ristorantevillafrancesca.com

39 MARE

★★★$$$$ Mare, pronounced *mah-ray,* is a coastal Italian trattoria located just 100 feet from Paul Revere's house on the Freedom Trail. Large dining-room windows open to the street in nice weather and there's a comfortable feel, even in the decidedly modern décor. Food is superior; consider butter-braised two-pound lobster, salmon with balsamic sorbet, or the barbecued octopus appetizer. Capacity is 56, plus four at the small bar. The chef uses certified organic seafood, hormone-free beef, organic free-range chicken and eggs, and organic wines. ♦ Italian ♦ Daily, dinner; F, Su, lunch. 135 Richmond St (at North St). 723.6273 &

40 V. CIRACE & SON

Jeff and Lisa Cirace are the third generation and the second brother-sister act to run this almost 100-year-old Italian wine establishment. About half of the store's 1,500-plus wines are Italian, and there's an extensive collection of Cognacs, cordials, grappa, and

---

Restaurants/Clubs: Red | Hotels: Purple | Shops: Orange | Outdoors/Parks: Green | Sights/Culture: Blue

several venerable vintages. This is not a self-service place, but the staff is friendly and helpful. The "V" in the name, by the way, is for Vincenza, the owners' grandmother. ◆ M-Sa. 173 North St (at Richmond St). 227.3193; www.vcirace.com

41 McLAUTHLIN BUILDING

The soft brownish-mauve façade of New England's first cast-iron building is adorned with lacy rows of arched windows crowned by fanlights. Built circa 1850, the structure was originally the home of the McLauthlin Elevator Company. Renovated in 1979 by Moritz Bergmeyer, it now houses condominiums. ◆ 120 Fulton St (between Richmond and Lewis Sts)

42 PURITY CHEESE COMPANY

Four people make all the marvelous ricotta and mozzarella sold fresh in this unobtrusive storefront, which is easy to miss unless you glance in and spot the giant, pungent wheels of Parmesan and tubs of olives. Grating cheeses, pastas, oils, and big serving bowls are available too. The business began in 1938, and the operation is as unfussy as ever. People come from all over for the high-caliber cheese choices. And it smells delicious inside. ◆ Tu-Sa. 55 Endicott St (between Cross and Morton Sts). 227.5060 ₺

43 DAIRY FRESH CANDIES

If you like sweets, it's impossible to pass by without stopping; once you're inside, it's all over. Those who suffer from chocoholism will tremble at the sight of loose chocolates of every sort, including massive chunks of the plain and simple sinful stuff and gorgeous

Boston is full of public squares that are named after someone, but the North End has an especially large supply, including Joseph S. Giambarresi Square, Arthur A. Sirignano Square, and Gus P. Napoli Square. Most honor Italian-American public figures, war heroes, and the like.

The first subway in the New World opened in Boston on 1 September 1897. Some 200 workers dug out by hand 67,000 cubic yards of dirt under Boston Common along Tremont Street. In the process, they unearthed nearly 1,100 skeletons of people who had been buried in the Central Burying Ground on the Common. Only about 75 could be identified by headstones. The remains were reinterred elsewhere in the cemetery. The newly opened subway had two stations, Park Street and Boylston Street. The two stations remain stops on Boston's present subway system, and the original station kiosks at Park Street are National Historic Landmarks.

packaged European assortments. The entire confection spectrum is here, including hard candies, old-fashioned nougats, and teeth-breaking brittles. But the amiable Matara family's retail and wholesale business, in operation for more than 30 years, goes way beyond candy, also selling Italian cakes and cookies, dried fruits, nuts, exotic oils and extracts, vinegars, antipasti, pastas, cooking and baking supplies, and more—an extravaganza of delicacies. You can assemble a wonderful gift box here. "Thank you, stay sweet," says the hand-lettered sign by the door. ◆ M-Sa. 57 Salem St (between Cross and Parmenter Sts). 742.2639, 800/336.5536 ₺

44 CAFFÈ PARADISO ESPRESSO BAR

★$ There are cheerier places to be on a bright summer day, but this is (by Boston standards) a night-owl spot, with the only 2AM liquor license on the street. Stop here on the night of a *festa* or other celebration—the whole neighborhood shows up and has a great time. The lively crowd keeps the jukebox cranking. There's a full line of Italian bitter aperitifs; pastries, homemade gelati, spumoni, and sorbetti; plus an enormous array of desserts that you won't see in any of the local bakeries. There are outdoor tables in the warm-weather months. ◆ Café ◆ Daily, 6:30AM-2AM. 255 Hanover St (between Mechanic and Richmond Sts). 742.1768. Also at 1 Eliot St (at Eliot Sq), Cambridge. 868.3240

Upstairs at the Caffè Paradiso Espresso Bar:

TRATTORIA À SCALINATELLA

★★★$$$ This small (10 tables) brick-walled walk-up is one of a growing number of gourmet restaurants in the North End. Wood beams and a fireplace help create a feeling of sanctuary. Owner Paolo Diecidue is happy to acquaint guests with the menu of seasonal local fare and fresh produce from his own farm. Try the *casarecci mara bosco* (pasta with arugula, porcini mushrooms, and farm-raised clams), crab cakes, or rack of wild boar. Leave room for Sicilian *bomba* (sponge cake made with ricotta, rum, marzipan, and chocolate chips). ◆ Italian ◆ Daily, dinner. Reservations recommended. 253 Hanover St 523.8865

44 MODERN PASTRY

Giovanni Picariellos Senior and Junior are renowned for their diabolically delicious homemade *torrone*, a nougat-and-almond confection drenched in chocolate. This ever-popular, more than 60-year-old *pasticceria* also offers great *sfogliatelle* (pastry shells filled with vanilla cream and egg), *pizzelle* (a light waffle), and cannoli. There are several tables for those who can't wait to sample their sweets. ♦ Daily. 257 Hanover St (between Mechanic and Richmond Sts). 523.3783; www.modernpastry.com

45 BRICCO

★★$$$ This much-praised, California-inspired Italian restaurant and wine bar offers a change from typical neighborhood fare. You can enjoy tapas-like appetizers called *cicchetti;* homemade pastas like *corzetti di stampati* with lobster, celery root, and walnut sauce; and entrées like roasted red snapper with caramelized onions, pine nuts, cauliflower, and parsley vinaigrette. Late-night diners are in luck; wood-oven pizzas are prepared for the lounge until 2AM. Valet parking is free. "Bricco," by the way, refers to the summit of a vineyard. ♦ Contemporary Italian. ♦ Daily, dinner. 241 Hanover St (near Cross St). 248.6800; www.bricco.com

46 MARIA'S PASTRY SHOP

What's a *pasticceria* without a display of marzipan in fruit and animal shapes, lurid with food coloring? You'll find that popular almond-sugar confection here, and plenty more. Butter, anise, and almond scent the air, and through the kitchen door you can see bakers taking cookies out of the oven. Try the *savoiardi napolitani* (citrus-layered cookies), or, at Halloween time, the intriguing *moscardini ossa di morta* (cinnamon cookies that really do resemble bones). The *sfogliatelli* (clam-shaped pastries) are creamy, citrony, and not too sweet. ♦ M-Sa; Su until 1PM. 46

Cross St (between Hanover and Salem Sts). 523.1196

46 TARANTA

★★$$$ Chef and owner José Duarte is from Peru. He learned Italian cooking in Venezuela and now has this much-praised, three-story Peruvian-Italian restaurant. It was a long journey, but Boston diners are winners. Duarte and his wife, Anna, mix Southern Italian with Peruvian cuisine to delicious effect, especially in dishes like shrimp ravioli in a pesto of pine nuts and Peruvian black mint. Reduced-rate validated parking nearby. ♦ Italian-Peruvian ♦ Daily, dinner. 210 Hanover St 720.0052; www.tarantarist.com ᕫ (first floor)

47 HANOVER STREET

The straightest and widest street in the labyrinthine North End runs through the heart of the district and boasts the greatest concentration of restaurants, bakeries, cafés, banks, services, and shops selling everything from religious articles to Italian leather goods. Two famous department stores began here in 1851. At No. 168, Eben Jordan started a dry-goods store that eventually became the Jordan Marsh Company; Rowland H. Macy opened a similar operation nearby that grew into the R.H. Macy Company. Block after block, four- and five-story buildings crowd in so closely that the Waterfront's nearness stays a secret until you reach the bend by Charles Bulfinch's **St. Stephen's Church.** Tourists stream along the narrow sidewalks as they follow the **Freedom Trail** to the **Old North Church** (see page 48) or seek out popular dining spots such as the **Daily Catch** (see page 54). But most of the street scene belongs to the people who live here. Even on a sleepy Sunday afternoon, this thoroughfare pulses with the vigor of Italian-American culture.
♦ Between Cross and Commercial Sts

ewcomers to Boston who have heard of its great maritime past are sometimes surprised to discover that its **waterfront area** is quite elusive. Hills that once overlooked **Boston Harbor** were leveled long ago, and the shoreline, for centuries Boston's lifeline, was sheared from the city's core by Atlantic Avenue, the old Central Artery, and a shield of modern buildings. But the Big Dig removed the Central Artery barrier by putting the formerly elevated highway below ground. Now you can easily cross the Rose Fitzgerald Kennedy Greenway to see where Boston began. And, on the South Boston waterfront, you'll see where much of the new Boston is rising (see page 202).

An urban treasure, the Waterfront is vibrant with light and color and the constant motion of water and air. The neighborhood's heyday is recorded in the street and wharf names, and captured in grand old buildings. The harbor itself, once among the nation's most polluted, has undergone a massive cleanup. Sludge dumping has ceased, and a primary sewage treatment plant was built on Deer Island, resulting in much-improved water quality. Eventually, the 34 harbor islands, which comprise a National Park Area, will have the sparkling setting they deserve. From little Gallops, Grape, and Bumpkin to big Peddocks and Thompson, the **Boston Harbor Islands** will entice you with picturesque paths, beaches, and views of the city (www.bostonislands.org).

In colonial times young Boston looked to the Atlantic Ocean for commerce and prosperity. Throughout the 17th, 18th, and 19th centuries profit-minded Bostonians tinkered with the shoreline, which originally reached to where **Faneuil Hall Marketplace** and **Government Center** are today, once the Town Dock area. Citizens built piers,

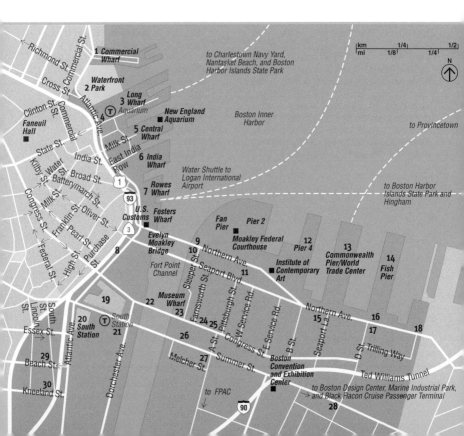

shipyards, warehouses, and wharves extending ever farther into the sea, until the shoreline resembled a tentacled creature reaching hungrily for trade. The ocean brought profitable European and Chinese trade and established the city's merchant princes.

One of Boston's most glorious times was the clipper ship era of the 1850s, when the harbor was alive with masts and sails. Toward the turn of the century, as rails and roads replaced sea routes and manufacturing supplanted maritime trade, fishing, and shipbuilding, Boston's liaison with the sea began to suffer, languishing for decades until the late 1960s, when the city began to reclaim it. Since that time the Waterfront has been resurrected gradually, its connections to the heart of Boston reforged. The working-harbor activities that remain have shifted elsewhere, primarily to **Charlestown** and the **Black Falcon Cruise Passenger Terminal** in Marine Industrial Park and the **Fish Pier** in South Boston. Boston is also reinterpreting the Waterfront's role as a place for leisure, luxurious residences and offices, pleasure boats, and waterside restaurants and hotels. Completion of the Moakley Federal Courthouse on the Fan Pier waterfront next to South Boston has spurred massive, ongoing redevelopment of what used to be a grungy stretch of piers, parking lots, and industry. The **Seaport/South Boston Waterfront** is approximately 1,000 acres wedged between the downtown financial area, residential South Boston, and what remains of the working port. Developers, politicians, and citizen groups quietly squabble over the future of the district. But when completed, with new hotels, condos, and offices, this will be Boston's first new neighborhood since the Back Bay was filled in more than 100 years ago. It's hard, without a map, to tell where the South Boston waterfront starts and the Seaport yields. To most of us, it's all the same thing; it's Boston. More changes are coming, but already the city's $800 million convention center and the $40 million Institute of Contemporary Art (see South Boston, page 202) have brought new life to the whole waterfront.

Excursion and commuter boats depart from the numerous wharves for the **Boston Harbor Islands, Provincetown** on Cape Cod, **Cape Ann,** and **South Shore** communities. The **Water Shuttle** (www.massport.com) serves travelers between **Logan International Airport** just across the harbor, the new courthouse, and **Rowes Wharf** on the downtown waterfront. **Harborwalk,** the pedestrian route along the Waterfront, is lengthening. It will stretch from the **Charlestown Navy Yard**—where Old Ironsides is open for your inspection—to **Fort Point Channel** and that **South Boston Waterfront,** linking with walks along Boston's second waterfront, the **Charles River Basin,** to create a pathway of more than 40 miles. Big Dig construction no longer gets in the way of a walk. Parts are still to be built, but you can take at least sections of a great stroll that begins at **Waterfront Park** and **Commercial Wharf,** proceeds past the **New England Aquarium** and around sumptuous Rowes Wharf, and crosses over the channel via the Northern Avenue Bridge (closed to vehicle traffic), past the federal courthouse and ICA on Fan Pier, up to the Fish Pier and beyond. Double back to **The Children's Museum** and the **Boston Tea Party Ship and Museum** before carrying on to **South Station,** and concluding with a brief meander in the **Leather District** (www.bostonharborwalk.com).

Fort Point Channel and the Leather District aren't part of the historic Waterfront per se, but are natural companions because they too reveal facets of Boston's workaday life. Developed during the late 19th century, the Fort Point Channel neighborhood was the center for Boston's fishing, shipping, warehousing, and manufacturing industries; during the same era, the garment and raw leather goods industries thrived in the Leather District. In both atmosphere and architecture, these two neighborhoods, like the Waterfront, have acquired new vitality as galleries, restaurants, condos, and shops move into restored buildings, following artists and other urban pioneers. Unfortunately, this gentrification and the steep rent hikes that follow drives out many artists. Walking the length of this far-flung neighborhood is an ambitious undertaking but is a great Boston experience.

WATERFRONT

1 COMMERCIAL WHARF

When Atlantic Avenue sliced through the Waterfront in 1868, it split a rugged 1834 building of Quincy granite and Charlestown brick in two. Now the western half of the building, renovated by Anderson Notter Associates in 1971, and the larger eastern half, renovated by **Halasz and Halasz** in 1969, houses offices and upscale apartments with enviable views. Original architect **Isaiah Rogers** also designed Boston's famed but long gone Tremont Hotel, the nation's first luxury overnight digs. If you walk to the wharf's end, you'll see ramshackle buildings, relics of days gone by. Now pleasure boats in the adjacent yacht marina crowd the pier and, if you look across to the South Boston waterfront, you'll see new buildings rising in that new waterfront neighborhood. ◆ Atlantic Ave (below Commercial St)

On Commercial Wharf:

BOSTON SAIL LOFT

★$ Is this the North End or the waterfront? Actually, it's both. Strange as it seems in a seaside city, there aren't many restaurants in Boston where you can sit and look out at the water. This is one of the few. Longtime residents fondly recall its predecessor, a quiet, run-down hole-in-the-wall called The Wharf. But things change; even if this is now a hopping touristy spot on the Happy Hour trail, you get a nice view of Boston Harbor along with your oversize portions of decent seafood. The fried clams are good and the Oreo jar on the bar is grand. ◆ American/Seafood ◆ Daily, lunch and dinner. No tank tops allowed. 80 Atlantic Ave. 227.7280. Also at One Memorial Dr (at Main St), Cambridge. 225.2222

2 WATERFRONT PARK

This friendly park, designed by **Sasaki Associates** in 1976, opened a window to the sea and drew Bostonians back to where their city began. In fact, the park was built to complete the **walk to the sea** that starts at City Hall Plaza in Government Center, proceeds through Faneuil Hall Marketplace, and then passes under the Central Artery to end by Boston Harbor. A

The first regularly issued American newspaper, *The Boston News-Letter,* began publication in 1704.

handsome trellis promenade—its greenery gradually is growing in—crowns the park's center, with huge bollards and an anchor chain marking the seawall. The park offers views of the harbor and wharves, and a sociable scene: From morning until late at night, this versatile oasis hosts sea gazing, ledge sitting, sun tanning, Frisbee throwing, dog walking, and romantic rendezvous. Watch the steady boat traffic, and planes taking off across the harbor at Logan International Airport. On a summer afternoon sit and read amid the grove of honey locust trees or in the **Rose Fitzgerald Kennedy Garden**, fragrant with her namesake blooms. **Quincy Market** is just a five-minute walk away; pick up some treats and picnic with the cool ocean breezes rustling by. ◆ Bounded by Boston Harbor and Atlantic Ave, and Long and Commercial Wharves

3 LONG WHARF

Boston was already America's busiest port when farsighted **Captain Oliver Noyes** constructed this wharf in 1710. The city's oldest wharf and now a National Historic Landmark, it was lined with warehouses and originally extended from what is now State Street far out into what was then Town Cove, creating a half-mile avenue to the farthest corners of the world. It was the Logan Airport of its day, where even the deepest-drawing ships could unload their cargo. The painter John Singleton Copley played here as a child, where his mother ran a tobacco shop. Landfill and road construction demolished most of the wharf by the 1950s, but the restoration of its remaining buildings and the arrival of the **Boston Marriott Long Wharf hotel** (see below) have made it a destination once more. Walk to the spacious granite plaza at the wharf's end for fresh air and lovely views. ◆ Atlantic Ave and State St

On Long Wharf:

BOSTON MARRIOTT LONG WHARF

$$$$ It's certainly pleasant to stay here at the city's edge in rooms surveying the lively Waterfront, with **Waterfront Park** next door, the **New England Aquarium** one wharf over, and the North End ristoranti and **Faneuil Hall Marketplace** mere minutes away. Many of the 400 rooms, all renovated in 2001, have good views, and two luxury suites have outside decks. The Concierge Level offers premium services; on-site amenities include a business center, an indoor swimming pool, other exercise facilities, and a

game room. This 1982 hotel, designed by **Cossutta and Associates,** has a couple of counts against it as a Waterfront neighbor, however: It crowds what should have remained a generous link in the Harborwalk (although there's a walkway around the hotel), and the architects' attempt to mimic Waterfront warehouses and the lines of a ship resulted in an awkward, aggressively bulky building. The hotel's red-garbed porters are a striking sight, though. Be sure to see the 19th-century fresco depicting Boston Harbor that is mounted in the lobby upstairs. Relax by a window or (in warm weather) on the outside harbor-front terrace **Waves Bar & Grill;** there is also the formal **Oceana** restaurant and a more casual café. (And check the bar at **Tia's,** a restaurant just outside the hotel.) ♦ 296 State St. 227.0800, 800/228.9290; fax 227.2867 ₲

THE CHART HOUSE

★★$$$ The **Gardner Building,** a simple and solid circa-1763 brick warehouse—the Waterfront's oldest, renovated in 1973 by Anderson Notter Associates—was recycled for this chain restaurant. Inside, rustic bricks and beams recall the building's former life. Steak, prime rib, and seafood are the ticket, with children's plates available. Lots of stories circulate about the building's history—some possibly true—claiming it was called "Hancock's Counting House" because John Hancock had an office here, and that tea was stored here prior to the Boston Tea Party. The free valet parking is a great boon in a neighborhood born long before the days of autos. ♦ Seafood/American ♦ Daily, dinner. 60 Long Wharf. 227.1576

CUSTOM HOUSE BLOCK

Before his writing career finally freed him from ordinary pursuits, **Nathaniel Hawthorne** spent two years (1838-1840) recording cargoes in the cramped predecessor to this building, demolished in 1847. The "new" structure, designed by **Isaiah Rogers** and restored as a National Historic Landmark by **Anderson Notter Associates** in 1973, was never used for customs collection. Nonetheless, this building bears the signature eagle and a misleading sign on its granite façade. It now accommodates offices and apartments.

4 SEL DE LA TERRE

★★★$$$ French for "salt of the earth," this sunny restaurant offers the rustic cuisine of Provence—perfect bouillabaisse, country roasts, omelets, hams, and pâtés. There's also a children's menu with dishes like pasta with butter and parmesan ($7). Sister restaurant to the Back Bay's L'Espelier. Room for 115 in the dining room and 20 at the bar.♦ Provençal ♦ M-Sa, lunch; daily, dinner; Sunday brunch.

Valet parking available after 5PM. Parking garage next door. 225 State St. (at Atlantic Ave). 720.1300, fax 227.1569; www.seldelaterre.com ₲

5 CENTRAL WHARF

In the early 19th century Boston rebounded from the devastating economic effects of the American Revolution and became a booming seaport once again. The daring developer **Uriah Cotting** formed the Broad Street Association to modernize the dilapidated waterfront. With architect **Charles Bulfinch** designing, the association created broad streets flanked by majestic four-story brick-and-granite warehouses, and completed this pier and **India Wharf** (see page 66) in 1816. Only a fragment of the original wharf remains, with a handful of its structures stranded across the expressway. ♦ Atlantic Ave and Milk St

On Central Wharf:

NEW ENGLAND AQUARIUM

The aquarium takes visitors on a trip around the world from Boston Harbor to the Amazon River, with exhibits of fish and other aquatic creatures in re-created habitats. The complex boasts more than 70 exhibit tanks and is home to more than 28,000 fish, birds, and mammals. Among the major exhibits are the spectacular four-story, 200,000-gallon **Giant Ocean Tank,** which offers multi-angle views of sharks, sea turtles, moray eels, and tropical fish; the **Ocean Tray,** home to African and rockhopper penguins; the **Edge of the Sea** hands-on tidal pool; the floating pavilion **Discovery,** where sea lions appear in shows that combine entertainment and education; and the **Aquarium Medical Center,** where visitors can watch staff veterinarians and biologists examine and care for sick sea animals. There are also issue-oriented changing exhibits.

The boxy concrete building (designed by **Cambridge Seven** in 1969) is somewhat like a sea creature grown too big for its shell. Opened in 1969, the aquarium has grown, notably in 1998, with an expanded **West Wing** for an outdoor seal exhibit and a two-level gallery for special exhibits. Designed by **Schwartz/Silver Architects,** the wing has a multi-angled exterior meant to call to mind stony outcroppings or shards of ice; it is covered with stainless-steel panels that create a shimmering "fish scale" effect. In 2002, an IMAX 3D movie theater/auditorium was added. There is a separate admission fee for

---

Restaurants/Clubs: Red | Hotels: Purple | Shops: Orange | Outdoors/Parks: Green | Sights/Culture: Blue

the theater (886/815.4269). There are plans for a marine-mammal pavilion in the future. ♦ Admission. Daily. 973.5200; www.neaq.org ⟞

NEW ENGLAND AQUARIUM WHALE WATCHING

Because the aquarium considers the whales that live at **Stellwagen Bank,** a rich feeding ground 25 miles due east of Boston, to be yet another of its many exhibitions, it organizes trips to visit the massive mammals in the spring, summer, and early fall. During the five- to six-hour voyage (round-trip), aquarium naturalists tell whale tales and describe other marine life. Whales frequenting New England coastal waters include humpbacks, finbacks, and, occasionally, right whales. Blue whales, the largest creatures ever to live on earth, have been sighted off Cape Cod.

Be sure to dress warmly in layers—even in summer—and bring waterproof gear, rubber-soled shoes, and sunscreen. The boat offers a full-service galley. Children under 36 inches tall aren't permitted on board. ♦ Apr-Oct; call for schedule. Reservations by credit card; payment in cash only. 973.5200, recorded information 973.5277; www.neaq.org ⟞

6 INDIA WHARF

Another success of the Broad Street Association's 19th-century scheme to revamp the Waterfront, this wharf (begun in 1805) was once a half-mile stretch of piers, stores, and warehouses designed by **Charles Bulfinch.** The last vestiges of the handsome structures were leveled to make room for the upstart **Harbor Towers** (see below). ♦ Atlantic Ave and East India Row

On India Wharf:

HARBOR TOWERS

Whereas Boston's historic Waterfront buildings stretched like fingers into the harbor, waves lapping among them, these modern towers aren't so involved in the maritime scene. The standoffish pair (designed by **I.M. Pei** in 1971) is more intrigued by the sky. At their nascent stage, the 40-story interlopers brought dramatic new style and scale to this part of town. Originally somewhat alienating, the towers have acquired a kind of folk appeal, partly because newer buildings more brazen and far less clever have pushed their way in, such as **International Place** across the Greenway. The towers are more exciting to live in than to look at; the residents enjoy stunning views. David von Schlegell's *India Wharf Project,* a stark 1972 sculpture composed of four folded planes, stands at the edge of the harbor-side terrace. The flat surfaces clad in stainless steel also ignore the harbor and reflect what's happening above instead.

7 ROWES WHARF

Many Bostonians consider **Skidmore, Owings & Merrill**'s grand, redbrick complex—luxury condos, offices, shops, a 38-slip marina, and a hotel—the best addition to Boston in years. The 15-story development was built in 1987 on the 1760s' **Rowes and Fosters Wharves.** Many don't realize its relative youth, because unlike **Harbor Towers,** the complex takes its inspiration from the past. The ornamental overkill borders on kitsch, but the building is generous, capable of grand gestures—for example, a resplendent six-story arch lures pedestrians from Atlantic Avenue to the water's edge. Rowes Wharf has further privatized the Waterfront, yet gives back to Bostonians the heroic arch, an observatory, open space, a splendid **Harborwalk** extension leading past enormous yachts, and best of all, an entry to the city via the **Water Shuttle** that zips between Logan International Airport, the new South Boston waterfront, and the wharf. This speedy journey is worth taking just for the sake of enjoying the most picturesque approach to Boston and seeing the flipside view through the monumental portal. It's not a cheap thrill, but do it once (see "Orientation" for more information). ♦ Atlantic Ave (between Northern Ave and East India Row). www.som.com/html/rowes_wharf.html

On Rowes Wharf:

BOSTON HARBOR SAILING CLUB

Sail in the harbor and among the islands that once witnessed the stirring arrivals and departures of Boston's majestic clipper ships. In a city known for its exclusive clubs, this is not a club per se, but rather a private enterprise founded in 1974 to offer sailing classes taught by experts. The one-week courses are popular, attracting novices from all over. Properly certified visitors can rent boats from a fleet of 65, ranging in length from 26 to 39 feet. ♦ Daily May-Oct. In the marina at Rowes Wharf. 720.0049; www.bostonharborsailing.com

BOSTON HARBOR HOTEL

$$$$ This 230-room hotel's public spaces are tranquil and attractively dressed in warm woods, pearly grays, and subdued burgundies, with companionable textures and tapestry patterns. Cove lighting adds a subtle glow and paintings by Massachusetts artists decorate the first two floors. It may be worthwhile to pay more for a room where you can gaze out at **Boston Harbor**. Deluxe rooms have separate sitting areas and all but a few rooms have king-size beds. All rooms are soundproofed. Amenities include a posh health club and spa with a pristine three-lane lap pool (fees apply), 24-hour room service, rooms for nonsmokers and people with disabilities, and pet services from catnip to

SHORT TRIPS TO THE BOSTON HARBOR ISLANDS

The 34 islands that dot the inner and outer harbors offer wonderful respite from city crowds and new perspectives on Boston's connection to the sea.

These "away from it all" islands, only a few miles from, and within sight of, Boston's downtown skyline, may have been used more enthusiastically 150 years ago as venues for summer excursions than they are today. Then, public steamers carried passengers to the islands for picnics or fancier meals at the flourishing summer resorts on several of the islands. Gambling and illegal Sunday boxing matches on other islands added to the allure. Boston's harbor islands, now part of the National Park system and only 45 minutes by ferry from downtown, are still the settings for a wide range of activities.

Georges Island, the hub of the chain, is dominated by **Fort Warren,** a massive 19th-century granite fortification where Confederate soldiers were imprisoned during the Civil War. Restored and now a National Historic Landmark, it is an explorer's delight, with drawbridge, dungeons, and cavernous vault-ceilinged common rooms. Guided tours and programs are offered by park staff six (warm) months of the year. The 30-acre island is a good place for a picnic within sight of a distant city, and has rest rooms, an information booth, public food grills, and a first-aid station. There's a free water shuttle to other islands from here.

Sixteen-acre **Gallops Island** also has picnic grounds, plus a pier with a large gazebo, shady paths, meadows, and remnants of a World War II maritime radio school. **Lovell Island,** 62 acres large, offers a supervised swimming beach, a picnic area with hibachis and tables, campsites, and walking trails.

One of the harbor's biggest islands, 188-acre **Peddocks** also has picnic and camping areas and the remains of **Fort Andrews** occupying its East Head. Because the West Head is a protected salt marsh and **wildlife sanctuary,** access beyond recreational areas is restricted to organized tours or by permission of park staff.

Tranquil **Bumpkin Island** offers trails to the ruins of an old children's hospital and a stone farmhouse, and its rocky beach is popular for fishing. Wild rabbits and raspberry bushes proliferate. Some campsites are available. **Grape Island,** named for the vines that grew here in colonial times, feeds many birds with its wild bayberries, blackberries, and rose hips. Come here for birding, picnicking, camping, and meandering. Although rugged **Great Brewster Island** can only be reached by private boat, it offers 23 pristine acres and splendid views of **Boston Light,** the country's oldest lighthouse, which is located on nearby **Little Brewster.** The lighthouse on Little Brewster (www.lighthousefriends.com)

began blinking in 1716. Destroyed by a 1751 fire, rebuilt, destroyed by the evacuating British in 1776, and rebuilt again, Boston Light is visible 16 miles out to sea. The last manned (by the Coast Guard) lighthouse in the country, the 89-foot-tall structure was automated in 1989. The first light keeper, George Worthylake, drowned with most of his family and their slave, Shadwell, when his boat capsized on the way back to Little Brewster in 1718. Benjamin Franklin wrote a poem about the tragedy. The names of the present and former keepers are etched on island rocks. The interior of the lighthouse is closed to the public. Owned by the nonprofit Thompson Island Outward Bound Center (328.3900; www.thompsonisland.org), 204-acre Thompson Island is open on a limited basis for guided tours, hiking, picnicking, educational programs, and conferences. You must call ahead. The center provides boat transportation to the island.

No fresh water is available on Gallops, Lovell, Bumpkin, Grape, and Great Brewster Islands. Day-use permits are required for large groups; permits are also necessary for camping and for alcohol consumption on some islands. A number of the islands belong to the **Boston Harbor islands State Park** and can be reached via **ferries** departing from Long Wharf or Rowes Wharf on the Waterfront. Privately operated, the ferries charge fees and mostly sail to Georges Island, where free water taxis depart for five other islands. For more information or to obtain permits for Georges, Lovell, Gallops, Bumpkin, Grape, Great Brewster, and Peddocks Islands, call the state Department of Conservation and Recreation (727.7676). Georges, Bumpkin, and Thompson Islands are wheelchair accessible.

Friends of the Boston Harbor Islands (740.4290, www.fbhi.org), a nonprofit organization dedicated to preserving the islands' resources, sponsors year-round public education programs, history tours, and boat trips.

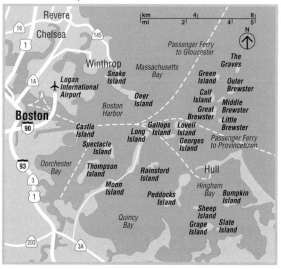

counseling. There's easy access to the airport **Water Shuttle,** whose embarkation point is directly in front of the hotel. Indoor parking and marina slips are also available.

In the hotel's **Magellan Gallery** is a largely undiscovered treasure: a private collection of early maps and charts depicting New England and Boston. Owned by The Beacon Companies, developers of the Rowes Wharf complex, the display includes Virginia captain John Smith's 1614 map of the New England coast, the first produced, which later guided the Pilgrims to Plymouth. Another fascinating map (created in 1625 by Sir William Alexander) records the Council of New England's scheme to turn the region into an elite association of English estates, which was ultimately scuttled by competition from the Massachusetts Bay Colony and support for the Puritan cause. There are also two restaurants (see below). The **Rowes Wharf Bar** is located in the hotel lobby; it makes up for its lack of views with blissful quiet and an excellent array of single-malt Scotch labels. ◆ No. 70. 439.7000, 800/323.7500; fax 330.9450; www.bhh.com &

Within Boston Harbor Hotel:

MERITAGE RESTAURANT

★★★★$$$$ The views here are only exceeded by the excellent food and highly professional service. Chef Daniel Bruce—who came from New York's 21 and Le Cirque and has demonstrated his considerable talent in places like Venice and Paris—performs with equal distinction in Boston. The American menu, which changes daily, includes seafood and meat dishes with a hint of France. An added touch is a prix fixe menu with a wine matched to each dish. Recent offerings have included an appetizer of smoked salmon served with a crisp potato cake topped with crème fraîche and caviar, and an entrée rack of veal with wild mushrooms and roasted red potatoes. Desserts are creative and delicious. The atmosphere is one of sophistication, and patrons leave feeling pampered and satisfied. ◆ American ◆ Tu-Sa, dinner; Su, brunch 10:30AM-2PM. 439.3995; www.meritagetherestaurant.com &

INTRIGUE

★★★$$ This comfortable café, furnished with wing chairs and sofas, is less formal than its big sister. Also under the expert supervision of chef Daniel Bruce, it serves up American dishes in a room that overlooks the hotel's harbor-front terrace. ◆ Café ◆ Daily, breakfast, lunch, dinner, and snacks (until midnight). 439.7000 &

FORT POINT CHANNEL

Most Bostonians have yet to stumble upon this fascinating place, and those who love it hope that won't change too much. This no-nonsense neighborhood, bordering the Financial District and South Boston, exposes some of the city's practical inner workings. The narrow channel is now all that divides the original Shawmut Peninsula from South Boston, once a far-off neck of land. In the 1870s the Boston Wharf Company cut the channel and erected warehouses on the South Boston side to store lumber, sugar, coal, imported fruit, wool, raw pelts, and ice. **Fish Pier** and **Commonwealth Pier** were built on landfill, the second becoming the center of the Boston fishing industry. By the 1890s the area was the major transfer point for raw materials fueling most New England industries, and was bursting with wharves, machine shops, iron foundries, glassworks, wagon factories, soap producers, brickyards, and printing trades. Business boomed through the early 20th century, and then slackened as the fishing and wool industries, shipping, and manufacturing declined. Construction of the now underground Central Artery isolated the area further.

Artists rediscovered the neighborhood in the 1970s, creating a SoHo-like atmosphere that early on earned the district the affectionate nickname "NoSo," short for North of South Boston. Now many of the artists have moved on, pushed out by the boom that brought lost leases, new buildings, and new city priorities. The new **Institute of Contemporary Art (ICA)** on the Waterfront may give some a new lease on their Boston artistic life. (See also www.friendsoffortpointchannel.org).

The **Seaport World Trade Center** and the massive **Boston Design Center**, the latter New England's major showroom for the interior-design trade, have comfortably settled in, too. What port activity remains in Boston is along Northern Avenue and at Fish Pier, home of the **New England Fish Exchange** (574.4600). Those renewal plans for long-vacant **Fan Pier** nearby gave us the **Moakley federal courthouse** at 1 Courthouse Way. The view of downtown Boston from the courthouse is magnificent. The new Institute of Contemporary Art shares Fan Pier with the courthouse. A slew of developments, often slowed by politics, court challenges, and planning procedures, are either in the works or planned. For now, there's some of the old industrial flavor left. Beyond the parking lots, look for the **Boston Wharf Company**'s architecturally inventive warehouses on Summer and Congress Streets. Trucks and tractor-trailers rule some of the roads in this part of town. Back across the channel, skyscrapers spread like weeds; here, while new hotels and office and residential towers are going up, low-rise buildings and empty lots still let light flood in. Unfamiliar vantage points show off the city's skyline. Down Summer Street on the way to South Boston is **Marine Industrial Park** and Boston's state-of-the-art **Black Falcon Cruise Passenger Terminal.**

8 INTERCONTINENTAL BOSTON

$$$$ The 22-story Intercontinental Boston Hotel opened in fall of 2006 across Fort Point Channel in the Financial District, but the tone is new-neighborhood Waterfront. The $330 million luxury hotel has 424 rooms and suites, with 130 luxury condos on the upper floors. Hotel management says the building is on the actual site of the 1773 Boston Tea Party. Triple-glazed blue thermal glass sheathing the

building reflects the harbor during the day and lets reddish tones shine out at night. ♦ 500 Atlantic Ave (between Congress St and Seaport Blvd). 747.1000, fax 273.8095; www.intercontinentalboston.com ☺

9 DAILY CATCH

★★$$ An offspring of the popular North End hole-in-the-wall, this Seaport incarnation serves the same great seafood. Try one of the many calamari dishes; the owners love to turn people on to their favorites. ♦ Seafood ♦ Daily, lunch and dinner. Two Northern Ave on the Harborwalk (at Sleeper St at the foot of the old Northern Ave Bridge). 338.3093. Also at 223 Hanover St (between Lothrop Pl and Prince Sq). 523.8567; and 441 Harvard St (at Coolidge St), Brookline. 734.2700; www.dailycatch.com

10 THE BARKING CRAB

★★$$ Take a hard right rudder after the Northern Avenue Bridge and you'll find this fun urban clam shack. They've extended traditional clambake fare with all kinds of fried, boiled, steamed, and grilled seafood. Sit at tables under the giant heated tent, with a wonderful view juxtaposing lobster boats and the city skyline. ♦ Seafood ♦ Daily, lunch and dinner. 88 Sleeper St (at Northern Ave). 426.2722 ☺

11 OUR LADY OF THE GOOD VOYAGE CHAPEL

In addition to regular weekend masses, an annual **Blessing of the Animals** service is held the first Sunday in October at this humble little chapel. ♦ Services: Sa, 7PM; Su, 11:30AM, 7 and 8PM. 65 Northern Ave (between Northern Ave and Sleeper St). 542.3883

12 ANTHONY'S PIER 4

★$$$ Anthony's may move to make way for a waterfront park in the not-too-distant future. Though tourists and old-timers love it, there are better places to go in Boston for an expensive seafood dinner. Still, Anthony's is worth a visit to experience a big-time restaurant formula that keeps 'em coming. It's on Pier 4, adjacent to the new Institute of Contemporary Art on Fan Pier and surrounded by the buzz of new buildings, planned or going up. The late owner, Anthony Athanas, an Albanian immigrant, started as a shoeshine boy, built a successful restaurant, and wound up ruling a fiefdom of seafood houses. Enjoy towering popovers, raw oysters or clams, steamed lobster, or simply cooked seafood. Big views of Boston Harbor steal the show.

Note the walls crammed with old photos of Anthony and the Pope, Anthony and John F. Kennedy, Anthony and Frank Sinatra, Anthony and Liz Taylor, Anthony and Gregory Peck. ♦ Seafood/ American ♦ Daily, lunch and dinner. Jacket required and tie requested for main dining room at dinner; no jeans, sneakers, or gym attire in evening. Reservations recommended. Valet parking available. 140 Northern Ave (at B St). 423.6363; www.pier4.com

13 COMMONWEALTH PIER/SEAPORT WORLD TRADE CENTER

Excursion boats depart from this pier for Provincetown, the Harbor Islands, and other points. The monumental, beflagged business center accommodates all kinds of enormous functions. A pedestrian walkway connects the Trade Center with the Seaport Hotel and Conference Center across the street. ♦ Northern Ave (between Seaport La and B St). 385.4212

14 FISH PIER

Two long, arcaded rows housing fish-related businesses stretch more than 700 feet out onto the water, with the heroic **Exchange Conference Center at Fish Pier** (formerly the New England Fish Exchange) dominating the far end. The century-old building's arch is crowned with a wonderful carved relief of Neptune's head. No longer the center of New England's—let alone America's—fish industry, Boston's catch keeps shrinking, with more and more fish brought in by trucks, not boats. ♦ Northern Ave and D St Extension

At Fish Pier:

NO-NAME

★$$ Once upon a time this eatery had a name, but it sure doesn't need one now. The hungry hordes know where to find this big-business restaurant, which has been cooking for fishers and pier workers since 1917 (though now the crowd is heavy on tourists and folks in from the suburbs): It's in the right-hand building of Fish Pier, just past the arcade's first curve. It's family and kid friendly. Hope for a table in the back overlooking the pier. Sit elbow-to-elbow at boisterous communal tables, fill up on "chowdah" and big portions of fresh seafood, boiled lobster, broiled or fried fish, fish of the day, and homemade pie. Expect to wait in line; they don't take reservations. ♦ Seafood ♦ Daily, lunch and dinner. No. 15½. 338.7539 ☺

Restaurants/Clubs: Red | Hotels: Purple | Shops: Orange | Outdoors/Parks: Green | Sights/Culture: Blue

15 SEAPORT HOTEL AND CONFERENCE CENTER

$$$$ In the heart of the Waterfront district overlooking **Boston Harbor,** this ultramodern hotel is tailor-made for the businessperson. Each of the 427 deluxe rooms features such extras as individual air-conditioning controls, a mini-bar, office supplies (Post-it notes and floppy disks), an in-room safe large enough to hold a laptop computer, color TV with on-demand movies and a separate channel for airport arrival and departure information, fluffy bathrobes, a hair dryer, and an iron and ironing board. Telephones are equipped with two lines, fax capability, speakerphone, and voice mail, and there's high-speed Internet access in each room and in the hotel's 24-hour business center. Other amenities include concierge service and complimentary transportation to the Financial District. On-site facilities include a restaurant (see below), a fitness center and spa, and an indoor heated lap pool. There's also free Wi-Fi Internet access, in all public areas and guest rooms, including 250,000 square feet of meeting and function space, including the Trade Center's 120,000-square-foot exhibition hall. Note: This is a gratuity-free hotel—no tips are accepted. Ground and Water Shuttle services to the airport are available for a fee, as is an executive sedan service. ◆ 1 Seaport La (between Congress St and Northern Ave). 385.4000, 877/SEAPORT; fax 385.5090; www.seaporthotel.com &

Within the Seaport Hotel:

AURA

★★$$$$ The menu is American but eclectic, with an emphasis on seafood. Entrées include pan-roasted lobster with steamed clams and cod fritters, grilled red snapper with citrus baby beets, applewood-roasted venison with black pepper and plum chutney, grilled aged sirloin with potato and roasted-garlic flan, and spring vegetable pot-au-feu with barley crisps and herbs. The dining room is accented with cherry wood screens, a mural depicting the spice trade between New England and the Far East, and specially commissioned pieces by local and national artists and craftspeople. There's also a bar with floor-to-ceiling windows overlooking the harbor. ◆ American/Seafood ◆ Daily, breakfast and lunch; Tu-Sa, dinner. Reservations recommended. 385.4000; www.aurarestaurant.com &

16 JIMMY'S HARBORSIDE RESTAURANT

This famous seafood icon started in 1924 serving Fish-Pier workers and fisherman. Over the years, they served fresh seafood and a much-praised chowder, and the crowd included tourists, celebrities, and politicians, including President John F. Kennedy and members of Congress. But the restaurant stayed pretty much the same and the regular crowd aged. In 2006 the grand old restaurant was closed for renovation and plans for another new-seafront location were discussed. That may happen, but the president of Legal Sea Foods bought the restaurant's vital liquor license with plans to use it in 2007 in a new, casual restaurant called Legal C-Bar & Grill in the nearby Westin hotel at the Convention and Exhibition Center. 242 Northern Ave (between Trilling Way and Fish Pier).

17 LTK BAR AND KITCHEN

★★★$$$ This ostensibly hipper update of **Legal Seafoods** is part of the wave of restaurants pioneering in the new Seaport district. LTK stands for Legal's Test Kitchen, which is aimed at a younger, more tech-savvy crowd. There's a stylish emphasis on tapas-style plates and new ways to present Boston classics. There's a lobster roll on grilled flatbread, for example, instead of on a hot-dog bun, with bacon and avocado. The sleek-looking restaurant has plasma TVs scattered about, digital menus, and tableside iPod docks. Food ranges from sushi to fusion, and includes Asian-influenced seafood and salads, soups, and shellfish. ◆ Multicultural Seafood ◆ Daily. 255 Northern Ave (across Northern Ave/Seaport Blvd from Fish Pier). 330.7430; www.ltkbarandkitchen.com &

18 HARPOON BREWERY

★★$ The brewery produces more than 70,000 barrels of beer yearly. Holiday parties and regular events take place here. Free tours, which take 30 to 45 minutes, are offered. Families are welcome, but you must be at least 21 with proper ID to sample the brew, and samples are offered only during tour times. ◆ Tours, Tu-Th 3PM and F, Sa 11AM and 3PM. Groups of 15 or more can schedule private tours by calling 888/HARPOON, ext 522. The Silverline bus from South Station stops in front of the brewery. ◆ 306 Northern Ave in the Marine Industrial Park next to the white-tented Bank of America Pavilion (still called Harborlights by locals), near Jimmy's Harborside Restaurant and the Black Falcon Ship Terminal). www.harpoonbrewery.com

19 FEDERAL RESERVE BANK OF BOSTON

Whether you think this building (designed by **Hugh Stubbins & Associates** in 1977) resembles an old-fashioned washboard, goalposts, or a radiator, its shimmering aluminum- sheathed form is remarkably visible from many vantage points. The bank's **art gallery** on the ground floor is an alternative space where nonprofit New England–based artists and arts organizations mount professional-level exhibitions. A **performance series** is held in the adjacent auditorium September through December and March through June; call for program information. Security is tight, but educational workshops are conducted for school and civic groups. ♦ 600 Atlantic Ave (between Summer and Congress Sts). 973.3453; www.bos.frb.org. Workshop information 973.3451; www.economicadventure.org &

20 SOUTH STATION

When construction on this station (designed by **Shepley, Rutan, and Coolidge**) at Dewey Square was completed in 1900, it was the world's largest railroad station. By 1913, the station handled 38 million passengers a year, making it the busiest one in the country—even topping New York City's Grand Central Terminal. In peak year 1907, some 876 trains plied the rails on weekdays. The majestic five-story edifice, its shapely curved façade adorned with a nine-foot-wide clock surmounted by a proud eagle, proclaimed Boston's important place in the world. In its heyday, the station's comforts included a theater that screened newsreels and Our Lady of the Railways Chapel. But when airplanes, trucks, and cars eclipsed trains, the station slid into decrepitude. Eventually, most of it was demolished, except for the handsome headhouse, which nearly gave up the ghost in the 1960s but was saved and is now on the National Register of Historic Places.

Now modern construction, respectful restoration, and intelligent planning have made the terminal a pleasant destination once more, with pushcart vendors, a large food hall, coffee bar, newsstand, bank, and other services to lure pedestrians from nearby streets. Look for the old tin ceilings and beautiful carved details. More than 200 commuter trains and dozens of Amtrak runs, including the high-speed Acela Express, come and go on the busiest travel days. With the Red Line subway on site, travelers are linked to the rest of Boston and the suburbs. With the addition of a commuter and long-distance bus terminal, even changing modes of transport has become convenient. Unfortunately, we must still schlep to North Station to board commuter trains to the north and northwest. ♦ Atlantic Ave and Summer St. Tourist information at 330.1230

21 US POSTAL SERVICE– SOUTH POSTAL ANNEX

Boston's general mail facility looks like a 1920s ocean liner berthed alongside the channel. Always open, this is the mail-processing hub for the Boston Division, with more than 1.2 million square feet of space and 12 miles of conveyors. Groups of 10 or more (minimum age 13 or eighth grade) can take a guided tour of the automated and mechanized facility and see how employees sort a daily average of 9 million pieces of mail with the help of optical character readers, letter-sorting machines, bar-code sorters, and other sophisticated equipment. ♦ Free. Tours Tu-F Jan-Nov; call at least one week in advance to arrange a tour. 25 Dorchester Ave (just south of Summer St). 654.5081 &

22 BOSTON TEA PARTY SHIP AND MUSEUM

The Boston Tea Party took place near here on long-gone Griffin's Wharf (its site is now landfill on Atlantic Avenue between Congress Street and Northern Avenue). On a cold December 16th night in 1773, colonists dressed as Indians came from the Old South Meeting House, boarded ships, and dumped 340 chests of costly British tea into the harbor to protest a tea tax. The British responded by blockading the harbor. The *Beaver* II, a Danish brig resembling one of the three original Tea Party ships, was long moored alongside the Congress Street Bridge. Kids and adults climbed aboard the 110-foot-long vessel, listened to costumed guides, and helped toss a bale of tea defiantly over the side (the fact that the bale was roped to the ship and hauled up again didn't lessen the thrill). On the adjacent pier, a small museum had exhibits, films, ship models, and memorabilia, with printed information available in seven languages. Tax-free tea was served at all times. ♦ The ship, heavily damaged by a wharf fire, is being rebuilt, the wharf-side museum expanded, and two more tall ships added. Extensive repairs and expansion are scheduled to be finished by summer 2007. ♦ Congress St Bridge. 338.1773; www.bostonteapartyship.com. Also see www.boston-tea-party.org

23 THE MILK BOTTLE

$ A landmark in its own right, this vintage 1930s highway lunch stand (pictured below) was installed in front of the **Children's Museum** (see page 72) in 1977, having first been sawed in half and floated down the

Charles River. Donated to the museum by the H.P. Hood Company, the 40-foot-tall wooden bottle would hold 50,000 gallons of milk and 860 gallons of cream if filled. Served from within is a variety of soups (the chowder is good) and salads, and, of course, ice cream. The milk bottle, closed during Children's Museum expansion, should reopen in summer 2007. ♦ American ♦ Daily, Apr-Oct; closed Nov-Mar. Congress St and Fort Point Channel. 426.7074 &

23 THE CHILDREN'S MUSEUM

Closed from January 2007 and reopens April 2007

This is a lively and participatory place for kids, being renovated and expanded from 2006 through spring 2007 with trees, decking, and a parking area removed to make way for an addition and a park. In exhibits for toddlers to teens, kids can blow bubbles, race golf balls in the **Science Playground**, interact with Arthur and Friends (from books and PBS cartoons), and see what life was like in a Japanese silk merchant's reconstructed home in old Kyoto, Boston's sister city. An exhibit popular with the 440,000 yearly visitors is **Climbing the Walls**, with three climbing walls, one with slides for ages two to five. The others are for older kids, and all are on padded floors. There are knot-tying stations and videos of pro rock climbers at play. For the three-and-under crowd, there's a supervised second-floor **Play Space**. The **Pop-Up Train** is a toy train on a table with holes placed so kids can pop up in the middle and push child-powered trains past little bridges, towns, and trees. In the **Messy Play** area, tykes in smocks experiment with shaving-cream art, watercolors, and play clay. There's a clear plastic wall for watercolor painting. The noise of 30 or 40 toddlers at play is pleasure for some parents, perhaps. For very small kids, there's **Crawler Space**, stocked with soft toys. They can also safely roll around on a plush-covered, sunken water bed built into a padded area. Older children enjoy the **Construction Zone**, the museum's own Big Dig, with plastic mini-trucks, backhoes, and jackhammers. Kids wear hard hats and climb on full-size (but nonrunning) earthmovers. They can balance on a steel beam against a Boston-skyline backdrop. The **Hall of Toys** has dolls and lots of Americana antique toys. The **Museum Shop** has unusual gifts, toys, and books. The museum is the country's second largest (Indianapolis's is larger) and second oldest (Brooklyn, New York, has the oldest

children's museum). Closed for renovation from January 2007; scheduled to reopen April 2007. ♦ Admission, Tu-Su and school holidays. Reduced admission F, 5-9PM. 300 Congress St (at Fort Point Channel). Recorded information 426.8855; www.bostonkids.org &

24 BOSTON FIRE MUSEUM

This chunky 1891 granite-and-brick firehouse is now owned by the Boston Sparks Association, which welcomes visitors. Exhibits include a 1783 hand-drawn, hand-operated pumper and an 1860 ladder truck. Reconstruction of the Congress Street Bridge, expected until late 2007, makes getting to the museum difficult. Use local streets. The website gives directions. ♦ Free. Th-Sa, April through Oct. 344 Congress St (at Farnsworth St). 482.1344; www.bostonfiremuseum.com &

25 MOBIUS

Mobius is an artist-run nonprofit organization that has provided a home since 1977 for experimental work in all media. The group programs work at theaters, galleries, and public sites in performance, installation, sound art, new music, film, video, and dance. ♦ 374 Congress St, No. 611 (at Stillings St). 542.7416; www.mobius.org

26 MARCO POLO CAFE

★$ Frequented by employees of local architecture offices, this stylishly sparse cafeteria-style lunch spot serves great coffee and Mediterranean fare, ranging from minestrone to moussaka. Most everything is made on the premises, including from-scratch morning muffins. ♦ International/Takeout ♦ M-F, breakfast and lunch. 274 Summer St (east of Fort Point Channel). 695.9039 &

27 A STREET DELI EXPRESS

$ While the rest of the city's asleep, get a hearty breakfast with lots of good grease to jump-start your day. For lunch, the food is of the pizza, soup, and salad variety—cheap, basic, and tasty. From here, walk up Melcher Street to see its gracefully curving warehouses. ♦ American ♦ M-F, breakfast and lunch. 324 A St (at Melcher St). 338.7571 &

28 WESTIN BOSTON WATERFRONT HOTEL

$$$$ This new-in-2006 luxury convention hotel is actually two blocks from the waterfront. But you can't get much closer to the sprawling **Boston Convention & Exhibition Center**. The smoke-free Westin, with 17 floors, 793 rooms, and a three-story lobby, is connected to the convention center next door

by a glass-enclosed walkway. It was the biggest hotel to open in Boston since the Marriott Copley Place, with 1,147 rooms, and the 803-room Westin Copley Place in 1984. (Five more hotels with 1,400 rooms are scheduled to open by 2009). There's 24-hour room service, wireless Internet access in every room (there's a charge), indoor heated pool and health club, two presidential suites, and on-site parking for 400 vehicles. There are two ballrooms and 100,000 square feet of retail and restaurant space. 425 Summer St (between West Side Drive and D Street). 532.4600; fax 532.4630; www.westin.com &

Within the Westin Boston Waterfront:

SAUCIETY

★★$$$ The 130-seat restaurant's name derives from the 15 sauces available with fish, chicken, and meat dishes. ◆ American ◆ Daily, breakfast, lunch, and dinner

BIRCH BAR

The lobby lounge, styled rather like part of an airport terminal, seats 80 and sports a water-fall and plastic birch trees as part of the décor. The trees look good, considering, and the bar menu is a scaled-down reflection of Sauciety's yummy offerings. ◆ Daily

LEATHER DISTRICT

Like the Fort Point Channel area, this tiny appendage to the Financial District has a businesslike personality and lots of integrity. You can cover the seven-block neighborhood in a one-hour stroll. When Boston's **Great Fire of 1872** swept clean more than 65 acres, it wiped out the city's commercial and wholesale centers, including the dense leather and garment district concentrated here. But slowly, businesses rose from the ashes and built sturdy new warehouses and factories, most along Lincoln and South Streets, some Romanesque in style and quite distinguished. Except for a few firms, the leather warehousing industry long ago departed for other countries. In the 1970s artists and urban pioneers began to move in, followed by art galleries, shops and services, and restaurants. Now, many of the artists have been driven out by high rents, high real-estate prices, and conversions to luxury condos. The neighborhood, in short, is trendy.

29 SOUTH STREET

Fifteen years ago, this street was thriving as a venue for art galleries and intriguing shops. But what a difference a few years can make! One of the reasons seems to be that because of popular and populous Boston's perpetual paucity of affordable housing, many of the buildings have been renovated for residential occupancy. Located within easy walking distance of Boston's business districts—and convenient to Chinatown, Downtown, the Waterfront, and other sections of Boston— South Street seems destined to become the new residential neighborhood. Art gallery tenants are understandably upset over this change. They lose their leases, and the street floors of many buildings, once rehabbed, are leased commercially to restaurants and shops—and perhaps galleries. ◆ Between Kneeland and Summer Sts

On South Street:

LES ZYGOMATES

★★$$$ Located in the 1888 Beebe Building, this wine bar and bistro brings an authentic touch of Paris to downtown Boston. The atmosphere is casual and very French, including the zinc-topped bar, where more than 30 wines are served by the glass. The menu changes seasonally; among the favorite items are tuna au poivre with Dijonaise sauce, venison, and terrine au foie gras. There are also vegetarian offerings. Live jazz is featured on Sunday nights. ◆ French ◆ M-F, lunch and dinner; Sa, Su, dinner. Reservations recommended for dinner. No. 129 (between Beach and Tufts Sts). 542.5108; www.winebar.com

30 NEWS

★$ News keeps hunger away until 5AM. Don't expect gourmet grub, and count on a mob after 2AM, but be happy there's food at that hour. The late-night breakfast menu is nice after a bout of clubbing, and the place is popular after work. Among choices: steak tips and Alaskan herb-encrusted salmon. ◆ American ◆ Daily, breakfast, lunch, and dinner; drinks until 2AM. 150 Kneeland St (at Utica St). 426.6397; www.newsboston.com

---

Restaurants/Clubs: Red | Hotels: Purple | Shops: Orange | Outdoors/Parks: Green | Sights/Culture: Blue

FINANCIAL DISTRICT/DOWNTOWN

This on-the-go neighborhood is bounded by Boston Common and Tremont Street to the west, the Rose Fitzgerald Kennedy Greenway to the east, Government Center and Faneuil Hall Marketplace to the north, and Chinatown and the Theater District to the south. Celebrating the city's economic health, the bumper crop of skyscrapers found here transforms the Boston skyline. The **Downtown Crossing** shopping area is cheerfully chaotic, if sometimes a bit tacky, with pedestrians, pushcarts, and outdoor performers luring shoppers to the famous **Filene's Basement** and dozens of other stores and boutiques.

History's imprint is here as well: Important **Freedom Trail** stops such as the **Old State House** and the **Old South Meeting House** impart a vision of a Revolution-era "Main Street." The **Custom House Tower, State Street Block,** and surviving wharf buildings designed by **Charles Bulfinch** speak of early wealth from the sea. Come during weekday work hours, when everything is open and in full swing. Walk along the profusion of twisty, tiny colonial lanes that have turned into busy arteries shadowed by architectural giants, creating windy, shady New York City–style canyons. Businesslike street names—State, Court, Broad, Federal, School—reflect the neighborhood's no-nonsense character. Numerous commercial palaces bear carved or fading traces of their original names, paying tribute to past lives.

From the city's earliest days, **State Street** was Boston's business artery—the most

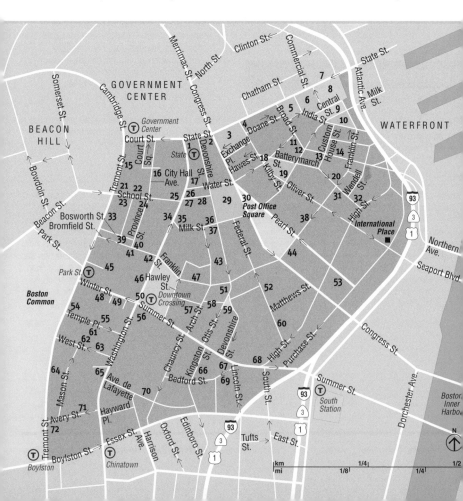

prestigious and spacious in town. Called King Street until the Revolution, State Street stretched 800 feet from the Old State House to **Long Wharf,** the noble pier that once served as the city's highway to the sea. The intersection of State Street and Washington Street was the epicenter of Boston's commercial and financial life.

An old Indian trail, **Washington Street** is now the major downtown commercial way, with great streetscapes down the Ladder Block side streets toward the Common. Always an important thoroughfare, in the 17th and 18th centuries it was the only road that ran the full length of Boston, linking the Old State House with the town gate at the neck of the Shawmut Peninsula. The street was renamed to honor George Washington's visit to the city in 1789. It loses some luster beyond Temple Place as it heads south toward the almost gone **Combat Zone,** the old red-light district. Much of the existing Washington Street area was built after the **Great Fire of 1872,** which leveled 65 acres bounded by Washington, Broad, Milk, and Summer Streets, destroyed the heart of major New England industry, and left thousands without jobs. Many buildings still show scars and burns from the conflagration, which stopped just short of a number of Boston's historical treasures. Although the neighborhood was rapidly rebuilt, its residents had fled and commercialism took over. Boston's publishing and newspaper concerns flourished along **Newspaper Row,** where Washington Street meets State and Court Streets, and insurance, banking, retail, garment, manufacturing, and other industries continue to call the area home. The famous **Omni Parker House** hotel and **Locke-Ober** restaurant also persevered in the face of change.

Economically, Boston was a Sleeping Beauty from 1895 until around 1965, when its prince arrived in the form of a building boom. Early skyscrapers are in short supply, but Boston does have its pleasing Custom House Tower, Art Deco **Batterymarch Building,** and lithe and lovely **Winthrop Building.** "If it ain't broke, don't fix it" is a Yankee credo, and Bostonians have a talent for recycling old structures. The city's fiscally conservative streak even influences new architecture. Unlike Chicago, where buildings shoot up to the sky, Boston usually prefers a modest scale for towers, so they politely accommodate older neighbors. Developers are subjected to stringent regulations and reviews. Some new buildings are dressed to the nines in decoration, but many are quite plain, even dowdy. It's as if the city were just getting used to its stature and doesn't quite know how to dress the part.

---

1 OLD STATE HOUSE

This lovable 1713 brick building has survived centuries of tumult and transformation, witnessing more than its share of dramatic moments in local and American history.

A National Historic Landmark, the building has been remodeled and restored so often (**Goody, Clancy & Associates** performed the shoring-up in 1992) that its parts date from many eras. Situated at the head of State Street, the so-called Temple of Liberty originally commanded a clear view to the sea, and in the mid-18th century became the political and commercial center of the Massachusetts Bay Colony. Its first floor was a merchants' exchange, with the wheels of government turning on the floors above. Even the site occupied an important place in the town's history, for the earliest Boston market square was located here, as were the stocks, pillory, and whipping post used to mete out 17th-century Puritan justice. The building started life as a meeting place used by the British crown's provincial governor, and was the seat of the government after the Revolution sent the British packing. The fantastical cavorting lion and unicorn on the older edifice's gable, emblems of the hated crown, were frowned upon and removed. (They have since been restored to their original home.)

The ceremonial balcony at the east end overlooks the site—within a circle of cobblestones—where on 5 March 1770, frightened British soldiers fired on a large, angry mob of Bostonians, killing former slave **Crispus Attucks** and four others in the **Boston**

Massacre. From this same balcony, the Declaration of Independence was first read to Bostonians on 18 July 1776. Every year since, the Declaration has been read from the same spot on the Fourth of July. John Hancock was inaugurated here as the first governor under the new state constitution. And when George Washington visited Boston in 1789, he surveyed the great parade in his honor from here. But after the new State House was built on Beacon Hill, this monument became a jack-of-all-trades building, used and abused as a commercial center, newspaper office, and, for a decade, Boston's City Hall.

The outcast's cause was championed just in time in 1881, when a nonprofit organization called the Bostonian Society organized to restore the building and preserve the rich history it had witnessed. Ever since, the society has called it home and maintained a marvelous museum featuring changing and permanent exhibitions on the Revolutionary era, maritime history, and other important chapters in the city's life. The history of the building is chronicled too. Paintings, portraits, figureheads, military and domestic artifacts, and other treasures tell the tale of this city. A vial of the original tea from the Boston Tea Party is on view, for instance, as is the coroner's report on Crispus Attucks. Look for John Hancock's family Bible and some of his clothing, and for Fitz Hugh Lane's painting *View of Boston Harbor.* A lovely spiral staircase leads to where inaugurations, daily government, and momentous meetings took place. For those who want to dig deeper, the society's splendid library, across the street on the third floor of the Visitor Center (see right), comprises more than

6,000 volumes and a thousand maps and architectural plans, plus rare manuscripts and broadsides. The library also owns more than 10,000 Boston views in photographs, prints, watercolors, and drawings. Happily, the Old State House has flourished under the society's care. Unicorn and lion now prance with pride, copies elevated to the original animals' lofty perches. Another testament to the building's resilience: the presence of the State Street subway station tucked underneath. ♦ Admission. Daily. 206 Washington St (at State St). 720.3290

2 VISITOR CENTER

Located around the corner from the **Old State House,** the center is operated by the Boston National Historic Park Service, which also runs the Old South Meeting House, Faneuil Hall, Paul Revere House, Old North Church, Bunker Hill Monument, Charlestown Navy Yard, and Dorchester Heights. In addition to offering information about these places, including a brief slide-show presentation, the center's staff of park rangers and volunteers answers questions about Boston and the entire National Park system. Find out about tours, many of which start from here. Pick up free **Freedom Trail maps** and pamphlets about all kinds of places, activities, and events. The center also sells books and souvenirs—and, equally important, has well-kept rest rooms, water fountains, and telephones, public conveniences hard to come by in Boston. There are also places to sit and rest weary bones. ♦ Daily. 15 State St (at Devonshire St). 242.5642 &

Old State House

3 EXCHANGE PLACE

Opinions vary wildly about this blending of old and new. Actually, all that remains of the original 1891 Stock Exchange Building designed by **Peabody and Stearns** is a 60-foot segment of its worthy granite façade on the State Street side; the rest of the building is now engulfed by a glassy tower added in 1984. From some vantage points, its dark reflective surfaces shimmer interestingly, but overall the newer building is, well, tacky. A handsome restored marble staircase is the atrium's incongruous centerpiece. This was the site of the historic **Bunch of Grapes Tavern,** located at the head of Long Wharf during the 19th century. A favorite watering hole for patriot leaders before the Revolution, the tavern reputedly served the best bowl of punch in Boston. ♦ 53 State St (between Kilby and Congress Sts)

4 75 STATE STREET

This unabashedly gilded and gaudy showpiece, erected in 1988 by **Graham Gund Associates,** is loved by some and hated by others. The lobby looks like an example of tender loving care gone too far, with its plethora of patterns, types of marble, and fancy fixtures—but the vast atrium lets in plenty of pure, unadulterated light. ♦ At Kilby St

5 BOARD OF TRADE BUILDING

This elaborate, urbane building designed in 1901 by **Winslow and Bradlee** has aged well. Its allegorical figures and vigorous stone carvings harken to seafaring days gone by, especially the galleons rushing forward into the viewer's space. ♦ 131 State St (between India and Broad Sts)

6 CUSTOM HOUSE TOWER

This preposterous marriage of convenience between a Greek Revival temple dating from one century (**Ammi Young** was the architect in 1847) and a tower plunked on top during the next (**Peabody and Stearns** added it in 1915) originally appalled many Bostonians. After all, the proud Custom House was once the focal point of the thriving waterfront.

Situated at the base of State Street, the important colonial route that once led from the Old State House and neighboring financial establishments out onto the wharves, the original structure was mammoth, with each of its 32 Doric columns a single 42-ton shaft of Quincy granite. Before Atlantic Avenue was created, the building was so close to the waterfront that the bows of ships would bump the windows facing the harbor. As the 20th century progressed and skyscrapers sprouted in other cities, Boston was mired in an economic slump. The federal government forked over the funds for the addition of the 495-foot tower; built between 1912 and 1917, it was the city's first skyscraper and for decades was New England's tallest structure.

Bostonians eventually became attached to their peculiar landmark, now a familiar friend. No matter how many new structures crowd the skyline, the steadfast tower is the most memorable silhouette, its 22-foot-wide clock (repaired and refurbished in 1997) aglow at night.

The lobby beneath the original building's rotunda—skylit until the tower leaped on top—deserves a look.

The city bought the entire edifice from the federal government in 1987, but later leased it to developers. Today it is a time-share property owned by the Marriott Corporation (see below). ♦ State St (between McKinley Sq and India St)

Within the Custom House Tower:

MARRIOTT'S CUSTOM HOUSE

$$$ Opened in 1997, this time-share complex offers accommodations to short-term guests (reservations are required). Overlooking Boston Harbor and just a short distance from **Faneuil Hall Marketplace,** the **New England Aquarium,** and the waterfront hotel and shopping complexes, the property has 84 units, all one-bedroom suites with skyline and harbor views. Each has a wet bar, microwave, TVs, and a VCR/DVD. Amenities include concierge service, $7 on-site or $35 valet parking, and an exercise room, but there's no restaurant, and pets are not allowed . ♦ 3 McKinley Sq (between Central and State Sts). 310.1600, 800/881.6824; fax 310.6301 ⑤

Brookstone®

7 BROOKSTONE

The brainchild of engineer Pierre de Beaumont, a frustrated hobbyist who sought unusual tools that weren't available, this specialty store stocks more than a thousand well-made, practical, and sometimes pricey, tools and gifts. The inventory focuses on unusual, hard-to-find items, and includes shop and gardening tools, small electronics, house wares, personal-care items, exercise and sports equipment, indoor and outdoor games, office supplies, and travel and automotive accessories. De Beaumont started simply with a mail-order catalog business, then launched the innovative retail system that resulted in more than

---

Restaurants/Clubs: Red | Hotels: Purple | Shops: Orange | Outdoors/Parks: Green | Sights/Culture: Blue

BOSTON BY BIKE: PLUM PATHS FOR PEDAL PUSHERS

Thanks to the many feckless drivers who dominate Boston's streets, bicycling in the city can be akin to navigating the Indianapolis 500. But in an effort to make the city—which is naturally conducive to two-wheelers with its relative flatness and compact layout—more bicycle friendly, Boston's Transportation Department has begun implementation of an official city bicycle policy. The purpose is to encourage bicycling for both recreation and commuting to and from work by linking neighborhoods with bike trails, publicizing safety regulations, and instituting a repair and maintenance program for the city's existing bike paths.

Student-packed **Cambridge,** across the Charles River, has a head start on Boston in bicycle-friendly streets. It has designated bicycle lanes and is a leader in providing bicycle paths and parking. Cambridge actively promotes bicycle-safety guidelines and enforces a law that makes it illegal to ride bicycles on sidewalks in designated business districts, including Harvard and Central Square. Cambridge puts out an excellent brochure on alternative forms of transportation in the city, including bicycling. For a free copy of *How to Get Around Cambridge,* call 349.4600.

Lobbying groups have made progress in making Boston more welcoming to two-wheelers, primarily by promoting bike paths. The centerpiece is the **Dr. Paul Dudley White Charles River Bike Path,** a 14-mile loop that's increasingly bucolic the farther from downtown you get. This trail hugs both banks of the Charles from the Museum of Science to Watertown Square. Shorter in-town stretches include the **Southwest Corridor Park Bike Path** (five miles in reclaimed South End parkland), the wooded **Riverway Bike Path** (from Boston's Park Drive to Brookline's Brookline Avenue), and the scenic **Jamaicaway Bike Path** (landscape architect Frederick Law Olmsted's former bridle path along the Muddy River).

The **Minuteman Bikeway** is an 11-mile swath linking the Alewife T Station in Cambridge (the outermost Red Line subway stop) to the towns of Arlington, Lexington, and Bedford. Former congressman Joseph Kennedy, an avid biker, managed to eke out $1.2 million in federal funds to connect the Minuteman Bikeway with the Dudley Bike Path. That hasn't happened. You'll often see riders making their own way from Alewife over to Massachusetts Avenue, then turning right and pedaling down Mass Ave to Harvard Square. They follow Mass Ave to JFK Street, take a right to the river, cross the Charles, then connect to the Dudley path on the Boston side.

All subway lines except the Green Line (which is usually about as roomy as a sardine can) will accommodate bikes, but not during rush hours, morning and evening; call the Massachusetts Bay Transportation Authority (722.3200, 800/392.6100) for details or see the excellent Mass Bike web site at www.massbike.org.

To find out about other trails, including some to Provincetown on Cape Cod, contact the **Massachusetts Department of Environmental Management** (Division of Forests and Parks, Saltonstall Building, 100 Cambridge St, Boston, MA 02202, 727.3180). You can rent wheels at the **Community Bike Shop** (496 Tremont St, at E Berkeley St, 542.8623) or **Back Bay Bicycles & Boards** (333 Newbury St, between Hereford St and Massachusetts Ave, 247.2336). For general tips on bike trails, rules of the road, and rentals or repairs, check the massbike.org web site, (run by the **Bicycle Coalition of Massachusetts**). **American Youth Hostels** (1020 Commonwealth Ave, between Babcock St and Winslow Rd, 731.6692) and the **Appalachian Mountain Club** (5 Joy St, between Beacon and Mount Vernon Sts, 523.0636, www.amcboston.org) organize cycling trips.

100 outlets nationwide. Mail-order catalogs are available too. ♦ Daily. Marketplace Center, 200 State St (between Atlantic Ave and Commercial St). 439.4460. Also at Copley Place, 100 Huntington Ave (between Garrison and Dartmouth Sts), 267.4308

8 STATE STREET BLOCK

Gridley J.F. Bryant, one of the architects for the Old City Hall on School Street, not to mention Boston City Hospital in the South End and the Charles Street Jail on Cambridge Street, also built large granite warehouses that once extended to the harbor. He designed this massive granite block in 1858. Look for the big granite globe squeezed under the arched cornice facing the Custom House Tower. The mansard roofs were added later. ♦ Bounded by the Rose Kennedy Greenway and McKinley Sq, and Central and State Sts

Within State Street Block:

DOCKSIDE

$ At one of Boston's popular sports bars, fans have their choice of TVs and big screens to watch the games. The drinks, rah-rah décor, camaraderie, and customers are the draw, not the cuisine. Expect bar-food basics like pizza, barbecue, and burgers. Sports figures have been known to drop by. One memorable night, Jack Nicholson tended bar. ♦ American ♦ Daily, lunch and dinner. 183 State St. 723.7050

Harborside Inn of Boston

$$ Victorian period furnishings characterize this small hotel housed in a renovated granite mercantile building. The 54 rooms and suites also offer queen-size beds, private baths, individual climate control, voice mail, and free local phone calls. Some rooms have convertible sofas. There's no on-site restaurant, but many are located nearby. ♦ 185 State St. 723.7500, 888/723.7565

9 Central Wharf Buildings

This humble but handsome row of eight brick buildings between India Street and the now-underground expressway are all that remain of the 54 designed by **Charles Bulfinch,** which together extended nearly 1,300 feet to where the **New England Aquarium** now stands. All of the structures, built in 1817, originally opened onto the water to receive goods from the ships docked out front. ♦ Milk St (between Atlantic Ave and India St)

10 Flour and Grain Exchange Building

This commercial castle brings a surprising fillip of fantasy to the hard-nosed Financial District. The conical roof of the exchange's curvaceous corner is bedecked with pointy dormers that look like a crown. Architect Henry Hobson Richardson's influence is palpable in this 1893 design by his successors, **Shepley, Rutan, and Coolidge,** who also built the impressive **Ames Building** on Court Street. Look for the extraordinary cartouche adorned with an eagle straddling a globe and cornucopias spilling fruit and coins. The exchange was built for the Chamber of Commerce and once housed a large trading hall on the third floor. Now architects hold court within. The original lobby was renovated into oblivion. With its lanterns and scattering of trees, the building's triangular **plaza** is an oasis ♦ 177 Milk St (at India St)

11 Broad Street

Indefatigable developer **Uriah Cotting** led his Broad Street Association in many ambitious 19th-century urban redevelopment schemes, of which this street was but one by-product. Laid out about 1805 according to **Charles Bulfinch**'s plans, it quickly became a handsome commercial avenue to the sea, bordered by Federal-style Bulfinch buildings, such as that at **No. 104.** A scattering still stand among more recent but distinguished structures such as **No. 52,** which was

completed in 1853. With its many low-rise buildings, this street is one of the neighborhood's most open, sunny spots. A historical note: In a store located on this thoroughfare, Francis Cabot Lowell, one of Cotting's partners, developed a power loom that revolutionized American textile manufacture. ♦ Between the Rose Kennedy Greenway (over now-underground 1-93) and State St

11 Bakey's

★★$ This appealing upscale delicatessen with a full bar serves all sorts of sandwiches for lunch and supper, plus an extensive continental breakfast. There are two pleasant dining rooms, one called The Snug, named for the room women retired to when it wasn't considered proper for the sexes to mingle in bars. The wooden bars and booths were imported from England. Be sure to notice The Snug's cozy little square bar, antique lighting, Oriental rugs, fresh linen, and flowers. ♦ American/Deli ♦ M-F, lunch and dinner. 45 Broad St (at Water St). 426.1710 &

12 Sakura-bana

★★★$$ Sushi is the house specialty—as you might guess if you notice the poem by the entrance extolling "sushi rapture"—and you can even order "Sushi Heaven," a sampler of more than two dozen varieties of sushi and sashimi. If you order à la carte, you can be as daring or timid as you wish, staying with salmon, tuna, and mackerel, or exploring flying fish roe and sea urchin. The daily *bento* (lunch box) specials served with soup, salad, rice, and fruit are also good choices. For dinner, try seafood *teppan yaki* (broiled with teriyaki sauce and served on a sizzling iron plate). Not only is this trim and tidy restaurant's cuisine outstanding, its prices are reasonable and portions generous. The name, by the way, means "Cherry Blossom." ♦ Japanese ♦ M-Sa, lunch and dinner; Su, dinner (closed first Sunday of the month). Reservations recommended for dinner. 57 Broad St (at Milk St). 542.4311 &

13 Mr. Dooley's Boston Tavern

★★$ A cut above other area Irish pubs for the the service and the crowd. It can look and feel like a bar scene out of the old *Ally McBeal* TV show. Entertainment nightly, except Thursdays. ♦ Hearty Pub Food ♦ Daily; Su, breakfast. 77 Broad St (at Custom House St). 338.5656

Restaurants/Clubs: Red | Hotels: Purple | Shops: Orange | Outdoors/Parks: Green | Sights/Culture: Blue

14 SULTAN'S KITCHEN

★$ Located in a remnant of **Charles Bulfinch**'s 19th-century Broad Street development, this self-service restaurant cooks up fresh and delicious renditions of Middle Eastern and Greek favorites for the lunch crowd: kabobs, stuffed grape leaves, Greek salad, baba ghannouj, egg-lemon-chicken soup, falafel, and tabbouleh. If too many dishes tempt you, order sampler plates. ♦ Middle Eastern/Takeout ♦ M-Sa, lunch. 72 Broad St (at Custom House St). 338.7819, recorded menu 338.8509

15 REBECCA'S CAFE

★$ They're all over Boston, offering made-from-scratch hot entrées, pastas, soups, salads, sandwiches, pastries, and dreamy desserts. ♦ Café/Takeout ♦ M-F, breakfast, lunch, and dinner; Sa, breakfast and lunch. 18 Tremont St (between School and Court Sts). 227.0020 & Also at 112 Newbury St (between Clarendon and Dartmouth Sts), 267.1122; Prudential Center, 800 Boylston St (between Exeter and Dalton Sts), 266.3355; 560 Harrison Ave (between Waltham and Randolph Sts), 482.1414

16 BOSTON PUBLIC LIBRARY, KIRSTEIN BUSINESS BRANCH

This branch of the Boston Public Library, designed by **Putnam and Cox** in 1930, specializes in noncirculating business and financial references. It's off the beaten trail on a pedestrian lane connecting School and Court Streets. An interesting feature of the building is its Georgian Revival façade, which replicates the central pavilion of daring **Charles Bulfinch**'s architecturally innovative (for America) and financially disastrous Tontine Crescent residential development, built on Franklin Street in 1794 and demolished in 1858. It was this speculative real-estate scheme's failure that cost Bulfinch his inheritance and turned him from an architect by choice into one by necessity. Several blocks away, part of Franklin Street still follows the footprints of the vanished Tontine's curve. ♦ M-F. 20 City Hall Ave (at Pi Alley). 523.0860

16 PI ALLEY

The printer's term *pi,* meaning spilled or jumbled type, is probably the origin of this alley's name. As the story goes, type would spill from printers' pockets as they went to and from a popular colonial tavern at the alley's end. A less common account claims the alley is actually Pie Alley, paying tribute to the tavern's popular pies. ♦ East of City Hall Ave

17 MERCHANTS WINE & SPIRITS

This former bank now houses liquid treasures. One of the city's finest wine and spirits shops, it carries unusual vintages as well as inexpensive drinkable specials. Rare Cognacs and superior Burgundies are a specialty; there's also a large California section. Tastings are held regularly in the old bank vault, its walls still lined with safety-deposit boxes. The cheese department sells superb cheeses from small New England farmsteads, plus imports. ♦ M-Sa. 6 Water St (between Devonshire and Washington Sts). 523.7425

18 LIBERTY SQUARE

At this triangular intersection is another of Boston's quaintly misnamed "squares" squeezed into a busy block. This one commemorates the 14 August 1765 destruction of the British Stamp Tax office that was here. (A year later, England repealed the Stamp Act.) The square was formally named in 1793 in a gala ceremony honoring the French Revolution, complete with extravagant feasting and 21-gun salute. It is dominated by Gyuri Hollosy's memorial to the Hungarian Revolution of 1956, dedicated in 1986. For those who love old urban pockets lingering in modern cities, this site is a treat. It's surrounded by businesslike 19th-century buildings that reveal curious and delightful details, if you take time to notice. The old street pattern's turns and angles provide interesting vistas. ♦ At Batterymarch, Kilby, and Water Sts

18 THE VAULT BISTRO & WINE BAR

★$$$ The atmosphere and service (both excellent) matter most in this plush former bank, although the wine is good and the food is not at all bad. Many young professionals meet here after work. ♦ American ♦ M-Sa, lunch and dinner. 105 Water St, on Liberty Sq. 292.3355; www.thevaultboston.com

19 APPLETON BUILDING

Coolidge and Shattuck designed this powerful, austere Classical Revival edifice in 1924; Irving Salsberg renovated it in 1981. Named for Samuel Appleton, a Boston insurance magnate, the building's most expressive gesture is its generous curve to accommodate converging streets on Liberty Square, its best side. (The Milk Street façade is far less interesting.) All else is measured, pragmatic, restrained—just right for the industry it housed. But the more you study the structure, the more inventive it appears, especially its syncopated window patterns and entrance façade friezes depicting a violin maker, carpenter, glassblower, sculptor, draftsman, and other artisans. Peek into the elliptical lobby with its elegant gilded ceiling. ♦ 110 Milk St (at Oliver St)

20 BATTERYMARCH BUILDING

Named for the street it adorns—once part of a marching route for military companies from **Boston Common** to now-leveled Fort Hill—this heroically optimistic Art Deco assemblage designed by **Henry Kellogg** in 1928 is wonderful to behold in the midst of a district becoming ever more crowded and shadowed by impersonal modern giants. The three slender towers linked by third-story arcades undergo a marvelous transformation as they push through the crowded block to the sky. Their dark brown brick at ground level gradually lightens in color until it becomes a glowing buff at the top, as if bleached by sunlight (the one commodity always in short supply in congested downtowns). Under the handsome entrance arches, look for the charming reliefs of boats, trains, planes, stagecoaches, and clipper ships. Unlike the heavy-handed gilding of nearby **75 State Street,** this building's discreet touches of gold enhance rather than bedizen its fine form. The second floor of the building is a conference center for Northeastern University. ♦ 60 Batterymarch St (between Franklin St and Batterymarch Arm)

Within the Batterymarch Building:

BOSTON WYNDHAM DOWNTOWN HOTEL

$$$ Opened in 1999 when this was chaotic Big Dig territory, the hotel uses the arched 89 Broad Street entrance as its impressive front door. (There's an entrance on Batterymarch too.) There are 362 rooms and 62 suites with full amenities (including 24-hour room service) in the fully refurbished, 14-story Art Deco building. Guests are greeted by lots of marble, mahogany paneling, and brass railing through the lobby level. Broad Street is filled with Irish pubs and restaurants and Northeastern University still uses the second floor, but guests have a lobby bar and library and the California/Italian **Caliterra** restaurant (★$$$) in the hotel for breakfast, lunch, and dinner daily. Children under 12 with an adult

stay free. ♦ 89 Broad St. 556.0006, 800/695.8284; fax 556.0053; Caliterra 348.1234; www.wyndham.com ᕮ

21 KING'S CHAPEL

The original 1688 chapel stirred Bostonians' ire, since it was the city's first place of worship for Anglicanism, the official Church of England that had driven Puritans from their homeland. The plain wooden structure was built at the behest of Sir Edmund Andros, the royal governor who took the reins when the Massachusetts Bay Colony charter was revoked—one early link in the long chain of events leading to the Revolution. To avoid interrupting services, the substantial 1754 Georgian chapel of Quincy granite standing today (a National Historic Landmark) was erected around the original building, which was then dismantled and heaved out the windows of its replacement. If the chapel seems squat, it's because the stone steeple that architect **Peter Harrison** envisioned atop its square tower was never built; funds ran out. But in one splendid finishing touch, the façade was embellished with a portico supported by Ionic columns.

The Georgian interior has weathered the centuries well. Its raised pulpit is the oldest in America still in use on its original site. The pew dedicated to early royal governors' use later accommodated George Washington on his Boston visits, as well as other American worthies. Slaves sat in the rear gallery on the cemetery side, and condemned prisoners sat to the right of the entrance for a last sermon before being hanged on the Common. After the Revolution, once the British and Loyalists had evacuated Boston, the chapel was converted (around 1789) into the first American Unitarian church. Some of the rich presents given to the earlier chapel by William and Mary of Britain are still in use, but most are displayed at the **Boston Athenaeum.**

One of the church's other treasures is **Paul Revere's largest bell,** which he called "the sweetest bell we ever made." Come hear the resonant **Charles Fisk organ,** a replica of the church's 1756 original. There are free musical recitals Tuesdays at 12:15PM; every Wednesday there's an organ prelude before the worship service. On Thursday there are free poetry readings in "the King's English."

Near the Old State House, a bookshop once stood where the first Bibles printed in America were sold and where Edgar Allan Poe's first volume of verse was published. No copies of Poe's work were sold here, a first blow among the many that darkened his view of life.

Restaurants/Clubs: Red | Hotels: Purple | Shops: Orange | Outdoors/Parks: Green | Sights/Culture: Blue

No tours are offered, but guides are on hand to answer questions during summer months. ♦ Tu-Sa; May-Oct until 4PM, Nov-Apr until 2PM. 58 Tremont St (at School St). 227.2155 ♿

Adjacent to King's Chapel:

KING'S CHAPEL BURYING GROUND

The first resident of Boston's earliest town cemetery was Isaac Johnson, who owned the land and was buried here in his garden in 1630. So many Boston settlers so quickly followed suit that some wag noted, "Brother Johnson's garden is getting to be a poor place for vegetables." A pleasant neighbor today, the church next door was erected on land seized from the burying ground. Burials continued until 1796, although a gravedigger complained in 1739 that this and two other local graveyards "are so fulled with dead bodies that we are obliged oft times to bury them four deep."

As in other Boston cemeteries, grave markers were moved about to accommodate newcomers, an unsettling practice that caused Oliver Wendell Holmes to complain: "The upright stones have been shuffled about like chessmen and nothing short of the Day of Judgment will tell whose dust lies beneath. . . . Shame! Shame! Shame!" The burying ground's inhabitants include governors **John Winthrop** and **John Endicott.** On the chapel side, look for the 1704 gravestone of **Elizabeth Pain,** who supposedly bore a minister's child and probably was Nathaniel Hawthorne's model for Hester Prynne in *The Scarlet Letter.* Also buried here is Sons of Liberty courier **William Dawes,** who rode through the night just as bravely as Paul Revere, but didn't have the posthumous good fortune to be lionized in a Longfellow poem. And for a sample of the Puritans' pessimistic stance on the snuffing of life's candle, look for **Joseph Tapping**'s marker. Stone rubbings are not allowed. ♦ Open daily 9AM-5PM, late spring, summer, and early fall; winter, closed at 3PM ♿

22 OLD CITY HALL

Replaced by modern City Hall at Government Center, this empress dowager is an exuberantly ornamental artifact of a more flamboyant era. The days when colorful Boston

politicos like James Michael Curley held sway are long gone. Retired in 1969, the 1865 hall designed by **Gridley J.F. Bryant** and **Arthur Gilman** is no longer in the thick of things. For many, it's a surprise to discover this French Second Empire edifice tucked away from the street. Still graced with ample arched windows and an imposing pavilion, the National Historic Landmark building now accommodates offices and a restaurant; the foyer contains a nice trompe l'oeil reminder of its former finery by muralist Josh Winer, and further embellishments are planned. The exterior was painstakingly renovated by Anderson Notter Associates in 1970.

On either side of the entrance stand Richard S. Greenough's 1855 statue of Benjamin Franklin and Thomas Ball's 1879 statue of Josiah Quincy, Boston's second mayor, who built Quincy Market and served as president of Harvard College. Franklin's likeness was the first portrait statue in Boston. Embedded in the sidewalk in front of the hall's cast-iron fence is Lilli Ann Killen Rosenberg's appealing 1983 mosaic, **City Carpet,** which commemorates the oldest public school in the US. Erected near this site in 1635, the Boston Public Latin School gave School Street its name and contributed influential alumni to American history books, including Franklin, John Hancock, Charles Bulfinch, Charles Francis Adams, and Ralph Waldo Emerson. The respected school is now at 78 Avenue Louis Pasteur, between the Fenway and Longwood Medical Area. Rosenberg also created the mosaic located on the wall side of

Old City Hall

The Best

Arthur Dion

Director/art dealer, Gallery Naga

After luxuriating in the city's great art galleries (the **Institute of Contemporary Art,** the **Museum of Fine Arts,** the **Isabella Stewart Gardner,** and the **Albert and Vera List Visual Arts Center**), walk around **Newbury Street** and environs.

The King & I has the best Thai cuisine in town—classic pad Thai, beautiful chicken basil.

Davio's, for haute Italian, irresistible homemade sausages, and supernal soups and sauces.

The holiday lights in the trees of **Boston Common** on a winter night during December.

The views driving along **Storrow Drive** or **Memorial Drive** along the Charles River day or night, to/from the Museum of Science; it's almost worth renting a car or bike.

Ice-skating on the Lagoon in the Public Garden (I've never done it, but it looks great).

The **Charles River Esplanade** is just gorgeous, especially if it's the first Sunday in June and you've just finished the 10K From All Walks of Life, which raises millions of dollars for AIDS care and research.

The **Museum of Afro American History**—a gem.

The **Cyclorama** at the Boston Center for the Arts is a huge, odd, wonderful exhibition space.

The amazing **flower beds in the Public Garden.**

On spring and fall weekends a large number of Boston's **artists' studios** are open to all. (Check the paper or call a gallery for details.) Fort Point Channel, the South End, and Vernon Street, to name only the biggest, are all primers to the city's art world.

---

the Green Line's outbound platform in Park Street Station, offering a pictorial account of Boston's first subway. ♦ 45 School St (between City Hall Ave and Tremont St)

Within Old City Hall:

Ruth's Chris Steak House

★★$$$ The wheeling and dealing of Old City Hall belong to the past. Now there's a casual Ruth's Chris steak house within these hallowed walls. It's one of 90 nationwide, but the steaks here get good reviews. The restaurant's bar, **Curley's,** is named for the city's iconic first Irish mayor, James Michael Curley, the "Rascal King." ♦ American ♦ M-F, daily, lunch; dinner. 742.8401. $14 for valet parking, or use nearby garages.

Old City Hall is also home to Boston Harborfest, 227.1528; www.bostonharborfest.com, and preservation-oriented groups like the Architectural Heritage Foundation, 523.8678; Boston Preservation Alliance, 367.2458, www.bostonpreservation.org; and Preservation MASS, 723.3383, www.preservationmass.org.

23 Omni Parker House

$$$ Boston's genteel dowager hotel proclaims itself "the choice of legends since 1854," and it's true: US presidents and celebrities of every stripe, from Joan Crawford to Hopalong Cassidy, have made themselves at home here. This oldest continuously operating hotel in America was treated to a long-overdue multimillion-dollar face-lift in 2000. This ambitious undertaking resulted in restoration of the hotel's beautiful centerpiece lobby, fashioned in original oak woodwork, crystal chandeliers, and carved gilt moldings. The hotel represents the success story of Maine native Harvey D. Parker, who came to Boston with less than a dollar and became its leading hotelier. Rebuilt numerous times, the current structure dates to 1927 and attracts a mainly business-oriented clientele. There are 500 rooms on 14 floors, including rooms for people with disabilities and floors for nonsmokers. Along with deluxe rooms, the hotel offers dollar-wise economy rooms.

Starting around 1855, the erudite **Saturday Club** met here on the last Saturday of every month, its circle including American literary and intellectual luminaries such as Nathaniel Hawthorne, John Whittier, Ralph Waldo Emerson, and Henry Wadsworth Longfellow; a spin-off group founded *The Atlantic Monthly* in 1859. Charles Dickens stayed at the hotel and joined the club's congenial gatherings, often fixing gin punch for his pals. The sitting-room mirror before which Dickens practiced his famous Boston readings now hangs on the mezzanine. On a more somber note, just 10 days before assassinating Abraham Lincoln, actor John Wilkes Booth stayed here while visiting his brother Edwin, also an actor, who was performing nearby. John spent some time practicing at a nearby shooting gallery. The hotel was the site of Senator John F. Kennedy's announcement of his candidacy for the presidency.

Parker's Bar is known for its classic martini, and live music is played here Wednesday

---

Restaurants/Clubs: Red | Hotels: Purple | Shops: Orange | Outdoors/Parks: Green | Sights/Culture: Blue

BOSTON IN FACT . . . AND FICTION

With its long and distinguished literary tradition, it's understandable Boston has become the subject of and/or setting for many a volume. Here are some of the best titles.

Nonfiction

AIA Guide to Boston by Susan and Michael Southworld (Globe Pequot Press, 1991). The official American Institute of Architects survey of over 500 notable landmarks is informative and entertaining.

Boston, A Topographical History by Walter Muir Whitehill (Belnap Press of Harvard University Press, 1968). An urbane discourse on Boston's history describing the changing face of the city, and the society that changed with it, over 300 years.

Boston Boy by Nat Hentoff (Alfred A. Knopf, 1986). Growing up Jewish in Roxbury in the '30s and '40s, when Roxbury had only kosher butcher shops, Hentoff came to know the Boston Latin School, jazz, rampant anti-Semitism, heroic editors, and the rascal king, Mayor James M. Curley.

The Boston Irish by Thomas H. O'Connor (Northeastern University Press, 1995). The history of the Irish immigration to Boston and how the Irish helped mold the city into what it is today.

Death at an Early Age: The Destruction of the Hearts and Minds of Negro Children in the Boston Public Schools by Jonathan Kozol. (Penguin, 1967, 1985) National Book Award winner. Kozol spent his first year of teaching in an inner-city Boston public school, where he found a segregated, spirit-killing system that warehoused black children.

Irish America: Coming into Clover, the Evolution of a People and a Culture by Boston Globe reporter Maureen Dezell (Doubleday, 2000). Boston-Irish herself, Dezell examines the stereotypes and realities of Irish Americans—the ethnic loyalty, overextended humility, humor, sometimes pious intolerance, and the changing relationship with the Catholic Church. You'll find no green beer or plastic shamrocks here, but much insight and wit.

On Common Ground: A Turbulent Decade in the Lives of Three American Families by J. Anthony Lukas (Alfred A. Knopf, 1985). A vivid portrayal of the era of court-ordered school busing in Boston.

Fiction

All Our Yesterdays by Robert B. Parker (Delacorte Press, 1994). Filled with Boston settings and lore, this sprawling saga spans the 20th century and reaches from Ireland's IRA to Boston's Beacon Hill mansions. Parker, a Cambridge resident, is the author of the acclaimed Spenser detective stories.

April Morning by Howard Fast (Crown, 1961). An admirable fictional historical re-creation of the events at Lexington and Concord on 19 April 1775, as observed by a 15-year-old boy who signed the muster roll of the Lexington militia.

Divine Inspiration by Jane Langton (Penguin, 1993). One of 10 locally set Homer Kelly mysteries (others include *Memorial Hall Murder* and *God in Concord*), this story has a Back Bay church as a backdrop.

The Friends of Eddie Coyle by George V. Higgins (1972, reissued 1987; Viking/Penguin). This and several other mysteries in the ongoing series—*The Patriot Game, Cogan's Trade, Impostors, Outlaws, Penance for Jerry Kennedy*—are set in Boston. The focus is on small-time crooks and Irish politics.

The Godwulf Manuscript by Robert B. Parker (Dell Publishing, 1973). This is the first in the many-book series of detective novels featuring literature-quoting tough-guy private eye Spenser. Parker is a native Bostonian and Boston and its environs play a significant role in each book.

Johnny Tremain by Esther Forbes (Dell Publishing, 1987). This young person's classic is set in 18th-century Revolutionary Boston.

The Last Hurrah by Edwin O'Connor (Little, Brown and Company, 1956). Considered one of the most entertaining novels ever written about American politics, and twice made into a film, it's the story of Frank Skeffington, making his final race for mayor. The character is based on the real-life Boston mayor James M. Curley.

The Late George Apley by John P. Marquand (1937, reissued 1967; Little, Brown and Company). A novel told in the form of the memoir of the character Horatio Willing, who satirizes himself as he recounts the life of a conventional and somewhat pathetic Bostonian. It was awarded the Pulitzer Prize.

Make Way for Ducklings by Robert McCloskey (1941, reissued 1976; Penguin). This is the beloved children's picture book about Mr. and Mrs. Mallard and their eight ducklings, who settle in Boston's Public Garden.

The Rise of Silas Lapham by William Dean Howells (1885, reissued 1991; Random House). A self-reliant businessman who has become wealthy moves to Boston and learns about pretention and social and ethical standards on Beacon Hill.

The Scarlet Letter by Nathaniel Hawthorne (1850, reissued 1992; Alfred A. Knopf). Hester Prynne, condemned to wear the scarlet embroidered letter "A" as punishment for adultery, refuses to reveal the name of her child's father.

through Saturday. The famous soft "Parker House roll" was first created here, as was the tasty but very unpielike Boston cream pie. Both are available in the restaurants and to take out. ♦ Paid valet parking available. 60 School St (at Tremont St). 227.8600, 800/843.6664; fax 742.5729; www.parkerhouseboston.com

Within Omni Parker House:

PARKER'S RESTAURANT

★★$$$ With vaulted ceilings and high, wing-back chairs, the restaurant is tranquil, roomy, and timeless. The good, reliable American cuisine—accompanied by those famous rolls—is undeservedly overlooked. ♦ American ♦ M-Sa, breakfast, lunch, and dinner; Su, brunch. Jacket required at dinner, requested at lunch. Reservations recommended. Valet parking available. 227.8600 &

THE LAST HURRAH! BAR AND GRILL

★$$ Renovated and restored, the walls are plastered with political memorabilia harking back to when Old City Hall down the street was in full swing. You can dine as well as drink here, but the food is nothing special. The bar is popular with the State House and City Hall sets. ♦ American ♦ M-Sa, lunch and dinner; Su, brunch and dinner. Reservations recommended. 227.8600

24 SKYLIGHT JEWELERS

Edward Spencer, an old-fashioned artisan with a gift for modern design, has been a neighborhood fixture for more than three decades. His display cases suggest his range and feature fluid settings for organic shapes (freshwater pearls are a specialty, as are moonstones—feldspar carved into moon faces). He's happy to accommodate your design suggestions. ♦ M-Sa. 44 School St (at Province St). 426.0521; www.skylightjewelers.com & (will assist)

25 3 SCHOOL STREET

This redbrick, gambrel-roofed building—now on the National Register of Historic Places—was built circa 1711 for Thomas Crease, who opened Boston's first apothecary shop within. In 1828 Timothy Carter, a bookseller, took over, installed printing presses, and opened the Old Corner Bookstore. Thus began the building's long career as the locus of Boston's publishing industry and literary life.

Here Ticknor & Fields published works by Harriet Beecher Stowe, Charles Dickens, Alfred, Lord Tennyson, Elizabeth Barrett Browning, Henry David Thoreau, Nathaniel Hawthorne, William Makepeace Thackeray, Julia Ward Howe, and Ralph Waldo Emerson, helping to establish a native literature. Gregarious Jamie Fields in particular gained respect as counsel, friend, and guardian to writers, and was especially loved as an innovator who believed writers ought to be paid for their

pains. Here, too, *The Atlantic Monthly* was founded and rose to cultural eminence. *The Boston Globe*'s downtown offices once occupied the building, whose preservation the newspaper ensured by opening its namesake, the Globe Corner Bookstore, in 1982. Sadly, the bookshop at this location closed in 1998, although it remains in Cambridge. The building now houses a bank, shops, and the offices of Globe-Pequot Press. ♦ At Washington St

26 WINTHROP BUILDING

Boston's first building with a steel skeleton instead of load-bearing masonry walls; this sliver slips gracefully into a tapering lot. Conceived in 1893 by one of Boston's more adventurous architects, **Clarence H. Blackall,** the gently curving building flows between Spring Lane and Water Street. Now on the National Register of Historic Places, its golden airiness and dressy decoration, especially on the lower levels, delight the eye. Blackall's Chicago training was a fantastic boon to Boston. He designed a number of majestic theaters and other public buildings. Among Boston's other early steel-frame office buildings are a charming pair nearby: **Cass Gilbert**'s **Brazer Building** of 1896 and **Carl Fehmer**'s **Worthington Building** of 1894, standing side by side at 27 and 33 State Street. ♦ 276-278 Washington St (between Spring La and Water St)

Within the Winthrop Building:

MRS. FIELDS COOKIES

Ultrarich, chewy, and chocolaty cookies bring a steady stream of sweet-toothed customers to this cookie cove, one of hundreds in the national chain. Choose from the rich repertoire of chocolate-chip varieties, or try oatmeal raisin or cinnamon sugar. The brownies and muffins are equally tempting. ♦ Daily. 264 Washington St (at Water St), 523.0390 & Also at: Copley Place, 100 Huntington Ave (between Garrison and Dartmouth Sts), 536.6833; Marketplace Center, 200 State St (between Atlantic Ave and Commercial St). 951.0855

27 FANNY FARMER

A Boston classic, this shop has been selling chocolates, fudge, and other candy, ice cream, and nuts on this site for more than 50 years. It is part of the huge national chain named for Fanny Merritt Farmer, Boston's acclaimed cookbook author. Among other innovations, Fanny introduced the level measurement system that revolutionized food preparation. The company also owns all rights to Fanny's immensely popular *The Boston*

Restaurants/Clubs: Red | Hotels: Purple | Shops: Orange | Outdoors/Parks: Green | Sights/Culture: Blue

Cooking-School Cook Book, which can be purchased here. ◆ Daily. 288 Washington St (between Milk St and Spring La). 542.7045. Also at: 3 Center Plaza, Tremont, and Cambridge Sts. 723.6201

28 9 SPRING LANE

In 1643 this corner was the site of Governor Winthrop's home, conveniently located by Great Spring, for which the street was named. (The spring itself ran dry in the mid–19th century.) ◆ M-Sa. 9 Spring La (between Devonshire and Washington Sts).

29 JOHN W. McCORMACK POST OFFICE AND COURT HOUSE

A commanding Art Deco building with plenty of ornament and vertical window ribbons, this post office (designed in 1931 by **Cram & Ferguson** with **James A. Wetmore**) has a nicely weathered gray façade. ◆ Congress and Milk Sts (main entrance at 90 Devonshire St, at Water St). 654.5676

30 POST OFFICE SQUARE

This popular public space tops a 1,400-car garage. One of the busiest and most visually exciting pockets in the city, it's surrounded by the Art Deco post office and telephone company headquarters, and affords wonderful views of the city's most eclectic architecture— a delightful hodgepodge of new and old. The square was landscaped by Craig Halvorson, and harbors 125 species of plants, including seven different species of vines climbing an elegant 143-foot-long trellised colonnade. **Harry Ellenzweig** designed the sparkling glass quarters of the **Milk Street Cafe** (see page 88); sculptor Howard Ben Tre designed the handsome green-glass fountains. ◆ Bounded by Pearl, Congress, and Franklin Sts

At Post Office Square:

ANGELL MEMORIAL PLAZA

At the triangle's tip opposite the post office is a pocket park dedicated to George Thorndike Angell, founder of the Massachusetts Society for the Prevention of Cruelty to Animals and the American Humane Education Society. A sculpture of a small pond and its inhabitants is located in the middle of a brick circle inset with reliefs of birds, beasts, and bugs. Look for Angell's wise words: "Our humane societies are now sowing the seeds of a harvest which will one of these days protect not only the birds of the air and beasts of the field but also human beings as well." Looming near the pond is the fountain designed by Peabody and Stearns as a watering place for horses in 1912.

31 UMBRIA

★★$$$$ Umbria has five floors devoted to fine dining and dancing. Managed by the people who made **Bricco** a success in the North End, Umbria offers earthy Italian cuisine from the Umbrian region. Think boar sausages and pasta with truffles. Sunday brunch is lavish (and relatively inexpensive). Italian steak-house entrées, hardwood grilled and finished in a brick oven, have been added to the menu. ◆ Regional Italian M-F, lunch; M-Sa, dinner. Lounge and nightclub F, Sa (and Sundays of three-day weekends). 295 Franklin St (between Broad and Batterymarch Sts). 338.1000; www.umbriaristorante.com

31 BRANDY PETE'S

★★ $$ During Prohibition thirsty Bostonians flocked here after a flip of the venetian blinds signaled a new shipment of booze. When that dry period ended, owner Peter Sabia transformed his speakeasy into a restaurant. Today Bostonians come to the large brass-and-mahogany-appointed pub, especially after work, where the menu features good, simple dishes, including scrod, chicken potpie, and basic pub food. There's also dining for eight on the patio. ◆ American ◆ M-F, lunch and dinner. 267 Franklin St (between Batterymarch and Oliver Sts). 439.4165

32 CHADWICK LEADWORKS

Though one-upped by the bulky neoclassical **International Place,** a nearby high-rise, this forceful structure still holds its own on the Financial District fringe. Built in 1887 by Joseph Houghton Chadwick, once described as the "Lead King of Boston," it was designed by **William G. Preston,** who also created the former New England Museum of Natural History in Back Bay (now the upscale Louis, Boston clothing store). Handsome three-story arches with a graceful ripple of spandrels are topped by a row of little windows and a bold parapet. A gargoyle glares from one corner, and other grotesques and dragonlike lizards cling to the façade. At the back is the square **shot tower,** inside which molten lead was poured from the top, cooling into shot before reaching the bottom floor. ◆ 184 High St (at Batterymarch St)

33 NINE ZERO HOTEL

$$$$ Opened in 2002, this 19-story redbrick building, billed as a 190-room luxury business hotel, is on the Freedom Trail and overlooks Boston Common, a block away. It has a concierge, 24-hour room service, in-room work areas, and high-speed Internet access. The Cloud Nine penthouse suite features a Jacuzzi, dining room, bar, office, floor-to-ceiling windows, and a telescope. ◆ 90 Tremont St (at Bosworth St) close to the Park Street Red Line T station. 772.5800; fax: 772.5810; www.ninezerohotel.com ♿

The Best

Susan Park

President, Boston Harborfest

Trinity Church (Back Bay): Organ concerts on Friday in the winter.

Commonwealth Avenue (Back Bay): Walking up the avenue in the spring with the magnolias in bloom.

The Cyclorama (South End): Attending the flea markets and finding a treasure.

Symphony Hall (Fenway): Attending a concert.

Within Nine Zero Hotel:

Spire Restaurant

★★★$$$ Patrons facing the floor-to-ceiling windows of this 72-seat restaurant can look out onto Tremont Street while they enjoy fine American food with a French accent. ♦ American/French ♦ Daily, breakfast, lunch, and dinner. Second floor. Accessible from the hotel lobby and through the entrance on Tremont. 772.0202; www.spirerestaurant.com ᷄

33 Tremont Temple

The fanciful Venetian stone façade of this structure, made of 15 delicate shades of terra-cotta, incongruously hides an office and church complex inside. It gets more and more curious with the added adornment of several elaborate balconies. The 1895 building, designed by **Clarence H. Blackall,** stands on the site of the famous Tremont Theater, where illustrious 19th-century thespians, performers, lecturers, and politicians—including Abe Lincoln—enthralled the public. ♦ 88 Tremont St (between Bosworth and School Sts). 523.7320

34 Borders Books, Music, Cafe

With more than 200,000 book, music, and video titles, along with an extensive selection of periodicals and newspapers from 55 US cities and 25 foreign countries, this Borders occupies some 39,000 square feet of a former bank. Adding on to the Renaissance-style structure (originally designed in 1926 by **Parker, Thomas & Rice**), architects **Kallmann and McKinnell** created a dynamic building. The firm's 1972 addition gracefully adapted to a tricky site and earned the building its place in one of Boston's most historic quarters. A corner of the building was cut away, creating an open urban area in front that offers breathing space from Washington Street crowds, as well as good views of its 18th-century neighbor, the **Old South Meeting House** (see right). In true Borders tradition, the store hosts free community events like readings, musical performances, and book signings. The staff is knowledgeable and helpful. On a mezzanine balcony overlooking the enormous light-filled and multiwindowed ground floor, there's an in-store **Café.** ♦ Daily. 10-24 School St (at Washington St). 557.7188

35 Old South Meeting House

This is Boston's second-oldest church (the **Old North Church** in the North End predates it). Built in 1729 by **Joshua Blanchard,** the National Historic Landmark is a traditional New England brick meetinghouse fronted by a solid square wooden tower that blossoms into a delicate spire. When nearby **Faneuil Hall**'s public meeting space grew too cramped, Bostonians congregated here for town meetings peppered with fiery debate to prepare for the coming Revolution and plan such events as the Boston Tea Party of 1773. That cold December night, more than 5,000 gathered within to rally against the hated tea tax. Three ships filled with tea to be taxed were anchored at Griffin's Wharf, and the royal governor refused Bostonians' demands that the tea be sent back to England. Samuel Adams gave the signal igniting the protest that turned Boston Harbor into a teapot. During the British occupation, Redcoats struck back at the patriots by using their meeting place for the riding school of General "Gentleman Johnny" Burgoyne's light cavalry, complete with an officers' bar. By the time the British had evacuated, the church was in a sorry state. The congregation finally moved back in, then decamped in 1875 to the new **Old South Church** in Copley Square. Among the early congregation members were Phillis Wheatley, a freed slave and one of the first published African-American poets; Elizabeth Vergoose, aka "Mother Goose"; and patriots James Otis, Samuel Adams, and William Dawes.

After escaping destruction by the **Great Fire of 1872,** the edifice was nearly demolished in a plan to make room for commercial businesses. But Bostonians, including Julia Ward Howe and Ralph Waldo Emerson, contributed funds to purchase and restore the historic property, which has been maintained as a national monument and museum by the Old South Association ever since. A three-year, $7 million restoration took place in the late 1990s. Step inside and experience restful simplicity. Because the British stripped the interior in 1776, only the sounding board and corner stairway are original. The award-winning permanent multimedia exhibition "In Prayer and

Restaurants/Clubs: Red | Hotels: Purple | Shops: Orange | Outdoors/Parks: Green | Sights/Culture: Blue

Protest: Old South Meeting House Remembers" includes audio programs that emanate from the walls, tapes with reenactments of the Boston Tea Party debates, a scale model of colonial Boston, profiles of famous churchgoers, and artifacts. The museum shop sells cards and theme souvenirs such as pennywhistles, quill pens, and soldiers' dice made from musket balls. An excellent series of concerts and Thursday lectures on American history and culture runs October through April. Events are free with museum admission. The church also hosts public debates, forums, and announcements of candidacies for office. During July and August, re-creations of 18th-century Boston town meetings are staged every Saturday on the plaza across the street, and bystanders are encouraged to participate. Outside on the corner is one of Boston's largest and prettiest flower stands. ♦ Admission. Daily. Tours for groups of 10 or more by reservation. 310 Washington St (at Milk St). 482.6439 www.oldsouthmeetinghouse.org &

36 MILK STREET CAFE

★$ Downtown shoppers and Financial District denizens love this crowded cafeteria, and many a politician stops in for kosher dairy, vegetarian home-style cooking that includes muffins and bagels, soups, pizzas, pastas, quiches, salads, and sweet treats. ♦ Café/ Takeout ♦ M-F, breakfast and lunch. 50 Milk St (at Devonshire St). 542.3663 also in the park at nearby Post Office Square, Devonshire Stand Milk St. 350.7275 &

37 INTERNATIONAL TRUST COMPANY BUILDING

Max Bachman's allegorical figures *Commerce* and *Industry* adorn the Arch Street side, while *Security* and *Fidelity* are ensconced on Devonshire Street, adding a fanciful representation of business rectitude modern buildings sorely lack. This edifice, built in 1893 by William G. Preston, enlarged in 1906, and now listed on the National Register of Historic Places, incorporated the remains of a building partly destroyed by Boston's terrible 1872 fire. ♦ 39-47 Milk St (between Devonshire and Arch Sts)

38 LANGHAM HOTEL

$$$$ Formerly known as Le Meridien Boston, this former Old Federal Reserve Bank is a luxury hotel but at a reasonable price. A Renaissance Revival palazzo designed by **R. Clipston Sturgis** in 1922, it overlooks the park at Post Office Square and has a reputation for attentive, friendly service. Pets are allowed. The 325 guest rooms have a contemporary elegance; look for marble and granite in the bath. The lobby and public spaces feature restored original architectural details. Because a glass mansard roof was

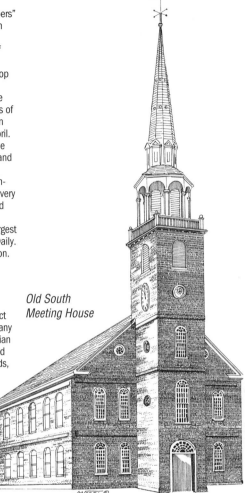

Old South Meeting House

MARJORIE VOGEL, RHODE ISLAND ORIGINALS

plunked on top of the old structure to provide additional floors, many rooms feature sloping glass walls, offering great views. Suite 915 is especially popular, as are the loft suites. Specially equipped rooms are available for people with disabilities, and floors are reserved for nonsmokers. There's a posh health club on the third floor (featuring a pool, whirlpool, sauna, massage services, and exercise equipment), a full-service business center, and 13 meeting rooms. Other amenities include a multilingual staff, valet parking, 24-hour concierge and room services, high-speed Internet access, and express laundry and dry cleaning.

The big plus for guests is the location in the heart of the Financial District; it's an easy walk from here to many popular attractions (five blocks to Faneuil Hall) and the Theater District. Adjoining the hotel is **One Post Office Square**, a 41-story tower added in 1981 by **Jung/Brannen Associates and Pietro Belluschi** that houses conference rooms and offices. ♦ 250 Franklin St (between Oliver and Pearl Sts). Paid parking offered in the adjacent 400-car garage. 451.1900; www.langhamhotels.com/langham/boston ⟨b⟩

Within Langham Hotel:

JULIEN

★★★$$$$ Named for Boston's first French restaurant, which opened on this same site in 1794, this restaurant draws a predominantly business clientele. Yet the restaurant's lofty, refined splendor and creative French cuisine make it a good choice for a serious evening out. Chef de cuisine Brian Corbley combines fresh native ingredients with French/Mediterranean touches in dishes such as black peppercorn–crusted yellowfin tuna steak with sweet red pearl onions, raisins, and snow peas; rack of New Zealand lamb with asparagus, artichokes, radishes, and olives in a garlic-and-thyme sauce; and grilled Atlantic salmon with marinated mushrooms, wrapped in a spinach leaf and topped with lemon zest. Desserts are equally inspired, and the wine list is exceptional.

The vast dining room is in the high-ceilinged hall that once served as the bank's boardroom; tables are generously spaced and diners settle into Queen Anne wingback chairs, promoting privacy and conversation. The **Julien Bar,** with gilded coffered ceilings and wonderful carved details, provides background piano music. Look for the pair of **N.C. Wyeth murals** portraying Abraham Lincoln and George Washington. ♦ French ♦ M-Sa, dinner. Jacket required at restaurant. Reservations recommended. Complimentary valet parking at dinnertime. 451.1900 ⟨b⟩

CAFE FLEURI

★★$$$ Situated beneath the six-story atrium in One Post Office Square, connected to the hotel, this airy and open café features Mediterranean-style cuisine and New England favorites. It is popular for business breakfasts and lunches, and for the spectacular Sunday jazz brunch. Attention all chocoholics: On Saturday afternoons (except in the summer) the café puts on a sumptuous all-you-can-eat Chocolate Bar buffet, a truly decadent display of cakes, pies, tortes, fondues, mousses, cookies, brownies, and the like. ♦

Café ♦ Daily, breakfast, lunch, and dinner. Reservations recommended. Valet parking available. 451.1900

39 PROVINCE HOUSE STEPS

From Province Street, mount the weathered steps that once led to the gardens of a 17th-century house, the luxurious official residence of the royal governors of Massachusetts Bay. Renamed Government House after the Revolution, the mansion was inhabited until 1796. Here General Gage ordered Redcoats to Lexington and Concord. Here, too, General Howe ordered his men to flee after Washington fortified Dorchester Heights, aiming big guns at the British. Years later, Nathaniel Hawthorne wrote about the by-then-decaying tavern and inn in *Twice-Told Tales.* Only these steps remain. ♦ Province and Bosworth Sts

39 CAFE MARLIAVE

★$$ Dressed up with bits of wrought iron and balconies, this restaurant has stood on its corner for so long—more than a century—that many Bostonians forget it exists. However, a cadre of loyalists keeps coming back. The Italian-American cooking is average, but it's reasonably priced, with plenty of choices. The same family has run the place since 1935. The café sits high above the street, at the top of the Province House Steps; dine on the second floor by the windows and become part of the streetscape. ♦ Italian-American ♦ Daily, lunch and dinner. 10 Bosworth St (at Province St). 423.6340

39 BROMFIELD STREET

This short, narrow street was once the location of Revolutionary hero Thomas Cushing's residence, where the Massachusetts delegates to the first Continental Congress assembled, among them Samuel and John Adams and Robert Treat Paine. Today it's a commercial street, packed with small establishments specializing in cameras, antiques, collector's coins and stamps, jewelry, watches, and pens. Pawnshops are also on the street, along with great old buildings, such as **Nos. 22** and **30** of 1848 and the 1870 Wesleyan Association Building at **No. 36,** all made of granite. ♦ Between Washington and Tremont Sts

39 BROMFIELD PEN SHOP

Accustomed to inexpensive, use-and-abuse disposable pens? Wander into this little shop, gaze upon gleaming rows of new and antique pens, and reconsider your choice of writing instrument. Imagine what that handsome handful of a lovingly restored Bakelite pen might do for your prose. In addition to brands like Parker and Sheaffer, Mont Blanc, Lamy, Pelikan, Yard-O-Led of England, S.T. Dupont,

Restaurants/Clubs: Red | **Hotels: Purple** | **Shops: Orange** | **Outdoors/Parks: Green** | **Sights/Culture: Blue**

89

Waterman, Omas of Italy, delicate glass pens and ink varieties are in stock. Engraving is free. It's the best store of its kind in New England. They also sell the never-fail inexpensive pen used by Boston traffic cops. The shop also stocks art supplies. ♦ M-Sa. 39 Bromfield St (between Province and Tremont Sts). 482.9053 &

39 J.J. Teaparty Coin

Numismatists take note: Owner Ed Leventhal has been buying and selling coins at Bromfield Street's premier coin shop since 1963. Both casual collectors and serious investors come by to drop some coins of their own for proof sets, mint sets, and bullion coins like the American Eagle and Canadian Maple Leaf. ♦ M-F; Sa until 2PM; closed Sa July-Aug. No credit cards accepted. 51 Bromfield St (between Province and Tremont Sts). 482.2398, 800/343.6412; www.jjteaparty.com

40 Kennedy's Midtown

★★$$ This upscale Irish restaurant and pub is patronized by adults and young adults past the age of spilling beer and shouting. Comfortably plush décor is like Dublin's best, staff and patrons are friendly, and the food is quite good. The place is especially popular at lunch and after work. ♦ Irish/Pub ♦ Daily, lunch and dinner. 42 Province St (between Bromfield and School Sts). 426.3333; www.kennedysmidtown.com &

41 Bruegger's Bagel Bakery

$ Ten varieties of excellent bagels—Boston's best—are baked throughout the day at this family business and are never more than a few hours old. Bruegger's own factory also produces nine different cream cheeses to spread on top. If you want a more filling meal, try a sandwich on a bagel, accompanied by freshly made soup. Bruegger's décor is fast-food basic, but the restaurant is neat and clean, with plenty of seating. ♦ Bagels/Take-out ♦ Daily, breakfast and lunch. 32 Bromfield St (between Washington and Tremont Sts). 357.5577 &. Also at numerous locations throughout the Boston area

42 Jewelers Building

Though stripped of its frilly original copper trim, this Beaux Arts–inspired early "skyscraper" designed by **Winslow and Bigelow** in 1898 still serves the trade it was designed for, housing nearly 100 jewelry dealers, most of whom sell retail as well as wholesale. In the lobby, you can't miss a crude but informative bronze bas-relief depicting the history of diamond mining and cutting. ♦ M-Sa. 379 Washington St (between Winter and Bromfield Sts) &

43 Arch St. Deli

$ For years known as Hole in the Wall, one of the district's tiniest tidbits of real estate, this diminutive deli turns out a huge assortment of breakfast and lunch items to go. You'd be hard-pressed to think of a hot or cold sandwich that isn't served here (okay, so there's no peanut butter), not to mention the salads, soups and stews, egg combos, burgers, and snacks. Join the line at the outside counter, or step inside to watch how skillfully counter staff dart past each other in close quarters. A passerby's remark—"Look at that hole in the wall"—gave the 12-by-4-foot deli its original appellation. Take a moment to examine Richard Haas's trompe l'oeil mural across the street, painted on the back of 31 Milk Street, which portrays a cutaway of the actual façade. Haas also painted the well-known mural on the Boston Architectural Center in Back Bay. ♦ Deli/ Takeout ♦ M-F, 5:30AM-4PM. 24 Arch St (between Franklin and Milk Sts). 423.4625 &

44 Verizon

A 1947 design by **Cram & Ferguson,** this step-top Art Deco throwback occupies its place with pride. **Goody, Clancy & Associates** renovated the façade in 1992 in a spiffy homage; check out the spiky beacons, echoed in the phone booths on either side. (Everything has been touched with a Deco wand, from the garden guardrails and trash receptacles right down to the sidewalk pattern.) Off the main lobby, you can see a re-creation of inventor **Alexander Graham Bell's garret.** Dean Cornwell's frenzied and colorful Norman Rockwell-esque mural circles the lobby. Called *Telephone Men and Women at Work,* the 160-foot-long, action-packed painting depicts 197 lifesize figures in dramatic groupings. Painted in 1951, it lionizes not only Bell and other telephone pioneers, but also employees on the job and those risking life and limb in disaster. Cornwell was an old hand at this sort of thing, having created murals honoring steelworkers, pioneers in medicine, various states' histories, and the like.

Bell's laboratory is a painstaking replica of his original studio at 109 Court Street in old Scollay Square, where he electrically transmitted the first speech sounds over a wire on 3 June 1875. (The following March, in a different lab, Bell succeeded in sending not just sounds but intelligible words, when he issued his famous line, "Mr. Watson, come here, I want you.") The studio was saved from demolition, dismantled, and eventually brought here in pieces and rebuilt. On display are models, telephone replicas, drawings, references, and historic artifacts, plus a wonderful diorama of the view of

Scollay Square from Bell's window. Pamphlets about Cornwell's creation and Bell's garret are usually available. ◆ Free. M-F. 185 Franklin St (between Congress and Pearl Sts). 743.4747 ৬

45 ORPHEUM THEATRE

Originally called the Music Hall, this worldly theater, built in 1852 by **Snell and Gregorson,** has seen a thing or two. It housed the fledgling New England Conservatory and witnessed the Boston Symphony Orchestra's debut concert in 1881. The Handel and Haydn Society performed here for years. **Tchaikovsky**'s first piano concerto had its world premiere, **Ralph Waldo Emerson** and **Booker T. Washington** lectured, and **Oscar Wilde** promoted a Gilbert and Sullivan operetta here. Today the theater mostly books rock concerts. ◆ Box office: M-Sa. No credit cards accepted at box office. Hamilton Pl (southeast of Tremont St). Recorded information 482.0650, Ticketmaster 931.2000 ৬

46 BARNES & NOBLE BOOKSTORE

This big general bookstore specializes in reduced-price best-sellers and discounted paperbacks and hardcovers, as well as publishers' overstocks. It also sells children's books, magazines, board games, cards, and local maps, plus classical and jazz records, tapes, and CDs. ◆ Daily. 395 Washington St (between Winter and Bromfield Sts). 426.5502 ৬ Also at 660 Beacon St (between Raleigh St and Kenmore Sq). 267.8484; 603 Boylston St (between Clarendon and Dartmouth Sts). 236.1308

47 LONDON HARNESS COMPANY

Fine leather goods are the focus. You'll find only the finest in proper gifts for travel, home, office, and personal use, tastefully arrayed amid the shop's gleaming old wooden fixtures. The oldest operating retailer in the country, the shop has done business in this general location since the 1700s. Benjamin Franklin was among the early shoppers and traveled with trunks purchased here. Honor momentous occasions (weddings, graduations) or get yourself something indispensable that will last forever. There are other gift items too. Perhaps you'd like a wooden box with "Fenway Park" hand-painted on it, or a chess set, or an umbrella that will stand up to Boston's gusty winds. There are clocks, luggage, wallets and accessories, leather frames and photo albums, jewelry boxes, briefcases, bookends, desk sets, old prints and maps, and more. ◆ M-Sa. 60 Franklin St (between Arch and Hawley Sts). 542.9234 ৬ (through rear entrance)

48 MOJITOS

★★$$ Doors to this Latin nightclub open in the evening, but dancing gets hot from 10:30 to 2 AM. Before that, a well-dressed, mixed-age crowd enjoys the lounge and cocktail area. Look for the mural of Latin legends like Celia Cruz, Tito Puente, and Juan Luis Guerra. The name Mojitos is from the classic Cuban drink, which contains rum, fresh lime, and mint leaves, the club's signature drink. ◆ Cover charge and proper dress required. Reduced-rate parking at nearby Lafayette Garage with Mojitos' validation. 48 Winter St (between Tremont St and Winter Pl). 988.8123; www.mojitoslounge.com

48 ORIGINAL TREMONT TEAROOM

Yeah, we know that psychics often have a dodgy reputation, but this one has been around for more than 60 years. Tea-leaf and palm reading, tarot cards, rune stones, astrology, Reiki treatments, and a generally New Age attitude are offered here. Fifteen minutes for $25. ◆ Daily from 11AM (noon on Sundays). They also offer wedding services and gay and lesbian commitment ceremonies. Downtown Crossing at 48-50 Winter St, third floor (between Tremont St and Winter Pl). 338.8100; www.tremont-tearoom.com ৬

49 LOCKE-OBER

★★★$$$ The old is new again. Locke-Ober has kept the storied tradition even as it jumped happily into the 21st century. This now-updated bastion of Brahmin dining, under star chef Lynda Shire, retains its oysters and Indian-pudding charm, but offers such dishes as Black Angus filet mignon and sauté of rum foie gras with golden pineapple.

After trying his hand at numerous occupations, Louis Ober, an Alsatian, opened Ober's Restaurant Parisien in 1870 in this tiny residential alley. In 1892 Frank Locke opened a wine bar next door. Ober's successors combined the two and their founders' names, an ingenious partnership that has flourished to this day. For nearly a hundred years, the **Men's Cafe** downstairs was reserved for men; escorted women were admitted only on New

The Old Corner Bookstore, site of the one-time home of Anne Hutchinson, subsequently housed several publishing firms, one of which was Ticknor & Fields. In order to lure fine American writers and to secure exclusive American publishing rights for English authors, Fields formulated the royalty system, which gave authors both the standard manuscript sum and 10 percent of retail sales.

Restaurants/Clubs: Red | Hotels: Purple | Shops: Orange | Outdoors/Parks: Green | Sights/Culture: Blue

Year's Eve and on the night of the Harvard–Yale game. (If Harvard lost, the nude painting of Yvonne in the first-floor barroom was draped in black.) But modern times came knocking and this hallowed enclave reluctantly began admitting women. Both sexes now enjoy its Victorian splendor, rich Yankee-European cuisine, and discreet black-tie, Old World service. Some waiters have been at Locke-Ober for 40 years.

You may share the dining room with Kennedy or those ubiquitous Harvard students who come from across the Charles River to toast their graduations. The famous downstairs is dark-wood splendor, the hand-carved bar agleam with German silver, but the revamped and gilded upstairs is nice also. Private dining chambers are available for a fee. You'll see plenty of loyalists, mostly male, sitting in their customary places and dining on such delicious old favorites as oysters, lobster Savannah, steak tartare, filet mignon, Dover sole, roast beef hash, rack of lamb, calf's liver, Indian pudding, and baked Alaska. The café's lock-shaped sign, by the way, was inspired by one that adorned Locke's original establishment. ◆ Continental ◆ M-F, lunch and dinner; Sa, Su, dinner (hours vary in July and August). Jacket and tie required. Reservations recommended. Valet parking available after 6PM. 3-4 Winter Pl (at Winter St). 542.1340

50 FILENE'S

The owners of **Macy's** stores bought the many Filene's department stores, vowing to close most and rebrand the remaining as Macy's. It is unlikely that this one—the original 1912 Filene's designed by Chicago architect **Daniel Burnham**—will keep the old name, and city officials want the entire block redeveloped into a mixed-use (commercial, residential, hotel, and office) space. Developers talk of keeping the Filene's building and erecting offices, luxury condos, and at least one new hotel on the landmark-status block. Filene's founder, William Filene, opened his first retail business in 1851. The present building was the first—and probably only—department store to have a zoo on its roof, with an elephant, lions, monkeys, and other wild animals. Sixty thousand children visited the zoo before it was destroyed by the 1954 hurricane that toppled Old North Church's steeple. ◆ Daily. 426 Washington St (at Summer St). 357.2100

Below Filene's:

FILENE'S BASEMENT

Now an independent company unaffected by changes upstairs, America's first off-price store became more famous than its parent. It opened in 1908 and there are replicas in nine states, but nothing equals the original. Inventory includes designer-label and bargain clothing and accessories for men, women, and children, and house wares. Retail stock from such prestigious stores as Saks, Brooks Brothers, Bergdorf Goodman, and Neiman Marcus is regularly featured.

Because of its automatic markdown policy, the Basement offers shoppers a treasure hunt. The price tag for each item also carries the date of the day it came on the selling floor. Fourteen days from that date the item is marked down 25 percent. Seven days after that, it drops an additional 25 percent. After another seven days, it is marked down another 25 percent, making that a total of 75 percent off. After another seven days, you may still buy the item at 75 percent off, but you must take it to the Customer Service desk and pay for it by making out a check to one of the listed charity organizations. Any items remaining on the floor after that are donated directly to charities.

Many a quickie course has been offered on how to come away laden with low-cost treasures from the legendary emporium. The simple formula: perseverance, skill, and luck. Strike it lucky and you might bring home a wedding dress, winter coat, business suit, evening attire, luggage, lingerie, goose-down comforter, fine linen, or even a diamond ring for a fraction of its original price. Crowds gather on the popular "Big Sale" days, when doors open early. Try to flip through a local Sunday paper, since many sales begin Monday. If you watch, you'll see how veterans work the room; you'll also see neat piles and racks of clothing and goods reduced to colorful, chaotic heaps, and glassy-eyed, overstimulated novices escaping to the upper levels in defeat. A women's dressing room was added in 1991 after complaints of sexism (the men's department had been equipped with changing rooms for years). However, true shopping mavens won't stand for the lines and instead take advantage of the liberal return policy (14 days, with receipt) for home tryouts. Many use the time-honored method of slipping stuff on in an out-of-the-way aisle.

The Basement has two levels; it may be entered from Filene's proper, or underground from the Downtown Crossing subway station (on the Red and Orange Lines). ◆ Daily. 542.2011 ♿ (enter from Filene's; use the elevator)

51 WHIPPOORWILL

Formerly at home in Faneuil Hall, this standout independent crafts shop specializes in the whimsical. Mixed in among kaleidoscopes, chimes, woven clothes, and other staples are such oddities as Josh and Michael Cohen's heart-bedecked ceramic condom boxes. This is a good place to look for one-of-a-kind tokens of affection. ◆ Daily. 93 Franklin St (between Arch and Devonshire Sts). 422.0025

52 BANK OF AMERICA

Campbell, Aldrich & Nulty designed this ungainly brown tower with a big belly in 1971. It quickly earned a famous nickname: "The Pregnant Building." ◆ 100 Federal St (between Matthews and Franklin Sts). 434.2200 &

53 MARTIN'S TOWNHOUSE

★$ A friendly and basic place for enjoying beer, good burgers, and pub food, especially at lunch. The crowd includes bankers and phone-company employees. From 6 to 10PM on Fridays, karaoke is the big draw. ◆ American ◆ M-Th, lunch and dinner to 11PM; F, lunch and dinner; open until 2AM. 137 Pearl St (between High and Purchase Sts). 423.4792

54 CATHEDRAL CHURCH OF ST. PAUL

Most of Boston's old buildings mingle comfortably enough with their modern neighbors, but this dignified edifice looks uncomfortable sandwiched between two towering commercial structures, as if wondering what happened to the spacious rural town that surrounded it back in the 1820s. Once surrounded by handsome homes, the simple gray granite Episcopalian cathedral—Boston's first example of Greek Revival architecture, and today on the National Register of Historic Places—is now situated in Boston's workaday district. The massive sandstone Ionic columns supporting its porch add conviction to a stretch of street that can use it. Architect **Alexander Parris,** an avid practitioner of the Greek Revival style, also designed **Quincy Market.** If the temple's tympanum looks strangely blank, that's because the bas-relief figures intended for it were never carved—another example of a Boston building where ambitious aspirations exceeded funds. Visit the starkly impressive interior, which was revised somewhat by architect Ralph Adams Cram in the 1920s. ◆ M-F, noon service. Free organ concerts Th, 12:45-1:15PM. 138 Tremont St (between Temple Pl and Winter St). 482.5800; www.stpaulboston.org & (enter through the side entrance)

Within Cathedral Church of St. Paul:

CATHEDRAL CROSSING

This full-service bookshop, which is operated by the Society of St. John the Evangelist and the Episcopal Diocese of Massachusetts, specializes in religious books, primarily with a liberal Christian focus. There are also children's books, ministry resources, icon reproductions, and gifts. ◆ Tu-Sa. Entrance also at 28 Temple Pl (between Washington and Tremont Sts). 423.4719

55 STODDARD'S

Open since 1800, the country's oldest cutlery shop sells plenty of other invaluable items too: row upon row of nail nippers (who'd ever think so many kinds existed?), pocket knives, corkscrews, clocks, manicure sets, mirrors, magnifiers, binoculars, brushes, scissors, lobster shears, fishing rods and lures, and almost anything else that could possibly come in handy. A great source for practical presents, this place is also one of only a handful remaining where cutlery is sharpened by hand—the only way to give blades their proper edge. An expert grinder works upstairs, giving scissors and such a new lease on life. ◆ M-Sa. 50 Temple Pl (between Washington and Tremont Sts). 426.4187 & Also at Copley Place, 100 Huntington Ave (between Garrison and Dartmouth Sts). 536.8688

55 MANTRA

★★★$$$$ This site used to be a bank, and the restaurant inherited the high ceilings and marble. The décor includes such touches as laser-cut steel mirrors, chain-mail drapery, and leather floors. The Indian-French cuisine is pricey but very good. The restaurant has been uneven since its 2001 opening, but a new chef in 2006 put it back on the quality track. Try the curried scallop salad with mango dressing, seared veal tenderloin, and saffron coconut soup, and investigate the unusual blue-cheese ice cream. There's also a *très* hip bar scene. You'll find Mantra just east of Boston Common. ◆ Indian/French ◆ M-F, lunch and dinner; Sa, dinner. Valet parking available. 52 Temple Pl (between Washington and Tremont Sts). 542.8111; www.mantrarestaurant.com &

56 MACY'S

Although the Macy's sign was raised in 1996, Bostonians will always think of this place as **Jordan Marsh.** The slogan "A tradition since 1851" referred to the department store's beginning as a small, high-quality dry-goods establishment, founded in Boston by Eben Dyer Jordan and partner Benjamin L. Marsh. Interestingly, Macy's also was founded in 1851 and has grown to a chain of 85 full-service department stores nationwide, offering both trendy and fashionable goods. ◆ Daily. 450 Washington St (at Summer St). 357.3000 &

Restaurants/Clubs: Red | Hotels: Purple | Shops: Orange | Outdoors/Parks: Green | Sights/Culture: Blue

57 VINALIA

★★$$$ Hailing from Dallas, this clubby-looking dining spot does big business in Boston, attracting the briefcase crowd at lunchtime and the *Playbill* crowd in the evening. The menu's focus is on American grill with a Southwestern accent. Many dishes are good and colorfully presented: Try the calamari, venison-sausage quesadillas, onion rings, gulf seafood chowder, tortilla soup, roast chicken, or lamb chops. Desserts are intensely rich, and the freshly made breads pleasantly fragrant. Sit in the elevated bar area and look over the fast-paced dining room, spiffed up with marble, ceiling fans, Roman shades, and club chairs.

The restaurant inhabits the second level of a 21-story office tower called **101 Arch Street,** which preserved under glass a section of the façade of **34 Summer Street** (an 1873 commercial palace) as a decorative piece in the lobby. And, if you're arriving by T, look for a vintage wooden escalator—more than 90 years old—on the outbound Chauncy Street side of the Red Line's **Downtown Crossing** stop. The grooved slats are so slanted, it's a challenge to ascend. ♦ American ♦ M-F, lunch and dinner. Reservations recommended. Valet parking after 5:30PM on the Summer Street side. 101 Arch St (between Arch and Winter Sts). 737.1777; www.vinaliaboston.com &

58 WINTHROP LANE

This short-and-sweet brick lane would be unremarkable except for the florist and **Boston Coffee Exchange** shops at one end, and an imaginative work of public art called ***Boston Bricks: A Celebration of Boston's Past and Present,*** created by Kate Burke and Gregg Lefevre in 1985, at the other. The artists have inset dozens of bronze brick reliefs amid the lane's bricks from start to finish. Each relief tells a piece of Boston's story. Some images and references are familiar: the Custom House Tower, Boston Common's cows, the Boston Pops, the city's ethnic groups, the Underground Railroad, the Boston Marathon, the Red Sox, whale watching, rowers on the Charles River, swans in the Public Garden, and an amusing representation of the notorious Boston driver. Others may keep you puzzling. Collectively, the clever bricks present a good likeness of the city. ♦ Between Devonshire and Arch Sts

59 ONE WINTHROP SQUARE

Ralph Waldo Emerson's nephew, **William Ralph Emerson,** is responsible for several vigorously unconventional Boston structures, including the **House of Odd Windows** on Beacon Hill and the **Boston Art Club** in Back Bay. In this collaborative effort carried out with **Carl Fehmer** in 1873, William Emerson's influence dominates in the eccentric mixing of architectural motifs. Originally a dry-goods emporium and later headquarters for the *Boston Record-American* newspaper, the building has been adapted to offices. Out front, where trucks once loaded up with newspapers, is an attractive park with Henry Hudson Kitson's bronze of Robert Burns briskly striding along, walking stick in hand and collie at his side. ♦ At Otis St

60 UNITED SHOE MACHINERY CORPORATION BUILDING

Now renovated, placed on the National Register of Historic Places, and renamed "The Landmark," Boston's first Art Deco skyscraper—built in 1929 by **Peter, Thomas, and Rice**—forms a handsome ziggurat crowned by a pyramid of tiles. At street level, look for the fine cast-metal storefronts set into limestone. Rude buildings shove against this proud bulwark, which recalls the era when shoes were big business in Boston. ♦ 160 Federal St (between High and Matthews Sts)

61 RICK WALKER'S

Horseback-riding outfitters since 1932, Walker's carries a selection of Western duds (Stetson hats, cowboy shirts, jeans, jackets, and pointy boots). There are long horns on the wall and scorpion-motif belt buckles in the display cases. There's also motorcycle gear and what Rick calls Rock 'n Roll threads. ♦ Daily. 21 Temple Pl (between Washington and Tremont Sts). 482.7426; www.rickwalkers.com &

61 IVY

★★$$ A well-dressed but casual clientele has discovered Ivy for after-work relaxing. There's quality dining on two floors, with a choice of large or small-plate items, and an intriguing downstairs lounge called **Cava.** Lunch and dinner are quite reasonable (try oven-roasted chicken with grilled asparagus and a thyme-lemon succo for dinner). Wine, regardless of choice, is capped at $26 a bottle. Downstairs, brick and granite walls are lined with tea lights with parts of birch trees behind the bar. There are Sunday-night wine tastings in the restaurant. ♦ Italian. Daily, dinner; M-F, lunch; Th-Sa, lounge. 49 Temple Pl (between Washington and Tremont Sts).

451.1416; fax 426.1535;
www.ivyrestaurantgroup.com &

62 FAJITAS & 'RITAS

★$ Unabashedly fun, this ultraloose joint attracts a surprising number of buttoned-up types. Not content to scribble on the paper tablecloths (crayons are provided), diners have spread doodles and graffiti across every surface; the whole place is a communal work of art in progress. When you fill out your own order forms for assorted fajitas and other Tex-Mex dishes, you can also check off a 'rita (that's *marga*rita) or beer or wine, including sangria by the liter. ♦ Tex-Mex/ Takeout ♦ M-Sa, lunch and dinner. 25 West St (between Washington and Tremont Sts). 426.1222; www.fajitasandritas.com &

63 BRATTLE BOOK SHOP

Foreign and domestic bibliophiles find their way to this humble-looking establishment. Not only is it one of America's few surviving urban-based bookshops of its kind, it's also successor to the country's oldest operating antiquarian bookshop (founded in 1825). For a good part of the 20th century, this literary establishment was run by the late George Gloss, a former fruit peddler who once exchanged a bunch of grapes for a paperback Dickens novel. Gloss earned the nickname "The Pied Piper of Book Lovers": At one time, he drove a wagon through the city, tossing free books to passersby. His son Ken now runs the place, having worked here since age five. The three-level shop holds all sorts of used and rare books, with fine selections on Boston and New England and a wealth of autographs and photo albums. The resilient store has risen from the ashes of two fires and relocated numerous times. Treasures have passed through these portals, including a well-read copy of *The Great Gatsby* given by F. Scott Fitzgerald to T. S. Eliot and containing Fitzgerald's misspelled inscription and Eliot's annotations. Peruse the outdoor racks, where you'll be under the watchful eyes of 18 influential authors (from Leo Tolstoy to Gish Jen) painted by South End artists Jeffrey Hull and Sarah Hutt. Valuable volumes are appraised here and helpful staff members are book sleuths. Two of them are appraisers on PBS's *Antiques Roadshow*. ♦ M-Sa. 9 West St

"Boston," an elision of "Botolph" in St. Botolph's Town, was named after the English Lincolnshire town, which in turn was named for the patron saint of fishing, whose name was derived from *bot* (boat) and *ulph* (help).

(between Washington and Tremont Sts). 542.0210, 800/447.9595; www.brattlebookshop.com &

63 15 WEST STREET

This three-story town house, described as "Mrs. Peabody's caravansary" by Nathaniel Hawthorne, was home to the Peabody family from 1840 to 1854. In the rear parlor, Hawthorne married his beloved Sophia, the Peabodys' youngest daughter, and Mary Peabody wed Horace Mann, the founder of American public education. In the front parlor, headstrong and brilliant Elizabeth Peabody opened Boston's first bookstore selling foreign works. Elizabeth was a fervent abolitionist, an early advocate of kindergartens in America, and the model for the formidable Miss Birdseye in Henry James's novel *The Bostonians*. Here, with Ralph Waldo Emerson, Elizabeth published *The Dial*, the quarterly journal of the Transcendentalists. And each Wednesday local ladies came to hear journalist Margaret Fuller's "Conversations"—landmark lectures in the history of American feminism. These days, the town house is given over to the **West Street Grill** (see below). ♦ Between Washington and Tremont Sts

Within 15 West Street:

WEST STREET GRILL

★★$$ Especially popular with a late-night crowd, this spot offers three levels of dining and drinking. The downstairs bar seats about 15, but there are always plenty of standees here and at the smaller upstairs bar. Among the favorite creations are goat cheese fondue; calamari *fritti* with ginger-spiced cilantro sauce; Old Bay crab cake sandwich; and pizza with Portobello mushrooms, roasted garlic, artichoke hearts, and asiago cheese. ♦ American ♦ M-F, lunch and dinner; Su, dinner. 423.0300

64 SANTACROSS DISTINCTIVE SHOE SERVICE

In business since 1917, this shop will heal your footwear woes. Walk-in repairs, shoe shines, and handbag repairs are done on the premises. Orthopedic shoes are a specialty here. ♦ M-Sa, 7:30AM-4:45 PM. 151 Tremont St (between Avery and West Sts). 426.6978 &

65 OPERA HOUSE

The 1928 Opera House has been restored to its 1920s grandeur after years, beginning in

---

1991, of being shuttered. This grand show-place now offers a variety of visiting performers, music, time-tested Broadway shows—some quite enjoyable—and popular local productions like *The Nutcracker*. The Opera House shows what historic theaters should be, although you might need a tele-scope to see the stage from the upper balcony and the cheap seats.

The Opera House and the 1932 **Paramount Theater** next door were designated for preservation on the National Registry of Historic Places. The area's renewal is shown most notably in the 2002 opening of the 1.8-million-square-foot **Ritz-Carlton Hotel and Towers**, adjacent to the Paramount. Emerson College and the city agreed in 2005 to rede-velop the Paramount, vacant since 1976, and nearby properties into an Emerson-run performing arts center and student housing. But few things are sure in Boston's realty world, especially deals involving small, old theaters.

The Opera House was first named the B.F. Keith Memorial Theatre to honor the show-biz wizard who coined the term "vaudeville." Keith introduced performances of high-quality variety acts for family viewing to contrast with the low-life entertainment offered at Scollay Square's notorious Old Howard Theater. He owned 400 theaters, after which movie "picture palaces" were modeled. This one was called the Savoy Theatre. Later it was home to Sarah Caldwell's Boston Opera Company. The Spanish Baroque terra-cotta façade is best seen from Avenue de Lafayette across the way. ◆ 539 Washington St (between Avery St and Harlem Pl). 880. 2442. ♿ (Up-front seats for visually and hearing-impaired patrons are available in pairs by request.)

66 PROCTOR BUILDING

On sunny days it's bathed in light and is the preferred perch for many pigeons. On any day, the small Spanish Renaissance–style building, built in 1897 by **Winslow and Bigelow,** is an orchestra of ornament crowned by a tiara-like cornice. Shells, birds, flowers, garlands, cherubs, urns, and more parade across the curving cream-colored façade. ◆ 100-106 Bedford St (at Kingston St)

67 CHURCH GREEN BUILDING

This fine addition to the city's stock of 19th-century granite mercantile buildings is named for **Church Green,** the triangular intersection of Summer, Lincoln, and Bedford Streets, which in turn was named for the lovely **Charles Bulfinch**–designed church that once stood here—just another example of how history haunts many Boston place names. The building was built circa 1873, and though its architect is unknown, it is widely attributed to **Jonathan Preston.** Behind this structure rises red-roofed **99 Summer Street,** a 1987 interloper by **Goody, Clancy & Associates** that tries mightily to fit in. Across the way is **125 Summer Street,** a 1990 building by **Kohn Pederson Fox,** lurking behind an eclectic row of commercial façades now belonging to **No. 125.** A swath of old streetscape has been nicely preserved, but the huge modern tower bursting from its midst is a little disconcerting in contrast. ◆ 105-113 Summer St (at Bedford St)

68 RADIUS

★★★★$$$$ Chef Michael Schlow's much-praised modern French cuisine showcases dishes like seared Maine scallops with wild mushrooms and Vermont pheasant with baby turnips and kumquats. There's fine dining in the circular dining room and a popular, posh after-work bar. ◆ Modern French ◆ M-F, lunch, M-Sa, dinner. Reservations recommended. Valet parking after 5PM. 8 High St (between Federal St and Milton Pl). 426.1234; fax 426.2526; www.radiusrestaurant.com/Clients/Radius. ♿ (with staff assistance)

69 BEDFORD BUILDING

Red granite, white Vermont marble, and terra-cotta blend well on the Ruskinian Gothic-style façade of this 1876 **Cummings & Sears** creation, renovated in 1983 by the **Bay Bedford Company** and placed on the National Register of Historic Places. The proud building lost its original clock, but its stained-glass timepiece (created by Cambridge artisan Lynn Hovey) is particularly striking at night. ◆ 89-103 Bedford St (between Lincoln and Columbia Sts)

70 HYATT REGENCY BOSTON

$$$ Formerly called Swissotel Boston, the 500 rooms and suites on the hotel's 22 floors have been refurbished by the new owner and are more sumptuous and

---

Charles Dickens was one of Boston's greatest admirers. Said Dickens: "Boston is what I would like the whole United States to be." On the other hand, Edgar Allan Poe was perhaps the city's greatest detractor. Poe said he was "heartily ashamed to have been born in Boston" and referred to his native city as "Frogpondium."

Popular illustrations to the contrary, early New Englanders did not dress in black with steeple-crowned hats. They actually preferred bright colors for their clothing, furniture, and wall hangings.

contemporary in décor than the impersonal exterior might imply. Guest services include a concierge, fee parking, a multilingual staff, same-day laundry and valet services, an indoor swimming pool, a steam room, exercise equipment, and two-line phones in all rooms. There are rooms for people with disabilities plus floors for nonsmokers. Pets allowed. There's a lobby bar and the hotel's reasonably priced American-menu restaurant, **Avenue One**. ♦ 1 Ave de Lafayette (at Chauncy St). 912.1234; fax 451.2198; www.regencyboston.hyatt.com

71 RITZ-CARLTON BOSTON COMMON HOTEL

$$$$ Until 2007, Boston had two Ritz-Carltons: the original Ritz at the Public Garden and Newbury Street and this contemporary luxury Ritz across the park in what, years ago, was called the Combat Zone. The old Brahman-Yankee Ritz has become the luxury Taj Boston. This new Ritz, opened in 2001, is part of a project that also contains a 19-screen Loews Boston Common theater complex and a large sports club, spa, fitness, and sports facility with swimming pool. There are 193 guestrooms, including 43 suites at the **Ritz-Carlton Towers** and 300 condominiums. Among the guest perks are large marble soaking bathtubs, separate showers, and original hanging art. Pets accepted with nonrefundable per-animal cleaning fee of $125 per stay, maximum two pets ♦ 10 Avery St (between Washington and Tremont Sts). 574.7100, fax 574.7200, reservations 800-509-5507; www.ritzcarlton.com/hotels/boston_common

Within the Ritz-Carlton Boston Common:

JER-NE

★★$$$$ Pronounced "journey," this attractive, modern-design restaurant on the second floor has a showcase kitchen in the middle of a dual-level dining room. The quality comfort food includes such dishes as filet mignon and Maine lobster tail with turnips and herb butter. A lavish Sunday brunch offers children's portions. There's also a casual-attire cocktail lounge in the lobby, next to a large fireplace, for drinks or afternoon tea (reservations required for tea). The **JER-NE bar** is on the street level (12 Avery Street or through the hotel lobby) and offers a light menu. A steel-and-textured-glass winding staircase leads from the bar to the restaurant. ♦ Contemporary American ♦ Daily, breakfast, lunch, and dinner; Su, brunch.

72 TEATRO

★★★$$$ The vaulted ceiling in the dining room could produce feelings of eating in a museum, but the heavenly pastas, Northern Italian rustic entrées, and sophisticated thin-crust pizzas are absolutely first-rate. Popular with diners bound for nearby theaters. ♦ Italian Rustic ♦ Dinner; closed W-Th. dinner. 177 Tremont St (between Boylston and Avery Sts). 778.6841; www.teatroboston.com

CHINATOWN/THEATER DISTRICT

This checkered neighborhood's story has had many acts, characters, triumphs, and tribulations over the years. Here, in a geographically awkward and angular fringe of the city, three principal dramatis personae converge and sometimes collide: the **Theater District**, what used to be called the **Combat Zone** (Boston's old red-light district), and **Chinatown**.

Beginning in the 1920s, Boston was a favorite tryout city for Broadway-bound plays, a glittering, glamorous place when all the big stage names were in town. After movies outstripped theater in popularity and suburbs swelled, playhouses like the **Wilbur** and the **Majestic** deteriorated. As roofs leaked, walls crumbled, and paint and plaster peeled, the shadow of the wrecking ball loomed. But Boston's 1980s boom, known as the "Massachusetts Miracle," rescued a number of theaters. The small Wilbur was repaired and has hosted such hits as *Stomp* and *The Vagina Monologues*, the **Shubert** was refurbished and has touring Broadway shows, the Cutler Majestic was resuscitated and renamed the **Emerson Majestic**, and the **Colonial** shines. Today, Boston's rialto is clustered around Tremont and Stuart Streets.

The once-sleazy Combat Zone, an "adult entertainment" district concentrated on lower Washington Street, doesn't really exist anymore. It flourished during the pre-Internet, pre-DVD 1970s as home to X-rated movie houses and dozens of strip joints, peep shows, and porn shops. All over the country, many strip clubs have morphed into upscale "gentlemen's clubs" that are more expensive, if no less tacky. Rising real-estate prices, neighborhood-association pressure, and cultural change have strangled the old Zone, reducing it from seven blocks to a few doorways. Shady sorts can still hang out here, however, so it's still not safe late at night.

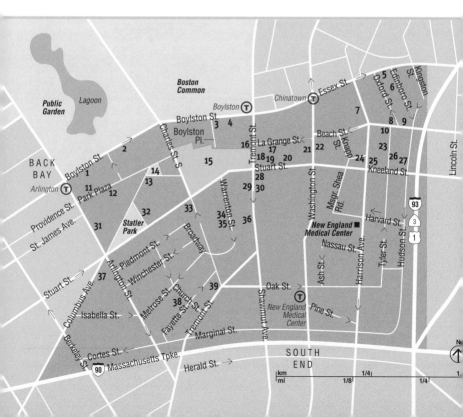

Chinatown's official entry point is a massive **ceremonial gateway** on Beach Street, but pedestrians approach this quarter from every which way. Bounded by Interstate 93 and Washington, Kneeland, and Essex Streets, this four-block-wide neighborhood is known for its restaurants and colorful storefronts. Cramped it may be, but Chinatown is always full of activity, and exudes a festive ambience with subtitled signs and banners and pagoda-topped phone booths. Popular events are **Chinese New Year** and the **August Moon Festival,** when local martial-arts groups don dragon costumes and dance through the streets amid exploding firecrackers and crowds. Jammed into these dense blocks are more than 100 restaurants (some open as late as 4AM), bakeries, gift and curio shops, and markets selling live poultry, fresh fish, and vegetables. The remains of the textile and garment industry (Chinatown's economic mainstay before restaurants and grocery wholesalers took the lead) are located where Harrison Avenue intersects Kneeland Street. **Tyler Street** is the showiest thoroughfare, with the most flamboyant storefronts, while **Beach Street** harbors the workaday scene.

Chinatown is struggling to preserve its ethnic character. The first Chinese came to Boston soon after the Revolution. The subsequent China trade brought workers to the seaport, but a permanent community wasn't established until 1875, when laborers were imported to break a shoe-industry strike. With liberalization of immigration laws in the mid-1960s, Chinatown ballooned, but then lost half its land to highway expansion, downtown encroachment, and the **New England Medical Center.** Today, the population has swelled, with Vietnamese, Laotians, and Cambodians enriching the ethnic composition.

Bursting at the seams, troubled by refuse-strewn streets, and demoralized by proximity to the then crime-ridden Combat Zone and a lack of affordable housing, not long ago Chinatown faced a grim future. In recent years, however, there have been signs of change. A Neighborhood Council now acts as liaison to the mayor's office and reviews plans for development; in fact, little happens in Chinatown without the council's involvement. A denouement to the neighborhood drama is an urban megadevelopment called the **Midtown Cultural District,** restoring historic theaters, ensuring Chinatown's prosperity and the New England Medical Center's growth, and boosting downtown nightlife in the two-square-mile, mixed-use community of office towers, department stores, hotels, restaurants, clubs, and cultural space. It encompasses Park Square, the Theater District, the old Combat Zone, and Downtown Crossing (the intersection of Washington Street and Winter/Summer Streets). **Emerson College** relocated dormitories from Kenmore Square to the Little Building next to the Colonial theater at Boylston and Tremont, in what was the Combat Zone.

In the midst of these changes, Chinatown and the Theater District will undoubtedly remain the places to go in Boston for great performances in gorgeous old theaters, Asian culture and cuisine, and innovative meals in sophisticated restaurants.

---

1 THE HERITAGE ON THE GARDEN

One of Boston's more accommodating architectural presences is this mixed-use complex of retail and commercial space and luxurious residential condos designed by The Architects Collaborative in 1988. A number of upscale shops and restaurants are located on the premises (albeit with confusingly varied street addresses), including **Sonia Rykiel Boutique** (280 Boylston St, 426.2033), **Villeroy & Boch** (288 Boylston St, 542.7442), **Escada** (308 Boylston St, 437.1200), and **Hermès** (320 Boylsoton St, 482.8707). ♦ 300 Boylston St (between Hadassah Way and Arlington St) &

Within The Heritage on the Garden:

Le Pli at the Heritage

Six kinds of massage, facials, body wraps, manicures, aerobics classes, and pampering for your body, skin, or hair are available to the public (for a fee) at this ultrachic and expensive European-style spa/health club/salon. Only the workout facilities and the three-lane lap pool are limited to members or guests of member hotels. Plenty of special packages with the works are available, some including hotel accommodations and food. Schwartz/Silver Architects designed the pristine interior, collaborating with artist Stephen Knapp. The same owners operate **Le Pli spa** in Cambridge (547.4081). ♦ 28 Arlington St. Spa 426.6999, salon 482.2424

2 Four Seasons Hotel Boston

$$$$ Half of the 288 rooms and the restaurants at this luxurious hostelry feature views of the lovely Public Garden. Celebrities who have stayed in the posh Presidential Suite include Bruce Springsteen, Glenda Jackson, Luciano Pavarotti, and John Williams. Maybe they like the friendly and solicitous staff or the hotel's concern for niceties. Every child's crib is equipped with a teddy bear, and kids get bedtime milk and cookies and kits with cameras or magic tricks. The concierge distributes duck and squirrel treats for feeding park denizens, and the hotel will pack picnic baskets for guests on request. For joggers, a pair of running shoes is provided, with maps outlining trails that start outside the front door. Accommodations are on eight floors, with special rooms for people with disabilities and rooms for nonsmokers. Additional amenities include concierge services, around-the-clock room service, same-day laundry and 24-hour valet and pressing services, valet parking, and business services. The health spa has a lap pool, Jacuzzi, sauna, and on-call trainers. ♦ 200 Boylston St (between Charles St S and Hadassah Way). 338.4400, 800/332.3442 in the US, 800/268.6282 in Canada; fax 426.9207. www.fourseasons.com/boston &

Within the Four Seasons Hotel:

AUJOURD'HUI

Aujourd'hui

★★★$$$$ A refined setting for an elegant meal—and an expensive one: Aujourd'hui has a reputation as the most expensive restaurant in Boston—this restaurant is the most pleasant when light lingers in the Public Garden beyond (be sure to reserve a window-side table). The acclaimed menu is complemented by a lengthy international wine list. Specialties range from Mediterranean and classic French cuisine to regional American favorites. Among the potential offerings are juniper-roasted venison chop with sweet potato and turnip cake and cider-glazed chard; Maine lobster with spicy Thai ginger sauce, crusty potato wonton, and snow peas; and red-pepper pasta with marinated vine-ripened tomato, basil olive oil, and garlic. Reduced-calorie and sodium- and cholesterol-free dishes are also available. Local designers and shops are featured at lunchtime fashion shows Tuesdays (September through June). Theatergoers pressed for time may opt for the prix-fixe pretheater menu. For a cozy party, reserve one of two private dining rooms. ♦ Continental ♦ M-F, breakfast, lunch, and dinner; Sa, breakfast and dinner; Su, brunch and dinner. Jacket and tie requested at dinner. Reservations recommended. Valet parking available. 451.1392 &

The Bristol Lounge

★★$$ Pick one of the discretely positioned clusters of chairs and sofas for lunch, afternoon tea, cocktails, before- or after-theater supper, or dessert (there's a lush Viennese dessert table from 9PM to midnight on Friday and Saturday). A children's menu is offered. Pianists provide classical music and soft jazz in the afternoon and evening. A fireplace warms the place during the cold winter months, and afternoon tea is served daily from 3 to 4:30PM. ♦ Continental ♦ Daily. Reservations recommended for lunch. 338.4400 &

ADESSO

Adesso

The owners bring up-to-the-moment furniture and lighting from France, Italy, Germany, Holland, and Austria (and some from the US). Called "new classics" by the store, these smashing, versatile pieces are often architect-designed and may be available only to the trade in other cities. They'll ship anywhere. ♦ M-Sa; Th until 8PM. 451.2212 &

3 Boylston Place

Located off Boylston Street along Piano Row, this pedestrian cul-de-sac reputedly was where football was born in 1860, when a student of Mr. Dixwell's Private School organized the first game. The rubber sphere used for a ball is in the Society for the Preservation of New England Antiquities' collections. Enter via a fanciful arch with theatrical and local allusions, and pass through a phalanx of nightspots popular with a young, partying crowd, such as **Sugar Shack** (No. 1, 351.2510), **Envy** (No. 2, 423.3832), and **The Big Easy** (see below). At the end, a pedestrian passage leads through the Transportation Building to Stuart Street, a handy shortcut. www.alleyboston.com

On Boylston Place, also known as The Alley:

THE BIG EASY

This two-story, Cajun-theme playhouse with a spacious dance floor (that gets mobbed) is one of the city's most popular dance and party spots. A DJ spins a mix of Top 40 and rock 'n' roll burners to a crowd that tends to be upscale, generally ranging in age from mid-20s to mid-40s. ◆ Cover. F, Sa. No sneakers or ripped jeans. No one under 21 admitted. Valet parking on weekends. No. 1. 351.7000 ᕴ

ALLEY CAT

This club hosts bachelorette parties, karaoke, hip-hop, pop-radio promotions, comedians, and young patrons singing and dancing, and dancing some more. Guests get a free pass into the Big Easy. ◆ Cover charge. Th-Sa. 351.7000; www.alleycatboston.com

SWEETWATER CAFE

$ When you want to be casual and anonymous, try this laid-back, cheap-eats place for big portions of items like burger baskets, steak tips, and gravy fries. There are Thursday-night concerts and Tuesday-night trivia. There's a bar on the second level, but the downstairs has booths. Jukeboxes—one stocked with old 45s—crank out tunes. You can eat outdoors in nice weather. ◆ American ◆ Daily, dinner until 2AM. No. 3. 351.2515

THE TAVERN CLUB

Don't knock. This exclusive private club, which barred women until the late 1980s, has resided since 1887 in three quaint brick row houses built in the early to mid–19th century. For generations the club has been famed for its private performances of outrageous plays starring club members. ◆ Nos. 4-6. 338.9682

3 GYPSY BAR

$$ Formerly known as Pravda 116, this plush dance club retains the 30-meter bar and often attracts a Euro crowd (especially Wednesdays) partying under low lighting. It's more upscale, better dressed, and older (mid-20s to mid-30s) than some nearby college-age clubs. Restaurant on premises. ◆ $10 admission after 10PM. Club W-Sa, 10PM-2AM; restaurant 5PM-2AM. 116 Boylston Pl (at Boylston St). 482.7799

4 COLONIAL THEATRE

Built in 1900, the most grand theater in Boston is also one of the most handsome in the country. Actually, this is a very uncolonial-style structure, a 10-story office building with a theater tucked in. It does, however, brim with classical ornament, gilded and mirrored. H.B. Pennell's interiors feature glittering chandeliers, lofty arched ceilings, sumptuous frescoes and friezes, and allegorical figures. Yet the 1,658-seat theater is also intimate and comfortable, with excellent sight lines and acoustics. Architect **Clarence H. Blackall**'s other local credits include the nearby **Wilbur Theater** and **Metropolitan Theater** (now the Wang Center), as well as the **Winthrop Building** downtown. Thankfully, Blackall and Pennell's masterpiece has been lovingly preserved.

The Colonial books major productions, often musicals, many on their way to (or from) Broadway. In the theater's years in business, Flo Ziegfeld, Irving Berlin, Rodgers and Hammerstein, Bob Fosse, and Tommy Tune have launched shows here. Ethel Barrymore, Frederic March, Helen Hayes, Katharine Hepburn, Henry Fonda, Fred Astaire, Eddie Cantor, W.C. Fields, the Marx Brothers, Will Rogers, Danny Kaye, and Barbra Streisand have trod the boards. 106 Boylston St (between Tremont St and Boylston Pl). 426.9366 ᕴ (There are no elevators, but the main floor is wheelchair accessible. Wheelchair seats, at the rear of the orchestra, are half price. Full-price seats for visually and hearing-impaired patrons, typically located in front of the theater, are held for special-needs patrons. They are sold only in pairs.)

4 BOYLSTON STREET

The slice of this thoroughfare facing Boston Common was once known as Piano Row for its concentration of piano-making and music-publishing establishments—enterprises in which music-loving Boston led the nation during the 19th and early 20th centuries. Only one firm is left. The **Wurlitzer Company** (now in Nashville as a division of Gibson Musical Instruments) was at No. 100, with its elegant, elaborate storefront designed by **Clarence H. Blackall;** the building is also home to the **Colonial Theatre.** M. Steinert & Sons (426.1900), authorized dealer for the **Steinway Piano Company,** has been in the Beaux Arts-style No. 162 since 1896, when it was designed by **Winslow and Bigelow.** Steinert Hall, called America's oldest music retail location, houses the corporate offices, recital space, a piano repair and restoration

Chinatown—originally composed of tents—was born when Chinese workers were imported from the West to break a shoe-industry strike in the 1870s.

Restaurants/Clubs: Red | Hotels: Purple | Shops: Orange | Outdoors/Parks: Green | Sights/Culture: Blue

SIGHTS FOR SORE EYES

Whether you see them at ground level while on foot, boat, or bike, or from above, maybe while you're dining, the views in and of Boston are among the great pleasures of the city.

To see Boston at its best, go beyond its borders to the Cambridge side of the Charles River. From **Harvard Bridge** on Memorial Drive, look toward the Royal Sonesta Hotel; you'll be gratified by a stunning view of Back Bay, Beacon Hill, and the gleaming gold-domed State House, with Downtown and the Financial District's skyline behind. Late afternoon offers the best lighting.

For far-reaching views from high above Boston, try the **Prudential Tower** (800 Boylston St, between Exeter and Dalton Sts, 236.3318), in the heart of Back Bay.

Downtown, there's a heart-stopping view from the **Custom House Tower,** now **Marriott's Custom House** (3 McKinley Sq, between Central and State Sts, 310.1600), and from the **Bay Tower Room** (60 State St, at Congress St, 723.1666), where there's dining and dancing. In Cambridge, stop in at the **Spinnaker Italia,** the region's only revolving restaurant, high atop the Hyatt Regency Cambridge (575 Memorial Dr, at Amesbury St, 492.1234, 800/233.1234).

If you're up to the climb to the top of the **Bunker Hill Monument** in Charlestown, you'll be rewarded with a fine view of Boston. If you find your way to **Castle Island** in South Boston, walk by the harbor to view the traffic in Boston Harbor's main shipping lane, planes landing at Logan International Airport, and the harbor islands. Even Boston's **subway system** offers a view—between the Charles/MGH and Kendall stops on the MBTA Red Line, the subway car rises aboveground to cross the Charles River, and offers terrific views.

shop, a piano classroom, private piano and voice studios, and four floors of showrooms. Nearby Boston Organ and Piano closed in 2005 to concentrate on suburban locations.

While you're on this stretch, look for the **Little Building,** No. 80, a 1916 commercial edifice designed by Blackall's firm with a Gothic-influenced terra-cotta façade, now part of Emerson College. Then cross Tremont Street to see No. 48, the eye-catching Ruskinian Gothic **Young Men's Christian Union of 1875,** by **Nathaniel J. Bradlee,** listed on the National Register of Historic Places.

A few steps farther is the **Boylston Building,** an 1887 edifice designed by **Carl Fehmer,** architect of many Boston office buildings and homes, including the grandiose **Oliver Ames Mansion** in Back Bay. It's now home to the China Trade Center, an office/ arcade complex, and is on the National Register of Historic Places. The Boston Architectural Team carved out an appealing atrium, decorated with a mosaic walkway and wall plaque by Lilli Ann and Marvin Rosenberg, elucidating the Chinese lunar zodiac. Several food shops are on the premises, and on some afternoons actors perform on a small stage in the atrium's well. ♦ Between Washington St and Charles St S

5 CHAU CHOW CITY

★★$ Imagine three floors of delightful Cantonese food, what one local critic calls three floors of seafood heaven. Unless you come off-hours, count on a busy place. Arriving before 11AM is the trick for otherwise crowded Saturday and Sunday dim sum brunch. The dim sum sessions are especially popular with groups of people who like to share a bit of this and a bit of that. The Chau Chow restaurants are owned by the same people who operate the very successful Super 88 Asian-food supermarkets that have spread throughout the Boston area. ♦ Cantonese/Seafood, 83 Essex St (between Oxford and Edinboro St). 338.8158

6 MOON VILLA

$ By no means the romantic place its name implies, this hangout for hungry night owls serves family-style Cantonese dishes while the rest of the city snoozes. For dim sum, however, you have to come Saturday or Sunday during the day. The waiters tend to be brusque. ♦ Chinese/Take-out ♦ Daily, lunch and dinner until 4AM. 15-19 Edinboro St (between Kingston and Essex Sts). 423.2061

7 NORTH END FABRICS

Not only is the largest selection of fake "fun furs" around offered here—great for a come-as-you-were-half-a-million-years-ago party—but there's just about everything else in the way of fabrics you could possibly want. Professional dressmakers, designers, and home sewers all frequent this shop, around now for some 40 years. ♦ M-Sa. 31 Harrison Ave (between Beach and Essex Sts). 542.2763

8 YAN'S BEST PLACE

★★$ Yan's is a gem that stands out from the crowd. It's a well-appointed storefront offering authentic Cantonese, Szechuan, and Hong Kong cuisine. The food is inexpensive, tasty, and served in good-sized portions, and almost everything is several cuts above the norm. ◆ Chinese/Takeout ◆ Daily, lunch and dinner until 4AM. 52 Beach St (between Oxford St and Harrison Ave). 338.6223

9 IMPERIAL SEAFOOD RESTAURANT

★$ Right at the gateway to Chinatown, this noisy, cavernous restaurant is a good choice for its second-floor dim-sum parlor, where a fleet of carts laden with arrays of little treats—pork dumplings, shrimp balls, bean curd, stuffed meat buns, braised chicken's feet, and so forth—whiz past the packed tables. Point to your selection and it's whisked onto your table. Usually crowded, the tearoom attracts a mixed clientele. There's often a short wait. Downstairs, order traditional Cantonese dishes from the regular menu. ◆ Chinese/Takeout ◆ M-Th, Su, breakfast, lunch, and dinner until 3AM; F, Sa, breakfast, lunch, and dinner until 4AM. Reservations recommended for large parties at dinner. 70-72 Beach St (between Kingston and Oxford Sts). 426.8439 &

10 C.W.H. COMPANY

Step inside this small neighborhood grocery store for plenty of local flavor. Stock up on everything from herbs and candies to freshwater and vacuum-packed dried fish. Also available are large selections of tea, rice, noodles, and frozen items, including Peking raviolis. ◆ Daily. No credit cards accepted. 55 Beach St (at Tyler St). 426.3619

10 GRAND CHAU CHOW SEAFOOD

★★$ For the price, you can't do better. The seafood is out of this world, but the bill isn't. Try the delicate steamed striped bass with ginger, the spicy fried salted squid, or a plate of sizzling noodles with seafood. Presentation and service here are outstanding. ◆ Chinese ◆ Daily lunch and dinner. Reservations recommended. 45 Beach St (between Tyler St and Harrison Ave). 292.5166

11 VIA MATTA

★★★$$ There's a see-and-be-seen atmosphere here. Simple ingredients are elegantly prepared, and don't miss the desserts. Patrons can choose the large dining room, a casual café with a lighter menu, the popular bar, or the outdoor patio, though there's not much to see. ◆ Italian ◆ M-F, lunch and dinner; Sa, dinner. Valet parking. 79 Park Plaza (across from the **Boston Park Plaza Hotel**). 422.0008; www.viamattarestaurant.com &

12 BEN & JERRY'S ICE CREAM

This franchise dishes up delicious ice cream, shipped from the Vermont factory. Chocolate Chip Cookie Dough, Coconut Milk Chocolate Almond, and Cappuccino Chocolate Chunk are among the perennial favorites. All flavors are available in sundaes, shakes, cones, and ice-cream cakes, as well as between brownies and cookies. Coffee and muffins baked on the premises are sold in the morning until they run out. ◆ Daily. No credit cards. 20 Park Plaza (between Columbus Ave and Arlington St). 426.0890 & Also at 174 Newbury St (between Dartmouth and Exeter Sts), Back Bay. 536.5456

13 MAGGIANO'S LITTLE ITALY

★★$$$ This is one of the better local incarnations of a national chain. Seating 230 people on two floors in six rooms, it's a big restaurant with big portions, red-checkered tablecloths, and good service. The North End has more authentic Italian cuisine, but this is a convenient location. Children's menu available. ◆ Italian-American ◆ Daily, lunch, and dinner. 4 Columbus Ave. 542.3456

14 THE GREAT EMANCIPATOR

Across the street from the **Boston Park Plaza Hotel** (see page 107) stands a statue Boston could do without. This 1879 hero-worshiping homage to Abraham Lincoln, copied from the Washington original and sponsored by legislator Moses Kimball, portrays the president anointing a kneeling former slave, with the inscription "A race set free / A country at peace / Lincoln rests from his labors." From today's vantage point, the work appears paternalistic. ◆ Park Plaza and Columbus Ave

15 MASSACHUSETTS STATE TRANSPORTATION BUILDING

The architectural firm of **Goody, Clancy & Associates** designed this enormous (it occupies an entire city block) state transportation office complex with the participation of local business, cultural, and neighborhood groups, to relate to the surrounding low-rise brick structures. The redbrick exterior, with asymmetrical cantilevers, is fairly self-effacing. The excitement awaits within, where an atrium with exposed endoskeletal support beams vaults above a pedestrian mall with shops and restaurants. Noontime music concerts entertain lunchtime crowds, and a small art gallery operated by the Artists Foundation adds an avant-garde frisson. ◆ Gallery, Tu-Sa afternoons. Stuart St (between Tremont St and Charles St S)

Within the Massachusetts State Transportation Building:

Rock Bottom

★★$$ Rock Bottom, part of a 15-state restaurant chain, replaced the old Brew Moon here and patrons seem to be quite happy. There's a lot of brass and wood and a variety of good beers. Service is quick and friendly, and the hearty American menu—burgers to steaks to garlic tenderloin—fits with the casual, adult atmosphere. ♦ American ♦ Daily, lunch and dinner. 115 Stuart St. 742.2739 &

16 Emerson Majestic Theatre

Originally famous for its musicals and opera performances, this extravagantly ornate Beaux Arts–style theater, designed by **John Galen Howard** in 1903, was bought in the 1950s by a movie-theater chain that slapped tacky fake materials on top of marble and neoclassical friezes. Emerson College rescued the theater in 1983, spent millions on renovations, and has made it "majestic" once more. The name changed from the Cutter Majestic to the Emerson Majestic. Today the 859-seat multi-purpose performance center serves as a stage for nonprofit groups, including Dance Umbrella, Boston Lyric Opera, the New England Conservatory, and Emerson Stage. Patrons favor the theater for its sense of excitement and inclusion with performers; entertainers like the space for its rococo high style and fine acoustics. This was the first theater in Boston to incorporate electricity into the building's design. ♦ Box office daily. 219 Tremont St (between Stuart and Boylston Sts). 824.8000 &

17 Centerfolds

What would have been called a strip club when this was the old Combat Zone is now a "gentlemen's club." Patrons, if not entertainers, are better dressed. Centerfolds is advertised as Boston's only such gentlemen's club, although a stretch of Route 1, north of the city, has lower-rent versions. ♦ Free buffet, noon-2PM. Amateur nights Tuesdays. ♦ 12 La Grange St (between Washington and Tremont Sts). 292.2600

18 Jack's Joke Shop

Pick out your latest disguise at Harold Bengin's wholesale/retail emporium for tricksters. Or make an impression with a gift from an inventory topping 3,000 items, including backward-running clocks, instant worms, garlic gum, sneeze powder, or the gross but ever-popular severed heads, fake wounds, and worse. Open since 1922 (it's the oldest shop of its type in the US), this is one of the city's more colorful institutions. Halloween is the shop's biggest selling season, naturally, but kids and adults stream in throughout the year for jokes, tricks, magic, novelties, complete costumes, masks, wigs, beards, flags of all countries, and other oddities. Bengin has been there since 1951. ♦ M-Sa. 226 Tremont St (across from the Emerson Majestic Theatre). 426.9640; www.jacksjokes.com &

19 Montien

★★$$ A favorite with theatergoers, businesspeople, and staff from the nearby medical complex, Montien serves classic Thai favorites, plus specials like *kat-thong-tong* (a crisp pastry shell filled with ground chicken, onions, corn, and coriander, with a sweet dipping sauce). The tamarind duck and fried squid are superb. Service is efficient and prompt, so you'll make that curtain. ♦ Thai/Takeout ♦ M-Sa, lunch and dinner; Su, dinner. Reservations recommended for large parties. 63 Stuart St (between Washington and Tremont Sts). 338.5600; www.montien-boston.com. Also in Inman Square, Cambridge (1287 Cambridge St), 868.1240; www.montiencambridge.com &

20 Jacob Wirth

★$$ This restaurant serves hearty traditional German fare—bratwurst, knockwurst, sauerbraten, and sauerkraut, accompanied by heady, specially brewed dark beer—as it has since opening in the same bowfront row house in 1868. The 1845 house is on the National Register of Historic Places, and the furniture and fixtures—globe lighting, brass rails, dark paneling—are original. The cavernous beer hall is a great place to bring a crowd and sample the long list of lagers. You can get a pitcher of Pabst for $4. Big appetites might attempt the German boiled dinner: pigs' feet, pork roast, ribs, and cabbage. Sing along with piano music on Friday. ♦ German ♦ Daily, lunch and dinner. Patrons offered two hours of parking at the adjacent lot. 37 Stuart St (between Washington and Tremont Sts). 338.8586, www.jacobwirth.com &

21 Hayden Building

Modest-sized and easily overlooked, this 1875 office building at the head of LaGrange Street isn't one of **Henry Hobson Richardson**'s finer works, but it displays his characteristically vigorous Romanesque Revival approach. The building is on the National Register of Historic Places and is on what was once a thriving mercantile stretch with hatters, tailors, shoemakers, and such. ♦ 681 Washington St (at La Grange St)

22 Penang

★★★$$ Malaysian cooking is a hit in Boston, and this restaurant, like **Tiger Lilly** near **Symphony Hall,** provides some of the best. Think Thai or Vietnamese cooking, only with richer flavors. Try beef *rendang* (which actually

Child's Play

With its parks, waterfronts, and participatory museums, Boston is a city for family sightseeing. Just don't hard-sell the educational/historic sites. (It's usually the adults who romanticize such events as the midnight ride of Paul Revere and the Boston Tea Party.)

USS *Constitution* Board "Old Ironsides," the oldest commissioned ship afloat. Doing so will make you feel like a seafarer—and convince you that life at sea was anything but glamorous.

The Museum of Science It's actually in Cambridge. You can get there by taking the subway (the Green Line T, to Science Park). For older kids, there's the Planetarium, great movies in the wraparound Imax theater, and the shocking—and kind of scary—electricity shows that flash real lightning overhead. Dinosaurs, wave tanks, sophisticated math games, hands-on computer activities, and a casual, child-friendly restaurant area make for a full day of enjoyment.

New England Aquarium Watch creatures of the deep swim round and round in the giant, 187,000-gallon ocean tank. If you're lucky, you'll see SCUBA divers feeding the creatures inside the tank.

Freedom Trail This is truly a fun way of tracing the role of Boston in the American Revolution. The three-mile journey covers 16 sites—remember to wear your athletic shoes!

The Children's Museum *Touch* is the magic word here. The hands-on museum features exhibits such as the Recycle Room, where leftover materials get an artistic makeover. Don't miss the climbing structure for older kids.

The Milk Bottle Refreshment awaits outside the Children's Museum, where a snack stand shaped like a giant milk bottle serves up sandwiches, salads, and ice cream.

Franklin Park Zoo Spend a day in the **African Tropical Forest,** home to more than 150 animals—among them gorillas, leopards, pygmy hippos, and monkeys. Or watch the big cats in the **Kalahari Kingdom** section.

Public Garden Take a ride on a **Swan Boat** or, in winter, a spin on ice skates. Be sure to see the knee-high brass statues of **Mrs. Mallard** and her brood, characters in the children's classic *Make Way for Ducklings*.

originated in Sumatra), a rich, flavorful coconut, lemongrass, and currylike dish of tender beef chunks. Seafood abounds too, and there's beer and wine. ♦ Malaysian ♦ Daily, lunch and dinner. Washington St (between Kneeland and Beach Sts). 451.6373; www.penangusa.com ♿ Also at 57 John F. Kennedy St (Harvard Sq), Cambridge. 234.3988

23 China Pearl

★★$$ It pays to get past the glitz, past the bright reds and golds, for the reliable Cantonese food—and lots of it. The menu is shamelessly long, but the best thing for many visitors is the dim sum. Full bar. Beware: Sunday brunch is mobbed. ♦ Cantonese ♦ Daily, breakfast, lunch, and dinner. 9 Tyler St (between Kneeland and Beach Sts). 426.4388

24 Dong Khanh

★$ Come to this clean and bright establishment for Vietnamese-style fast food, including more than a dozen great noodle-soup dishes. The *bi cuon* (meat rolls) are tasty, as are the fish in spicy soup and assorted barbecue meats with vermicelli. Be daring and try a durian juice drink, made from the Asian fruit that looks like a hedgehog and smells overly ripe but has plenty of fans for its flavor. ♦ Vietnamese ♦ Daily,

breakfast, lunch, and dinner. No credit cards. 83 Harrison Ave (at Knapp St). 426.9410

25 Siam Square

★$ Positioned at Chinatown's edge, Siam Square offers its own distinctive Thai tastes. Lemongrass infuses a dish of steamed mussels; a pepper-garlic sauce spices frogs' legs; the squid *pik pow* is at once spicy and sweet; and Thai seasonings lend a signature kick to *chow foon* (fat noodles). ♦ Thai ♦ Daily, lunch and dinner. 86 Harrison Ave (between Kneeland and Beach Sts). 338.7706

26 Golden Palace

★★$ Many Chinatown restaurants are so innocuous-looking that they're easy to miss, but not this one, which has the fanciest façade around. The main attraction is excellent dim sum—among Boston's best—served daily until 3PM. There's no menu; when the carts roll up, select whatever tidbits strike your fancy in the sea of little plates loaded with dumplings, fried and steamed pastries, and noodle dishes. Try *har gao* (shrimp dumplings), spareribs in black-bean sauce, steamed *bao* (meat-filled buns), *shu mai* (pork dumplings), or curried squid. This sprawling place—aglitz with reds, golds, pinks, and painted and carved dragons—is a noisy neighborhood favorite. People come to

Restaurants/Clubs: Red | Hotels: Purple | Shops: Orange | Outdoors/Parks: Green | Sights/Culture: Blue

eat, not unwind, so the service is hurried and the atmosphere minimal. But the dim sum are piping hot, and there are loads of superior dishes, including abalone and squab treatments. ♦ Chinese/Takeout ♦ Daily, breakfast, lunch, and dinner. Reservations recommended for 10 or more. 14-20 Tyler St (between Kneeland and Beach Sts). 423.4565

27 NEW SHANGHAI

★★★$$ The chef prepares an extraordinary Peking duck; another favorite is scallops with black pepper. Top off the meal with a dessert of banana fritters. It's all served in the sleekest of settings. ♦ Chinese ♦ Daily, breakfast, lunch, and dinner. 21 Hudson St (between Kneeland and Beach Sts). 338.6688

28 WILBUR THEATRE

This distinguished Colonial Revival theater has witnessed its share of dramatic debuts, including the pre-Broadway production of Tennessee Williams's *A Streetcar Named Desire* starring Marlon Brando and Jessica Tandy. Another of Boston's **Clarence H. Blackall** treasures, built in 1914 and now on the National Register of Historic Places, this stage endured dark days and decay; its nadir was a brief (and unsuccessful) stint as a cabaret. But the lights are on again: The proud (but small at 1,200 seats), fan-shaped theater has rebounded and was renovated to accommodate Broadway and Off Broadway–style productions. Rumors forecast its possible future as a comedy club, but nothing like this had happened at press time. Look up at the façade and note the three theatrical masks grinning, grimacing, and agape above the upper windows. Half-price tickets are offered for people with disabilities (plus one companion). ♦ Box office open daily. 246 Tremont St (between Oak and Stuart Sts). 423.4008 &

28 ARIA

$$$ Lavish dance club Aria is so chic, marketed to the beautiful and the international. If you're neither, or only one, wear your most expensive, trendy clothes and a young Eurotrash attitude might get you in to relax on the red couches. Admission. Doors open 10PM or later. ♦ W-Sa. 246 Tremont St (attached to the Wilbur Theater). 338.7080

28 HUB TICKET AGENCY

Located in a trailer parked on a corner, this agency sells sports and theater tickets, including those for events in New York City; Providence, Rhode Island; and Worcester, Massachusetts. Many local performances are sold out well in advance, so call first. The day of the game or performance is a good time to check on last-minute availability. Those who plan ahead should order by mail; the ZIP code

is 02116. ♦ M-F; Sa until noon. 240 Tremont St (at Stuart St). 426.8340; www.hubticket.com

29 SHUBERT THEATRE

In 1910 **Hill, James & Whitaker** designed this refined 1,680-seat theater with a graceful marquee; today it's listed on the National Register of Historic Places. It's part of the famous chain, but has a fine reputation in its own right among both actors and audiences. The illustrious Sir Laurence Olivier, John Barrymore, and Sir John Gielgud performed on this stage, as did Sarah Bernhardt, Mae West, Humphrey Bogart, Ingrid Bergman, Cary Grant, and Helen Hayes. Discounted tickets are offered for persons with disabilities (plus one companion). ♦ Box office open daily. 265 Tremont St (between Charles St S and Stuart St). 482.9393 &

30 THE WANG CENTER FOR THE PERFORMING ARTS

It's worth the ticket price just to see the inside of this former motion-picture cathedral. Predating New York City's Radio City Music Hall, this mammoth entertainment palace, designed by **Blackall, Clapp and Whittemore,** was considered the "wonder theater of the world" when it opened in the Roaring Twenties, built to pack in huge crowds four times daily for variety revues and first-run movies. An architectural extravaganza, the 7-story, 3,800-seat theater boasts a succession of dramatic lobbies bedecked with Italian marble columns, stained glass, bronze detailing, gold leaf, crystal chandeliers, and florid ceiling murals, culminating with the five-story **Grand Lobby.** In the theater's early days, the four ornate lobbies had billiards, Ping-Pong, card parties, and other games to occupy the crowds until the next show got started.

First called the Metropolitan Theater and later the Music Hall, it was expanded by **Jung/Brannen Associates** in 1982, renamed for benefactor An Wang in 1983, and renovated by **Notter, Finegold & Alexander** in 1990 to accommodate a variety of performing arts, including opera, ballet, and Broadway musicals. Additional painstaking restoration work done later brought back more of the auditorium's former splendor and updated its facilities and theater technology. On the National Register of Historic Places, it has one of the world's largest theater stages. For plays, try to get down-front center seats in the orchestra, where the sight and sound are best.

Reduced-rate tickets are available, and many events are free; call to inquire. The theater also brings back a hint of its past history with films shown on one of the world's largest screens. The **Boston Ballet** makes its home here, and visiting companies such as the Alvin Ailey American Dance Theater and the Bolshoi Ballet often perform. The center's Young at Arts educational outreach program involves Boston children in the visual and performing arts through workshops and performances in the theater's lobbies. ♦ 268 Tremont St (between Oak and Stuart Sts). General information 482.9393, Ticketmaster 931.2000; www.wangcenter.org &

31 BOSTON PARK PLAZA HOTEL AND TOWERS

$$$ The elegant lobby is dazzling. Steps away from the theaters and one block from the Public Garden, this 1927 hotel, a member of Historic Hotels of America, has 941 renovated rooms and 22 suites. Décor and room sizes vary considerably: Of special interest are the hotel's "double/double" rooms, featuring two double beds and two baths. All rooms feature individual voice mail; other pluses include a weight room and 24-hour room service. The hotel is nonsmoking, except for half a floor set aside for those who just must. You can order breakfast and check out via video. The 15th floor pampers guests in its 81 rooms and suites with things like a lounge, breakfast and snacks, lots of marble in the baths, and free high-speed Internet access. Within or adjacent to the hotel are restaurants and lounges, including **Finale,** a lovely dessert restaurant. **Swans Court** in the lobby, where Liberace began his career, serves tea and pastries and offers a full bar, and **MJ O'Connor's** pub offers an Irish-themed refuge and a pint. The hotel has international recognition for its Environmental Action Program, which focuses on waste reduction, reuse, and recycling. ♦ 64 Arlington St (between Columbus Ave and Park Plaza). 426.2000; fax 654.1999; www.bostonparkplaza.com

Within Boston Park Plaza Hotel and Towers:

PF CHANG'S CHINA BISTRO

★★$$ Guests often have to wait for a table at this very popular Boston outlet of the PF Chang chain. The food is quite tasty and service is good, although a local critic pointed out that Chang's is best for a group in which not everyone wants Chinese food. Walk a few blocks to Chinatown if you want authentic. ♦ 8 Park Plaza. 573.0821; www.pfchangs.com

WHISKEY PARK

Cindy Crawford's husband, Rande Gerber, opened this high-end bar in 2000. A well-dressed, well-heeled crowd has been happy to pay $10 to $13 per drink in the plush confines ever since. The staff is tight-lipped about celebrity visits, but the prospect is there. No live music but lots of comfortable brown leather, candles, and polish. Hotel guests get priority but must enter through the Arlington Street door with everyone else. ♦ Light dinner menu until 10PM daily. Reservations advised. 54 Arlington St. 542.2286; fax 542.1482 &

McCORMICK & SCHMICK'S SEAFOOD

★★$$ Classic seafood is featured here with a menu that offers more than 40 varieties. Also pasta, poultry, and beef. ♦ Daily, lunch and dinner. Entrance in the hotel or at 34 Columbus Ave, 482.3999; www.mccormickandschmicks.com &

TODD ENGLISH'S BONFIRE

★★$$$ Billed as a steak house with European influences, the restaurant features steak preparations from around the world, with many from Argentina. There's some fine showmanship as you watch your beef being prepared. ♦ Steak house ♦ Daily, dinner. Reservations recommended. 262.3473

32 LEGAL SEA FOODS

★★$$$ "If it isn't fresh, it isn't Legal!" is the slogan at this multistate fleet of seafood restaurants. Many agree, as witnessed by the lines. And this is one place where it's safe to eat raw clams and oysters; every batch is tested at an in-house laboratory. The extensive wine list lives up to the long menu. This is not a spot for lingering conversation, however. They take reservations only for large groups, so there can be a long wait for a table. The dining rooms can get noisy and jammed, and the policy is to bring food to tables when it is ready, so you may get your meal before or after your companions. Still, superb seafood is worth some concessions. If you can't wait or don't like crowds, get your **seafood to go.** ♦ Seafood ♦ Daily, lunch and dinner. 26 Park Pl (off Columbus Ave). 426.4444; www.legalseafoods.com &

Also at Prudential Center, 800 Boylston St (between Exeter and Dalton Sts). 266.6800; Copley Place, 100 Huntington Ave (between Garrison and Dartmouth Sts). 266.7775; Long Wharf, 255 State St (near Quincy Market). 227.3115; on the plaza at the Charles Hotel, with outdoor seating, 20 University Rd (Harvard Sq), Cambridge. 491.9400; 5 Cambridge Center,

---

Restaurants/Clubs: Red | Hotels: Purple | Shops: Orange | Outdoors/Parks: Green | Sights/Culture: Blue

Main St (between Kendall Sq and Fulkerson St). 864.3000. There are also on-the-fly restaurants for travelers at Logan Airport terminal B (568.2811) and C (568.2800)

33 RADISSON HOTEL BOSTON

$$$ This 24-story former Howard Johnson hostelry is conveniently located and features 356 refurbished rooms, two restaurants and a bar, an indoor heated pool, a sauna, a sundeck, room service, and indoor parking with direct access to the hotel. Rooms are available for those with disabilities, as are nonsmoking floors. ♦ 200 Stuart St (at Charles St S). 482.1800, 800/468.3557; fax 451.2750; www.radisson.com/bostonma ♿

Within the Radisson:

RUSTIC KITCHEN BISTRO & LOUNGE

★★$$$ Taking the place of the 57 Restaurant in the fall of 2006, this newest site of the local mini-chain provides tasty, uncomplicated Italian/Mediterranean food in a warm-toned, 250-seat (but comfortable) setting. ♦ Italian ♦ Also in Cambridge and Hingham. ♦ Valet parking or validated self-parking. Daily, lunch and dinner. 423 5700; www.rustickitchen.biz.

33 PIGALLE

★★$$$ There are 54 seats in the dining room (and six in the full-menu bar), yet Pigalle has an intimate, romantic, antique feel. French jazz and cabaret music play softly and the wine list is heavy on Southern France (there's also a selection of good American wines). ♦ Contemporary and Classic French ♦ Daily, dinner. 75 Charles St S (next to the Radisson Hotel). 423.4944; fax 423.6766; www.pigalleboston.com ♿

34 NICK'S ENTERTAINMENT CENTER

A fixture on Boston's entertainment scene that has survived by changing with the times, this spot once had a cabaret/dinner theater, a comedy club, and a sports bar. Now it is home to **Nick's Comedy Stop,** a club featuring local and national comics. ♦ Cover. Shows W, Th, Su, 8:30PM; F, Sa, 8:15, 10:15PM. 100 Warrenton St (between Charles St S and Stuart St). 482.0930; www.nickscomedystop.com

35 CHARLES PLAYHOUSE

The Theater District's oldest playhouse—built by **Asher Benjamin** in 1843, renovated by the Cambridge Seven in 1966, and listed on the National Register of Historic Places—began life as a church and today is a rental facility for private productions, all managed separately. Blue Man Group, with three enig-

matic bald and blue characters, seems destined to last and last. And on Stage II, *Shear Madness*—which opened in 1980—is likely to go on as long as new visitors come to town. It has already made the Guinness Book of Records for longest-running non-musical play. The audience-participation comedy whodunit, set in a beauty salon on Newbury Street in the Back Bay, often stars good local professional actors. The solution to the murder mystery changes nightly, and new improvisations, local color, and topical humor are added continually. ♦ Box office daily; shows Tu-Su. No credit cards accepted at box office. 74-78 Warrenton St (between Charles St S and Stuart St). Stage I 426.6912, Stage II 426.5225, Charge-Tix 542.8511

36 THE TREMONT BOSTON

$$$ Built as the national headquarters for the Benevolent and Protective Order of Elks, this 322-room, 15-floor big-city hotel is now operated by Marriott and has been restored to its 1926 business-travel best, with marble columns, sculpted ceilings, and crystal chandeliers. Guests get complimentary high-speed Internet access and a business center. With the **Wang Center** across the street and theaters all around, the hotel attracts a theater crowd (both casts and spectators). There are nonsmoking rooms and a fitness center, and the Courtyard Café offers break-fast. ♦ 275 Tremont St. 426.1400; fax 482.6730; www.marriott.com ♿

36 THE ROXY

If you want to kick loose, this may be just the place. It's a gorgeous setting for any kind of dancing, but you must have high energy. You can watch the action from any of seven bars or the stunning balcony. There are Latin Saturdays, hip-hop and R&B Fridays, and Chippendale's dancers frequently perform. ♦ Cover. F, Sa, from 10PM. No jeans, T-shirts, or sneakers allowed. 279 Tremont St (between Charles St S and Stuart St). 338.7699; www.roxyplex.com ♿

37 PARK PLAZA CASTLE

The imposing granite "Castle" was built in 1897 by **William G. Preston** as an armory for the First Corps of Cadets, a private Massachusetts military organization founded in 1741 and commanded at one time by John Hancock. The Victorian fortress, now on the National Register of Historic Places, was a social center for prominent Bostonians in the late 1800s, and its luxurious, clubby interior was the site for billiards, fine wine, and the popular Cadet Theatricals. The corps now operates a private military museum in Back Bay. The lofty hexagonal tower, turrets, crenel-lated walls, lancet windows, and drawbridge create the illusion of a strong structure ready for medieval-style combat. But much calmer events transpire at this exhibition and convention center, now owned by the Park Plaza Hotel. Bostonians flock to the **Crafts at the Castle** sale in early December, sponsored by Family Services of Greater Boston. In the castle is **Smith & Wollensky's Seafood** (423.1112; also at Faneuil Hall). Next door, at 162 Columbus Ave (357.1620), is the fine **Grillfish Seafood Restaurant**—built in 1886 as Carter's Ink Factory—which boasts an impressive terra-cotta and brick façade. ♦ 130 Columbus Ave (at Arlington St). For events information, call Boston Park Plaza Hotel's sales office, 426.2000 &

38 BAY VILLAGE

For the flavor of 19th-century Boston, take a 15-minute stroll along this insular nook on Winchester, Church, Melrose, and Fayette Streets. Difficult to find by car and easy to miss on foot, the tight cluster of short streets bordered by diminutive brick houses was mostly laid out during the 1820s and 1830s. Many of the artisans, housewrights, and carpenters who worked

on fashionable Beacon Hill's prestigious residences built their own small homes here. The neighborhood's residents once encompassed other colorful professions: sailmakers, paperhangers, blacksmiths, harness and rope makers, painters, salt merchants, musical instrument makers, and cabinetmakers. **Edgar Allan Poe** was born in a lodging house in the vicinity in 1809; his parents were actors in a stock company playing nearby. Because it's so close to the Theater District, Bay Village gradually acquired a bohemian flavor and spillover nightlife. On Fayette Street, look for brief **Bay Street** with its single house. ♦ Bounded by Charles St S, Broadway, Arlington, Tremont, and Piedmont Sts and Marginal Rd

39 BEACON HILL SKATE

You can rent or purchase Rollerblades, skates, skateboards, and safety equipment here to whiz along the esplanade bordering the Charles River. In winter, you can get ice skates to skim over the Public Garden lagoon while it's vacated by ducks and Swan Boats for the season. ♦ Daily. 135 Charles St S (at Tremont St). 482.7400

DREAMS OF FREEDOM CENTER

The 2000 census showed that Boston has become a minority-majority city, although many of the newest immigrant and ethnic groups have yet to gain substantial political power. The Dreams of Freedom Center celebrates Boston's immigrant history—Irish and the many others—in multimedia exhibits that include a moving gangplank, passport stations, talking walls, photo exhibits, and immigrant memorabilia. Kennedy family patriarch Patrick Kennedy is represented, along with Ben Franklin (who was born on the site of the center), anarchists Sacco and Vanzetti, and other famous immigrants. ♦ Admission charge. 1 Milk Street,

across from Old South Meeting House, adjacent to Famine Memorial (At Milk and Washington Sts). 338.6022. www.dreamsoffreedom.org &

A map of the Irish Heritage Trail is available at Dreams of Freedom Center and at the Boston Commons and Prudential Center visitor centers. You can see a calendar of special activities relating to the Irish of Massachusetts at the website www.irishmassachusetts.com/events.html. There's also a valuable research resource on many immigrant ethnic groups and Boston neighborhoods at www.bostonfamilyhistory.com.

BACK BAY

Boston's sumptuous centerpiece of illustrious institutions and architecture is also the best place in the city for extravagant shopping sprees and leisurely promenades. Back Bay attracts a stylish international crowd that's as fun to look at as any of Newbury Street's artful windows. It is also a comfortable, compact neighborhood of gracious streets bordered by harmonious four- and five-story Victorian town houses. Its residents are well-to-do families, established professionals, footloose young people, and transient students for whom the **Public Garden** is an outdoor living room and the **Charles River Esplanade** a grassy waterside backyard.

In the 19th century Boston's wealthy old guard and brash new moneymakers together planted this garden of beautiful homes and public buildings, creating a cosmopolitan, Paris-like quarter wrapped in an aura of privilege and prosperity. The lingering mystique has even tricked some Bostonians into believing Back Bay is one of the city's oldest neighborhoods, when it's really one of the youngest. What began as Boston's marshy wasteland was transformed in the late 1800s into its most desirable neighborhood by a spectacular feat of urban design.

In the 1850s Boston boasted a booming population and exuberant commercial growth. Railroads and manufacturing supplanted the sea as the city's primary source of capital. The nouveaux riches were hungry for spectacular domiciles, but the almost waterbound city was already overcrowded on its little peninsula. The problem: Where to get land? In 1814 a mile-and-a-half-long dam had been built from the base of Beacon Hill to what is now Kenmore Square to harness the Charles River's tidal flow and power a chain of mills. The scheme failed, and the acres of water trapped by the dam became a stagnant, stinking, unhealthy tidal flat called Back Bay. This became the unlikely site that developers clamored to fill with daring urban design schemes. To do so, land had to be reclaimed from the water by an ambitious landfill program.

Meanwhile, design work began. Inspired by the Parisian boulevard system Baron Haussmann had built for Emperor Louis Napoleon, architect **Arthur Gilman** proposed Back Bay's orderly layout. Starting at the Charles River, the principal east–west streets are Beacon Street, Marlborough Street, Commonwealth Avenue, Newbury Street, and Boylston Street, all intersected by eight streets named alphabetically after English peers (from Arlington Street to Hereford Street). Sixteen-foot-wide public alleys, originally designed for service and deliveries, interlace these blocks and provide access to the rear of buildings. Gilman's rational grid remains a startling departure from Old Boston's labyrinthine tangles.

In 1857 the landfill wave began its sweep across the marshland block by block, from Arlington Street at the Public Garden's western edge toward Fenway. As soon as a lot was ready, another architectural beauty debuted. By the time the wave subsided in 1890, 450 acres and more than 1,500 new buildings had been added to the 783-acre peninsula. Gone was the eyesore; in its place was a charming neighborhood of the same name. Completed in just 60 years, Back Bay is an extraordinary repository of Victorian architectural styles, perhaps the most outstanding in America. As an urban design scheme, it was surpassed in its era only by Pierre Charles L'Enfant's plan for Washington, DC.

The newborn Back Bay became Boston's darling, a magnificent symbol of civic pride and the city's coming of age. No Puritan simplicity or provincialism here. Affluent Boston had learned how to stage a good show, from **Copley Square**'s lofty cultural monuments to **Commonwealth Avenue**'s architectural revue of fancy brickwork, stained glass, cut granite, ornate ironwork, gargoyles, and other European conceits. In Back Bay's golden hours, the city's leading financiers, authors, industrialists, artists, architects, and legendary Brahmins lived here. But as the city's economy soured late in the 19th century, the ostentatious single-family dwellings were gradually converted to more modest uses. Though Back Bay's shining moments as a residential district faded after the Great Depression, the neighborhood has resiliently adapted to 20th-century incursions of shops, offices, and apartments. Beginning in the 1980s with the emergence of condominium conversion, it has become regentrified.

1 THE GIBSON HOUSE MUSEUM

Façades can only reveal so much, so here's your best chance to peer into family life during Back Bay's early years. Three generations of Gibsons lived in decorous luxury in this Victorian residence, one of the neighborhood's oldest. It was built in 1860 for Catherine Hammond Gibson and bequeathed nearly a century later to the Victorian Society in America by her grandson Charles, to be made into a museum enshrining his family's life and times. It's not much to look at on the outside, but the interior is a six-story repository of perfectly preserved Victoriana. The Gibsons' ghosts would be content to wander through their dim rooms (sunshine was considered "common" then), still crowded with the ornaments, overstuffed furniture, fixtures, keepsakes, and curios they amassed and passed down to one another. The tour includes the kitchen, laundry, and other service areas, giving visitors a full portrait of daily life at the Gibson home. ♦ Admission. Tours W-Su afternoons May-Oct; Sa-Su afternoons Nov-Apr. Groups of 12 or more by appointment only. 137 Beacon St (between Arlington and Berkeley Sts). 267.6338; www.thegibsonhouse.org

2 GOETHE-INSTITUTE INTER NATIONES, GERMAN CULTURAL CENTER

New England's branch of the Munich-based institute inhabits a 1901 Italian Renaissance Revival building designed by **Ogden Codman.** It was built to house Boston financier Eben Howard Gay's formidable Chippendale and Adams furniture collection, parts of which are now in the Museum of Fine Arts (Gay donated the collection displayed in the MFA's Chippendale Wing). The institute library of more than 5,000 volumes and 40 periodicals and newspapers is open to the public, though only cardholders may check out materials. The institute offers language programs and film series, exhibitions, and other cultural events. ♦ Offices and library M-F. 170 Beacon St (between Berkeley and Clarendon Sts). 262.6050

3 MARLBOROUGH STREET

This peaceful, shady residential street in the midst of the Back Bay is humbler than Commonwealth Avenue, and more picturesque with its brick sidewalks, gaslights, and tidy little black-iron-fenced front gardens. Some houses are still single-family town houses, but the majority have been converted to condominiums. ♦ Between Arlington St and Massachusetts Ave

---

"The Pledge of Allegiance" was written by Francis Bellamy, who lived at 142 Berkeley Street (now known as "The Pledge of Allegiance House").

Fanny Merrit Farmer introduced modern measurements, such as the teaspoon, to American cooking. Her cooking school, founded in 1902, occupied 40 Hereford Street (now the site of condominiums) for years. Farmer's *Boston Cooking-School Cook Book* was a smash hit, and her books are still a staple in kitchens all across America.

3 THE FRENCH LIBRARY AND CULTURAL CENTER

Ever since the dashing young Marquis de Lafayette won Bostonians' hearts during the Revolutionary War, the city has had a special fondness for things French. Since its founding in 1946, Boston's center for French language and culture has grown. Today it has more than 45,000 books and hundreds of CDs, cassettes, records, and periodicals (only members may borrow). A special treat is its collection of *bandes dessinées* (comic books for mature readers), which provide readers with a good workout in idiomatic and colloquial French. The library offers language lessons, lectures, exhibitions, concerts, children's activities, and many other events. Every 14th of July, this block of Marlborough Street is closed for the library's **Bastille Day celebration,** an evening of dining, music, and dancing that Bostonians enjoy with French flair. The library has a cozy reading room and a theater where **French films** are regularly screened. ♦ Tu-Th until 8PM; F, Sa. 53 Marlborough St (at Berkeley St). 266.4351; www.frenchlib.org

4 FIRST AND SECOND CHURCH

The First Church burned down in 1968, but the fire spared some of the 1867 structure (designed by **William R. Ware** and **Henry Van Brunt),** remnants that architect **Paul Rudolph** incorporated into this 1971 hybrid. Rudolph is known for Yale University's School of Art and Architecture. Even using coarse, striated concrete—the material that is his trademark—Rudolph creates poignant connections with the ruined fragments, particularly the square stone tower and rose window. Unitarian Universalist services Sundays at 11AM. ♦ M-F (call first). 66 Marlborough St (at Berkeley St). 267.6730; fscboston.org &

5 FIRST LUTHERAN CHURCH

Entering from Berkeley Street, enjoy a quiet moment in the small landscaped courtyard nestled against this modest brick church, designed by **Pietro Belluschi** in 1959. ♦ 299 Berkeley St (at Marlborough St). 536.8851; www.flc-boston.org

6 COMMONWEALTH AVENUE AND MALL

This expansive street served as Bostonians' first major clue that the new Back Bay wouldn't resemble older mazelike districts. Modeled after Paris's grand boulevards, "Comm Ave"—its undignified, unpunctuated nickname—was the first street of its kind in America, setting a chic French example for the rest of Back Bay to follow. The boulevard is 240 feet wide, with a 100-foot-wide central mall that Winston Churchill deemed one of the world's most beautiful. The avenue is shaded with elm trees and dotted with statues memorializing the famous and forgotten. In spring, when the magnolias are in bloom, it's a pleasant place indeed. This Victorian promenade was once the place for the fashionable to stroll and be seen. Today a more casual collection of Bostonians ambles along, including plenty of dog walkers and young mothers wheeling infants. Before you get to Massachusetts Ave, the avenue boasts block after block of handsome buildings that were once aristocratic town houses but have since become luxury condos, apartments, and headquarters for firms and clubs. Unfortunately, a number of the buildings have had suburban-looking roof decks and unsympathetic stories tacked on, ruining many a graceful roofline. The boulevard's northern, sunny side was the most desirable residential stretch in Back Bay, and many grandly residential showplaces remain. Comm Ave later runs through Kenmore Square, past sprawling **Boston University,** and heads west for distant **Boston College.** But it's most charming closer to the **Public Garden.** ♦ Between Arlington St and Massachusetts Ave

6 BAYLIES-GAMBLE MANSION

In the early 1900s, textile industrialist Walter C. Baylies moved to Boston, married into a wealthy family, and promptly metamorphosed into a full-fledged Brahmin. He tore down an 1861 house to build this showy Italianate mansion (designed by **Thomas and Rice** in 1912), adding a fabulous Louis XIV ballroom for his daughter's debut. A site for glittering society events, the room did its stint of civic service too: Bandages were rolled here during World War I. Since 1941 this has been the home of the **Boston Center for Adult Education.** Many of the mansion's original ornaments and interior finishes remain

untouched. ♦ 5 Commonwealth Ave (between Arlington and Berkeley Sts)

7 HARBRIDGE HOUSE

In 1893 Boston's grande dame and arts patron Mrs. J. Montgomery Sears combined 12 Arlington Street, a formidable five-story French and Italian–style mansion built by **Arthur Gilman** in 1860, with 1 Commonwealth Avenue, creating a small palace to house her art collection and music room. Pianist Ignace Paderewski and violinist Fritz Kreisler visited Mrs. Sears here, as did John Singer Sargent, who executed a portrait of his patron and her daughter at home. Today the building has been broken up into condominiums. Gilman also designed **Arlington Street Church** down the block. ♦ 12 Arlington St (at Commonwealth Ave)

8 CHURCH COURT CONDOMINIUM

In 1978 an up-and-coming young architect named **Graham Gund** caused a furor when he purchased the burnt-out shell of Mount Vernon Church for commercial development, but this elegant amalgam—with a clerestory topped by sculptor Gene Cauthon's ethereal bronze angel—set a brave standard for creative reuse. ♦ 490 Beacon St (at Massachusetts Ave). 353.0971

9 OLIVER AMES MANSION

The original owner was president of the Union Pacific Railroad, head of the Ames Shovel Manufacturing Company, a philanthropist, owner of the Booth Theatre in New York, and a Massachusetts governor. Naturally, a man like Ames would command Back Bay's biggest mansion. Henry Hobson Richardson prepared a sketch for the house, but it was rejected, and **Carl Fehmer** took over in 1882. Note the frieze panels portraying the activities that occurred in the rooms behind. Now an office building, the mansion served as the longtime headquarters of the National Casket Company. ♦ 355 Commonwealth Ave (at Massachusetts Ave)

10 BURRAGE MANSION

Not all Bostonians were willing to surrender their highfalutin aspirations to fit Back Bay's decorous mold. Certainly not Albert Burrage; his theatrical 1899 limestone mansion simultaneously pays homage to the Vanderbilts' Fifth Avenue mansions and Chenonceaux, the French château on the Loire. A multitude of strange carved figures peer down from and crawl across the highly ornamented façade. Burrage once cultivated orchids in the splendid glass-domed greenhouse at the rear. The mansion is now a luxurious retirement

---

Restaurants/Clubs: Red | Hotels: Purple | Shops: Orange | Outdoors/Parks: Green | Sights/Culture: Blue

home. Peek inside to see how enthusiastically the interior, with its sculpted marble staircase and abundant embellishments, competes with the exterior. ♦ 314 Commonwealth Ave (at Hereford St)

11 NICKERSON HOUSE

Architects **McKim, Mead & White**'s last Back Bay residence offers one monumental gesture in the sweep of its bulging granite bowfront. The 1895 building is a model of chilly restraint, but enjoyed a brief fling as the site of two of Boston's most lavish debutante balls, held by Mrs. Pickman, wife of the house's second owner, for her daughters. It's still a private residence. ♦ 303 Commonwealth Ave (between Gloucester and Hereford Sts)

12 ALGONQUIN CLUB

It would be hard to find a haughtier façade in the city than this one by **McKim, Mead & White,** with its overblown frieze and projecting pair of falcons. The Italian Renaissance Revival palace, built in 1887 for the private club still based here, certainly catches the eye with its self-confident, flamboyant architectural maneuvers. ♦ 217 Commonwealth Ave (between Exeter and Fairfield Sts). www.algonquinclub.com

12 1ST CORPS OF CADETS MUSEUM

Military history buffs won't want to miss this place. Established in 1726, the First Corps of Cadets is one of America's oldest military organizations, and its members have served in most US wars and conflicts. The corps originally acted as bodyguards to the royal governors of the Province of Massachusetts Bay; **John Hancock** served as a colonel in 1774. The museum has extensive displays of armaments dating back to King George II, many of which were brought back from action by corps members. Also featured are flags, uniforms, drums, and paintings. ♦ Free. Tours by appointment only. 227 Commonwealth Ave (between Exeter and Fairfield Sts). 267.1726

13 ADMIRAL SAMUEL ELIOT MORISON STATUE

In Penelope Jencks's statue, the sailor and historian is seated on a rock by the sea, binoculars in hand, dressed in oilskins with a jaunty yachting cap on his head. Notice the coppery lichen on his stony perch, and the sand crabs on the beach below. Smaller rocks are inscribed with quotes from Morison's books, such as, "Dream dreams then write them / Aye, but live them first." Just across the street is the exclusive **St. Botolph Club** (199 Commonwealth Ave), to which Morison belonged. ♦ Commonwealth Mall (between Exeter and Fairfield Sts)

Ames-Webster House

14 AMES-WEBSTER HOUSE

This mansion was built by Peabody and Stearns in 1872 for railroad tycoon and US congressman **Frederick L. Ames.** Its massive pavilion and porte-cochere were added 10 years later by **John Sturgis,** and the whole was renovated in 1969 by the architectural firm **CBT/Childs Bertman Tseckares.** The exterior is impressive enough, with wrought-iron gates, a two-story conservatory, a monumental tower, and a commanding chimney. But inside is the extraordinary grand hall bedecked with elaborately carved oak woodwork. The theatrical staircase ascends toward the skylit stained-glass dome, past murals by French painter Benjamin Constant. There's a compact jewel of a ballroom decorated in celery green and gilt, and delicately proportioned, particularly its "heavens," the balcony where musicians played. Now housing private offices, the building, unfortunately, is no longer accessible to the public. ♦ 306 Dartmouth St (at Commonwealth Ave)

15 WILLIAM LLOYD GARRISON STATUE

In Olin L. Warner's posthumous (1885) rendition, Boston's famed abolitionist looks as though he had been intently reading when the artist interrupted and asked him to pose. The statue suggests a man taut with energy, feigning relaxation, stretching back in his armchair with his books and papers hastily stuffed underneath. His profile is truly memorable. The fiery inscription—"I am in earnest—I will not equivocate. I will not excuse. I will not retreat a single inch, and I will be heard!"—expresses all of Garrison's unquenchable conviction. It's taken from the inaugural manifesto of *The Liberator*, a journal he founded and edited. ♦ Commonwealth Mall (between Dartmouth and Exeter Sts)

16 THE VENDÔME

You'd think the marsh-bottomed Back Bay would sag under the weight of this magnificent monster, a hybrid of **William G. Preston**'s 1871 corner building and **J. F. Ober**'s main building, both renovated in 1975 by **Stahl Bennett**. For 100 years, this was Boston's most fashionable hotel, the only place where Sarah Bernhardt would deign to lay her weary head. Presidents Ulysses S. Grant and Grover Cleveland, John Singer Sargent, Oscar Wilde, Mark Twain, and countless other worthies stayed here as well.

During its heyday, the hotel boasted previously unheard-of luxuries: It was the first public building in the city to have electric lighting, powered in 1882 by a plant Thomas Edison had designed. Every room featured a private bath and fireplace, as well as steam heat. Inevitably, the hotel's glory days passed, and it became a run-down white elephant. In the 1970s the interior décor was obliterated during renovation, and a terrible fire destroyed portions of the roof and building in 1972. (A black granite memorial to the nine firefighters who died in that blaze is located on the Commonwealth Avenue Mall between Clarendon and Dartmouth Streets.) Now a condominium complex, The Vendôme has accepted its comedown as gracefully as possible. To the left at Dartmouth Street is Preston's original structure, forced to play a supporting role to Ober's enormous addition on the right. The duo's conjoining marble façades ripple with ornamentation.
♦ 160 Commonwealth Ave (at Dartmouth St)

Within the Vendôme:

BARLOLA TAPAS LOUNGE

★$$ Operating below street level, BarLola offers cocktails, sangria, and tapas and attracts a younger crowd, but is hardly competition for Spanish places like Dali or Tasca. There's a sunken outside patio on Commonwealth Avenue, and location counts.
♦ Spanish ♦ Daily, dinner; Sa, Su, brunch. Valet parking available. 266.1122; www.barlola.com ♦

17 FIRST BAPTIST CHURCH

Henry Hobson Richardson was just starting to flex his creative muscles when he won the commission for this 1871 pudding-stone church (originally called New Brattle Square Church) in a competition. Its marvelous campanile springs into the air to create one of Back Bay's most striking silhouettes. The belfry's frieze was modeled in Paris by **Frédéric-Auguste Bartholdi,** sculptor of the Statue of Liberty (Bartholdi had a way with drapery), and its scenes depict the sacraments of baptism, communion, marriage, and last rites. Some of the sculpted faces supposedly belong to famous Bostonians, including Hawthorne, Emerson, and Longfellow. Protruding proudly from the corners, the angels' trumpets won the figures the irreverent nickname "The Holy Bean Blowers." Come at sunset to admire their profiles etched crisply against a darkening sky. Unfortunately, the original congregation disbanded and funds ran out, so Richardson's lofty plans for the church interior never came to be. Still home to a Baptist congregation, the church is fairly unremarkable inside, with lots of dark wood. ♦ M-F; Su service 11AM. 110 Commonwealth Ave (at Clarendon St). 267.3148. www.firstbaptistchurchofboston.org

18 THE CAPITAL GRILLE

★★$$$$ Top-grade steak—dry-aged in plain view on the premises—is this upscale restaurant's raison d'être. Straightforward seafood is also served. The décor is modeled after an old-fashioned men's club: lots of dark paneling (lifted from a 16th-century Welsh castle), marble floors, and a long brass bar with private wine lockers. It attracts a prosperous crowd whose business image requires a certain conspicuous consumption.
♦ American ♦ Daily, dinner. Reservations recommended. Valet parking available after 5 PM. 359 Newbury St (between Hereford St and Massachusetts Ave). 262.8900 www.thecapitalgrille.com ♦

18 BHINDI BAZAAR INDIAN CAFÉ

★★$ Good and varied Indian cooking, casual atmosphere, substantial portions, and moderate prices draw students from nearby Berklee College of Music, but the quality attracts fans of all ages and backgrounds. Tulip-shaped lamps, bright colors, big windows, and no buffet table make it feel unlike many local Indian restaurants. Good sauces and selections, wine and beer. ♦ Indian ♦ Daily, lunch and dinner. Metered street parking. 95 Masachusetts Ave (at Newberry St). 450.0660. www.bhindibazaar.com ♦

18 JOHNSON PAINT COMPANY

Look for the sign with bright multicolored stripes and real gold leaf. The Johnson family's business has occupied this former carriage house—where horses owned by wealthy Back Bay residents once slept—for more than 50 years. In addition to selling good old-fashioned paint products (they've carried the same lines of paint since 1936),

---

Restaurants/Clubs: Red | Hotels: Purple | Shops: Orange | Outdoors/Parks: Green | Sights/Culture: Blue

Boston on Screen

Renowned as the setting for the TV classic *Cheers,* Boston is also a thriving film production venue. Here are flicks featuring the city and environs.

Amistad (1997) tells of an 1839 mutiny aboard a slave ship and the Africans who were put on trial for the murder of the ship's crew. Set in New England, it was partially filmed in Boston and Quincy, Massachusetts, and in Providence and Newport, Rhode Island. Anthony Hopkins, Morgan Freeman, Matthew McConaughey, and Djimon Hounsou star in this Steven Spielberg film.

Blown Away (1993) offers high action when an explosion jolts downtown Boston. An ex-bomb squad expert is brought back to work on the case. Starring Jeff Bridges, Tommy Lee Jones, and Lloyd Bridges. It was filmed in Boston and Gloucester.

The Bostonians (1984), based on the novel by Henry James, is set in 1876 Boston, where the cause of female emancipation wrecks a relationship. Starring Vanessa Redgrave, Christopher Reeve, and Jessica Tandy, it captures settings in Boston and other Massachusetts locations.

The Boston Strangler (1968) is a semifactual account of the maniac who terrified Boston in the 1960s. Tony Curtis, Henry Fonda, and George Kennedy star.

Coma (1978), based on the novel by Robin Cook, stars Genevieve Bujold, Richard Widmark, and Michael Douglas. A doctor in a Boston hospital discovers that patients suffer irreparable brain damage when surgery takes place in a particular operating room.

The Crucible (1996) features Daniel Day-Lewis, Winona Ryder, Paul Scofield, Joan Allen, and Jeffrey Jones in Arthur Miller's original play (he also wrote the screenplay) about the 1692 Salem Witch Trials.

The Departed (2006) from director Martin Scorsese is bloody, violent, treacherous, obscene, and absolutely riveting. Scorsese nails the subculture of Boston-Irish hoodlums, Boston-Irish cops and poor Boston-Irish street life. Jack Nicholson is stunning as a bent Whitey Bulger archetype, an aging South-Boston Irish-Mafia boss. Martin Sheen, Matt Damon, Leonardo DiCaprio, Mark Wahlberg, Vera Farmiga, and top character actors ring true, even down to the accents.

Fever Pitch (2005) A Farrelly brothers romantic comedy made in the glow of the 2004 Red Sox World Series victory, this light film has Drew Barrymore dealing with her Red Sox–obsessed boyfriend (Jimmy Fallon). With Fenway Park footage, Red Sox players, and veteran Boston comic Lenny Clarke.

The Firm (1993) traces the career of a Harvard Law School graduate who joins a small yet corrupt Memphis law firm. The movie features Tom Cruise, Gene Hackman, and Jeanne Tripplehorn.

The Friends of Eddie Coyle (1973), based on a novel by George V. Higgins, is about an aging hoodlum who becomes a police informer and is then executed by his associates. It stars Robert Mitchum, Peter Boyle, and Richard Jordan.

Glory (1989), filmed at Old Sturbridge Village, Boston Common, the South End, and Ipswich, is a rich historical spectacle chronicling the first black volunteer infantry unit in the Civil War. Stars Denzel Washington, Matthew Broderick, and Jane Alexander.

Good Will Hunting (1997) tells the story of a mathematically gifted MIT janitor (Matt Damon), his best friend from the old neighborhood (Ben Affleck), a washed-up shrink who is trying to help him achieve his dream (Robin Williams), and his new love (Minnie Driver). There are plenty of recognizable Boston and Cambridge sites. The film won two Academy Awards: for best supporting actor and for best screenplay.

Hocus Pocus (1992) stars comedic Bette Midler, Sarah Jessica Parker, and Kathy Najimy as 17th-century Salem witches conjured up by pranksters.

Little Women (1994) is the classic Louisa May Alcott novel about four sisters. Starring Winona Ryder and Susan Sarandon. It was filmed in Deerfield.

Malcolm X (1992) Director Spike Lee's account, with Denzel Washington in the lead, of the charismatic African-American figure who spent his young-adult years in Boston. A street hustler at times, the then Malcolm Little also worked at the Parker House.

Mrs. Winterbourne (1996), with Ricki Lake, Shirley MacLaine, and Brendan Fraser, is a romantic comedy about a woman who pretends to be the widow of a wealthy Bostonian.

Mystic River (2003) A Clint Eastwood movie from a Dennis Lehane novel, the film had hundreds of locals as extras, along with stars like Sean Penn, Tim Robbins, Kevin Bacon, Laurence Fishburne, and Laura Linney. It's a gritty tragedy set in a working-class Irish neighborhood, with extremely gifted actors.

Now, Voyager (1942) is a classic variation on Cinderella. Claude Rains plays a psychiatrist who enables a repressed Back Bay resident (Bette Davis) to become an attractive, vibrant woman.

The Paper Chase (1973) captures the scholarly environment of Harvard Law School with stars John Houseman, Timothy Bottoms, and Lindsay Wagner.

The Perfect Storm (2000) is an impressive man-against-the-sea blockbuster based on the book of the same name by Sebastian Junger and filmed in Gloucester. It pits George Clooney, Mark Wahlberg, and the crew of the fishing boat *Andea Gail* against a monster 1991 storm that eventually sends the boat to the bottom. True story and great special effects.

Sabrina (1995) is the remake of the great romantic comedy in which two brothers fall in love with the same woman. Shot on Martha's Vineyard, the film stars Harrison Ford and Julia Ormond.

The Thomas Crown Affair (1967) is a visual travelogue of Boston. Steve McQueen and Faye Dunaway star in this story of a multimillionaire who decides to plot and execute the perfect crime.

The Witches of Eastwick (1986) is about three New England women (Susan Sarandon, Cher, and Michelle Pfeiffer) and their liberation by Jack Nicholson. It was filmed in Cohasset, Marblehead, and Ipswich.

the store is a fixture in the fine-arts community, stocking what the staff refers to as "fancy painting stuff"—imported brushes, easels, tables, pads, powdered pigments, and art books. If you have a tricky wall color to match, this is a good place to come. The color mixer has worked here for more than 30 years and is better than a computer at matching samples. Classes on faux painting, glazing, gilding, and other techniques are also held here. T-shirts with the store's gaily colored emblem are available. ♦ M-F; Sa until 1PM. 355 Newbury St (between Hereford St and Massachusetts Ave). 536.4244 &

19 SONSIE

★★$$$ Complete with bar and brick oven, this fashionable bistro offers bustling sidewalk tables or more quiet, elegant dining at inside booths. Not to be outdone in originality, chef Bill Poirier prepares dishes that will satisfy any number of palates. Among the stunning pizza variations are a tasty delight with spicy shrimp, peppers, ricotta, and leeks, and one topped with lime chicken, salsa, guacamole, and Monterey Jack cheese. Entrées include sake-steamed salmon fillet with cucumber nori rolls and toasted sesame, and white lasagna with chicken, eggplant, and sweet marjoram. Vegetarian choices include whole roasted onion soup, wild mushroom tamale, orecchiette with broccoli and extra-virgin olive oil, and a vegetable mixed grill. Many of the dishes are low fat, dairy products are used sparingly or not at all, and special dietary preferences are accommodated. There's outdoor dining in season. ♦ International ♦ Daily, breakfast, lunch, and dinner. 327 Newbury St (at Hereford St). 351.2500; www.sonsieboston.com

20 L'ESPALIER

★★★$$$$ This refined and sophisticated establishment started Boston's restaurant revolution in 1978, yanking the city out of its culinary doldrums into an era of posh cuisine. Frank McClelland, successor to the original owner, leans a bit more toward contemporary American cuisine and uses native products. But dinner here is as rarefied an event as ever. Set in a stately 1873 town house, the stunning dining rooms allow guests to imagine that

they're feasting back in Back Bay's heyday. The prix-fixe menu might include sautéed yellowfin tuna steaks, squab and fig salad, grilled partridge, or duck breast coupled with foie gras. Every dish is tenderly treated and gorgeously presented in modest portions. The service is exceedingly proper. ♦ Contemporary American ♦ M-Sa, dinner; tea, Sa 2-3 PM. Jacket and tie recommended. Reservations required weekends. Valet parking available. 30 Gloucester St (between Newbury St and Commonwealth Ave). 262.3023; www.lespalier.com

20 CASA ROMERO

★$$$ The prices are steep, though there's compensation in the picturesque dining rooms brightened with hand-painted tiles and Mexican handicrafts. A number of dishes are outstanding, including the avocado soup, chicken with *mole poblano* (a rich garlic, onion, chili pepper, and chocolate sauce), and *puerco adobado* (pork with smoked chilies). Enter at the public alley that runs between Gloucester and Hereford Streets. ♦ Mexican ♦ M-F, lunch and dinner; Sa, Su, dinner. Reservations recommended. 30 Gloucester St (between Newbury St and Commonwealth Ave). 536.4341; www.casaromero.com

21 LUIGI & ROSCOE'S

★★$$ This casual spot, with sidewalk tables, is a good place to stop with a family or a date when you want to enjoy the street's ambience. And it's open until midnight Friday, Saturday, and Sunday. (Luigi and Roscoe were executive chef Steven Beadle's grandfathers.) ♦ Italian ♦ Daily, dinner; F-Su, lunch. 279A Newbury St (at Gloucester St). 536.9321; fax 536.9892

22 NEWBURY GUEST HOUSE

$$ Located in adjoining 1880s town houses, this four-story charmer offers pleasant accommodations in the heart of Boston. The interior

Commonwealth Avenue, with its double street and long parklike mall between—a span of 240 feet—is slightly wider than Paris's Champs-Elysées.

Restaurants/Clubs: Red | Hotels: Purple | Shops: Orange | Outdoors/Parks: Green | Sights/Culture: Blue

boasts polished hardwood floors and several distinctive touches, including original Tiffany glass windows. Guests have use of the bay-windowed lobby lounge. All 32 rooms feature modern bath, cable TV, and telephone (no charge for local calls). All but two rooms, on the top floor, are nonsmoking and there's free wireless Internet access. Rates include continental breakfast, which is served in the large dining room. For added convenience, $15 parking is provided behind the house. ♦ 261 Newbury St (between Fairfield and Gloucester Sts). 437.7666; www.newburyguesthouse.com

23 EXETER STREET THEATRE BUILDING

This Victorian gem of granite and brownstone, the 1884 work of **H.W. Hartwell** and **W.C. Richardson,** was built as a temple for the Working Union of Progressive Spiritualists. It had a long run as a repertory movie theater, but in 1984 was converted to impressive retail space. A greenhouse extension was appended to its street level during a 1975 renovation by **CBT/Childs Bertman Tseckares Casendinon** that became home for a chain restaurant and bar. In 2005 the Back Bay's **Kinsgley Montessori School** moved elementary-school classes to three floors in the brownstone. ♦ 26 Exeter St (at Newbury St). 247.1417; www.kingsley.org

24 NIELSEN GALLERY

Nina Nielsen has run this gallery for more than three decades, and exhibits contemporary works by Joan Snyder, Jake Berthot, Harvey Quaytman, Jane Smaldone, and Porfirio DiDonna. Not a trend-chaser, Nielsen looks for artists—many young, awaiting their first break—whose work expresses highly personal, often spiritual viewpoints. She also shows work by such famous 20th-century artists as Jackson Pollock and David Smith. Nielsen likes what she likes and has many clients who feel the same way. She doesn't shy away from making one of her biggest interests—the continuum of spiritual substance in art—apparent. Says Nielsen about purchasing art: "Buy for love after talking to knowledgeable people." ♦ Tu-Sa. 179 Newbury St (between Dartmouth and Exeter Sts). 266.4835; www.nielsengallery.com よ (with advance notice)

24 MARCOZ

Something splendid always graces the show windows here. The two handsomely preserved floors of a Victorian town house make a divine setting for furniture and decorative items from the 18th to the early 20th century. The hard-to-find accent pieces are imported from En-gland or France, or purchased from New England estates. Knowledgeable and friendly,

Mr. Marcoz will tell you all about whatever strikes your fancy, be it the 17th-century Madonna and Child processional figures, a 19th-century French *boule de petarque* (boccie-style ball), exquisite engravings, ivorine and sterling-silver napkin rings, a desktop inkwell, a pocket watch, or other finds. ♦ M-Sa. 177 Newbury St (between Dartmouth and Exeter Sts). 262.0780; www.marcozantiques.com

24 THE SOCIETY OF ARTS AND CRAFTS

Stop in here for a special handmade, one-of-a-kind something or other. The oldest nonprofit craft association in America, oper-ating since 1897, the society promotes established and up-and-coming artisans by putting their wares before the public. All work is selected by jury; merchandise includes jewelry, ceramics, glass, quilts, woven items, wood and leather pieces, collages, clothing, accessories, and furniture (always especially noteworthy). Themed exhibitions are held on the second floor. ♦ Daily. 175 Newbury St (between Dartmouth and Exeter Sts). 266.1810; www.societyofcrafts.org

24 PUCKER GALLERY

This gallery displays local and international contemporary artists' graphics, paintings, sculptures, and porcelains. It also carries modern masters such as Chagall, Picasso, and Hundertwasser. Israeli art is a gallery specialty; works by Samuel Bak, David Sharir, and others are shown. ♦ M-Sa. 171 Newbury St (between Dartmouth and Exeter Sts). 267.9473; www.puckergallery.com

25 KITCHEN ARTS

At this wonderful resource for cooks, expert and far-from, you can pick up any kitchen tool your culinary sleight-of-hand requires. The emphasis here is on performance tools, not pretty-to-look-at gifts. These wares are ready to go to work immediately—slicing, dicing, decorating, coring, chopping, cracking, grinding, and so on. Kitchen cutlery and knife sharpening are subspecialties. ♦ Daily. 161 Newbury St (between Dartmouth and Exeter Sts). 266.8701

26 AUTREFOIS ANTIQUES

The name means "yesteryear" in French, and 18th- and 19th-century France is captured here in fine imported hardwood furnishings such as armoires, tables, chairs, chandeliers, and mirrors. Other epochs and places of origin also slip in, with the biggest shipments of new merchandise arriving in the spring and fall. The expert owners, Charles and Maria Rowe, will do on-site restoration and adapt old furnishings for modern needs. Updating lighting is their specialty. ♦ Tu-Su. 125 Newbury St (between Clarendon and Dartmouth Sts). 424.8823 &. Also at 130 Harvard St (between Harvard Ave and Auburn St), Brookline. 566.0113

27 CUOIO

For women only, this store showcases fashionable boots and shoes (the name means "leather" in Italian), many imported from Italy, and jewelry, hats, and fabulous hair ornaments. Many of these styles aren't available elsewhere in the city. ♦ Daily. 115 Newbury St (ground floor, between Clarendon and Dartmouth Sts). 859.0636 &. Also at Faneuil Hall Marketplace, South Market. 742.4486

27 PAVO REAL

Custom-designed, hand-knit sweaters from Peru and Bolivia are a highlight here. For men and women, the richly colored garments are made with luxurious alpaca wool and pima cotton. Also available are jewelry, hats, gloves, scarves, wallets, and pocketbooks—some whimsical in design—that make wonderful gifts. ♦ Daily. 115 Newbury St (2nd floor, between Clarendon and Dartmouth Sts). 437.6699

28 ÖKW

Irene Kerzner and Henry Wong (the "o" in ökw, pronounced *oh-koo*, is the initial of a departed partner) are the designers of choice for prominent businesswomen and socialites too discriminating to buy off the rack. Their

creations are compellingly playful yet impeccably crafted of opulent fabrics. ♦ By appointment. 234 Clarendon St (between Newbury St and Commonwealth Ave). 266.4114 &

29 TRINITY CHURCH RECTORY

The massive arched entry bellows the name of the 1879 rectory's masterful architect, **Henry Hobson Richardson,** who designed its parent **Trinity Church** at Copley Square. The building is now on the National Register of Historic Places. Look at its surface, vigorously alive with twisting flowers and ornament. A third story was, unfortunately, added by HHR's successor firm after his death. ♦ 233 Clarendon St (between Newbury St and Commonwealth Ave). www.trinitychurchboston.org

30 NEW ENGLAND HISTORIC GENEALOGICAL SOCIETY

Many searchers for information on a family tree have zeroed in on this private, nonprofit research library, the oldest of its kind in the nation and the first in the world. The mission: to plumb the past, to root out those roots. Housed in a former bank and founded in 1845, the society now holds 200,000 volumes and more than a million manuscripts dating as far back as the 17th century. The organization's dedication to the study and preservation of family history has resulted in records and histories for all US states and

IRISH BOSTON

Despite its Yankee-Puritan heritage, Boston has become a capital of Irish America. Waves of immigrants and continuing close ties between Boston and Ireland have produced a town particularly open to things Irish. The Kennedys, former House Speaker Tip O'Neill, rascal mayor James Michael Curley, and many others have represented Irish-Americans and all of Boston.

This cluster of Irish-oriented memorials near the **Old South Meeting House** are all worth seeing.

Irish Famine Memorial

Boston's Irish community commemorates the tragic famine in Ireland that, beginning in 1847, cost a million Irish lives and drove another million to emigrate, many of them to America. Life-size bronze sculptures across from the Old South Meeting House and along

the Freedom Trail show a starving, desperate woman looking to heaven and a family arriving in Boston with hope and determination. At Washington and School Streets near Downtown Crossing, just blocks from where the Irish refugees first crowded into tenements along Boston's waterfront. ♦ www.boston.com/partners/famine_memorial/ &

Irish Heritage Trail

Anchored by the Famine Memorial, this self-guided, three-mile walking tour moves through Boston's downtown, North End, Beacon Hill, and Back Bay. Statues, memorials, parks, and cemeteries capture the Irish story in Boston, ranging from Revolutionary and Civil War figures to 19th-century artists and 20th-century politicians. ♦ 888/749.9494; www.irishheritagetrail.com &

Restaurants/Clubs: Red | Hotels: Purple | Shops: Orange | Outdoors/Parks: Green | Sights/Culture: Blue

Canadian provinces, plus Europe. There's no better place to try to document one's heritage. Members have online access to the archives. Visitors pay a half- or full-day research fee. ◆ Tu, W-Th until 9PM; F, Sa. 101 Newbury St (between Berkeley and Clarendon Sts). 536.5740; www.newenglandancestors.org

30 JOHN LEWIS, INC.

Wave upon wave of silver strands swinging in the window lure passersby into this serene 1876 brownstone, where veteran Newbury Street proprietors John and Louise Lewis design jewelry. Working with solid precious metals and natural stones, the couple turns out a glittering array of imaginative designs. Some are simple marriages of rich materials and careful artisanship. Others are more intricate, such as the Lewises' line of Victorian-inspired jewelry embellished with cherubim, scrolls, flowers, and bows. ◆ Tu-Sa. 97 Newbury St (between Berkeley and Clarendon Sts). 266.6665; www.johnlewisinc.com ♿

31 MARTINI CARL

The Ventola family's boutique stocks sophisticated European apparel for men and women ranging from very casual to very dressy, with all the requisite accessories. The designer and private labels emphasize rich fabrics and leathers, superb tailoring, and enduring styles. ◆ M-Sa. 77 Newbury St (between Berkeley and Clarendon Sts). 247.0441 ♿

32 CHURCH OF THE COVENANT

R.M. Upjohn designed this 1867 Gothic Revival treasure house, which is on the National Register of Historic Places. To many, the steeple—which Oliver Wendell Holmes said "to my eyes seems absolutely perfect"—resembles the famed spire at England's Salisbury Cathedral. Within the church is the largest collection of work in the world by

Built on landfill (as was all of Back Bay), Trinity Church was constructed on a foundation of four massive granite pyramids with 35-foot-square bases. Below these is a subterranean safety net of 4,502 wooden pilings. Carefully monitored since its construction in 1877, the foundation held firm until the early 1970s, when the adjacent John Hancock Tower was begun. The Hancock construction damaged Trinity, a National Historic Landmark, twisting the church and cracking parts of its foundation, walls, some precious stained glass, and a La Farge mural. Trinity sued John Hancock for $4 million in 1975, and when the case was finally settled in 1987, the church received $11.6 million—the damage award plus 12 years of interest.

stained-glass master Tiffany, including 43 windows, some 30 feet high, and clerestories. Especially noteworthy is the sanctuary lantern with seven angels, originally wired for electricity by Thomas Edison. It was designed by Tiffany's firm for the Tiffany Chapel exhibited at the World's Columbian Exposition of 1893 in Chicago, then installed here. Also look for the Welte-Tripp pipe organ, a five-keyboard, manual, 3,530-pipe instrument, completed in 1929 as the last installation of that German firm, and unique in Boston as a surviving example of and a testament to the firm's orchestral pipe building and voicing. A complete restoration of the organ in 2001 was a major achievement for a church of only 200 members. The Presbyterian church has a long history of giving generously to the community; the well-known Women's Lunch Place shelter is resident in the basement. The church also founded the **Back Bay Chorale** and the **Boston Pro Arte Chamber Orchestra,** which perform regularly here and at Harvard University. ◆ M-Th 10AM-1PM, subject to staff availability. 67 Newbury St (at Berkeley St). 266.7480; www.churchofthecovenant.org ♿

Within the Church of the Covenant:

GALLERY NAGA

Director Arthur Dion mounts interesting exhibitions of contemporary painting, sculpture, photography, and prints by the known and unknown. He likes to bridge the division between fine art and craft, sometimes showcasing furniture and glass. Exhibits have included the work of Peter Brooke, Reese Inmann, Henry Schwartz, James Gemmill, and Irene Valincius, and furniture designers such as Tom Loeser and Judy Kensley McKie. The gallery occupies a generous 1,400-square-foot swatch—in the church, whose progressive congregation has given art a boost by making a long-term space commitment to the gallery. ◆ By appointment. 267.9060; gallerynaga.com

33 MILANO'S ITALIAN KITCHEN

★$ Wood-fired oven specialties enjoy ever-widening popularity in Boston, and they are as good here as anywhere. Panini, pasta, salads, and the antipasti are also worth a try. Start with the polenta cup (a polenta shell filled with a ragout of vegetables covered with pesto sauce, served with broccoli, peppers, and sun-dried tomatoes in a marinara sauce) or the popular antipasti Milano (Genoa salami, prosciutto, mozzarella, and marinated mixed vegetables drizzled with extra-virgin olive oil). Jugs of Chianti are placed on every table, and patrons are on the honor system to keep track of how many glasses they drink. ◆ Italian ◆ Daily, lunch and dinner. 47 Newbury St (at Berkeley St). 267.6150

34 29 NEWBURY

★★★$$ This popular bistro, a favorite with modeling, hair salon, music, and media types, serves contemporary cuisine that's considerably priced. Certain dishes sing, and even the burgers are prepared as they should be. The semisubterranean dining room also doubles as an art gallery, and deep-set booths ensure privacy. More sociable types crowd around the bar or, in good weather, spill onto the sidewalk patio. Sunday brunch. ♦ American ♦ M-Sa, lunch and dinner; Su, brunch and dinner. Reservations recommended. 29 Newbury St (between Arlington and Berkeley Sts). 536.0290; www.29newbury.com

34 EMMANUEL CHURCH

Its uninspired rural Gothic Revival architecture (an 1862 effort by **Alexander R. Estey,** enlarged by **Frederick R. Allen** in 1899) doesn't do justice to this Episcopal church's lively, creative spirit. Dedicated since the 1970s to "a special ministry through art," the church organizes a variety of music and cultural events. A professionally performed Bach cantata accompanies the liturgy every Sunday from September through May. Jazz celebrations are held periodically. ♦ Su, 10AM service. 15 Newbury St (between Arlington and Berkeley Sts). 536.3355; www.emmanuel-boston.org ⅊ (a portable ramp is available with advance notice)

Within Emmanuel Church:

LESLIE LINDSEY MEMORIAL CHAPEL

This 1924 Gothic chapel was commissioned by Mr. and Mrs. William Lindsey as a memorial to their daughter, Leslie, who with her new husband was bound for a European honeymoon on the ill-fated RMS *Lusitania.* Sometime after the boat sank, Leslie's body supposedly washed ashore in Ireland, still wearing her father's wedding gift of diamonds and rubies; they were sold to help pay for her memorial. The chapel is sometimes called the "Lady Chapel" for its marble carvings of female saints. It was designed by **Allen & Collens,** nationally renowned at the time for the Riverside Church in New York City.

35 DOMAIN

It's fun to prowl through this mecca of home embellishments, a fantasy habitat for antique, traditional, and designer pieces, none commonplace or conventional. The aim is to mass-market one-of-a-kind–looking furnishings. A multitude of quirky accessories crowd in among the beds, tables, and sofas. ♦ Daily (call for summer evening hours). 7 Newbury St (between Arlington and Berkeley Sts). 266.5252; www.domain-home.com ⅊

35 RITZ-CARLTON HOTEL— TAJ BOSTON

$$$$ Many Bostonians will always call that quietly luxurious hotel across from the Public Garden the Ritz-Carlton. But the hallowed Ritz, a reminder of old, Yankee Boston, is to become part of one of Asia's largest luxury-hotel groups in January, 2007.

A $170-million agreement by India's Taj Hotels Resorts and Palaces to buy the Ritz was announced in late 2006. Taj owns the Pierre on Fifth Avenue in New York and some 75 other luxury hotels around the world. The Ritz will be renamed the Taj Boston, although the new and old owners insist that most everything else will stay the same. Since the hotel name had not changed by press time, we'll call what will be the Taj Boston by its Ritz name for this edition. The other Boston Ritz, a newer venture on the other side of Boston Common [called the Ritz-Carlton, Boston Common], was not sold by owner Millennium Partners and is not affected by its sale of the venerable, original Ritz.

The refurbished, refreshed grande dame had a $50 million face-lift in 2002. The nationwide Ritz hotel chain's reputation for luxury, elegance, and service is exemplified at this, the oldest Ritz-Carlton in the country. Taj continues this. Built in 1927 by **Strickland and Blodget,** and subtly expanded by **Skidmore, Owings & Merrill** in 1981, the Boston landmark provides all the niceties proper Bostonians love so well—the elevator attendants, for example, wear white gloves. There's nothing flashy or eye-catching about this building, except for its parade of vivid blue awnings, but it has become a timeless, steadfast fixture. The 278 rooms and suites at the original are simply and traditionally appointed in European style and offer safes, locking closets, and windows that open. The 41 suites have wood-burning fireplaces. Request a room with a view of the **Public Garden**. The hotel boasts a venerable dining room, a café, a lounge, and a bar. There's a small health club, and guests may use (at no charge) the fancy spa at the **Heritage,** a block away. Other amenities include 24-hour room service, twice-daily housekeeping, valet parking, same-day laundry service, a multilingual staff, babysitting and massage services, a concierge, a barber shop, and a shoe-shine stand. Rooms for nonsmokers and people with disabilities are available. Pets are allowed if they are leashed. ♦ 15 Arlington St (between Newbury St and Commonwealth Ave). 536.5700, 800/241.3333; fax 536.1335; www.tajhotels.com www.ritzcarlton.com/hotels/boston

The Dining Room

★★$$$$ New hub restaurants open every day, but there will never be another dining room like this. It's the hotel's showpiece, with cobalt-blue Venetian crystal chandeliers and matching table crystal, a gold-filigreed ceiling, regal drapery, and huge picture windows overlooking the Public Garden. There's no better place for wedding proposals, anniversaries, and other momentous occasions. Piano music and an occasional harpist add to the spell. Such timeless classics as rack of lamb and chateaubriand for two commune with a few more stylish offerings on the menu. But the chef introduces innovations very carefully; old-guard patrons would rise in arms if Boston cream pie and other old-time favorites were seriously challenged. Entrées low in sodium, cholesterol, and calories are available, as is a children's menu. Chamber music accompanies the fabulous Sunday brunch. ♦ French ♦ M-Sa, lunch and dinner; Su, brunch and dinner. Jacket and tie required. Reservations required. 536.5700 ♿

The Ritz Cafe

★★$$$ With its views of Newbury Street, its quiet vanilla décor, and its cordial service, this café offers respite during a hectic day. When you've had it with the world, come for a restorative touch of civility. Since you can't see the Public Garden from here, it has been reproduced in a mural. On weekday mornings, many of Boston's business heavy hitters breakfast here. At night the café caters to the after-theater crowd. Children may order from a special menu. ♦ American ♦ Daily, breakfast, lunch, and dinner. Jacket and tie required evenings; no denim allowed. Reservations recommended at lunch. 536.5700 ♿

The Ritz Lounge

★★★$$ Perch in a high-backed chair in this soothing second-floor drawing room as a harpist plays and you sip your way through afternoon tea and its accompanying dainty delights (see "Boston's Tea Parties" on page 44). This is also a lovely spot for evening drinks. ♦ Lounge ♦ Daily. Jacket suggested; no denim or athletic shoes allowed. 536.5700 ♿

The Ritz Bar

★★★$$ On a snowy evening, the gorgeous view of the Public Garden from this cozy street-level bar is right out of a storybook. Inside, there's welcome serenity and a crackling fire in the hearth. A selection of soups, club sandwiches, pasta dishes, and salads is served at lunch. The bar is famous for its perfect martinis; ask for the special martini menu. Boston mystery writer Robert B. Parker's fictional sleuth Spenser has quaffed many a beer here. ♦ American ♦ M-Sa, lunch. Bar: M-Sa, 11:30AM-1AM; Su, noon-midnight. Jacket requested. 536.5700 ♿

36 Newbury Street

With some of the highest retail rents in the US, this thoroughfare aspires to the highest commercial heights. It's increasingly fashionable the closer you are to the Arlington Street end, where you can feel underdressed just strolling along. In addition to boutiques and galleries offering art, literature, antiques, and costly geegaws, there are dozens of hair "designers," tanning and facial salons, and modeling studios along this stretch, as well as a thriving local café society. ♦ Between Arlington St and Massachusetts Ave

36 360 Newbury Street

An early-1900s warehouse designed by **Arthur Bowditch** was metamorphosed into a dramatic iconoclast by architect **Frank O. Gehry** with the assistance of **Schwartz/Silver Architects** in 1989. The building towers over the Massachusetts Avenue end of Newbury Street. Viewed from the Massachusetts Turnpike and many Back Bay angles, it is a challenging, eye-catching presence, critically lauded if not universally beloved. Its brash projecting struts, canopy, and cornice make it appear scaffolded and still in process, as if the building hasn't quite decided what it wants to be yet. The top five floors, formerly office space, have been converted to 54 high-end loft-style condominiums. A 40,000-square-foot Virgin Megastore selling CDs, records and entertainment goodies that filled the bottom of the building was shuttered in fall of 2006. Another retail store is expected to fill the space. ♦ At Massachusetts Ave.

Trident Booksellers & Cafe

37 TRIDENT BOOKSELLERS & CAFE

★★★$ "Boston's alternative bookstore" sells fiction, but is particularly strong in Jungian psychology, acupuncture, poetry, Eastern religions (particularly Buddhism), and women's and metaphysical works. Scented oils, tarot cards, and bonsai trees are also on sale. The café is a popular neighborhood meeting place for a broad spectrum of Bostonians, who come for its no-fuss, down-to-earth menu of homemade soups, salads, sandwiches, bagels, dinners like shepherd's pie and desserts like carrot cake, plus coffees, juices, wine, and beer. ♦ Café ♦ Daily, 9AM-midnight. 338 Newbury St (between Hereford St and Massachusetts Ave). 267.8688

37 NEWBURY COMICS

This successful store started as a comic-book outpost in 1976, then branched into anything music-related. They still sell comics—graphic novels, including some aimed at adults—but the eclectic inventory now encompasses independent-label and import CDs, music and comic T-shirts, music videos and books, posters, jewelry, and novelties. Students flock here for hard-to-find recordings. ♦ Daily. 332 Newbury St (between Hereford St and Massachusetts Ave) and 25 other stores throughout New England. 236.4930 &

38 BOSTON ARCHITECTURAL CENTER (BAC)

This bulky building is a 1967 exemplar of Brutalism by **Ashley, Myer & Associates,** the architectural firm now called Arrowstreet. It is an amiable addition to Back Bay, but don't let the contemporary look fool you: It houses an architecture school founded in 1889. The school began as a free atelier run by the Boston Architectural Club, where deserving youth were given drawing lessons. Today it is

the only architecture school in the US that requires most students to work full-time as fledgling architects while taking evening classes from a mostly volunteer faculty. The inviting, glass-sheathed ground floor is a public space for student work and art and architectural exhibitions. On the building's exterior west wall, New York artist Richard Haas painted one of his best murals in 1977. It has since become a Back Bay landmark. This six-story trompe l'oeil is a cross-sectional view of a French neoclassical palace in the Beaux Arts style. Look for the mural's teasers: the shadow of a man against a corridor wall, a foot disappearing through a closing door, and a man in a doorway on his way to the rotunda. ♦ Gallery M-Th until 10:30PM; F-Su., call. 320 Newbury St (at Hereford St). 536.3170; www.the-bac.edu &

STEVE'S
GREEK & AMERICAN CUISINE

39 STEVE'S GREEK & AMERICAN CUISINE

★$ Locals, students, and conventioneers from the Hynes Convention Center come to this cheerful restaurant. On one side is takeout, on the other, a simple, pleasant plant-entwined dining room overlooking Newbury Street. The menu offers Greek and Middle Eastern favorites as well as burgers and omelets and vegetarian-friendly dishes. ♦ Greek/ American ♦ Daily, breakfast, lunch, and dinner. 62 Hereford St (at Newbury St). 267.1817

40 JOHN FLUEVOG

If you want your feet to make a particularly hip or up-to-the-minute fashion statement, get your footwear here. European-made in plenty of colors, with crests and bows and buckles and tapestry, the quality leather shoes are all ready for action of some sort. With a cool web site too. ♦ Daily. 302 Newbury St (between Gloucester and Hereford Sts). 266.1079; www.fluevog.com

41 CAFE JAFFA

★$ An inviting storefront with picture windows and bare brick walls, this modest café has authentic, affordable Middle Eastern fare. Order hummus, falafel, *shawarma* (ground roasted lamb or chicken), and other traditional dishes. ♦ Middle Eastern/Takeout

♦ Daily, lunch and dinner. 48 Gloucester St (between Boylston and Newbury Sts). 536.0230 ♿

42 TAPEO

★★★$$$ Tapas—especially garlic shrimp, salmon balls with caper sauce, and beef tenderloin with pimiento on toast—and sangria on the patio are reasons enough to stop by this popular spot. But a good and affordable wine list, along with main dishes like *pescado a la sal* (fish baked in coarse salt), *lomo de buey a las frutas* (beef tenderloin with dried figs, apricots, and prunes in a cream brandy sauce), and, of course, paella are other reasons. There's a cozy brick dining room on the ground floor; the second-floor dining room has rustic Spanish décor and a fireplace. There's a $10-per-person food minimum. ♦ Spanish ♦ M-F, dinner; Sa, Su, lunch and dinner. Reservations recommended. Valet parking available. 266 Newbury St (between Fairfield and Gloucester Sts). 267.4799; www.tapeorestaurant.com

43 MATSU

Skirts, sweaters, jewelry, leather handbags, and chic accessories of all kinds are offered in a high-end, aromatic little store with saffron walls. ♦ Daily. 259 Newbury St (between Fairfield and Gloucester Sts). 266.9707; www.matsuboston.com

44 CIAO BELLA

★★$$$ Convivial singles like to lunch at the bar, looking out at Newbury Street. In the evening the dressy dining room draws a chic clientele. Choose from the appealing selection of appetizers, then turn to pasta or a simple meat dish like the veal cutlet. Dine on the patio in nice weather. ♦ Italian ♦ Daily, lunch and dinner. Reservations recommended F-Su. Valet parking. 240A Newbury St (at Fairfield St). 536.2626; reservations online at www.ciaobella.com

45 VOSE GALLERIES OF BOSTON

Established in 1841, this is the oldest continuously run art gallery in America, and is now under the direction of the fifth generation of Voses. Well over 30,000 paintings have passed through here since 1896, and they've sold works to nearly every major American museum. The family specializes in 18th-, 19th-, and early 20th-century American painting, and frequently show paintings by artists of the Hudson River School and the Boston School, as well as Luminists and American Impressionists (including Childe Hassam and John Henry Twachtman). Since 2001, they've also had a contemporary wing. ♦ M-Sa. 238 Newbury St (between Exeter and Fairfield Sts). 536.6176; www.vosegalleries.com

45 PIATTINI

★★$$ The name means "small plate" in Italian. Diners have a choice of a small-plates menu, allowing them samples to taste, or dinner and brunch menus with traditionally sized dishes. The charming original Piattini on Newbury Street has a 14-table (they call it intimate) dining room and secluded patio offering regional Italian cuisine (delicious, crispy calamari can be had for under $8) and more than two dozen wines by the glass. The newer and larger **Piattini Wine Bar** on Columbus Avenue, near the Park Square Castle, has front patio tables, Italian and Mediterranean dishes, a larger dining room, full bar, and a more extensive wine list. ♦ Italian ♦ 226 Newbury St (between Fairfield and Exeter Sts). Daily, dinner; M-F, lunch, Sa, Su, brunch. 536.2020. Piattini Wine Bar, 162 Columbus Ave (between Berkeley and Arlington Sts). Daily, lunch and dinner. 423.2021; www.piattini.com

46 STEPHANIE'S ON NEWBURY

★★$$$ Serving what the owner calls sophisticated comfort food, the restaurant and café is a warm and clubby space with a bar and a conversation area next to full-length windowed doors that can open onto a large sidewalk seating area. Earth tones abound in all the dining rooms. Specialties include lobster pot pie and home-style macaroni and cheese. ♦ Café ♦ Daily, breakfast, lunch, and dinner. Reservations recommended for dinner. 190 Newbury St (between Dartmouth and Exeter Sts). 236.0990; www.stephaniesonnewbury.com

47 THE COPLEY SOCIETY OF BOSTON

The oldest art association in America, this nonprofit society was founded in 1879 to promote access to art (particularly new European trends) and to exhibit the work of its members and other artists of the day. Members **John Singer Sargent** and **James McNeill Whistler** showed their work in galleries run by the society. In 1905 the organization mounted **Claude Monet**'s first American exhibition, a controversial event, and in 1913 **Marcel Duchamp**'s *Nude Descending a Staircase* was shown here, creating a furor. Today the society has more than 800 committee-selected members

For all of Back Bay's French influences, its street names are strictly British.

from around the world, though most are New Englanders. It operates two floors of galleries, with individual artists renting space upstairs and an ongoing members' show downstairs. The society has become somewhat mired in tradition, although recently it has focused more attention on contemporary work. Though the shows are uneven in quality, works by noted and rising artists are often on view, so the galleries here are worth investigating. ♦ Tu-Su. 158 Newbury St (between Dartmouth and Exeter Sts). 536.5049; www.copleysociety.org

47 BOSTON ART CLUB

This artful 1881 assemblage is the work of Ralph Waldo Emerson's clever nephew, **William Ralph Emerson,** also creator of the fascinating **House of Odd Windows** on Beacon Hill. Emerson let loose his entire artillery of architectural forms and ornament on the Queen Anne–style façade: From every angle, there's something peculiar or interesting to see. A school occupies the building. ♦ 270 Dartmouth St (at Newbury St)

47 NIKETOWN

One of the first of many Niketowns around the country, this shiny, expensive, and popular sneaker store, created by **Ruhl Walker and BOORA** architects in 1997, offers exactly what many people want. It's a multimedia-filled, 9,000-square-foot corner emporium where you'll pay full retail prices, should you want to buy. Displays and promotions are often linked—for obvious reasons—to the Boston Marathon. The store is chaos on marathon day. 200 Newbury St (at Exeter St). 267.3400

48 PAPA RAZZI

★★$$ This inviting, busy Italian trattoria, complete with a wood-burning pizza oven, has a menu that leans toward rustic Northern Italian dishes with California overtones. Hearty fare includes an array of splendid crispy-crust pizzas, polenta with grilled Italian sausages, and bountiful antipasti and pastas. ♦ Italian ♦ Daily, lunch and dinner. 271 Dartmouth St (between Boylston and Newbury Sts). 536.9200

49 SERENELLA

Women come to this small, friendly boutique to invest in luxurious, classic, timeless clothes that will serve them for years. The emphasis is on European designer daytime wear, with some accessories and shoes. Owner Ines Capelli does all the buying. ♦ M-Sa. 134 Newbury St (between Clarendon and Dartmouth Sts). 262.5568; www.serenella-boston.com &

49 RICCARDI

The latest in European fashion for men and women is on sale here, all made in Italy, but based on designs and influences from throughout Europe. Designers include Ann Demeulemeester (Belgium), Comme des Garçons (Japan), and Dolce e Gabbana and Romeo Gigli (Italy). The shoes and accessories are multinational, too. An entire department is devoted to sporting wear. The staff is up-to-date and informative on fashions. This is one of Boston's most worldly shops; they even accept JCB, the Japanese credit card. ♦ M-Sa. 128 Newbury St (between Clarendon and Dartmouth Sts). 266.3158; www.riccardiboston.com

50 REBECCA'S CAFE

★$ Everything is made fresh daily at this gourmet take-out place. Lines form all day long for homemade muffins and scones, fresh salads, hot entrée specials, and the desserts and pastries. The chocolate mousse cake and the fresh-fruit tarts are pure pleasure. There are a few tables at the back. ♦ Café/Take-out ♦ Daily, breakfast, lunch, and dinner. 112 Newbury St (between Clarendon and Dartmouth Sts). 267.1122

Trinity Church's resplendent interior illustrates architect Henry Hobson Richardson's penchant for the Romanesque style; he often enlisted celebrated artists and sculptors to collaborate on the decoration of his houses, churches, schools, libraries, hospitals, bridges, and railroad stations. The stamp of such craftsmen can be seen in many of his works.

51 LOUIS, BOSTON

Until the New England Museum of Natural History moved to its current site straddling the Charles River and changed its name to the Boston Museum of Science, it was jammed into this French Academic structure, designed in 1863 by **William G. Preston**. The museum was one of Back Bay's pioneers. When it vacated, part of the moving-day chaos included lowering a stuffed moose from an upper-story window, a scene captured in a photograph that the museum now prizes. Bonwit Teller then resided here for decades until this astronomically priced clothier took over in 1987 and gave the building a much-needed restoration. Three floors are dedicated to men's apparel and one to women's—everything of exceptional quality. Also on the premises is the **Mario Russo** women's hair salon (424.6676). The building's splendid isolation makes it appear even more magnificent. Inside, its spaciousness makes for enjoyable browsing. ♦ M-Sa. 234 Berkeley St (between Boylston and Newbury Sts). 262.6100 ♿

Within Louis, Boston:

L

★★★$$$$ The clothier's café deserves a special visit. High-ceilinged and formerly furnished with lacquered bamboo chairs and tapestry banquettes as Café Louis, it is today just "L." It's a modded-up, hip (and expensive) place to be. Not that it matters if you're shopping at Louis Boston, but a glass of fine wine will set you back $13. It's possible to use the café's main entrance off the parking lot, but more fun to stroll through the store, past $1,000 sweaters and $200 scarves. Inside, the menu marries Asian and French flavors. You can eat outdoors at tables on the cement landing, though the view of the parking lot and the New England Life Building across the way isn't breathtaking. ♦ Café/Takeout ♦ M-Sa, lunch; Tu-Sa, dinner. 266.4680 ♿

52 ALAN BILZERIAN

The dramatic clothes in this store's striking display windows need few props; they speak for themselves. A native of Worcester, Massachusetts, Bilzerian started out with a college student clientele more than two decades ago, then began selling to rock stars. Now his is the local name in fashion best known outside of Boston. In fact, New Yorkers with the fashion world at their feet still make special trips, and lots of celebrities drop in when in town—Cher and Mick Jagger among them. Featured are art-to-wear fashions, accessories, and shoes for men and women: the work of such European and Japanese designers as Yohji Yamamoto, Michele Klien, Issey Miyake, Katharine Hamnett, Rifat Ozbek, Jean Paul Gaultier, Azzedine Alaia, and Romeo Gigli, to name a few. Complementing the other collections are Bilzerian designs for men and designs for women by his wife, Bê. Of course, outlandishly stylish wear commands outlandishly high prices. ♦ Daily. 34 Newbury St (between Arlington and Berkeley Sts). 536.1001 ♿ (The staff will carry wheelchairs up the stairs; once inside, there's an elevator to the second-floor women's department.)

53 CHARLES SUMNER

This head-to-toe boutique carries great imported and American women's designer apparel by Donna Karan, Valentino, Louis Ferraud, Missoni, Akris, and others, plus shoes, handbags, makeup, hosiery, jewelry, gloves, and hats. The enthusiastic salespeople try hard to work with customers and make them feel at home. ♦ M-Sa. 16 Newbury St (between Arlington and Berkeley Sts). 536.6225 ♿

53 ALPHA GALLERY

The best free art shows in town are often on display here. A family affair, the gallery is owned by Alan Fink, managed by his daughter Joanna, and often shows work by his wife, Barbara Swan, and son Aaron Fink, both of whom merit the attention. The gallery specializes in 20th-century and contemporary American and European painting, sculpture, and prints. The work of such distinguished artists as American painters Milton Avery, Bernard Chaet, and Fairfield Porter, and Europeans Mimmo Paladino and Georg Baselitz has been exhibited here. Other shows have featured Massachusetts realist Scott Prior and such gifted young artists as T. Wiley Carr. Over its 30-year history the gallery has mounted major exhibitions of work by John Marin, Max Beckmann, and Stuart Davis as well as Picasso's complete Vollard Suite. ♦ Tu-Sa. 14 Newbury St (between Arlington and Berkeley Sts). 536.4465

53 BARBARA KRAKOW GALLERY

Don't pass by this fifth-floor gallery, which you can zero in on by locating the eye-catching marble bench carved with enigmatic messages by Jenny Holzer on the sidewalk out front. After selling art for more than 30 years, it is perhaps Boston's most important art gallery, and it uses its prestige to benefit numerous worthy causes. Many of the most significant contemporary artists are shown here, among them Jenny Holzer, Agnes Martin, Cameron Shaw, Jim Dine, Donald Judd, and Michael Mazur. Despite the superstars on the walls, this is a very hospitable, unpretentious place, combining sure taste with a willingness to take risks—showing work created by high-school kids, for example. ♦ Tu-Sa. 10 Newbury St (between Arlington and Berkeley Sts). 262.4490 ♿

Café de Paris

54 CAFÉ DE PARIS

★$ This is some kind of a fast-food joint, with velvet banquettes, burled paneling, and Art Deco sconces. The food is a cut above, too, ranging from croissants and omelets to true Parisian pastries. Grab a booth or place an order to go and cross over to the Public Garden for breakfast in the park. ♦ French/Takeout ♦ Daily, 7:30AM-9PM (7PM in winter). 19 Arlington St (at Newbury St). 247.7121

55 DILLON'S

★★$$ Located in a former police station, this lively bistro is aimed at 20- and 30-something Back Bay hipsters (and those who like the image). With ceiling fans and a friendly staff, it offers burgers, steak tips, and pizza, along with a seafood and a tapas menu. There's a hidden patio that makes for fun dining in nice weather. ♦ American ♦ Daily, dinner. Valet parking. 955 Boylston St (at Hereford St). 421.1818 ♿

56 THE CACTUS CLUB

★$ The American Southwestern motif is so out of hand here, it must be parody (intense aqua everywhere, O'Keeffe-esque skulls, a buffalo over the bar). But as the big, high-ceilinged rooms fill up, the design assault recedes. Beneath this garishly cheerful disguise lurks a fern bar. The nouvelle Southwestern cuisine highlights ribs, grilled fish and meat, pasta, barbecue, and the like, with such welcome accents as fresh coriander and chipotle peppers. If you have a penchant for swimming in fishbowl-size glasses, you'll like the drinks. This has become a popular hangout for a youngish crowd. The restaurant inhabits the handsome **Tennis and Racquet**

Club building (constructed in 1904), which has a splendid gate in its lobby that prevents access to upstairs offices after hours. ♦ Southwestern ♦ Daily, lunch and dinner. 939 Boylston St (at Hereford St). 236.0200 ♿

57 BOYLSTON STREET

This once-unkempt road bordering Boston's rail yards is today a fashionable stretch with new shops and restaurants scattered among imposing historic, cultural, and religious institutions. ♦ Between Arlington St and Massachusetts Ave

58 ABE & LOUIE'S

★★★$$$$ Good, old-fashioned steak and seafood in a casual and comfortable setting. There are leather booths, bronze chandeliers, and a vaulted ceiling, and a crowd that tilts toward maturity. A 24-ounce prime porterhouse lists for only $37. Reservations recommended. ♦ Steak House/American. Daily, lunch and dinner. 793 Boylston St (at Fairfield St). 536.6300; www.abeandlouies.com

58 THE FAMOUS ATLANTIC FISH COMPANY

★$$ With a long menu and better prices than many seafood houses in Boston, this is a reliable choice for a casual meal. And the patio is so nice in summer. Fried-clam lovers will be particularly content here. At lunchtime, meals are guaranteed to arrive within 12 minutes after ordering, so there's always a crowd of time-is-money professionals. ♦ Seafood ♦ Daily, lunch and dinner. 777 Boylston St (between Exeter and Fairfield Sts). 267.4000 ♿

59 VOX POPULI

★★$$$ This Back Bay sidewalk café restaurant, with red and yellow umbrellas over a few people-watching tables out front, is especially popular in summer. There's a bar/fireplace lounge on the first floor, and another bar on the second floor overlooking Boylston Street, with adjacent dining. ♦ M-Sa, lunch and dinner; Su, brunch 11AM-3PM. 755 Boylston St (between Exeter and Fairfield Sts). 424.8300, fax 424.1016; www.voxboston.com ♿

60 EMPORIO ARMANI

Obviously no longer a fashion backwater, Boston has earned a third outpost of the imperious designer's coterie of stores. (The others are **Giorgio Armani** at 22 Newbury Street and **Armani A/X** at Copley Place.) This one claims 24,500 square feet in the rehabbed United Business Services office building. ♦ Daily. 210-212 Newbury St

---

Restaurants/Clubs: Red | Hotels: Purple | Shops: Orange | Outdoors/Parks: Green | Sights/Culture: Blue

(between Exeter and Fairfield Sts). 262.7300; www.emporioarmani.com &

60 ARMANI CAFÉ

★★★$$$ This café is much more than an adjunct to the expensive clothing store. The location provides great people-watching, especially at the outdoor tables. New management arrived in 2002, and the dining is, well, quite fine. The old crowd seems largely to have been replaced by a kinder, gentler variety. Though the place has been redone, it has the same outdoor café tables, umbrellas, and chairs.♦ Italian ♦ Daily, lunch and dinner. Reservations recommended. 214 Newbury St (between Exeter and Fairfield Sts). 437.0909

61 MORTON'S OF CHICAGO

★★$$$$ This restaurant's stock of tender, prime-grade, dry-aged beef is flown in fresh daily from Chicago. One of a chain of restaurants, the place has a fabulous way with steak, especially the 24-ounce porterhouse, its hallmark. Come famished enough to eat a side of beef, a flock of chickens, or a school of fish—even the baked potatoes are behemoths. There are some smaller cuts of meat, but most people will still consider them huge. A favorite of business folk,

it's just the place for a power meal. Private meeting/dining "boardrooms" are available. The steak house is set in what Bostonians have derisively dubbed "The Darth Vader Building"—the architectural equivalent of a bad haircut, the structure sticks out in all the wrong places. ♦ Steak house/American ♦ Daily, dinner. Reservations recommended. Valet parking. 1 Exeter Plaza, at Boylston and Exeter Sts. 266.5858 &

62 NEW OLD SOUTH CHURCH

The Old South Church moved here from its 18th-century meeting house on Washington Street (better known as the **Old South Meeting House** on the Freedom Trail). The Northern Italian Gothic structure, executed by **Cummings & Sears** in 1874-1875 and now a National Historic Landmark, is pleasingly picturesque, with its multicolored ornamentation, tall campanile, and copper-topped Venetian lantern. On the entry portico's right wall, look for the tombstone remnant, in concrete, that records the death of John Alden, congregation member and eldest son of John and Priscilla Alden of the Plymouth Colony. With a subway station entrance and newsstand located near its porte cochere, the church is witness to comings and goings. Sunday services at 9 and 11 AM. The United Church of Christ periodically hosts musical programs. ♦ M-F; Su until 2PM. 645 Boylston St (between Dartmouth and Exeter Sts). 536.1970; www.oldsouth.org

62 COPLEY SQUARE NEWS

Max has run this newsstand next to the New Old South Church for more than 70 years. He carries periodicals in English, Spanish, French, Italian, and German. ♦ M-Sa, 3AM-6:30PM. Boylston St (between Dartmouth and Exeter Sts). 262.1477 (a pay phone; Max or a helper will answer)

New Old South Church

COURTESY OF BOSTONIAN SOCIETY

63 WHITE STAR TAVERN

★$$ Owner Frank Bell changed the name from Small Planet Bar and Grill to White Star Tavern, but the attractive, lively atmosphere of a neighborhood bistro remains. The menu is heavy on local seafood, steaks and chops, sandwiches and burgers, and beer (of course), plus a wide wine selection in half-bottles, which Bell calls his answer to overpriced by-the-glass wine. There's also a selection of vegetarian dishes. ◆ American ◆ Daily, lunch and dinner, food to midnight and bar to 1AM. 565 Boylston St (between Clarendon and Dartmouth Sts). 536.4477 &

64 PARISH CAFÉ

★★$$ This drinks-and-sandwiches café near the Public Garden affords diners a great patio perch from which to watch the passing parade. Many of the pricey sandwiches are inventive, even exotic, but having a nice place to meet a friend or people-watch is what counts. ◆ Daily, 11:30AM-2AM. 361 Boylston St (between Berkeley and Arlington Sts). 247.4777 &

65 ARLINGTON STREET CHURCH, UNITARIAN UNIVERSALIST

This church's most striking feature is its shapely tower, inspired by St. Martin-in-the-Fields in London. The first building erected in Back Bay (completed in 1861), the simple brownstone structure by **Arthur Gilman** is quite conservative in style, as if unsure of its leadership role in storming the mudflats. The outspoken minister **William Ellery Channing** served here for years; his statue just across the way in the Public Garden keeps watch still. A staunch abolitionist, Channing invited Harriet Beecher Stowe and William Lloyd Garrison to address his congregation. During the Vietnam War, the church was active in the peace movement. Attendance skyrocketed with the arrival of Reverend Kim Crawford Harvie—a woman—who is now senior minister. Inside, look for the Tiffany windows. ◆ Su services at 11AM. Sanctuary tours May-Sept; call for details. 351 Boylston St (at Arlington St). 536.7050; www.ascboston.org &

66 BERKLEE PERFORMANCE CENTER

Associated with the highly regarded **Berklee College of Music,** the world's largest independent music college, this center hosts popular performances of all types of contemporary music, especially jazz and folk. Check the web site for performances. ◆ Admission. Box office M-Sa. 136 Massachusetts Ave (between Belvidere and Boylston Sts). 747.2261, recorded concert information 266.7455; www.berklee.bpc.com/calendar.html

67 JOHN B. HYNES VETERANS MEMORIAL CONVENTION CENTER

Commonly called "The Hynes," this popular convention facility is ordinarily not open to the public. Cross to the opposite side of Boylston Street to study the impressive façade and ground-floor loggia, then peek inside at the magnificent main rotunda. A much admired structure, rebuilt in 1988 by **Kallmann McKinnell & Wood Architects** (who also designed Boston's unusual **City Hall**), the center is so conciliatory toward its surroundings that it's easy to forget it can handle a convention of 22,000. Bankers, dentists, lumberers, and teachers—even the Association of Old Crows—have passed through its handsome portals. The center is connected to Copley Place through the Prudential Center by an enclosed glass walkway. It shares convention duties with the new, larger **Boston Convention and Exhibition Center** on the South Boston waterfront. ◆ 900 Boylston St (between Exeter and Dalton Sts). 954.2000; www.mccahome.com &

After graduating from Harvard College in 1859, Henry Hobson Richardson, a Louisiana native, studied architecture at the Ecole des Beaux Arts in Paris. Returning to the United States seven years later, Richardson created works that were at once robust and monumental. He began his practice in New York, then moved to Boston upon winning the Trinity Church commission.

In 1913, the nation's first credit union was opened by Boston's Women's Educational and Industrial Union.

Restaurants/Clubs: Red | Hotels: Purple | Shops: Orange | Outdoors/Parks: Green | Sights/Culture: Blue

68 PRUDENTIAL CENTER

Former home of the insurance giant, "The Pru" is a sprawling 27-acre complex—encompassing six million square feet of offices, apartments, hotels, and stores in a network of elevated blocky buildings and windy plazas. It was plopped down here in the 1960s by **Charles Luckman and Associates** and **Hoyle, Doran, and Berry** to cover the Boston & Albany rail yards. At the time, the structure introduced a new scale to Back Bay, and stirred hopes for a rejuvenated modern Boston. It's worth a visit to grasp the radical 1960s concept of American urban renewal. Once the city's tallest skyscraper, the inelegant 52-story **Prudential Tower** has been outraced to the heavens by its rival, the sleek John Hancock Tower. Still, Bostonians have grown used to the homely smaller tower. Take an elevator up to the **Skywalk,** the observation deck on the fiftieth floor, and see what's happening for miles around. A new hotel—the **Mandarin Oriental**—was under construction here in 2006. There are also interesting exhibits in the Center on Boston history and contemporary life. At Christmastime, an enormous tree, a gift to Boston from Nova Scotia, is illuminated on the south plaza in front of the tower, facing Huntington Ave. ♦ Admission to Skywalk. Daily, 10AM-10PM. 800 Boylston St (between Exeter and Dalton Sts). 236.3314; www.prudentialcenter.com &

Within Prudential Center:

TOP OF THE HUB

★★★$$$$ Visitors go for the view, or maybe romance, but the food is surprisingly good. Floor-to-ceiling windows flank two sides of the restaurant and bar, offering dramatic 52nd-story views of Back Bay, the Charles River, and Boston Harbor. Attractive "sails" on the ceiling not only decorate but act as sound absorbers, allowing comfortable conversation even when the restaurant is full. Among the recommended dishes are Maine crabmeat spring roll with melon, baby green oak-leaf salad, aged Black Angus sirloin, *médaillons* of venison, and seared yellowfin tuna with Asian spices. The wine list is augmented by a selection of dessert wines, Cognacs, and vintage ports. Live jazz nightly. Dressy casual attire. ♦ American ♦ M-Sa, lunch and dinner; Su, brunch and dinner. Reservations recommended. 536.1775; www.topofthehub.net &

69 THE LENOX HOTEL

$$$ When this historic hotel opened in 1900, it stood alone in the midst of railroad tracks. That year the *Boston Sunday Post* said the edifice would "scrape the sky and dally with the gods." In its heyday, Enrico Caruso stayed here. Later, like its city, the hostelry fell on hard times. But today, having undergone a multimillion-dollar renovation, it has all the luxury of a newcomer and all the charm of a European-style *pensione*. Rates can run from under $200 to $,1500, and a personal touch is still present. The 214 classically decorated rooms line spacious corridors and feature high ceilings, hand-carved gilt moldings, separate sitting areas, and walk-in closets. The corner rooms with working fireplaces are favorites. One of the 11 floors is set aside for smokers, and the hotel's Irish bar, **Solas,** is welcoming. Amenities include an exercise room, valet service, valet parking, and babysitting. No pets. ♦ 710 Boylston St (at Exeter St). 536.5300, 800/225.7676; fax 266.7905; www.lenoxhotel.com &

AZURE

★★★★$$$$ Blue, of course, is a central color here. Somehow the healthy portions and fine food go together in the spacious room under iron chandeliers. The menu, which changes daily, is heavy on fresh seafood. Confirmed meat eaters can get the likes of roast rack of lamb in a nut crust.♦ American/ Fusion ♦ Daily, dinner. Reservations recommended. Diagonally across the lobby is the trendy **City Bar.** Look for leather sofas and dark paneling, well-dressed hotel guests, and an equally dressy over-25 local crowd. There's an extensive selection of single malts and Cognacs and a variety of martinis. Entrance through the hotel and from 61 Exeter St. 933.4800; www.azureboston.com & (through lobby chair lift)

70 BOSTON PUBLIC LIBRARY

Boston boasts the oldest municipally supported library system in the world (founded in 1852) and, with some 15 million volumes, the third-largest system in the US. (The Library of Congress and Harvard University have more). It serves more than two million people each year. The city's first library was located in a former schoolhouse on Mason Street, but in keeping with its self-image as the "Athens of America," Boston demanded a splendid main library building that would set an example for the nation. A "Palace for the People" was what the library's trustees had in mind, and that's precisely what architect Stanford White, in Charles Follen McKim's firm of **McKim, Mead & White,** achieved. This coolly serene Italian Renaissance Revival edifice, built in 1895 and on the National Register of Historic Places, enshrines and celebrates learning. The library's decoration and design brought together the most magnificent crew of architects, artisans, painters, and sculptors ever assembled in the US until that time. Materials alone reflect the nothing-but-the-best attitude of its creators; for instance, a palette of more than 25 different types of marble and stone was used. Years of

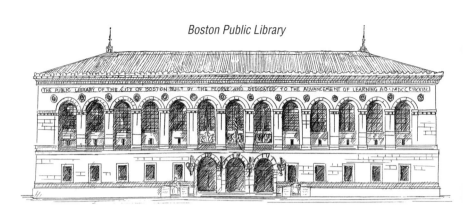

Boston Public Library

neglect eventually diminished much of the building's beauty, but a massive $65 million restoration project has returned much of the library to its original glory. Flanking the Dartmouth Street entrance are Bela Pratt's huge 1911 bronzes of two seated women personifying Art and Science, their pedestals carved with the names of artists and scientists. Prickly wrought-iron lanterns bloom by the doorways, looking startlingly Halloweenish. Note the library parapets carved with the names of important people in the history of human culture. There are 519 names in all; the carvers mistakenly repeated four. When one local newspaper reported that McKim, Mead & White had amused themselves by working the firm's name into the first letters in three of the panels, enough taxpayers were incensed that the architects had to erase their clever acrostic.

Pass through the bronze portals and enter the main entrance hall. Everywhere you turn there are more inscriptions, dedications, and names of the forgotten great and zealous benefactors. Brass intarsia of the zodiac signs decorate the marble floor, while mosaics adorn the ceilings. A grand staircase of tawny Sienna marble leads past a pair of lions to the second-floor gallery, which features enormous contemplative Arcadian allegories by Puvis de Chavanne (artist of the poetic murals in the Hôtel de Ville in Paris).

Adjacent to the gallery is **Bates Hall,** a cavernous reading room (218 feet long) with a barrel-vaulted ceiling 50 feet high. To the right is the former **Delivery Room,** where Bostonians once waited for their requested books to arrive, transported from the stacks by a small hidden train. In the library's remotest reaches on the third floor resides one of Boston's forgotten treasures: the **Sargent Gallery.** Few people find their way up the gloomy stairs to this poorly lit place, yet John Singer Sargent

considered this gallery the artistic apex of his career. He devoted 30 years to planning the historical Judaism- and Christianity-themed murals and designing the entire hall where they were placed. The gallery wasn't quite complete when he died in 1916. The somber murals deserve attention. Also on the third floor is the **Wiggin Gallery,** which mounts exhibitions of local artists, and the **Cheverus Room,** housing library treasures such as the Joan of Arc Collection. The most satisfying way to end any trip to the BPL is to visit its peaceful **central courtyard** with reading material in hand. (Nonresidents will have to bring their own books.) Pull up a chair between the stone columns of the cloister, modeled after the one in the Palazzo della Cancelleria in Rome. Even on a rainy day this is a pleasant, restful place to read. ♦ Free. M-Th, 9AM-9PM; F, Sa, 9AM-5PM; Su, 1-5PM Oct-May. One-hour art and architecture tours M, 2:30PM; Tu, W, 6:30PM; Th, Sa, 11AM. Dartmouth St (between Blagden and Boylston Sts). 536.5400; www.bpl.org &

Within the Boston Public Library:

Two lovely restaurants are on the first floor of the library. **Novel** (M-F, lunch) overlooks the Italianate courtyard with its Bacchante statue and fountain. **Sebastians Map Room Café** (M-Sa, breakfast and lunch) is in the space opened in 1895 as a map room. Reservations at 385.5660

BOSTON PUBLIC LIBRARY ADDITION

When the Boston Public Library outgrew McKim, Mead & White's palatial structure, this annex was added in 1972. In materials and monumentality, **Philip Johnson**'s addition echoes the original structure, yet has a colder, starker feel. The interior connection between the new and old buildings is circuitous: You reach the old from the new by turning left just beyond the entry turnstiles and following a corridor past Louise Stimson's appealing dioramas to an innocuous door that leads back to the original building. Nevertheless, Bostonians use the "new" building like mad; its stacks are open, so there's immediate access to the books. Exhibitions are held regularly in the lofty central space. In the basement is a comfortable **theater,** where regular readings are held and a free film series offers weekly screenings.

The **Access Center** on the concourse level serves people with disabilities, offering special equipment and materials. There are large rest rooms in the basement here (a plus in a city with a dearth of public bathrooms), as well as telephones. ♦ Free. Daily; closed Su, June-Sep. 666 Boylston St (between Dartmouth and Exeter Sts). 536.5400 ♿

71 COPLEY SQUARE

Once called "Art Square" for the galleries, art schools, and clubs clustered around it, the plaza's modern name honors **John Singleton Copley,** Boston's great colonial painter. Originally an unsightly patch created by the disruption of Back Bay's grid by two rail lines, the square blossomed after the **Museum of**

Fine Arts opened its doors there. (The museum stood at the site of today's **Copley Plaza Hotel** before moving to its current Huntington Avenue address in the Fenway, after which its old residence was demolished.) **Trinity Church** (see right) and the **Boston Public Library** (see above) were spectacular additions, and the presence of numerous ecclesiastical and academic institutions nearby enhanced the square's reputation (in Bostonians' minds least) as the "Acropolis of the New World." ♦ Bounded by Clarendon and Dartmouth Sts, and St. James Ave and Boylston St
Within Copley Square:

BOSTON ATHLETIC ASSOCIATION BOSTON MARATHON MONUMENT

Unveiled in 1996, the medallion-shaped granite monument lies flush to the ground near the northwest corner of Copley Square and is a short distance from the finish line of the 26.2-mile annual event. The eight varieties of marble and the eight crests in the monument honor the eight cities and towns through which the marathon route runs. Measuring 15 feet in diameter with a sculpted center, the medallion consists of two concentric rings that contain the names of male and

ROMANTIC RETREATS

For a city that's briskly businesslike, Boston has hidden charms that deserve slower savoring. While everyone else goes about their appointed rounds, you and your loved one can meander at a private pace, enjoying your own sweet *folie à deux.*

Many of Boston's better hotels offer specially priced weekend packages, with amenities ranging from champagne and roses to spa privileges and limo service. And **Julien,** at the Langham Hotel (250 Franklin St, between Oliver and Pearl Sts, 451.1900) offers outstanding French fare, luxurious service, and intimacy not matched elsewhere, thanks to comfy, encompassing armchairs. The area tends to shut down at night (all the better for focusing on each other), but by day it is convenient to Beacon Hill, the North End, Fort Point Channel, and the Leather District.

Traditionalism has its piquancy, too, and if that's more your style, try the **Ritz-Carlton Hotel** in the Common (15 Arlington St, between Newbury St and Commonwealth Ave, 536.5700, 800/241.3333), a bastion for Boston's old guard. Ask for a room overlooking the Public Garden, and with any luck you'll get a Childe Hassam–like landscape suffused with slanting light. The bar is a cosseting world unto itself, but the elegant dining room, alas, lacks culinary verve. Instead, head outside to explore. The romantic **75 Chestnut** (75 Chestnut St, between Brimmer and River

Sts, 227.2175), near the Public Garden, is a charming choice in a Beacon Hill town house. Another good choice for a romantic dinner for two is the **Top of the Hub** restaurant on the 52nd floor of the Prudential Tower (Boylston St, between Exeter and Dalton Sts, 536.1775), which offers splendid views over Back Bay and the Charles River. After a night at the Ritz, browse the Newbury Street shops and galleries or take in a concert at the **Isabella Stewart Gardner Museum** (280 The Fenway, at Palace Rd, 566.1401), always an indulgence for the senses.

Cambridge attracts couples intent on reliving (or prolonging) their youth. The **Charles Hotel** (1 Bennett St, between Eliot St and University Rd, 864.1200, 800/882.1818) draws on the bustle of Harvard Square while keeping just enough distance. It's calm, pampering, and pretty, with patchwork quilts on the pine beds and a premier jazz club, the **Regattabar.** Street performers, cafés, and bookstores in Harvard Square are perfect for peaceful sojourns. (For love sonnets, search out **The Grolier Poetry Book Shop,** 6 Plympton St, between Bow St and Massachusetts Ave, 547.4648).

And don't forget, one of the area's most romantic pleasures is one of its simplest: a stroll along the banks of the **Charles River,** hand in hand.

female champions of the open, masters, and wheelchair divisions since the inaugural BAA Marathon; the outer ring has room for the names of future champions. Designed by landscape architect Mark Flannery, it is encircled by a laurel wreath, the symbol of victory.

THE TORTOISE AND THE HARE

A whimsical tribute to the Boston Marathon is this sculpture by Nancy Schon, who also sculpted the Mrs. Mallard and her brood of eight ducklings in the Public Garden. Unveiled near the fountain in Copley Square in 1995, the fabled tortoise and hare honor the runners. Children, enjoy sitting on the figures.

TRINITY CHURCH

Approach Copley Square from any direction, and your eyes will be drawn to this grandiose French Romanesque–inspired edifice. A National Historic Landmark, it is one of the great buildings in America, losing none of its power to fascinate in the century and more that has passed since it first graced the city. Like a wise and tolerant elder, it offers a model of urbane dignity and grandeur that has not been equaled in Boston. The church is nicely complemented by the handsome old **Boston Public Library** across the way.

Henry Hobson Richardson was at the summit of his career when he designed this ecclesiastic edifice in 1877. In the 1860s its leaders decided to move the parish from Summer Street (downtown) to the Copley Square site. In retrospect their decision seems prescient:

One of Boston's great conflagrations destroyed the Summer Street building in November 1872. In March of that year, six architects had been invited to submit designs for the new structure. Thirty-four years old at the time and a New York City resident, Richardson had already contributed one admired piece to the emerging Back Bay fabric, the New Brattle Square Church (now the **First Baptist Church**), then under construction on Clarendon Street.

The cruciform church's fluid massing is an inimitable Richardson tour de force, especially the leaping exterior colonnade. To contend with the awkward triangular site, he designed the great square tower as the central element. Assisting Richardson with the tower was apprentice **Stanford White,** later of McKim, Mead & White, the Boston Public Library architects. The church's vitality comes from the tension between Richardson's powerful vision of the whole and his spirited treatment of its parts. Elegant bands of red sandstone hold the coarse granite's brute force in check. Inside and out, the church is richly polychromatic in wood, paint, glass, and stone—another Richardson signature. **John La Farge** decorated the majestic interiors with the aid of six assistants, most notably young **Augustus Saint-Gaudens.** Look for La Farge's 12 oil paintings in the arches beneath the vaulted ceilings below the tower, 103 feet above the nave. La Farge orchestrated production of the stained-glass windows (see the diagram below), among them glowing creations of his own—look for the lancet windows on the west wall—and some jointly

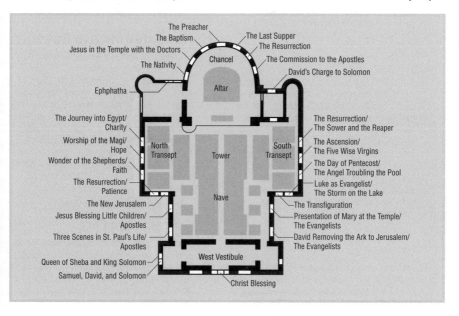

executed by Edward Burne-Jones and William Morris and Company. The interior resembles a gigantic tapestry woven in intricate patterns of gold and rich colors.

Outside, Saint-Gaudens added a fine flourish: On the church's northeast corner stands his dramatic depiction of Phillips Brooks, the Copley Square Trinity's first rector, the Episcopal Bishop of Massachusetts, and author of "O Little Town of Bethlehem." A somber, shrouded Christ stands behind the bishop. It was the daring Brooks who convinced his congregation to move to the new frontier of Back Bay. Saint-Gaudens died before his design was sculpted; assistants completed the statue in 1910, and it was set into a marble canopy designed by **McKim, Mead & White.** The cloistered colonnade to your left overlooks a pretty enclosed garden with a humbler statue of St. Francis of Assisi. The most wonderful time of the year to visit is Christmas, when the church is filled with candlelight and carols during special services. Free half-hour **organ recitals** are at noon Fridays from September through June. Located in the vestibule is a gift desk with books, cards with pictures of the church, and recordings by the choir. ◆ Su services at 8AM, 9AM, and 11AM with choir music, and 6PM. Tours available following the 11AM service and by arrangement. Reception desk at 206 Clarendon St (at St. James Ave). 536.0944; www.trinitychurchboston.org ᵔ

72 500 BOYLSTON STREET

Called "a sort of box covered with architectural clothes" by architect/*Boston Globe* architectural critic Robert Campbell, this 1988 building designed by **John Burgee** and **Philip Johnson** is an overblown, outscaled complex that houses fancy shops and offices. Its famous architects must have lost interest during the project—the building is unimaginative kitsch that turns a cold shoulder to its inviting neighbor, **Trinity Church.** The bowling-ball spheres and urns along the parapets look ready to topple. Johnson was the architect of the Boston Public Library Addition, and Johnson and Burgee designed International Place near South Station in the Financial District, another graceless building that dismays many Bostonians. Local citizens tried to halt the construction of this building—to no avail. ◆ At Clarendon St

Within 500 Boylston Street:

SKIPJACK'S

★$$ This Art Deco and neon restaurant with an underwater motif looks like what it is: an upstart rival to Boston's venerable seafood establishments. A favorite of many younger Bostonians, it purveys 33 different types of fish and shellfish, all available not just broiled or fried, but prepared in more adventurous ways, including

the restaurant's signature coating of lemon, soy, and spice. It draws long lines and gets hectic; if you feel daunted when you arrive, you can opt for a take-out dinner. They'll deliver to Boston, Cambridge, and Brookline. Live jazz accompanies the Sunday brunch. ◆ Seafood/Takeout ◆ M-Sa, lunch and dinner; Su, brunch and dinner. Valet parking available in the evenings. Second entrance at 199 Clarendon St (between St. James Ave and Boylston St). Restaurant 536.3500, takeout 536.4949 ᵔ. Also at 2 Brookline Place, Route 9 (between Brookline Ave and Harvard St), Brookline. 232.8887

73 FAO SCHWARZ BRONZE BEAR

Beginning in 1991, children enjoyed a three-ton, 12-foot-tall bronze teddy bear in the plaza in front of the famous toy store at Berkeley and Boylston. Bankruptcy intervened, but before closing its doors, the retailer donated the bear to the **Tufts University Floating Hospital for Children** in the South End (750 Washington St). The hospital with the unusual name began in 1894 as a hospital on a ship, sailing around Boston Harbor to treat sick infants and children. 636.5911

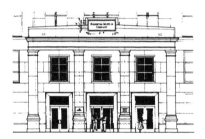

74 HOUGHTON MIFFLIN BUILDING

Posh digs for Boston's venerable publisher (and several other tenants), this 22-story high-rise designed by **Robert A.M. Stern** turns inward for luxury, unlike its ostentatious neighbor, **500 Boylston Street** (see left). The outside is all clean, tasteful lines; the interior is creamy marble with a five-story skylighted "winter garden" complete with splashing fountains, tables and chairs, and a café on a mezzanine off the foyer—a secret indoor retreat in the heart of Back Bay. ◆ 222 Berkeley St (between St. James Ave and Boylston St)

Within the Houghton Mifflin Building:

COTTONWOOD CAFE

★★$$ Bountiful, robust Southwestern fare is served in an evocative, pared-down setting that suggests the desert at sunset, even at high noon. Indulge in the delicious Rocky Mountain lamb (mesquite-grilled, with raspberry chipotle sauce on one half of the enormous platter, cilantro pesto on the other), available in the café, which is more like a bar with some tables, or in the restaurant proper, where a booth is your best choice. Lunch is not served in the café, but otherwise the menu is the same in both rooms, and both are informal. The service is attentive but nonintrusive, and the fresh-fruit margaritas are heavenly. ♦ Southwestern ♦ Restaurant: daily, lunch and dinner. Café: daily, afternoon snacks and dinner. Reservations recommended. 247.2225; cottonwoodboston.com &

CITY SPORTS

A popular local outfitter, this chain has chosen to decorate its flagship store with raw beams and exposed ducts, and somehow the stripped-away aesthetic is effective. The high-energy music pumping through doesn't hurt. ♦ Daily. 267.3900 &

75 BERKELEY BUILDING

Stand on the opposite side of the street to get a full view of this striking Beaux Arts–inspired office building, designed in 1905 by **Codman & Despredelle.** Look for its spectacular cornice and colorful banners waving. Clad in enameled terra-cotta, the steel frame supports five-story towers of glass edged in sea-foam green. There's only one elegant embellishment of gilt, over the front door—the façade is dressy enough. Parisian architect Desiré Despredelle taught design classes across the street, where the Massachusetts Institute of Technology School of Architecture was located. ♦ 420 Boylston St (at Berkeley St)

76 WOMEN'S EDUCATIONAL AND INDUSTRIAL UNION (WEIU)

Designed by **Parker, Thomas & Rice** in 1906 and restored in 1973 by **Shepley, Bulfinch, Richardson & Abbott,** this local institution boasts a gilded swan floating above its decorative entry. It was chosen as a logo because the union was launched in 1877, the same year the Swan Boats settled in the Public Garden's lagoon. At press time, the WEIU was scheduled to merge in 2006 with Crittenton, a Boston nonprofit human-service organization, to form The Crittenton Women's Union. The new organization will continue helping low-income and at-risk families achieve self-sufficiency.

A small group of women established the WEIU to further employment and educational opportunities for women and to help the elderly, disabled, and poor. In 1891 **Julia Ward Howe** became the first president of the union's Traveler's Information Exchange, which began as a secret underground organization for women travelers, unaccompanied

by men, to share information. Today men participate in all of the organization's programs. In 1926 **Amelia Earhart** found a job as a social worker through a career services program here. Her application carried the note "Has a sky pilot's license???"

The genteel **retail shop** run by this private social service organization offers an avant-garde mix of antiques and crafts and is a favorite with Bostonians, particularly at holiday time. Staffed by friendly volunteers, the store is filled with handmade articles of all kinds, books and toys for children, knitting and craft supplies, stationery and wrapping paper, and household treasures. There's also a pastry counter. Be sure to visit the **antiques consignment shop** on the upper level, where great finds often surface. There's a flower stand outside. ♦ M-Sa. 356 Boylston St (between Arlington and Berkeley Sts). 536.5651 &

77 SHREVE, CRUMP & LOW

Since 1800, Boston brides have registered at this renowned institution, and countless marriages have been launched with jewelry, sterling, crystal, and china from this jeweler of choice. They've been at this location since 1929. They created the Davis Cup trophy (1899) and the Cy Young trophy (1908). You can pick up a baby-size silver cup here or order personalized stationery. The antiques department displays 18th- and 19th-century English and American furniture and prints; China-trade furniture and porcelain; and English, Irish, and American silver. The service is expert and assiduous. ♦ M-Sa. 330 Boylston St (at Arlington St). 267.9100; www.shrevecrumpandlow.com

78 COPLEY SQUARE HOTEL

$$ One of Boston's oldest, this modest-size, family-owned 1891 hotel is a Back Bay bargain and attracts an international clientele. It's not fancy, but has a pleasantly low-key, informal European style. Rooms and suites, which received a recent $8 million renovation, vary greatly in size, but all 148 feature wireless Internet access, coffeemakers, individual climate control, closet floor safes, and windows you can open. The nearby Westin Hotel's health facilities are available to guests for a small fee. Dining options include an inexpensive coffee shop. Other perks include a currency exchange, nonsmoking rooms, and inexpensive adjacent parking; airport limo service is available for a fee. There's a café for breakfast and lunch. ♦ 47 Huntington Ave (at Exeter St). 536.9000, 800/225.7062; fax 267.3547; www.copleysquarehotel.com &

Within Copley Square Hotel:

SAINT

★$$$ Pricey, mildly spicy Asian-influenced food is served on small plates on small tables in an *über*-glitzy nightclub, which opened in 2002 in the hotel's lower level. It's the former home of Cafe Budapest and George Wein's famed Storyville. Saint draws a comfortable older crowd, some actually beyond 40. The décor features black, gray, and red hues, padded walls, and flattering colored lights. Enjoy the full bar. ◆ Daily, 5PM-2AM. Valet parking available. Entry from street and hotel lobby. 90 Exeter St. & (by elevator from lobby)

79 THE FAIRMONT COPLEY PLAZA HOTEL

$$$$ The empress dowager of Boston's hotels embodies the mature, full-flowered Back Bay. It not only draws business and international guests, but also lovers of grand epochs gone by. Opened in 1912, it was designed by **Clarence Blackall** and **Henry Hardenbergh** (the latter was the architect of the Plaza Hotel in New York and the Willard Hotel in Washington, DC). It was built on the original site of The Museum of Fine Arts. This Italian Renaissance Revival structure has endured well.

The six-story building's exterior includes French and Venetian Renaissance elements; terra-cotta accents decorate the limestone façade. The European interior is nothing short of grand. The 5,000-square-foot lobby contains period antiques and numerous flamboyant architectural touches. Towering over the lobby is a gilded ceiling festooned with trompe l'oeil paintings of the sky. The **Grand Ballroom** and the **Oval Room** are equally opulent.

The 383 guest rooms, including 17 suites, are decorated in a luxurious classic English style and contain such amenities as marble bathrooms, mini-bars, hair dryers, clock radios, voice mail, Internet access ($13.95 daily), and irons and ironing boards. Rooms for people with disabilities are available. As part of a $34 million renovation of the entire hotel, managers added what they call **Fairmont Gold,** a luxury (and extra-cost) hotel within a hotel.

The Fairmont offers guests a fitness center, a business center, laundry and dry-cleaning service, a barber shop, child care, a concierge, and 24-hour room service. Pets are allowed (with a $95 surcharge). ◆ 138 St. James Ave (between Trinity Pl and Dartmouth St). 267.5300, 800/527.4727; fax 247.6681; www.fairmont.com/copleyplaza &

Within The Fairmont Copley Plaza Hotel:

OAK ROOM

★★★$$$ Fine steaks, chops, and seafood are what you will find at this staid and upscale hotel dining room along with a 30-foot ceiling, Waterford crystal chandeliers, and lots of windows. The menu offers all the traditional favorites. Appetizers include oysters, clams casino, oysters Rockefeller, shrimp lobster cocktail, crab cakes, steak tartare, and lobster bisque. Among the entrées are chateaubriand; grilled aged steaks, lamb, veal, and pork chops with a choice of sauces (béarnaise, mint jelly, chutney, red wine demiglace); seafood including shrimp, scallops, lobster, halibut, haddock, salmon, and swordfish; and roast chicken. For dessert there's—what else?—Boston cream pie. A pianist and a jazz trio play during dinner. ◆ American ◆ Daily breakfast, lunch, and dinner. Jacket requested at dinner. Reservations recommended. 267.5300 &

OAK BAR

★★$$$ At the end of Peacock Alley, which runs off the lobby, you'll find great specialty martinis. Business deals and romance seem to go well here. Ceiling fans twirl lazily high overhead, just as they did years ago when a circular bar in the room's center turned slowly. You can see a photo of the old Merry-Go-Round Bar as you enter from the lobby. With poles and a canopy (but no horses), it was powered by a merry-go-round mechanism. Guests sitting around the bar got a ride too. Today the large martinis (and the steaks) are the attraction—they're some of the best in town. There's a raw bar, and patrons can order from the same menu as in the Oak Room. Music Fridays and Saturdays. (Trivia: Part of the 1996 movie *Celtic Pride* was filmed here.) ◆ Daily. 267.5300 &

80 JOHN HANCOCK TOWER

When towering new edifices invade historic neighborhoods, they often try to gain public acceptance with lame gestures—by aping local architectural modes or bribing with street-level shops, skimpy parks, or outdoor art. Making no such overtures, in 1976 **I.M. Pei & Partners** designed this cool, aloof, and inscrutable tower, with its own style, well away from the spire-crowded financial district. Bostonians have grown fond of this skyscraper as the years passed. A 62-story glass rhomboid, it has a shimmering surface that serves as a full-length mirror for **Trinity Church** while also reflecting the shifts of New England weather. The tower's crisp form is mesmerizing from all angles, whether you glimpse the broad faces or razor-blade edges standing two-dimensional against the sky. The Hancock is now New England's tallest structure, but in 2006 Mayor Thomas Menino called for construction of a 1,000-foot building in the financial district.

The now-popular Hancock Tower had a rocky start: Its construction caused serious structural damage to architectural landmark Trinity Church across the street, and inadequate glass was used in its sheathing—windowpanes popped out randomly due to wind torquing and rained onto the square below. Sidewalks had to be cordoned off to protect pedestrians. All 13 acres of the 10,344 glass panels were replaced; today the panes are continuously monitored for signs of potential breakage. Making matters worse, a later engineering inspection revealed that the building was in danger of toppling, which required reinforcing its steel frame and installing a moving weight on the 58th floor to counter wind stress. Once Bostonians could walk by the tower without flinching, however, they began to notice what a dazzling addition it is to the Boston skyline. 572.6000 ♦ 200 Clarendon St (between Stuart St and St. James Ave).

81 DAVIO'S NORTHERN ITALIAN STEAKHOUSE

★★★$$$$ A favorite with Bostonians, Davio's makes its own pasta and sausages, and they lavish attention on soups, seafood, venison, and veal. Some outstanding entrées include butternut squash fettuccine with red pepper, goat cheese, and toasted bread crumbs, and grilled rosemary chicken with mushrooms, artichokes, lemon, and Pinot Grigio. A good wine list completes the dining experience. ♦ Italian ♦ M-F, lunch; daily, dinner. Reservations recommended. 75 Arlington St (between Stuart St and St. James Ave). 357.4810; www.davios.com &

82 THE LYRIC STAGE

The oldest resident professional theater company in Boston now performs in spacious quarters within the YWCA and mounts such neglected classics as George Bernard Shaw's works. Led by artistic director Ron Ritchell, the company is one of the few non–university-sponsored theaters in the area to warrant critical attention. ♦ 140 Clarendon St (between Columbus Ave and Stuart St). 437.7172 &

83 HARD ROCK CAFE

★$ Here's Boston's branch of the aging, famous chain of restaurants where rock 'n' roll is family fare. There's a menu of surprisingly good bar food starring burgers and barbecue.

The rock 'n' roll theme plays itself out all over: The bar is shaped like a guitar; stained-glass windows honor Elvis Presley, Jerry Lee Lewis, and Chuck Berry; and one wall is covered with bricks taken from the demolished Cavern Club in Liverpool, England, where the Beatles got their start.

Like its siblings, the café overflows with memorabilia: Roy Orbison's autographed Gibson, John Lennon's original scribbling for "Imagine," an Elvis necklace, and objects belonging to other stars. But why come here unless you like din with dinner, want to personally experience a legendary marketing coup, or have a young friend who's hot on the idea? ♦ American ♦ Daily, lunch and dinner. 131 Clarendon St (at Stuart St). 424.7625 &

84 33 RESTAURANT & LOUNGE

★★★$$$ They've added a blue-steel bar, a plasma music-video system, and tons of steel on the walls downstairs, but concentrate on the rich French and Italian cuisine, especially lobster and Kobe beef carpaccio and thin-crust pizzas. This chic meeting spot on the edge of the South End also offers disco in the basement and a late-night bar scene. ♦ French/Italian ♦ Daily, lunch and dinner. Complimentary valet parking. 33 Stanhope St (three blocks from Copley Sq). 572.3311; www.33restaurant.com &

85 JURYS BOSTON HOTEL

$$$$ Run by the Irish hotel group, Jurys opened in 2004. It is one of only two Jurys hotels in the US (the other is in Washington, DC). It's located in what used to be Boston Police Headquarters and offers guests 222 elegant rooms, three suites, free wireless Internet, and 24-hour room service. There's a business center, valet parking, and proximity to the Hancock Tower and Back Bay conventions. Fifteen rooms are reserved for smokers. Discounts and packages are often available. ♦ 350 Stuart St (at Berkeley St). 266.7200; fax 266.7203

Within Jurys Boston Hotel:

STANHOPE GRILLE

★★$$$ This three-meals-a-day, cosmopolitan restaurant serves freshly prepared selections from hearty Irish breakfasts to a full à la carte dinner selection.

CUFFS

Taking its name from the police HQ location, this (truly) Irish bar offers light dining and good drinks. Clientele is a mix of hotel guests, neighborhood folk, and businesspeople.

86 GRILL 23 & BAR

★★$$$$ A sea of white linen, mahogany paneling, banker's lamps, and burnished brass give this place a formal demeanor—the ideal setting for a festive but seemly occasion. During the week you'll see more wheeling-and-dealing Boston professionals than tourists here. Famous for its sure touch with red meat, especially the perfectly aged and charbroiled 18-ounce New York sirloin, the restaurant turns out splendid seafood and poultry, too. The old-fashioned American practice of topping off hearty fare with equally hearty sweets is enthusiastically followed here; the dessert list features apple pie and New York cheesecake. Be sure to come famished, but be forewarned: With few rugs on its wooden floors and an open kitchen, the dining room gets noisy.

The restaurant is in the renovated **Salada Tea Building,** designed by **Densmore, LeClear, and Robbins** in 1929. On your way out, be sure to look for the fantastic bronze doors at the Stuart Street entrance. Cast from Englishman Henry Wilson's design, they depict exotic scenes from the tea trade and won a silver medal at the 1927 Paris Salon. Elephants and solemn human figures protrude dramatically in bas-relief from the bronze doors and their carved stone setting. ♦ American ♦ Daily, dinner. Jacket and tie required. Reservations recommended. 161 Berkeley St (at Stuart St). 542.2255; www.grill23.com ♿

87 CLUB CAFÉ

★★$$ Attracting a predominantly (though not exclusively) gay clientele, this spot is good for a light meal. The menu ranges from burgers to roast beef tenderloin. Also on the premises is an intimate setting for occasional (and often stellar) musical performances. The bar is especially crowded Thursdays. ♦ International ♦ Café: daily, lunch and dinner. Bar: Th-Sa, 9PM-2AM. 209 Columbus Ave (at Berkeley St). 536.0966; www.clubcafe.com ♿

88 MISTRAL

★★★★$$$$ One of the city's top restaurants, Mistral is what a fine restaurant should be. Awards and a record of media praise fill an entire page. Service is attentive and gracious. Wines are wonderful. The dining choices are stunning. Located on the edge of the South End, Mistral is sophisticated without

stuffiness. The dramatic, high-ceilinged dining room comes alive with well-dressed diners seven nights a week. The bar, set off from the main dining room, has 40 seats and seems always busy. Valet parking ($15). ♦ French, Mediterranean ♦ Reservations recommended. 223 Columbus Ave (between Berkeley and Clarendon Sts). 867.9300; mistralbistro.com

89 COPLEY PLACE

This upscale indoor-mall complex covers 9.5 acres of land and air rights above the Massachusetts Turnpike. With 3.7 million square feet of space, it is the size of 2,500 average American homes, 822 football fields, or more than two John Hancock Towers. It includes two hotels—the **Westin** and the **Boston Marriott** (see page 139)—more than 100 upscale shops and restaurants, four office buildings, 1,400 parking places, and 104 residences. In the central atrium, 1,000 gallons of water per minute cascade over Dimitri Hadzi's 60-foot-high water sculpture made of more than 80 tons of travertine and granite.

Plunked down at one corner of Copley Square, the behemoth has become a formidable barrier to the neighboring **South End.** But as bland, anonymous, and prefab-looking as the exterior is, inside, it's marble, marble everywhere, and hardly a bench to sit on. Shoppers are meant to come with laden pockets (among its tenants are the new-in-2006 **Barney's, Neiman Marcus, Tiffany, Armani Exchange, Gucci,** and **Louis Vuitton**) and be ready to empty them in shops that are, with a few exceptions, identical to those in many other cities. By and large, visitors should stick to Newbury Street unless the weather is bad, because although prices are exorbitant there too, it's much more genuinely Boston. ♦ Daily. 100 Huntington Ave (between Garrison and Dartmouth Sts). 375.4400 ♿

Within Copley Place:

WESTIN HOTEL COPLEY PLACE

$$$$ One of Boston's many major chain hotels, this hostelry has 803 rooms and suites on 36 floors, with good views to be had above the 11th floor and two specialty suites on the 36th floor. There are floors designed for people with disabilities and others reserved for nonsmokers. Other amenities include 24-hour room service, a bilingual concierge, valet parking, a health club with an indoor pool, a car-rental desk, many stores, and five restaurants, including **Turner Fisheries** (see right), the **Palm** restaurant, **Osushi Sushi,** and **Bar 10,** a favorite with executives. Small pets are allowed. ♦ 10 Huntington Ave (at Dartmouth St). 262.9600, 800/228.3000; fax 424.7483

When the land-filled Back Bay was laid out, its main open space was named Art Square, since it fronted the original building of the Museum of Fine Arts. In 1883 the square was renamed for Boston artist John Singleton Copley.

Within the Westin Hotel Copley Place:

TURNER FISHERIES

★$$$ This softly lit, spacious restaurant is quiet enough that you can enjoy conversation along with absolutely fresh, simply prepared seafood. The clam chowder has been elevated to the citywide annual Chowderfest's Hall of Fame. For a quick, light meal, take a seat at the oyster bar or sit in the lounge and order the smoked-bluefish appetizer. There's live music nightly. ◆ Seafood ◆ Daily, lunch and dinner. Reservations recommended. 424.7425 ৬

ARTFUL HAND GALLERY

Representing US artists, the crafts featured here are contemporary, sophisticated, and eclectic, and available at a wide range of prices. On a $20 budget, you could take home handmade earrings, beeswax candles, a glazed ceramic mug, or a wooden letter opener. The prohibitively expensive glass sculptures by Orient and Flume are exquisite, as is the ceramic jewelry. ◆ Daily. First floor. 262.9601

BOSTON MARRIOTT COPLEY PLACE

$$$$ This massive 38-story hotel complex rode into town in 1984 with the Copley Place mega-development (so there are plenty of shops right next door). The highest-up of the 1,147 rooms and suites offer pleasing views; comfortable guest rooms have cable TV and individual climate control. There are units designed for people with disabilities, and all but three floors are nonsmoking. The two-story concierge level costs more and includes such extras as breakfast, a private lounge, and special concierge service. The hotel also boasts a four-story atrium with a gushing mall waterfall, along with restaurants including **Gourmeli's** (American), **Champions Sports Bar** (burgers and sandwiches), and a popular little sushi bar. Other features include 24-hour room service; valet parking and on-site parking; valet service; an indoor swimming pool; a fitness/health club with masseuse, Jacuzzi, and exercise machines; a car-rental agency; meeting facilities and business services; an exhibit hall; and ballroom that will accommodate 3,600. The building is connected to **Prudential Center** and the **Hynes Convention Center** by an enclosed footbridge. The hotel is directly above the Massachusetts Turnpike, although a tunnel insulates guests from noise and pollution. ◆ 110 Huntington Ave (between Garrison and Stuart Sts). 236.5800, 800/228.9290; fax 424.9378 ৬

90 BACK BAY HILTON

$$$$ A stone's throw from the **Hynes Convention Center,** this unassuming 25-story hotel caters assiduously to the business traveler. All 385 rooms are soundproofed, with small bathrooms and high-speed Internet access, and decorated in soothing pastels. Many have balconies and bay windows you can open. Amenities include a steak-house restaurant (see page 140), a year-round swimming pool, a renovated fitness center, 24-hour room service, a parking garage, valet parking, meeting and banquet rooms, a 24-hour business center, and smoking rooms (only on the eighth floor). ◆ 40 Dalton St (at

Restaurants/Clubs: Red | Hotels: Purple | Shops: Orange | Outdoors/Parks: Green | Sights/Culture: Blue

Belvidere St). 236.1100, 800/874.0663; fax 236.1506 &

Within the Back Bay Hilton:

BOODLES OF BOSTON

★★$$$ A sillier name for such an earnest grill room would be hard to find. The English décor is a little ponderous, but appropriate to the main business at hand: expertly grilling massive cuts of meat over hardwoods, including sassafras and hickory. Seafood and vegetables take many a pleasant turn on the grill here, too, and there are oyster dishes galore. You can dress up the entrées by choosing from 20 butters, sauces, and condiments. ◆ Steak House/American ◆ Daily, breakfast, lunch, and dinner. Reservations recommended for dinner. 266.3537 &

91 SHERATON BOSTON HOTEL

$$$$ Recently renovated, the Sheraton is popular with business travelers and families visiting the city. There's a new lobby, three new ballrooms, upgraded guest rooms, and lots of behind-the-scenes improvements. Pre-symphony drinks at the lobby's **Turning Point Lounge,** which also has a tapas menu, allow for a relaxed stroll through the Christian Science Center to **Symphony Hall** a block away. The hotel, across from the Hilton, has New England's largest indoor/outdoor pool (with a clear, retractable roof to cover it in nasty weather). This is also where sports teams stay, with a staffer dedicated to their needs and wants. The 1,215-room property abuts the **Hynes Convention Center,** which convention-eers can enter without going outdoors. Rooms on upper floors offer splendid views of the Charles River. The hotel also has a restaurant (see following), a health club with Jacuzzi, and a business center. For those who want more luxury, four floors (the club level) offer free access to the health club, breakfast and snacks

in the 29th-floor lounge, and one of those fluffy robes to use after a shower. Small pets are welcome. ◆ 39 Dalton St (at Belvidere St). 236.2000, 800/325.3535; fax 236.6061 &

Within the Sheraton Boston Hotel:

APROPOS

★$$$ As busy hotel restaurants go, this is pretty good. The relaxed, casual setting is perfect for a breakfast business meeting, and kids can order from a children's menu. There's an open kitchen and the space is comforting, with lots of earth tones. ◆ American ◆ Breakfast, lunch, and dinner daily. 236.2000 &

92 CHRISTIAN SCIENCE INTERNATIONAL HEADQUARTERS

It's easy to overlook the little acorn from which this gigantic oak grew. **Franklin J. Welch's** original 1894 Romanesque **Christian Science Mother Church,** which founder Mary Baker Eddy called "our prayer in stone," is now dwarfed by a behemoth extension. The 1906 addition designed by **Charles E. Brigham** (with Solon S. Beman and Brigham, Coveney and Bisbee) soars to a height of 224 feet. This Renaissance basilica bears the weight of its towering dome like giant Atlas holding the world upon his shoulders. Designed to seat 3,000, it boasts one of the world's largest working pipe organs, a 13,595-pipe Aeolian Skinner manufactured locally. Located on what was the outer edge of respectability, the old and new sections of the church clung together in the midst of tenements and crowded residential blocks until 1973, when I.M. Pei's master plan carved a great swath of 22 acres out of the neighborhood, populating its core with monumental church administration buildings. The

Christian Science International Headquarters

THE BEST

John Drew

Executive Vice President of ABCD (Action for Boston Community Development)

Standing on **Castle Island** in South Boston; especially on July 4 when the USS *Constitution* makes its annual turnaround. And I love going out there at dusk, watching ships going in and out of the harbor, planes coming low into Logan, and people enjoying the evening.

The Esplanade, where the water and the canal meet by the **Arthur Fiedler footbridge**. You can sit on the benches there and watch the sailboats and the river and Cambridge on the other side. It's a great view.

The Museum of Fine Arts on Saturday morning, before the rest of the crowd gets there.

Locke-Ober restaurant. It's the ambience. You could probably go elsewhere for better food, but this is the place if you want to touch past Boston. It's got the bar Jackie Gleason used to drink at and a sense of old-style dining: the wood, the waiters in black and white, the maître d'. It gives you some sense of old Boston.

financially troubled church is now cutting back on its properties.

Strategically flanking the church are the 28-story **Church Administration Building,** the fan-shaped **Sunday School,** and the low-slung **Colonnade Building.** They surround a vast public space dominated by a 670-foot-long, 100-foot-wide reflecting pool rimmed with red granite, a pleasant feature with a hidden agenda: to cool water from the air-conditioning system. The circular fountain at one end is dull when shut off, but gushing on hot days, it becomes a hectic playground and contributes a badly needed note of spontaneity to this austere, overplanned setting. With rows of manicured trees, flowerbeds, and water, the plaza is a popular lunchtime spot. But in the winter the wind can whip through here fiercely, treating the office tower as a sail.

To one side of the church is the **Christian Science Publishing Society** building, home of the well-regarded *Christian Science Monitor,* founded in 1908. Inside, look up at the two extraordinary glass globe lanterns suspended from the lobby ceiling; one lights up to tell the time, the other the date. Follow signs to the fabulous **Mapparium,** a vividly colored stained-glass globe 30 feet in diameter, traversed by a glass bridge. Since glass doesn't absorb sound, you can stand at one end and send whispered messages echoing eerily across the way to a partner. Made of more than 600 kiln-fired glass panels, the Mapparium is illuminated from behind by 300 lights. Designed by the building's architect, **Chester Lindsay Churchill,** the globe was completed in 1932 and has not been altered since. It's outdated, but all the more interesting for its pre–World War II record of political boundaries. Ten-minute guided tours of the Mapparium are offered, as are guided tours of the original church and the extension. Concerts on the 18-bell chime keyboard in the original church tower are given daily. ◆ Free. Mother Church: daily. Concerts: M, Tu, noon; W, 7PM; Th-Sa, noon; Su, 9:30AM, 6:30PM. Mapparium: M-Sa; closed Su and holidays. Mother Church: 175 Huntington Ave (between Massachusetts Ave and Belvidere St). Mapparium (within the Christian Science Publishing Society Building): 1 Norway St (at Massachusetts Ave). General information 450.2000

93 HORTICULTURAL HALL

Founded in 1829, the Massachusetts Horticultural Society sponsors the nation's oldest annual spring flower show. It's a spectacular event, but has bloomed too large for the society's hall, designed in 1901 by **Wheelwright and Haven** and now on the National Register of Historic Places. The six-acre show now takes place at the Bayside Expo Center in Dorchester. Likewise, the Horticultural Society is now based in suburban Wellesley. It launched America's school-gardening movement, which brings gardening studies into schools and spreads a love of growing things. In addition to operating the world's largest independent horticultural library, the society runs a shop selling seeds, books, and prints. Horticultural Hall has been owned by the Christian Science Church since 1992 and is home to the Museum of Fine Arts library, *Boston Magazine,* and other organizations. It makes a striking couple with **Symphony Hall** across the street. ◆ 300 Massachusetts Ave (at Huntington Ave). 933.4929; www.masshort.org &

Restaurants/Clubs: Red | Hotels: Purple | Shops: Orange | Outdoors/Parks: Green | Sights/Culture: Blue

KENMORE SQUARE/FENWAY

This section of Boston befuddles even Bostonians, who regularly scramble references to **Fenway Park** (the famous baseball stadium), **The Fenway** (a parkway), **the Fens** (part of the park system designed by **Frederick Law Olmsted**), and **Fenway**, the district containing all three. **Kenmore Square** is also a section of Fenway, encompassing Longwood Medical Area, a dense complex of world-renowned medical and educational establishments that includes **Harvard Medical School**. A student mecca, Kenmore Square is practically a city unto itself. (And it is a city changing rapidly as development blossoms.) Unlike Beacon Hill or Back Bay, Fenway lacks a cohesive personality, and its indeterminate boundaries are a constant source of confusion to visitors and residents alike. But it's worth navigating the helter-skelter neighborhood to explore its attractions: the **Museum of Fine Arts, Isabella Stewart Gardner Museum, Symphony Hall**, Olmsted's famous **Emerald Necklace**, and, of course, **Fenway Park**, home of the Red Sox.

Fenway was the last Boston neighborhood built on landfill, and only emerged after the noxious **Back Bay Fens** was imaginatively rehabilitated by Olmsted. Like the original Back Bay, whose stagnant tidal flats metamorphosed into the city's most fashionable neighborhood, the Back Bay Fens was considered an unusable part of town, a stinking, swampy mess that collected sewage and runoff from the Muddy River and Stony Brook before draining into the Charles River. The problem worsened after Back Bay was filled in and the Fens' unsanitary state became a concern for the city. A group of commissioners assembled to address its drainage problems and to simultaneously develop a park system for Boston, an idea that gained momentum in the 1870s. Co-creator of New York City's Central Park and founder of the landscape-architecture profession in America, Olmsted was called in as consultant and ultimately hired in 1878 to fix the Fens and create the **Boston Park System.** His ingenious solution involved installing a tidal gate and holding basin, and using mud dredged from the refreshed Fens to create surrounding parkland. Developers quickly recognized the neighborhood's new appeal, and it was "Westward ho!" once again for overcrowded Boston.

The transformed Fens became the first link in Olmsted's Emerald Necklace, the most important feature in the Boston Park Department's plan for a city-scaled network of green space, and the first of its kind in the nation. Instead of a New York–style central park (inappropriate given Boston's topography), Boston wanted a system of open spaces, offering breathing room to residents. Olmsted envisioned interconnected parks, recreation grounds, boulevards, and parkways that would not only beautify the environment and enhance public health and sanitation, but also direct urban expansion, population density, and the local economy. Boston and Olmsted were ideally matched: City officials appreciated not only his talents and civic-mindedness, but also his interest in solving practical problems through landscape design.

Olmsted's plan succeeded, as cultural, medical, educational, and social institutions began relocating to the Fenway area. Boston's devastating downtown fire of 1872 and advances in public transportation also encouraged many to move. During the 1890s and early 1900s the **Massachusetts Historical Society,** Symphony Hall, **New England Conservatory of Music, Simmons College,** the Museum of Fine Arts, and Harvard Medical School were built. Another neighborhood pioneer was **Fenway Court,** the fashionable residence where Isabella Stewart Gardner installed the magnificent personal museum of art that now bears her name. Other institutions have followed; **Northeastern University** and **Boston University** now dominate the district. Fenway's resident educational and medical institutions have played the largest role in shaping its contemporary character. Today the Kenmore Square/Fenway area claims a huge concentration of college students and young adults. It has the lowest median age of all Boston neighborhoods and a transient feel. Originally an extension of prestigious Back Bay, with fine hotels, offices, and shops, Kenmore Square is now largely geared toward its student population, with many fast-food joints and cheap-eats delis, good ethnic restaurants, clubs, and music shops.

Traffic is awful on Red Sox home-game days. Forget parking on the street, and parking lots can be expensive.

1 PARADISE ROCK CLUB

This club, west of Kenmore Square, is one of Boston's best places to dance and to see national and international groups in concert. Pop and rock are the mainstays, but jazz, folk, blues, and country are also frequently booked. Get tickets in advance, since few are left for performances by popular groups on the days of the shows. On Saturday nights when there's not a show, patrons dance to DJ-mixed music. There's a full bar, and minimum age requirements vary by shows. Take the B Green Line to the Pleasant Street stop. ◆ Admission. Box office M-Sa. Doors open at 8PM for shows; sometimes there are two per night. Cash only at the door; credit cards accepted at box office and bar. 969 Commonwealth Ave (between Gaffney and Babcock Sts). Recorded information 562.8804, Ticketmaster 931.2000; www.thedise.com

2 MUGAR MEMORIAL LIBRARY OF BOSTON UNIVERSITY

Few outside the university community know about this library's marvelous and massive Department of Special Collections, dedicated to scholarly research but also open to the public. Preserved and exhibited here are rare books, manuscripts, and papers pertaining to hundreds of interesting people, famous and not, from the 15th century onward (the 20th-century archives are especially strong).

Of particular note are the large collections of **Theodore Roosevelt**'s and **Robert Frost**'s papers and memorabilia, and the archives of Boston University alumnus **Dr. Martin Luther King Jr.,** some of which are displayed in the third-floor King Exhibit Room. The papers of numerous journalists, politicians, mystery writers, film and stage actors, musicians, and others are housed here. Browse awhile and you'll find material by and about Frederick Douglass, Bette Davis, Florence Nightingale, Albert Einstein, Tennessee Williams, Irwin Shaw, Arthur Fiedler, Eric Ambler, Walt Whitman, Michael Halberstam, Rex Harrison, Fred Astaire, and Abraham Lincoln. ◆ Library: daily. Special Collections: M-F. Tours by reservation. 771 Commonwealth Ave (between Granby St and University Rd). 353.3696 &

3 GUITAR CENTER

Across Commonwealth Avenue from Boston University's Marsh Chapel is a storehouse of guitars, amps, keyboards, electronics, and music accessories. You can *carefully* try, say, a $3,000 vintage Martin or Gibson and pretend you can afford it. Some young musicians grouse that it's part of a national chain, but they come anyway. The selection is too great to ignore. ◆ Daily. 750 Commonwealth Ave (between University Rd and St. Mary's St). 738.5958; www.guitarcenter.com &

4 PHOTOGRAPHIC RESOURCE CENTER (PRC)

One of the few centers for photography in the country, this nonprofit arts organization leases space from Boston University and houses three galleries and a nonlending photography library. The 1985 building's intelligent, award-winning design (by **Leers, Weinzapfel Associates/Alex Krieger Architects**) evokes the mechanical process of photography and its manipulation of light, particularly in the architects' use of industrial materials and glass. The exhibitions emphasize new and experimental photography from the US and abroad and frequently feature works by students and members. Check local papers or call to find out about the center's regular lectures/slide presentations; Chuck Close, Mary Ellen Mark, John Baldessari, and William Wegman have all spoken here. ◆ Admission. Tu-Su; Th until 8PM. Call in advance to arrange a tour. 602 Commonwealth Ave (at Blandford St). 353.0700; www.bu.edu/prc &

5 HOWARD JOHNSON KENMORE

$$$ Just beyond Kenmore Square on Boston University's campus, this bustling stopover is convenient to Fenway Park, western Boston, and Back Bay. Lots of tour groups stay here. An older but well-kept hotel, it has 180 rooms on seven floors, including an executive section offering such extras as larger rooms, VCRs, and complimentary coffee and newspapers. Also on site are a restaurant, lounge, and indoor swimming pool. Rooms for nonsmokers and free parking are available. ◆ 575 Commonwealth Ave (between Kenmore Sq and Sherborn St). 267.3100, 800/654.2000; fax 864.0242

6 HOTEL BUCKMINSTER

$$ Built in 1897, the Buckminster is a not among Boston's fancier hotels, but there's class and history here. The Kenmore Square location is amazing, and the price is right. It's two blocks from Fenway Park, Boston University is at the doorstep, guests can easily walk to Newbury Street, and the neighborhood is filled with fun places to dine. The hotel was the site, in 1929, of the first network-radio broadcast, and local lore says early plotting for the 1919 Black Sox baseball scandal took place in the lobby. Famed architect **Stanford White,** three years after designing the Boston

Public Library, designed this six-story, redbrick hotel in the triangle where Commonwealth Avenue, Beacon Street, and Brookline Avenue come together. The lobby was restored in 2006, and the hotel wisely retained the chandeliers and marble flooring. Coin laundry and kitchen on each floor. **Pizzeria Uno** and **Maluken,** a Japanese restaurant, are in the building. ◆ 645 Beacon St (at Commonwealth Ave). 800/727.2825, 236.7050; www.bostonhotelbuckminster.com ⑁

7 BARNES & NOBLE AT BOSTON UNIVERSITY

You won't have trouble locating this store, since Kenmore Square's famous landmark, the **CITGO Sign** (see below), is on top of the building. This is one of the largest bookstores in New England, with three floors of books. The store sponsors frequent events, including author signings and children's story readings. In addition to books, this six-story department store offers specialty shops selling clothing and accessories, chocolates, stationery, housewares, office supplies, flowers, electronics and cameras, and more. There's even a travel agent. ◆ Daily. 660 Beacon St (between Raleigh St and Kenmore Sq). 267.8484; www.bu.bkstore.com ⑁. Also at 395 Washington St (between Winter and Bromfield Sts), 426.5502; 603 Boylston St (between Clarendon and Dartmouth Sts), 236.1308

At Barnes & Noble at Boston University:

CAFE AT BARNES & NOBLE

★$ There are many places to grab a quick bite in Kenmore Square, but few are as serene as this pretty café. ◆ Café/Takeout ◆ Daily breakfast, lunch, and dinner. First floor. 236.7423

CITGO SIGN

The 60-square-foot, double-sided electric sign, with two miles of blinking red, white, and blue neon tubing, dates from 1965. An immediate Pop Art hit, the sign inspired one filmmaker to create a short film called *Go, Go CITGO,* in which the sign did its off-and-on routine to music. The sign was turned off during the energy crisis of the 1970s and came close to being torn down in 1982. It was saved by protesting fans. Eventually, CITGO agreed to keep Kenmore Square's illuminated heartbeat plugged in and maintained.

8 COMMONWEALTH HOTEL

$$$ Opened by nearby Boston University in 2003, the Commonwealth replaced a block of aging town houses and bars. Design critics

and neighbors called the hotel garish, so the original bright coloring was toned down a bit. BU then agreed to spend some $3 million for more design changes. The changes were worth the price; it's a good-looking, comfortable hotel. Some of the 150 guest rooms have a view of nearby Fenway Park. Rooms for people with disabilities are available. Street parking is difficult, and near impossible on Sox home-game days. Valet and on-site parking and retail plaza. ◆ 500 Commonwealth Ave (at Kenmore St). 933.5000

Within the Commonwealth:

GREAT BAY

★★$$$ This much-praised contemporary American restaurant offers relaxed fine dining with a seafood theme. ◆ Contemporary American/Seafood ◆ Daily, breakfast, lunch, and dinner. First floor. 532.5300 ⑁

EASTERN STANDARD

★★$$$ A sidewalk café and a chic two-level lounge/restaurant indoors offer breakfast, lunch, and dinner, and dining for Sox games. ◆ 528 Commonwealth Ave. 532.9100

FOUNDATION LOUNGE

Offering what managers call a sophisticated, mature experience, the plush lounge serves cocktails, champagne, martinis, and Zensai (Japanese appetizers), with recorded and live music. ◆ Daily, 5PM-2AM; Japanese appetizers and small bites until 12:30AM

9 NUGGETS

Looking for old (or new) vinyl records? Nuggets has new, used, rare, and out-of-print records, CDs, tapes, and 12-inch dance singles, along with posters, T-shirts, and magazines. ◆ M-F until 8PM; Sa, noon-7PM. 486 Commonwealth Ave (between Charlesgate W and Raleigh St). 536.0679

For all its substantial contributions to American history, education, and culture, Boston is a geographically small city. If Los Angeles, for instance, were overlaid on Boston, it would stretch from Plymouth to the New Hampshire border.

Writer John Updike, a die-hard Red Sox fan, calls Fenway Park "a lyric little bandbox of a park. Everything is painted green and seems in curiously sharp focus, like the inside of an old-fashioned peeping-type Easter egg."

Restaurants/Clubs: Red | Hotels: Purple | Shops: Orange | Outdoors/Parks: Green | Sights/Culture: Blue

10 PETIT ROBERT BISTRO

★★$$ Chef Jacky Robert's popular, affordable French bistro—think drinks and beef bourguignon, pâtés, and escargot—also has a lower-level pastry bar with dreamy desserts like warm lemon soufflé with blueberry compote or chocolate praline mousse. (The bistro has been so successful that Robert opened another in 2006 in the South End at 480 Columbus Avenue.) ♦ Daily. 468 Commonwealth Ave (between Charlesgate West and Kenmore St). 375.0699; www.petitrobertbistro.com

11 THE ELIOT HOTEL

$$$$ Located on the edge of Back Bay, this all-suite hotel built in 1925 (and extensively renovated in the mid-1990s) used to be primarily a convenient place to stay. It's minutes from **Symphony Hall** and the **Museum of Fine Arts,** and a five-minute walk from **Fenway Park** and the **Public Garden.** There used to be a pack of historic hotels along Commonwealth Avenue—the Vendôme, the Tuilerie, and the Somerset, to name a few—but this hostelry is the sole survivor. It has been redone to a quiet elegance. There are 95 rooms on nine floors, all swathed with traditional English-style chintz fabrics and further decorated with authentic botanical prints and antique furnishings. Lovely French doors separate the living rooms from the bedrooms. Amenities include Italian marble baths, two TV sets with a free movie channel, and pantries with coffeemakers, microwave ovens, and stocked minibars. The overall ambience is quiet and luxurious, with the old-fashioned intimacy of a European hotel. There's also an excellent restaurant on the premises (see below). Nonsmoking rooms and paid parking are available. ♦ 370 Commonwealth Ave (at Massachusetts Ave). 267.1607, 800/44ELIOT; fax 536.9114; www.eliothotel.com

Within the Eliot Hotel:

CLIO

★★★★$$$$ This French-American eatery has been winning raves since it opened in 1997. Owned by award-winning restaurateur Ken Oringer, the plush Parisian-style supper club serves excellent food at high prices. Among the highlights of the appetizer selection are the puree of sweet potato soup; the bone-marrow custard with corn, mushrooms, and fresh black truffles; and the smoked salmon terrine with fennel salad and marinated clams. Notable entrées include garlic-rubbed organic chicken with a cassoulet of spring vegetables, smoked bacon, and potato gnocchi; filet mignon of veal with melted veal cheeks, fava beans, and morel mushrooms; and butter-basted Maine lobster with baby

spring turnips, purple kohlrabi, and Vidalia onion puree. ♦ French ♦ Tu-Sa, dinner; Su, brunch and dinner. Reservations required. 536.7200

11 ISLAND HOPPER

★★$ Though billed as "Pan-Asian," the menu more accurately represents the cuisines of Indonesia, Singapore, Thailand, Burma, and Vietnam, and includes many Malaysian treats. Dining here is relaxed and casual, with banquettes, exposed brick walls, high ceilings, and a wall of windows. Nice wines and imported beers are available. ♦ Daily, lunch and dinner. Street parking. 91 Massachusetts Ave (at Newbury St). 266.1618; www.islandhopperrestaurant.com &

12 BOSTON BEER WORKS

★$$ Yet another on-site brewery complete with gleaming tanks, this one is unusually well situated, a stone's throw from the ballpark. The menu is ambitious, with such interesting entries as onion-and-ale soup, barbecued Cajun andouille sausage, shark shish kebabs, and beer-basted burgers. There's brunch each Sunday, except when the Red Sox are at home in nearby **Fenway Park.** ♦ American ♦ M-Sa, lunch and dinner; Su, brunch and dinner. 61 Brookline Ave (near Beacon St). 536.2337 &

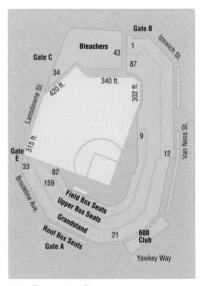

13 FENWAY PARK

The Sox finally beat the curse in 2004 to triumph in the World Series. But even without that stunning victory, Fenway Park would be a wonderful place to visit. Fans are thrillingly close to the players at the country's smallest major-league baseball stadium, which now seats 38,000 people. Unfortunately, it also has the highest-priced tickets in major-league baseball. New ownership has replaced the longtime, unloved owners. Hundreds of seats have been added and even put atop the old "green monster" scoreboard in left field. There's a circus atmosphere outside and in the park on game days, with food stands and beer available. In what becomes a concourse on Yawkey Way there are stilt walkers in Red Sox uniforms, live music, magicians, and sometimes old baseball players signing autographs. Legends including Carl Yastrzemski, Ted Williams, Dwight Evans, and Roger Clemens have all dominated the famous diamond. Babe Ruth made his debut as a Red Sox pitcher here on 11 July 1914. He was later traded.

Built in 1912 and rebuilt in 1934, the park is a classic, with plenty of quirks that enhance its battered charm. One odd characteristic is the legendary "green monster" wall that looms 37 feet high in the outfield. Thanks to the wall, players who hit a high fly ball here score one of the shortest home runs in any major-league ballpark. But if the hit isn't high enough to clear the wall, a line drive that might have been a homer in any other park could wind up a mere double here. The park still has real green grass, and its idiosyncratic shape is the result of an awkward site—the surrounding lots weren't for sale when the ballpark was embedded in the city. Come for the baseball or the show—just sitting among Boston's demanding, impassioned, vocal fans is fun. (For those who prefer to avoid overly raucous spectators, there's an alcohol-free reserved zone; tickets are available on a first-come, first-served basis.)

The ballpark opens 1½ hours before game time. Ask about youth, senior, and family discounts available for designated dates. Souvenirs are sold on all sides of the park—look for the amazing **Souvenir Store** (19 Yawkey Way, 421.8686) across from the box office. Before and after the games, crowds flock to the **Cask 'n' Flagon** sports bar (62 Brookline Ave, at Lansdowne St, 536.4840) and other neighborhood watering holes. ♦ Box office: M-F. 4 Yawkey Way (between Van Ness St and Brookline Ave). Tickets 267.1700, recorded information 267.8661; www.redsox.mlb.com &

14 AVALON

This mammoth dance club holds up to 1,500 mostly young people for a rotating roster of music. There's a full bar, but no food is served. Expect to wait in line at the door, but barring late arrival, everyone gets in eventually. ♦ Cover. Th-Su until 2AM. Patrons must be 21 or older. No sneakers, jeans, or athletic wear allowed. Credit cards accepted at bar only. 15 Lansdowne St (between Ipswich St and Brookline Ave). 262.2424 &

14 AXIS

Music changes nightly and includes progressive, punk, funk, heavy metal, hard rock, and alternative dance tunes, sometimes with live bands, sometimes with DJ spins. Creative dress is encouraged; "When in doubt, wear black" is the club's advice. On Sunday, this smaller club (800 capacity) connects with its next-door neighbor for gay/lesbian night—enter through Avalon. ♦ Cover. Tu-Su until 2AM. Call for information on age minimums and shows. 13 Lansdowne St (between Ipswich St and Brookline Ave). 262.2437 &

14 KARMA CLUB

The former Venus de Milo now strives for an exotic ambience, with lots of Shiva, Buddha, and goddess carvings. Wednesday is gay night, Thursday is jazz night, Friday and Saturday feature international music. ♦ Cover. W-Sa until 2AM. Patrons must be 21 or older. No jeans or sneakers permitted. 9 Lansdowne St (between Ipswich St and Brookline Ave). 421.9595 &

15 JAKE IVORY'S

Audience participation is prized at this spot, where there are dueling pianos and sing-alongs after many Red Sox games. "If you don't have a good time here, it's your own fault," says The Boston Globe. ♦ Cover. W-Sa until 2AM. 1 Lansdowne St (at Ipswich St). 247.1222 &

15 JILLIAN'S BILLIARD CLUB

Get behind the eight ball at one of 50 tournament-quality billiard, pocket billiard, and snooker tables—and you'll find darts, shuffleboard, a batting cage, Ping-Pong tables, video games, virtual sports, and wide-screen TVs, too. Café fare, beer, and wine are served, and on the first floor the **Atlas Bar and Grill** offers innovative American fare. ♦ Fee. M-Sa, 11AM-2AM; Su, noon-2AM. Only those 18 and over are admitted after 8PM. No hats, tank tops, sweats, or cutoffs allowed. 145 Ipswich St (at Lansdowne St). 437.0300

---

16 THE MASSACHUSETTS HISTORICAL SOCIETY

The first historical society founded in the New World (in 1791) is housed in an 1899 National Historic Landmark designed by **Edmund March Wheelwright.** It largely operates as a research center for the study of American history and in that role is surpassed only by the Library of Congress. The focal point is the library, which contains some 3,200 collections of manuscripts and several hundred thousand books, pamphlets, broadsides, maps, early newspapers, and journals, including the papers of Governor John Winthrop and the Adams family, **Paul Revere**'s accounts of his famous ride, two copies of the **Declaration of Independence** (one written in John Adams's hand, the other in Thomas Jefferson's), and a staggering quantity of other such treasures. The society's rare-books collection includes most of the important early books printed in America or about discovery and settlement of the US. Government, politics, women's history, slavery, the China trade, railroads, science and technology—the breadth of topics addressed is immense. The society also owns prints, engravings, furniture, antique clocks, personal belongings, and several hundred works of art, as well as the first map produced in British North America, an 18th-century Indian archer weather vane by Deacon Shem Drowne (maker of Faneuil Hall's grasshopper weather vane), a list of Americans killed in the Battle of Concord, and Jefferson's architectural plans for Monticello. But there's a catch: To use the library, you must fill out a form in advance, demonstrating that you are a "serious" person with a "worthy" pursuit. ♦ Free. M-F. Free guided tours are given if requested in advance. 1154 Boylston St (between Hemenway St and The Fenway). 536.1608 ♿

17 BOSTON INTERNATIONAL AMERICAN YOUTH HOSTEL (AYH)

$ There's no cheaper lodging available in the city, and it's near the **Museum of Fine Arts.** Offering 150 beds in the winter and 220 in the summer, the hostel accommodates men and women of all ages in six-bunk, dormitory-style rooms, separated by sex. Every floor has showers and bathrooms, and there are laundry facilities and two kitchens (with utensils) on the premises. Sleeping bags are not allowed; you can rent a sleep sheet for a modest fee and deposit. The hostel fills up quickly from May until fall. The fee is lower if you're a member, and you can join on the spot. Only members can get bunks in summer. Bikes and packs can be stored securely on the premises. No alcohol is allowed, there is no smoking, and there's a four-night limit per 30-day period. Reservations can be made by phone with a credit card; 25 percent of the beds are reserved for walk-ins. ♦ 12 Hemenway St

(between Haviland and Boylston Sts). 536.9455, fax 424.6558; www.bostonhostel.org

Other Boston hostels: The 100-bed, great-location **Boston–Back Bay Summer Hostel** at 512 Beacon Street has dorm-style and private rooms and accepts some credit cards (mid-June to mid-August); off-season 531.0459; fax 424.6558, attn: Back Bay Hostel; www.bostonhostel.org). The independent (and somewhat grittier) **Irish Embassy Hostel** at 232 Friend St (973.4841; www.angelfire.com/ ma/IrishEmbassy) is close by Hooter's bar/restaurant (222 Friend St, 557.4555) and the Banknorth Garden and requires cash or traveler's checks from its backpacking guests, but no membership card is needed. Guests get showers, kitchen, laundry, and 48 dorm-style beds, plus free admission to some of the nearby pubs, including the Irish Embassy.

17 LOONEY TUNES

This music emporium is a good source for both serious and dilettante collectors of used and out-of-print jazz, classical, and rock records, some rare. The shop also sells movie soundtracks, Broadway cast recordings, comedy, country, blues, and opera LPs and 45s, plus cutouts (discontinued recordings), CDs, cassettes, and videos. They carry a few new items, too, and also buy and trade. ♦ Daily. 1106 Boylston St (between Massachusetts Ave and Hemenway St). 247.2238 ♿ Also at 1001 Massachusetts Ave (between Dana and Ellery Sts), Cambridge. 876.5624

18 BANGKOK CUISINE

★$ A favorite with students and people who work nearby, Boston's oldest Thai restaurant is still turning out great beef and chicken satay (marinated, skewered, and grilled or broiled) and other treats. The long, narrow dining room empties and fills quickly, but service is sometimes slow, so allow extra time if you have a concert or movie ahead. ♦ Thai/Takeout ♦ M-Sa, lunch and dinner; Su, dinner. 177A Massachusetts Ave (between Westland Ave and Haviland St). 262.5377 ♿

19 SOL AZTECA

★★$$ Dinner begins with some of the best salsa and chips, and progresses to marvelous Mexican fare like chiles rellenos (chili peppers stuffed with cheese), camarones al cilantro (shrimp seasoned with cilantro), and puerco en adobo (pork tenderloin with spicy red peppers). Enjoy excellent sangria or Mexican beer; afterward, try coffee flavored with cinnamon and coffee-flavored flan. The rustic dining rooms are festively decorated with hand-painted tile tables and handicrafts. ♦ Mexican ♦ Daily, dinner. Reservations recommended S-Th, 5PM-10PM; F, Sa, 5PM-11PM. 914A Beacon St (between Park Dr and St. Marys St). 262.0909 ♿

20 SAVOY FRENCH BAKERY

One owner of this savory spot (just over the border in Brookline) was trained by a French baker, so the goods are classic French. Go out of your way to sample the fantastic apple-and-almond, apricot, chocolate, plain, and other croissant varieties baked here. Equally delicious are the decorative fresh-fruit tartlets, mini-cakes such as hazelnut frangipane, the assortment of cookies (try the traditional French palmier, nick-named "elephant's ear"), and the breads, including baguettes, batards, and petit pain (rolls). Truffles are also a taste treat. ♦ Daily. No credit cards. 1003 Beacon St (at St. Marys St), Brookline. 734.0214

21 LINWOOD GRILL

★$ This bar, almost across from **Thornton's Fenway Grill,** is more than 70 years old and looks it. But pool and darts are available, and the nighttime music by up-and-coming bands can be good; there's a small cover charge. The daytime baseball talk is usually educated. Red Sox great Ted Williams used to hang out here. ♦ Daily, breakfast, lunch, and dinner. M-Sa, 10AM-2AM; Su, noon-2AM. 69 Kilmarnock St. 267.8644 ᕕ

22 THORNTON'S FENWAY GRILL

★★$ Though there are many grilled dishes on the menu, this place is known for its generous sandwiches and supersalads. Come to the sprawling corner restaurant for a summer supper and some beer or wine before or after a Red Sox game. ♦ American ♦ M-Sa, break-fast, lunch, and dinner; Su, brunch and dinner. 100 Peterborough St (at Kilmarnock St). 421.0104 ᕕ

22 SORENTO'S

★★$$ The décor is pretty dramatic for a neighborhood pizza place: Everything is black and white, including the harlequin tile floor. This is no ordinary pizza either, not with toppings like imported prosciutto, fried eggplant, and Fontina cheese. Try the chicken al Abruzzi (pâté sautéed with basil and spinach and served over cappellini). It's just one of a full array of luscious pasta dishes that share star billing here. ♦ Italian/Takeout ♦ Daily, lunch and dinner. 86 Peterborough St (between Jersey and Kilmarnock Sts). 424.7070; www.sorentos.com ᕕ

23 BUTECO RESTAURANT

★$ Don't be put off by the shabby façade; good food lurks inside. With Latin music pulsing in the background (a band plays on Monday), a diverse, youngish clientele packs the tiny dining room. Plates get piled with such spicy Brazilian dishes as mandioca (fried cassava root with carrot dipping sauce), hearts-of-palm salad, black-bean soup, picadinho a carioca (beef stew with garlic), vatapá a Baiana (sole baked in coconut milk and served on shrimp with peanut paste), and churrasco (mixed grill). On weekends order feijoada, the Brazilian national dish—a hearty stew with black beans, pork sausage, beef, collard greens, and orange. ♦ Brazilian ♦ M-F, lunch and dinner; Sa, Su, dinner. Reservations recommended Sa, Su. 130 Jersey St (between Park Dr and Queensberry St). 247.9508 ᕕ

24 TIGER LILLY

★★$$ Before or after a concert at **Symphony Hall** or an art-filled film at the **Museum of Fine Art,** you can dine on fine Malaysian cuisine, fiery or delicate, at this quiet refuge behind the hall. Try the udang kelapa (jumbo prawns fried in a light coconut batter) or the originally Sumatran beef rendang (beef chunks in spicy coconut curry). ♦ Malaysian ♦ Daily, dinner. 8 Westland Ave (between St. Stephen and Hemenway Sts). 267.8881. ᕕ (bar dining area only)

25 SYMPHONY HALL

Deep-pocketed Brahmin philanthropist and amateur musician Henry Lee Higginson, who founded the **Boston Symphony Orchestra** (BSO) in 1881, wanted his creation's new home to be among the world's most magnifi-cent, so he commissioned **McKim, Mead & White** as architects. The building, completed in 1900, is on the National Register of Historic Places. However, the hall's enduring fame stems not from its restrained Italian Renaissance style, however distinguished, but rather from its internationally acclaimed acoustics, which have led to it being called the Stradivarius of concert halls. It is one of only a handful of near acoustically perfect halls in the world, and the only one in the Western Hemisphere.

This was the first concert hall to be built according to an acoustical engineering formula, the work of **Wallace Sabine,** an assistant professor of physics at Massachusetts Insti-tute of Technology who probed the scientific basis of acoustics. The 2,625-seat auditorium is basically a shoebox-shaped shell built to resonate glorious sound to astound the ears. The best seats are in the second balcony center, from which it is possible to hear the proverbial pin drop on the stage.

The BSO is one of the world's preeminent orchestras. It is in residence here from October through April; in July and August it performs at **Tanglewood,** an open-air facility

---

Restaurants/Clubs: Red | Hotels: Purple | Shops: Orange | Outdoors/Parks: Green | Sights/Culture: Blue

THE HOUSE THAT MRS. JACK BUILT

The larger-than-life Isabella Stewart Gardner (1840-1924) was a charismatic, spirited, and independent New Yorker who married into Victorian Boston's high society but never bowed to its conventions. (Her husband, John, was known as Jack to close friends, hence her nickname, "Mrs. Jack.") Though she became a prominent private art collector and flamboyant socialite, many proper Bostonians forever dismissed her as a brash outsider. But Isabella didn't give a hoot. A passionate woman, she loved the spotlight, so much so that she built a showcase mansion that is now a museum (see page 154) to enshrine her collections and to throw gala parties.

Gardner delighted in upstaging her critics and creating a stir with outrageous behavior, but with a regal awareness of her lofty social stature. Among her many pleasures were art, literature, and music, and she surrounded herself with the most fashionable talents of her time. However, most of her tremendous energy went toward acquiring fabulous art objects.

When their posh Back Bay mansion on Beacon Street became too small for Isabella's treasures, the Gardners started planning for a museum. After John's death in 1898, she built **Fenway Court,** a 15th-century Venetian-style palazzo that proudly towered alone in the unfashionable Fenway. While "Mrs. Jack's Palace" was under construction, Gardner was always on the scene, and often got into the action, at one point climbing on scaffolds to daub the paint to her liking on the courtyard walls. She was accompanied by a trumpeter who summoned workers when she wanted to confer with them: one note for the architect, another for the plumber, and so on. Anyone ignoring the summons was fired.

Gardner held court among her collections, blurring the distinction between residence and museum in an extraordinary, idiosyncratic way. Signs of her presence remain—a table is set for tea as if she were in the next room. Prevented by gender from the prestige and power for which she was suited by temperament, Gardner found in the museum the stage, cultural forum, artistic medium, and professional avocation denied her by her times. Look for the plaque she first affixed over the door in 1900, giving her home its official name. Then find the seal designed for her achievement—carved in marble and set into the museum façade's brick wall, it bears her motto, *"C'est mon plaisir"* (it is my pleasure)—and a phoenix, a symbol of immortality. Henry James thought Isabella resembled "a figure on a wondrous cinquecento tapestry." John Singer Sargent's portrait of Gardner started a scandal when it was first unveiled in 1888 at the private, then all-male St. Botolph Club to which her husband belonged. Isabella had posed bare-armed in a clingy décolleté gown, which so shocked proper Bostonians that her husband became infuriated, threatened to horsewhip any gossipers, and forbade the picture to be publicly displayed. But today you can see it through 21st-century eyes at Isabella's museum, where it finally found its niche in 1924.

in Lenox in western Massachusetts. The hall is also home to the **Boston Pops,** who perform here from May through June. Formerly conducted by **Arthur Fiedler** and then by Oscar-winning composer John Williams, the Pops is now under the baton of Keith Lockhart. For Boston Pops concerts, seats are removed from the main floor and replaced by tables and chairs, and food and drink are served. The **Handel & Haydn Society,** America's oldest continuously active performing arts organization, performs here, too, as do many other local, national, and international musical ensembles and musicians. The hall also boasts a magnificent 5,000-pipe organ. No one should miss the chance to experience a concert here, a delight music-loving Boston has always cherished. ♦ Box office M-Sa. To reserve and charge seats for BSO or Pops performances, call Symphony Charge at 266.1200 or go to the web site, www.bso.org some same-day, one-per-customer discounted seats for BSO performances are available for Tuesday and Thursday evenings and Friday afternoons. The line forms near the box office Tuesday and Thursday at 5PM, and at 9AM on Friday. 301 Massachusetts Ave (at Huntington Ave). 266.1492 ♿

26 BOSTON UNIVERSITY THEATRE

The acclaimed **Huntington Theatre Company** (HTC), the professional company-in-residence, puts on five plays annually at this charming 1925 Greek Revival theater, which seats 850. The focus here is both classic and contemporary, ranging from Shakespeare and musicals

Symphony Hall

to new plays. Discounts are offered for senior citizens, students, and groups; subscriptions are also available. ♦ 264 Huntington Ave (between Gainsborough St and Massachusetts Ave). Ticket information 266.0800; www.huntingtontheatre.org &

27 JORDAN HALL AT THE NEW ENGLAND CONSERVATORY OF MUSIC (NEC)

Like **Symphony Hall,** only smaller and more intimate, this venue is an acoustically superior concert space, ideal for chamber music. Designed in 1903 by **Wheelwright and Haven,** the hall was funded by Eben Jordan, founder of the Jordan Marsh department stores. An extensive $8.2 million restoration project in 1995 preserved its exceptional acoustics. The NEC was established in 1867 as the first music college in the country and is internationally renowned for its undergraduate and graduate music programs. Some 450 faculty and student concerts take place here annually, most free and held during the school term. In addition, a number of musical groups perform here, including the Juilliard Quartet, Tokyo String Quartet, Boston Symphony Chamber Players, Cantata Singers, and the Boston Chamber Music Society. ♦ Box office M-Sa; tickets may be purchased by mail or telephone. 30 Gainsborough St (at St. Botolph St). Box office 536.2414, concert information 262.1120 &

28 GREATER BOSTON YMCA

$ The first of the nationwide association's outposts, the Greater Boston branch was founded in 1851. Stays are limited to 10 days, and guests must be at least 18 years old with a picture ID and luggage. There are 49 single and double rooms with shared baths and a suite with a private bath. Children can stay with a parent. Breakfast is free, as is use of the gym, indoor track, pool, and sauna. A cafeteria-style restaurant and laundry facilities are also on the premises. Smoking is allowed only in the guest rooms. A modest key deposit is required. Reserve two weeks in advance; walk-ins are accepted daily after 12:30PM. ♦ 316 Huntington Ave (between Gainsborough and Forsyth Sts). 536.7800; www.ymcaboston.org &

29 WHEELOCK FAMILY THEATRE

Boston's only Actor's Equity theater company serving younger audiences staunchly upholds a nontraditional casting policy and mounts ambitious, polished productions in February, April, and October. It seats 650. ♦ Box office: M-F, noon-5:30PM; Sa, Su, noon-2PM. 180 Riverway (between Longwood and Brookline Aves). 734.4760; www.wheelock.edu/wft &

30 MUSEUM OF FINE ARTS (MFA)

The first exhibitions under the auspices of this institution were displayed upstairs at the **Boston Athenaeum** on Beacon Hill; the works were moved in 1876 to the museum's ornate Gothic Revival Copley Square quarters, since demolished. In 1909 the museum made the trek out to the newly fashionable Fenway area, joining a number of pioneering public institutions seeking more spacious sites than Boston proper could offer. Here the museum has remained, housed in an imposing, if dull, Classical Revival edifice designed by **Guy Lowell** in 1909. The original structure, with a majestic colonnade on the Fenway side and a

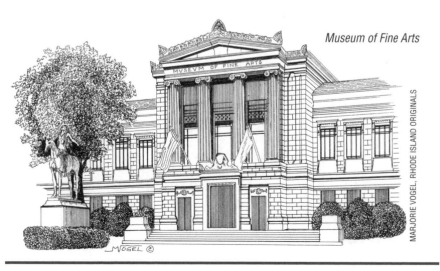

Museum of Fine Arts

MARJORIE VOGEL, RHODE ISLAND ORIGINALS

Restaurants/Clubs: Red | **Hotels: Purple** | **Shops: Orange** | **Outdoors/Parks: Green** | **Sights/Culture: Blue**

MUSEUM OF FINE ARTS

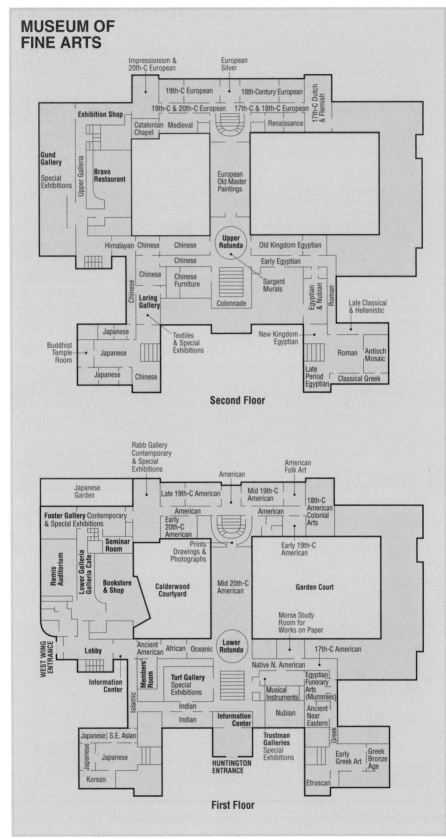

Second Floor

Impressionism & 20th-C European
European Silver
19th-C European
18th-Century European
17th-C Dutch & Flemish
19th-C & 20th-C European
17th-C & 18th-C European
Exhibition Shop
Catalonian Chapel
Medieval
Renaissance
Gund Gallery
Special Exhibitions
Upper Galleria
Bravo Restaurant
European Old Master Paintings
Himalayan
Chinese
Chinese
Upper Rotunda
Old Kingdom Egyptian
Chinese
Early Egyptian
Chinese
Chinese Furniture
Sargent Murals
Loring Gallery
Colonnade
Egyptian & Nubian
Roman
Late Classical & Hellenistic
Buddhist Temple Room
Japanese
Textiles & Special Exhibitions
New Kingdom Egyptian
Roman
Antioch Mosaic
Japanese
Japanese
Chinese
Late Period Egyptian
Classical Greek

First Floor

Rabb Gallery Contemporary & Special Exhibitions
American
American Folk Art
Japanese Garden
Late 19th-C American
Mid 19th-C American
18th-C American Colonial Arts
Foster Gallery Contemporary & Special Exhibitions
American
American
Early 20th-C American
Prints Drawings & Photographs
Early 19th-C American
Seminar Room
Remis Auditorium
Lower Galleria
Galleria Cafe
Bookstore & Shop
Calderwood Courtyard
Mid 20th-C American
Garden Court
Morse Study Room for Works on Paper
WEST WING ENTRANCE
Lobby
Ancient American
African
Oceanic
Lower Rotunda
17th-C American
Native N. American
Information Center
Members' Room
Islamic
Torf Gallery Special Exhibitions
Musical Instruments
Egyptian Funerary Arts (Mummies)
Indian
Ancient Near Eastern
Nubian
Greek
Japanese
S.E. Asian
Indian
Information Center
Trustman Galleries Special Exhibitions
Japanese
Japanese
HUNTINGTON ENTRANCE
Early Greek Art
Greek Bronze Age
Korean
Etruscan

temple portico on the Huntington Avenue side, is now flanked by two big wings, the newest designed in 1981 by **I.M. Pei & Partners**. Standing in the front courtyard is Cyrus Edwin Dallin's *Appeal to the Great White Spirit*, a statue of a mounted Indian gazing skyward, appealing for aid against the white man's invasion. It won a gold medal at the 1909 Paris Salon and attracted many admirers when it was erected here in 1913, but today it looks somewhat odd in this ordered setting.

The museum's somber starkness ends abruptly indoors, where an embarrassment of riches begins, much of it acquired through the generosity of wealthy Victorian Bostonians committed to creating a cosmopolitan cultural repository. It is one of the country's greatest museums and deserves repeated exploration (see floor plan on page 152). Begin with a dose of familiar sights and historic names and faces in the **American collections.** More than 60 works by John Singleton Copley, including his portrait of Paul Revere and his famous silver Liberty Bowl, and paintings by local boy Winslow Homer, Gilbert Stuart, Edward Hopper, John Singer Sargent, Fitz Hugh Lane, Mary Cassatt, James McNeill Whistler, and Thomas Eakins are permanently on exhibit here. Holdings range from native New England folk art and portraiture to works by the Hudson River School, American Impressionists, Realists, Ash Can School, and New York's Abstract Expressionists. The **Department of American Decorative Arts and Sculpture** is particularly noteworthy for its pre–Civil War New England items, including furniture, silver, pewter, glass, ceramics, sculpture, and folk art. The collection progresses from the rustic functional creations of early colonial times to the elegant pieces popular in the increasingly prosperous colonies. The **Department of Twentieth-Century Art** is a Johnny-come-lately, emphasized only since the 1970s, but includes works by Jackson Pollock, David Smith, Robert Motherwell, Helen Frankenthaler, Morris Louis, Joan Miró, and Georgia O'Keeffe.

The museum owns superb works from all major periods of European painting from the 11th to the 20th centuries, with a particularly rich representation of 19th-century French works. On display in the **Evans Wing** galleries are many of the museum's 38 Monets—considered the largest collection outside of France—and more than 150 Millets, including his best-known painting, *The Sower*, as well as works by Corot, Délacroix, Courbet, Renoir, Pissarro, Manet, Gauguin, and Cézanne. Other celebrated artists shown in this wing are van Gogh, van der Weyden, Il Rosso, El Greco, Rubens, Canaletto, Turner, and Picasso.

The MFA's extraordinary assembly of Asiatic art—the largest under any one museum roof worldwide—features one of the greatest **Japanese collections** in existence, and important objects from China, India, and Southeast Asia. The **Egyptian and ancient Near Eastern art galleries** are a favorite with kids—they love the mummies—and are also treasure troves of jewelry, sculpture, and other objects from throughout Asia's western regions. The array of Old Kingdom sculpture is equaled only by the Cairo Museum; the MFA cosponsored excavations in Egypt for 40 years with Harvard University. And it is apt that the "Athens of America" boasts a superb representation of ancient Greek, Roman, and Etruscan objects, including bronzes, sculpture dating from the sixth to the fourth centuries BC, and vases painted with fascinating figures and vignettes by some of the greatest early Greek artists.

Another highlight is the **Department of European Decorative Arts,** which features a collection of antique musical instruments that includes lutes, clavichords, harps, and zithers, replicas of which are often played in special concert programs. The **Department of Textiles** displays an international collection of tapestries, batiks, embroideries, silk weavings, costume materials, and other textiles. The Boston area was the capital of the textile industry in the late 19th century, and this was the first museum in America to elevate textiles to the status of art. Its collection ranks among the world's greatest. The **Department of Prints, Drawings and Photographs** has works of the past five centuries to today, including particularly outstanding 15th-century Italian engravings and 19th-century lithography; many works by Dürer, Rembrandt, Goya, the Tiepolos, and the German Expressionists; Picasso's complete Vollard Suite; the M. and M. Karolik Collection of American Drawings and Watercolors from 1800 to 1875; a growing collection of original photographs, and more.

Special exhibitions are mounted in the modern light-filled **West Wing,** where you'll find **Bravo, Galleria Cafe,** and **Cafeteria** (see page 154) as well as a wonderful **Museum Shop.** The popular MFA First Fridays, a 4:30PM–9:30PM social event for ages 21 and older, attracts many Boston singles. The ads say "Come for the art/Stay for a drink." There's live music, cocktails, tapas, exhibition highlights, and an elegant atmosphere. Admission is free with museum admission.

Restaurants/Clubs: Red | Hotels: Purple | Shops: Orange | Outdoors/Parks: Green | Sights/Culture: Blue

Changes are in the works. The MFA began another part of its $425 million expansion campaign in 2006. That will mean a new, multilevel gallery for the American art collections, a glassed-in courtyard for public gatherings, and reopening of an entrance facing the Fenway. ♦ Admission; voluntary donation. 4PM-9:45PM (select galleries closed during this time); members and children under six free; reduced admission for students and seniors. Sa-Tu, 10AM-4:45PM; W-F, 10AM-9:45PM (select galleries open after 4:45PM). Free guided tours; free introductory walk in Spanish the first Wednesday of every month; in French every Wednesday; in Russian every 1st and 3rd Wednesday of the month. Paid parking available on Museum Road. 465 Huntington Ave (between Forsyth Way and Museum Rd). 267.9300; TTY/TDD 267.9703; concerts, lectures, film information 267.3300 (parking for people with disabilities near West Wing entrance) ♿

Also in the neighborhood: the **School of the Museum of Fine Arts** (230 The Fenway, at Museum Rd, 267.6100) and the **Massachusetts College of Art** (621 Huntington Ave, at Longwood Ave, 232.1555), both of which maintain galleries. And not far away, in the Back Bay, is the **New England School of Art & Design** (75 Arlington St, 573 8785).

Within the Museum of Fine Arts:

BRAVO

Bravo features a light, eclectic, and contemporary menu and a stylish bar offering snacks, light lunch, and dinner, signature cocktails, and an extensive list of wines by the glass or bottle. It is often a destination for people who are not planning to visit the rest of the MFA. Lunch: M-F, 11:30AM-3PM; dinner: W-F, 5:30-8:30PM; brunch: Sa, Su 11:30AM-3PM. ♦ Continental ♦ Second floor, opposite the Gund gallery

GALLERIA CAFE

★$ Refuel for another foray with a light meal, fruit, cheese, or dessert, accompanied by a cappuccino or a glass of wine, at this informal, open café. ♦ Café ♦ Sa-Tu, 11AM-4PM; W-F, 11AM-8:45PM. West Wing, first floor. 267.9300 ♿

CAFETERIA

$ If you're on a budget, this is the best option for a quick meal, and there's rarely a wait. ♦

Boston proper is 48.6 square miles; the Greater Boston area covers some 2,100 square miles. Boston has 790 miles of streets, 43 miles of waterfront, 349 bridges, 8 historic or preservation districts, and 8 major medical research centers.

American ♦ Sa-Tu, breakfast and lunch, 10AM-4PM; W-F, breakfast, lunch, and dinner, 10AM-5:30PM. Lower level. 267.9300 ♿

31 ISABELLA STEWART GARDNER MUSEUM

On New Year's Day 1903, Isabella Stewart Gardner held a glorious gala-to-end-all-galas to unveil her private art collection in its opulent new Fenway Court home. No one could pass up this event, including those who typically snubbed flamboyant Isabella. Fifty Boston Symphony musicians played a Bach chorale, and when the crowd caught sight of the now-famous flower-filled palace **Courtyard,** a collective gasp was followed by awed silence. Admirers and detractors alike were wowed by Gardner's resplendent array of paintings, sculpture, tapestries, and objets d'art, all displayed in such a dazzling setting. An admiring Henry Adams wrote: "As long as such a work can be done, I will not despair of our age. . . . You are a creator and stand alone." Gardner herself described her home, after 20 years of residence, as "very nice, very comfortable, and rather jolly."

In keeping with Gardner's wishes, after her death in 1924 the mansion became a museum (see floor plan on page 155). Her will, however, stipulates very demanding terms for the museum's operation: Everything has to remain exactly as it was upon her death, or else everything will be sold and the proceeds given to Harvard University. This accounts for the hodgepodge manner in which the works of art are displayed here—Gardner's preferences have been preserved into perpetuity. Until recently the museum director lived rent-free in Gardner's own lush apartment; the most liberal reinterpretation of her will to date was to transform these fourth-floor living quarters into office space, a controversial move. More recently, a tiny new gallery (17 by 22 feet) was reclaimed from storage space and deemed a "reasonable deviation" from the will. Museum curators have also initiated an artists-in-residence program to perpetuate Gardner's own predilections as a patron of the arts.

For countless Bostonians and visitors, Gardner's museum has no equal, and many return again and again for another heady dose of her compelling creation. The museum's appeal is in the total impression it creates. In a series of singular stage-set galleries—the **Veronese Room, Gothic Room, Dutch Room, Titian Room**—works by Botticelli, Manet, Raphael, Rembrandt, Rubens, Matisse, Sargent, Titian, La Farge, and Whistler line the walls. Nearly 2,000 objects are on display, spanning more than 30 centuries, with emphasis on Italian

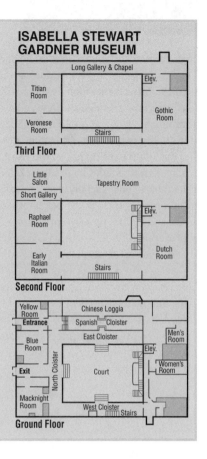

ISABELLA STEWART GARDNER MUSEUM

Third Floor
- Long Gallery & Chapel
- Titian Room
- Elev.
- Gothic Room
- Veronese Room
- Stairs

Second Floor
- Little Salon
- Tapestry Room
- Short Gallery
- Raphael Room
- Elev.
- Early Italian Room
- Dutch Room
- Stairs

Ground Floor
- Yellow Room
- Chinese Loggia
- Entrance
- Spanish Cloister
- East Cloister
- Men's Room
- Blue Room
- Elev.
- North Cloister
- Women's Room
- Exit
- Court
- Macknight Room
- West Cloister Stairs

Empty spaces were created on the walls of her museum on 18 March 1990. Thirteen uninsured paintings and artifacts valued at $200 million were stolen by two thieves disguised as policemen in what the *Boston Herald* dubbed "the Heist of the Century." The most famous of the stolen works, *The Concert* by Jan Vermeer, cost Gardner $6,000 at an 1892 auction in Paris; it is now priceless. Also stolen were two Rembrandts, *The Storm on the Sea of Galilee* (his only known seascape) and *A Lady and Gentleman in Black*. The stolen paintings have not been recovered. In gentler times, Gardner often acted as her own security guard. Today the museum has a state-of-the-art security system and the collection is insured. (Also see "The House That Mrs. Jack Built" on page 150.) The museum is planning its first addition since the Gardner opened. When completed, probably in 2010, a multifloor gallery will triple the exhibition space. Italian architect **Renzo Piano** is to design the addition. ◆ Admission; members and children under 12 free; reduced admission for senior citizens and students; additional fee for concerts. Tu-Su. Public guided tour F at 2:30PM. 280 The Fenway (at Palace Rd). 566.1401, recorded concert information 734.1359; www.gardnermuseum.org ♿ (limited because of narrow spaces; museum provides wheelchairs that fit everywhere)

Within the Isabella Stewart Gardner Museum:

THE CAFE AT THE GARDNER

★★$$ This little café (and it is little) serves excellent lunches, including quiches, salads, sandwiches, and the most delicious desserts. Weather permitting, dine on the outdoor terrace overlooking the museum gardens. ◆ Café ◆ Tu-Su, lunch. 566.1088 ♿

32 BEST WESTERN INN AT LONGWOOD MEDICAL

$$ Smack dab in the middle of the Longwood Medical Area (Children's Hospital is across the street, near Beth Israel Medical Center), this economical 152-room hotel attracts many guests connected with the hospitals in the neighborhood. The **Museum of Fine Arts** and **Isabella Stewart Gardner Museum** are also nearby, and it's less than 15 minutes to **Back Bay** via the Green Line. Rooms for people with disabilities are available, and there is a restaurant as well as room service. The hotel is connected to a galleria of fast-food shops, a health club, and other services. ◆ 342 Longwood Ave (at Binney St). 731.4700, 800/528.1234; fax 731.4870; www.innatlongwood.com ♿

Renaissance and 17th-century Dutch Masters. Objects from different periods and cultures are liberally intermixed in the eclectic manner favored by the mistress of the mansion.

With its soft natural light, cloudy pink walls, picturesque balconies, quiet fountain, and fragrant fresh flowers and plantings supplied by the museum's own greenhouse, the four-story skylighted interior Courtyard is one of Boston's most serene and beloved places. It features authentic architectural and decorative elements collected by Gardner from throughout Europe and Egypt. Of note, too, is the **Tapestry Room**, where classical music concerts are held on Saturday and Sunday from September through April. Also worth perusing is the **Blue Room,** which has a display of Gardner's correspondence with her distinguished friends—including John Singer Sargent, who twice painted her portrait, and the illustrious art historian Bernard Berenson, who advised her on what works to buy.

Restaurants/Clubs: Red | Hotels: Purple | Shops: Orange | Outdoors/Parks: Green | Sights/Culture: Blue

SOUTH END

This part of Boston is often overlooked by sightseers, who favor neighboring Back Bay with its Copley Place and Prudential Center developments. But it does attract those who like to stray from the beaten tourist track. Enticements include block after block of undulating Victorian bowfront town houses, intimate residential parks, vibrant street life, out-of-the-ordinary shops, and restaurants of excellent quality. The South End is now one of the hottest neighborhoods for quality restaurants, with some great new ones appearing in that once-rough section of the South End/Roxbury called **SoWa** (South of Washington). And, as in South Boston, real estate values have skyrocketed.

The South End is one of Boston's most diverse neighborhoods—racially, economically, ethnically, and religiously. After a brief flowering as a genteel enclave, the neighborhood became home to Boston's immigrant populations. It still exudes port-of-entry flavor in places (that is changing rapidly). Some blocks are predominantly Lebanese, Irish, Yankee, Chinese, West Indian, African-American, Greek, or Hispanic. The neighborhood also has a bohemian side, attracting visual artists, architects, writers, performers, designers, craftspeople, and musicians. Many of Boston's gay residents live here. There's a thriving gay culture, reflected in theaters, restaurants, bars, and many aspects of everyday life. Over the past 40 years young middle-class professionals have moved in, gentrifying more and more of this crazy quilt. This gentrification, and the higher prices that came with it, is often blamed for the dispersion of many gay, but not wealthy, residents to other parts of the Boston area, including parts of nearby Dorchester.

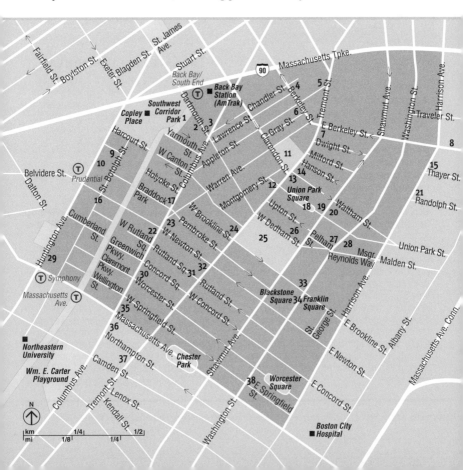

Like Back Bay, the entire South End rests on landfill. The neighborhood was originally marshland bordering **Washington Street,** which was once a narrow neck that linked the peninsula to the mainland. By the mid-19th century upwardly mobile Bostonians wanted fashionable new quarters, and from 1850 to 1875 the South End emerged as speculators filled in blocks of land and auctioned them off. While Back Bay is French inspired and cosmopolitan in style, the South End follows more traditional English patterns. To attract buyers, developers created London-style residential squares such as **Worcester, Rutland,** and **Union Park,** oases loosely linked by common architecture. **Boston City Hospital** was also built in the South End during this period. Founded in the 1860s, it is now the oldest institution on **Hospital Row,** a dense cluster of university and municipal medical buildings located near Roxbury.

Many of the structures built during the South End's genesis still stand. Within this scant square mile is the largest **Victorian row-house district** extant in the US, with more than 3,000 original buildings intact. Boston made the neighborhood a city landmark district in 1983, and it is listed on the National Register of Historic Places.

The South End rose and fell from grace in less than a decade, eclipsed by glamorous Back Bay and the allure of streetcar suburbs. By 1900 prosperous Bostonians had abandoned handsome South End row houses, which were then divided into multiple units and lodging rooms to accommodate waves of immigrants and working-class families. Industries and businesses sprang up. The South End also became the largest lodging-house district in the country, gaining a reputation for harboring dens of vice and unsavory pursuits. Finally declared a federal urban renewal area in 1965, the South End was torn apart, setting the stage for development and gentrification.

Today the neighborhood endures, changeable and fascinating as ever. While suffering all the trials and tribulations that gentrification can bring—the demolition of historic buildings, the construction of unpopular developments, tensions between old-time residents and newcomers—the neighborhood has seen many buildings and blocks being recycled and renewed. Residents and community groups take active roles in healing old wounds—the **Southwest Corridor Park** is but one attractive result.

Explore **Columbus Avenue** and **Tremont Street** for the greatest concentration of good shops and restaurants. Take a walk through tiny Rutland Square or tranquil Union Park, both hugged by carefully restored residences. Stroll along **Chandler, Lawrence,** and **Appleton Streets,** lined with appealing, smaller-scale brick houses. From block to block, the architecture changes from down-in-the-dumps to resplendently restored. And with each block you'll sense the presence of the neighborhood's different populations—the African-American community to the south, for example, and the Middle Eastern and Armenian enclaves along **Shawmut Avenue** to the east.

A cautionary note: The South End's changeable nature means that shops and restaurants come and go quickly, and those that stay sometimes keep erratic hours. The best approach is to call ahead when possible, be prepared for occasional disappointments, and be alert to interesting new finds.

---

1 SOUTHWEST CORRIDOR PARK

Where an ugly gash once slashed the South End, a ribbon of attractive parkland now curls. In the early 1970s more than 100 acres of housing in the South End and adjoining Roxbury and Jamaica Plain were demolished to make way for a highway project. Community protests killed that plan, but the blight remained, a sore spot awaiting healing. In 1977, 52 acres of this area were reclaimed for parkland to reknit divided neighborhoods. More than a decade in the making, the park, landscaped by Roy B. Mann, has become a valued part of the city. Twenty-three architectural and engineering firms worked with more than 15 community groups to chart the course of the new green trail. The result: 4.7 miles of walkways and bike paths graced with young trees and plantings and dotted with tot lots, street-hockey rinks, and basketball and tennis courts. The lauded fingerlike park is as narrow as 60 feet in spots and as wide as a quarter mile in others, and continues all the way to **Franklin Park,** the **Arnold Arboretum,** and **Forest Hills Cemetery.** An adjunct project, the 13-acre, community-run **Southwest Corridor Farms,** provides plots of land and training to urban gardeners.

Starting behind Copley Place, stroll as far southwest as your fancy takes you, and see how intensely used the well-loved park has become by all ages, races, and economic groups. Along the way, note the words of 18 local writers chiseled on walls near T stops. The park is just one piece of the enormous and controversial $750 million–plus **Southwest Corridor Project.** The project also involved relocating Boston's old elevated MBTA Orange Line and constructing nine new rapid-transit stations, including two in the South End. The **Back Bay/South End Station** is a well-crafted structure designed by **Kallmann McKinnell & Wood Architects.** It extends a full block from Dartmouth Street, across from the park's northeastern end, to Clarendon Street. In its heroic navelike concourse, vaulted by massive wooden arches and illuminated by clerestory windows, the station recalls the sense of grandeur of Victorian railway stations. The **Massachusetts Avenue Station,** by **Ellenzweig, Moore and Associates,** is a sleek, sinuous brick, glass, and aluminum structure located where the park intersects Massachusetts Avenue.

Another aspect of the Southwest Corridor Project is the creation of development parcels intended to revitalize neglected Boston neigh-

borhoods by providing employment and development opportunities. A city police department and a shopping mall have been built as a result of this effort. ♦ Dartmouth St (between Columbus Ave and Stuart St)

2 TENT CITY

The construction of affluent **Copley Place** across the way was the catalyst that brought African-American community activists to this site to protest the South End's gentrification. This forced Boston to alter plans to put a parking lot here and to build affordable housing instead. The result, designed by **Goody, Clancy & Associates** in 1988, is a gentle addition to the neighborhood. One quarter of the units in the cheerful patterned-brick complex of apartments and row houses are market rate, one quarter are for low-income residents, and one half are for moderate-income residents. The biggest surprise is the name, which preserves the political moment when activists set up tents here in protest. It was among the earliest in the wave of tent cities that spread across the country as the homelessness crisis worsened. ♦ Dartmouth St (between Columbus Ave and Stuart St)

3 THE CLADDAGH

★$ This Irish pub offers just the sort of filling, unfussy food you'd expect to find in a neighborhood bar. You're best off with burgers, chicken, stews, and other straightforward items. The walls are adorned with Irish family crests. ♦ Irish-American/Takeout ♦ Daily, lunch and dinner. 335 Columbus Ave (between Clarendon and Dartmouth Sts). 262.9874

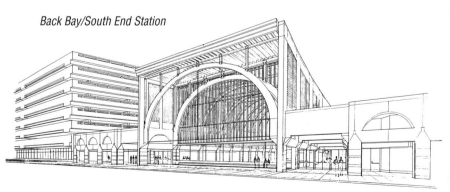

Back Bay/South End Station

COURTESY OF KALLMAN MCKINNELL & WOOD ARCHITECTS

JEWISH BOSTON

Before the North End became the Italian North End around 1920, Yiddish was common on the narrow neighborhood streets.

Tenements that had housed Irish-Catholic immigrants since the beginning of the Great Famine in the 1840s filled in the 1870s with poor Jews from Eastern Europe, who were not always welcomed by the city's long-established German Jewish community. The Irish, of course, had replaced native white Protestants and others—who had not always welcomed them.

Roxbury, now a predominantly African-American urban neighborhood just south of the trendy South End, was what writer **Nat Hentoff** calls a Jewish ghetto when he grew up there in the 1930s and 1940s. Hentoff took the bus from Roxbury to the merit-admission Boston Latin School on Louis Pasteur Avenue in the Fenway and went on to write about jazz, politics, and civil liberties. In his 1986 memoir, *Boston Boy*, he writes of Jewish Roxbury as a world of bagels, Talmudists, herring men, and radical politics. Large parts of Dorchester, now Irish and African-American, were likewise primarily Jewish. Between 1915 and 1950, Roxbury and Dorchester were centers of Boston Jewish life.

Michael A. Ross of Belmont, author of *BostonWalks' The Jewish Friendship Trail* guidebook, points to places like the **Charles Playhouse** in the theater district (74-78 Warrenton St), which began life as a Unitarian church but was Temple Ohabei Shalom from 1859 to 1874. He notes the Beacon Hill houses of US Supreme Court Justice **Louis Dembitz Brandeis** (6 Otis Place and 114 Mt. Vernon St) and **Edward Filene,** the first president of what has grown to be Filene's department stores (12 Otis Place). The **African Meeting House** at 8 Smith Court, off Joy Street, was the Libawitz synagogue for some 70 years, beginning in the 1890s. And the **AME Zion Church** at Columbus Avenue and Northampton Street was Temple Israel from 1884 to 1906. The **West End,** on the back of Beacon Hill, filled with Jewish immigrants from the 1890s to the 1930s. Most of it was demolished in the 1960s to make way for urban renewal and Massachusetts General Hospital, although some landmarks remain. Ross says there were settlement houses, 15 synagogues, and a school system that was, at peak, 70 to 80 percent Jewish.

The Boston Jewish community is widely dispersed now, with some concentration in Newton, Sharon, and Brookline. There are delicatessens of varying quality all over, of course (Harvard professor and attorney **Alan Dershowitz** started a short-lived one in Harvard Square a few years ago), but Ross recommends the downtown kosher dairy at the **Milk Street Cafe** (50 Milk St and 0 Post Office Square). Or take a short ride from Boston on the T's Green Line subway to Brookline's Coolidge Corner to enjoy kosher Chinese food at **Taam China** (423 Harvard St) or kosher deli fare at **Rubin's** (500 Harvard St).

4 CHANDLER INN HOTEL

$$ This hotel is clean, safe, and a steal. The 56 rooms boast all the basic amenities, including air conditioning, and there's a bar (but no restaurant) on the premises. It has a large gay clientele and is genial to all, especially the budget-conscious traveler. ♦ 26 Chandler St (at Berkeley St). 482.3450, 800/842.3450; www.chandlerinn.com

5 ICARUS

★★$$$ The mood is muted and relaxed, the décor and cuisine eclectic. Beneath a ceiling edged with neon, a statue of winged Icarus surveys the two-tiered dining room, where a diverse clientele enjoys chef/co-owner Chris Douglass's seasonal inspirations. The menu might include polenta with wild mushrooms and thyme, lobster in ginger-cream sauce on homemade noodles, grilled tuna with wasabi and sushi, pork loin with mango and jalapeño salsa, caramel-apple tart, and cherry-chocolate-chunk ice cream with icebox cookies. The lengthy wine list is superb. ♦ International ♦ M-Sa, dinner; Su, brunch; closed Su in summer. Reservations recommended F-Su. Valet parking available W-Sa. 3 Appleton St (between Tremont and Berkeley Sts). 426.1790

5 MASA

★★$$$$ Sophisticated Southwestern cooking in a comfortable, art-filled room of creams, natural tones, and mahogany. Try the skillet-

---

Restaurants/Clubs: Red | **Hotels: Purple** | Shops: Orange | **Outdoors/Parks: Green** | Sights/Culture: Blue roasted duck breast with cranberry chili sauce. The $1 tapas are a treat too. ♦ Southwestern ♦ Tu-Su, dinner. Valet parking available. 439 Tremont St (between E Berkeley and Herald Sts). 338.8884; www.masarestaurant.com ♿

6 BERKELEY RESIDENCE CLUB

$ Run by the YWCA, this 200-room residence for women combines features of a hotel, dormitory, and old-fashioned rooming house. The clientele is an interesting mix: tourists, students, and working and professional women, some of them long-term residents. The rooms are tiny—just the basics—with some doubles available. Each well-kept bathroom is shared by 13 to 16 women. There's a library, sitting room, laundry room, TV room, and pretty outdoor courtyard. The dining room serves two full meals a day (extra charge), with takeout available. Conveniently located, the residence is affordable and secure. Inquire about the rules, which aren't excessive and are designed to protect residents. The second floor has a less restrictive policy on gentleman callers. There are nightly and weekly rates; short-term guests also pay a nominal fee for temporary membership. ♦ 40 Berkeley St (at Appleton St). 375.2524 ♿

7 OLDE DUTCH COTTAGE CANDY

This labyrinthine shop is notable for its kitschy atmosphere and eclectic merchandise, an odd mix of antiques, bric-a-brac, and handmade chocolate. ♦ Daily, noon-5PM. 518 Tremont St (at Dwight St). 338.0233

8 MEDIEVAL MANOR

★$$$$ What to say about this inexplicably popular and long-running themed theater/restaurant? An evening here involves a gargantuan three-hour, eat-with-your-fingers, fixed-price feast of sorts, with bawdy musical comedy starring singing wenches, oafs, strolling minstrels, and a sexist "Lord of the Manor." The whole thing's participatory, which means you can get into the action if you so choose—joined by many others from the typically vocal audience. Students pack the place. Though the feast is heavy on roast meat and chicken, vegetarians can join in, too, with 48 hours' advance notice. Parties of 4 to 8 are recommended, and no party of more than 10 is accepted if all male, all female, or all Harvard. There are more numbers-related rules; call to inquire. By car: Take I-93 south to the Albany Street exit, then turn right onto East Berkeley Street. ♦ American ♦ Admission. Call for show times. Reservations required. 246 E Berkeley St (between Albany St and Harrison Ave). 423.4900; www.medievalmanor.com

9 COPLEY INN

$$$ Set in a European-style three-story brick town house, this hotel has 20 contemporary studio units, each with a kitchenette, private bath, cable TV, and telephone with voice mail. The inn is located on the corner of an attractive Victorian-era residential street convenient to Back Bay's **Copley Square.** There are no public rooms, no meal service, and no elevator. Children under 12 stay free. ♦ 19 Garrison St (at St. Botolph St). 236.0300, 800/232.0306; fax 536.0816; www.copleyinn.com

10 THE COLONNADE HOTEL

$$$ Named for the columns that cross its concrete Bauhaus façade, this modern luxury hotel has gracious public rooms and 285 rooms and suites with city views and marble bathrooms. On the premises is **Brasserie Jo** restaurant, serving Alsatian French cuisine. Other amenities include a lounge, fitness room, outdoor rooftop pool, indoor parking, a multilingual staff, 24-hour room service, same-day valet service (for an additional fee), and foreign currency exchange. ♦ 120 Huntington Ave (between W Newton and Garrison Sts). 424.7000, 800/962.3030; fax 424.1717; www.colonnadehotel.com ♿

11 BOSTON CENTER FOR THE ARTS (BCA)

Since 1970, the city has subsidized art and cultural events at this three-acre complex. In addition to studios for some 60 artists chosen by their peers, there is office and performance space for various theater and dance groups. One of the complex's many converted buildings is the **Cyclorama,** a beautiful, shallow, steel-trussed dome built by **Cummings & Sears** in 1884. Its original raison d'être was to house a novel tourist attraction: a 400-by-50-foot circular mural of the Battle of Gettysburg by Paul Philippoteaux, which is today exhibited in Gettysburg. Subsequently, the building served as a skating rink; a track for bicycle races; a gymnasium and workout ring for boxers, where Boston's famous prizefighter **John L. Sullivan** fought; Alfred Champion's garage, where he invented the spark plug; and a flower market from 1923 to 1968. The Cyclorama currently houses three theaters and is the site of annual art and antiques shows, flea markets, and other large-scale events. The theaters (the **BCA Theater, The Black Box,** the **BCA Plaza Theater,** and the **Calderwood Pavilion at the BCA,** including the Virginia Wimberly Theatre and the Nancy and Edward Roberts Studio Theatre) have hosted dozens of Greater Boston performing arts groups, which have presented new and classical works here. The attractive kiosk out front was originally a cupola atop a Roxbury building designed by Gridley J.F. Bryant, architect of the Old City Hall, the original Boston City Hospital building, and other Boston landmarks. ♦ 539 Tremont St (between Clarendon and Berkeley Sts). 426.5000, recorded information 426.7700, TTY/TTD 348.2926; www.bcaonline.org &

Boston Ballet Center

Corps of ballerinas leapt for joy when work was completed in 1991 on this splendid and spacious **Graham Gund**-designed dance center, the largest in New England. The foyer itself is like a stage set, with a grand pair of bifurcating staircases. The largest of the studios duplicates the dimensions of the Wang Center stage, so that *The Nutcracker*—the most popular rendition in the world—can be rehearsed under authentic conditions. ♦ Tours can be arranged through the volunteer office. 19 Clarendon St (at Warren Ave). 695.6950 &

Hamersley's Bistro

★★★★$$$$ Ambitious in cuisine, modest in décor, Gordon and Fiona Hamersley's restaurant is one of the most appealing in Boston. In the exposed kitchen, Gordon and his crew don baseball caps and deftly turn out favorites inspired by French country cooking—lemon and garlic chicken (Hamersley is famous for his chicken), tenderloin of beef with wild mushroom tart and porcini sauce, and an amazing Mediterranean sea bass braised in Champagne with black truffles. The cozy dining rooms are filled with an interesting assortment of neighborhood people, suburban visitors, and artists, actors, musicians, architects, and other creative folk. ♦ French ♦ Daily, dinner. Reservations recommended. Valet parking available. 553 Tremont St. 423.2700; www.hamersleysbistro.com &

Picco Pizza and Ice Cream

★$ There's more than pizza and ice cream in this busy, retro-looking restaurant in the base of the expensive Atelier 505 building. You can have a real brown-cow ice-cream soda, a pie, or a sandwich at a table or, better yet, the counter, complete with chromed, red-cover stools. There are also sidewalk-patio tables. ♦ American ♦ Daily, lunch and dinner. 513 Tremont St (between Dwight and E Berkeley Sts). 927.0066; piccorestaurant.com &

Sibling Rivalry

★★$$ The brother chefs here offer fare like spit-roast chicken with chive crepe filled with sausage, sage, and fontina cheese, with Madeira-thyme sauce and vegetables. There's an open feel to the place (with an open kitchen), a great location next to the Calderwood Pavillion, and an attractive, lively clientele. Across Tremont is Milford Street, lined with three-story vintage town houses that are in the process of being remodeled. ♦ American ♦ Daily, dinner; Sa, Su, lunch. 525 Tremont St (between Dwight and Milford Sts). 338.5338; www.siblingrivalryboston.com

12 Garden of Eden

★★$ All the fixings for a proper tea are prettily presented at this café, which is decorated with dried flowers and garden statuary. They carry top-notch teas, coffees, and jams, and such stellar baked goods as hearty whole-wheat loaves, rosemary focaccia, fruit tarts, and a full range of French pastries. In addition, superb pastas, soups, and salads are available to eat on site or to take home. Try the coq au vin or garlic-parsley-basil pasta tossed with sun-dried tomato–basil sauce and fresh pine nuts. The most popular summer soup is the creamless cream of asparagus soup, thickened with puree of white rice. Sandwiches are topped with endive, watercress, romaine, or radicchio. It's the perfect place to grab a meal on the run or to linger and stock a larder. ♦ Continental/Takeout ♦ Daily, breakfast and lunch. 577 Tremont St (between Dartmouth and Union Park Sts). 247.8377; www.goeboston.com

13 Aquitaine

★★$$$ One of the better French bistros in Boston, with yummy steak and fries. More complex fare involves dishes like magret of duck with Anjou pear, basted monkfish with spring peas, and pork and foie gras with lentil cream. There are high ceilings, leather booths, an open kitchen, and windows looking onto Tremont Street, as well as ambitious (and pricey) French and California wine offerings. ♦ French ♦ Daily, dinner; Sa, Su, brunch. 569 Tremont St (between Union Park and Clarendon Sts). 424.8577; fax; 424.0249; www.aquitaineboston.com &.

Restaurants/Clubs: Red | Hotels: Purple | Shops: Orange | Outdoors/Parks: Green | Sights/Culture: Blue

14 ADDIS RED SEA ETHIOPIAN RESTAURANT

★★$ Adventurous diners sit around a *mesob* (woven table) and use bits of *injera* (crepelike bread) to scoop up morsels of chicken, lamb, beef, or vegetables. There are two basic preparations to choose from: *watt* (spicy) dishes are infused with *berbere* (cayenne pepper) sauce, while the *alicha* (yellow pepper) choices tend to be a bit milder. Wash your dinner down with Ethiopian beer or wine. ♦ Ethiopian ♦ M-F, dinner; Sa, Su, lunch and dinner. 544 Tremont St (between Waltham and Hanson Sts). 426.8727; www.addisredsea.com

14 B&G OYSTERS

★★$$$ Oysters and seafood, but mostly oysters, are the stars here. There's a white-marble oyster bar surrounding the open kitchen, oyster shuckers, and 12 varieties of oysters from which to choose. Or you might like a lobster B.L.T. Barbara Lynch, executive chef and co-owner of **No 9 Park,** is the one behind this fun, casual, quality place. ♦ Seafood. ♦ Daily, lunch and dinner. 550 Tremont St (at Waltham St). 423.0550; www.bandgoysters.com &

15 BROMFIELD GALLERY

Boston's oldest artist-owned cooperative gallery exhibits contemporary art in a variety of media, realist to abstract, by member artists as well as emerging and established visiting artists. Exhibits (solo or group shows) change once a month. ♦ W-Sa, noon-5PM. 450 Harrison Ave (at Thayer St). 451.3605

16 ST. BOTOLPH STREET

Stroll down this pleasant stretch of street, which New York City's Ash Can School painter George Benjamin Luks portrayed in *Noontime, St. Botolph* (on view in the Museum of Fine Arts). Look for the **Musician's Mutual Relief Society Building** at No. 56, an 1886 commercial hall designed by **Cabot and Chandler** that was renovated and suitably ornamented for the society's use in 1913 (it now houses apartments). Separated by stone lyres beneath the cornice are composers' names. At the Cumberland Street intersection is an attractive schoolhouse dating from 1891, converted to condominiums in 1980 by **Graham Gund Associates.** ♦ Between Gainsborough and Harcourt Sts

17 CHARLIE'S SANDWICH SHOPPE

★★$ Family run for more than 50 years, this unpretentious luncheonette is a melting pot, attracting all types of folks in search of a hearty breakfast or lunch. Owner Christi Manjourides stays up all night baking pies and muffins, while sons Chris and Arthur wait tables by day. Relax among the awards, accolades, and smiling photos taken at the eatery since opening day in 1927. Start your day with a platter of cranberry pancakes or a Cajun omelette with spicy sausage. Lunch specials include cheeseburgers, Greek salad, turkey hash, frankfurters and beans, fried clams, hot pastrami on a bulky roll, sweet-potato pie, and more. It's pleasant to linger —that is, if you can ignore the lines of people waiting for a table. Duke Ellington and other famous African-American musicians were welcomed here in the 1940s, when people of color were barred from most Boston restaurants. ♦ American ♦ M-Sa, breakfast and lunch. No credit cards accepted. 429 Columbus Ave (between Braddock Park and Holyoke St). 536.7669

18 UNION PARK

Designed in the 1850s, the first square to be finished in the South End remains one of its most special places. Enclosed by an iron fence, the elliptical park is lush and shady and accented with fountains and flowers. It's bordered by big brick town houses dating from the neighborhood's brief shining moment before Back Bay became the place to lay out one's welcome mat. The handsome houses and perfect park commune harmoniously in their own little world. Regrettably, gauche modern hands have tacked on unsightly extra stories to the houses here and there, marring an otherwise splendid composition. ♦ Between Shawmut Ave and Tremont St

19 JOE V'S

★★$$ The monkey logo used by Joe V's shouldn't obscure the fact that there's good, reasonably priced food in this friendly bistro a few strides from Union Park. There are thin-crust pizzas, including the astounding "I Just Worked Out" with pepperoni, sausage, meatballs, mushrooms, red onions, and red peppers. Entrées include more sophisticated dishes like lobster ravioli in tomato vodka cream sauce. The wine list is pioneering and classifies wines as either cheap or decent. You'll find metered parking on nearby Washington Street, but beware the resident-only parking signs on Shawmut. ♦ American bistro ♦ Daily, dinner; Su, brunch. 315 Shawmut Ave (at Union Park). 338.5638

20 FRANKLIN CAFÉ

★★$$ This small, casual-chic neighborhood restaurant and bar is the real South End, says South End resident and Franklin patron Chris Haynes. The clientele is a mixture of straight and gay, of businesspeople, artists, actors, and young professionals—there's usually a crowd meeting and greeting around the long bar. The décor is blacks and greens with lots of candles, and nine booths look out two big windows onto Shawmut Avenue. Chef David DuBois's cooking is award-winning—a bargain of SoHo-style eating. You'll find paper napkins and no desserts, but look for the seared soy-marinated chicken livers with bacon and horseradish-fennel salad, and for the gourmet turkey meat loaf with Turkish figs for the gravy. ♦ Contemporary American. ♦ Daily, dinner with full menu to 1:30AM. No reservations accepted. 278 Shawmut Ave (at Waltham St). 350.0010; fax 350.5115; www.franklincafe.com. Also at The Franklin Cape Ann, a sister café on the North Shore, which opened in 2001. Full dinner menu (with dessert) daily until midnight. 118 Main St, Gloucester. 978/283.7888 &

20 SOUTH END BUTTERY

A relaxed neighborhood coffee shop with good breads, muffins, pastries, and desserts (try the signature cupcakes). There's breakfast, of course, but sandwiches and salads rule at lunch. Takeout too. ♦ Daily. No credit cards accepted. 314 Shawmut Ave (at Union Park St). 482.1015 &

21 ARS LIBRI

On the first floor of this converted brick factory building is a quiet shop renowned internationally for its large and comprehensive inventory of rare and out-of-print books and periodicals about the fine arts, including architecture and photography. A visitor might encounter such treasures as Francisco de Goya's *Los Caprichos* or drawings by Albrecht Dürer. The owners buy and sell out-of-print and rare scholarly works, exhibition catalogs, print portfolios, and books with original graphics dating from the 16th century onward. Most business is conducted via subject-oriented catalogs sent to universities, libraries, museums, and individuals. The **Mario Diacono** contemporary art gallery is within Ars Libri. ♦ M-Sa. 500 Harrison Ave (at Randolph St). 357.5212; www.arslibri.com &

22 UNION UNITED METHODIST CHURCH

Designed by **Alexander R. Estey,** the architect of **Emmanuel Church** in Back Bay, this 1877 Gothic Revival creation has the gracious proportions and picturesqueness of a rural parish church. Its demure size makes it all the more friendly and inviting. ♦ Daily. 485 Columbus Ave (at W Rutland Sq). 536.0872

23 PETIT ROBERT

★★$$ Chef Jackie Robert, who made his reasonably priced, high-quality French bistro a success on Commonwealth Avenue in Kenmore Square, has brought the concept here to the former home of Rouge. It's across from the Union United Methodist Church. ♦ French Bistro ♦ Daily, lunch and dinner. 480 Columbus Ave (between W Newton and Pembroke Sts). 867.0600

24 TREMONT 647

★★$$ An attractive young professional crowd frequents this South End bistro, which offers good food and very nice wines. Dishes include Singapore-style chicken with rice and golden pineapple. The restaurant is popular for brunch. ♦ American/Eclectic ♦ Daily, dinner; Su, brunch. 647 Tremont St (at W Brookline St). 266.4600; www.tremont647.com &

25 VILLA VICTORIA

Built in 1976 by **John Sharratt Associates,** this housing complex is a local success story. The South End's Puerto Rican community not only participated in every stage of its development, but also collaborated with the architect so that residents' cultural values and traditions would be expressed with dignity. While the complex is by no means beautiful, given limited funds, it has developed its own strong identity. ♦ Bounded by Shawmut Ave and Tremont St, W Brookline and W Dedham Sts

26 BUTECO II

★$ This easygoing hole-in-the-wall (its name is Portuguese slang for "joint") serves authentic Brazilian dishes like *mandioca frita* (fried cassava root with carrot sauce), *moqueca de peixe* (fish in spicy coconut sauce), and, Saturday and Sunday only, the popular *feijoada* (black-bean stew with sausage, dried beef, pork, rice, collard greens, and orange). Some traditional Spanish dishes are offered too. The lively restaurant attracts an appreciative South American clientele. ♦ Brazilian/Spanish ♦ M-Sa, lunch and dinner; Su, dinner. Reservations recommended for

On the eve of the Civil War, and following the Irish migrations beginning with the Great Hunger of 1846, Boston's population was one-third Irish.

Restaurants/Clubs: Red | Hotels: Purple | Shops: Orange | Outdoors/Parks: Green | Sights/Culture: Blue

THE EMERALD NECKLACE

Ponds and parks strung together by parkways form Boston's prized Emerald Necklace, which, when charted on a map, looks like it's dangling from Boston Harbor like a chain around a slender neck. Executed by the Boston Park Commission in 1895, landscape architect **Frederick Law Olmsted**'s design encompasses more than 2,000 acres of open land, its main artery the five-mile-long "necklace."

The largest continuous green space through an urban center in the country, the Emerald Necklace crosses a number of communities and is adorned with five major parks—**Back Bay Fens, Muddy River Improvement, Jamaica Park, Arnold Arboretum,** and **Franklin Park**—all connected by parkways. Olmsted's necklace was further embellished by the joining of **Boston Common** and the **Public Garden.** The **Charles River Esplanade** is often considered an additional jewel on the chain, although it wasn't built until 1931, long after Olmsted's death. The necklace has missing links (which the city promises to eventually fix), the most important of which is the never-realized **Columbia Road extension,** by which Olmsted intended to connect Franklin Park with **Marine Park** in South Boston.

The only way to see the entire Emerald Necklace at one time is to drive its length along the parkways, but the twisting route will offer only fleeting glimpses of greenery and water—not at all the restful communion with nature Olmsted had in mind. Instead, pick a fair-weather day and jog, bicycle, walk, or ride a horse through a segment of the park system.

The Emerald Necklace starts at **Boston Common** (1), proceeds through the **Public Garden** (2), then continues along **Commonwealth Avenue Mall** (3) to **Charlesgate** (4), the original connection forged between the Mall and the **Back Bay Fens** (5), where the Muddy River entered the Charles River Estuary. Charlesgate's open wetlands were largely destroyed when elevated overpasses to Storrow Drive were built during the 1960s, but it still provides a tenuous link between the Mall and the Fens.

Olmsted's first contribution to Boston's park system, the Back Bay Fens (named after the marshlands of eastern England) originally embodied the designer's love of idyllic English rural landscapes. Dredging, draining, and land-scaping rescued the area from its reeking muddy past and made way for tranquil salt-marsh meadows. The damming of the Charles River in 1910 changed the water from salt to fresh, however, and destroyed Olmsted's original scheme. Years of neglect have also taken their toll. Yet the park is still a pleasant spot to wander among willows, dogwoods, lindens, and hawthorns. The **Victory Gardens** planted during World War II and the spectacular **Rose Garden** behind the Museum of Fine Arts, as well as an athletic field, have settled in to stay. And the pudding-stone bridge where Boylston Street crosses the river is a poetic charmer, designed in 1880 by Olmsted's friend **Henry Hobson Richardson.** A cautionary note: Don't walk in the Fens after dark and never stray into the stands of debris-laden tall reeds.

The **Muddy River Improvement** (6) is the next ornament in the chain, although its connection to the Fens via the Riverway was obliterated by construction of the former Sears, Roebuck building. Make your way around the building to reach this meandering riverside park with graceful bridges, placid ponds, lush plantings, and bridle, walking, and running paths. The Improvement—unpoetically named for the spruce-up job it accomplished—widens at a section now called **Olmsted Park,** where Leverett, Willow, and Wards Ponds are located. Just south of these is **Jamaica Park** (7), its centerpiece the largest freshwater pond in Boston. Fringed by a tree-shaded promenade lit by gas lanterns, **Jamaica Pond** is popular for sailing, rowing, walking, jogging, and fishing. Edmund March Wheelwright designed the decorative 1913 boathouse and gazebo.

From Jamaica Pond, Arborway leads to the world-renowned **Arnold Arboretum** (8) (details on page 205), which belongs to the Boston park system but is administered by Harvard University. Charles Sprague Sargent, a landscape gardener and the arboretum's first director, collaborated with Olmsted in 1878 in designing this living museum of trees.

Linked to the arboretum by the Arborway, the Emerald Necklace's massive pendant is **Franklin Park** (9), named for Benjamin Franklin. One of Olmsted's three greatest parks, its design expresses his precept that the natural world offers the ideal antidote to the dehumanizing quality of urban living. Within this 500-acre tract straddling Dorchester, Jamaica Plain, and Roxbury, Olmsted preserved and enhanced existing natural features. Franklin Park is a great green swath of rolling hills and broad fields and meadows, with hickory, hemlock, locust, oak, and tulip trees, as well as a myriad of other plants, enormous boulders, and park ornaments fashioned from Roxbury pudding stone. But because the park is four miles from the heart of Boston and tricky to reach, it never achieved the popularity it deserved, and languished from the 1940s until the present. And like the Fens, changes have been made that spoil the integrity of Olmsted's original plan. It's still a gem, though, a sanctuary from the city where one can walk, jog, picnic, bird-watch, play golf or baseball, visit the zoo, and generally let loose a little. The 18-hole, par-70 golf course is the country's second-oldest municipal course. Although it will take time for Franklin Park to shake its unfair poor reputation, it is actually one of the city's safer parks. Nonetheless, don't linger after dark or stray into the overgrown areas.

The Necklace breaks after Franklin Park, but it should have led via Columbia Road through Upham's Corner and on to **Marine Park** (10). (A lack of funds kept Columbia Road from becoming the spacious green boulevard Olmsted intended.) Eclipsed long ago by suburban beaches, Marine Park no longer draws crowds, but the sea breezes and harbor views are worth an outing, and this is where you can look at the shiny bellies of the big jets as they descend to Logan International Airport. It's best to drive here; there's always plenty of parking.

Now missing from the Emerald Necklace, **Charlesbank** was a pioneering neighborhood park (designed by Olmsted in the 1890s) that once bordered the Charles River near Massachusetts General Hospital. The park was intended to alleviate the overcrowding suffered by residents of the West End, a neighborhood largely wiped out by urban renewal in the 1960s. Charlesbank featured the city's first playgrounds and America's first sandboxes, called "sand courts." Today Charlesbank is mostly buried under a tangle of roadways.

Boston's park rangers direct all kinds of activities throughout the Boston park system: historical tours,

educational programs, nature walks through the Arnold Arboretum, bird-watching along the Muddy River, fishing on Jamaica Pond, an architectural exploration of Commonwealth Avenue, and more. Some events require reservations; all are free. For information, call the **Boston Parks and Recreation Department** (635.4505) or the **Boston Park Rangers** (635.7383 or 635.7488).

Additional **recreational and educational programs** are planned for kids during the summer, including golf clinics at Franklin Park, "Sox Talk" with Red Sox players, and sailing on Boston Harbor and Jamaica Pond. Call the **Parks and Recreation Activities Eventline** (635.3445) for daily updates. Boston parks are officially closed from 11:30PM to 6AM.

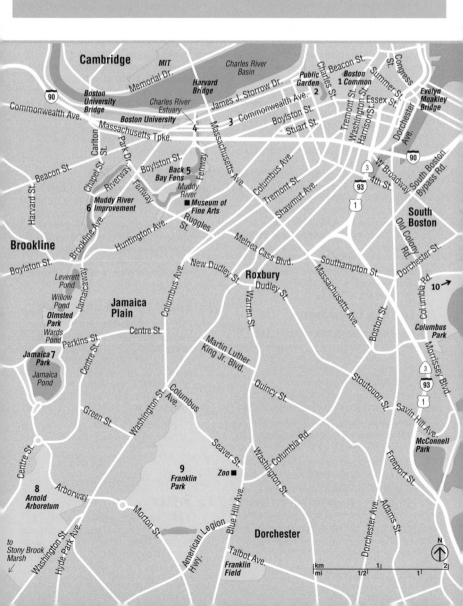

groups of five or more. 57 W Dedham St (between Shawmut Ave and Tremont St). 247.9249 &

27 CAFÉ UMBRA

★★★$$$ A sign that a neighborhood is hip (aside from expensive real estate and difficult parking) is the presence of award-winning chef and owner Laura Brennan. Her Umbria, in the shadow of the Cathedral of the Holy Cross, attracts food fans from the city and beyond. There are dishes like *panino*, roasted leg of lamb, herbed goat cheese, and baby spinach, served with Vidalia onion rings. There's hand-made buffalo mozzarella, organic and local produce, and a serious wine list. A late-hours lounge menu helps the tardy and hungry. ◆ French, Italian ◆ Daily, dinner; Su, brunch. 1395 Washington St (at Union Park St). 867.0707

28 CATHEDRAL OF THE HOLY CROSS

A sight along this gentrifying stretch of Washington Street in Roxbury, which developers now call SoWa—South of Washington—in the South End, is this heroic Gothic Revival struc-ture, completed in 1875 by **Patrick C. Keely.** New England's biggest church, and the largest Catholic church in the country when it was built, the cathedral recalls an era when Irish Roman Catholic immigrants were a dominant presence in the South End. The Roxbury pudding-stone cathedral seats 3,500 and accommodates 7,000 when you include standing room. It's still the principal church of the Archdiocese of Boston but is now used mainly for special occa-sions. The front vestibule's arch contains bricks from a convent in Somerville (then called Charlestown) that burned during anti-Catholic rioting in 1834. As is true of so many Boston ecclesiastical edifices, the intention was to surmount the two towers with spires, but that never happened. ◆ Daily. Washington and Union Park Sts. 542.5682

29 THE MIDTOWN HOTEL

$ A well-kept secret, this two-story, 159-room hotel is older and far less fashionable

than the numerous luxury hotels located nearby, but also much less expensive. It's frequented by families, tour groups, and businesspeople. The rooms are spacious, and there's free parking, an outdoor pool with a lifeguard (in season), and a multi-lingual staff. Children under 18 stay free with parents. Winter packages are available on request. The restaurant **Tables of Content** is located on the premises. ◆ 220 Huntington Ave (between Massachusetts Ave and Cumberland St). 262.1000, 800/343.1177; fax 262.8739 &

30 JAE'S CAFE AND GRILL

★★$$ The healthful Korean/Japanese fare served in this crowded, bustling restaurant has attracted the trendies; there's almost always a line. Consider pan-seared Chilean sea bass. A full array of sushi and sashimi awaits, along with soups, satays (skewered meat or poultry with various sauces), and rice specials such as yuk hai bi bim bab (shredded raw beef marinated in seasoned sesame oil). ◆ Korean/Japanese ◆ Daily, lunch and dinner. Valet parking available. 520 Columbus Ave (between Worcester St and Concord Sq). 421.9405. & Also at 1223 Beacon St, Brookline, 739.0000, & and 711 Boylston St in the Back Bay, 236.1777 www.jaescafe.com

31 RUTLAND SQUARE

Ⓟ Bracketed by two rows of three-story bowfronts, this shady, slim, elliptical park is one of the South End's most intimate oases. A number of façades break from the neighbor-hood pattern of warm red brick, and instead are prettily painted and detailed in light colors. Only one block long, the square is a lovely sliver of green. ◆ Between Tremont St and Columbus Ave

32 ENCORE BED & BREAKFAST

Price varies depending on the season and length of stay—minimum two nights on weekends, three nights during peak season. Amenities include queen-size beds, air conditioning, DVD, and cable TV. Photos are on the website. No elevator. ◆ 116 W Newton St (between Tremont St and Columbus Ave). 247.3425; www.encorebandb.com

Stella

33 STELLA

★★$$ The popular restaurant and bar is named for the owners' young daughter, not Tennessee Williams's character. It's a casual neighborhood destination, a place to relax

During the American Revolution, when churches associated with Tory sentiments were regarded as enemy outposts by many colonists, Trinity Church—predecessor to the Trinity Church that now stands in Copley Square—was the only Anglican church that remained open in Boston. Christ Church (today's Old North Church) closed in 1775, and the ministers of King's Chapel and Trinity fled north to Halifax, Nova Scotia, during the British evacuation of 1776. But Trinity's assistant minister, Samuel Parker, kept the parish doors open, wisely agreeing to delete prayers for the British king from the church's liturgy. He also endorsed the patriot cause.

with pleasing food. There's room inside for 60, but the terrace is the place to be in nice weather. Choices include pastas, ornate pizzas, and antipasti like spicy mussels in saffron-cream with peppers, white wine, and garlic. Dinners include grilled half chicken with a chile-citrus glaze and Parmesan polenta. ♦ Italian ♦ Daily, dinner, with late menu to 1:30AM; Su, brunch. 1525 Washington St (just off Blackstone Square, between W Brookline and Mystic Sts). 247.7747; www.bostonstella.com

34 BLACKSTONE AND FRANKLIN SQUARES

Divided by Washington Street, both squares were built in the 1860s but originated in an 1801 plan to which **Charles Bulfinch,** then chairman of Boston's Board of Selectmen, was a major contributor. Although they have lost something to time, the squares' original grandeur remains palpable. Look for the brownstone houses overlooking the square on **West Newton Street.** These exemplars of old-world architectural elegance will transport you into the neighborhood's genteel past. At 11 East Newton Street stands the **Franklin Square House** apartments for the elderly. Built in 1868, the lumbering French Second Empire building—equipped with two steam-powered elevators—was originally the St. James Hotel, once considered the South End's poshest lodging place. At the height of the hotel's brief eminence, President Ulysses S. Grant stayed here. ♦ Bounded by St. George St and Shawmut Ave, and E Newton and Brookline Sts

35 HARRIET TUBMAN HOUSE

Named for the "Moses of the South," a runaway slave and Underground Railroad organizer, this iconoclastic complex greets the street with a sense of spirit and purposefulness. It's home to United South End Settlements, a social service organization responsible for vital community programs. The architect, **Don Stull Associates,** deserves applause for doing a lot with a small budget. Incidentally, the house stands on the site of one of Boston's famous jazz clubs, The Hi Hat, which burned down. ♦ Daily. 566 Columbus Ave (at W Springfield St). 536.8610 &

35 WALLY'S CAFE

★★★$ Just three blocks from **Symphony Hall** and open since 1934, Wally's bar and jazz club has some of the best jazz and break-out jams in the city. Young musicians you don't know, and veterans you might, pack in late-night crowds. The area was home in the 1940s and 1950s to jazz clubs like the Hi Hat, Savoy Ballroom, Chicken Lane, the Wig Wam, and Mr. M. They're gone, but Wally's still delights. In the crowd or on stage, you'll often find students (and faculty) from the nearby Berklee College of Music, Boston Conservatory, and New England Conservatory. Live music 365 days of the year. Be warned: This place, on the edge of the South End, can be a bit gritty, like the neighborhood. If you want genteel jazz, go to **Scullers, Top of the Hub,** or the **Regattabar.** ♦ No cover charge. One-drink minimum. Daily. 427 Massachusetts Ave (at Columbus Ave). 424.1408; fax 424.8340; www.wallyscafe.com

36 BOB'S SOUTHERN BISTRO

★★$$ A friendly young crowd (many from nearby Northeastern University) come here for good and live jazz with close-up musicians. Located four blocks from Symphony Hall, the café (formerly called Bob the Chef's Jazz Café) has brick walls and steam tables, serving dishes like Creole jambalaya and barbecued spareribs. There's an all-you-can-eat Sunday buffet brunch, accompanied by gospel and live jazz. ♦ Southern/Cajun/Soul ♦ Daily, lunch and dinner; Su, brunch. 604 Columbus Ave (near the corner of Massachusetts Ave). 536.6204; www.bobthechefs.com &

37 PIANO CRAFT GUILD

When new in 1853, the Chickering piano factory was reputedly the second-largest building in the country, dwarfed only by the US Capitol building. The surprisingly graceful industrial structure is enlivened by a sprightly octagonal tower. It was renovated in 1972 by **Anderson Notter Associates** with **Bruner Cott Associates** and now houses artists' studios and living spaces. The project was one of the first and largest mill conversions in the state, an early example of the creative lengths local artists have gone to obtain affordable housing. The two-story gallery shows works by residents. ♦ Call for hours. 791 Tremont St (at Northampton St). 437.9365

38 TORO

★★★$$$ Chef Ken Oringer, who has won praise for his top-dollar restaurant **Clio** and sashimi bar **Uni** in the Back Bay's Elliot Hotel, opened this popular spot featuring Spanish dishes and Barcelona-style tapas in 2006. Two blocks from Boston Medical Center, it's a welcome and relatively unusual sight in the South End: a combination of quality fare and affordable prices. No reservations are taken, so go early or expect a wait. Street and valet parking. ♦ Daily, dinner; Su, brunch. 1704 Washington St (at Springfield St). 536.4300 &

Restaurants/Clubs: Red | Hotels: Purple | Shops: Orange | Outdoors/Parks: Green | Sights/Culture: Blue

Paths, playgrounds, lagoons, and lawns lace the Charles River Basin and its esplanade. Together they form a lovely urban water park and the most spectacular section of the **Charles River Reservation.** Of all Boston's landmarks, this waterway is the most visually striking, especially the views of the downtown and Back Bay skylines and Beacon Hill from the Cambridge side. In this majestic, romantic setting, Bostonians congregate for promenades, outdoor concerts, picnics, jogging, bicycling, games, sailing, sculling, canoeing, and feeding the hungry ducks made famous in Robert McCloskey's 1941 children's book *Make Way for Ducklings.* In winter the riverside is still and quiet, and the Cambridge shoreline seems far away. But in fall, spring, and summer the two-mile length of the esplanade from Beacon Hill to Boston University brims with activity and the river sparkles with white sails. As the days heat up, free concerts draw enormous crowds to the **Hatch Shell,** where the pièce de résistance is the traditional **Fourth of July Boston Pops concert,** which attracts hundreds of thousands.

The lazy brown-green Charles casually zigs and zags, coiling left and right, even appearing at times to change its mind and turn back, while traversing an 80-mile course from Hopkinton to Boston Harbor, a distance of less than 30 miles as the crow flies. In general, the sluggish Charles is not an impressive river, shrinking to a stream in some places. But the Charles River Basin is the splendid lakelike section nine miles long from

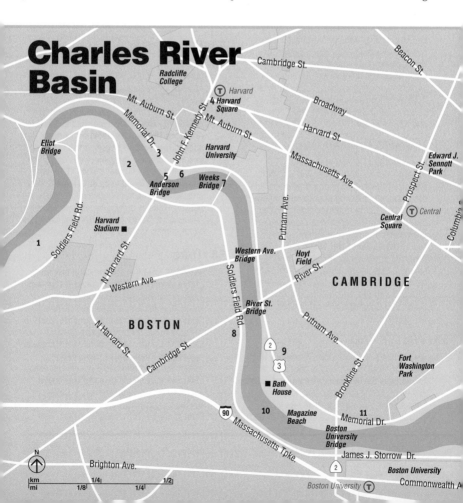

Charles River Basin

Radcliffe College

ⓣ Harvard
4 Harvard Square

Cambridge St.

Beacon St.

Broadway

Mt. Auburn St.

Memorial Dr. **3**

John F. Kennedy St.

Mt. Auburn St.

Harvard St.

Eliot Bridge

2

Harvard University

Massachusetts Ave.

Edward J. Sennott Park

Prospect St.

5 6 Anderson Bridge

Weeks Bridge **7**

ⓣ Central
Central Square

Columbia

Soldiers Field Rd.

Harvard Stadium ■

1

N Harvard St.

Western Ave. Bridge

Hoyt Field

River St.

CAMBRIDGE

Western Ave.

Putnam Ave.

Soldiers Field Rd.

River St. Bridge

Putnam Ave.

N Harvard St.

BOSTON

Cambridge St.

8

⑵ **9**
⑶

Brookline St.

Fort Washington Park

■ Bath House

⑼⁰

10 Magazine Beach

Memorial Dr. **11**

Boston University Bridge

James J. Storrow Dr.

Massachusetts Tpke.

⑵

Boston University

N

km   1/4   1/2
mi   1/8   1/4

Brighton Ave.

Boston University ⓣ   Commonwealth A

Watertown, past **Harvard University** and the **Massachusetts Institute of Technology** (MIT), and on to the Atlantic Ocean. Here the Charles has been sculpted into a splendid urban waterway.

The river got its name 15 years before the Puritans arrived, when explorer Captain John Smith sent early maps of New England home to 15-year-old Charles Stuart, the future **King Charles I,** and asked him to give its prominent features good English names. Throughout the 18th and 19th centuries, industries on the Charles included gristmills, sawmills, spinning and weaving companies, and manufacturers of paper products, leather, and chocolate. But intense industrialization polluted the river, and its estuary shrank from landfilling. At low tide, the Charles was a malodorous eyesore with mudflats bordering wealthy **Back Bay,** which is why the neighborhood appears physically to turn its back to the river.

In the early 1900s a long crusade to make the lower Charles healthy and attractive gained momentum. Prominent Boston and Cambridge residents, including landscape architect Charles Eliot (a colleague of Frederick Law Olmsted and founder of the Trustees of Reservations, a nonprofit conservation group) and philanthropists James J. Storrow and Henry Lee Higginson (founder of the Boston Symphony Orchestra) led the drive to build the **Charles River Dam** in 1908. This created the freshwater basin, with an embankment extending from **Charlesgate West** (where the Back Bay Fens meets the river) to the old **West End.** In the early 1930s Arthur A. Shurcliff, landscape architect of

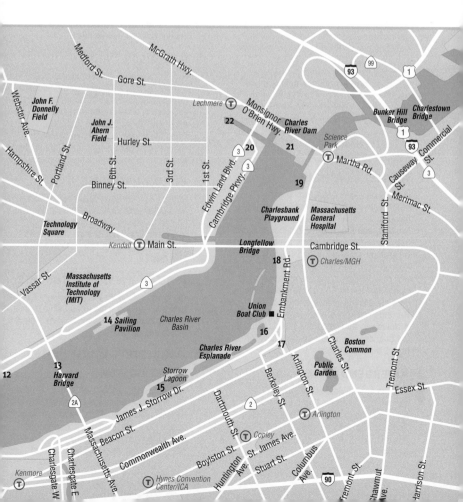

Colonial Williamsburg, greatly embellished the embankment, designing the picturesque esplanade and its lagoons with funding provided by Storrow's widow, Helen Osborn Storrow. In 1951 Boston's **Museum of Science** took up residence astride the Charles River Dam on the Boston-Cambridge boundary. In the early 1950s **Storrow Drive,** the autoway, was built on the original embankment and, ironically, named for James Storrow, the avid supporter of the park it shouldered aside. It carries more than 100,000 vehicles a day, but extensive renovation of a vital underpass by the Esplanade should snarl traffic beginning in 2007. Construction delays could last up to four years. Storrow Drive's counterpart along the Cambridge side of the river is **Memorial Drive.**

The Charles River has been rebounding from abuse and pollution since the late 1970s. But while above Watertown the river is rated Class B (okay for swimming and fishing), below Watertown it is only approaching swimmable. To see the river in its most protected natural state, visit the Massachusetts Audubon Society's **Broadmoor Wildlife Sanctuary,** a 600-acre tract along the Charles in South Natick and Sherborn (280 Eliot St, between South and Lake Sts, South Natick, 508/655.2296), about 18 miles from downtown Boston.

1 THE PUBLICK THEATRE INC.

Boston's oldest resident professional theater company has been staging performances under the stars for more than 33 years. Productions have included *A Little Night Music, Macbeth*, and *The Beard of Avon*. The company's season runs from late May to early September. Purchase tickets online or at the on-site outdoor box office after 7PM on performance nights, or charge by phone; tickets are also available at **BosTix** outlets (see "Tickets" on page 12). The theater seats 200, and free parking and picnic facilities are nearby. ◆ Shows W-Su, weather permitting, late June to early September. Soldiers Field Rd and Everett St in Allston. 782.5425; www.publicktheatre.com &

2 NEWELL BOATHOUSE

Harvard University's first permanent boathouse, with red-slate walls and delicate finials, dates from 1900 and was designed by **Peabody and Stearns.** The boathouse is dedicated to varsity teams, who often train for the US Olympic team or England's Henley Royal Regatta. Harvard's passion for rowing began with the founding of the country's first boat club in the 1840s. The oldest intercollegiate crew meet in the country is the annual Harvard--Yale competition, first held in 1854. ◆ Hours vary throughout the year. Located on the Charles River across Soldiers Field Rd from Dillon Field House

3 RIVERBEND PARK

On Sundays during daylight saving time, Memorial Drive on the Cambridge side of the river is closed to traffic from Western Avenue Bridge to Eliot Bridge, creating what is called Riverbend Park. ◆ Sundays 24 April to 13 November annually

4 HARVARD SQUARE

On the Cambridge side of the river near Harvard University, it's only a few minutes' stroll up John F. Kennedy Street to Harvard Square's restaurants and shops. ◆ Open daily. Bounded by Harvard St, John F. Kennedy St, and Cambridge St

5 ANDERSON BRIDGE

In 1911 a special act of Congress closed the Charles River to navigation so the Anderson Bridge could be built without a drawbridge. To a "father by a son," a tablet reads: Larz Anderson, US ambassador to Belgium, dedicated the bridge to his father, Nicholas Longworth Anderson, also a Harvard graduate. ◆ Joins N Harvard St to John F. Kennedy St

6 WELD BOATHOUSE

Harvard's picturesque boathouse, designed by **Peabody and Stearns,** was built in 1907 and houses Radcliffe College and intramural shells as well as single sculls. ◆ On the Charles River on the corner of John F. Kennedy St and Memorial Dr

7 JOHN W. WEEKS FOOTBRIDGE

The graceful John W. Weeks Footbridge is the best place to watch the Head Of The Charles Regatta in October. ◆ Joins Soldiers Field Rd and Memorial Dr

8 DOUBLETREE GUEST SUITES HOTEL BOSTON

$$$ The site is right by the Cambridge/Allston exit of the Massachusetts Turnpike (I.90), but the 308 units on 16 floors are all two-room suites, most with good views (request one facing the river and Cambridge). Some bilevel suites are available on upper floors, and suites

for nonsmokers and people with disabilities are available. There's an indoor pool, sauna, whirlpool, and exercise room, and $20 on-premises parking. Complimentary van service is provided to downtown Boston and Cambridge. Ask about the hotel's special weekend rates. ♦ 400 Soldiers Field Rd (at Cambridge St). 783.0090, 800/424.2900; fax 783.0897 &

Within the Doubletree Guest Suites Hotel Boston/Cambridge:

SCULLERS JAZZ CLUB

If you're seeking jazz and light fare, then this comfortable listening room will fit the bill. Local and national jazz and cabaret acts are booked here, with an emphasis on vocalists, and the crowd runs the age range from 25 to 75. ♦ Cover. Tu-Sa; two shows nightly. Reservations recommended. 562.4111; www.scullersjazz.com &

BOATHOUSE GRILL

★★$$ Seafood, including a great bouillabaisse, is featured here. Another highlight is the marvelous river view. ♦ Seafood ♦ M-Sa, breakfast, lunch, and dinner; Su, breakfast and dinner. Reservations recommended. 562.4114 &

9 RADISSON HOTEL CAMBRIDGE

$$ Most of the rooms in this modern high-rise (202 in all) have lovely views. Most folks prefer to overlook the river, although the Cambridge skyline is nice too. There's an indoor pool, $20 guest parking, and the **Bisuteki Japanese Steakhouse** and two other restaurants. It's about a 20-minute walk along the Charles (best by day) to Harvard Square. Rooms for nonsmokers are available. No pets. ♦ 777 Memorial Dr (at Pleasant St), Cambridge. 492.7777, 800/333.3333; fax 492.6038; www.radisson.com &

10 HEAD OF THE CHARLES REGATTA

The annual Head Of The Charles Regatta, on the next-to-last Sunday in October, is the world's largest single-day regatta and the oldest head-style racing event in the US. The course extends upstream from the Boston University Bridge to a half mile above Eliot Bridge. This is computer timed, with boats departing at 10- to 12-second intervals. A good place to watch this event is in Cambridge, around the Eliot Bridge across from the Buckingham, Browne & Nichols school.

11 HYATT REGENCY CAMBRIDGE

$$$$ This glitzy, glassy, ziggurat-shaped hotel, nicknamed the "Pyramid on the Charles," has 469 rooms, some with outdoor terraces overlooking the river and Boston. The atrium rises 14 stories, with balconies, trees, fountains, and glass-cage elevators that offer a view. The skylit health spa has an indoor pool, sauna, whirlpool, exercise room, and sundeck, plus a retractable ceiling and walls. There's also an outdoor basketball court. The hotel rents adults' and children's bicycles, so you can take a leisurely riverside journey. The place is popular with families (there's a 50% discount for a second room when traveling with children) and with locals seeking weekend luxury as well as the usual business and convention crowds. Choose between valet or self-parking. A free van shuttles guests to Harvard Square, Kendall Square, Faneuil Hall Marketplace, Boston Common, and Copley Place. Accommodations for people with disabilities and for nonsmokers are available. Pet friendly. ♦ 575 Memorial Dr (at Amesbury St), Cambridge. 492.1234, 800/233.1234; fax 491.6906; www.cambridge.hyatt.com &

Within the Hyatt Regency Cambridge:

ZEPHYR

★$ A sleek, redesigned dining lounge with a lower-floor view of the Charles, Zephyr serves breakfast, lunch, and dinner (and drinks) daily. An innovation of sorts is a focus on tapaslike small plates, should you want them. Regular portions are available too. ♦ Eclectic. ♦ Daily, breakfast, lunch, and dinner, 6:30AM to 1AM. Dress casual. 492.1234 &

12 MIT'S HAROLD WHITWORTH PIERCE BOATHOUSE

Massachusetts Institute of Technology's Harold Whitworth Pierce Boathouse was built in the 1960s and is considered one of the nation's best. It has an eight-person rowing simulator in which water pumped at 125,000 gallons a minute produces a 10-mph current for crew practice. ♦ Located along Memorial Dr

13 HARVARD BRIDGE

The Harvard Bridge, which carries Massachusetts Avenue between Boston's Back Bay and Cambridge, confuses residents and visitors because it actually arrives in Cambridge at the threshold of the Massachusetts Institute of Technology's campus, not Harvard University's. Harvard Bridge was built in 1891 and was rebuilt in 1990. The bridge is 364.4 Smoots and one

The first ferry on the Charles River began operating between the Boston and Charlestown peninsulas in 1631.

Restaurants/Clubs: Red | Hotels: Purple | Shops: Orange | Outdoors/Parks: Green | Sights/Culture: Blue

ear long. A Smoot equals the length of the late Oliver Reed Smoot (five feet seven inches), who was an MIT student from 1958 to 1962. Originally a fraternity prank, the paint marks counting off Smoots along the bridge have become famous—so much so that they were restored when the bridge was rebuilt. You can see a Smoot mark in the MIT Museum collection. ♦ Joins the Boston and Cambridge sides of Massachusetts Ave

14 WALKER WOOD SAILING PAVILION

Modern college sailing was spurred on by the construction of the Massachusetts Institute of Technology's Walker Wood Sailing Pavilion in 1935. ♦ Along Memorial Dr (Rte 3), adjacent to the Charles River Basin

15 STORROW LAGOON

A particularly pretty spot along the esplanade is Storrow Lagoon, enclosed by a slender outer island joined to the mainland by little stone bridges. The fingerlike island is a delightful detour. ♦ Located off James J. Storrow Dr

16 THE HATCH SHELL

Built in 1940 of concrete, the Hatch Shell is one of Boston's best-known Art Deco pieces. To find out about free outdoor summer concerts at the shell, including the **Boston Pops Esplanade Orchestra series,** check the **Boston Globe**'s entertainment sections. ♦ 20-minute walk from the MBTA's Park Street Red and Green Line stations or 10 minutes from the Charles/MGH Red Line station. Adjacent to Storrow Dr

17 THE ARTHUR FIEDLER MEMORIAL FOOTBRIDGE

Named for the late Boston Pops conductor, this footbridge is a sinuous pink structure of poured concrete connecting the esplanade to Back Bay at Beacon Street, near Arlington Street.

18 COMMUNITY BOATING INC.

America's oldest and largest nonprofit public sailing organization offers sailing instruction at affordable prices. Its impressive fleet includes sailboats, kayaks, and windsurfers. See also "Water Play: Activities On and Along the Charles," on page 173. ♦ 21 Embankment Rd (between Storrow Dr and Charles St). 523.7038; TTY 523.1038; www.community-boating.org &

19 LUNA AND VENUS

These are a pair of retired old tugboats that worked Boston Harbor for half a century. In 1936 Luna led an entourage that escorted the Queen Mary into New York Harbor on her maiden American voyage. Hardie Gramatky's classic tale Little Toot regales children with Luna's adventures. You can see the boats docked here near the Museum of Science. ♦ Adjacent to Charlesbank Playground, along Embankment Rd. 367.4935

20 ROYAL SONESTA HOTEL BOSTON/CAMBRIDGE

$$$ Ask for a room facing the river and look across at the gold dome of the **State House** gleaming above Beacon Hill. The hotel, which boasts an excellent modern art collection with pieces by Frank Stella, Andy Warhol, and Robert Rauschenberg, has 400 contemporary rooms on 10 floors. On-site facilities include an indoor pool, fitness center, and two restaurants (see below). A courtesy van goes to Harvard and Kendall Squares and Boston. The hotel provides guests with free ice cream, bicycles, and cameras during the summer, and vouchers for a free narrated river tour are available from early June to mid-September. There are rooms for nonsmokers and for people with disabilities. The hotel is near the **CambridgeSide Galleria** shopping mall and next door to the **Museum of Science.** ♦ 5 Cambridge Pkwy (at Commercial Ave), Cambridge. 806.4200, 800/766.3782; fax 661.5956, www.royalsonestaboston.com

Within the Royal Sonesta:

DANTE

★★$$$$ New in 2006, this 250-seat hotel restaurant offers lovely views of the Charles and Boston. ♦ Mediterranean ♦ Daily, breakfast, lunch, and dinner. 497.4200; www.restaurantdante.com

GALLERY CAFÉ

★$$ It's easy to relax at this casual eatery, where seafood dishes are served. The room is bright and comfortable and there's riverfront patio dining in season. Children's menu. ♦ Continental ♦ M-F, breakfast, lunch, and dinner; Sa, Su, lunch and dinner. 806.4122

21 MUSEUM OF SCIENCE

One of Boston's most familiar sights is this museum's 1950s silhouette above the Charles River. Streams of families and fleets of school and tour buses arrive all day long. If you're with kids, you can be sure they'll have a great time. If not, you might wish the crowds would thin and the decibels lower, but you'll still squeeze past many interesting exhibits.

The museum was the Boston Society of Natural History, founded in 1830, then the New England Museum of Natural History, residing in an imposing edifice in Back Bay. In 1951 the museum moved to modern quarters on this site straddling the Charles River Dam

WATER PLAY: ACTIVITIES ON AND ALONG THE CHARLES

The Charles River is one of Boston's favorite places to enjoy outdoor sports and activities. Many people run, skate, and bicycle along the banks of the river while numerous canoes, sailboats, and rowing shells ply its waters.

Sailing

Sailing vessels bearing passengers and freight, and later tugboats, tankers, and barges, once navigated the river, but today recreational craft rule: canoes, rowboats, sailboats, and powerboats. The river is dotted with numerous boathouses and yacht clubs—many dating from the late 19th and early 20th centuries—that offer classes and rentals of various conveyances, and sponsor competitions.

Community Boating Inc. is a nonprofit that offers sailing and instruction for everyone at low prices. Hundreds of kids 10 to 18 learn to sail each summer for $1 each. Adults learn to sail too, and their memberships subsidize the youth program. Some members race seriously; others take part in moonlight sailing on the Charles. And some just want to enjoy a river sail. The CBI fleet includes sailboats, windsurfers, and kayaks. This is America's oldest and largest public sailing program and offers different membership options, including short-term visitor packages. (21 Embankment Rd, between the Hatch Shell and the Longfellow Bridge, next to the Charles Circle footbridge, 523.1038; TTY 523.7406; www.community-boating.org &

Canoeing and Rowing

More than 60 of the Charles River's 80 miles can be explored by canoe, although a few portages are required. The **Charles River Watershed Association** (781/788.0007), a private, nonprofit conservation group founded in 1965, recommends the *Charles River Canoe Guide*; on the last Sunday in April, it sponsors a set of popular races called the Run of the Charles. www.crwa.org

The Massachusetts Audubon Society's **Broadmoor Wildlife Sanctuary** (280 Eliot St, between South and Lake Sts, South Natick, 508/655.2296; www.massaudubon.org) is a very popular destination for canoers. Many say the waterway is at its prettiest there.

Rowing and the Charles have had a long, romantic liaison. A single figure sculling gracefully over the river's surface is a common early-morning sight in the pleasant-weather months. So too are "eights," crew boats with exhorting coxswains, which skim past and then disappear beneath the next bridge. Each year rowers from around the world and from a variety of American colleges compete in the **Head Of The Charles Regatta** on the next-to-last Sunday in October (www.hocr.org). It starts at the Boston University DeWolfe Boathouse and winds three miles upriver to Artesani Playground in Brighton. Use public transportation if you go; shore traffic is awful.

Rent canoes, kayaks, and rowing shells on the river at the **Charles River Canoe and Kayak Center** (2401 Commonwealth Ave, Newton, between Islington Rd and I-95, 965.5110). The center offers canoeing, kayaking, and rowing classes for all levels. Closer to downtown Boston, the center has a rental kiosk in Herter Park by the river in Allston (1100 Soldiers Field Rd, 462.2513).

For group or private rowing instruction, contact **Community Rowing Inc.** (1400 Soldiers Field Rd, between Telford St and Western Ave, 964.2455; www.communityrowing.org). Open to the public from April through October, it charges reasonable monthly fees. Community Rowing also organizes adaptive rowers' groups for people with disabilities.

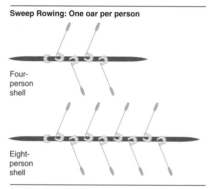

Sweep Rowing: One oar per person

Four-person shell

Eight-person shell

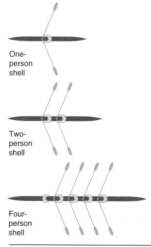

Sculling: Two oars per person

One-person shell

Two-person shell

Four-person shell

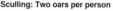

and changed its name to reflect the forward-looking attitude that has made it so innovative. Under director **Bradford Washburn,** a renowned explorer, mountaineer, and mapmaker, the museum embraced modern science and the demands of today's sophisticated visitors, becoming a flexible, participatory place.

The **Exhibit Hall**'s 600-plus exhibits date from 1830 to today, covering astronomy, astrophysics, natural history, and much more. All-time favorites are the **Plexiglas Transparent Woman** with light-up organs, the chicken hatchery, the world's largest Van de Graaff generator spitting 15-foot lightning bolts, a space capsule replica, and the 20-foot-high model of *Tyrannosaurus rex.* Walk on the moon or fly over Boston at the *Science Live* stage, or see how an ocean wave is made. Other popular features are the **Charles Hayden Planetarium** and **Mugar Omni Theater** with its domed, five-story screen.

The museum sponsors educational programs for families, schools, and communities. Special events include the **Inventor's Weekend Exhibition,** in which students' inventions—such as an automatic baseball-card stacker—are exhibited along with the creations of adults.

There are four cafeteria-style restaurants, some with captivating views of Boston on one side of the Charles, Cambridge on the other, and boats passing through the dam below and cruising upriver. Also be sure to explore the **Museum Shop,** which has a fantastic inventory of science-related projects, gadgets, toys, jewelry, books, and T-shirts. ♦ Admission: discounts for seniors and children 3 to 11; children under 3 free. Separate admission fees for the Planetarium and Mugar Omni Theater; combination discount tickets available. There's a service charge, but you can buy tickets online. Exhibit-hall-only admission: adults and teens $15, kids 3 to 11 $12, 60 or over $13. Daily, F until

9PM. Parking available for a fee. Monsignor O'Brien Hwy (between Charles St and Commercial Ave). 723.2500, TDD 589.0417; www.mos.org &

Within the Museum of Science:

CHARLES HAYDEN PLANETARIUM

A $2 million Zeiss planetarium projector and multi-image system create enthralling programs on what's happening in the heavens: everything from the seasonal skies over Boston to phenomena like black holes and supernova. There are also special laser shows—not recommended for children under four. ♦ Admission; discounts for senior citizens and children 3 to 11. M-Th, Sa, Su; F, 9AM-9PM. Call for show times. 723.2500 &

MUGAR OMNI THEATER

In Massachusetts's first OMNIMAX theater, a tilted dome 76 feet in diameter and four stories high wraps around the audience, and state-of-the-art film technology makes viewers feel as though they're surrounded by the images on the screen. Films project viewers into locales like the tropical rain forest or Antarctica, inside the human body, on a rocket to outer space, or on a roller-coaster-like tour of Boston. Not recommended for children under four. ♦ Admission; discounts for seniors and children 4 to 14. Daily. Call for show times. Reservations recommended. 723.2500 &

22 CHARLES RIVERBOAT COMPANY

Canal Park, behind the Cambridge-side Galleria, is the departure point for Charles Riverboat Company's reasonably priced 60-minute narrated river cruises. Group charters are available, as are charming sunset cruises. ♦ On Cambridge side of Monsignor O'Brien Hwy. 621.3001; www.charlesriverboat.com

CRUISING ALONG THE CHARLES RIVER

The favorite places to run and bicycle in Boston are the paths on both sides of the Charles River. Roller- and in-line skating and skateboarding are popular here too. Skates can be rented from the **Beacon Hill Skate Shop** (135 Charles St S, between Melrose and Stuart Sts, 482.7400). For more information on bicycling, see "Boston by Bike: Plum Paths for Pedal Pushers" on page 78.

CAMBRIDGE

Across the Charles River is Boston's Left Bank, the intellectual, self-assured neighbor of Cambridge. Boston and Cambridge are crowded with college campuses, but Cambridge exudes a true Ivy League ambience. Many identify Cambridge with **Harvard University,** the nation's first college, which is as old as the city itself. Others associate it with the prestigious **Massachusetts Institute of Technology** (MIT), which moved here from Boston in 1916.

The two giant institutions have a total of more than 28,000 students, hailing from nearly 100 nations. Since World War II, MIT and Harvard, with government and industry support, have made Cambridge a world-renowned research center that focuses on military and aerospace industries, artificial intelligence, and genetic engineering. These partnerships have spurred the growth of related industries in Cambridge and other Massachusetts cities, creating the state's high-tech economy.

In 1630 Newtowne village was founded by the Massachusetts Bay Colony, led by Governor John Winthrop. Eight years later the settlement was nostalgically renamed Cambridge, after the English university where many Puritans had been educated. That same year, the college founded here two years earlier by the colony's Great and General Court was named Harvard College to memorialize John Harvard, a young Charlestown minister who bequeathed his 400-volume library and half his estate to the fledgling school. And in 1639 the New World's first printing press was established in Cambridge, publishing the first American document, *Oath of a Free Man.* No other settlement in the colony was permitted a press until 1674, so Cambridge became the earliest publishing center of the hemisphere, ensuring its prominence as a place of ideas.

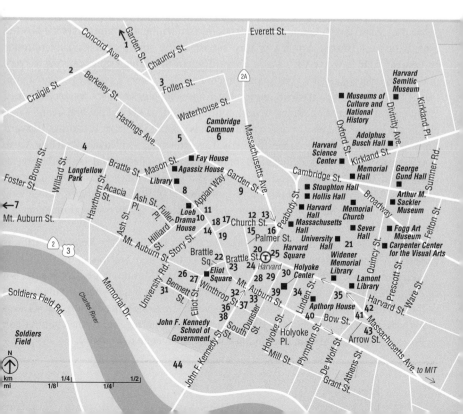

Today Cambridge is still a place of ideas. The engine of academia drives this 6¼-square-mile city of more than 101,000 "Cantabrigians" (as Cambridge residents are known), half of whom are affiliated in some way with the local universities. But that is by no means the whole story. Cambridge has traditionally been a place for progressive politics and lawmaking, where generations of residents have embraced such causes as the abolition of slavery, women's rights, the antinuclear movement, environmentalism, opposition to the Vietnam War and US foreign policy in Latin America, and many other concerns. So strong is its reputation as a bastion of liberalism that some people of a more conservative political bent call Cambridge an enclave of eggheads and bleeding hearts.

But, political name-calling aside, the city is known for cultural diversity as well, for it is full of people from somewhere else. The cafés, bookstores, shops, and restaurants here reflect a multicultural mix—a mélange of Yankee gentry, blue-collar workers, conservatives, liberals, immigrant newcomers, and long-established ethnic groups. They live in Brattle Street mansions, crowded triple-deckers, chic condos, and subsidized housing. In 1846 Cambridge officially became a city when Old Cambridge joined with the industrial riverside communities of East Cambridge and Cambridgeport. Today the city consists of several distinctive but loosely defined neighborhoods: **Kendall Square, East Cambridge, Inman Square, Central Square, Cambridgeport, Riverside, Mid-Cambridge, North Cambridge, West Cambridge**, and the famous **Harvard Square**. **Massachusetts Avenue,** which connects Boston with Cambridge via the Harvard Bridge across the Charles River, runs the entire length of Cambridge through MIT's campus to Harvard Square and northward (www.cambridgema.gov).

It would take weeks to fully comb Cambridge, so most visitors head directly to Harvard Square (commonly referred to as "the Square"), the city's centerpiece and the heart of Old Cambridge. Overdevelopment and the invasion of franchises have eroded some of its quirky charm, but you can still sit in cafés and browse in bookstores, overhearing amazing conversations among an extraordinarily eclectic group. On a warm afternoon sit at an outdoor café and watch Cambridge stroll by. In summer the nighttime street life bustles, especially near **Brattle Square** (a tiny square-within-the-Square), where outdoor entertainers hold forth every few yards. Harvard Square boasts bookstores catering to every interest, and many stay open late. Among the commercial landmarks are the **Harvard Coop, Out of Town News,** and **Charles Square,** a hotel-and-shopping complex. Student-oriented cheap eats as well as fine dining opportunities abound, as do vintage and avant-garde clothing boutiques and housewares and furnishings stores. Experience the aura of **Harvard Yard,** then walk up Brattle Street (formerly Tory Row) and visit lovely **Radcliffe Yard.** You'll see plenty of historic edifices and some interesting modern architecture. The Square offers good theater, movies, and music in a variety of settings, plus Harvard's great museums. Along with MIT and other local colleges and institutions, Harvard hosts a long menu of lectures, exhibitions, symposia, and cultural and sports events throughout the academic year.

To get to Cambridge from Boston, take the MBTA Red Line: The **Kendall Station** is closest to MIT and is also near East Cambridge. The **Lechmere Station** on the Green Line is even more convenient to East Cambridge. The **Central Station,** in Central Square, is a five-minute walk from Inman Square; the **Harvard Station** brings you right to the heart of the Square; the **Porter Station** is nearest to North Cambridge. In addition, **Bus #1** runs along Massachusetts Avenue from Harvard Square in Cambridge across the Charles River to Boston's Back Bay, continuing on Massachusetts Avenue to Roxbury.

1 HARVARD COLLEGE OBSERVATORY

Built in 1843 as the appearance of "the Great Comet" sparked interest in astronomy, the observatory now opens its doors to the public once a month. **Observatory Nights** feature an hour-long lecture/film program geared toward teens and adults; afterward, if the sky is clear, visitors have the chance to look through some nifty telescopes. The domed pavilion is the only surviving element of the original building, designed by **Isaiah Rogers** in 1851. ♦ Free. Open to the public the third Thursday of every month; doors open at 7:30PM, lecture at 8PM. 60 Garden St (between Bond St and Garden Terr). 495.7461; cfa-www.harvard.edu/obsnight.html

2 CRAIGIE STREET BISTROT

★★★★$$$$$ On residential Craigie Circle, a 15-minute walk from Harvard Square, this intimate jewel of modern French cooking is in what was the basement of a vintage apartment building. The chef relies on fresh local ingredients and there are some fine wines. The menu changes daily, depending on what's good at the market. Consider entrées like Pain d'Épice-crusted chops of wild boar with roasted shallot-tamarind jus, or try the Neighborhood Menu, a three-course prix-fixe bargain, available. Wednesday, Thursday, and Sunday, and after 9PM Friday and Saturday. Limited on-street parking. ♦ W-Su, dinner. Reservations recommended, by phone or online. 5 Craigie Circle (off Craigie St, between Concord St and Buckingham Ave). 497.5511; www.craigiestreetbistrot.com

3 LONGY SCHOOL OF MUSIC

Founded in 1915 and housed in the 1889 **Edwin Abbot Mansion** (listed in the National Register of Historic Places), this is a very active and esteemed music school. It hosts a wide array of notable concerts of every era and style in intimate **Pickman Hall**. ♦ 1 Follen St (at Concord Ave). 876.0956; www.longy.edu ♿

4 HENRY WADSWORTH LONGFELLOW HOUSE

During the Siege of Boston from 1775 to 1776, **George Washington** moved his head-quarters from Wadsworth House near Harvard Yard to this stately Georgian residence, built in 1759 by a wealthy Tory, John Vassall, who fled just before the Revolution. Longfellow rented a room here in 1837, then was given the house by his wealthy new father-in-law upon marrying heiress Frances Appleton in 1843. (She died here tragically years later, burned in a fire in the library.) Longfellow wrote many of his famous poems in this mansion, including *The Song of Hiawatha* and *Evangeline: A Tale of Acadie*. He lived here for 45 years, with prominent literary friends often gathered around. The house has been restored to the poet's period, with thousands of books from his library, plus many of his possessions. Wood from the spreading chestnut tree that inspired him was made into a carved armchair, presented to the poet on his 72nd birthday by Cambridge school-children and now on display.

The home stayed in the Longfellow family until 1973, and is now operated by the National Park Service as a National Historic Site. Visitors can see the house during tours, which are given throughout the day. Special events are held here regularly, including children's programs, a celebration of the poet's birthday in February, and poetry readings and concerts on the east lawn in the summer. A bookstore offers most of the Longfellow books in print, plus books on his life, the literary profession, poetry, and more. ♦ Admission: free for those under 16 and over 62. Open daily mid-March to Oct. Guided tours only; reserve in advance for groups. 105 Brattle St (between Mason and Craigie Sts). 876.4491; www.nps.gov/long ♿ (staff will assist)

5 SHERATON COMMANDER HOTEL

$$$ Near **Cambridge Common** and a short walk to the Square, this gracious old reliable often welcomes prominent political figures. The 175 understated but pleasant rooms include nine "executive king" suites, each with a sitting area, small dining area, canopy bed, and whirlpool bath. Hotel amenities include a fitness room, multilingual staff, a concierge, and a business center. Rooms for people with disabilities and for nonsmokers are available. **The Cafe at 16 Garden Street** serves conti-nental fare. Reservations recommended. ♦ 16 Garden St (between Mason and Berkeley Sts). 547.4800, 800/325.3535; fax 868.8322; www.sheratoncommander.com ♿

6 CAMBRIDGE COMMON

ⓟ The site of General Washington's main camp from 1775 to 1776 is now a grassy park for relaxing students and tourists. ♦ Bounded by Massachusetts Ave, Garden St, and Waterhouse St

On Cambridge Common:

DAWES ISLAND

ⓟ Look for the bronze horseshoes embedded in the sidewalk here, marking William Dawes's ride through town on the way to warn the populace in Lexington with the famous cry

---

Restaurants/Clubs: Red | Hotels: Purple | Shops: Orange | Outdoors/Parks: Green | Sights/Culture: Blue

THE LITERARY TRAIL

This self-guided tour winds through Boston, Cambridge, and Concord's rich literary territory, visiting sites related to some of the nation's greatest authors and poets. The five-hour journey includes the **Boston Public Library,** a poet's Back Bay mansion, Louisa May Alcott's **Orchard House,** and Thoreau's **Walden Pond.** A background book, brochures, and admission tickets can be purchased at the **Omni Parker House** hotel (60 School St), where Ralph Waldo Emerson and his group met in the mid-19th century (and where the trail begins). Information at 621.4020; www.literarytrailofgreaterboston.org.

"The British are coming!" The shoes were given to the city of Cambridge by Dawes's descendants as a US Bicentennial gift. ♦ Garden St and Massachusetts Ave

7 MOUNT AUBURN CEMETERY

This serene spot is worth seeking out for a sunny afternoon stroll, a picnic, and some fine bird-watching. Now one of its illustrious residents, Henry Wadsworth Longfellow once called Mount Auburn the "city of the dead." When it was founded in 1831, the cemetery introduced a new concept of interment to the US. Before, burial grounds were rustic grave-yards where the dead were buried in an erratic fashion. Grave markers were frequently moved about along with bodies, with the dead's remains even shuttled from one burial ground to another. (Boston's cemeteries offer plenty of evidence of these casual practices.) But with the creation of this cemetery, the idea of commemorating an individual with a permanent, unencroachable burial place was instituted. A ritual of memory took root in America, with personal gravesites becoming a new status symbol. Oliver Wendell Holmes, Isabella Stewart Gardner, Mary Baker Eddy, and Winslow Homer are among the more than 70,000 people buried here. The first garden cemetery in America, it has 170 verdant acres planted with unusual native and rare foreign trees (more than 3,000 in all) and flowering shrubs. To take a self-guided tour, stop by the office and pick up maps and audiotapes; a horticultural tour and a tour of the cemetery's notable memorials are available. The Friends of Mount Auburn sponsors special walks, talks, and other activities. ♦ 580 Mount Auburn St (between Coolidge Ave and Cottage St). 547.7105; www.mountauburn.org &

8 RADCLIFFE YARD

Radcliffe College was founded for women in 1879 and named for Harvard's first female benefactor, **Ann Radcliffe.** It was Harvard's sister school until 1975, when the two colleges were united, their administrations merged, and equal admission standards adopted for men and women. Radcliffe remains an independent corporation with its own president, but students share housing, classes, facilities, and degrees.

Stroll through Radcliffe's pretty campus green and note the college's first building, **Fay House,** an 1806 Federal mansion. Other noteworthy Radcliffe Yard buildings include the stately **Agassiz House,** where the Harvard Gilbert and Sullivan Players put on operettas, and the **Arthur and Elizabeth Schlesinger Library,** which has the country's most extensive collection of books, photographs, oral histories, and other materials related to women's history. ♦ Brattle St (between Appian Way and Mason St)

Within Radcliffe Yard:

LOEB DRAMA CENTER

Harvard University's theater, built in 1959 by **Hugh Stubbins,** is home to the prestigious **American Repertory Theatre** (ART), a nonprofit professional company affiliated with the university that presents new American plays, neglected works from the past, and unconventional interpretations of classics. The ART has premiered works by Jules Feiffer, Carlos Fuentes, Marsha Norman, Milan Kundera, Larry Gelbart, and David Mamet. The student **Harvard-Radcliffe Dramatic Club** is also based here.

The center's main theater seats 556 people and boasts the first fully flexible stage in the country, which can easily be converted into different configurations. Free student performances are held in the experimental theater; information is available at the box office. Infrared hearing amplifiers available on request. ♦ Daily. 64 Brattle St (at Hilliard St). 547.8300; www.amrep.org &

9 CHRIST CHURCH

America's first trained architect, **Peter Harrison,** designed this church as well as **King's Chapel** in Boston. Cambridge's oldest church, the former Tory place of worship later served as barracks for Connecticut troops, who melted down the organ pipes for bullets during the Revolution. **Theodore Roosevelt** taught Sunday school here while at Harvard.

Like the Boston chapel, the church's interior is simple. ♦ Garden St (between Massachusetts Ave and Appian Way)

10 CLOTHWARE

Mix and match carefully selected, uncommon women's garments made from natural fibers, especially cottons and silks, at this small, well-known shop. The designer lines, including the private label of one of the original owners, focus on graceful, classic, and fun-to-wear styles. The lingerie selection here is especially tempting. The shop also carries some accessories, including leggings, tights, scarves, hats, socks, jewelry, wallets, and handbags. There are regular sales, but this is not the place for a bargain-hunting excursion. ♦ Daily. 52 Brattle St (at Story St). 661.6441

10 HI-RISE PIE CO.

★$$ "Under a spreading chestnut tree / The village smithy stands / The smith a mighty man is he / With large and sinewy hands." The smithy in **Henry Wadsworth Longfellow**'s famous poem "The Village Blacksmith" lived in this old yellow house dating from 1811, the **Dexter Pratt House.** A stone nearby marks the former site of the famous chestnut tree. There's been a bakery on the premises for more than 45 years, although it has changed hands a couple of times. Baker Rene Becker makes wonderful breads and creates tempting sandwiches. Enjoy lunch or just a snack. The house belongs to the Cambridge Center for Adult Education, which offers courses, lectures, seminars, films, and cultural activities. ♦ Bakery/Café/Takeout ♦ Bakery: daily. Café: M-Sa, breakfast, lunch (until 5PM), and tea; Su, brunch. 56 Brattle St (between Story and Hilliard Sts). 492.3003 &

10 BURDICK CHOCOLATE CAFE

A homey shop and café, Burdick's is often crowded with people of all ages, but the hot chocolates, teas, coffees, and chocolate cakes and pastries are worth it. Hot chocolate is thick and delicious. The warm raspberry tart with cream is divine. ♦ Daily, 8AM-10 or 11 PM. 52-D Brattle St (between Hilliard and Story Sts). 491.4340; www.burdickchocolate.com &

10 DESIGN RESEARCH BUILDING/ CRATE & BARREL

Benjamin Thompson built this architectural equivalent of a giant glass showcase in 1969 for Design Research, the store he founded to introduce Americans to international modern design products for the home. The store was taken over by Crate & Barrel in the mid-1970s. He certainly knows how to put together an interesting display—as a later project, **Faneuil Hall Marketplace,** attests. ♦ M-W, F, 10AM-7PM; Th, 10AM-9PM; Sa, 10AM-6PM; Su, noon-6PM. 48 Brattle St (between Story and Hilliard Sts). 876.6300; www.crateandbarrel.com

11 COLONIAL DRUG

This 50-year-old establishment produces more than 900 essences, using natural ingredients according to centuries-old formulations. Also look for a complete line of cosmetics, skin and hair products, Kent brushes, and other high-quality personal care items. ♦ M-Sa. No credit cards accepted. 49 Brattle St (between Church St and Appian Way). 864.2222

12 CAMBRIDGE 1

★★$$ In what was Cambridge's first firehouse, this upscale pizza parlor and sports bar draws a casual young-professional crowd with prices that keep strapped students at bay. Exotic thin-crust pizza, salads, pitchers of quality beer, and lots of exposed brick and wood make for a fun atmosphere. Sports, of course, are on the large-screen TVs. ♦ Daily, lunch and dinner. 27 Church St (between Brattle St and Massachusetts Ave). 576.1111 &

13 FIRST PARISH CHURCH AND OLD BURYING GROUND

This wooden Gothic Revival church, the 1833 creation of **Isaiah Rogers,** was partly funded by Harvard in return for pews for students' use. Numerous Revolutionary War veterans—including two African-American slaves, Cato Stedman and Neptune Frost, who fought alongside their masters—and Harvard's first eight presidents are buried in the adjacent cemetery. ♦ 3 Church St (between Massachusetts Ave and Brattle St)

Within the First Parish Church:

NAMELESS COFFEEHOUSE

New England's oldest volunteer-run coffeehouse is a neighborly venue where local folk musicians play. **Tracy Chapman** sang here during her days as a Harvard Square street performer. ♦ Monthly entertainment; call for schedule. 864.1630; www.namelesscoffeehouse.org

14 BRATTLE HOUSE

This 1727 frame house, on the National Register of Historic Places, belonged to William Brattle, a Tory who fled in 1774 and for whom the street is named. **Margaret**

Restaurants/Clubs: Red | Hotels: Purple | Shops: Orange | Outdoors/Parks: Green | Sights/Culture: Blue

Fuller, the feminist editor of *The Dial*, lived here from 1840 to 1842. The house is now headquarters for the **Cambridge Center for Adult Education** (547.6789; www.ccae.org), which sponsors a heady array of courses as well as a well-attended holiday-season crafts fair. ♦ 42 Brattle St (at Story St)

14 THE BRATTLE THEATRE

This more-than-a-century-old independent movie house extraordinaire has struggled to preserve its identity in the midst of increasingly commercial Harvard Square and in an era of movie-chain monopolies. Renovated from top to bottom, but retaining its rare rear-screen projection system, this is one of the country's oldest remaining repertory movie houses. If it doesn't look much like a movie house, that's because it opened as Brattle Hall in 1890, founded by the Cambridge Social Union as a place for literary, musical, and dramatic entertainments. From 1948 to 1952 the **Brattle Theatre Company** put on nationally acclaimed performances from Shakespeare to Chekhov with many notable stars, including Jessica Tandy and Hume Cronyn. The theater made a policy of hiring actors blacklisted during the US government's political witch hunts of the era, including Zero Mostel. Subsequent financial difficulties inspired Harvard grads Bryant Haliday and Cyrus Harvey Jr. (who brought the first films of Fellini, Antonioni, Bergman, and Olmi to America) to convert it to an art cinema in 1953. A local Humphrey Bogart cult was born here in the 1950s when owners Harvey and Haliday screened neglected Bogie movies during Harvard exam time, drawing college students and other fans in droves. As the revived Bogie mystique spread across the country, a weeklong Bogart series became an annual tradition.

The movie house has shared its quarters with a variety of retail businesses since the 1960s. Today a faithful following comes for classic Hollywood and foreign movies, independently made films, new art films, staged readings, and concerts. Financially hard-pressed but fundraising furiously, the theater offers double features nearly every night. Movie lovers are drawn by the attractive lineup and two-shows-for-one-price admission. A free two-month calendar of events is available in front of the theater. ♦ Daily. 40 Brattle St (at Story St). 876.6837; www.brattlefilm.org &

Within The Brattle Theatre building:

ALGIERS CAFE

★★$ Head upstairs to this domed hideaway to sip minted coffee and feast on baba ghannouj or tabbouleh. This café made out like a bandit in the Brattle Theatre rehab: once a grungy (if atmospheric) underground café, it's now airy and gorgeous, with balletic little tables and prize rugs on the walls. Best of all, you're still left in peace to converse or cogitate. ♦ Middle Eastern ♦ Daily. 492.1557 &

CASABLANCA

★★$$ Long the last word in student romance, this Bogie classic's namesake has graduated from mostly bar to full-scale restaurant while keeping its oversize rattan chairs-for-two and David Omar White's movie-homage murals—even though it meant moving whole walls. The menu offers dishes from Spain, Portugal, Turkey, and Provence. Specialties include braised beef short ribs with star anise, Turkish lamb and vegetable kabobs, and garlic chicken soup with almonds and bread. ♦ Mediterranean ♦ Daily, lunch and dinner. 876.0999; www.casablanca-restaurant.com &

15 CLUB PASSIM

★$ One of America's oldest and best-known coffeehouses, this below-street-level venue began featuring folk music around 1971 and today is a nonprofit club. Latin for "here and there," the name is pronounced *Pass-im*, although just about everybody says *Pass-eem*. Original owners Bob and Rae Donlins have always been true-blue friends to local folk and bluegrass performers; among those they helped boost to fame are Jackson Browne, Tracy Chapman, Suzanne Vega, and Tom Waits.

The club has weathered well, and continues to showcase acoustic music. It's small (50-person capacity), unpretentious, and has no liquor license. It serves light, surprisingly good pizzas and flatbreads, and vegetarian and vegan cooking from the in-house **Veggie Planet** restaurant (661.1513; www.veggieplanet.net). Seating is first-come, first-served, and the admission prices are low. ♦ Coffeehouse/Café ♦ Cover for performances. Restaurant: daily from 11:30AM. Call for show times. 47 Palmer St (between Brattle and Church Sts). 492.7679; www.clubpassim.org

16 CURIOUS GEORGE GOES TO WORDSWORTH

This charming children's book and toy store across from the Harvard Square T station specializes in books and toys featuring the simian children's-book character, along with dolls, cuddly animal figures, puzzles, and other kids' books. This is the remnant of what was once the independent, influential WordsWorth bookstore, driven out of business in 2004 by competition from online booksellers and big-box stores. ♦ 1 John F. Kennedy St (at Brattle St). 498.0062; www.curiousg.com & (Staff will assist. No elevator to lower level.)

17 CAMBRIDGE ARTISTS' COOPERATIVE

This casual and funky shop, which represents some 200 artists (most regional), covers three floors with handmade arts and crafts. The unusual, fun, and interesting selection of eclectic wares features jewelry, pottery, clothing, and glassware. Prices range from $20 earrings to quilts at more than $1,000. There is usually at least one artist at work in the store. ◆ Daily. 59A Church St (between Massachusetts Ave and Brattle St). 868.4434; www.cambridgeartistscoop.com

18 JASMINE/SOLA

Moderately expensive women's clothing and accessories are featured here, as are women's shoes (which range widely in price), including some hard-to-find brands. The couture runs from casual to dressy, with an emphasis on unusual rich fabrics and striking styles. The jewelry is fun, much of it produced by independent and emerging jewelry makers. Also here is Sola Men, a modest selection of great-looking men's clothing and shoes, often European in style. ◆ Daily. 37 Brattle St (between Appian Way and Church Sts). 354.6043; www.jasminesola.com &

19 MOTTO/MDF

Side by side are two small shops with different wares but the same distinctive aesthetic. Both are owned and operated by Jude Silver, whose own art background has influenced her preference for modern, functional, and sophisticated creations. Motto sells abstract avant-garde jewelry of striking materials, textures, compositions, and tones. They may suggest European élan, classical coolness, industrial efficiency, or Southwestern warmth. MDF (Modern Design Furnishings) offers personal and home and office accessories, lamps, small furniture, and men's jewelry, all fabricated from nontraditional materials. Brides-to-be can register at this store, and both stores will gladly take special orders, pack, and ship all over the country. ◆ Daily. 17-19 Brattle St (between Church and Brattle Sts). Motto 868.8448, MDF 491.2789 &

19 BERTUCCI'S

★$ One of many in a chain that serves delicious pizzas along with pasta and Italian entrées. The family-friendly menu, casual atmosphere, and reasonable prices make it a good bet with kids. ◆ Italian ◆ Daily. 21 Brattle St (between Brattle and Church Sts). 864.4748; www.bertuccis.com. Also at

numerous other locations in Boston and Cambridge

20 HARVARD COOPERATIVE SOCIETY (THE COOP)

Students angered at local merchants' price gouging founded this society in 1882. Their enterprise sold goods to faculty and students, and gradually blossomed into the largest college cooperative in the US, today universally known as "The Coop" (pronounced like the chicken abode). The store is owned by its members: Harvard and MIT students, faculty, employees, and alumni.

Barnes & Noble took over management of The Coop in 1996, and created a new look inside, but the institution essentially remained the same. Some departments were expanded (books, music), some closed (housewares, sports equipment, fashions, electronics, luggage), and some remain as they've always been (New England's best selection of posters, prints, and frames; basic clothing; stationery products; basic furnishings for apartments and dormitory rooms; and, of course, anything and everything imaginable emblazoned with Harvard colors and the Veritas seal). Sidewalk sales are often set up on Palmer Street, between the original building facing the Square and its annex. Happily, you can find rest rooms here, the only public ones in the Square. Try the **COOP Café**, 499.2240, for fair-trade coffee and light lunch fare. Also, there's the **COOP for Kids**, for children's books. ◆ M-Sa. 1400 Massachusetts Ave (at John F. Kennedy St). 499.2000 &

21 HARVARD UNIVERSITY

The first and foremost of the famed Ivy League schools was originally founded to train young men for the ministry. The university's seal, incorporating the Latin word *Veritas* ("truth"), was adopted in 1643. Harvard College gradually moved from Puritanism to intellectual independence and became a private institution in 1865. In the mid-19th century the college became the undergraduate core of a burgeoning modern university, with satellite professional schools. Today there are 11 Harvard graduate schools: Arts and Sciences, Business Administration, Dental Health, Design, Divinity, Education, the Extension School, Government, Law, Medicine, and Public Health. With 400-odd buildings on 380 acres of land in the Cambridge/Boston area, the university and its Cambridge surrounds are so entwined that it's hard to tell where town ends and gown begins. The current endowment of $25.9 billion (give or take many millions) represents the largest of any

Restaurants/Clubs: Red | **Hotels: Purple** | **Shops: Orange** | **Outdoors/Parks: Green** | **Sights/Culture: Blue**

181

university in the world. Harvard "houses," where students live after their freshman year, dot the Square toward the river and include lovely Georgian-style brick residences with courtyards. Most memorable are the River Houses, best seen from the Charles; www.news.harvard.edu/guide

Within Harvard University:

HARVARD UNIVERSITY INFORMATION CENTER/HOLYOKE CENTER

Located on the ground floor of Holyoke Center, in the arcade, the center distributes maps, pamphlets, self-guided walking tours, and other materials (some free, some sold) on the university and area events. Tickets for university events are sold here, too. Get a free copy of the *Harvard University Gazette*, which lists activities open to the public. Students also offer free one-hour tours (departing from the Information Center) that give visitors a good general introduction to the university. ♦ Information Center: M-Sa. Campus tours: M-F, 10AM and 2PM; Sa, 2PM during the academic year; daily in summer. 1350 Massachusetts Ave (between Holyoke and Dunster Sts). 495.1573; www.hno.harvard.edu/guide/to_do &

HARVARD YARD

Verdant and dappled with sun and shade, its great trees sentinels to the education of generations, this expanse—now on the National Register of Historic Places—exudes an aura of privilege and prestige, the very essence of the institution. Anyone is welcome to relax on its grassy lawns, although when late spring arrives the air becomes thick with lawn fertilizer and noisy with machinery as the university starts sprucing up for another commencement. Summer mornings are particularly tranquil here; early fall heralds the return of the students and faculty with their brisk, purposeful traffic to and from classes.

The university's oldest buildings date from the early 18th century; its newest were built yesterday. From Holyoke Center, cross Massachusetts Avenue and enter the gate, where you'll find the **Benjamin Wadsworth House,** an attractive yellow clapboard house built in 1726, where Harvard presidents resided until 1849. It briefly served as **General George Washington**'s headquarters when he took command of the Continental Army in Cambridge in 1775. Walk through the western side of the yard (considered the "Old Yard"); to the left is Early Georgian **Massachusetts Hall,** the oldest university building, dating from 1720, where the president's offices are now located. Patriot regiments were once housed here and in

several other buildings nearby. Opposite is **Harvard Hall** (built in 1766); between the two halls is **Johnston Gate** (erected in 1889), the main entrance, which was designed by **McKim, Mead & White.** Standing at attention by the gate is a bit of frippery, a tiny guardhouse designed by **Graham Gund.** Next on the left is **Hollis Hall** (completed in 1763), where John Quincy Adams, Ralph Waldo Emerson, and Henry David Thoreau roomed. Beyond is **Holden Chapel** (built in 1742), a High Georgian gem, complete with a family coat of arms. Once called "a solitary English daisy in a field of Yankee dandelions," it has been tarnished through constant alterations. Next is **Stoughton Hall,** designed in 1805 by Harvard graduate **Charles Bulfinch.**

Opposite Johnston Gate on the right stands **University Hall,** designed by Bulfinch in 1815. It was this building that created the illusion of an academic enclave, instead of merely clusters of buildings facing outward. In front stands Daniel Chester French's 1884 statue of **John Harvard** (French also sculpted the statue in the Lincoln Memorial in Washington, DC). This statue is famous for the three lies set forth in its plaque, which states "John Harvard, founder 1638." It is the image of an 1880s Harvard student, not of Harvard himself; Harvard was a benefactor, not a founder, and the college was founded in 1636. Nevertheless, the false John is nearly always surrounded by tourists and visitors.

Behind University Hall, in the "New Yard," is **Memorial Church** (constructed in 1932), with its soaring needle-sharp spire. By school regulations, the church's wonderful **University Choir** only performs during religious services here. Installed in the church is a glorious organ, a creation of the late C.B. Fisk of Gloucester and one of the greatest American instruments built according to Baroque principles. Many international organists have vied to play it. Looming opposite is the massive **Harry Elkins Widener Memorial Library** (see right), which lies across from the grassy **Tercentenary Theatre,** where the university's commencements are held with all the traditional ruffles and flourishes—even a Latin oration. As you head in that direction you'll pass Romanesque Revival **Sever Hall** on your left, designed by **Henry Hobson Richardson** in 1880, a National Historic Landmark and one of his greatest buildings. Study its brilliantly animated and decorative brickwork.

Alongside Widener Library are **Pusey Library,** where the university's archives and map and theater collections are stored, and **Houghton Library,** home to its rare books and manuscripts,

Harvard College was the only college in North America until 1693.

INNOVATION ODYSSEY

This tour links six areas of Boston's greatest innovations: technology, education, finance, health care, information technology, and biotechnology. An actor/guide plays a dozen roles during stops at places like the **Ether Dome** at **Massachusetts General Hospital** (where doctors performed the first surgery using anesthesia), the **Pioneer Telephone Museum** (at City Hall Plaza, next to where Alexander Graham Bell invented the telephone), and **Harvard University.** The 2½-hour, $25 coach tour travels through the heart of Boston and Cambridge. Weekly from State Street Orange Line T station, State and Congress Sts. Reserve at 350.0358, or by e-mail at info@bostonhistorycollaborative.org. The web site is www.bostonhistorycollaborative.org.

including memorabilia and furnishings from Emily Dickinson's Amherst home, and the single book remaining from John Harvard's library. Pusey often exhibits selections from its theater collection on the first floor, and Houghton offers public displays of some of its many treasures, with an emphasis on fine bookmaking. Near **Lamont Library,** which is tucked in the corner, is a **Henry Moore** sculpture called *Four-Piece Reclining Figure.* ♦ Bounded by Quincy and Peabody Sts, Massachusetts Ave, Broadway, and Cambridge St

Within Harvard Yard:

HARRY ELKINS WIDENER MEMORIAL LIBRARY

A more triumphal and imposing entrance than this would be hard to find, with its massive Corinthian colonnade and grand exterior staircase. Chilly gray and austere, this library (built in 1915) is the patriarch in Harvard's family of nearly 100 department libraries campuswide. It was named for Harry Elkins Widener, who went down with the *Titanic*; a plaque inside the entrance tells the story.

It has more than three million volumes on more than five miles of bookshelves; the collection of books found here is surpassed only by the Library of Congress and the New York City Public Library. (The entire Harvard library system contains more than 15 million items: books, manuscripts, microforms, maps, photographs, slides, and other materials.) The building is open to the public, but access to its stacks is limited to cardholders with Harvard affiliation and those with special permission. In the resplendent **Harry Elkins Widener Memorial Room,** bibliophile and collector Harry's books are on display, including a Gutenberg Bible, one of only 20 complete copies remaining, and a First Folio of Shakespeare's plays dated 1623, the first collected edition. Look for the dioramas depicting Cambridge in 1667, 1775, and 1936, and for the John Singer Sargent murals in the main stair hall. ♦ Daily when school is in session; M-F during school vacations. 495.2411 &

HARVARD SCIENCE CENTER

The largest building on Harvard's campus (built by **Sert, Jackson and Associates** in 1973) looks like a giant Polaroid Land Camera, with a complex and multiterraced exterior. Science buffs, take note: On the center's lower level you'll find Harvard's **Collection of Historical Scientific Instruments,** a repository for scientific apparatus used for Harvard teaching and research in astronomy, surveying, physics, geology, electricity, navigation, and other subjects since 1765, with additional devices donated to the university dating back to 1450. On view are telescopes, sundials, clocks, vacuum pumps, microscopes, early computing devices, and more. There are occasional exhibitions of private collections as well. Outside, the **Tanner Fountain,** designed by sculptor Peter Walker, is a jet-misted cluster of rocks that's always alluring to children. ♦ Free. Tu-F; closed June through August. Oxford and Kirkland Sts. 495.2779 &

MUSEUMS OF CULTURE AND NATURAL HISTORY

Sharing one roof are four separate Harvard University museums dedicated to the study of archaeology, botany, comparative zoology, and minerals. The most famous exhibition is the **Botanical Museum**'s **Blaschka Glass Flowers collection,** handblown by Leopold and Rudolph Blaschka in Dresden, Germany, from 1887 to 1936 using a process that was lost with their deaths. More than 840 plant species are represented, though a few have been irrevocably lost when shattered by sonic booms. Another odd Botanical Museum exhibit is Rosalba Towne's 19th-century series of paintings depicting every plant and flower mentioned in the works of Shakespeare. Particularly wondrous is the **Mineralogical** and **Geological Museum**'s collection of gemstones, minerals, ores, and meteorites. Look for the giant Mexican crystals.

The **Peabody Museum of Archaeology and Ethnology** is the oldest museum of its kind in this hemisphere, with treasures from pre-historic and historic cultures from all over the world. Founded in 1866 by George Peabody, the museum owns many items brought back from Harvard-sponsored expeditions. The Peabody's largest collections focus on North, Central, and South American Indian cultures. The **Hall of the North American Indian,** for example, boasts some 500 artifacts, including magnificent towering totem poles, peace pipes, a Plains Indian ceremonial outfit, warriors' longbows, and a number of items brought back by the Lewis and Clark expedition. The exceptionally comprehensive collection includes objects from 10 different Indian cultures over five centuries. ♦ 11 Divinity Ave. 496.1027; www.peabody.harvard.edu &

Tracing the evolution of animals and man, the **Museum of Comparative Zoology** delights kids with such treasures as whale skeletons, a 180-million-year-old *Paleosaurus,* the 25,000-year-old Harvard mastodon, the giant sea serpent *Kronosaurus queenslandicus,* George Washington's pheasants, the world's oldest egg (225 million years old), and the largest known fossilized turtle shell. The museum also displays a skeleton of the coela-canth, a fish thought to have been extinct for 70 million years until fishermen began to catch some live in 1938. Visit the museums' **gift shop,** a largely undiscovered treasure trove. The Peabody has a separate gift shop, also excellent. ♦ Admission (one fee for all four museums); free Sa, 9-11AM; children under 5 free; reduced fee for senior citizens, students, and children 5 to 15. Daily. 24 Oxford St (between Kirkland and Hammond Sts). 495.3045; www.hmnh.harvard.edu & (inquire at admission desk)

HARVARD SEMITIC MUSEUM

Founded in 1889, this museum participated in the first US archaeological expedition to the Near East that year and the first scientific excavations in the Holy Land, from 1907 to 1912. The museum closed during World War II and reopened in 1982, and now presents special exhibitions drawn from its archeolog-ical and photographic collections, which include 28,000 photographs of 19th-century life in the Near East. ♦ Admission. Tu-Sa, 10AM-4PM; Su, 1-4PM; 6 Divinity Ave (north of Kirkland St). 495.3123; www.fas.harvard.edu/~semitic

ADOLPHUS BUSCH HALL

Named for the famous beer baron, this noble hall was formerly the Busch-Reisinger

Museum. It is now the home of Harvard's **Center for European Studies.** Designed by a German architect and completed in 1917, the medieval-style edifice was built to house the university's Germanic collections. Full of carved heroes, solemn inscriptions, and other lavish details, it was created to laud German culture. The hall and its purpose have been influenced by wars and changes in international opinion toward Germany. Much of the former museum's 20th-century German art was collected during the rise of Hitler, when the works were declared degen-erate, banned by the Nazis, and shipped to the US.

The Busch-Reisinger's Renaissance, Baroque, and modern holdings have been moved to the newer **Werner Otto Hall,** the creation of architects **Gwathmey and Siegel,** located behind the **Fogg Art Museum** (see page 185). It is not open to the public. Still displayed in Busch Hall are medieval statuary, stained glass, metal, and other works. Overlooking the wonderful courtyard garden are carved stone heads depicting characters in Wagner's *Ring of the Nibelungen.* Across Kirkland Street from the hall is a Gothic Swedenborgian church, a little jewel. ♦ Courtyard M-F, 11AM-3PM; collection 1-5PM second Sunday every month. 29 Kirkland St (at Divinity Ave).

MEMORIAL HALL

Just north of Harvard Yard looms this Ruskinian Gothic giant. With its square tower, pyramidal multicolored slate roofs, gargoyles, and colorful ornamentation, the cathedral-like structure has pomp and circumstance to spare. Designed in 1878 by Harvardians **Henry Van Brunt** and **William R. Ware,** the hall was built as a monument to university alumni who died in the Civil War—on the Yankee side, of course. Their names are inscribed in the transept inside. Some of the stained-glass windows were produced in the studios of **Louis Comfort Tiffany** and **John La Farge.** Innumerable momentous events (depending on one's perspective) have occurred here, from college registration and examinations to major lectures and concerts. Fine as the building was, until a major renovation was completed in 1996 it had been a drab-looking structure. But a rebirth as a student commons and freshman dining hall, coordi-nated by oft-time controversial Philadelphia architect **Robert Venturi,** has restored its original glory. Busts and portraits retrieved from storage, new chandeliers copied from lost gas-lamp originals, stained-glass win-dows, and a painted azure ceiling can now be seen in the building's **Annenberg Hall. Loker Commons,** in the basement of Memorial Hall, is a food and schmooze

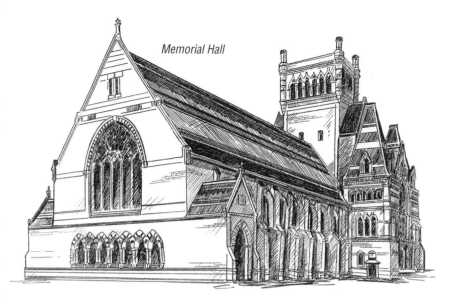

Memorial Hall

court, also open to the public. ♦ Cambridge St (between Quincy St and Massachusetts Ave) &

Within Memorial Hall:

SANDERS THEATRE

Celebrated painter **Frank Stella** and many other illustrious figures have lectured in this richly carved wooden theater, which seats 1,160. National performers such as the **Beaux Arts Trio** have also appeared here, as have many local music groups, including the Pro Arte Chamber Orchestra of Boston, the Cantata Singers, the Cecilia Society, and the Cambridge Society for Early Music. Festive **Christmas Revels** is an annual event. ♦ Admission for most events. General information 496.2222, recorded information 495.4595; www.fas.harvard.edu/~memhall/sanders.html & (use the Kirkland St entrance)

GEORGE GUND HALL

Home of the Harvard Graduate School of Design, this modern concrete building, completed in 1972 by **John Andrews,** is notable for the striking nighttime silhouette created by its stepped-glass roof, beneath which design students toil at their drawing boards late into the night. Within this hall is the **Frances Loeb Library** and its architecture and urban design collections (not open to the public. The first-floor gallery hosts changing architecture exhibits. ♦ Gallery: daily, 9AM–11PM. 48 Quincy St (at Cambridge St). 495.4731 & www.gsd.harvard.edu

ARTHUR M. SACKLER MUSEUM

Across Broadway from the **Fogg Art Museum** (see below) is this relative newcomer to Harvard. Except for its brick stripes, interesting window arrangements, and touches of bright lime paint, the chunky postmodern building is quite ordinary-looking. It was designed in 1986 by British architect **James Stirling,** who aptly called Harvard's campus "an architectural zoo." Exhibited here are Asian and Islamic art, including the world's finest collections of ancient Chinese jades, cave reliefs, and Chun-ware ceramics, and an exceptional selection of Japanese wood-block prints. Special exhibitions are also mounted here, and the **Harvard University Art Museum Shop** is on the first floor.

The Fogg Art Museum, the **Busch-Reisinger Museum,** and the Arthur M. Sackler Museum, which together comprise the Harvard University Art Museums, are set for extensive renovations after 2007. During renovation the museums will move almost everything to an interim home across the Charles River in what was a bank building at 1380 Soldiers Field Road in Allston. There has been talk of creating a Harvard arts and culture complex in Allston. ♦ Admission (includes Fogg Art Museum); free Sa, 10AM–noon; free for those under 18; reduced fee for senior citizens and students. Tu–Su. Free tours Sa at 1PM. 485 Broadway (at Quincy St). 495.9400; www.artmuseums.harvard.edu/ &

FOGG ART MUSEUM

Founded in 1891, Harvard's oldest art museum houses a comprehensive collection

---

Restaurants/Clubs: Red | Hotels: Purple | Shops: Orange | Outdoors/Parks: Green | Sights/Culture: Blue

representing most major artistic periods in the history of Western art from the Middle Ages to the present. In this 1927 **Coolidge, Shepley, Bulfinch, and Abbot** design, art galleries on two levels surround an Italian Renaissance courtyard modeled after a 16th-century canon's house. The French Impressionist, British, and Italian holdings are especially strong; look for works by Whistler, Rossetti, Géricault, Fra Angelico, Rubens, Ingres, Beardsley, and Pollock, as well as Monet, Renoir, and Picasso, as well as the **Wertheim Collection** on the second floor.

Also on the second floor is Harvard's first permanent gallery of decorative arts, which rotates treasures from the university's vast collection of furniture, clocks, chests, Wedgwood, silver vessels, and other household goods bequeathed by alumni and others over the past 300 years. Probably the most famous item is the **President's Chair,** a knobby, uncomfortable-looking triangular-seated chair made in England or Wales in the 16th century and brought to Harvard by the Reverend Edward Holyoke, college president from 1737 to 1769. Since Holyoke (who is shown seated in the chair in a portrait by John Singleton Copley), the President's Chair has supported every Harvard president during commencement. ◆ Admission (includes Sackler Museum); free Sa, 10AM-noon; free for children under 18; reduced fee for senior citizens and students. Daily; free tours at 11AM. 32 Quincy St (between Massachusetts Ave and Broadway). 495.9400 ఉ

Carpenter Center for the Visual Arts

Coolly surveying Harvard Yard across the way, this sculptural edifice is the only structure in North America designed by **Le Corbusier.** It was built in 1963 and is on the National Register of Historic Places. The iconoclastic concrete-and-glass form carries on an interesting dialogue with the sedate Fogg Art Museum next door and other conservative architectural neighbors. The building, which contains Harvard's Department of Visual and Environmental Studies, also hosts lectures and the **Harvard Film Archive** (which runs a wonderful film series), and has two public galleries that offer a rotating program of contemporary art exhibits. The center also houses a photography collection and studios. ◆ Daily. 24 Quincy St (between Massachusetts Ave and Broadway). 495.3251, recorded information on film showings 495.4700; www.harvardfilmarchive.org ఉ

Apthorp House

This 1760 structure, now surrounded by newer buildings, was built for the first rector of Christ Church, **East Apthorp.** Its extravagance so shocked Puritans that they dubbed the house "The Bishop's Palace," sparking a controversy so fierce that Apthorp quickly returned to England. The building now houses Harvard undergraduates; it is not open to the public. ◆ 10 Linden St (between Bow St and Massachusetts Ave)

22 Cardullo's

This crowded gourmet shop has been in Harvard Square since 1950, offering heavenly imported chocolates, wines, Champagne, caviar, gift baskets, marzipan, tea and coffee, and New England products. But the chocolates, of course, dominate. ◆ Daily. 6 Brattle St. 491.8888, 800/491.8288; www.cardullos.com

23 Brattle Street

Called **Tory Row** in the 1770s because its residents were loyal to King George, this glorious avenue still retains its share of magnificent homes (they were once country estates whose spacious grounds spilled right to the river's edge). In the summer of 1775 the patriots under George Washington appropriated the homes. Today the thoroughfare is far more densely inhabited, but its sumptuous properties secure its reputation as one of the country's poshest streets. **Henry Hobson Richardson** designed the **Stoughton House** at No. 90 in 1882; it's still a private residence. No. 159 is the **Hooper-Lee-Nichols House**, parts of which date back to the 1600s; it's now the headquarters of the Cambridge Historical Society. The building is open to the public on some afternoons and the society offers tours of Tory Row and the Old Burial Ground (call 497.1630). **John Bartlett,** the Harvard Square bookseller who compiled the famous *Bartlett's Familiar Quotations*, lived at **No. 165;** the house was erected for him in 1873. It is still a private home. ◆ Between Harvard Sq and Fresh Pond Pkwy

24 Urban Outfitters

This chain store is popular with students and an under-30 crowd that shops here for the latest in men's and women's attire, fashion accessories, housewares, and a slew of trendy novelties. You'll find lots of popular name brands and the store's own label. A bargain basement sells vintage clothing too. ◆ Daily. 11 John F. Kennedy St (between Mount Auburn and Brattle Sts). 864.0070; www.urbanoutfitters.com. Also at 361 Newbury St (at Massachusetts Ave), Boston. 236.0088

25 Harvard Square

Not really a square at all, it's officially located where Massachusetts Avenue turns and widens into a big triangle, on which the 1928

GOING FOR THE LAURELS: THE BOSTON MARATHON

Those who know Boston would agree it's a walker's city. However, each year in mid-April it becomes a runner's town, thanks to its remarkable marathon. Known formally as the Boston Athletic Association (BAA) Marathon, but simply as "Boston" to the running world, the annual event celebrated its hundredth running in 1996. The 36,748 starters in the centennial race (of whom 35,810 finished) made it the largest single running event in history. There were 22,517 entrants in 2006, representing 94 countries and all 50 states.

It's the oldest marathon in North America and one of the most prestigious races in the world. But the annual event is more than a race: For spectators as well as runners, it is one of Boston's best-loved traditions, with a mystique all its own and some grumbling from local residents.

The first Boston Marathon was run on 19 April 1896, after Tom Burke dug a line in the dirt with his heel at Metcalf's Mill in Ashland, about 25 miles southwest of Boston, and shouted "Go" to 15 men in heavy boots to protect their feet from the rutted roads. John McDermott of New York won the race in less than three hours, losing 10 pounds in the process.

Since that first race, the Boston Marathon has been run on Patriots' Day, a holiday commemorating the beginning battles of the American Revolution. (Today Patriots' Day is celebrated and the Boston Marathon is run on the third Monday in April.) The starting point of the race, however, was changed in the early years of the last century, when the standard length of a marathon was changed from 25 miles to 26.2 miles.

There's a story as to how the standard marathon course came to be lengthened. At the Olympic Games in London in 1908, illness in the Royal Family was going to prevent several of its members from attending the much-touted marathon. So Olympic officials brought the starting line to them, at Windsor Castle. This

extended the course one mile and 385 yards, and the new distance stuck. The Boston course was adjusted by moving the starting line to the town of **Hopkinton,** where it remains today.

Another innovation was introduced in the 1996 marathon, when computer chips were tied to the runners' shoelaces. The chips calculate how long it takes each athlete to run the 26.2-mile course—a time that was difficult to gauge in the past, since many thousands of runners are still at the starting line long after the race starts at noon. While each runner's official time begins when the starting gun is fired, runners may use their computer-chip time to qualify for the following year's race.

What sets the Boston course apart is that at about 20 miles into the race, when a runner's body begins to undergo traumatic chemical changes (known as "hitting the wall"), runners also hit the hills of **Newton.** These hills are not very high—the third and final one, the infamous **Heartbreak Hill,** rises only 90 feet from sea level—but their location makes Boston's one of the most challenging marathon courses in the world. The course record for men, set in 2006 by Robert Cheruiyot of Kenya, is 2:07:14; the women's record time, set in 2002 by Kenyan Margaret Okayo, is 2:20:43.

Women have run officially in the Boston Marathon since 1972, though they had to wait till 1984 before a women's marathon was added to the Olympic games. In 1975 Boston became the world's first major marathon to allow wheelchair racers to compete.

The winner in each division is crowned with a wreath of laurel leaves made of branches cut from groves in Marathon, Greece. But most spectators and runners agree that in the Boston Marathon, just to finish is to win. For information, contact the BAA (131 Clarendon St, at Stanhope St). 236.1652; www.bostonmarathon.org.

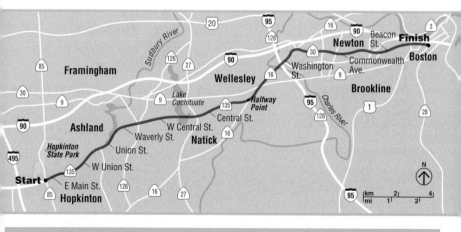

landmark kiosk, **Out of Town Newspapers** (see below), is located. On one side of this triangle is Harvard University; on the other two lies commerce. But to students and Cantabrigians, "the Square" always refers to the much larger area radiating from this central point, with most shops, restaurants, clubs, and services concentrated on Brattle, John F. Kennedy, and Mount Auburn Streets, as well as on many small side streets like Church, Plympton, Dunster, and that whimsical pair, Bow and Arrow Streets. All around the Square, sidewalks are crowded with college students, professors, canvassers, protesters, businesspeople, and entertainers—in fact, you can safely assume you're heading beyond the Harvard Square area when the foot traffic around you starts to dwindle. ♦ Bounded by Massachusetts Ave, Brattle St, and John F. Kennedy St

Within Harvard Square:

OUT OF TOWN NEWSPAPERS

Busy from opening to closing, this National Historic Landmark newsstand—always called Out of Town News—sells newspapers from every major American city and many large cities worldwide, plus a huge array of magazines, maps, comic books, and Harvard T-shirts. Many a rendezvous is kept at this ornate kiosk. Also on this traffic island is sculptor Dimitri Hadzi's 21-foot-tall *Omphalos* (Greek for "navel"), signifying the center of the universe. Generations of Harvard students and Cantabrigians have considered the Square precisely that. ♦ Daily. No credit cards accepted. 354.7777 ♦ (use the rear entrance)

25 RAVEN USED BOOKS

Raven is smallish, but its discounts on quality books are big. More than 13,000 volumes, many scholarly, are somehow here. Selections are prime in art and architecture. You must navigate several steps to enter. ♦ Daily. 52B John F. Kennedy St (between South and Winthrop Sts). 441.6999

26 HARVARD SQUARE HOTEL

$$ In the heart of the Square, this low-key, friendly hotel was refurbished in 2003 and has 73 simple, basic rooms on four floors. Lots of visiting parents and professors at the nearby **John F. Kennedy School of Government** stay here. It offers free Wi-Fi and all the amenities of a small business hotel. There's no room service, but the many restaurants in

the neighborhood make up for that. ♦ 110 Mount Auburn St (between Eliot St and University Rd). 864.5200; fax 864.2409; www.harvardsquarehotel.com ♦

27 CAFFÈ PARADISO

★★$ Students, faculty, and lovers of Italian coffees and delicacies have known Paradiso for years (the original has been at 253 Hanover Street in Boston's North End since 1962). Sunny and usually filled with conversation at the small tables, the café is an oasis from the bustle of Harvard Square. Light lunches are served; the gelato (Italian ice cream) is delicious, the rich cakes divine. Italian soccer games play quietly on satellite TV, and there's fascinating people-watching through the big windows or from tables outside. ♦ Café/Italian ♦ Daily, 7AM-11:30PM. 1 Eliot St (at Eliot Sq). 868.3240; www.caffeparadiso.com ♦

28 THE GARAGE

A fun complex of youth-oriented stores and restaurants, this urban minimall is filled with high school- and college-age kids, especially on weekends. There's a **Starbucks**, **Ben & Jerry's** ice cream, clothing stores, **Newbury Comics**, a tattoo and piercing shop, **Crazy Dough's** pizza, and a public rest room. There's also **Hootenanny**, a goth/punk/alternative clothing store where rebel kids shell out big bucks to fight the establishment, and **Le's** (formerly **Pho Pasteur**) (★★$), a lovely, casual Vietnamese restaurant. ♦ Daily. 36 John F. Kennedy St (at Mt Auburn St). You can also enter from Dunster Street, up a short flight of stairs. 492.4881 ♦

29 JOHN HARVARD'S BREW HOUSE

★★$ Six brews are made on the premises along with out-of-the-ordinary pub fare, which may include grilled sausages with fresh spaetzle and buttermilk fried chicken with spiced corn bread. The place is often noisy, but look for a series of Hogarthian panels conceived by muralists Josh Winer and John Devaney that depicts a semispurious (but funny) biography of John Harvard, the infamous brewmaster. ♦ American ♦ Daily, lunch and dinner. 33 Dunster St (between Mount Auburn St and Massachusetts Ave). 868.3585 ♦

29 LA FLAMME

A classic eight-seater, this old-fashioned barber shop (women welcome) has shorn such a distinguished head as Henry Kissinger's. ♦ M-Sa. 21 Dunster St (between Mount Auburn St and Massachusetts Ave). 354.8377 ⅙

29 HERRELL'S ICE CREAM

Steve Herrell is generally credited with starting the whole gourmet ice-cream boom at his out-of-the-way Somerville shop in 1972. He made his fame selling his first name (**Steve's Ice Cream**), and then started up again with a chain of stores bearing his last name. His hand-made ice cream, dense and intense and in luscious flavors like moccacino and choco-late pudding, is still among the best. The "back room" here—a former bank vault painted to resemble a grotto—is the coolest place in Cambridge on a hot summer evening. ♦ Daily, noon-midnight. 15 Dunster St (between Mount Auburn St and Massachusetts Ave). 497.2179

30 AU BON PAIN

★$ The mass-produced croissants are surpris-ingly tasty and the café also sells muffins, sandwiches, and soups. But the real reason to be here is to relax outside on the large terrace in nice weather and watch humanity flow to and from the Square. Singers, jugglers, and promoters of various causes often hold forth alongside the café. A local chess master regularly plays against the clock for a small sum at one of the café's chess tables, attracting aficionados. ♦ Café ♦ Daily, 6AM-midnight. 1360 Massachusetts Ave (at Dunster St). 497.9797

31 THE CHARLES HOTEL

$$$$ Harvard University guests, entertainment- industry folk, and business travelers who like to be near the late-night liveliness of the Square stay here, many on a long-term basis. The hotel is also popular with writers, and sponsors readings. Part of the **Charles Square** complex, which features shops, condominiums, a health club, and restaurants, the 299-room, 10-story hotel offers many rooms overlooking the **John F. Kennedy Memorial Park** and the **Charles River,** with Shaker-style furniture, telephones and TVs in all bathrooms, and a patchwork down quilt on every bed. The King Charles minisuites have four-poster beds. The public areas have eighteenth-century quilts and New England antiques. **Noir,** a sleek bar off the lobby, has a sultry 1940s theme and special-izes in martinis and classic cocktails. The bar menu was created by the chef at Rialto, in the hotel. There are also two restaurants and a popular jazz club (see page 190) on the premises. A concierge, a multilingual staff, complimentary overnight shoe shines, 24-hour room service, valet parking, and special rooms for people with disabilities and for nonsmokers are among the amenities. Guests have complimentary access to the exercise equipment and pool at the neighboring **Wellbridge Athletic Club** (441.0800). ♦ 1 Bennett St (between Eliot St and University Rd). 864.1200, 800/323.7500; fax 864.5715 ⅙

Within The Charles Hotel:

RIALTO

★★★$$$$ This formal dining room features subdued lighting in a living-room-like setting of moss green banquettes, crisp white table-cloths, and black blinds that add a touch of drama. As prepared by chef Jody Adams (winner of the 1997 James Beard Award for Best Chef in the East), the seasonal menu is shaded with hints of French, Italian, and Spanish cuisine. Start off with Provençale fisherman's soup with rouille, Gruyère, and basil oil, or a plate of chicken and duck liver and country pâtés garnished with porcini mushrooms, currants, Jerusalem artichokes, and pickled red onions. Entrées include seared scallops on a shredded potato cake

---

Restaurants/Clubs: Red | Hotels: Purple | Shops: Orange | Outdoors/Parks: Green | Sights/Culture: Blue

with cider sauce and hazelnuts; seared peppered venison with semolina gnocchi layered with Gorgonzola dolce, toasted walnuts, grilled Portobello mushrooms, and Cabernet sauce; and sole poached in white wine with chanterelle mushrooms and mussels. Desserts are as appealing: Try the hot chocolate cream and malted vanilla ice cream, or Breton butter cake with warm spiced pears, currants, and whipped crème fraîche. ♦ American ♦ Daily, dinner. Reservations required. 661.5050 ♿

Henrietta's Table

★★$$ The motto is "fresh and honest," and that's exactly what diners get from the open kitchen in this place. Menu highlights include Yankee pot roast, apple-wood-smoked Maine salmon, chicken potpie, stuffed cabbage, and rotisserie-roasted Vermont pheasant with lingonberry sauce. An extensive list of regional ales, beers, and wines is also available. There is outdoor dining in season. ♦ American ♦ M-Sa, breakfast, lunch, and dinner; Su, brunch and dinner. Reservations recommended for groups of six or more. 661.5005; www.henriettastable.com

The Regattabar

Here's a comfortable spot to listen and dance to local and nationally acclaimed jazz acts. The George Shearing Duo, the Milt Jackson Quartet, Gary Burton, Herbie Hancock, Ahmad Jamal, Pat Metheny, Herbie Mann, and the Four Freshmen have all performed in this popular venue. Tickets for Friday and Saturday sell out fast, so plan a week in advance. Hotel guests are admitted free to all shows Tuesday through Thursday and to any 11PM show; sign up with the concierge. All customers get 50% off the price of the second show if they stay for both shows on one night. ♦ Cover. Tu-Sa, evenings. No jeans, tank tops, or sneakers allowed. 876.7777; www.regattabarjazz.com ♿

31 The Shops at Charles Square

Among the establishments at this stark modern shopping complex are a branch of **Legal Sea Foods,** the elegant **Le Pli Salon** spa (547.4081), and some national chain stores. Originally viewed by locals as an unwelcome upscale intruder, this complex has proved to be a congenial addition to the neighborhood, thanks in part to such public events as courtyard concerts, but mainly because the design is low-key and browser-friendly. The Charles Square Parking Garage is open 24 hours—convenient for late-night revelers. ♦ Daily. Bennett St (between Eliot St and University Rd). 491.5282 ♿

32 Red House

★★$$$ The red-painted cottage across Winthrop Street from Upstairs on the Square is in stark contrast. Upstairs has elegance and slickness. Little Red House, circa 1802, has plank floors, low ceilings, and four dining rooms (and small bar) spread over two stories. It also has very good food in a charming, casual setting. Menu varies by season. Outdoor patio. ♦ International ♦ Tu-Su, lunch and dinner. 98 Winthrop St. 576.0605; www.theredhouse.com ♿

33 The Globe Corner Bookstore

An outpost of the Boston original, this shop specializes in books, maps, and guides for New England and world travel, and also carries travel-oriented novelties, games, and accessories. ♦ Daily. 90 Mt Auburn St (between Dunster and JFK Sts). 497.6277; www.globecorner.com

34 The Hasty Pudding Building

This little theater is home to the undergraduate **Hasty Pudding Theatricals,** a dramatic society established in 1795 and renowned for its annual Hasty Pudding Awards to the Man and Woman of the Year. The celebrity recipients—Halle Berry, Kevin Costner, Jodie Foster, and Martin Scorsese are past winners—are honored with parades through Cambridge in February, accompanied by male club members in female attire. The guest is then treated to an irreverent performance and comedic roast, and presented with a ceremonial pudding pot. ♦ 12 Holyoke St (between Mount Auburn St and Massachusetts Ave). Box office 495.5205; www.hastypudding.org

34 Sandrine's

★★$$$ A comfortable French bistro featuring traditional Alsatian dishes like *choucroute* and *flammekueche*, an Alsatian tarte/pizza. There's a classic French touch with dishes like roasted venison loin or trout Grenobloise. Chef Raymond Ost also puts a California influence into lunch sandwiches, and the french fries that accompany the sandwiches are excellent. In keeping with the menu, the décor melds country French and California elements, and the mood is casual and low-key romantic with cozy banquettes and warm colors. ♦ French/Alsatian ♦ Daily, dinner; M-Sa, lunch. Reservations recommended. 8 Holyoke St (between Mount Auburn St and Massachusetts Ave). 497.5300; www.sandrines.com ♿

35 Bartley's Burger Cottage

★$ A fixture in the Square since 1960, the Bartleys (and their son, Bill) have helped several generations of ravenous college students through their undergraduate years. According to the owners, their roasted, marinated chicken is "a degree above the rest," but the real draw is the big juicy burger—available in 30 standard variations plus a dozen or so topical guises, such as the Madonna ("a naked burger stripped of its roll"). The place is chockablock with tiny tables and decorated with odd remnants of popular culture—for instance, a vintage ad with Ronald Reagan hawking cigarettes. ◆ American ◆ M-Sa, lunch and dinner. 1246 Massachusetts Ave (between Bow and Plympton Sts). 354.6559 &

35 COMEDY STUDIO

An offbeat, sometimes silly, sometimes brilliant little comedy club on the third floor (stairway only) of the Hong Kong, an otherwise unremarkable Chinese restaurant that supplies the casual club's food. A variety of comedians experiment with new material. ◆ Th-Su, 8PM. 1236 Massachusetts Ave. 661.6507; www.thecomedystudio.com

35 HARVARD BOOK STORE

Open since 1932, this family-run Cambridge institution is a general-interest bookstore that emphasizes scholarly works and customer service. It's particularly strong in philosophy, literary theory and criticism, psychology, African-American and women's studies, classics, and books from university presses, and puts out a monthly newsletter. People flock in for the great remainders selection and the basement inventory of used paperbacks, hardcovers, and texts. ◆ Daily. 1256 Massachusetts Ave (at Plympton St). 661.1515; www.harvard.com & (street level only)

35 THE GROLIER POETRY BOOK SHOP, INC.

This all-poetry bookshop was founded in 1927 as a rare-books store, then converted to its specialty in 1974 by poetry-loving owner Louisa Solano. She has 15,000 poetry titles today, including books and CDs, first editions, small-press publications, and little magazines. Solano cosponsors a poetry-reading series, hosts autograph parties about once a week from September through May, and keeps a mailing list and bulletin board going as well as a photo gallery of the store's poet patrons. The shop is also a meeting place; lots of visiting poets use it as an information center and sounding board. ◆ M-Sa, noon-6:30PM. 6 Plympton St (between Bow St and Massachusetts Ave). 547.4648, 800/234.7636; www.grolierpoetrybookshop.com

35 GRAFTON STREET PUB & GRILLE

★★$$ With a great street view, this is one of the better people-watching places in Harvard Square and a good meeting and drinking spot. Irish barmen and an attentive wait staff in the roomy, multilevel dining area provide fine service. There's lots of dark wood and a variety of beers. Good casual food includes steamed Prince Edward Island mussels and sirloin steak with fingerling potatoes and a green peppercorn demiglace. The lunch menu offers crisp fish and chips. ◆ American ◆ Daily, lunch and dinner. 1230 Massachusetts Ave (at Bow St). 497.0400; www.graftonstreetcambridge.com

36 GRENDEL'S DEN

★$ The food is basic, but it's plentiful and cheap—and the all-ages clientele can be fascinating. The funky bar and restaurant is downstairs, with the entrance from Winthrop Park. ◆ International ◆ Daily, lunch and dinner noon to 1AM. 89 Winthrop St (between John F. Kennedy and Eliot Sts). 491.1160 & (staff will assist)

36 UPSTAIRS ON THE SQUARE

★★★★$$$$ Theatrical, romantic, and first class. When Harvard forced Upstairs at the Pudding to move from the **Hasty Pudding Building** in 2002, the renowned restaurant landed here, a few blocks away, in the former home of the Market Theater. Expect zebra stripes, pastels, chandeliers, and fine, rich American food with a flourish, such as Colorado lamb. In the impressive **Soiree Room**, entrées are expensive, but the **Monday Club** bar on the first floor is informal, more affordable, and jumping with a bar scene. Critics praise even the grilled cheese sandwich. ◆ American ◆ Daily, lunch and dinner until midnight. Valet parking is available as well as difficult street parking. 91 Winthrop St (between John F. Kennedy and Eliot Sts). 864.1933; fax 864.4625; www.upstairsonthesquare.com &

36 BOMBAY CLUB

★$$ Decked out in authentic Indian artifacts, this dining room overlooks a small park just off Harvard Square. Try *sheemi kabob* (deep-fried ground lamb patties) or *boti* (barbecued lamb chop). ◆ Indian ◆ Daily. Reservations recommended. 57 John F. Kennedy St (between Eliot and Winthrop Sts). 661.8100; www.bombayclub.com &

Restaurants/Clubs: Red | Hotels: Purple | Shops: Orange | Outdoors/Parks: Green | Sights/Culture: Blue

37 TAMARIND BAY

★★$$ A cozy and well-appointed Indian/Pakistani restaurant with bronze-and-copper décor and subtle spices. It's in the basement, but diners hardly notice. ♦ Indian ♦ Daily, lunch and dinner. 75 Winthrop St (at John F. Kennedy St). 491.4552; www.tamarind-bay.com

38 RED LINE PUB & GRILL

★★$$ Run by the same talented Irish group that helms the nearby **Grafton Street Pub & Grille** and Temple Bar, this downstairs pub boasts more than a dozen beers, decent casual American food, and an interesting mix of people, especially after work. ♦ American ♦ Daily. 59 John F. Kennedy St (between Eliot and Winthrop Sts). 491.9851 &

39 FINALE

★★$$ This dessert shop and bakery—a dieter's tempting fantasy—serves lunch and light dinners and has a full liquor license. Skip takeout and go directly to the plated desserts, especially Just Peachy: peach sorbet between layers of almond shortbread, with fresh raspberries, Chardonnay wine sauce, and sweet pesto. ♦ Daily, lunch and dinner. 30 Dunster St (between Mass Ave and Auburn St). 441.9797; www.finaledesserts.com &. Also in Boston in the 20 Park Plaza office building, 1 Columbus Ave. 423.3184

39 SCHOENHOF'S FOREIGN BOOKS, INC.

Writer John Updike, Harvard economist John Kenneth Galbraith, and chef Julia Child have all shopped here. And soon after arriving in the United States, many of Boston's foreign-born residents and students head to this understated basement shop. The reason: It's the best foreign-language bookstore in the country, with more than 35,000 titles—original works, not translations—representing 200 languages. Founded in 1856 by Carl Schoenhof to serve Boston's German community, this store tries to bring together people and books of all nationalities. The sales staff is fluent in several languages and work together to choose books, with an emphasis on history, philosophy, literature, and literary criticism. The biggest selections are in French, Spanish, German, Italian, and Russian. There's a great department of reference works, tapes, and CDs for language learning, and there are children's books too. The wholesale/retail store runs a mail-order service and is tenacious in tracking down the most esoteric special orders—a French book on termites or a $5,000 German edition on Freud, for example. ♦ M-Sa, 10AM-6PM; Th to 8PM. 76A Mount Auburn St (between Mass Ave and Auburn St). 547.8855; www.schoenhofs.com

40 HARVARD LAMPOON CASTLE

Cambridge's most whimsical building—designed by **Wheelwright and Haven** in 1909—is home to the offices of the *Harvard Lampoon*, an undergraduate humor magazine that inspired the **National Lampoon** (although there's no formal affiliation). "Poonies" have long been known for their pranks, from stealing the Massachusetts State House's Sacred Cod in 1933 to hiring an actress in 1990 to hold a press conference and pretend she was Donald Trump's then-girlfriend. Pick out the eyes, nose, mouth, and hat on the entrance tower. Atop is a statue of an ibis, frequently taken by *Harvard Crimson* staffers. William Randolph Hearst, who once served as the *Lampoon's* business manager, donated the land. ♦ Mount Auburn St (between Plympton and Bow Sts)

Within Harvard Lampoon Castle:

STARR BOOK SHOP

This academic bookstore purveys antiquarian sets and scholarly works in literature, philosophy, classics, history, biography, and general subject areas. They carry current reviewers' copies too. Graduate and undergraduate students frequent the shop. ♦ Daily. 29 Plympton St (at Bow St). 547.6864

41 CAFE PAMPLONA

★$ Patrons linger, drinking espresso and writing, reading, or talking. The tiny café is on the lower level of a snug red house, with an outdoor terrace where people hang past midnight in the summer. In addition to teas and coffees of all kinds, the café serves gazpacho, sandwiches, and specials, plus desserts. ♦ Spanish ♦ M-Sa, 11AM-1AM; Su, 2PM-1AM. No credit cards accepted. 12 Bow St (between Arrow St and Massachusetts Ave). No phone

42 THE INN AT HARVARD

$$$ **Graham Gund**'s 1992 design earned a "Worst New Architecture" award from *Boston Magazine*, but the redbrick boutique hotel fit

---

The first printing of a book in English in the colonies took place in Cambridge in 1640. The *Bay Psalm Book* was printed by the Puritans to replace the disliked English version of the psalms.

The building of bridges—particularly the West Boston Bridge of 1793 and the Craigie Bridge of 1809—turned Cambridge into a more viable city by opening direct routes to Boston.

LOBSTER LOGISTICS

Indulging in your first lobster? Anxious to develop the knack of cracking this tasty crustacean? There's hardly a better place to learn than in Boston, where the critters are often caught and served the same day. Getting the meat out of a lobster takes practice, patience, and a little perseverance. This guide covers the basics, but it's best to take an experienced lobster-cracking friend along for encouragement and coaching. And despite how funny you may look, wear a bib—you're going to get more than a little messy.

1 Twist off the claws.

2 Crack each claw with a nutcracker.

3 Separate the tailpiece from the body by arching the back until it cracks.

4 Bend back the flippers and break them off the tail-piece.

5 Insert a fork where the flippers broke off and push the meat out.

6 Unhinge the back from the body. This contains the tomalley (or liver), which some folks are known to consume.

7 Open the remaining part of the body by cracking it sideways (the meat in this section is particularly good).

8 The small claws are good eating—just suck the meat out as illustrated here.

in as time passed. Drop in and decide for yourself. There are 113 basic rooms plus a Presidential Suite. The four-story atrium—furnished with couches, tables, and shelves of up-to-date books—functions as a living room and salon. It also serves as the hotel's only dining room, with meals and bar service available. Wi-Fi is available for a fee, and a fitness center for guests was added in 2006. ♦ 1201 Massachusetts Ave (at Quincy St). 491.2222, 800/458.5886; fax 491.6520; www.theinnatharvard.com &

43 ZERO ARROW THEATER

A few blocks away, the Zero Arrow Theater is the ART's flexible-space second stage and an incubator for new works. The 300-seat theater, completed in 2004 and bankrolled by philanthropist Greg Carr, features new works, young artists, and theater, dance, and music at affordable prices. The vintage-appearing building is also home to two human-rights organizations, the Carr Foundation and Physicians for Human Rights. ♦ 0 Arrow St (at Massachusetts Ave). 547.8300 &. Close to the Harvard Square T station. Valet parking by Grafton Street Pub & Grill, a block away, and at Charles Hotel Garage, 1 Bennett St.

44 JOHN F. KENNEDY MEMORIAL PARK

Well maintained, this big, grassy park is wonderful for lounging, and many students take advantage of it on nice days. It's behind the John F. Kennedy School of Government and The Charles Hotel (see page 189), with the river just across the street. Look for the fountain inscribed with JFK quotes. ♦ John F. Kennedy St and Memorial Dr &

KENDALL SQUARE

Visitors who arrive at Kendall Square via the MBTA Red Line are in for a treat. Located in the station is a **kinetic musical sculpture** by artist/inventor Paul Matisse (grandson of Henri) consisting of three pieces titled *Pythagoras*, *Kepler*, and *Galileo*. *Pythagoras* has wall handles on either side of the subway tracks that when cranked set large teak hammers into motion, which strike 16 tuned tubular chimes and produce melodious bell-like music. Pull the handle on *Kepler* a number of times and a triple-headed steel hammer strikes an aluminum ring, producing a low F-sharp note. *Galileo*'s mechanism makes rumbling, windlike music. When operated in unison by passersby, the pieces produce a pleasing concert that soothes impatient T riders.

The Kendall stop is the closest T station to the **Massachusetts Institute of Technology (MIT)**, which dominates this section of Cambridge. MIT was founded in 1861 on the Boston side of the river by natural scientist William Barton Rogers. He envisioned a pragmatic

institution fitted to the needs of an increasingly industrialized and mechanized America. The modest technological school, then called Boston Tech, moved to its current site in 1916, comfortable with its industrial surroundings. MIT has never aspired to Harvard's picturesque Olympian aura, but has focused on scientific principles as the basis for advanced research and industrial applications. Appropriately, the school's motto is "*Mens et Manus*" (Mind and Hand). The institute grew rapidly and played a significant research role with the onset of World War II. In hastily assembled laboratories, Harvard and MIT scientists developed the machinery of modern warfare. One of MIT's most significant contributions was the development of radar. In peacetime, the labs have produced instrumentation and guidance devices for NASA and nuclear submarines. The institute has an international identity, and graduates have founded local, national, and multinational high-tech and biotechnology companies. It has schools of Engineering, Sciences, Architecture and Planning, Management, Humanities, Health Sciences and Technology, and Social Science.

For general information on MIT or to join one of the free student-guided campus tours, lasting an hour and offered weekdays, stop by the Information Center (Rogers Bldg, 77 Massachusetts Ave, between Memorial Dr and Vassar St, 253.4795), open Monday through Friday, 9AM to 5PM. Arrange tours in advance by calling 253.1875. You can also fashion your own campus tour, ambling across the 150-acre campus. MIT gives the arts elbow room, too, and has excellent museums as well as some superb modern architecture, like the 2004 **Stata Center**, and public art. Take a chance on getting lost for a bit in the domed neoclassical **Rogers Building** with its factory-like maze of hallways.

The **MIT Museum** (265 Massachusetts Ave near MIT Campus and Central Square) is the city's only museum dedicated to science and technology. It displays holograms, robots, and temporary exhibits. The museum also hosts regular, interactive programs and talks for students and adults. It has everything from an exhibit on Artificial Intelligence to the country's largest display of

South Boston is famed, among other things, for its "L Street Brownies." This group of people "of a certain age" have for years taken a much-publicized swim off Columbus Park's Carson Beach on New Year's Day, plunging into the frigid waters dressed only in bathing suits and caps. They get an annual picture in Boston newspapers for their daring.

Thomas Brattle—the early Harvard College treasurer for whom Brattle Street was named—ensured himself a spirited send-off by bequeathing "a half crown bill to each of the students of Harvard College that shall come to my funeral."

The first published American poet was Anne Bradstreet, who lived at what is now 1348 Massachusetts Avenue, the heart of today's Harvard Square. Her work was printed in England in 1650.

Boston by Sea

A 1½-hour cruise on Boston harbor uses live theater performances, sea chanties, and video to bring the harbor's history to life. You'll hear true stories of pirates, clipper ship races, the USS *Constitution*, immigration, Boston Harbor Islands, Boston Light (the country's oldest continuously manned lighthouse), and the Boston Tea Party. From Long Wharf, May through October. Contact **Boston Harbor Cruises,** 227.4321; www.bostonharborcruises.com.

Arthur Ganson's gestural sculptures to the cutting-edge **Emerging Technologies Gallery**. A small museum store is on site (http://web.mit.edu/museum). Other MIT galleries include the **Hart Nautical Galleries** in Building 5, where you can see ships' models and plans representing vessels from all over the world (Rogers Bldg, first floor, 253.5942). The **Compton Gallery** in building 10 under MIT's big dome features science, technology, architecture, and history (253.4444; http://web.mit.edu/museum). The **Albert and Vera List Visual Arts Center** (Wiesner Bldg, 20 Ames St, between Amherst and Main Sts, first floor, 253.4680; http://web.mit.edu/lvac) has two galleries that display challenging art and design in diverse media. Science buffs will enjoy a walk through **Strobe Alley** (Rogers Bldg, fourth floor), for a demonstration of high-speed stroboscopic equipment and photographs by the late Harold E. "Doc" Edgerton, class of 1927. Admission is free to all but the MIT Museum. Call for days and hours; many of the galleries close during the summer.

MIT's **East Campus,** on the east side of Massachusetts Avenue, has an impersonal, businesslike look, thanks in part to the new office and research buildings that have sprouted around Kendall Square since the 1980s. In the last few years, Main Street at Kendall Square has been spruced up with the arrival of a major hotel and cafés and restaurants. But MIT has, fortunately, preserved a network of big green spaces, where fine outdoor art can be found. In Killian Court behind the Rogers Building is **Henry Moore**'s *Three-Piece Reclining Figure*, erected in 1976. (Another Moore work, *Reclining Figure*, is located off Ames Street between Whitaker College and **I.M. Pei**'s Weisner Building.) Michael Heizer's sculpture *Guennette* stands opposite.

The **Great Dome**, MIT's architectural focal point, looms over Killian Court. From this grassy expanse, the view to the river and Boston beyond is magnificent. At McDermott Court, look for I.M. Pei's **Green Building**, the 1964 Center for Earth Sciences. In front is the giant black-steel sculpture *La Grande Voile* (*The Big Sail*), designed by **Alexander Calder**. Nearby is a 1975 black-steel sculpture by **Louise Nevelson** called *Transparent Horizon*. At the end of Main Street near the Longfellow Bridge is a small outdoor plaza adorned with a controversial creation called *Galaxy* by MIT artists. The focal point is a meteorite-like stainless-steel globe encrusted with strange topographic textures and patterns, clouds of steam billowing from below. The globe is ringed by 12 smaller ones that cast unusual illuminations at night. **Picasso**'s *Figure Découpée*, 1963, stands in front of the Hermann Building at the far east end of campus. A five-mile system of underground passages, the "infinite corridor," connects East Campus buildings.

The most striking, whimsical buildings at MIT—and maybe in all of Cambridge and Boston—make up the **Stata Center** on the northeast edge of the campus. Designed by architect **Frank Gehry** and dedicated in 2004, the humorous, tilting buildings on Vassar Street (between Massachusetts Ave and Main St, 258.7971) are something never before seen on campus. Multi-colored and built with walls angling as much as 30 degrees, the towers and connecting buildings house classroom, offices, and research facilities on 2.8 acres. There's also a pub and fitness center tucked in. Officially named the Stata Center for Computer, Information and Intelligence Sciences, the two C-shaped, nine-story towers are home to the Computer Science and Artificial Intelligence Laboratory, the Laboratory for Information and Decision Systems, and the Department of Linguistics and Philosophy. Hundreds of MIT events—music, dance, theater, author readings—are open to the public, and most are free. For details, check http://web.mit.edu/arts.

This area has several bookstores suited to the university. The **MIT Press Bookstore** (292 Main St, between Hayward and Dock Sts, 253.5249) sells books and journals on engineering, computer science, architecture, philosophy, linguistics, economics, and more. The **MIT Coop** (3 Cambridge Center, Main St, between Kendall Sq and Fulkerson St, 499.3200) is the scion of the Harvard Coop. **Quantum Books** (4 Cambridge Center, Broadway, between Kendall Sq and Fulkerson St, 494.5042) is a technical bookstore with one of the largest collections of computer books and periodicals in the world.

Just across the Longfellow Bridge from Boston, on the former site (1895 to 1993) of Engine Company Seven of the Cambridge Fire Department, is the **Kendall Hotel** ($$; 315 Main St, 577.1300, 866/566.1300, fax 577.1377; www.kendallhotel.com), opened in 2003. The couple who run it and operate the **Mary Prentiss bed-and-breakfast** (6 Prentiss St, between Harvard and Porter squares) turned the historic firehouse into a warm, 65-room boutique hotel with modern amenities, antiques, a lobby fireplace, and extra space. The MIT location is convenient, the price is right, and the décor is

Restaurants/Clubs: Red | Hotels: Purple | Shops: Orange | Outdoors/Parks: Green | Sights/Culture: Blue

tasteful and nonchain. In the Kendall is the casual **Black Sheep Café**, with 10 tables and a small bar. Off the hotel's front lobby, the café has a street view through what were once giant doors that opened for horse-drawn fire engines. Antique fire hats are part of the low-key décor.

Also in the neighborhood is a branch of **Legal Sea Foods** (★★★$$$; 5 Cambridge Center, Main St, between Kendall Sq and Fulkerson St, 864.3400). All kinds of fresh fish are served just about any way you can imagine in this crowded and noisy restaurant. For a variety of other dining options, visit the **One Kendall Square** development (Hampshire St and Broadway), a handsomely renovated factory complex. It's home to **The Blue Room** (★★★★$$$$; 494.9034), a jazzy modernist boîte featuring good cooking; **Tommy Doyle's Pub & Restaurant** (★★$; 225.0888; www.tommydoyles.com); and the **Cambridge Brewing Company** ($$; 494.1994), a comfortable pub/restaurant that serves up the company's own beers and ales. Adjacent to the parking garage of One Kendall Square is the **Kendall Square Cinema** (494.9800), an art movie house with six high-tech theaters showing first-run films.

Nearby is **The Hotel at MIT** ($$$; 20 Sidney St, at Massachusetts Ave, 577.0200, 800/222.8733; www.hotelatmit.com). Part of the 27-acre mixed-use University Park at MIT complex, it has 183 rooms and 27 suites with two-line telephones, dataports, Wi-Fi, and workstations. There's also an exercise facility and **Sidney's Grill**, serving American regional cuisine. Other pluses include valet and self-service parking and 24-hour room service. The **Cambridge Center Marriott** ($$$; Two Cambridge Center, Broadway in between Kendall Sq and Fulkerson St). 494.6600, 800/228.9290; fax 494.0036; marriott.com/property/propertypage/BOSCB) is another lodging option. It offers 431 rooms and 12 suites; a pool; a 24-hour health club; an Italian restaurant, **Maria's Cambridge Square**; and a sports bar, on 26 floors. No pets.

MIT's **West Campus**, west of Massachusetts Avenue, has a more residential and relaxed atmosphere. Look for **Kresge Auditorium** (48 Massachusetts Ave, between Amherst and Vassar Sts), designed in 1955 by **Eero Saarinen**, unmistakable with its curving roof, one eighth of a sphere resting on three abutments and floating free of the auditorium structure beneath. Also designed by Saarinen, the exquisite interfaith **MIT Chapel** is illuminated by a skylight that focuses light on the altar and is surrounded by a small moat that casts reflections upward on the interior walls. **Harry Bertoia** designed the sculpture behind the altar. Sought after as a site for weddings, the cylindrical structure is topped

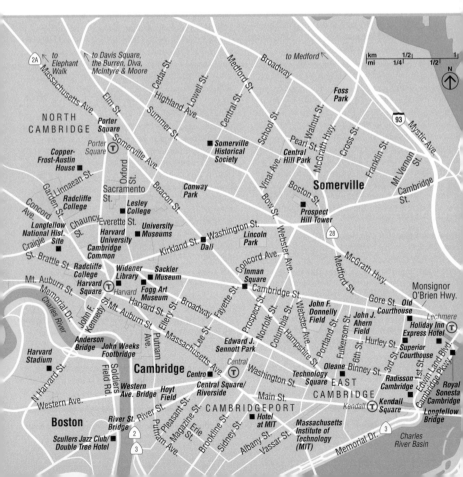

by **Theodore Roszak**'s aluminum bell tower and bell. Free Thursday noon concerts take place in the chapel during the school year. Nearby is **Baker House** (362 Memorial Dr, between Danforth and Endicott Sts), a 1949 **Alvar Aalto**–designed dormitory whose serpentine form cleverly maximizes views of the Charles, and the **Miracle of Science Bar & Grill** (★$$; 321 Massachusetts Ave, at State St, 828.2866), a fun eatery and drinkery modeled (loosely) on a chem lab.

A few doors toward MIT from the Miracle of Science is **Royal Bengal India** (★★$; 313 Massachusetts Ave, 491.1988 &). Bengal and Northern Indian dishes with great sauces and subtle seasonings abound under the blue awning in this deceptively plain storefront. There are vegetarian dishes too.

One of the better **thrift stores** in the Boston area is across from the Miracle of Science, namely the **Salvation Army store** (328 Massachusetts Ave, 354.9159), loaded with donated treasures and often crowded with students and others looking for bargains.

Up a block toward Central Square, the **Asgard** (★$; 350 Massachusetts Ave, at Sidney St, 577.9100, 888/955.6248 &) is a polished, Irish-themed restaurant and bar of the type you might find in a suburb. Hearty food and drink abound here for a primarily postcollege crowd and workers from nearby high-tech firms.

EAST CAMBRIDGE

This multicultural community—predominantly Italian and Brazilian/Portuguese—was once a prosperous Yankee enclave. In the 19th century, factories turning out glass, furniture, soap, boxes, woven hose, and other goods flourished here along the Charles, and "Quality Row," a line of fine town houses (now 83-95 Third St), sprang up. Then, slowly, the riverside industries declined. After suffering through decades as a backwater, East Cambridge underwent major urban renewal and development. Look for the magnificently restored **Bulfinch Superior Courthouse Building,** original site of the Middlesex County court system, now occupied by the **Cambridge Multicultural Arts Center** (41 Second St, at Otis St, 577.1400), which has two spacious galleries and a theater.

A 1990 addition to the neighborhood is the **Cambridge-Side Galleria** on First Street, where you'll find **Filene's** (621.3800), **Sears** (252.3500), and **Best Buy** (225.2004) along with **J. Crew, Ann Taylor, Banana Republic,** and other shops; restaurants like the chain **Cheesecake Factory** (252.3810); and services. A shuttle bus runs every 15 minutes Monday through Saturday between One Kendall Square and the Galleria.

Nearby is pleasant **Lechmere Canal Park** with its lagoon and 50-foot geyser. It's the pickup point for picturesque cruises on the Charles River basin with the **Charles Riverboat Company** (621.3001).

Just a block along First Street from CambridgeSide Galleria is **Helmand** (★★★$$; 143 First St, between Bent and Rogers Sts, 492.4646 &), the area's first Afghan restaurant. There's a warm, inviting atmosphere and comfortable surroundings. The food is a subtle variant on Indian or Turkish and the service is attentive. Lamb and chicken dishes are excellent, and vegetarian alternatives are available. Their homemade bread shines.

New in 2003 was the eight-story **Hotel Marlow** (25 Edwin Land Blvd, across from the Royal Sonesta Hotel and next to the CambridgeSide Galleria, 868.8000, 800/825.7140; www.hotelmarlowe.com &). You'll find bellhops in straw hats, an oversize fireplace, a vaguely nautical theme, and 236 tastefully decorated rooms, some overlooking the Charles River and the Museum of Science. The hotel is pet-friendly and there's 24-hour room service and attention to business travelers. Also in the Marlow is the **Bambara** (★★$$), a restaurant with bar that offers regional American dishes with New England ingredients. There's 24-hour room service for hotel guests.

A convenient if not overly charming hotel (near the Museum of Science and the Lechmere T stop) is the **Holiday Inn Express Hotel and Suites** ($$; 250 Monsignor O'Brien Hwy, just west of Sciarappa St, 577.7600, 800/HOLIDAY; fax 354.1313). Each of the 112 rooms and suites has a microwave oven, refrigerator, coffeemaker, minibar, cable TV, free Wi-Fi, and telephone with voice mail. There are smoking and nonsmoking floors, and a restaurant.

Nearby and across the busy street from the Lechmere Green Line T station (to downtown Boston) is the seven-story **Hampton Inn** ($$; 191 Monsignor O'Brien Hwy, next to the **Cambridge Antiques Center,** 661.5600, 800/HAMPTON; www.hiltonhamptoninn.com, click on Cambridge &). The reasonably priced 114 rooms are unadorned, and there's free underground parking. No restaurant.

CENTRAL SQUARE/ RIVERSIDE

Central Square is a sprawling area located straight down Massachusetts Avenue from Harvard Square toward Boston. This section of Cambridge, which has been most resistant to gentrification, is now becoming more attractive, thanks to an influx of city and federal funds. From a visitor's point of view, it's noteworthy for the concentration of international restaurants and interesting clubs.

Close to Harvard Square, and relatively upscale, **Cafe Sushi** (★★$$$; also at 1105 Massachusetts Ave, between Trowbridge and Remington Sts, 492.0434) offers a spectrum of sushi and sashimi, and a wide

The first chocolate manufacturer in the New World was Walter Baker of Dorchester. Baker's Chocolate is still in existence today.

Restaurants/Clubs: Red | **Hotels: Purple** | **Shops: Orange** | **Outdoors/Parks: Green** | **Sights/Culture: Blue**

197

choice of other dishes. **Dolphin Seafood** (★★$$; 1105 Massachusetts Ave, between Trowbridge and Remington Sts, 661.2937) is a friendly little family place serving good and reasonably priced seafood.

In Central Square proper, **The Middle East Restaurant & Nightclub** (★★$$; 472 Massachusetts Ave, at Brookline St, 492.9181, 354.8238; mideastclub.com) books interesting eclectic acts and serves traditional Middle Eastern fare. There's rock nightly and a young crowd at the separate, downstairs club called **Middle East Downstairs**. A restaurant offering casual international dining is **ZuZu** (★★$$; 474 Massachusetts Ave). **Mary Chung** (★★$$; 464 Massachusetts Ave, between Sidney and Brookline Sts, 864.1991) is a modest-looking place with superb Mandarin and Szechuan specialties. Central Square also has lots of noteworthy Indian restaurants, the best of which is **India Pavilion** (★$$; 17 Central Sq, 547.7463).

For some of the best ice cream, stop by **Toscanini's** (899 Main St, between Bishop Richard Allen Dr and Columbia St, 491.5877). For superb regional American cuisine, visit **Salts** (★★$$; 798 Main St, between Windsor St and Massachusetts Ave, 876.8444). For home-style Italian cuisine, try **La Groceria** (★$$; 853 Main St, between Bishop Richard Allen Dr and Columbia St, 876.4162). A little out of the way, but worth the effort for a drink or for dinner, **Green Street Grill** (★★★$$$; 280 Green St, between Pearl and Magazine Sts, 876.1655) serves flamboyant dishes with Caribbean/American influences in a neighborhood setting. Dinner daily.

Evening entertainment in Central Square centers on music of all kinds, with clubs ranging from neighborhood-casual to somewhat chic. Coffeehouses to sample: **Carberry's Bakery & Coffee House** (74-76 Prospect St, between Bishop Richard Allen Dr and Harvard St, 576.3530 ♿), and **Liberty Cafe** (479B Massachusetts Ave, between Main and Douglass Sts, 492.9900). If you're looking to sip a pint in an authentic Irish pub, visit **The Field** (20 Prospect St, between Massachusetts Ave and Bishop Richard Allen Dr, 354.7345) or **Phoenix Landing** (512 Massachusetts Ave, between Brookline and Pearl Sts, 576.6260). The tiniest and rowdiest of the area's Irish pubs is **The Plough and Stars** (912 Massachusetts Ave, at Hancock St, 576.0032; www.ploughandstars.com), which features live Irish, blues, country, and bluegrass music. It serves lunch Monday through Friday and Sunday brunch. You can hear local bands and dance the night away at the slightly seedy but fun **Cantab Lounge** (738 Massachusetts Ave, between Central Sq and Pleasant St, 354.2685; www.cantab-lounge.com ♿), or **T.T. the Bear's Place** (10 Brookline St, between Green St and Massachusetts Ave, 492.2327), a homey rock 'n' roll club that showcases local talent.

INMAN SQUARE

A 15-minute walk east on Cambridge Street from Harvard Square (or the same distance north on Prospect Street from Central Square), Inman Square is a quieter residential district with a surprising array of great restaurants, both ethnic and American. The square is slowly being gentrified, shedding much of its character as a family neighborhood with a variety of ethnic populations. It's definitely worth making a dinnertime journey here.

S&S Restaurant Deli (★$$; 1334 Cambridge St, between Prospect and Hampshire Sts, 354.0777), an Inman Square old-timer, extensively renovated, is popular all day. The nationally known and very popular **East Coast Grill** (★★★$$$$; 1271 Cambridge St, between Prospect and Oakland Sts, 491.6568) will satisfy cravings for barbecue and great grilled fare. For Southern Cajun cooking, try **Magnolia's** (★★$$$; 1193 Cambridge St, between Tremont and Prospect Sts, 576.1971). Come with a ravenous group to family-run **Casa Portugal** (★ $$; 1200 Cambridge St, between Tremont and Prospect Sts, 491.8880) to enjoy heaping helpings of excellent Portuguese cuisine. For a fine contemporary Mediterranean dinner in a fashionable Cambridge-casual setting, try **Oleana** (★★★★$$$$; 134 Hampshire St, between Elm and Norfolk Sts [between Inman Square and MIT], 661.0505; oleanarestaurant.com ♿). There's garden dining in nice weather. Open daily.

For after-dinner entertainment or a great Sunday brunch, go to **Ryles** (212 Hampshire St, at Inman St, 876.9330; www.rylesjazz.com), a casual and comfortable jazz club that books top local and national acts, or the publike **Druid Restaurant** (1357 Cambridge St, between Oak and Springfield Sts, 497.0965) for Irish music. For dessert, visit **Rosie's** (243 Hampshire St, between Cambridge and Dickenson Sts, 491.9488) for "chocolate orgasm" brownies and other shockingly delicious treats. Rosie's is also in Porter Square at 1796 Massachusetts Avenue (902.2029) and at South Station in Boston (439.4684).

At **ImprovBoston** (1253 Cambridge St, 576.1253; www.improvboston.com) you'll find improv comedy in an intimate space. It's often funny. Brilliance doesn't always

There is some dispute over the origin of the name Jamaica Plain. The *Dictionary of Place Names* suggests that the neighborhood's name originated with an Indian tribe called the Jamaco or Jameco (Algonquin for "beaver"). A booklet issued by the City of Boston for the US Bicentennial, however, indicates that the name is related to the Jamaican rum trade, through which many prominent local families made their fortunes. And an apocryphal local legend tells of an Englishwoman whose husband told her he was heading for Jamaica—on her way to track him down, she found him, quite by chance, in the Boston neighborhood that now bears the name.

happen, but you'll laugh anyway. You're close to the young performers, and the cost is reasonable. Take a cab because parking is difficult.

Bukowski Tavern (★$; 1281 Cambridge St, 477.7077 ♿) is in-your-face poetic plain, like the smaller Boston Back Bay **Bukowski** behind the Berklee School of Music (50 Dalton St, 473.9999). The menu offers "beerfly food" such as burgers, roasted garlic goat cheese, and White Trash Cheese Dip. Next door is the charming and casual **Montien Thai** restaurant and lounge (★★$; 1287 Cambridge St, 868.1240; www.montiencambridge.com).

NORTH CAMBRIDGE/ PORTER SQUARE

Cambridge's neighborhoods offer an almost mind-boggling selection of international eateries. Head northward on Massachusetts Avenue toward Porter Square for still more. French bistro **Chez Henri** (★★★$$$$; 1 Shepard St, at Massachusetts Ave, 354.8980; www.chezhenri.com) offers top-quality French food with a Cuban flair. The bouillabaisse is wonderful, but try the venison with chile and cocoa à la Oaxaca. **Forest Café** (★★$$; 1682 Massachusetts Ave, 661.7810; www.theforestcafe.com ♿) is Cambridge casual, with a lively bar on one side and a much-praised Mexican restaurant on the other. **Temple Bar & Grill** (★★$$$; 1688 Massachusetts Ave, 547.5055) has slick décor and young professionals. There's metered parking on the street and too few parking spaces. **Changsho** (★★$$; 1712 Massachusetts Ave, at Martin St, 547.6565) offers a wide array of Chinese dishes. **The Elephant Walk** (★★★★$$$;

THE ELEPHANT WALK

2067 Massachusetts Ave in an otherwise undistinguished stretch north of Porter Square, between Hadley and Russell Sts, 942.6900; www.elephantwalk.com ♿) serves marvelous Cambodian and French cuisine and heavenly desserts on two levels in what was once a baby-carriage factory. Brick walls, beams, high ceilings, and elephant images create the atmosphere. Parking is easy and there's even a celiac (gluten-free) menu available.

A branch is also near Kenmore Square, Boston (900 Beacon St, about 50 feet from the Brookline border, 247.1500). Under the same ownership is the all-Cambodian **Carambola** restaurant (★$; 663 Main St, Waltham, 781/899.2244, www.carambola.com).

This stretch of Massachusetts Avenue also offers interesting shopping, including international clothing boutiques, shops purveying natural foods and products, and antiques. At **Porter Exchange**, an old Sears, Roebuck building (1815 Massachusetts Ave, at Roseland St), there's a collection of Japanese shops, small sushi cafés, and noodle shops. Also at Porter Exchange, with an entrance on Massachusetts Avenue, is **Rustic Kitchen**, an Italian-Mediterranean bistro (354.7766; www.rustickitchen.biz. Also at Faneuil Hall and the Radisson Hotel, Boston). **Joie de Vivre** (1792 Massachusetts Ave, between Lancaster and Arlington Sts, 864.8188) is a delightful shop selling unusual and artful trinkets and gifts. Keep on going until you reach **Kate's Mystery Books** (2211 Massachusetts Ave, between Chester and Day Sts, 491.2660; www.katesmysterybooks.com), an eccentric "Murder-Mystery Central" for all of New England.

Some of the best new local and touring musicians play at the **Lizard Lounge,** downstairs at the Cambridge Common restaurant (1667 Massachusetts Ave, between Harvard and Porter Sqs, 547.0759; www.lizardlounge-club.com). More good live local music almost every night and a lively late-night bar scene can be found at **Toad** (1912 Massachusetts Ave, in Porter Sq, 497.4950).

For elegant digs, try **A Cambridge House B&B** ($$$; 2218 Massachusetts Ave, between Rindge Ave and Haskell St, 491.6300, 800/232.9989; fax 868.2848; www.acambridgehouse.com). Built in 1892 and listed on the National Register of Historic Places, it has 16 rooms (12 with private baths), all of which are handsomely restored and decorated. An elaborate breakfast is included. The family-owned and -operated **Mary Prentiss Inn** ($$$; 6 Prentiss St, between Frost St and Massachusetts Ave, 661.2929; fax 661.5989; www.maryprentissinn.com) is an 1843 Greek Revival-style estate built by a prominent Cambridge housewright. A large, airy, high-ceilinged foyer with Victorian and Federal-era details leads to the parlor lounge with fireplace. Breakfast is served in the dining room or on the sunny garden deck. Twenty rooms are spread over three floors and vary in size, décor, and price. Six additional sleeping-loft duplexes are in an attached wing. All rooms have baths, telephones, cable TV, and air conditioning; a number have four-poster beds.

On the outer edges of Cambridge, near the Arlington town line and located between the Fresh Pond shopping center and the Alewife T station, there's **Jasper White's Summer Shack** (★$$; 149 Alewife Brook Pkwy, Rte 2, 520.9500; www.summershackrestaurant.com), a much-hyped and popular casual, usually crowded, loud restaurant. There's a jammed bar, picnic tables, decent seafood, and pretend beach/clam-shack décor. Also at Boston Back Bay, upstairs from **Kings,** a popular bowling alley and bar (50 Dalton St, 266.2695).

Boston's outer neighborhoods have distinctive personalities. And that makes sense, because most of them developed independently before being absorbed by Boston. Over the years, annexation has increased the city's size even more than landfilling. Boston was an overcrowded seaport in 1850, but by 1900 the metropolis had flung itself across a 10-mile radius and engulfed 31 other cities and towns. Public transportation—horse cars, followed by electric trolleys—made it possible for people to live in "streetcar suburbs" within easy traveling distance to their workplaces. Immigrant families and the expanding middle class began moving beyond Old Boston, rapidly swelling the commuter ranks. As a result these Boston neighborhoods and nearby suburbs are largely residential, with a smattering of important historical, recreational, and cultural attractions.

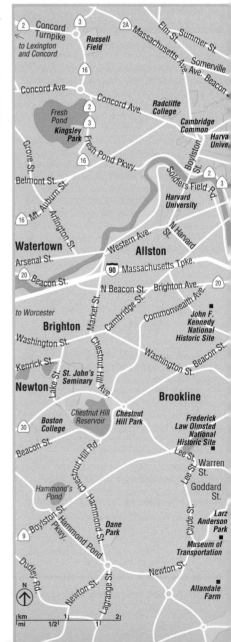

CHARLESTOWN

The North End and this neighborhood stare at one another across the mouth of the **Charles River.** Now a small satellite that's rather tricky to get to—reached by crossing the Charlestown Bridge by car or on foot, departing by boat from Long Wharf in the summer, or riding an MBTA bus—Charlestown was settled one year before Boston, in 1629. Most of the harborside town was burned by the British during the **Battle of Bunker Hill** in 1775, then rapidly rebuilt as a flourishing port where wealthy captains and ship owners lived in grand mansions on the hillsides.

The **Charlestown Navy Yard** brought jobs and prosperity from its opening in 1800 into the early 20th century, as waves of European immigrants moved in while well-to-do families moved out. Charlestown was annexed to Boston in 1874. Maritime activities began shrinking in the following years, and the Great Depression increased the neighborhood's economic woes.

The Navy Yard was shut down by the federal government in 1974, but the neighborhood has been rebounding steadily since, transforming the beautifully sited yard into residential, office, retail, and medical-research space. Many have recognized the charm of Charlestown's narrow colonial streets, which are bordered by neat little residences. A predominantly white, Irish-American enclave since the turn of the century, Charlestown is still a family-oriented neighborhood entrenched in tradition. Many young professionals have moved in, however, and it appears that gentrification will further open up Charlestown.

The enormous Navy Yard is now a National Historic Park under the direction of the National Park Service (242.5601; www.nps.gov/bost), and serves as a physical record of American shipbuilding history. Founded to build warships, the yard evolved over 170 years to meet the Navy's changing requirements. Among its 19th-century structures are the **Ropewalk**—

the last in existence—designed by **Alexander Parris** in 1836 and nearly a quarter mile long, where all rope for the navy was made for 135 years; the ornate **Telephone Exchange Building,** completed in 1852; the **Commandant's House,** an 1809 Georgian mansion; and **Dry Dock Number 1,** tied with a Virginia dry dock as the first in the US and called Constitution Dock because the **USS Constitution** (see below) was the first ship to dock here. Visitors can also board the **USS Cassin Young,** a World War II destroyer of the kind once built here.

The USS *Constitution* itself is one of Charlestown's main tourist attractions. Ordinarily visible from Copp's Hill in the North End, it's the oldest commissioned ship afloat

in the world, still on active duty and maintained by the US Navy. Launched in Boston on 21 October 1797, it served in Thomas Jefferson's campaign against the Barbary pirates and won 42 battles in the War of 1812, never losing once. Nicknamed "Old Ironsides" for its combat-proven wooden hull rather than for any actual iron plating, the ship is permanently moored at **Constitution Wharf** in the Charlestown Navy Yard. It makes one tour of the harbor—called the "turnaround"—every Fourth of July to remain a commissioned warship and to have a different side of the ship face the weathering effects of the ocean.

The **Constitution** received an extensive overhaul and

restoration for its two-hundredth anniversary in 1997. It's open for daily free tours led by Navy personnel dressed in uniforms from the War of 1812 era (call 242.5670 for information). The **Constitution Museum** (Constitution Wharf, 426.1812) screens a film revealing more about the ship and its history. Originally a pump house, the museum also displays original documents and other artifacts from the historic vessel; it is open daily, and there is an admission charge. Before leaving the museum area, visit **Shipyard Park** to the east.

Every American schoolchild learns how the Battle of Bunker Hill was really fought on Breed's Hill, where Solomon Willard's **Bunker Hill Monument** (242.5641), visible from many Boston locations, now points to the sky. The hill rises from the midst of formal Monument Square and its handsomely preserved 1840s town houses. Climb the grassy slope to the monument, part of the **Boston National Historical Park.** The Marquis de Lafayette laid the cornerstone in 1825, visiting the US for the first time since his days as a dashing youthful hero. The monument was finally completed in 1843, and Daniel Webster orated at the dedication. The 220-foot-tall obelisk of Quincy granite rises from the area where, on 17 June 1775, Colonel William Prescott reportedly ordered his citizens' militia not to fire "until you see the whites of their eyes." The redcoats ultimately seized the hill but suffered more than 1,300 casualties, a devastating blow that boosted the colonists' morale. Climb the 295 steps to the monument observatory for fine views; back at the bottom, notice the dioramas portraying the battle. The monument is open daily; there's no admission charge. Boston park rangers offer free talks in the summer. At the Navy Yard Visitor Center is the **"Whites of Their Eyes" exhibit** (55 Constitution Rd, between Warren and Chelsea Sts, 241.7575), a multimedia show that re-creates the Battle of Bunker Hill. It's open daily March through November.

Leave Monument Square and descend serene Monument Avenue to **Main Street.** If you visit the Bunker Hill Monument late in the afternoon and then dawdle, you can plan on enjoying a wonderful dinner at **Olives** (★★★★$$$$; 10 City Sq, at Park and Main Sts, 242.1999; www.toddenglish.com). The bistro-style restaurant is friendly, noisy, and known for such creatively rustic dishes as savory tarts, bouillabaisse, spit-roasted chicken, and butternut-squash raviolini; many of the specialties are cooked in a wood-burning brick oven. Reservations are recommended. Or while away some time at the nearby circa-1780 **Warren Tavern** (Two Pleasant St, at Main St, 241.8142), which offers drinks, fine chowder, and plenty of atmosphere. Named for the Revolutionary War hero General Joseph Warren, who died in the Battle of Bunker Hill, the tavern reputedly was the first edifice rebuilt in Charlestown following the massive destruction of that battle. A few blocks away, the modestly priced **99 Restaurant and Pub** (31 Austin St, between Main St and Rutherford Ave, 242.8999; www.99restaurants.com) offers relaxed lunch, dinner, and drinks daily. There are scores of 99s in New England.

Continue on Main Street up Town Hill to **Harvard Mall**. The young minister John Harvard and his family lived near this site, which is now on the National Register of Historic Places. When Harvard died at 31, he bequeathed half of his fortune and all of his library to the college in Cambridge that adopted his name in thanks. At the mall's edge is **Harvard Square**—not to be confused with the square in Cambridge—and its modest mid-19th century dwellings.

Development of the Charlestown waterfront between Shipyard Park and I-93 is seen in the **Residence Inn Boston Harbor at Tudor Wharf** ($$$; 34-44 Charles River Ave, just off Constitution Rd, 242.9000, fax 242.5554). There's no on-site parking at the eight-floor, tan-brick hotel. But since parking in Charlestown is next to impossible, the hotel's valet parking might be worth the cost if you're burdened with a car. The 168-suite hotel is on the Freedom Trail, on the waterfront, and just down the block from Old Ironsides and the Old Navy Yard. The Bunker Hill Monument, the North End, and the TD Banknorth Garden (on the site of the old Boston Garden) are all within a half mile. Studios, one-bedrooms, and two-bedroom suites, all with kitchens, are available.

SOUTH BOSTON

Expanded by landfill since the 18th century, South Boston is now a peninsula of approximately four square miles, with broad beaches and parks. Founded in 1630 as part of Dorchester, it was largely undeveloped until annexed to Boston in 1804. The first bridge to the main part of the city was built the next year and with it came the real estate speculators. Soon Yankee gentry built handsome wooden houses along **East Broadway** and around Thomas Park on **Telegraph Hill.** The building of bridges to Boston, railways, and the growth of industry at century's end brought great numbers of Irish-Americans to South Boston, where they established a tight-knit neighborhood known as "Southie" today. Lithuanians, Poles, and Italians also settled here. Wealthy merchants moved out as immigrants moved in and Back Bay became the magnet for fashion seekers. They moved too early, of course, since real estate values in South Boston have skyrocketed and development plans are announced on a regular basis. The South Boston waterfront, now with a convention center, hotels, condos, a museum, and offices, is the focus of much of the city's high-dollar growth. It is a shiny and new residential neighborhood filled with outsiders. The view of downtown Boston from the once-battered waterfront is breathtaking.

The 2004 convention center, across the harbor from Logan Airport at 415 Summer Street, cost more than $800 million and gives the impression of a cruise ship on land. Officially called the **Boston Convention & Exhibition Center** and designed by **Rafael Viñolyit**, it was host to about half of Boston's big conventions in 2006 (954.2000; www.bostonconventioncenter.com). It shared that job with the older Hynes Convention Center in the Back Bay and, to a smaller degree, the Bayside Exposition Center in Dorchester.

The **Institute of Contemporary Art (ICA)** moved in 2006 from a converted firehouse in the Back Bay to its bold new steel, glass, and concrete home on the blossoming Fan Pier at 100 Northern Avenue, off Seaport

Boulevard on the South Boston waterfront (478.3100; www.icaboston.org). With the new museum building, the ICA tripled its space in a stunning 65,000-square-foot structure that juts its cantilevered top floor (containing galleries) out to the water and over the harbor walk at the water's edge. The harbor walk is to be a 47-mile public walkway along the water, connecting cultural, commercial, and historic sites. In the future the ICA, designed by architects **Diller Scofidio and Renfro,** should be in the immediate company of close-by parks, another hotel, condos, restaurants, and shops.

Like Charlestown, residential South Boston is primarily a white enclave with a family focus. More than half the neighborhood is of Irish ancestry, and a major local event is the annual **St. Patrick's Day parade** and festivities. As in other areas, the old ways are changing as more young professionals move into what were working-class neighborhoods.

Drive to South Boston for great views of the harbor and islands from Day Boulevard and Castle Island at **Marine Park.** On **Castle Island** (actually no longer an island, since it's linked to the mainland by causeways), visit star-shaped **Fort Independence** (727.5290), which is open afternoons from Memorial Day to Labor Day (free tours are offered). The fort is more than 200 years old (built in 1801), but the site it occupies—strategically at the entrance to Boston Harbor—has been fortified since 1634. Near the fort is a statue of Donald McKay, who designed Boston clipper ships, including the famous *Flying Cloud.* Castle Island, with its wide-open harbor views, is also a great place for a picnic. After your visit, walk along **Pleasure Bay,** designed by **Frederick Law Olmsted.**

From **Dorchester Heights,** patriots commanded a clear view of the redcoats during the Siege of Boston in 1776. Here **George Washington** and his men set up cannons, heroically hauled through the wilderness for three months by Boston bookseller-turned-general **Henry Knox.** The guns were trained on the British—powerful persuasion that convinced them to flee for good. Located in **Thomas Park** (between G and Old Harbor Sts), Dorchester Heights is now a National Historic Site. The park is open daily.

For a hearty meal or a quick pint, stop at **Amrhein's** (★$$; 80 W Broadway, at A St, 268.6189), a popular Irish bar near the Broadway T station. More than a century old and family run, it boasts the oldest beer-pump system in Boston and the oldest hand-carved, mirror-backed wooden bar in the country. People come from all over for great meat-and-potatoes meals, fabulous onion rings, and, of course, beer.

It's hard to believe, but there were no Polish restaurants in Boston for a long time. **Café Polonia** (★★$; 611 Dorchester Ave, at Devine Way, near the Andrew St Red Line T stop, 269.0110; www.cafepolonia.com) changes that. This not-fancy, six-table gem near Our Lady of Czestochowa church offers wholesome, delicious Polish cooking and daily specials at lunch and dinner. A sample plate has the likes of kielbasa, stuffed cabbage, and pierogis. Reservations are recommended.

The classic South Boston tavern seen in the movie *Good Will Hunting* is still a good neighborhood bar. **Woody's L Street Tavern** (★$; 58 E 8th St, 268.4335) has regulars at the bar, football games on TV, and the occasional tourist.

DORCHESTER

If it weren't part of Boston, racially, ethnically, and economically diverse Dorchester would be an important Massachusetts city in its own right. Originally it was even larger and included South Boston and Hyde Park. Dorchester is an area of intimate neighborhoods, like the close-knit **Polish Triangle,** and **Dudley,** home to Hispanic and Cape Verdean families. **Dorchester Avenue,** nicknamed "Dot Ave," is the community's spine, with lots of ethnic and family-owned businesses— Irish pubs and bakeries next to Southeast Asian markets alongside West Indian grocers selling curries and spices.

In 1630 the Puritans landed at Mattapannock, today called **Columbia Point,** and, fearing Indian attacks, established homesteads near a fort atop **Savin Hill.** The area now known as **Upham's Corner** was once called Burying Place Corner because of the cemetery founded there in 1633, the **Dorchester North Burying Ground** (open occasionally; call 635.4505 for information). Nearby is Boston's oldest standing house, the 1648 **Blake House** (735 Columbia Rd, between Dorchester Ave and E Cottage St, 265.7802); it's open from 2 to 4PM on the second and fourth Saturday of each month, except August. Both the burying ground and house are on the National Register of Historic Places. Atop Meeting House Hill is the 1905 **Mather School** (One Parish St, at Winter St), the oldest elementary school in the nation, founded in 1639 as a one-room schoolhouse.

Dorchester was an agricultural community into the 1800s. Gradually, rich Bostonians built country estates and summer residences on its southern hilltops. In the early 1800s commercial villages grew up along the Neponset River and the waterfront. With the electric tram's inauguration in 1857, Dorchester became a suburb of Boston, annexed in 1869. Lovely Victorians are sprinkled throughout this neighborhood, but the best-known architectural style in Dorchester is the distinctive three-family house called the "triple decker," which became the rage in the early 1900s. After World War II, though, the suburban ideal of single-family homes and shopping malls emerged, and Dorchester endured white flight and neglect. It's still not always a safe place to wander at night, but attempts are being made to upgrade its image. One sign of the neighborhood's vitality is the rejuvenation of the 1918 **Strand Theater** (543 Columbia Rd, between Hancock St and Cushing Ave, 282.8000), a former movie palace restored as a venue for the performing arts and community events. Dorchester is also home to *The Boston Globe* newspaper (135 William T. Morrissey Blvd, between Old Colony Terrace and Columbia Rd, 929.2653), which has been printed every day for more than 120 years. Free tours on

---

Restaurants/Clubs: Red | Hotels: Purple | Shops: Orange | Outdoors/Parks: Green | Sights/Culture: Blue

Tuesday and Thursday explain how. Reservations are required.

The **John F. Kennedy Library and Museum** (929.4500; www.jfklibrary.org), a 1979 design of **I.M. Pei & Partners,** couldn't find a home in Cambridge and landed out on Columbia Point—inconvenient for tourists but a dramatic site at the University of Massachusetts-Boston, with glorious unobstructed views of the ocean. The stark, magnificent building is the official repository of JFK's presidential papers, classified and declassified, as well as all of his speeches on film and video and many personal belongings. The library also houses **Robert F. Kennedy**'s senatorial papers. The museum displays exhibitions on JFK and RFK, with tapes and videos. In addition, the library possesses 95 percent of **Ernest Hemingway**'s works. A new wing to be built in 2007 is to safeguard the papers of Massachusetts Senator Edward Kennedy and documents from JFK's relatives and administration members. The library and museum are open daily except Thanksgiving, Christmas, and New Year's Day. There's an admission charge, with discounts for seniors and children under 16; children under 6 are admitted free. Next to the library is the **Massachusetts Archives** (220 William T. Morrissey Blvd, south of Mt Vernon St, 727.2816), and within which is the **Commonwealth Museum,** with exhibits on state history like the original Massachusetts charter. Reserve in advance to view the documents. Closed Sunday and holidays; admission is free.

Dorchester has become a destination for young people seeking relatively affordable housing. New condos and bars and restaurants are appearing, along with places like the casual **Ashmont Grill** (555 Talbot St, at Dorchester Ave, 825.4300). A still-reliable dining spot long enjoyed by old Dorchester is **Phillips Old Colony** restaurant (★★$$ 780 Morrissey Blvd, between Freeport St and Victory Rd, 282.7700). Politicians have functions here and families are drawn to Sunday brunch. Just across Morrissey Boulevard, in the Puritan Plaza

shopping center, is the **Boston Ice Cream Factory** (777a Morrissey Blvd, 436.2189). Run by Boston ice-cream pioneer Steve Cirame, the plain-looking storefront produces luscious frozen flavors like Guinness, Mudslide, and—only on July 4—the unlikely Clam Chowder. Exotic Durian ice cream is an Asian-resident favorite.

JAMAICA PLAIN

Originally part of neighboring Roxbury, Jamaica Plain ("JP" to Bostonians) was once fertile farmland. In the late 1800s it became a summer resort for wealthy Back Bay and Beacon Hill residents, who drove their carriages along the tree-shaded Jamaica Way to season at splendid estates surrounding **Jamaica Pond** ("The Pond"). On the other side of town, thousands of factory workers labored in JP's 17 breweries, all of which eventually closed. (**Boston Beer Company,** maker of Samuel Adams Lager Beer, took up the torch of tradition in 1984.) In the 1830s railroads began bringing well-to-do commuters who built Greek Revival, Italianate, and mansard-roofed residences; in the 1870s streetcars brought the growing middle class. Today JP is one of Boston's most integrated neighborhoods, its three square miles filled mostly with families.

Centre Street developed early as JP's main artery and retains its small-town character. Along its bumpy, narrow length are good, cheap ethnic restaurants, bodegas, Irish pubs, mom-and-pop stores, and a number of upscale establishments. A popular Centre Street spot is the spacious, spare **Today's Bread** (★★$$; 701 Centre St, between Thomas and Burroughs Sts, 522.6458), with its big windows on the street and wonderful croissants, muffins, desserts, quiches, salads, and sandwiches.

One of Boston's best Irish bars and a local institution is **Doyle's Cafe** (★$$; 3484 Washington St, between

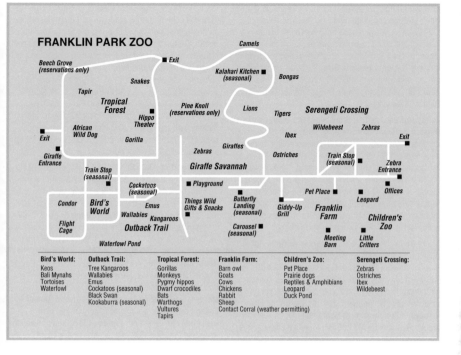

FRANKLIN PARK ZOO

Bird's World:	Outback Trail:	Tropical Forest:	Franklin Farm:	Children's Zoo:	Serengeti Crossing:
Keos	Tree Kangaroos	Gorillas	Barn owl	Pet Place	Zebras
Bali Mynahs	Wallabies	Monkeys	Goats	Prairie dogs	Ostriches
Tortoises	Emus	Pygmy hippos	Cows	Reptiles & Amphibians	Ibex
Waterfowl	Cockatoos (seasonal)	Dwarf crocodiles	Chickens	Leopard	Wildebeest
	Black Swan	Bats	Rabbit	Duck Pond	
	Kookaburra (seasonal)	Warthogs	Sheep		
		Vultures	Contact Corral (weather permitting)		
		Tapirs			

Williams and Gartland Sts, 524.2345), known for its clock logo, visiting politicians, high tin ceiling, and long bar. In a vintage setting full of memorabilia, try fine Irish coffee and Bloody Marys, abundant brunches, delicious basic food, and a variety of beers on tap.

For a somewhat younger crowd, there's the **Midway Café** (★$; 3496 Washington St, 524.9038; www.midwaycafe.com). Forget food; there's a big beer selection and good, loud live music many nights, and Thursday women's nights. Small cover charge on band nights. It's open daily from noon to 2AM.

Devoted fans have made **Ten Tables** (★★$$; 597 Centre St, 524.8810; www.tentables.net) a success. Small and friendly, the 24-seat restaurant has a French-influenced menu that changes often. Dinner daily.

Some of the loveliest sections of Frederick Law Olmsted's **Emerald Necklace** are in or border Jamaica Plain. Created in 1895, the **Arnold Arboretum** of Harvard University (125 Arborway, between Morton and Centre Sts, 524.1718) is the country's oldest arboretum and has more than 15,000 species of woody plants, trees, shrubs, and vines from throughout the world. Rare specimens abound. Along the Chinese Path are some rarer, older Asian specimens—among them the Dove Tree from China, a magical sight in spring when its creamy white bracts flutter like wings. Azaleas, magnolias, and fruit trees also bloom in profusion. Olmsted interlaced the park's 265 acres with walks and drives.

The arboretum is open daily; guided walking tours can be arranged for a fee.

Farther west, on poverty-plagued Blue Hill Avenue, is the 72-acre **Franklin Park Zoo** (1 Franklin Park Rd, at Blue Hill Ave, 541.5566; www.zoonewengland.com). Its prime attraction is the domed Tropical Forest, the largest in North America, with cliffs and caves, waterfalls, footbridges, and lush African vegetation. The three-acre environmental exhibit is home to gorillas, leopards, forest buffalo, bongo antelopes, crocodiles, scorpions, and exotic birds. There are 75 species and 250 specimens in all, with no cages and hidden barriers between animals and onlookers. There's also a Children's Zoo with a petting barn, where kids learn about New England farm animals. The zoo is open daily; there's an admission charge (children two and under free).

BROOKLINE

Actually, Brookline isn't part of Boston. When the cramped city began annexing towns to solve its land crunch, Brookline refused to be swallowed. It remains a suburban town with a somewhat high cost of living, fine schools, and an increasingly diverse population. **Coolidge Corner,** where Harvard and Beacon Streets meet, is a mini-Harvard Square with old-fashioned and new-fashioned establishments. The **Coolidge Corner Theatre** (290 Harvard St, 734.2500; www.coolidge.org)

Restaurants/Clubs: Red | Hotels: Purple | Shops: Orange | Outdoors/Parks: Green | Sights/Culture: Blue

was saved from development by movie lovers, and offers choice vintage and contemporary films in a restored, 1920s setting. A few blocks from the theater is the house where John F. Kennedy was born in 1917. The Kennedys lived here until 1921. Now called the **John F. Kennedy National Historic Site** (83 Beals St, between Harvard and Stedman Sts, 566.7937), it's open daily. There's an admission charge (except for seniors and children under 12).

An undiscovered gem in Brookline is the **Frederick Law Olmsted National Historic Site** (99 Warren St, between Lee and Walnut Sts, 566.1689), the rambling home and office named "Fairsted" by its owner, who was America's first landscape architect and founder of the profession in this country. The site is now open to the public Friday through Sunday, and by appointment on other days. On display here are valuable plans, photographs, and other documentation of the firm's work. The archives are open by appointment. There's no admission charge.

Also in Brookline is the **Larz Anderson Antique Auto Museum** (in an 1888 carriage house, in Larz Anderson Park, 15 Newton St, east of Goddard Ave, 522.6547). The oldest privately owned exotic antique car collection in America, it explores the auto's cultural impact on American society. Vintage car shows are on the lawn Sundays, mid-May through September. Open Tuesday through Sunday, 10 AM to 5PM; there's a small admission charge.

Stop for lunch at one of the town's excellent delis, including the **B & D Deli** (*$; 1653 Beacon St, between University and Winthrop Rds, 232.3727) and kosher **Rubin's** (★★$$; 500 Harvard St, at Kenwood St, 731.8787) on the Allston border. In the Brookline Village neighborhood, Tuscan cuisine rules at **La Morra**. (★★$$$ 48 Boylston St, between Harvard St and Walnut Path, 739.0007; www.lamorra.com &).

Parking in Brookline is limited to two hours during the day and is notoriously impossible overnight, when all visitors' cars on the street between 2AM and 6AM are subject to ticketing.

ALLSTON-BRIGHTON

Polyglot Allston-Brighton is Boston's most integrated district, where Irish, Italians, Greeks, and Russians are joined by growing numbers of Asians, African-Americans, Brazilians, and Hispanics. Most Bostonians associate this neighborhood with students from local universities, large numbers of whom live here. An agricultural community founded in 1635, the neighborhood later had huge stockyards, slaughterhouses, and meat-packing operations, then became industrialized. Since World War II there has been dramatic change led by the construction of the Massachusetts Turnpike. This further split Allston from Brighton, already divided by railroad tracks. Allston-Brighton has developed in a haphazard way that makes it confusing to navigate, but it has many pleasant streets with nice old homes, apartment buildings, and a cozy feel—along with ethnic restaurants and markets, pubs, interesting shops, and antiques stores.

More change is coming, as **Harvard University** expands from Cambridge across the Charles River into Allston.

The university is already established there, with the business school, dorms, stadium, and other operations on the Boston side of the Charles; the School of Public Health, Graduate School of Education, new science and research facilities, new student housing, and more are scheduled for what has been a large urban industrial/residential area. Harvard promises a green campus. A popular hangout is **Harper's Ferry** (156 Brighton Ave, between Harvard and Park Vale Aves, 254.9743), an established blues club and bar. The **Sunset Grill and Tap** (130 Brighton Ave, between Linden St and Harvard Ave, 254.1331) is known for its international selection of beers.

Across the street from Sunset Grill is the excellent **Le's** (formerly **Pho Pasteur**) Vietnamese restaurant (★★$; 134 Brighton Ave, 783.2340 &). There's wine and beer with your meal, if you choose. Also in Boston at, 123 Stuart St (742.2436), 682 Washington St (482.7467), and Harvard Square, Cambridge, in The Garage mall at 36 Dunster St at Mount Auburn St (864.4100). Up a few doors is the offbeat, student-casual **Herrell's Renaissance Café** (★★$; 155 Brighton Ave, at Harvard St, 782.9599), with some of the best ice cream in the Boston area. Eateries, taverns, shops, and college students line bustling Harvard Street toward Brookline. Parking is awful and traffic at rush hour and on weekends can be chaotic. **Tonic** (1315 Commonwealth Ave, Brighton, 566.6699) is an industrial-décor bar/restaurant popular with a 20-something crowd, with good bar food, mingling, and sports on the TVs.

And for quality Mexican cuisine, there's the reasonably priced **Zocalo Mexican** at 1414 Commonwealth Avenue (between Kelton and Alston Sts). Chiles rellenos and other specialties from Oaxaca and Veracruz (like a chocolate bread pudding) make it worthwhile. The Brighton Zocalo is an outgrowth of Zocalos in suburban Arlington (203a Broadway, 781/643.2299) and the mostly takeout, eight-seat Financial District **Andale** (125 Summer St; www.andaleboston.com).

There's also a relatively undiscovered—and romantic—gem in Brighton. But **Tasca** restaurant (★★★$$; 1612 Commonwealth Ave, at Washington St, 730.8002; www.tascarestaurant.com; & in upper section) is away from the bars and shops most people see, far along Commonwealth Avenue toward Boston College. A trip by car or Green Line T is worth it, though. Tasca is romantic. Quiet Spanish music (live classical guitar Thursdays) and good wines, delicious tapas dishes, and entrées like paella con mariscos—shrimp, scallops, mussels, and calamari with saffron rice cooked in lobster stock with red peppers and peas—make Tasca a treasure. Dinner is served daily, and there's free valet parking.

Public-TV powerhouse **WGBH** (125 Western Ave, between N Harvard St and Soldiers Field Rd; www.wgbh.org) is in the neighborhood close to Cambridge that will become part of Harvard University's Allston campus. In addition to broadcasting Boston's listener-supported Channel 2, Channel 44, and WGBH Radio, the station produces about one-third of the Public Broadcasting System's prime-time lineup. Programs originating here, such as *Nova* and *Masterpiece Theater*, are seen around the world. A Harvard research center is to be built where WGBH now stands and the more than 850 employees who work near the old, ivy-covered Harvard stadium are to move to a new seven-story headquarters, with new digital studios and a 200-seat theater, in nearby Brighton at Market and Guest Streets, sometime in 2007.

SOMERVILLE

Once primarily a working-class suburb, Somerville has become an increasingly popular place to live for students and people crowded (or priced) out of Cambridge. In keeping with this trend, the town has developed a growing restaurant/club scene. Try the wonderful **Dali Restaurant and Tapas Bar** (★★★$$$$; 415 Washington St, at Beacon St, 661.3254), an authentic and lively Spanish restaurant with irresistible tapas—great for satisfying multiple urges or for groups that are into sharing. Diners line up for the 5:30 opening. (Dali's sister tapas restaurant, **Tapéo**, is in Boston at 266 Newbury St, between Gloucester and Fairfield Sts, 267.4699.) **Redbones** (★★★$$; 55 Chester St, between Elm and Herbert Sts, 628.2200) stands out for its authentic Southern barbecue. And the intimate **Antonia's Italian Bistro** (★★★$$$; 37 Davis Square) looks out onto a well-used sculpture park across from the Somerville Theater. The Davis Square T station (Red Line subway) is next to the theater. The best home-style Mexican restaurant for miles around doesn't serve Tex-Mex. Close to Tufts University, there's sophisticated, real Mexican cuisine at the understated **Tu Y Yo**, (★★★$$; 858 Broadway at Powderhouse Square, 623.5411; www.tuyyomexicanfonda.com):

which serves Dinner daily. Try the *pollo yunkaax*, boneless chicken breast stuffed with *cuitlacoche* and spinach sauce. Catch some rock or blues in Davis Square at **Johnny D's Uptown** (17 Holland St, between Davis Sq and Winter St, 776.2004) or stop in at **The Burren** restaurant and pub (247 Elm St, 776.8696) for Irish music and a pint. Comic **Jimmy Tingle's Off Broadway Theater** (255 Elm St, 591.1616; www.jimmytingle.com) is next to The Burren. Or cross Elm Street to **Diva**, the lively and casual Indian bistro (246 Elm St, 629.4966). And remember **McIntyre & Moore Booksellers** (255 Elm St, 629.4840; www.mcintyre&moore.com), a source for scholarly and offbeat used books. You can browse daily until 11PM.

Somerville's **Union Square,** closer to I-93 and only blocks from Cambridge's Inman Square, has blossomed as an alternative dining and entertainment area. The cozy **TirNaNog** (366A Somerville Ave, 628.4300; www.thenog.com &) is one of the area's best Irish pubs for live music and friendly carousing. Look for the little place with a green front and a round Guinness sign. Street parking.

The Independent (★★★$$$; 75 Union Sq, 440.6021; www.theindependentbar.com &) is the most upscale restaurant in Union Square. Billed as an Irish pub and restaurant, it serves new American cuisine far above normal pub fare—dishes like saffron-scented tuna and roasted duck with candied ginger and kumquats. There's also a full menu in the cozy brick-walled pub, with good live music there many nights. Brunch is served on Sundays.

Closer to the Cambridge line and in a more casual food universe is **RF O'Sullivan's Pub** (★$; 282 Beacon St, between Porter Sq and Washington St). You will find beer signs, casual dress, a U-shaped bar, a neighborhood feel, and some 30 kinds of juicy burgers. They're juicy because the cooks don't squeeze them on the grill. And you can actually get a "rare" cheeseburger.

Restaurants/Clubs: Red | **Hotels: Purple** | Shops: Orange | **Outdoors/Parks: Green** | Sights/Culture: Blue

B oston is a wonderful place to explore, and it's easy to leave town for some stimulating day or weekend trips. In just an hour or two, public transportation or a car can take you to the rocky beaches of **Cape Ann** or the dunes of **Cape Cod;** it's just a bit farther to the green hills of the **Berkshires;** the beckoning mountains, lakes, and fall colors of **New Hampshire** and **Vermont;** or **Maine**'s coastal villages and idyllic islands. And if Boston begins to seem too large an urban center, in only an hour you can escape to the small-city pleasures of **Providence,** Rhode Island. Just a bit farther south is **Newport,**

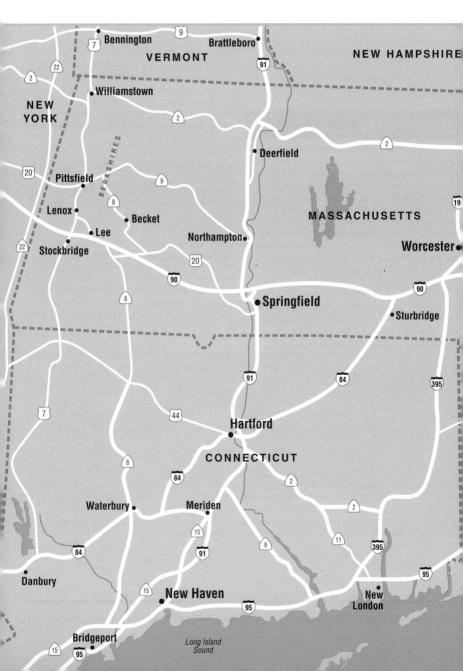

Rhode Island, site of the elaborate "summer cottages" of the Vanderbilts and Astors and still a popular yachting center.

A great source for guidebooks on travel throughout New England is **The Globe Corner Bookstore** (90 Mt. Auburn St, Cambridge, 497.6277). You can also get a wealth of free information (and discount coupons) on what to see and do in Massachusetts by calling or writing the **Massachusetts Office of Travel and Tourism** (10 Park Plaza, Suite 4510, Boston, MA 02116; M-F 800/227.MASS or 617/727.3201, daily 800/447.6277; www.massvacation.com).

The following are destination ideas rather than itineraries. Arm yourself with information on hours and prices before you go—or just head out with a good map or two

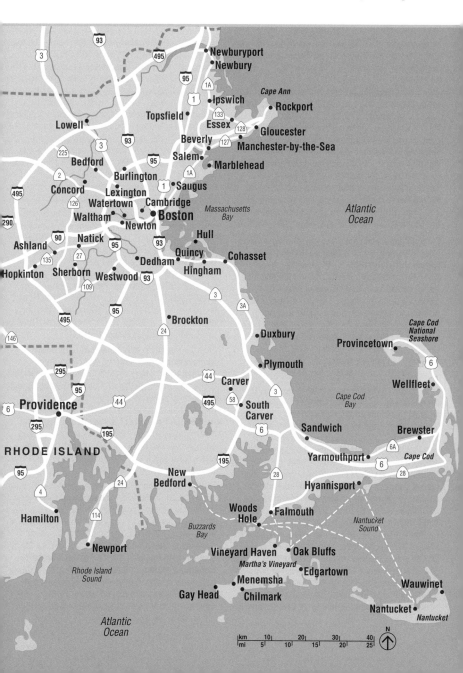

and a spirit of exploration. And keep in mind that the off-season can have its charms as well. Cape Cod and the islands in winter, for example, have their own compelling moods.

THE NORTH SHORE

Head north of Boston for the best **clams** in the world. While on the quest, there's plenty to see. The infamous **Saugus Strip** along Highway 1, for instance, is an eyesore to some and beloved by others for its garish roadside signs and attendant establishments, vintage kitsch inspired by America's love affair with the auto. This stretch of Highway 1 is home base for several of the biggest, gaudiest restaurants. A giant cactus sign and herd of life-size cattle heralds the **Hilltop Steak House,** affectionately called "The Hilltop" (★$$$; Hwy 1, southbound, 781/233.7700; www.hilltopsteakhouse.com), home of slabs of red meat, potatoes, and overeating. A Polynesian theme reigns at **Kowloon** ($$$; Hwy 1, northbound, 781/233.9719), located across from The Hilltop. For Chinese food in a Disney-like ambience, there's gargantuan **Weylu's** ($$$; Hwy 1, northbound, 781/233.1632). As you ride along, keep an eye out for a miniature golf course with a towering *Tyrannosaurus rex;* a ship-shaped restaurant; the **Prince Restaurant** ($$; Hwy 1 and Lynn Fells Pkwy, 781/233.9950), which is a pizza place shaped like the Leaning Tower of Pisa; and other quirky sights.

For a different historical slant, take the Main Street exit off Highway 1 to the **Saugus Iron Works National Historic Site** (244 Central St, 781/233.0050), a reconstruction of the first integrated ironworks in North America (created in 1646). The site includes a furnace, a forge, seven water-powered wheels, and a rolling and slitting mill. It's open daily; free admission. A well-kept Saugus secret is the **Breakheart Reservation** (177 Forest St, 781/233.0834), a park with 600 acres of oak-, hemlock-, and pine-covered hills, two freshwater lakes, 10 miles of trails, and lots of birds.

Take Route 1A north from Boston to Route 129 to **Marblehead,** a picture-postcard New England seaside town with early New World flavor and historical attractions, splendid views of the ocean, plus boutiques and good seafood restaurants. It's a perfect place for a leisurely day of walking and poking around. The Old Town predates the American Revolution and boasts Federal-style sea captains' homes and neat cottages. For more information, contact the **Marblehead Chamber of Commerce** (62 Pleasant St, 781/631.2868). **Salem,** "The Witch City," is a short drive west from Marblehead on Route 114 to Route 1A. The notorious witchcraft trials of 1692, one of the Massachusetts Bay Colony's most troubled chapters, caused 19 people to be hanged before the hysterical Puritan populace regained its reason. Pick up self-guided walking tour maps (and any other tourist information you may need) from the **Salem Chamber of Commerce** (32 Derby St, 978/744.0004).

Don't miss the **Salem Maritime National Historic Site** (174 Derby St, 978/740.1660), where American maritime history is enshrined in the Custom House, Derby House/Wharf, Bonded Warehouse, West India Goods Store, and lighthouse. The site is open daily except Thanksgiving, Christmas, and New Year's Day. There's no charge for admission, but they do charge a nominal fee for guided tours. Also visit **The House of the Seven Gables** (54 Turner St, 978/744.0991), the inspiration for Nathaniel Hawthorne's novel. It's open daily; there's an admission charge. The **Peabody Essex Museum** (East India Sq, Liberty and Essex Sts, 978.745.9500; www.pem.org) is also noteworthy for its period houses and collections covering three centuries of art and culture from around the world, maritime history and art, ethnology, natural history, architecture, and Asian trade. The Peabody Essex completed a major renovation and expansion in 2003. The Peabody is the oldest continuously operated museum in the US. It's open daily 10AM to 5PM; closed Thanksgiving, Christmas, and New Year's Day. There's an admission fee. If you don't want to direct your own steps, take the **Salem Trolley Tour,** run by Hawthorne Tours (978/744.5469); it departs from the Visitor Center.

Continue north on Route 1A to **Beverly** for an afternoon of vaudeville-esque entertainment. *Marco the Magi's Production of Le Grand David and His Own Spectacular Magic Company* plays at the 750-seat **Cabot Street Theatre** (286 Cabot St, 978/927.3677) on Sunday and at the more intimate 450-seat **Larcom Theatre** (13 Wallis St, 978/922.6313) for Saturday shows. Or catch a Broadway musical (often with Broadway stars) or a big-name concert at the **North Shore Music Theatre** (162 Dunham Rd, 978/922.8500).

En route northeast from Beverly to Gloucester is **Manchester-by-the-Sea,** the first North Shore summer resort, which catered to "Proper Bostonians" in the 1840s. The pretty-as-a-picture **Singing Beach** is a favorite of Boston day-trippers. To avoid the parking hassle, rise early and take a morning beach train on the **Rockport Line Commuter Rail** from North Station (978/722.3200). When you've had enough sunning, swimming, and clambering over rocks, it's a short, pleasant walk into town for a bite to eat before the train ride back.

To drive **Cape Ann**'s rugged shore, continue northeast on Route 127 to **Gloucester.** The largest town on the North Shore, Gloucester was settled as a fishing colony in 1623 and is still an important fishing port. The movie *Perfect Storm,* filmed in Gloucester, was based on bitterly true events. On its seafront promenade is the memorable **Gloucester Fisherman** statue, dedicated to "they that go down to the sea in ships." Unveiled in 1923 as part of Gloucester's tercentennial observances, the statue depicts a man in oilskins at a ship's wheel, eyes on the horizon. The local fishing fleet is blessed annually, with attendant colorful festivities in late June. **Whale-watching excursions** leave from here.

Visit the **Cape Ann Historical Association** (27 Pleasant St, 978/283.0455) to see the stunning collection of 19th-century American painter Fitz Hugh Lane's luminous views of Gloucester Harbor and islands. The museum is open Thursday through Saturday; there's an admission charge. Across town is **Rocky Neck,** the oldest artists' colony in the US. Perched on rocks overlooking the harbor is "Beauport," the **Sleeper-McCann House** (75 Eastern Point Blvd, 978/283.0800). Beauport was built in the early 1900s by architect/interior designer Henry Davis Sleeper, who greatly influenced contemporary tastes and style setters, including Isabella Stewart Gardner. The second owner of the mansion, Charles McCann, lived there with his wife, Helena Woolworth, of the five-and-dime empire. Within are 18th- and 19th-century decorative arts and furnishings. It's open Monday through Friday from 15 May to 15 September; daily 15 September to 15 October. There's an admission charge.

Then move on to the **Hammond Castle Museum** (80 Hesperus Ave, 978/283.2080, 800/283.1643). The medieval-style castle was the humble home of inventor Dr. John Hays Hammond Jr., whose brainstorms included shaving cream, the car starter, electrified toy trains, the forerunner of stereophonic sound, and the precursor to remote control—more than 437 patented inventions in all. Hammond's resplendent digs contain medieval furnishings, paintings, and sculpture. Monthly **organ concerts** are played on the 8,600-pipe organ, the largest in a private American home. Call in advance for a schedule of tours; there is an admission charge.

For dinner, fresh lobster is the way to go. Two Gloucester restaurants that are especially good are **Alchemy Cafe & Bistro** (★★$$; 3 Duncan St, 978/281.3997) and **White Rainbow** (★★$$$; 65 Main St, 978/281.0017). Afterward, spend an illuminating evening at the **Gloucester Stage Company** (267 E Main St, 978/281.4099), housed in a rehabbed fish factory. The plays of patron/resident playwright Israel Horovitz often deal with the local way of life.

A short drive up Cape Ann from Gloucester is tiny **Rockport,** a fishing community–turned-artists'-colony that can be happily meandered through in a day. (It's a dry town, by the way.) Parking can be difficult in the center of town unless you arrive as early as the birds, so take the commuter train from North Station (722.3200) in Boston if you can—it's a very pretty ride. Rockport's light is particularly beautiful at day's end and in early spring and late fall. The **Toad Hall Book Store** (51 Main St, 978/546.7323) is wonderful for old-time friendliness and services and has a large selection of books on local geography, history, and lore. The more touristy restaurants and shops are densely clustered on **Bearskin Neck** (closed to cars); for more interesting galleries and restaurants, walk along **Main Street** (where, inciden-

tally, the movie *Mermaids* was filmed). Just beyond town is a windswept haven and public park, the 68-acre **Halibut Point State Park and Reservation** (Rte 127, 978/546.2997). The acclaimed **Rockport Chamber Music Festival** (978/546.7391; www.rcmf.org) is held each June, with performances Thursday through Sunday evenings.

Inland on Route 133 from Gloucester is **Essex,** with a staggering concentration of antiques shops in a single-mile stretch. Stop for sustenance at supercasual, rambling **Woodman's** (★★$; Main St, 978/768.6451), a North Shore favorite, where Lawrence Woodman first dipped clams in batter and deep-fried them in 1916. Come early or late to avoid huge family crowds, but even if you can't, the steamers, lobsters, fried clams, scallops, chowder, etc., are worth a wait. Nearby is the town of **Ipswich,** also prized for its clams and more so for having more 17th-century houses than any other town in America (more than 40 of them were built before 1725). On Ipswich Bay, the **Crane Memorial Reservation** includes four miles of shoreline and an excellent sandy stretch at **Crane's Beach.** In the old Crane residence, the **Great House** (290 Argilla Rd, 978/356.4351), there are weekend concerts and art lectures during the summer, complemented by gorgeous Italianate gardens with sea views. The house is also open to the public on Wednesdays and Thursdays in summer; there's an admission charge.

Near the northeastern tip of Massachusetts, via Route 1A, is **Newburyport,** once a shipbuilding center and the birthplace of the US Coast Guard. Stroll along the waterfront park and promenade, and through the restored commercial district, an enclave of three-story brick and granite buildings. Many folks think the town has gone overboard gussying itself up for tourists, but it's a nice place to while away a few hours if you're in the mood for shopping, eating, or strolling.

A Massachusetts treasure is the **Parker River National and State Wildlife Refuge** on **Plum Island** (978/465.5753), which offers unsullied beauty, refreshing sea air, and glimpses of wildlife. From Newburyport, head south on Route 1A to Newbury and watch carefully for signs to Plum Island and the wildlife refuge. Headquartered at the old **Coast Guard lighthouse** at the island's northern end, the 4,662-acre refuge has six miles of sandy beaches, hiking trails, observation towers for spotting more than 300 bird species, saltwater and freshwater marshes, sand dunes, surf fishing, nature-study hikes, cross-country skiing, beach plum and cranberry picking, waterfowl hunting, and clamming. Come early on summer weekends because the refuge closes when its quota of 240 cars is reached, which often happens before 9AM. It reopens at 3PM, so if you're shut out early, spend the day in Newburyport and try again later. In late summer and autumn the marshland takes on rich, soft coloring and the sunsets are breathtaking. The island really empties out after the summer.

Restaurants/Clubs: **Red** | Hotels: **Purple** | Shops: **Orange** | Outdoors/Parks: **Green** | Sights/Culture: **Blue**

Northwest of Boston is **Lowell,** America's first successful planned industrial complex and now a National and State Historical Park. Located at the confluence of the Concord and Merrimack Rivers, Lowell was transformed from a sleepy agricultural village into an industrial powerhouse in 1822 by Boston merchant Francis Cabot Lowell and his fellow investors. Lowell's Boston Manufacturing Company had already successfully developed a textile mass-production system driven by water-powered looms in Waltham. Though Lowell (the town) played a pioneering role in the American industrial revolution, it gradually became a squalid environment where women mill workers and immigrants were exploited. Now revitalized by high-tech industries, its fascinating past has been preserved. Today you can tour the mill complexes, operating gatehouses, workers' housing, and a five-and-a-half-mile canal system. Guided interpretive mill and canal tours are offered numerous times daily during the summer; reservations are required. The **Lowell Heritage State Park waterpower exhibit** (25 Shattuck St, 978/970.5000) is open daily; there's an admission charge. Maps for **self-guided city tours** are available at the Visitors' Center (246 Market St, 978/970.5000), including one that points out sites related to native son **Jack Kerouac.** The town is also the birthplace of James Abbott McNeill Whistler. The **Whistler House Museum of Art** (243 Worthen St, 978/452.7641) displays 19th- and 20th-century American art, including works by Whistler. The museum is open Wednesday through Sunday from March through December; there's an admission charge.

Bostonians and visitors alike often travel beyond Massachusetts's northern border for fall foliage splendor, hiking, cross-country and downhill skiing, rock climbing, canoeing, shopping at factory outlet stores, and natural beauty and tranquillity. For more information, contact the **New Hampshire Office of Travel and Tourism** (603/271.2666), **Vermont Travel and Tourism** (802/828.3239), or **Maine Office of Tourism** (207/287.5710, 800/533.9595 out of state).

NEAR NORTHWEST

A few miles northwest of Cambridge on Route 2A are **Lexington** and **Concord,** historic towns where the first military encounters of the American Revolution took place. Concord grapes were first cultivated here, as were the ideas of Louisa May Alcott, Ralph Waldo Emerson, Nathaniel Hawthorne, and Henry David Thoreau. The most notable among the many historic sites is the **Lexington Battle Green** (or Common). Here the first skirmish of the Revolutionary War broke out on 19 April 1775 between the Concord-bound British troops and Colonial Minutemen, alerted earlier by messengers on horseback of the redcoats' approach. (A reenactment of the **Battle of Lexington** is staged on the green at dawn annually on the Monday closest to April 19, Patriot's Day.) The second battle of the day was fought in neighboring Concord, where the citizens' militia drove the British soldiers from North Bridge. Massachusetts artist Henry Hudson Kitson's *Minuteman* statue now stands guard at Lexington Green. The **Lexington Historical Society** (781/862.1703) sometimes offers tours of the green. For details, contact the **Lexington Visitors'**

THE BEST

Michael and Susan Southworth

Urban designers, planners, and authors of the *AIA Guide to Boston*

The ornamental wrought- and cast-iron fences, balconies, and door and window grilles of **Back Bay, Beacon Hill,** and the **South End.**

Friday afternoon at **Symphony Hall,** the Stradivarius of concert halls.

Exploring the **underground railroad stops** and the many other significant black history sites in Boston.

Candlelight concerts at the Isabella Stewart Gardner Museum.

The first day the **Swan Boats** paddle the pond in the Public Garden each spring (mid-April).

A Sunday afternoon walk through the **Back Bay Fens** with its tall rushes, winding waterway, and stone bridge (by Henry Hobson Richardson), followed by

visits to the **Museum of Fine Arts** and the **Isabella Stewart Gardner Museum.**

The **Robert Gould Shaw Memorial,** by Augustus Saint-Gaudens, honoring the first regiment of freed blacks to serve in the Civil War.

The Italian Renaissance Revival interiors of McKim, Mead & White's **Boston Public Library.**

Chiles rellenos at **Casa Romero,** an intimate Mexican restaurant that transcends tacos and smashed beans.

The **Peabody Essex Museum** in Salem, with its collection of important museum houses, furniture, and artifacts of the China trade.

Trinity Church by Henry Hobson Richardson, the best example of Romanesque Revival architecture in the country.

Saturday morning shopping at the **Italian street markets** in the North End.

The **Nichols House** and **Gibson House,** museums that transport us to domestic life in 19th-century Boston.

Center (1875 Massachusetts Ave, 781/862.1450; www.lexingtonchamber.org).

Minute Man National Historical Park, encompassing 750 acres in Concord, Lexington, and Lincoln, commemorates the start of the colonies' war for independence. The park is a narrow strip running on either side of Battle Road (a section of Route 2A), beginning beyond Lexington Center at the **Battle Road Visitors' Center** (Airport Rd, 781/862.7753) and ending in Concord at the **North Bridge Visitors' Center** (Liberty St, 781/369.6993). Though interpretive films and information relate the historical facts, you'll need a bit of imagination to conjure scenes of strife in this bucolic setting. For sustenance after your Revolutionary-era explorations, stop at the venerable (1716) **Colonial Inn,** which faces Concord's Monument Square (★★$$$; 48 Monument Sq, Concord, 978/369.9200; www.concordscolonialinn.com). It's a real inn, with guest rooms, a charming dining room, and, on warm afternoons and evenings, dining on the expansive old porch. Jazz and folk music can be heard in the pub after 8PM.

Concord's most precious asset—although it's sometimes not treated that way—is **Walden Pond Reservation** (Rte 126, 978/369.3254), open daily from 5AM to dusk. The quiet pond is 62 glimmering acres nestled in 333 woody ones. The transcendentalist and freethinker Henry David Thoreau lived and wrote in a 10-by-15-foot hand-hewn cabin alongside the pond from 1845 to 1847. Visitors to the reservation will find woods and pathways descending to smooth water, where sandbars slope to hundred-foot depths. Bostonians delight in this gentle place, so it gets overcrowded and overworked as summer progresses, but slowly recovers during fall and winter—the best time for waterside contemplation.

Architecture enthusiasts inevitably make the trek to **Gropius House** in nearby Lincoln (68 Baker Bridge Rd, 781/227.3956). Follow Route 2 west to Route 126 and watch for Baker Bridge Road. German architect Walter Gropius built the house in 1938, the year after he came to the United States. His iconoclastic modern residence introduced the Bauhaus principles of function and simplicity to this country. The house's industrial quality is derived from its commercial components, a revolutionary architectural approach at the time. The residence includes furniture designed by Gropius, Marcel Breuer, and others. It's part of the historic homes collection of the Society for the Preservation of New England Antiquities (SPNEA), which offers excellent guided tours. It's open to the public Wednesday through Sunday; there's an admission charge.

Nearby, and also located in Lincoln, is the **DeCordova Museum and Sculpture Park** (Sandy Pond Rd, 781/259.8355). The castlelike museum shows work by mostly New England contemporary artists in its galleries and 35-acre sculpture park. July and August feature **outdoor concerts.** This is a gorgeous spot for a picnic and stroll. The museum is open Tuesday through Sunday; there's an admission charge.

On the way back toward Boston (via Route 2 or Highway 20), stop in Waltham to take in a show at the **Rose Art Museum** (781/736.3434) at Brandeis University. It's open Tuesday through Sunday; admission is free. You also might want to check what's on stage at the college's **Spingold Theatre** (781/736.3400). The best restaurant in this area—it's up there in the Boston pantheon—is the **Tuscan Grill** (★★★★$$$$; 361 Moody St, Waltham, 781/891.5486).

THE BERKSHIRES

"The Berkshires" refers to the westernmost part of Massachusetts, a verdant region dappled with rivers, lakes, and gentle hills. It's a romantic and serene area with twin legacies: culture and leisure.

Nestled within mountains, the Berkshires offers hiking, camping, biking, fishing, canoeing, fall foliage, skiing, and welcoming country inns to retire to after the day's activities. From March to early April you can see **tree tapping,** watch sap reduce into real maple syrup, and savor the precious end product. The region is also home to several noted arts organizations. For information, call or write the **Berkshire Visitors' Bureau** (The Berkshire Common, Pittsfield, MA 01201, 413/443.9186, 800/237.5747; www.berkshires.org).

It's possible to take the **Massachusetts Turnpike** (Interstate 90) west from Boston all the way to New York State; the more northerly and scenic **Route 2** also traverses the state. A popular destination on the way to the Berkshires (about an hour west of Boston) is **Old Sturbridge Village** (508/347.3362; www.osv.org), perfect for a family outing. (Take Exit 9 off the Massachusetts Turnpike to Highway 20.) On more than 200 acres, the museum is a re-creation of an early 19th-century New England agricultural community, and features some participatory activities. There's a working farm, tended in the manner of the era, and gardens of culinary and medicinal herbs. Demonstrations explain crafts of 19th-century blacksmiths, shoemakers, potters, and coopers, while exhibits display period clocks, folk art, portraiture, and firearms and militia accoutrements. Open daily; there is an admission charge.

Farther west on the Turnpike, in the city of Springfield, kids who love the Cat in the Hat, the Grinch, and Yertle the Turtle (and many parents) will enjoy the **Dr. Seuss National Memorial Sculpture Garden** outside the Springfield Museums (220 State St, 800/625.7738; www.catinthehat.org). Dr. Seuss creator Theodor Seuss Geisel was born and raised in Springfield. The **Naismith Memorial Basketball Hall of Fame** (1000 W Columbus Ave, 413.781.6500; www.hoophall.com) is also in Springfield. Naismith, who was a physical education instructor at

---

Restaurants/Clubs: Red | Hotels: Purple | Shops: Orange | Outdoors/Parks: Green | Sights/Culture: Blue

Springfield College in the 1890s, is credited with inventing the modern game of basketball in a YMCA gym. There is an admission charge.

The Berkshires town of **Becket,** north of I-90 about three hours from Boston, is the summer home of **Jacob's Pillow** (413/243.0745; www.jacobspillow.org), the oldest dance festival in the country, which features performances by some of the world's most exciting companies. Picnic under the trees before a performance. Stay and/or dine nearby at the **Federal House** ($$$; 102 Main St, Lee, 413/243.1824).

Nearby Lenox is the site of **Tanglewood** (Rte 183, 413/637.5165, 617/266.1492 in Boston; www.tanglewood.org), the summer home of another acclaimed arts organization, the Boston Symphony Orchestra. The lush 200-acre estate is a popular destination for a day trip from Boston. Many listeners forgo seats in favor of a picnic on the grass while taking in the symphony. The world-renowned **Tanglewood Music Festival** is held here annually from July through August, and other events include a **Popular Artists Series** (throughout the summer) and **Labor Day Weekend Jazz Festival.**

Not far from Lenox is **Stockbridge,** a perfectly cast New England town known for its **Norman Rockwell Museum** (Rte 183, 413/298.4100). It's open daily; there's an admission charge. Folk singer Arlo Guthrie brought fame, of a sort, to his home town of Stockbridge with his Vietnam-era recording of "Alice's Restaurant." The town's landmark **Red Lion Inn** ($$$; Main St, 413/298.5545; www.redlioninn.com) has been in operation since 1773. The well-preserved inn offers rural charm year-round with a lobby fireplace, music from the grand piano, and a front porch lined with rocking chairs. For information on the town, click on www.stockbridgechamber.org.

Just west of Stockbridge is **Chesterwood** (4 Williamsville Rd, 413/298.3579), the former studio and summer residence of the prolific sculptor Daniel Chester French, who created Abraham Lincoln's famous image in the Washington, DC, memorial and the *Minuteman* statue in Concord, not to mention many works around Boston. Casts, models, tools, drawings, books, and French's personal belongings are displayed here. There's a garden and nature trail, too. It's open daily from 1 May through 31 October; there's an admission charge.

In 1903 the Boston Red Sox, then called the Boston Pilgrims, won their first pennant, and then went on to win the first ever baseball World Series against the Philadelphia Pirates.

The state drink of Massachusetts is cranberry juice, in testament to the state's number-one agricultural product. Over 400 growers work more than 12,000 acres, mostly in southeastern Massachusetts.

North from here on Highway 7 is **Williamstown,** home of **Williams College** and the **Sterling and Francine Clark Art Institute** (225 South St, 413/458.2303; www.clarkart.edu). The institute houses a wonderful collection of 15th- to 19th-century paintings, drawings, prints, and antique silver. It excels in 19th-century European and American painting, especially French Impressionists. It's open daily; there is an admission charge. The **Williamstown Theatre Festival** (1000 Main St, 413.597.3400; www.wtfestival.org) is like a summer camp for well-known stars of stage and screen. There are performances all summer long, but tickets to this popular series must be purchased in advance.

A detour on Highway 20 (west of Rte 7) leads to **Hancock Shaker Village** (413/443.0188), a restoration of the Shaker community founded in 1790. Twenty buildings have been restored, including a remarkable round stone barn. Shakers lived here until 1960. The village is open daily April through November; there is an admission charge.

THE SOUTH SHORE

Head for gentle surf on the South Shore, the coastal stretch that lies between Boston and Massachusetts's much more well-known beach area, Cape Cod.

Motor south on Interstate 93 to **Route 3A,** the winding shore road to **Hingham,** with its graceful town center. This is the site of the **Old Ship Meetinghouse** (Main St, 781/749.1679), the oldest wooden church in continuous use in America, built in 1681 and with pulpit, pews, and galleries dating from 1755. Then visit a rare pastoral setting of human design: **World's End Reservation** (Martin's La, 781/749.8956), a 250-acre part of a harborside estate designed by **Frederick Law Olmsted.** It's one of the Massachusetts Trustees of Reservations' beautiful park holdings. Here you'll forget about Boston's proximity until you reach the park's edge on the water, where you'll find unusual urban views. **Boston Light,** the oldest operating lighthouse in America, is easily viewed from **Nantasket Beach** on Nantasket Avenue in **Hull,** a teeny town at the end of a peninsula stretching north of Hingham into Boston Harbor. Nantasket Beach is a two-mile stretch of sand with a bathhouse, a playground, a promenade, a 1928 carousel, and the tiny **Hull Lifesaving Museum** (1117 Nantasket Ave, 781/925.5433). The museum is open daily; there is an admission charge. The beach is also accessible by **Bay State Cruises'** ferry (781/723.7800) from Long Wharf on Boston's waterfront. Continue south on Route 3A to Duxbury and **Duxbury Beach,** one of the finest barrier beaches on the eastern shore and a paradise for birders and walkers year-round.

Take Route 3 south to Exit 4 and Plymouth, former home of the pilgrims and now the site of **Plimoth Plantation** (137 Warren Ave/Rte 3A, 508/746.1622; www.plimoth.org), a "living museum" that re-creates 17th-century Plymouth. The plantation is open daily April through

November; there is an admission charge. The
famed rock and a replica of the *Mayflower* are
located at the center of town. Also in Plymouth is
Cranberry World (255 Water St, 508/747.2350),
with two outdoor working bogs, which are quite a
sight.

CAPE COD, MARTHA'S VINEYARD, AND NANTUCKET

Shaped like a large fishhook curving 75 miles into
the Atlantic and gleaming with hundreds of
freshwater ponds and lakes, **Cape Cod** was once a
prosperous fishing and whaling center. Today this
peninsula, bounded by the Atlantic Ocean on the
east and north, Buzzards Bay on the west, and
Nantucket Sound on the south, is lined with resort
communities offering beaches, clam shacks, summer
theater, and the like.

**Pilgrim
Monument &
Provincetown
Museum**

Much of the Cape has been intensely developed,
causing erosion to whittle away some lovely land, but
fortunately residents are forcing the pace to slow.
One of the state's great treasures is the **Cape Cod
National Seashore,** a protected 30-mile-long system
of pristine beaches, woodlands, and marshes, culminating in the magnificent Provincetown sand dunes.
For information, call the national seashore headquarters (99 Marconi Site Rd, Wellfleet, 508/349.3785).
For more on Cape Cod, including campsites, contact
the **Cape Cod Chamber of Commerce** (Mid-Cape
Hwy, Hyannis, MA 02601, 508/362.3225;
www.capecod.com).

From Boston, take Route 3 south and cross the
Sagamore Bridge over the imposing Cape Cod Canal
onto the Cape and Highway 6. (Warning: Traffic on
summer weekends can be brutal. Don't drive to the
Cape on a Friday afternoon or attempt to leave the
Cape Sunday afternoon.) A traffic-free alternative is
to take the 90-minute **Bay State Cruises** ferry
(457.1428, $68 round-trip; www.boston-ptown.com)
from Commonwealth Pier on Boston's
waterfront or, among others, **Boston Harbor
Cruises** from Long Wharf ($70 round-trip;
www.bostonharborcruises.com/ptown_main.html) to
Provincetown at the tip of Cape Cod. It's possible to
make a round-trip excursion in one day. Or, better
yet, stay at least one night and enjoy. Ferry service is
usually on a mid-May-to-October schedule.

Sightseeing on Cape Cod can be adapted to fit your
preference: For up-to-the-minute action, follow **Route
28** along the Cape's southern coast; for a quick trip
to Provincetown, take **Highway 6,** which bisects the
Cape; and for a sense of history, follow old **Route 6A**
along the north coast.

Also called the **Old King's Highway Historic District,**
Route 6A is protected from modern development by
strict laws. The road travels through several quaint

towns (including **Sandwich, Yarmouthport,** and
Brewster) that are home to a number of museums
and historic houses. Farther along the Cape, past
where Route 6A and Highway 6 merge, is **Wellfleet**
and the Massachusetts Audubon Society's **Wellfleet
Bay Wildlife Sanctuary** (Hwy 6, 508/349.2615),
one of Cape Cod's loveliest spots.

But perhaps the most interesting place to visit—the
timing depends on your tastes—is **Provincetown** at
the tip of the Cape, where the Pilgrims first landed
(www.provincetown.com). Home to a welcoming
year-round mix of artists and fishermen and their
families, Provincetown's population swells from
3,400 in the off-season to an estimated 60,000 in
summer. It's a gay haven, with a sensuous
atmosphere and active tourist life from Memorial Day
weekend until summer's end, but it has a quiet side
also. No matter what time of year, it feels
comfortable and safe here; return in winter when "P-
town" has shrunk and you'll feel as if you have the
town and an ocean to yourself. Endowed with the
loveliest National Seashore stretch, the town's
outskirts are wonderful for bicycling and jogging. For
a sweeping view of the tiny town and its ocean
setting, climb to the top of the **Pilgrim Monument**
(High Pole Hill Rd, 508/487.1310, 800/247.1620).
The tallest granite structure in the US, the tower
hovers high on the village skyline. Also consider the
guided canoe trips offered by park rangers at
Provincetown Outer Cape to places most tourists
never see (Province Lands Visitor Center,
508/487.1256).

Visit the funky, fascinating **Heritage Museum**
(356 Commercial St, 508/487.7098), which traces
the history of Provincetown. It's open daily from mid-
June through October; there's an admission charge.
Commercial Street is P-town's main street, where the

Restaurants/Clubs: Red | Hotels: Purple | Shops: Orange | Outdoors/Parks: Green | Sights/Culture: Blue

greatest concentration of restaurants, shops, and lodgings converge, and is the place for strolling and people-watching. The easiest way to find good accommodations and cuisine, including off-season listings, is to call or write the **Provincetown Chamber of Commerce** in advance (PO Box 1017, Provincetown, MA 02657, 508/487.3424; www.ptownchamber.com). The office is at 307 Commercial Street, on MacMillan Wharf.

Martha's Vineyard, an island south of Cape Cod, is another well-loved vacation spot; ferry reservations for cars are often sold out for summer weekends by Christmas. The Vineyard has wonderful beaches, sunsets, sailing, walking, picnicking, and bicycling. Its population balloons from 12,000 to perhaps 75,000 in the summer. Down-island (on the eastern side) you'll find **Vineyard Haven, Oak Bluffs,** and **Edgartown.** The latter is the most popular with tourists and has an array of architectural styles, from saltbox to Greek Revival. Up-island (the western side) are **West Tisbury, Chilmark,** and **Gay Head,** which is known for its varicolored clay cliffs. Like Cape Cod and Nantucket, the Vineyard is just as wonderful—or more so—out of season.

To get to Martha's Vineyard, you and your car can ride the **ferry** from Woods Hole at the southwest corner of Cape Cod (**Steamship Authority,** 508/477.8600). Seasonal, passengers-only ferries leave for the Vineyard from Hyannis (508/775.7185) and Falmouth (508/548.4800). Passenger ferries (**Cape Island Express Lines,** 508/997.1688) also operate year-round from **New Bedford** on the Massachusetts coast, about two hours south of Boston. New Bedford is a historic and still-important seaport, where you'll find the excellent **New Bedford Whaling Museum** (8 Johnny Cake Hill, 508/997.0046; www.whalingmuseum.org) and discount shopping too. The museum is open daily; there is an admission charge. You can also fly into **Martha's Vineyard Airport** (508/693.7022); flights leave from Logan International Airport and Hyannis.

For information on Vineyard events, places, and accommodations, call or write the **Martha's Vineyard Chamber of Commerce** (PO Box 1698, Vineyard Haven, MA 02568, 508/693.0085; www.mvy.com). The office is on Beach Road. One option is the 1891 **Harbor View Hotel,** which overlooks Edgartown harbor with a wraparound porch and 130 luxury rooms and suites (131 N Water St, 800/225.6005).

Eat fresh and delicious seafood at the elegant, expensive **L'Etoile** in Edgartown (★★★★$$$$; 22 N Water St, 508/627.5187) or en route to Gay Head at the **Beach Plum Inn** in Menemsha (★★$$; off North Rd, 508/645.9454). In Oak Bluffs, wander

among the **Carpenter Gothic Cottages,** a Methodist revival campground of Victorian Gothic cottages from the late 1800s, oddly ornate with filigree trim.

Located 30 miles south of Cape Cod, **Nantucket** is a historic whaling island known as the "Gray Lady of the Sea" for its gently weathering clapboards, and for the clothes worn by its early Quaker settlers. Nowadays, the island is a summer playground for the unflashy, monied crowd. When it's sweltering in Boston, the sea breezes keep Nantucket cool, with weathered beauty, gray-shingled houses and rose-covered cottages, moors of heather, cranberry bogs, and gnarled pines. There's no need for a car here—you can walk, bicycle, or ride a moped from one end of the island to the other. Arrive via **ferry** from Hyannis or Woods Hole. You can also fly to **Nantucket Memorial Airport** (508/325.5300) from Logan International Airport and Hyannis. For tourist information, call or write the **Nantucket Island Chamber of Commerce** (Main St, Nantucket, MA 02554, 508/228.1700; www.town.nantucket.ma.us).

The town of Nantucket is the picturesque and quaint center of activity, and is packed with interesting shops and restaurants. The deli-style **Espresso Café** (★$$; 40 Main St, 508/228.6930) is easy on the budget; **21 Federal** (★★★★$$$$; 21 Federal St, 508/228.2121) and the **Boarding House** (★★★$$$$; 12 Federal St, 508/228.9622) aren't, but they're worth every penny. For the ultimate in laid-back (if top-dollar) charm, plan a stay at the **Wauwinet** ($$$$; 120 Wauwinet Rd, Wauwinet, 508/228.0145, 800/426.8718, www.wauwinet.com), a historic inn surrounded by beaches at the edge of civilization. But as long as you reserve well ahead, you'll fare well at any of the island's reasonably priced bed-and-breakfasts. All of the island's beaches are dazzling and easily accessible.

PROVIDENCE AND NEWPORT, RHODE ISLAND

Beyond the commonwealth's southern border, yet within a one- to two-hour ride, are Providence and Newport, Rhode Island. Providence is the capital of the Ocean State and its industrial and commercial center as well as a major port. The city was founded by Roger Williams, who was banished from Boston by the often intolerant Puritans. A city guide and map of landmarks is available at the **Greater Providence-Warwick Convention and Visitors' Bureau** (30 Exchange Terr, Providence, RI 02903, 401/274.1636). To drive to Providence from Boston, take Interstate 93 south to I-95 and head south. Or take the train—Amtrak's **Acela Express** stops here, departing from Boston's South Station (800/872.7245). The **TF Green Airport** (www.pvd-ri.com) is just outside Providence in Warwick; many people now use it as an alternative to Logan International, with fewer hassles.

Cambridge is second only to Wales, in Britain, in the number of bookstores per capita in the world. The books sold in Cambridge range from manuscripts written in the 1200s to today's comic books.

CATAMARAN SAILS TO WITCH CITY

High-speed ferry service from Boston to Salem, the "witch city", takes 45 minutes on a 92-foot catamaran. The two-hulled, 150-passenger craft leaves daily from Central Wharf, home of the **New England Aquarium**, from 9 am to 9 pm (11 pm Saturdays). One-way fares to the North Shore city are $12 for adults, $8 children. In Salem, a trolley goes from the dock to downtown and places like the **Peabody Essex Museum**, the **House of Seven Gables**, and the **Salem Witch Museum**. The ferry runs Memorial Day weekend through 31 October. Call 978/741.0220; www.salemferry.com.

The skyline of Rhode Island's capital city features the tall, pointed spires of historic churches, plus the capitol building's white marble dome. Among the sights to see are the **State House** (82 Smith St, 401/277.2357), open Monday through Friday; **Waterplace Park,** an urban park built on the site of an old salt marsh; and the scenic half-mile **riverwalk.** The **Museum of Art** (224 Benefit St, 401/454.6500) offers a fine collection of works from ancient Greece, Rome, and Egypt through 20th-century Europe and America. It's open Tuesday through Sunday; there's an admission charge.

Providence's **College Hill** neighborhood is home to **Brown University** (Prospect St, 401/863.1000; www.brown.edu) and the **Rhode Island School of Design** (2 College St, 401/454.6100; www.risd.edu), both of which host plays, lectures, and cultural exhibits that are open to the public. Interspersed among the college buildings are splendid colonial homes, columned mansions, and gardens, some of which are open to the public.

Try to have dinner at one of George Germon and Johanne Killeen's renowned restaurants: **Al Forno** (★★★★$$$$) or **Lucky's** (★★★$$$$; both at 577 S Main St, 401/273.9760). Al Forno offers rustic Italian-style décor and food that's mainly grilled over hardwood or roasted in a brick oven; Lucky's tends toward French provincial in décor, but the cuisine is similar to that served at Al Forno. For an evening out, try the **Trinity Repertory Company** (201 Washington St, 401/351.4242), which is nationally renowned.

South of Providence is **Newport,** which still echoes its origins as a colonial seaport. The town has always been associated with opulence and the sea: yachts, the navy, competitive sailing, and seaside palaces of the rich. Annual celebrations include the star-studded **Newport Jazz Festival,** the country's oldest. The **Cliff Walk** is Newport's other most popular attraction, a three-and-a-half-mile shoreline path and a National Historic Walking Trail, with the Atlantic Ocean on one side and the famous summer mansions on the other.

Be sure to take a tour of one or more of these elaborate Victorian mansions (www.newportmansions review.com). **The Breakers** (Ochre Point Ave) is the most splendid of the very magnificent lot. Built in 1895 for Cornelius Vanderbilt, it resembles a Northern Italian Renaissance palace. Bellevue Avenue is the site of a magnificent line of "cottages" from the Gilded Age, including **Marble House,** completed in 1892 for William K. Vanderbilt and still boasting its original furnishings; **Château-sur-Mer,** built in 1852 and one of the finest examples of ornate Victorian architecture in the US; and **Rosecliff,** the 1902 palace designed by **Stanford White.** It was featured in the film *The Great Gatsby.*

For more information about mansions and other attractions, contact the **Newport County Convention & Visitors Bureau** (23 Americas Cup Ave, Newport, RI 02403, 401/845.9123, 800/326.6030; www.gonewport.com).

GAY BOSTON

The "Athens of America," Boston likes to call itself, and if an intellectual acceptance of homosexuality means anything, there might be some truth to the sobriquet. While some might say it's still Puritan at heart, this city of some 600,000 is nonetheless a sprawling multicultural mix with the third-largest lesbian and gay population in the country and every scene and type in the book: lesbian line dancing, pretty boys with attitude, leather clones, bookish dykes with baby strollers, and drag queens rubbing elbows with grunge rockers. In fact, a sort of bisexual chic has emerged at area colleges, with every other student around claiming to be "bi."

For a city founded by Pilgrim types—and later home to an Irish-Catholic political dynasty—there are a surprising number of places where you can comfortably hold a lover's hand while shopping for commitment rings. There's court-certified same-sex marriage, but only for Massachusetts residents. Sure, there are hot spots of hate—just listen to AM talk radio—but that ruling by the state's highest court makes Massachusetts the most

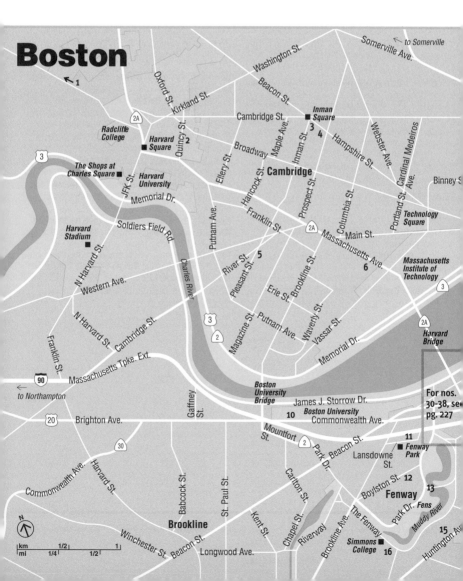

For nos. 30-38, see pg. 227

gay- and lesbian-friendly state in the US. Gay lives are lived pretty openly in most of the towns that make up Boston.

The major lesbian centers in the area are the Boston neighborhood of **Jamaica Plain,** southwest of downtown; **Dorchester;** and the cities of **Cambridge** and **Somerville,** across the **Charles River.** Gay clubs are also in Boston's downtown **Theater District** and along the **Fenway,** a green neighborhood named for the **Fens,** a parklike riverside area where naughty boys have sought furtive contact among the tall reeds for years. The practice has given rise to public debate over the appropriateness of outdoor sex—and to antigay violence as well.

This gay bashing is a reminder that homophobia can still leak out of places like **South Boston,** home of the no-organized-gays-allowed St. Patrick's Day Parade. In this culturally conservative but politically liberal town, however, bigotry usually does not go unchallenged. When the Supreme Court sided with South Boston's parade organizers, the mayor refused to march, and Cambridge organized an alternative event that keeps growing every year. Boston mayor Thomas Menino marches in the annual **Gay Pride Parade,**

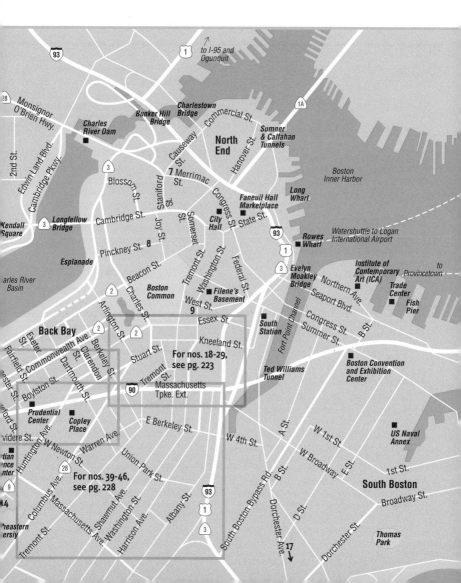

while the rainbow flag flutters proudly over **City Hall.** All of which is to say that, as these things go, the homo living is pretty good in these parts.

Here, as elsewhere, gays and lesbians sometimes seem to come from different planets (Mars and Venus, as they say) when it comes to partying. But in the real-life neighborhoods and suburbs, gay men and women do come together in church basements for line-dancing or parenting groups, in coffee shops to chat, or on local streets to train for the annual **Boston-New York AIDS Ride**–the gay world as it should be.

As for the youngsters, their scene would be lively by any standard, with some 50 colleges and universities in the area; but here even the high schools have active social and political gay student groups. A queer-straight alliance even got a gay student-rights bill passed and signed by former GOP governor William Weld (the typical Massachusetts Republican is a little left of center).

And so Bostonians have come a long way from the repression of the 1630s, when Governor John Winthrop courted the death penalty by writing love letters to his boyfriend. Today fags and dykes proudly deck their buildings with strands of pink bulbs every June, and Boston has become a city that, for the most part, defends its gay citizens and celebrates their lives—and can show visitors a pretty good time to boot.

Symbols

♂ predominantly/exclusively gay-male–oriented

♀ predominantly/exclusively lesbian-oriented

♂♀ predominantly/exclusively gay-oriented with a male and female clientele

1 WESTWAY

♀ Who said pool and darts are just guy things? Boston-area women shoot some and throw 'em (free, no less) on Thursdays and Sundays at this Cambridge spot (formerly called Upstairs at the Hideaway), hidden behind **Ma Magoo's** pizza place on a terrible Route 2 traffic rotary. It's a fun way to kill a lazy evening, though, sadly, it happens only twice a week. ♦ Cover. Th, 8PM-2AM, Su, 6PM-2AM. 20 Concord La (at Concord Ave). 661.8828

2 FOGG ART MUSEUM

Founded in 1891, **Harvard University**'s oldest museum houses a comprehensive collection covering much of the history of Western art. Amid the greater and lesser artistic lights (Picasso, Rubens, Monet, Pollock) is Boston's own flamboyant Cubist, Charles Demuth (1883-1935), who once described good painting as the "nth whoopee of life." No doubt that little gem came to him while doing his 1916 *Turkish Bath*, depicting the gay-frequented Lafayette Baths of New York City. For devotees of Martha Stewart, the museum

also offers rotating exhibits of elegant home furnishings, including a famed collection of Wedgwood. ♦ Admission; free Sa, 10AM-noon. Tu.-Su. 32 Quincy St (between Massachusetts Ave and Broadway), Cambridge. 495.9400; www.artmuseums.harvard.edu &

3 RYLES JAZZ CLUB

♀ There's an "Amazon Slam" poetry slam on the last Sunday of every month. Other times, it's a great place for live jazz, with the likes of Bucky Pizzarelli, Louie Bellson, and Slide Hampton. ♦ Tu-Sa, dinner; Su, jazz brunch. Free parking in Ryles lot nearby. 212 Hampshire St (at Inman St), Cambridge. 876.9330; www.rylesjazz.com

3 CITY GIRL CAFFÈ

♀ ★$ In Inman Square, near the S&S restaurant, this café offers a friendly atmosphere for all walks of dyke. You can hang out with friends—or alone—over coffee, sandwiches, pizza, light lunch, and dinner. ♦ Café/Takeout ♦ Tu-Su, lunch, dinner, and snacks. Closed M. 204 Hampshire St (at Inman St), Cambridge. 864.2809; fax 864.2806; www.citygirlcaffeandcatering.com

4 CENTER FOR NEW WORDS

♀ "Where women's words matter." Founded in 1974, the only remaining women's bookstore in the Boston area is lesbian owned and boasts 15,000 titles, ranging from children's books to separatist tracts. The shop also carries jewelry, posters, and CDs, and hosts regular readings by women authors. ♦ M-Sa; Su, noon-6PM. 186 Hampshire St (between Prospect and Armory Sts), Cambridge. 876.5310; www.centerfornewwords.org

5 WOMEN'S CENTER

♀ Lesbian visitors can stop by this women-only resource center to consult its listing of gay-friendly area establishments or to peruse its events bulletin board. The organization also hosts support groups for lesbians and bisexual women and sponsors lectures and women-oriented events. ♦ M-Th, 10AM-10PM; F, 10AM-8PM; Sa, 11AM-4PM. 46 Pleasant St (between Upton and Cottage Sts), Cambridge. 354.8807; www.cambridgewomenscenter.org

6 PARADISE

♂ Out-of-towners who think Cambridge is nothing but stuffy and cerebral should check out this not pretty, black-walled den by MIT, which caters equally to road-crew workers and future nuclear scientists. Strippers, porn stars, and touchy-feely dancers work the room on Wednesdays, while the down-stairs dance floor is grope-and-be-groped dark all week long. It's hot, it's cruisy, it's young and hurried. ♦ Cover. Daily, from 7PM. 180 Massachusetts Ave (at Albany St), Cambridge. 864.4130; www.paradisecambridge.com

7 119 MERRIMAC

♂ This denimish and leatherish joint is off by itself near North Station and the Banknorth Garden, only a 20-minute walk from the South End but miles away in attitude. Apart from a jukebox and pool table, the room is basically no-frills, but it's friendly, cruisy, and dark enough so that anyone looks good. (Does that read like a warning?) ♦ M-Sa, 10:30AM-2AM; Su, noon-2AM. 119 Merrimac St (at Lancastor St). 367.0713

8 PINCKNEY STREET

Some call this quiet lane of cobblestones and gas lamps the "Cinderella Street" of Beacon Hill. The oldest house on the street, **No. 5,** was built in 1786 by Revolutionary War hero George Middleton to share with his companion, Louis Clappion. One hundred years later, gay photographer F. Holland Day opened shop two doors down at **No. 9.** Credited with developing the style known as "aesthetic decadence," Day received visits from that most decadent of aesthetes, **Oscar Wilde.** The two houses are not open to the public. ♦ Between Joy and Charles Sts

9 TRIBE

Thursday is women's night at Tribe, a dance club for women at **Club Felt,** across from the Hyatt Boston. That means pool, a DJ, music, bars, and crowds. ♦ Cover. Th, 9PM-2AM.

533 Washington St (between Essex and West Sts). 350 5555; www.tribenightclub.com

10 MUGAR MEMORIAL LIBRARY

The massive **Department of Special Collections** may be one of **Boston University**'s better-kept semisecrets. Housed in this library, the collection has materials going back as far as the 15th century, including the papers of playwright Tennessee Williams and poet Walt Whitman, not to mention those of the fabulous Bette Davis. The library mounts fascinating changing exhibits, and it's easy to make an appointment to view whatever part of the collection is not on public display at the moment. ♦ Free. M-Th, 8AM-midnight; F, Sa, 8AM-11PM; Su, 10AM-midnight. 771 Commonwealth Ave (between Granby St and University Rd). 353.3696, tours 353.3710; www.bu.edu/library/mugar ♿

11 AVALON

♂ South End boy-gods boogie and cruise here on Sunday, making **"Citi"** (the official, but never-used, name of the club's gay night) Boston's biggest event on the gay dance circuit. The mammoth club (the biggest in Boston) opens up passageways to two adjacent clubs, **Axis** and **DV-8,** yielding three dance floors and a dozen bars to satisfy a very young crowd of 3,000. The music is up-to-the-minute and the pace frenetic, with the boys packed in like dancing sardines. ♦ Cover. Su, 10PM-2AM. 15 Lansdowne St (between Ipswich St and Brookline Ave). 262.2424 ♿

12 BOSTON RAMROD

♂ Park yer Harley on the sidewalk and strut through the heavy wooden door to join the butchy crowd inside (though not everyone here is necessarily as tough as they'd like you to think). On weekends, half of the club is reserved for shirtless or leather-clad patrons, who occasionally have been known to do naughty things in said half. For the tamer of heart, there's pinball, pool, video games, and even free pizza Monday night. ♦ Cover Su. Daily, noon-2AM. 1254 Boylston St (between Park Dr and Jersey St). 266.2986; www.ramrodboston.com

At Ramrod:

MACHINE

♂ This Saturday-night dance club in the base-ment of Ramrod offers a huge dance floor, a full bar, and music under the direction of a DJ that is loud, Loud, LOUD. The somewhat quieter lobby area has pool tables and lounging space. ♦ Cover. Sa, 10PM-2AM. 226.2986

Restaurants/Clubs: Red | Hotels: Purple | Shops: Orange | Outdoors/Parks: Green | Sights/Culture: Blue

BOSTON FESTIVALS

Gay Pride Week (officially called Gay, Lesbian, Bisexual, and Transgendered Pride Week; 739.4567) is Boston's biggest homosexual celebration. Held the first or second week of June, it begins with the **South End Pride Lighting,** in which a large tree in front of the Boston Center for the Arts (BCA; see page 228) is decorated with pink lights (as are many area businesses and residences). Numerous activities—harbor cruises, block parties, brunches, dances, etc.—are held throughout the week, and the festival ends with a big downtown **parade.**

Other annual events include **The Dinner Party,** a glamorous April benefit bash; the **Intercollegiate Queer Prom,** also in April; **From All Walks of Life** in June; and the **Boston–New York AIDS Ride** in September. The latter two are big AIDS fund-raisers (one for walkers, one for cyclists) that bring gay and straight Boston together. October sees **Out on the Edge,** a queer theater festival at the BCA, and in November the **AIDS Danceathon** takes place.

13 KATHARINE LEE BATES MEMORIAL

From the fruited pen of lesbian poet Katharine Lee Bates (1859-1929) sprang the immortal line "for purple mountains' majesty above the fruited plains." Inspired by the view from Pikes Peak, Bates wrote "America the Beautiful" in 1893. Here on the **Agassiz Bridge** in the Fens, a bronze plaque hails the Wellesley College grad and later head of Wellesley's English Literature Department as "scholar, patriot, poet." ♦ Agassiz Rd (between The Fenway and Park Dr)

14 JORDAN HALL AT THE NEW ENGLAND CONSERVATORY OF MUSIC (NEC)

This National Historic Landmark is one of New England's finest concert halls. Designed in 1903 by **Wheelwright and Haven,** it boasts austere Edwardian lines and world-famous acoustics ideal for chamber music. It's also the home of the versatile **Boston Gay Men's Chorus** (www.bgmc.org), whose repertoire ranges from classical to 1960s pop to new works by gay artists. Among other groups that perform here are the **Boston Symphony Chamber Players** and the **Boston Chamber Music Society.** The hall presents some 450 concerts annually. ♦ 30 Gainsborough St (between St. Botolph St and Huntington Ave). Box office 536.2412, 585.1100, chorus 424.8900; www.newenglandconservatory.edu &

15 MUSEUM OF FINE ARTS (MFA)

This museum houses diverse permanent exhibits that span time (and sexual orientations) from ancient Egypt to Andy Warhol. The collection of Greek antiquities is particularly noteworthy, and not just for the obvious reasons; its turn-of-the-century curator, Edward Perry Warren, once wrote that it was his "plea against that in Boston which contradicted my love." Special exhibits here often feature the work of contemporary gay artists—photographers Herb Ritts and Duane Michals are examples. The museum also hosts the annual **Gay and Lesbian Film Festival** every June in conjunction with the Harvard Film Archive and sponsors lectures by such queer luminaries as provocative scholar Camille Paglia. Three eateries offer something for every budget range. ♦ Admission; free Wednesday 4-9:45PM, except for the Graham Gund Gallery; reduced admission when only the West Wing is open; members and children under 6 free; reduced admission for students and senior citizens. M, Tu, Th-F, 10AM-4:45PM; W, 10AM-9:45PM; Sa, Su, 10AM-5:45PM (West Wing until 9:45PM). 465 Huntington Ave (at Museum Rd). 267.9300; www.mfa.org &

16 ISABELLA STEWART GARDNER MUSEUM

Boston's grand lady of culture, this mansion-turned-museum sits a block away from the **MFA** near the historically female **Simmons College.** Even by monied Victorian standards, Isabella was quite a diva: Her private home, built in 1903 to resemble an Italian palazzo, boasts paintings by Florentine fruit Michelangelo in addition to works by Rembrandt, Titian, Botticelli, Raphael, Degas, and Sargent. There's also a lavish year-round flower garden in a sunny courtyard, and for fans of flatware, an exhibition of Gardner's formal table settings. ♦ Admission; members and children under 12 free; reduced admission for seniors and students. T-Su. Free guided tour Friday 2:30PM; private tours available by reservation. 280 The Fenway (at Palace Rd). 566.1401; www.gardnermuseum.org &

17 D BAR

★★$$ What used to be just another Irish bar in Dorchester has taken on a new life as the D Bar, a cozy, nicely redecorated (lots of wood) place for the neighborhood's gay, lesbian, and straight residents to dine in the evening on dishes like seared, sesame-crusted tuna. Tables are moved aside after 10, when dancing could ensue. South Enders are known to make the short trip here. D Bar has its own parking lot. ♦ American. ♦ Daily, dinner. 1236 Dorchester Ave (between East and Hancock Sts). 265.4490; www.dbarboston.com &

18 BOSTON COMMON AND PUBLIC GARDEN

More than simple public parks, these cheek-to-cheek downtown oases are metaphors for the duality of the city's gay culture: day and night, good and naughty, out and not. The grass-and-concrete **Boston Common** is the oldest of the city's notorious late-night cruising spots—a place where men have come looking for men, and not to talk about needlework. Police are aware of this and still keep a close watch during the wee hours (in broad daylight, there's no action at all). The **Public Garden,** by contrast, is prim and proper, with manicured lawns, sprawling shade trees, and a dreamy pond where swans paddle about. This is a daytime place, where gay boys and girls and people of all stripes soak up the sun or take a summer ride on the Swan Boats, peddled by youths with calves thick as the nearby maple trees. **From All Walks of Life,** the annual AIDS walkathon, starts at the common and passes through the garden—giving the swans and tourists something to gander at. ♦ Bounded by Tremont, Park, Arlington, Boylston, and Beacon Sts

19 MARQUIS LEATHERS

The good Marquis is open until 11PM with XXX videos and a smorgasbord of goodies: restraints, leather rings, underwear, tops, lubes, and condoms. ♦ Daily, 10AM-11PM. 92 South St (above Calamus Books, between Beach and Tufts Sts). 426.2120

19 CALAMUS BOOKSTORE

There's a rainbow flag by the entrance and Walt Whitman on the window. Run by a dedicated John Mitzel, this friendly bookstore a block from South Station offers more than 9,000 books, videos, CDs, and DVDs. (Calamus was a son of the Greek river god Maeander. When his love, Carpus, drowned, the grieving Calamus was changed into a reed. The calamus plant, native to the northeastern US and a Whitman favorite, is found along river banks.) ♦ Daily. 92B South St. 338.1931; www.calamusbooks.com

FOUR SEASONS HOTEL
Boston

20 FOUR SEASONS HOTEL BOSTON

$$$$ Pricey but well worth it, this gay-friendly hotel will take you, your lover, and even your pet with a smile (just ask for the doggy room-service menu and a wicker bed for Fluffy). The contemporary décor is sprin-

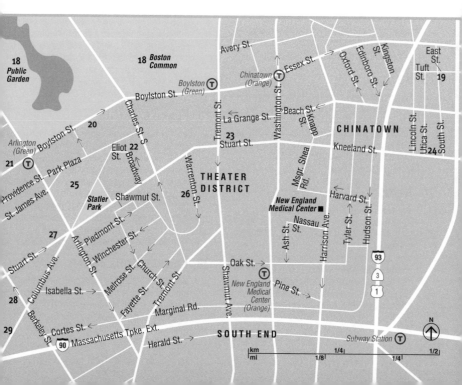

kled with antiques and oil paintings, but practical modern touches abound, like minibars and fax/dataports in all 288 rooms. For gym bunnies, the best part may be the eighth-floor health spa, offering stunning views over the **Public Garden** and Beacon Hill, plus a full workout room, complimentary personal trainer, and sunny swimming pool. All of which will get you in shape for dinner at **Aujourd'hui**, consistently rated among the best restaurants in Boston. ◆ 200 Boylston St (between Charles St S and Hadassah Way). 338.4400; fax 351.2051 ♿

21 PARRISH CAFÉ

♂ ★$ It's funky and casual, more restaurant than bar, with a busy lunch crowd of businesspeople and tourists. The most expensive item is a lobster roll. Across the street from the George tavern, the place gets much hipper after work and at night, when there's a gay and straight clientele, many headed past the original art walls for the outside patio. ◆ Daily, lunch and dinner. 361 Boylston St. 247.4777; www.parrishcafe.com

22 JACQUES

♂ With a nip, a tuck, and a stroke of marketing genius, this aging queen of the drag world has made herself a new life as, of all things, a venue for alternative rock. Sure, the girls still put the wigs on Wednesday through Saturday, but come Sunday night, the coolest local bands rock the tiny space. The crowd, of course, is half the fun, with guys in dresses, the blue-collar Joes who like to date them, college-age alternakids, and suburban girls doing bachelorette parties. ◆ Cover for shows. M-Sa, 10AM-midnight; Su, noon-midnight. 79 Broadway (at Eliot St). 426.8902; www.jacquescaberet.com

23 BUZZ

♂ **Aria,** at the Wilbur Theater, is taken over on Saturday nights by Buzz and shirtless lads who sweat and bop to trance and house noise inflicted by popular DJs Michael Shaenan and Maryalice. ◆ Cover. Sa, 10PM-2AM. 246 Tremont St (at Stuart St). 267.8969; www.buzzboston.com

24 NEWS

★$ News keeps hunger away until 5AM. Don't expect gourmet grub, and count on a mob after 2AM, but be happy there's food at that hour. The late-night breakfast menu is nice after a bout of clubbing, and the place is popular after work. Among choices: steak tips and Alaskan herb-encrusted salmon ($18.95). ◆ American ◆ Daily, breakfast, lunch, and dinner; drinks until 2AM. 150 Kneeland St (at Utica St). 426.6397; www.newsboston.com

25 BOSTON PARK PLAZA HOTEL

$$$ For those dying to stay near the South End gay scene (but who still want to be treated like a queen), this pricey, gay-friendly choice is heavy on the chintz and crystal. There are 960 delightful rooms. On the premises are two top-notch restaurants and the Grand Lobby's **Swans Court** lounge, a piano bar where Liberace began his career. Numerous gay events are held here, including, believe it or not, a queer college prom. ◆ 64 Arlington St (between Columbus Ave and Park Plaza). 426.2000; fax 426.5545; www.bostonparkplaza.com ♿

26 CHARLES PLAYHOUSE

The Theater District's oldest venue—built in 1843, renovated in 1966, and on the National Register of Historic Places—always has a gay hairdresser on hand to crack up the tourists in its long-running *Shear Madness,* a send-up of whodunits that has already made the *Guinness Book of Records.* Upstairs, an eclectic lineup of productions is staged—including Blue Man Group. ◆ 74 Warrenton St (between Warrenton Pl and Stuart St). 426.6912 ♿

26 VAPOR

♂ A wide gamut of college boys, regular Joes, drag queens, and old marrieds have been coming to this club, formerly Chaps, for years.
♀ Leather types are rarely seen. Darkish yet cheerful, it's a seven-nights-a-week party (rare for a dance club in Boston) with the guys coming to drink, dance, and gawk at the shirtless throngs. Overall, said throngs are quite good-looking, and variety keeps things lively, with different nights for Latinos (Wednesdays), go-go boys, AIDS benefits, and tea dances, to name but a few themes. The dance floor is not huge, but the tunes are discernible. ◆ Cover. M-Sa, 3PM-2AM; Su, noon-2AM. 100 Warrenton St (at Stuart St). 695.9500

27 FLASH'S

★$ Comfort foods like pulled-pork sandwiches and meat loaf are cheap, but the cocktail lounge specializes in classic cocktails—stingers, grasshoppers, Singapore slings, martinis, and Moscow mules—a draw for the mixed gay and straight crowd. To accompany the drinks there's a selection of tapas by the dark-wood bar. ◆ American ◆ M-Sa, lunch; daily, dinner. 310 Stuart St (between Arlington and Berkeley Sts). 574.8888 ♿

28 LAUREL GRILL & BAR

★★$$ A comfortable neighborhood restaurant and bar on the edge of the South End and Back Bay, Laurel offers reasonably priced American eclectic food to a mixed crowd. The green pastel walls and high windows give it a light-filled atrium feel. There are also vegetarian dishes, and they will ship their moist brownies. ♦ American ♦ Daily, dinner; M-F, lunch; Su, brunch. 142 Berkeley St (between Columbus Ave and Stuart St). 424.6711; www.laurelgrillandbar.com &

29 CLUB CAFÉ LOUNGE AND VIDEO BAR

♂ ★★$$ To put your finger on the pulse of
♀ gay Boston, grab a table at this romantic café at the heart of a small cluster of gay businesses just shy of the South End. A taupe color scheme, velvet drapes, and well-trained staff set the mood for a memorable repast, with pasta in subtle, complex sauces prominent on the menu. ♦ American ♦ M-Sa, lunch, dinner, and late-night snacks; Su, brunch, dinner, and late-night snacks. 209 Columbus Ave (between Clarendon and Berkeley Sts). 536.0966; www.clubcafe.com &

At Club Café:

MOONSHINE

♂ For postprandial hanging out, this lively video
♀ bar at the back of the restaurant really hits the spot. Occasionally, half the space turns into "Club Cabaret," with top-notch musical performers (such as popular local chanteuse Carol O'Shaughnessy) in the limelight. The thirty-something-and-up crowd here is the most professional and educated set you'll find at anything resembling a club in Boston. The place attracts a mixed gay and lesbian crowd, with the ratio of men to women changing each night of the week. ♦ W-Sa, 8PM-2AM. 536.0966 &

Below Club Café:

COLUMBUS ATHLETIC CLUB

This independently owned, 18,000-square-foot health and fitness club for men and women is overflowing with fitness equipment, trainers, and facilities for yoga, private training, and cross-fit training. It's below Club Café but has no affiliation. Before this place was redesigned in 2004, it was the very cruisy Metropolitan Health Club. But like much of the South End, it is now gay and straight with the primary emphasis not on pickups but on fitness. Young professionals looking for a neighborhood alternative to corporate health

clubs predominate. ♦ Daily. 536.3006; www.bostonfitness.com &

30 500 BOYLSTON STREET

This postmodern complex of offices, upscale shops, and restaurants, codesigned by gay architect **Philip Johnson**, has gotten mixed reviews since it went up next to **Trinity Church** in 1988. Some call its stone courtyard and archway beautiful, while others decry it as unimaginative kitsch. Whichever, it's a fun place to shop and eat. ♦ At Clarendon St. 536.3500

31 BOSTON PUBLIC LIBRARY ADDITION

Another **Philip Johnson** design, the 1972 addition to the palatial Florentine-style library echoes the original structure, but has a colder, starker, and more modern feel. Still, it is widely loved for its open stacks, exhibitions, and basement theater with free weekly readings and screenings. ♦ M-Th, 9AM-9PM; F, Sa, 9AM-5PM. Also Su, 1-5PM Oct-May. 700 Boylston St (between Dartmouth and Exeter Sts). 536.5400 &

32 463 BEACON STREET GUEST HOUSE

♂ $ No breakfast here, but then this brownstone
♀ hostelry is insanely cheap by Back Bay standards. Nonetheless, all 20 rooms have telephones, cable TV, and stoves or microwaves; most have private baths; and some even have fireplaces. Expect to see a few wayward straights among the clientele. Parking is a problem in these parts, so call ahead if bringing a car. Discount for military and US government. ♦ 463 Beacon St (between Hereford St and Massachusetts Ave). 536.1302; fax 247.8876; www.463beacon.com &

33 NEWBURY GUEST HOUSE

$$ The charm runs high at this popular gay-friendly bed-and-breakfast establishment squeezed in among the brownstones, with 32 rooms that manage to retain their Victorian grace despite the incursion of such conveniences as telephones and televisions. Private baths and queen-size beds, on the other hand, are welcome modern touches. Also appreciated are the tasty pastries served at breakfast. Most of the local gay attractions

Inspired, no doubt, by the French bordello theme, Judy Garland and Liberace would perform impromptu (and for free) at the old Napoleon's piano bar/nightclub whenever either was in Boston.

Restaurants/Clubs: Red | Hotels: Purple | Shops: Orange | Outdoors/Parks: Green | Sights/Culture: Blue

THE MAINE EVENT

Why, you ask, would anyone looking for a gay getaway choose a little place like **Ogunquit, Maine,** instead of Provincetown? Apart from the fact that it's closer to Boston (only a 75-mile drive north by car or Trailways bus; take Interstate 95 north to coastal Highway 1), it's much more low-key, less of a scene, and offers a quiet charm that appeals to lots of folks, especially "nesting" couples, both male and female. (www.ogunquit.org)

Founded in 1913 and a gay destination since the 1960s, this resort is known for its 30-mile stretch of beach and its 1¼-mile seaside walking path, called **Marginal Way.** It has a number of popular inns along Highway 1 (which becomes **Main Street** in town), including **The Gazebo** (Hwy 1, between Grasshopper La and Beach Plum Farm Rd, 207/646.3733), with eight rooms set in an 1865 house just north of town, and the 40-room **Yellow Monkey** (168 Main St, at Hoyts La, 207/646.9056), to name just two. The real charmer is **Moon Over Maine** (6 Berwick Rd, just west of Main St, 207/646-MOON, 800/851.6837), a nine-room inn restored to its original 1830s flair with beautiful hardwood floors and all the amenities, including balconies, flower beds, and an outdoor Jacuzzi. Drop your bags and walk the few blocks to Leanne Cusimano's **Amore Breakfast** (178 Shore Rd, between the center of town and Perkins Cove, 207/646.6661; www.amorebreakfast.com), a fresh-ingredients breakfast-only restaurant. A house specialty, only for the brave, is bananas Foster French toast with pecan-coated cream cheese stuffing and a side of bananas sautéed in rum. Or have a cappuccino at **Bread & Roses** (246 Main St, across from Club InsideOut, 207/646.4227; www.breadandrosesbakery.com), an excellent bakery proudly serving coffee from **Carpe Diem,** a lesbian-owned Maine beanery. Just down Main

Street is **Drop Anchor** (24 Main St, between Shore and Berwick Rds, 207/646.1615)—tellingly, the only place in town with Gay Pride paraphernalia—where chatty owner (and off-season college professor) Rod Joslyn plies shades and beachwear. The main gay club in town is **Club InsideOut** (237 Main St, between Shore and Berwick Rds, 207/646.6655; www.clubinsideout.com); the two-story bar and high-tech disco, with video games and pool tables, is open during the summer and Thursday through Sunday spring and fall (up to and including New Year's Eve). There's also a rooftop café and lounge. Adult-comedy shows are Thursday through Monday, and for variety, consider the piano-bar vibe at the **Front Porch** (9 Shore Rd in Village Square).

Follow **Shore Road** to the end and march left up the beach past the volleyball nets; stop when you spot the queers sunning themselves. Don't expect Fire Island—that a gay beach exists at all in a small Maine village is amazing enough. In truth, homophobia does rear its ugly head here, if subtly: The gay strand, for example, is but a fraction of the beachfront ("G" on the maps), and don't expect to feel welcome elsewhere among the guy-girl crowd. In fact, despite the town's huge gay tourist income, homosexual hand-holding in public is not completely accepted. There are lots of same-sex businesses on Main Street, but they seem to hide in plain sight, which is fine with the locals. (Keep in mind that in 1998, this state's voters chose to repeal Maine's gay-rights law.)

All that said, it's worth the trip just to end the day at **Arrows** (Berwick Rd, 1.8 miles west of Main St, 207/361.1100; www.arrowsrestaurant.com), a pricey restaurant serving innovative American cuisine in an 18th-century farmhouse. The gay chef and owners have been written up in magazines from *Boston* to *Gourmet* (be sure to reserve ahead in summer).

are within walking distance. Call ahead to arrange for parking. ♦ 261 Newbury St (between Fairfield and Gloucester Sts). 437.7666; fax 262.4243; www.newburyguesthouse.com

34 NASHOBA BROOK BAKERY

★$ This friendly, cozy neighborhood café serves award-winning sandwiches, salads, quiche, homemade bread, pastries, and cookies. It's open at 6:30AM weekdays and 8:30AM weekends. Look for the mural of Venus on one of the bright-yellow walls. ♦ Daily, breakfast and lunch. 288 Columbus Ave (at Clarendon St). 236.0777; www.slowrise.com &

35 PRAIRIE STAR

★$ Owned by executive chefs Russ and Sherry Berger and sister to their **Firefly** and

Laurel Grill & Bar, Prairie Star is a casual red-fronted restaurant that mixes what the owners call Health-Mex with Tex-Mex cooking. ♦ Tex-Mex ♦ Daily, dinner; M-Sa, lunch; late menu F, Sa. 111 Dartmouth St (between Columbus Ave and Massachusetts Tpk). 262.7575; www.prairiestarboston.com

36 CONDOM WORLD

Kitsch and sex are rolled into one colorful latex package here, with tacky "ice breakers" like rose bouquets made of condoms. There's also vanilla-flavored dusting powder, body oils that heat up on contact, a line of jewelry for those who have body piercings, and more practical stuff like dental dams and good old-fashioned condoms in dozens of styles. ♦ M-Th, 11AM-7PM; F, Sa, 11AM-8PM; Su, noon-6PM. 332 Newbury St (between Hereford St and Massachusetts Ave). 267.SAFE

36 Trident Booksellers & Cafe

★★★$ For many, the best place for coffee on Newbury Street is this "alternative," New Age, and gay-friendly bookshop and café. Check out the great selection of new and used books, as well as the hundreds of domestic and foreign periodicals (many of them gay). Then check out the equally great selection of coffees, fruit drinks, light dishes, and desserts. The cashew-vegetable chili is justly famous, and the Tibetan *momo* beef-filled dumplings make a great nosh. For late risers, breakfast is served all day. ♦ American ♦ Daily, 9AM-midnight. 338 Newbury St (between Hereford St and Massachusetts Ave). 267.8688; www.tridentbookscafe.com &

37 Fenway Community Health Center

Since 1971, the center has been a primary-care resource for gay, lesbian, bisexual, and transgendered people. Affiliated with Beth Israel Deaconess Medical Center, it works on HIV prevention, treatment, and research and concentrates on women's health, particularly the needs of lesbians. There's an alternative insemination program, family and parent-ing services, and an acupuncture detoxifica-tion program. All physicians have faculty appointments at Harvard Medical School. A volunteer-staffed help line is at 267.9001. ♦ 7 Haviland St (between Hemmingway St and Massachusetts Ave), or in the South End at 142 Berkeley St. 927.6000; www.fenwayhealth.org

38 Oasis

♂ $ Most notable perhaps for its proximity to the notorious (and dangerous) cruising grounds of the Fens, this inexpensive and functional 16-room bed-and-breakfast is set in two quaint brick town houses. There's Wi-Fi Internet access and no smoking. Basic rooms come with telephones, TV sets, and continental breakfast, but not all have private baths. There are also two decks for sunning; all-over tanning is not allowed. ♦ 22 Edgerly Rd (between Norway and Haviland Sts). 267.2262; fax 267.1920; www.oasisgh.com

39 Chandler Inn Hotel

♂ ♀ $$ This gay-owned hostelry in the South End plays host to the annual Gay Pride block party in June, so book way in advance for a ront-row view of the shirtless throngs. The 56 dormish rooms are definitely plain but comfy, with air conditioning, telephones, private baths, and TV sets. Continental breakfast is included in the room rate, but there's no restaurant. The front desk is open around the clock. ♦ 26 Chandler St (at Berkeley St). 482.3450, 800/842.3450; fax 542.3248; www.chandlerinn.com

At the Chandler Inn Hotel:

Fritz

♂ A sort of gay "Cheers," this neighborhood watering hole draws in a 30-ish and older bunch of guys. Weekdays after work are

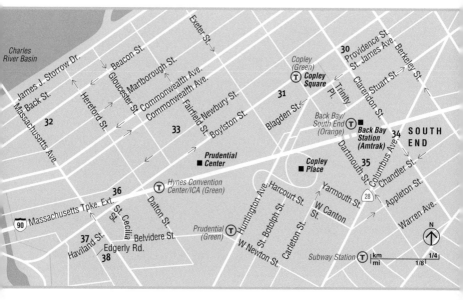

busiest, with a crowd of friendly locals catching sports on the plasma TVs over a few brews. Sundays, with brunch, are lively too. ◆ Daily, noon-2AM. 482.4428; www.fritzboston.com

40 ICARUS

★★$$$ Always ranked in Boston's top 10, this gay-owned restaurant of choice offers an elegant setting perfect for romantic dinners and special events. Beneath a cool band of neon, a hunky statue of winged Icarus surveys the two-tiered dining room, where a diverse clientele coos over chef (and co-owner) Chris Douglass's eclectic seasonal inspirations. With the likes of black pepper–rubbed duck with rhubarb and cherry compote, the menu is not for the tame of palate—or the lean of wallet. But make no mistake: The food is worth the splurge. ◆ American ◆ Daily, dinner. Reservations recommended F-Su. 3 Appleton St (between Tremont and Berkeley Sts). 426.1790; www.icarusrestaurant.com

41 BOSTON EAGLE

♂ While the straight world watches *Home Improvement* reruns to get their fix of friendly handymen, you can meet a real tool-belt kind of guy in the flesh at this one-room barroom with no attitude, no frills, and practically no lights. The mature guys here aren't big on trends, politics, or fashion, but can shoot a mean game of pool. Stop in to play some eight ball, chug a beer, and witness the primitive mating rituals at closing time. ◆ M-F, 3PM-2AM; Sa, 1PM-2AM; Su, noon-2AM. 520 Tremont St (between E Berkeley and Hanson Sts). 542.4494

42 BOSTON CENTER FOR THE ARTS (BCA)

The epicenter of the city's cutting-edge theater scene is set in a series of brick brownstones with a converted-factory feel. Spread over four acres, the center includes studio, performance, and office space for artists and performance and dance groups. One of the complex's converted buildings is the 23,000-square-foot **Cyclorama,** a beautiful, shallow, steel-trussed dome designed by **Cummings and Sears** and built in 1884. Large enough to accommodate a yearly lesbian dance and the annual Artists' Ball, the Cyclorama houses three theaters (the **BCA Theater,** the **Black Box,** and the **Leland Theater**) that have hosted more than 30 area performing arts groups. Among the companies that perform here are the **Coyote Theatre** (695.0659) and **Theater Offensive** (542.4214), the brainchild of half-drag diva/half-superman Abe Rybeck, which stages Out on the Edge, the annual gay theater festival, and Plays At Work, new queer plays by local writers. ◆ 539-551 Tremont St

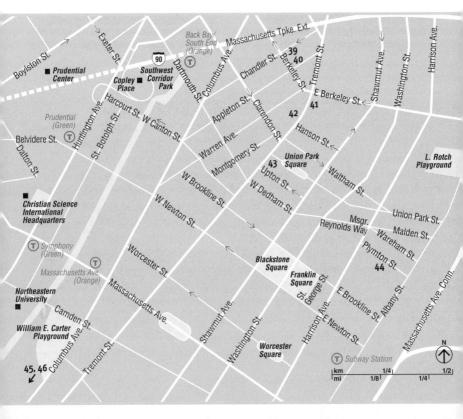

THE BEST

Arthur Leeth

Music librarian/former dancer, Boston Ballet

Surviving the lunch-hour shopping crush at **Filene's Basement.**

A Sunday walk in **Mt. Auburn Cemetery** in the fall.

Free concerts on the **Esplanade** in the summer.

A spring walk down **Commonwealth Avenue.**

Lilac Sunday in the **Arboretum.**

Taking the ferry to **Provincetown** for lunch and shopping.

Getting in the car and heading north to antique.

Attending the **Head of the Charles Regatta** in October.

A nice, quiet rainy afternoon at the **Museum of Fine Arts.**

Fall urban leaf watching around **Jamaica Pond.**

The **Duck Tours.**

Visiting Boston's great **museums.**

Going to the **Bunker Hill Monument.**

Lyric Stage and **ART (American Repertory Theater)** in Cambridge.

(between Clarendon and Berkeley Sts). 426.5000; www.bcaonline.org &

43 FRANCESCA'S

♂ ★$ If attitude isn't your cup of tea, try this
♀ lesbian-owned espresso bar and bakery. It's a tiny, cheery spot is on the casual side of queer, with a fun mix of boys and girls chowing down on pastries or lasagna, soups, sandwiches, and the like. The coffee concoctions are great. ♦ Coffeehouse ♦ M-Th, 8AM-11PM; F, Sa, 8AM-midnight; Su, 9AM-9PM. 564 Tremont St (at Union Park). 482.9026 &

44 BAY WINDOWS

This lively weekly is New England's largest GLBT newspaper and one of the country's best. It's a real newspaper, covering hard news affecting the community without the PR and puff pieces that clog too many weeklies. Much of the circulation is in Boston proper, but it is also in towns from Amherst to Provincetown to Worcester. The paper is available free in news boxes, restaurants, bars, bookstores, and even supermarket racks. ♦ 46 Plympton St (between Albany St and Harrison Ave). 266.6670; www.baywindows.com

45 PLUTO

♂ One-stop gay shopping has arrived.
♀ This double-storefront boutique in Jamaica Plain offers an awesome selection of greeting cards along with a fabulous array of clothes, housewares, toiletries, and other goodies that have "Gay!" written all over them. ♦ M-W, 11AM-6PM; Th, F, 11AM-7PM; Sa, 10AM-6PM; Su, noon-5PM. 603 Centre St (between Pond St and Goodrich Rd), 522.0054.

45 COFFEE CANTATA

★★★$$ Bach himself would have felt right at home amid the warm frescoes and classical tunes at this dykey Jamaica Plain spot. Besides the brews, no fewer than 25 kinds of sinful sweets are baked fresh daily (do try the voluptuous Queen of Sheba hazelnut torte). Service can be pokey and some of the staff clueless, but the eclectic dinner menu has fresh, handmade ravioli as a specialty. ♦ Café/Mediterranean/American ♦ M-W, Th, Sa, breakfast, lunch, and dinner 8AM-10PM; Su, breakfast and lunch 8AM-6PM. 605 Centre St (at Pond St). 522.2223

46 CENTRE STREET CAFÉ

★★$$ Gay men, lesbians, straights, and vegetarians of all stripes enjoy this Jamaica Plain institution for its cozy New Yorkish feel and fresh, simple entrées (like the excellent black-bean burritos). The brunch menu offers some nice surprises, too, including the eggs "Benny" (Atlantic salmon on toast with lime, scallions, and avocado). Vegetarian options. ♦ American ♦ M-F, lunch and dinner, Sa, dinner; Su, brunch. 669 Centre St (at Seaverns Rd and Green St). 524.9217 &

In the late 19th and early 20th centuries, the phrase "Boston marriage" was applied to the relationship between two "single" women setting up house with no apparent need for a man. Think of Olive Chancellor and Verena Tarrant in Henry James's 1886 novel The Bostonians (based on the real-life experience of the author's sister), and Rebecca and Lizzie in Louisa May Alcott's 1883 novel An Old-Fashioned Girl. A real-life "Boston marriage" was the 25-year partnership of Katharine Lee Bates (who penned "America the Beautiful") and fellow Wellesley College professor Katherine Conan.

Restaurants/Clubs: Red | Hotels: Purple | Shops: Orange | Outdoors/Parks: Green | Sights/Culture: Blue

HISTORY

1614 Captain John Smith explores the Boston/Massachusetts Bay area and calls it "a paradise"; thereafter the region becomes known as New England.

1620 The Pilgrims arrive on the *Mayflower* and establish the Plymouth Colony, the first permanent English settlement in New England.

1624 William Blackstone settles on Shawmut Peninsula (Boston) with 200 books and a Brahma bull.

1630 A group of Puritans led by John Winthrop, who sailed from England in a fleet of 11 ships, found Boston.

1632 Boston becomes the capital of the Massachusetts Bay Colony.

1635 Boston Latin School is established on 13 February, becoming America's first school; it remains open to this day.

1636 Harvard College is established to educate young men for the ministry.

1638 The first printing press in the English colonies is established at Cambridge by Stephen Day; four years later he publishes the *Bay Psalm Book*.

1639 The New World's first post office is established in the Boston home of Richard Fairbank.

1644 Gallows are erected on Boston Common.

1660 Boston's population reaches 3,000.

1684 The Massachusetts Bay Colony charter is annulled by the British court.

1685 The Dominion of New England is created by Britain's King James II and includes all New England colonies plus New York, New Jersey, and Pennsylvania. Rebellions by colonists and the overthrow of James II end this union.

1688 King's Chapel, the first Anglican church in the country, is established in Boston.

1689 On 18 April, a rebellion overthrows the British royal governor of New England, Sir Edmund Andros.

1691 A new Massachusetts charter abolishes church membership as a prerequisite for voting.

1692 "Witches" are tried in great numbers in Salem; the hysteria spreads, leading to the execution of 20 women and men.

1693 The first postal service is established between Boston and New York.

1704 The first successful newspaper in the colonies, the *Boston News-Letter*, is printed.

1712 The cornerstone is laid for the Old State House, the seat from which English governors ruled Boston prior to the Revolution.

1716 Boston Light is built on Little Brewster Island in Boston Harbor; it is destroyed by the British in 1776 and rebuilt in 1783. Today it's the oldest lighthouse in the US, and the only manned lighthouse on the East Coast.

1719 Thomas Fleet publishes *Tales of Mother Goose.*

1729 Construction of the Old South Meeting House is begun.

1742 Faneuil Hall, the "Cradle of Liberty," is built.

1765 The Stamp Act is passed by Britain's Parliament, levying taxes on American colonists for the first time. It is repealed one year later.

1767 The Townshend Acts are passed by Parliament, placing new import duties on glass, lead, paint, paper, and tea used by American colonists.

1770 The Townshend Acts are repealed by King George, except for taxes on tea. On 5 March five colonists are shot and killed by British soldiers outside the Old State House; the event becomes known as the Boston Massacre.

1773 The Tea Act is passed by Britain, giving the East India Company the rights to undersell American tea merchants. On 16 December the Sons of Liberty, disguised as Indians, dump 342 chests of tea shipped from England into Boston Harbor.

1774 On 31 March, Britain passes the Boston Port Bill, which closes the harbor in retaliation for the Boston Tea Party. Britain places limits on the powers of the Massachusetts legislature and prohibits town meetings without the consent of the governor. On 5 September the First Continental Congress meets in Philadelphia with delegates from all colonies and calls for a boycott on all British goods.

1775 The American Revolution begins. On 18 April, Paul Revere and William Dawes ride to warn the Minutemen that the British are marching. On 19 April the first engagements of the Revolution take place in the Battles of Lexington and Concord, where the "shot heard 'round the world" is fired. On 17 June the Battle of Bunker Hill takes place in Charlestown: The British win but suffer heavy casualties. George Washington takes command of the Continental Army at Cambridge. In retaliation, Britain prohibits all trade with the American colonies.

1776 British troops retreat from Boston. The Declaration of Independence is read for the first time in Boston from the balcony of the Old State House.

1781 The Massachusetts Medical Society is founded.

1784 The *Empress of China* makes her maiden voyage from Boston to the Orient; many local fortunes are built on the clipper ship trade out of Boston.

1792 The first *Farmer's Almanac* is published in Boston by Robert B. Thomas.

1793 Eli Whitney introduces the cotton gin in Boston.

1796 John Adams of Massachusetts is elected the second president of the US.

1797 The frigate USS *Constitution* (which becomes known as "Old Ironsides") is launched at Boston Naval Shipyard.

1798 The Massachusetts State House on Beacon Hill, designed by Charles Bulfinch, is completed.

1810 The Handel & Haydn Society, America's first musical and choral group, is formed.

1811 Massachusetts General Hospital is established.

1822 A city charter is granted to Boston.

1824 Massachusetts resident John Quincy Adams is elected sixth president of the US.

1825 The first city census is taken; Boston's population is 58,277.

1826 Quincy Market opens.

1829 On 16 October the Tremont House (today the Omni Parker House) opens as the first hotel in the US.

1831 William Lloyd Garrison publishes the first issue of *The Liberator*, a newspaper dedicated to emancipation.

1832 The New England Anti-Slavery Society is formed in Boston.

1833 The first US steam railway is built, running between Boston and Newton.

1835 Horace Mann creates the nation's first normal schools for the training of teachers.

1839 Charles Goodyear invents vulcanized rubber.

1840 The *Britannia*, the first transatlantic steamship of the Cunard Line, arrives in Boston. The first large influx of Irish arrives in Boston as a result of the potato famine.

1843 The 221-foot Bunker Hill Monument is dedicated on 17 July by US secretary of state Daniel Webster, former US senator from Massachusetts.

1845 The sewing machine is invented in Boston by Elias Howe.

1846 Anesthesia is used for the first time, at Massachusetts General Hospital.

1848 The Boston Public Library, the first free municipal library in the US, opens.

1851 The YMCA is organized in Boston; 15 years later the YWCA is formed.

1857 The first issue of *The Atlantic Monthly* magazine is published in Boston.

1859 The Public Garden is ratified as a garden forever public.

1862 Massachusetts sends the first all-African-American regiment to the Civil War.

1872 The Great Fire of Boston destroys all of what is today Boston's Financial District.

1874 The State House dome is gilded.

1875 The Cathedral of the Holy Cross opens in Boston's South End as the largest Roman Catholic church in North America, seating 7,000.

1876 Alexander Graham Bell successfully demonstrates the first telephone in Boston, starting a new era in communications.

1877 Trinity Church, the masterpiece of architect Henry Hobson Richardson, opens on Copley Square on the newly filled land of Back Bay. A fleet of Swan Boats is launched on the Public Garden lagoon.

1880 The Museum of Fine Arts is founded.

1881 The Boston Symphony Orchestra is founded.

1884 The Boston Cyclorama is built to house the gigantic circular painting *The Battle of Gettysburg*.

1892 The First Church of Christ Scientist, the mother church for the Christian Scientist religion founded by Mary Baker Eddy, opens.

1894 The Boston & Maine Railroad opens North Station.

1897 The first subway in the US opens in Boston, running beneath Tremont Street from Park Street to Boylston Street.

1900 Symphony Hall opens as the new home for the Boston Symphony Orchestra.

1903 The first World Series baseball game is played in Boston between the Boston Pilgrims (later the Boston Red Sox) and the Pittsburgh Pirates.

1909 The Museum of Fine Arts moves to its current home.

1912 Fenway Park opens as the home of the Boston Red Sox, who win the pennant and the World Series in their new stadium.

1915 A 495-foot tower is added to the Custom House, making it Boston's first skyscraper and the tallest building in New England. Albert Champion invents the first spark plug.

1927 Sacco and Vanzetti are executed in the electric chair in the state prison in Boston's Charlestown district, despite protests of their innocence; they were officially exonerated 50 years later.

1928 The world's first computer is developed at Massachusetts Institute of Technology.

1929 Arthur Fiedler organizes the first Esplanade Concerts, to become the Boston Pops in 1930.

1942 A fire in the Coconut Grove nightclub kills 491 people.

1946 Boston native John F. Kennedy is elected to the US House of Representatives from Boston's First Congressional District.

1947 Edward H. Land invents the Polaroid camera in Cambridge.

1950 On 17 January the infamous Brink's armored car robbery takes place.

1954 The steeple of the Old North Church is destroyed during a storm; its weather vane is sent on a national tour to raise money to help rebuild the historic landmark.

1955 The Beacon Hill Historical District is created.

1957 The Boston Celtics win the first of 16 National Basketball Association championships. The *Mayflower II* sails from Plymouth, England, to Plymouth, Massachusetts, on a voyage replicating that of the original *Mayflower*'s 1620 voyage.

1959 John F. Kennedy declares himself a candidate for president of the United States in Boston.

1962 The demolition of Scollay Square marks the beginning of the Government Center redevelopment project. Edward Kennedy begins his first term as US senator.

1966 Edward Brooke becomes the first African-American elected to the US Senate since Reconstruction.

1969 Boston City Hall is dedicated, with honors from the American Institute of Architects. The birthplace of John F. Kennedy in Brookline is declared a National Historic Site.

1972 Women are allowed to run in the Boston Marathon for the first time.

1976 The restored Faneuil Hall Marketplace opens, 150 years to the day after the original inauguration of the market buildings. Boston originates the "First Night" concept for the public celebration of New Year's Eve.

1980 A yearlong jubilee celebrates the 350th anniversary of Boston's settlement.

1990   Boston's population reaches 574,283, the first increase after four decades of decline. The Women's Heritage Trail is established.

1993   Thomas M. Merino is elected mayor, the first man not of Irish descent to hold the job in 63 years.

1994   Salem observes the 300th anniversary of the infamous witch trials.

1995   The beloved Boston Garden—home of the Boston Celtics and the Boston Bruins—closes its doors for the last time; its seats are sold to fans and collectors worldwide.

1996   The 100th running of the Boston Marathon takes place. Major additions and ongoing improvements to the Freedom Trail begin.

1997   Boston celebrates the 200th anniversary of the launching of the USS *Constitution*.

1998   The 200th anniversary of the State House is celebrated.

2004   The Democratic Party's National Convention is held.

2005 The $15 billion Big Dig construction project officially ends. Mayor Menino is elected to his fourth term in office.

2006 The Big Dig returns as faulty tunnel-roof construction results in the death of a car passenger crushed by falling cement. Closures bring massive traffic problems and repair bills mount.

After years of poor performance, Boston's public schools are recognized as getting better. The school system wins a half-million dollar award from the Broad Foundation as the urban school district making the greatest gains in student achievement. The award provides scholarships to graduating high school seniors.

After 16 years of Republican governors, Democrat Duval Patrick is overwhelmingly elected as governor. The former federal civil rights prosecutor became the first African-American governor in Massachusetts and the second African-American elected governor in the United States since Reconstruction.

INDEX

RESTAURANTS

Only restaurants with star ratings are listed below. All restaurants are listed alphabetically in the main (preceding) index. Always call in advance to ensure a restaurant has not closed, changed its hours, or booked its tables for a private party. The restaurant price ratings are based on the average cost of an entrée for one person, excluding tax and tip.

****An Extraordinary Experience
  ***Excellent
    **Very Good
      *Good

$$$$Big Bucks ($25 and up)
  $$$Expensive ($20–$25)
$$Reasonable ($15–$20)
  $The Price is Right (less than $15)

★★★★

★★★

HOTELS

The hotels listed below are grouped according to their price ratings; they are also listed in the main index. The hotel price ratings reflect the base price of a standard room for two people for one night during the peak season.

$$$$Big Bucks ($250 and up)
$$$Expensive ($180–$250)
$$Reasonable ($120–$180)
$The Price is Right (less than $120)

$$$$

$$$

$$

2

2

2